An Introduction to

Special Education

An Introduction to

Special Education

A Social Systems Perspective

Second Edition

Thomas M. Shea
Southern Illinois University—Edwardsville
University of Missouri—Saint Louis

Anne Marie Bauer
University of Cincinnati

Brown & Benchmark
PUBLISHERS

Madison, WI   Dubuque   Guilford, CT   Chicago   Toronto   London
Mexico City   Caracas   Buenos Aires   Madrid   Bogotá   Sydney

Book Team

Executive Publisher *Edgar J. Laube*
Managing Editor *Sue Pulvermacher-Alt*
Developmental Editor *Suzanne M. Guinn*
Production Editor *Terry Routley*
Designer *Christopher E. Reese*
Proofreading Coordinator *Carrie Barker*
Art Processor *Miriam Hoffman*
Photo Editor *Laura Fuller*
Visual Editor *Rachel Imsland*
Production Manager *Beth Kundert*
Production/Costing Manager *Sherry Padden*
Production/Imaging and Media Development Manager *Linda Meehan Avenarius*
Marketing Manager *Amy Halloran*
Copywriter *Jennifer Smith*
Proofreader *Mary Svetlik Anderson*

Basal Text *10/12 Clearface Regular*
Display Type *Bergell*
Typesetting System *Macintosh™ QuarkXPress™*
Paper Stock *50# Restorecote*

Brown & Benchmark
PUBLISHERS

Executive Vice President and General Manager *Bob McLaughlin*
Vice President, Business Manager *Russ Domeyer*
Vice President of Production and New Media Development *Victoria Putman*
National Sales Manager *Phil Rudder*
National Telesales Director *John Finn*

A Times Mirror Company

Cover design by Lisa Gravunder

Cover photograph by Vicki Roll

Copyedited by Mary Jean Gregory; proofread by Ann M. Kelly

The credits section for this book begins on page 463 and is considered an extension of the copyright page.

Copyright © 1997 by Times Mirror Higher Education Group, Inc.
All rights reserved

Library of Congress Catalog Card Number: 95–83925

ISBN 0–697–24439–3

Printed in the United States of America by Times Mirror Higher Education Group, Inc., 2460 Kerper Boulevard, Dubuque, IA 52001

10 9 8 7 6 5 4 3 2 1

This book is dedicated to Dolores, my best friend and wife, and to Keith, Kevin, and Jane; and to Riley and our children, Demian, Tarie, Christopher, Sarah, and Mickey.

Brief Contents

Contents

Contents

Contents

3

Learners Who Vary in Accessing the Environment   191

Chapter 9

Learners with Communication Disorders   193

Chapter 10

Learners with Physical Disabilities and Health Impairments   217

Chapter 11

Learners with Visual Impairments   243

Contents

4

Learners Who Vary in Their Learning Styles and Rates 297

Chapter 13

Contents

Contents

Chapter 16

Chapter 17

Contents

5

A Look Toward the Future 419

Chapter 18

Trends, Issues, and Directions 421

Contents

Preface

n the few years since the first edition of this text was published, significant change has continued in the fields of education and special education. Inclusion, discussed tentatively in the first edition, has become a reality for many children and youth. The recognition of both the social systems perspective and the development of the whole child has also become more common. Unfortunately, such challenges to our society as child maltreatment, substitute care, and prenatal drug and alcohol exposure have also become a reality for more and more families with children.

In this second edition, we again apply Urie Bronfenbrenner's ecological perspective. Through this perspective, we assume that learners with disabilities are learners first, who then vary in learning style, developmental rate, interactional style, and ability to access the environment through communication, mobility, vision, and audition. The issue of "disability" must be studied within the contexts in which the individual learner develops. Without studying the contexts, Bronfenbrenner's perception that developmental psychology is the study of the strange behavior of children in strange situations with strange adults for the briefest periods of time, remains valid.

Audience and Purpose

This introduction to special education acquaints undergraduate and beginning graduate students with the basic concepts of individual diversity as well as the impact of variations on interactions within the family, school, community, and society. Unlike the authors of many texts in the field of special education, we espouse a theoretical basis for our discussion and argue that without this framework, working with individuals with disabilities is a series of independent strategies and techniques rather than an integrated effort to enhance an individual's potential through interactions and relationships with others. Through this recognition of a theoretical base, we mirror the work of the Carnegie Report (1986) and the Holmes Group (1986), as well as professional organizations such as the National Association for the Education of Young Children and the National Council for the Accreditation of Teacher Education, in assuring that teachers function from a theoretical and knowledge base of child development and learning.

Organization

Section 1 of the text discusses the social systems contexts of learners with disabilities. Chapter 1 covers the nature of human development from the ecological or social systems perspective and the implications of this ecological development perspective for working with learners with disabilities. The following chapters in section 1 address issues that impact learners with disabilities regardless of the variations they demonstrate. These chapters include one on societal perceptions of learners with disabilities (chap. 2), one on schooling and learners with disabilities (chap. 3), and another on families having members with disabilities (chap. 4). The final chapters in this section address transitions learners with disabilities make between social subsystems (for example, home and school, or school and work, as in chap. 5) and family and community issues in contemporary society (chap. 6).

The next three sections of the text discuss the variations in human development referred to as "disabilities." Using the social systems perspective, we are able to discuss the full range of each variation rather than just those learners who are disabled by the variation. We are able to communicate the need for all teachers to recognize and celebrate the diversity among children, youth, and adults.

In section 2, we discuss learners who vary in their interactions, including learners identified as emotionally/behaviorally disordered (chap. 7) and learners from diverse ethnic, cultural, and linguistic groups (chap. 8).

Learners who vary with regard to accessing the environment are discussed in section 3. Chapters in this section are devoted to learners with communication disorders (chap. 9), physical disabilities and health impairments (chap. 10), visual impairments (chap. 11), and hearing impairments (chap. 12).

In section 4, we discuss learners who vary in learning styles and rates. Chapters are devoted to learning disabilities (chap. 13), mild or moderate mental retardation (chap. 14), mild disabilities (chap. 15), severe and multiple disabilities (chap. 16), and learners who are gifted, talented, or creative (chap. 17).

The fifth section and final chapter of the text looks to the future. Chapter 18 discusses emerging issues, trends, and directions in special education.

Within each chapter, we support learning through the use of objectives and key words and phrases. In this second edition, we have added exercises at the end of each chapter to support the reader in building his or her professional vocabulary and checking his or her comprehension of the content. The reader will find a glossary of terms at the end of the text.

In an effort to communicate our belief system regarding learners who vary from their peers, we have chosen our language with great care. We will not say "the retarded" or "visually impaired students"; we will refer to learners *with* mental retardation or learners *with* visual impairments. We especially recognize those students whose variations may be based on clinical judgment or the nature of instruction and schooling; we will refer to them as learners "identified as emotionally/behaviorally disordered" and learners "identified as learning disabled." We will describe ways to mediate the environment to provide equal benefit for these learners, rather than techniques or strategies to make the learner match the system. We fully recognize and apologize for any awkwardness of style this may pose to readers. We hope, however, that such awkwardness results in reader recognition of the learners rather than the variation that the learner presents.

New to the Second Edition

In this second edition, we have both updated and modified the text to support the learning of student users. Throughout the text, we have presented information from new research and instructional strategies. An increased emphasis on inclusion has been provided throughout. In addition, we have integrated much of the research (such as that previously presented about families), placing an emphasis on concepts and trends rather than facts and findings. A new final chapter explores issues that have emerged as the education of learners with disabilities becomes more inclusive, with information on the emerging paradigm shift in special education, assessment, and challenges to self-concept and identity related to the inclusion of learners with disabilities in general education.

In our effort to depict the social systems perspective, we have chosen to simplify the vocabulary related to Bronfenbrenner's developmental context. This new language, we feel, more clearly communicates the interrelatedness of the learner and the various settings in which he or she is engaged. By eliminating technical terms, such as *microsystem* and *macrosystem,* we feel students will more readily grasp the complexities of human development, particularly the development of learners who vary from their peers.

As teachers, we recognize the need for pedagogical supports in textbooks. In this second edition, we are including "A Closer Look" boxes to provide examples and clarifying information related to the content. "Guidelines for Practice" boxes provide ideas of how readers can apply the content to their own experiences or to the classroom. Icons relating content to *Annual Editions: Educating Exceptional Children* are provided for instructors who choose to use the DPG Publication as a supplement of additional readings. In addition, each chapter now concludes with exercises to build vocabulary and check comprehension. Finally, given the interest in using cases to teach preservice and in-service students, we are pleased to be the coauthors of a new casebook, *Cases in Special Education.*

Teaching Supplements

To help in teaching this course, several teaching supplements are available from Brown & Benchmark Publishers, including an Instructor's Manual, Test Item File, MicroTest III testing software, Transparency Masters, videotapes, and *Cases in Special Education,* a new book of cases by Boyle/Danforth/Shea/Bauer.

- **Instructor's Manual (IM)**—The IM contains lecture ideas, projects, discussion questions, objectives, related materials, and a NEW sample course syllabus.
- **Test Item File (TIF)**—For each chapter of the text the TIF offers numerous multiple choice, true/false, matching, and short answer questions (and responses).
- **MicroTest III**

The TIF is also offered on MicroTest III, a powerful but easy-to-use test-generating program by Chariot Software Group that is available for DOS, Windows, and Macintosh personal computers. With MicroTest III, the instructor can easily select the questions from the TIF and print a test and answer key. Questions, headings, and instructions can be customized; original questions can be added or imported; and the test can be printed in a choice of fonts. A copy of MicroTest III can be obtained by contacting the local Brown & Benchmark Sales Representative.

- **Transparency Masters**—Included in the IM are 25 masters showing key illustrations and tables from the text suitable for projecting.
- **Videotapes**

Qualified adopters can choose from several excellent videotapes that are available. Contact the Brown & Benchmark Sales Representative for more information about these videotapes.

- *Cases in Special Education* by Boyle/Danforth/Shea/Bauer—This NEW book of cases is available for student use. The cases are organized around a social systems perspective and cover persons with a variety of disabilities, of all different ages, and in various settings. Instructors can order a B&B CourseKit™—this text and the book of cases at substantial savings to students. Contact the Brown & Benchmark Sales Representative for more information.

Acknowledgments

This text is about social systems, and we must acknowledge those individuals in our personal social systems for their support of our efforts. To Dolores and Riley, a thanks for their constant support, and thanks to our children, Keith and Kevin, daughter-in-law Jane, Demian, Tarie, Christopher, Sarah, and Mickey, for their patience and understanding of our time at the computer. We appreciate and gratefully acknowledge the efforts of Sally Ann Zwicker and Shobha Chachie Joseph for their technical assistance related to the Deaf and deaf education in chapter 12, and to Sally Ann and Chachie as authors of chapter 18. We must recognize Sue Pulvermacher-Alt and the many members of the Brown & Benchmark book team for their understanding and support and their willingness to take a chance, not once but twice, with an introductory text that is a deviation from the commonplace. We also acknowledge the efforts of the reviewers of both the first and second editions, who provided insights to our work:

Peggy J. Anderson
  Wichita State University
Cynthia L. Baer
  Lamar Community College
Annette R. Clem-Robinson
  Seattle Pacific University
Ann Cranston-Gingras
  University of South Florida
Iva Dene McCleary
  University of Utah
Gail M. Drummer
  Michigan State University
Curt Dudley-Marling
  York University, Ontario, Canada
Craig Fiedler
  The University of Wisconsin–Oshkosh
Deborah Gartland
  Towson State University
Timothy L. Heaton
  Cedarville College
Jack J. Hourcade
  Boise State University
Richard M. Jackson
  Boston College
Janet Jamieson
  *University of British Columbia,
  Vancouver, British Columbia, Canada*

Robbie Ludy
  Northwest Missouri State University
Martha J. Meyer
  Butler University
Dr. Eric D. Moore
  Southwest Baptist University
Valerie Owen
  *National-Louis University,
  Chicago, Illinois*
Linda H. Parrish
  Texas A&M University
Kathy Jo Piechura-Couture
  Stetson University
Donald Stauffer
  *Slippery Rock University, Slippery
  Rock, Pennsylvania*
Sally M. Todd
  Brigham Young University
Ruth Violet
  *Vancouver Community College,
  Vancouver, British Columbia, Canada*
W. J. Ward
  Northeastern State University

Finally, we must thank the learners who vary from their peers and who challenge the educational system, for what they have taught us.

Thomas M. Shea
Anne M. Bauer

An Introduction to

Special Education

The Social Systems
Contexts of Learners
with Disabilities

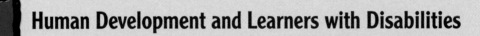

Chapter

Human
Development
and Learners
with
Disabilities

Objectives

After completing this chapter, you will be able to:

1. describe the social systems perspective of human development.
2. describe the impact of the social systems approach on learners who vary from their peers.
3. describe the application of the social systems perspective in the text.

Key Words and Phrases

accommodation
behavior
behavioral perspective
biophysical perspective
congruence
development
ecological contexts

milieu
psychoeducational perspective
social systems perspective
special education
transaction
transitions

Jamie is a seven-year-old boy with Down syndrome. His birth was unplanned. At the time of his birth, his mother was the single parent of two school-age children. When Jamie was an infant, she was unable to find affordable child care in the community. Because it was necessary that she return to work, she had to leave Jamie in the care of a young cousin.

A young man who was visiting the cousin's home physically abused Jamie because he would not stop crying. Jamie's mother, upon seeing her son bruised when she picked him up after work, took him to the hospital. As required by law, hospital personnel reported the case of suspected abuse to the authorities. The case was investigated by the Department of Human Services, and authorities prohibited Jamie's mother from leaving him in the cousin's home. During the three weeks that a caseworker was seeking appropriate day care for Jamie, his mother remained home from work. When she called her employer at the end of the third week to say she must remain out of work yet another few days, she was informed to return to work immediately or lose her job.

With no other resources (her family refused to help because she had "turned in" her cousin), Jamie's mother signed a voluntary agreement for her son to enter foster care. After Jamie spent thirty days in an emergency foster home, the courts ruled a temporary commitment to the custody of the Department of Human Services. Jamie left his emergency home for a long-term foster home. However because of his delayed development and behavioral problems, Jamie frequently changed foster homes.

When Jamie was five, his mother remarried. Her husband assumed responsibility for her two other children but did not want to attempt to parent a child with a disability. He urged Jamie's mother to terminate parental rights to Jamie. Jamie was placed in the permanent custody of the courts, and a social worker was assigned to find an adoptive home.

By the time Jamie was seven years old, he had lived in five different foster homes. No family has yet come forward to adopt him. At present, Jamie is socially withdrawn, has frequent temper outbursts, engages in limited play with a few toys, and has a speaking vocabulary of two words: "no" and "more."

Jack is a seven-year-old boy with Down syndrome. His birth was unplanned. His mother, with two school-age children, put her career on hold when Jack was born. This enabled her to care for him full-time and participate in infant stimulation and early intervention services with him.

While still in the hospital, upon learning that Jack had Down syndrome, his mother contacted the local Down Syndrome Association and was assigned a parent partner who not only provided social and emotional support but also information on Jack's disability and available community services. Jack's paternal grandparents, thrilled to have yet another grandchild, willingly cared for Jack at least one weekend a month so that other family members could have time for themselves and mother and father could have a "night out."

Jack has been in a variety of infant stimulation and early intervention programs since birth. He has participated in educational programs since he was six months old. At this time, Jack is an active and healthy boy who, with special education support, is in kindergarten in his neighborhood school. He has several friends and is on the swimming team with age-peers at the local YMCA. He communicates his needs effectively.

Introduction

This book is about learners with disabilities and special education. Learners with disabilities are individuals who, for various reasons, are seen by others as "different." They may vary from their peers in appearance, how they communicate, and how they move. They may vary in the manner in which they interact or relate with others, in the way they gain access to information in the environment, or in the rate and manner with which they learn.

Special education is essentially a subsystem of general education. It supports the education of learners with disabilities. In other words, **special education** is the part of general education that provides services for individuals who do not fit the system, that is, children who vary from the norm, or standard. Learners with disabilities are a challenge to an educational system designed to accept young children in preschool and kindergarten and, during the next thirteen to fourteen years, move them through high school into college, vocational training, or the workplace. Unlike the majority of children, learners with disabilities often do not move as quickly and unobtrusively through the system as their peers. More specifically, they challenge the system.

"Learners with disabilities" are first and foremost human learners. However, as learners with disabilities, they are often perceived to vary from peers to such an extent that something beyond that which usually occurs at home, in the classroom, and in the community must be provided for them if they are to be successful. In the educational system, that "something" is provided by special education. In the home and community, that "something" may be any one of a broad range of educational, therapeutic, and rehabilitation services offered by public and private medical and human service agencies.

In this text, we apply a social systems perspective to address the unique development experienced by each learner, typical or disabled. A **social systems perspective** is one in which the individual is seen as developing in a dynamic relationship with and as an inseparable part of the settings in which the individual functions over her or his life span. The particular perspective we apply is based on Bronfenbrenner's ecology of human development (1979). It may be referred to as an ecological perspective in that it is based on the relationship of humans and their environment (Thomas & Marshall, 1977).

A social systems perspective is not the only perspective through which human development and learners with disabilities can be viewed (D'Amato & Rothlisberg, 1992). There are many others, a few of which will be discussed briefly. However, it is important to understand that we, the authors, selected social systems theory as a framework because it is broad in scope and allows the integration of much of the information derived from other theories. It is a perspective that allows us to study and utilize all facets of the individual and the environment when explaining human development and learners with disabilities. The selection of a more restrictive theory would limit our discussion of various individual, behavioral, and environmental factors.

Among the other perspectives available for the study of development and learners with disabilities are the behavioral, psychoeducational, and biophysical theories. From the **behavioral perspective,** an individual's behavior is viewed as being maintained by the stimuli in the immediate environment in which the individual is functioning. Teaching involves manipulating those stimuli and managing the contingencies in the immediate environment to facilitate change in the individual's behavior. In this perspective, little consideration is given to factors within the individual or in the individual's extended environment. For example, if a student fails to turn in homework assignments, the teacher would arrange for a reward each time an assignment is turned in.

From the **psychoeducational perspective,** factors within the individual are seen as the primary cause of behavior. Emphasis is focused on the dynamic equilibrium of intrapsychic phenomena such as the id (basic instinct), ego (manager), and superego (conscience). In addition, emphasis is placed on the impact of the immediate and extended environments. Teaching involves accepting and interpreting the individual's behavior and encouraging new and more effective modes of interacting. An interview would be held with the student who fails to bring in homework assignments to explore the reasons the work is not returned. The student's feelings about the work and the relationship with the teacher and those who supervise the homework would be examined.

The **biophysical perspective** emphasizes neurological and other organic factors as the cause of behavior. Teaching involves providing ordered, controlled environments to assist the individual in neurologically processing stimuli. In addition, this perspective involves concern for nutrition, medication, and other medical interventions. Failure to bring in homework assignments may be viewed as a short-term memory problem, and strategies to improve retention would be employed.

We believe that these competing theories, though they do make a significant contribution to the understanding of human development and the learner with disabilities, are limited in scope and restrict our view of human development, of learners with disabilities, and of the factors involved in learning. The systems perspective does not rule out information derived from work regarding these theories, but rather provides a context for organizing vast amounts of information about individual diversity.

The Social Systems Perspective

In the systems perspective, **development** is the continual adaptation or adjustment of the individual and the environment to each other. It is a progressive, mutual accommodation that takes place throughout the life span between growing individuals and their changing environments. It is based on "the person's evolving conception of the ecological environment and his [or her] relationship to it, as well as the person's growing capacity to discover, sustain, or alter its properties" (Bronfenbrenner, 1979, p. 9). Thomas and Marshall (1977) relate this continual adaptation or development to the function of special education.

> The environment seldom adapts, and never completely to the specific needs of an individual with a handicap. Therefore, the ultimate purpose of any special education program is to assist that individual in adapting to the environment to [her or] his maximum capacity (p. 16).

Behavior is the expression of the dynamic relationship between the individual and the environment (Marmor and Pumpian-Mindlin, 1950). Behavior occurs in a setting that includes specific time, place, and object "props" as well as previously established patterns of behavior (Scott, 1980). By "previously established patterns of behavior," it is meant those ways of behaving that are characteristic of an individual and that he or she develops over time and brings to the setting in which the behavior is occurring. Understanding behavior requires more than the simple observation of an individual's behavior by one or two persons in a specific setting; it requires an examination of the systems of interaction surrounding the behavior and is not limited to a single setting. In addition, to understand behavior, those aspects of the environment beyond the immediate situation in which the individual is functioning that may impact the behavior must be taken into account (Bronfenbrenner, 1979).

Congruence is the "match" or "goodness of fit" between the individual and the environment. Thurman (1977) suggests that individuals we judge to be normal are operating in an ecology that is congruent. The "normal" individual's behavior is in harmony, or congruence, with the norms of the environment. Thurman further maintains that when there is a lack of congruence, the individual is viewed as either deviant (being out of harmony with the norms) or incompetent (lacking the necessary behaviors). Congruence between the individual and the environment results in maximum competence and acceptance. According to Poplin and Stone (1992), an individual may be identified as disabled when there is a mismatch between past and present experiences.

In summary, from the social systems perspective, human development is the progressive, mutual **accommodation,** or adaptation and adjustment, between an active, growing human being and the ever-changing settings in which the individual functions, as well as the relationships between those settings and the broader ecological contexts (the environments in which the individual develops) in which they are embedded. These relationships are emphasized, rather dramatically, in the cases of Jamie and Jack at the beginning of the chapter. The reader is urged to reread the two cases and note the significant disparity between the ecological circumstances to which Jamie and Jack were exposed and the potential impact these differences had on their development.

This systems perspective has many implications for the way in which we perceive individuals identified as learners with disabilities and thus describe them in this text. We accept the proposition that human development implies change in the characteristics of an individual and that this change implies reorganization over time and space. We accept the contention that human development is grounded in the **ecological contexts,** or settings, in which it occurs. In this manner, development is an individual's evolving concept of the environment and her or his relationship to it, as well as the person's increasing ability to discover, maintain, or change certain aspects of that environment.

The social systems approach is distinguished by its concern with the ongoing and progressive accommodation between the growing human learner and his or her immediate environment and the way in which this relationship is formed and reconciled by forces coming from more distinct aspects of the individual's social **milieu,** the individual's social surroundings.

Human Development from a Social Systems Perspective

Objective One

To describe the social systems perspective of human development.

Bronfenbrenner (1979) suggests that the ecological contexts, or settings, in which an individual develops are nested, one inside the other, like a set of Russian dolls (fig. 1.1). He argues that the nested nature of the context is decisive in the individual's development as events take place within them. For example, he suggests that a child's ability to read may be related to the nature of the relationship between the child's home and school, as well as to the methods used in school to instruct reading.

Any individual change must be viewed within the context of the larger social and cultural system (Riegel, 1975). From a special education perspective, the specific settings of most relevance to the development of the learner with disabilities are school, family, neighborhood, and community.

In the systems perspective, all individuals are viewed as growing, dynamic persons who progressively move into and restructure the settings in which they find themselves. As previously stated, these systems are nested. Kurdek (1981) calls the systems interdependent and states that the nature of this interdependence is dynamic. Bronfenbrenner refers to the ecological contexts as the microsystem, the mesosystem, the exosystem, and the macrosystem. In this text, we refer to these developmental contexts as the interpersonal relationships, relationships between settings, group interactions, society, and the learner (fig. 1.1).

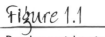

Figure 1.1

Developmental contexts.

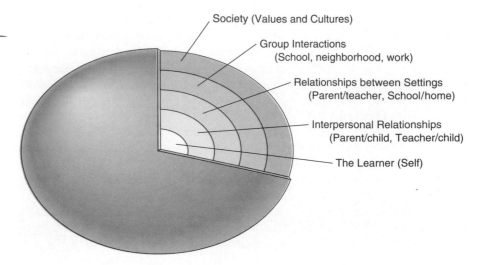

Society (Values and Cultures)

Group Interactions
(School, neighborhood, work)

Relationships between Settings
(Parent/teacher, School/home)

Interpersonal Relationships
(Parent/child, Teacher/child)

The Learner (Self)

Interpersonal relationships
between the developing
individual and teacher/care
giver make up a developmental
context for the learner.

Interpersonal Relationships

In the home, relationships occur between the parent and the child, the child and
each sibling, and between other pairs of family members. In the school, relationships
occur between the child and teacher as well as the child and each peer. Referral to
special education usually begins when there is a problem or lack of congruence in
child-teacher or child-peer interaction within these interpersonal relationships.

Relationships Between Settings

Relationships between settings may include the interrelations among home and
school, home and service agency, home and neighborhood, and school and peer
group. For example, students from diverse cultural, ethnic, and linguistic groups may
be challenged by the interrelationships between their home culture and the school
culture and as a consequence be overrepresented as a group in special education.
Parent-teacher collaboration and family-community service involvement are included
within this context. Relationships between settings includes consideration of transitions, or the movements of the learner with disabilities between learning settings.

Group Interaction

Group interaction settings do not involve the individual directly. However, events
affect or are affected by what happens to the individual. These settings include, for
example, a parent's workplace, a sibling's classroom, and the school system.
Factors such as the availability of special education service programs, the goals of
educational programs in the community, and the selection of school system-wide
instructional materials and textbooks are group interaction settings.

Society

Society includes the majority culture's belief system. This involves the broad social factors that impinge on the settings within which the individual is contained.
Society's general perspective of learners with disabilities, teachers, special education, the social role of students, and community values, for example, all impact
each student's education (Riegel, 1975).

The Learner

Belsky (1980) suggests that though Bronfenbrenner's ecological contexts provide an essential recognition of the complexity of human development, using
only these contexts fails to take into account the individual differences or variations that each learner brings to his or her primary interpersonal relationship

Accommodations provide learners with disabilities with equal access to the environment.

settings. He argues for the inclusion of the ontogenic system suggested by Tinbergen (1951) within the social systems perspective. We refer to this system as "the learner."

The learner includes the personal characteristics of the individual. Among these characteristics are the cognitive, communicative, social, and physical competencies that individuals bring to the settings in which they are functioning. Each individual has personal factors for coping with the environment, including personality attributes, skills, abilities, and competencies. As Gatlin (1980, p. 252) suggests, individuals do not deliberately make inappropriate behavioral decisions, but "attempt to satisfy their needs as they best understand them, while attempting to maintain some sense of personal and social integrity."

By including the learner in the perspective, human development must be viewed not as a series of cause-and-effect relationships between the individual and the environment, but as transactions among the individual and the environment. Sameroff (1975) contends the contact between the individual and the environment is a **transaction,** or communicative exchange, in which each is altered by the other. For example, the infant is influencing her or his caregiving environment at the same time that the caregiving environment is influencing the infant. Mothers with similarly behaving children may vary in their responses toward each child and thus cause different developmental outcomes. A child's development cannot be explained entirely by either biological or environmental factors. Rather, developmental and behavioral outcomes are due to the ongoing reciprocal interactions between the individual organism and the environment (Sameroff & Chandler, 1975).

Impact of the Social Systems Approach

As a result of our personal and professional experiences in education and special education, we conclude, as Bronfenbrenner (1979, p. 19) asserts, that as currently understood and practiced, developmental psychology is "the study of the strange behavior of children in strange situations with strange adults for the briefest possible periods of time." The use of a social systems framework forces us, as professionals, to seek above and beyond relationships between causes and instructional strategies. Rather, the social systems perspective insists that we recognize the complexity of the many issues related to individuals who are perceived as varying from

Objective Two

To describe the impact of the social systems approach on learners who vary from their peers.

their peers. Taking into account the transactions between the developing child and the environment, we can recognize how predictions resulting from the child's early assessment may be inadequate (Sameroff, 1975). For example, if a child is identified as demonstrating a disability, the parents may reduce their expectations for the child, thus limiting the child by their subconscious interaction style. Parents' perceptions of their child influence their behavior toward their child. Parents who perceive the child as limited interact with the child in a way which supports that perception. The same is true of the influence of teachers' perceptions of learners.

The social systems perspective also has an impact on professional practice. For example, assessment is a dynamic process that considers the learner's interactions with others within a variety of settings. Effective assessment procedures require the study of learner interactions in these various settings as well as the individual learner. In addition, the social systems perspective recognizes that changes in one setting may influence another setting, so understanding changes in the learner's home life is essential for the professionals with whom the learner is working. The social systems perspective requires the professional to view the learner as a particular individual rather than a person with whom the automatic use of certain assessment techniques is appropriate (Fine, 1992).

Objective Three

To describe the application of the social systems perspective in the text.

The Social Systems Perspective in the Text

The social systems perspective provides the framework for this text. It is used to organize the vast amount of information provided to college and university students in introductory courses in special education.

The first section of the text addresses in detail the developmental contexts introduced in this chapter. Information is provided on families and learners with disabilities, transitions between the various contexts, and schooling and learners with disabilities.

The next three sections of the text (chaps. 7–17) address primarily the learner. Sections are devoted to discussions of learners with disabilities who vary from their peers in how they interact with the environment, how they access the environment, and how they learn. However, as the systems perspective implies, it is impossible to discuss individuals without also describing the contexts in which they develop. Thus in each chapter information specific to individual variations is provided.

To assist the reader, a standard format is used for these chapters. Each chapter begins with an introduction, which sets the stage for the information provided in the chapter. The introduction presents basic issues with regard to the specific group of learners with disabilities under discussion. Next, each chapter addresses the ecological contexts of development as they apply to the group of individuals. A schemata depicting the developmental contexts as discussed in each chapter is presented in figure 1.2.

The first part of each chapter describes the personal characteristic of the group of learners being discussed. These include learning characteristics, language and communication skills, social and emotional characteristics, and psychomotor and physical characteristics. The second part of each chapter discusses the "professional" context applied to considerations of the characteristics discussed under the first objective, that is, definition, classification, prevalence and incidence, screening and identification, and assessment and evaluation. The third part of each chapter describes the impact of the disability within the home and classroom. Strategies and techniques for enhancing the individual's development within and among these settings are described in the fourth part of each chapter. This includes a discussion of the impact of the disability on participation in the larger social system of the school and the community. Each chapter concludes with a discussion of society's perceptions of individuals with the disability under discussion.

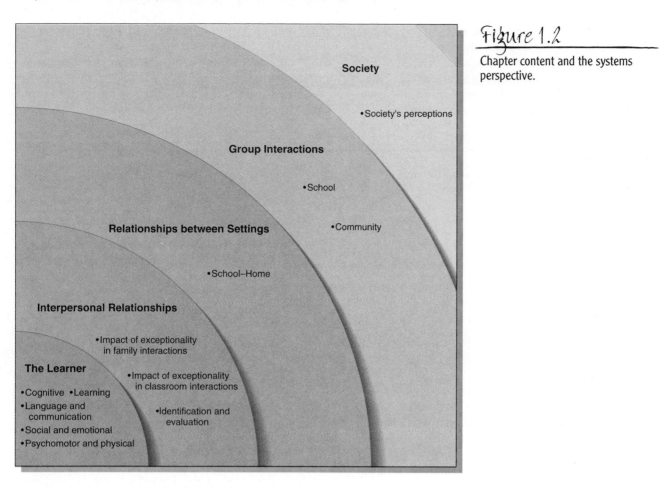

Figure 1.2
Chapter content and the systems perspective.

Society

• Society's perceptions

Group Interactions

• School

Relationships between Settings

• Community

• School–Home

Interpersonal Relationships

• Impact of exceptionality in family interactions

The Learner

• Impact of exceptionality in classroom interactions

• Cognitive • Learning
• Language and communication
• Social and emotional
• Psychomotor and physical

• Identification and evaluation

Summary

In this chapter, learners with disabilities and special education were defined and discussed. Learners with disabilities are individuals who are perceived by others as varying from their peers. They may differ in appearance, how they communicate, and how they move. They may vary in the ways in which they interact and relate to others, gain access to the environment, or the rate and manner in which they learn. In this chapter, we, the authors, emphasized that learners with disabilities are first and foremost learners, and these learners vary from their peers in some manner. Special education is presented as the subsystem of general education that is responsible for supporting learners with disabilities. Learners with disabilities are those individuals who challenge the general education system, which is designed primarily for learners who can move quickly and unobtrusively through the system.

The social systems perspective of disabilities and several terms essential to effective communication between reader and authors were presented. The social systems approach was defined as a perspective in which the individual is seen as developing in a dynamic relationship with and as an inseparable part of the social contexts in which the individual functions over her or his life span.

The social systems perspective was differentiated from other perspectives of human development and learning. It was applied in the text because it is broad in scope and allows the integration of much of the information derived from other theories (behavioral, psychoeducational, and biophysical).

The ecology of human development, originally presented by Bronfenbrenner and enhanced by others, was discussed. Each of the ecological contexts was defined and exemplified.

The impact of a social systems perspective on professional practice was discussed. In using the social systems perspective, the complex transactions among the learner, his or her interpersonal relationships, group relationships, the interaction among settings, and society's values are considered.

The implications of the ecological perspective for the study of learners with disabilities and special education were discussed. The social systems perspective requires the recognition of the complexity of the many issues related to individuals who are seen as differing from their peers.

The chapter concluded with an overview of the text and its chapters and their relationships to the ecological perspective. Essentially, the text is a blending of the social systems perspective (chaps. 1–6) with more traditional information on learners with disabilities and special education (chaps. 7–17).

The information in chapters 7–17 is presented using the ecological contexts as a framework.

The following five chapters are devoted to a detailed discussion of each of the ecological contexts introduced in this chapter. Chapter 2 focuses societal perceptions of learners with disabilities.

Building Your Professional Vocabulary

Match each word or phrase to its meaning.

_____ accommodation

_____ behavioral

_____ congruence

_____ ecological contexts

_____ psychoeducational

_____ transaction

_____ behavior

_____ biophysical

_____ development

_____ milieu

_____ special education

a. a subsystem of general education supporting the education of learners with disabilities
b. psychological factors within the individual are seen as the primary cause of behavior
c. the continual adaptation of the individual and the environment to each other
d. behavior is maintained by stimuli in the immediate environment

e. settings
f. behavior is caused by organic factors
g. expression of the dynamic relationship between the learner and the environment
h. goodness of fit
i. adaptation and adjustment
j. communicative exchange
k. the individual's social surroundings

Comprehension Check

Select the most appropriate response.
1. Prescribing medication for a learner whose behavior is disruptive in the classroom reflects
   a. the psychoeducational perspective.
   b. the social systems perspective.
   c. the biophysical perspective.
2. Assuming a social systems perspective
   a. allows for the complex interactions among environmental variables.
   b. ascribes cause and effect to behavior.
   c. allows for removing the individual from the context for consideration.
3. In the social systems perspective, development
   a. requires a positive change.
   b. is a mutual accommodation between the learner and the environment.
   c. follows stages consistent among learners.
4. In the social systems perspective, the learner with disabilities
   a. may be identified due to a lack of congruence between the learner and the environment.

   b. may be removed from the environment for assessment.
   c. may be readily identified by a single variable.
5. The social systems perspective is distinguished by
   a. emphasis on the personal characteristics of the learner.
   b. emphasis on the stimuli in the environment.
   c. emphasis on progressive accommodations between the learner and the environment.
6. In a transaction,
   a. an individual's behavior is altered by another.
   b. an individual's behavior is altered by and alters the behavior of another.
   c. an individual's behavior alters that of another.

References

Belsky, J. (1980). Child maltreatment: An ecological integration. *American Psychologist, 35,* 320–335.

Bronfenbrenner, U. (1979). *The ecology of human development.* Cambridge, MA: Harvard University.

D'Amato, R. C., & Rothlisberg, B. A. (Eds.). (1992). *Psychological perspectives on intervention: A case study approach to prescriptions for change.* New York: Longman.

Fine, M. J. (1992). A systems-ecological perspective on home-school intervention. In M. J. Fine and C. Carlson (Eds.), *The handbook of family-school intervention* (pp. 1–17). Boston: Allyn & Bacon.

Gatlin, H. (1980). Dialectics and family interaction. *Human Development, 23,* 245–253.

Kurdek, L. A. (1981). An integrative perspective on children's divorce adjustment. *American Psychologist, 36,* 856–866.

Marmor, J., & Pumpian-Mindlin, E. (1950). Toward an integrative conception of mental disorders. *Journal of Nervous and Mental Disease, 3,* 19–29.

Poplin, M. S., & Stone, S. (1992). Paradigm shifts in instructional strategies. In W. Stainback & S. Stainback (Eds.), *Controversial issues confronting special education.* Boston: Allyn & Bacon.

Riegel, K. F. (1975). Toward a dialectical theory of development. *Human Development, 18,* 50–64.

Sameroff, A. (1975). Transactional models in early social relations. *Human Development, 18,* 65–79.

Sameroff, A., & Chandler, M. J. (1975). Reproductive risk and the continuum of care-taking causality. In F. D. Horowitz, M. Heatherington, S. Scarr-Salapatek, & G. Siegel (Eds.), *Review of child development research, Volume IV.* Chicago, IL: University of Chicago Press.

Scott, M. (1980). Ecological theory and methods of research in special education. *Journal of Special Education, 4,* 279–294.

Thomas, E. D., & Marshall, M. J. (1977). Clinical evaluation and coordination of services: An ecological model. *Exceptional Children, 44,* 16–22.

Thurman, S. K. (1977). Congruence of behavioral ecologies: A model for special education programming. *Journal of Special Education, 11,* 329–333.

Tinbergen, N. (1951). *The study of instinct.* London: Oxford University Press.

2

Chapter

Societal
Perceptions
of Learners
with
Disabilities

Objectives

After completing this chapter, you will be able to:

1. describe the society in which learners with disabilities develop.
2. describe the evolution of current professional practices with individuals who vary from their peers.
3. describe issues related to societal perceptions that have an impact on the individual's development.

Key Words and Phrases

Americans with Disabilities Act
   of 1990 (ADA)
compensatory education
disability

handicap
inclusive education
stigma
the wild boy of Aveyron

he first clue that our society devalues us is the amount of an SSI [Supplementary Security Income] check. The solution to enforced poverty is to get more money to live on. In most cases, earning it through honest work—all of which is reported, of course—costs us our health care right off the bat. In a society which expects us to die or get well, Medicaid is the only third party payer in our health care system which covers most of the ongoing medical needs of people with disabilities. Therefore, we must be poor—at least on paper—to survive. Our struggle to earn honest, reportable money is further discouraged when every two dollars we earn not only reduces an SSI check by a dollar, but also adds a dollar to our (subsidized) rent and takes a dollar from our food stamps (Barbara Knowlen, an individual with physical disabilities, 1995).

Introduction

This chapter focuses attention on society's values and beliefs about disabilities and persons with disabilities. The belief system supported by the majority culture includes broad social factors that impact the settings within which the individual with disabilities functions. This context includes society members' general perceptions of individuals with disabilities, teachers, educational administrators, schools (including special education programs), and business and industry. According to Riegel (1975), society's general perspective of teachers, the social role of students, and community values all affect each student's education.

This chapter provides an overview of society's perceptions of individuals with disabilities, their status in society, their education, and their functioning in the workplace. Much of the information presented is derived from survey research conducted by individual researchers and research groups such as Louis Harris and Associates and the Gallup Organization. The evolution of current professional practices for treatment of individuals who vary from their peers is discussed. The chapter concludes with a discussion of the impact of societal perceptions on individual development.

Society and Learners with Disabilities

"Disability" versus "Handicap"

In 1975, Public Law 94-142 defined "handicapped children" as those who were mentally retarded, hard of hearing, deaf, speech impaired, visually handicapped, seriously emotionally disturbed, orthopedically impaired, other health impaired, deaf-blind, or multihandicapped, or who had specific learning disabilities. [In 1990, Public Law 101-476, The Individuals with Disabilities Education Act (IDEA) added learners with autism and traumatic brain injury to the disability categories.] To be considered handicapped according to Public Law 94-142, students had to require special education and related services as a consequence of their disabilities.

This prerequisite for identification as handicapped, that is, the need for special education and related services, drew a careful line of demarcation between disability and handicap. **Disability** referred to a reduction of function or the absence of a particular body part or organ, such as the loss of a limb (Blackhurst, 1985). A **handicap** was viewed as a disadvantage resulting from a disability that limits or prevents fulfillment of a role (McCarthy, 1984). This differentiation is consistent with Bronfenbrenner's position with regard to development in society, that is, "The direction and degree of psychological growth are governed by the extent to which opportunities to enter settings conducive to development in various domains are open or closed to the developing person" (1979, p. 288). This assertion is supported by Knowlen (1995), who has physical disabilities, in the opening statement of this chapter. The very way that society's support structure is established limits the opportunities available to persons with disabilities.

In an effort to remove the stigma of the term "handicapped," Congress changed the terminology to "disabilities" with the passage of Public Law 101-476. These amendments to Public Law 94-142 changed the name of the legislation from "The Education for All Handicapped Children Act" to "The Individuals with Disabilities Education Act." (Public Law 94-142, Public Law 101-476, and other legislation, as well as several judicial decisions having significant impact on the education of learners with disabilities, are discussed in chapter 3.)

In the remainder of this section, we will explore society's general beliefs and values regarding disabilities, including acceptance of persons with disabilities in the workplace and in the educational system as well as in the professional arena, by those who work with them.

Objective One

To describe the society in which learners with disabilities develop.

General Beliefs and Values

Yoshida, Wasilewski, and Friedman (1990) studied the content of five metropolitan area newspapers for a two-year period to determine the news coverage allowed to persons with disabilities. They found that the most frequently presented topic was the cost of developing community-based programs and providing services to persons with emotional disabilities. Budget expenditures, taxes, and housing for persons with disabilities as well as normalization and treatment in institutional settings were the topics next most likely to appear. Yoshida and associates found a paucity of articles on the actual education or instruction of individuals with disabilities, and the vast majority of articles concerned adults with disabilities.

Popular media may provide information to the public that is both erroneous and stereotypical. Rankin and Phillips (1995), recognizing that the reading materials people encounter in their daily lives affect their belief systems and may be held as "fact," suggest that educators ask themselves a series of questions as they read articles in the popular media. First, they should attempt to discern the major focus of the article, asking whether the intent is to provide general information, present new research, or describe personal experience. Second, educators should determine the perspective of the author, differences between the perspective of the article and that which parents see in their children's programs may be confusing for parents. Next, teachers should ask questions regarding the qualifications of the author and the research or "expert" support offered for the contentions put forth in the article. Finally, the educator should determine whether the article provides information on parental rights or provides other advice and recommendations. Rankin and Phillips caution that due to popular media, parents may make generalizations, be misinformed, or perform an "instant diagnosis" on their child.

The International Center for the Disabled (ICD) Survey of Disabled Americans (1986) was the first national survey designed to study the attitudes and experiences of disabled Americans. It sought to determine the impact of the individuals' disabilities on the quality of their lives, including work, social life, daily activities, education, and personal life. It explored the barriers persons with disabilities confront in their efforts to lead full and productive lives.

The survey, conducted through telephone interviews with one thousand persons with disabilities, focused on life changes in the past ten years, the personal meaning of disability, types of work available, barriers to work, social life and services, and government and employer benefits and policies. The survey also explored the perceptions of persons with disabilities as an underprivileged group and the emerging consciousness of persons with disabilities as a group.

Although the vast majority of those polled believed their lives had improved within the past ten years, their reports also indicate that disabilities have broad and varied repercussions. As a group, persons with disabilities have far less education than other Americans. They are poorer than other Americans. Persons with disabilities are generally unable to travel as they would like and have difficulty attending social events outside of the home, such as theater, concerts, and sports events. They are less likely than persons without disabilities to go to the movies, eat in restaurants, grocery shop, or to participate in general community life. Barriers to a full social life include fear that the disability will cause the individual to become sick, hurt, or victimized by crime; the need for help from other persons in getting around; difficulty in accessing public transportation or locating someone to drive them; and a lack of access to public buildings and restrooms.

According to the survey results, there are definite indications of an emerging group consciousness among persons with disabilities. They now perceive themselves as a minority and believe that equal rights legislation should be applied to persons with disabilities in the same way that it is applied to other minorities.

Technology has increased the mobility of individuals with disabilities.

Society's familiarity with individuals with disabilities has been challenged by this increasing awareness of the rights of persons with disabilities. The poster child, once perceived as a symbol of hope, is now viewed by many individuals with disabilities as a symbol of oppression. The disability, which impacts the individual daily, is depicted in the poster campaigns as something to be prevented, cured, or pitied.

Shapiro (1993) draws a parallel between the evolution of the poster child and the development of the Disabilities Rights Movement. The early poster-child campaigns were designed to suggest that the disability, tragic in innocent children yet unmentionable in adults, could be cured. But cures did not emerge, and prevention programs only created the impression that those who had disabilities were "damaged goods." Through hard work and determination, these individuals would always try to change this impression and to earn society's respect.

As realism overtook the optimism regarding prevention and cure of disabilities, the disability became something to be overcome, and images of the "inspirational disabled person" emerged. Shapiro indicates, however, that the Disability Rights Movement discards the notion that people with disabilities should be courageous or heroic superachievers, since most individuals with disabilities simply are trying to lead their own lives, not inspire anyone. In fact, within the disabilities rights culture, the term *supercrip* has emerged for individuals who attempt extraordinary feats to demonstrate that their disabilities can be "overcome."

Acceptance in the Workplace

Schafer, Rice, Metzler, and Haring (1989) surveyed both nondisabled co-workers of persons with disabilities and other nondisabled employees who worked in the same business, but not directly, with persons with disabilities. Co-workers of persons with disabilities expressed more comfort and acceptance about working with persons with mental retardations, and more respondents strongly agreed that such persons were friendly on the job and socially and vocationally competent than did nondisabled employees who did not work directly with persons with disabilities. The surveyors found that perceptions of co-workers of the social and vocational competencies of workers with severe disabilities were equal, and in many instances superior, to the perceptions of co-workers of workers with mild and moderate levels

Individuals with disabilities reported an improved quality of life in the last decade.

of mental retardation. Schafer and associates reported that co-workers expressed relative comfort and willingness to work with individuals identified as mentally retarded. However, the majority of the contact between workers who were disabled and those who were not was related to task performance; very little contact was reported among these groups of employees during work breaks and after work.

In 1986, Louis Harris and Associates conducted a nationwide survey of 920 employers for the ICD on the employment of Americans with disabilities (ICD, 1987). This survey, which remains the most recent large-scale study of the employment of persons with disabilities, was based on telephone interviews with 210 top managers or corporate executives, 301 equal opportunity employment managers, 210 department heads or line managers, and 200 top managers of very small companies. The survey results may not be generalized to particular groups, but they do provide a picture of persons with disabilities in the workplace.

The 1986 survey was a consequence of another survey conducted in 1985 for the ICD and the National Council of the Handicapped (ICD, 1986) in which it was found that two-thirds of all working-age persons with disabilities were not working, even though a large majority stated a willingness to work. The survey results indicate that work makes a considerable difference in the lives of persons with disabilities. Workers with disabilities are more satisfied with life, less likely to consider themselves disabled, and less likely to perceive their disability as a barrier to realizing their full potential as a person.

The survey results also suggest that cost should not be a barrier to employing persons with disabilities. Three-fourths of the managers stated that the cost of employing a person with disabilities was about the same as employing a person without disabilities. The managers indicated that making accommodations for employees with disabilities was not expensive; it was, in fact, within the range of the cost of accommodations for all employees. About 50 percent of the managers stated that their company had made accommodations for employees with disabilities, including the removal of architectural barriers, purchase of special equipment, adjustment of work hours, and restructuring of jobs.

Even though persons with disabilities have demonstrated excellent job performance, and employing them appears to involve limited additional cost, companies have not employed persons with disabilities in large numbers. Only 43 percent of the 301 equal employment opportunity managers surveyed stated that their company had hired a worker with disabilities in the year prior to the survey. Large corporations and companies with federal contracts, which mandate the employment of persons with disabilities, were more likely to employ such persons than were smaller companies.

The survey results indicate that the barriers to employing persons with disabilities are (a) a lack of qualified applicants, (b) the absence of company programs or policies relating to employment of those with disabilities, (c) a lack of awareness among middle management employers about employing persons with disabilities or about company policies concerning employment of persons with disabilities, and (d) managers' lack of consciousness with regard to persons with disabilities as a group. The survey reveals that discrimination on the job is a major barrier to the employment of persons with disabilities. Three in four managers felt that persons with disabilities would encounter discrimination on the job.

Approximately seven in ten managers believed that their company was making a sufficient effort to employ persons with disabilities and should not make a greater effort to employ them. Interestingly, the managers also thought that their company would make a greater effort to employ workers with disabilities in the following three years but anticipated that rehabilitation and placement agencies would assume responsibility for training qualified applicants. Managers were very supportive of proposed initiatives and policy changes suggested by employers, state and federal agencies, legislatures, and private rehabilitation and placement agencies and foundations. They favored (a) cooperative company and school or agency training programs, (b) part-time jobs and internships prior to full employment, (c) functional job descriptions presented by the employer rather than a teacher or vocational program personnel, (d) tax deductions for company expenses required to accommodate workers with disabilities, (e) salary subsidies for trial employment of persons with severe disabilities, (f) technical assistance and counseling for employees with disabilities, and (g) voluntary employment targets. All managers agreed that civil rights laws that protect minorities against discrimination should apply to persons with disabilities. Equal employment opportunity managers were the most supportive of this concept; top managers were the least supportive.

The acceptance of workers with disabilities in the workplace is marked with paradox. Though both co-workers and employers report comfort and willingness to work with individuals with disabilities, two-thirds of individuals with disabilities, according to one survey, are not working. Though managers report good or excellent job performance, employment of persons with disabilities is limited. Though managers and employers express an openness to employing persons with disabilities, that openness apparently is rarely put into practice.

Shapiro (1993) describes the Hockenberry Rule regarding the employment of persons with disabilities. John Hockenberry was the National Public Radio West Coast correspondent. His assignments included a range of events, including political races and the eruption of Mount Saint Helens. When he arrived at the national NPR office, his fellow correspondents were amazed to find that he used a wheelchair. They also realized that, had they known of his disability, he would not have received his challenging assignments—his colleagues would have assumed that he was unable to cover them. The Hockenberry Rule states that society automatically underestimates the capabilities of people with disabilities.

Employment remains very difficult for individuals with disabilities. Working means the loss of essential health insurance and Social Security benefits (Shapiro, 1993). The monthly check for an individual on Supplementary Security Income is about $400; the check for an individual on Disability Insurance is about $600. Both programs stop providing income when an individual consistently earns $500 or more a month. In addition, public income support problems are linked to health insurance (Medicare and Medicaid) eligibility. Society's support system itself creates disincentives for persons with disabilities to work, and in many cases makes employment impossible (Greenbaum, 1995).

Perceptions of Professionals

Professionals' perceptions of persons with disabilities and their families are affected by the roles those professionals assume. Marsh, Stoughton, and Williams (1985) found significant differences in the ratings of the impact of the disability on the individual and the family among clinical psychologists, school psychologists, teachers, and parents. Clinical psychologists and school psychologists tend to imbue many childhood behaviors with greater psychological significance than do either teachers or parents. According to Marsh and associates, both the role and the age of the professional rating a child's behavior can significantly influence his or her assessment of the child's mental health status.

Professionals may make unwarranted inferences with regard to the magnitude of the challenges that confront the families of children with disabilities. Blackard and Barsch (1982) examined the extent to which professionals were able to accurately predict parents' responses to questionnaire items concerning the impact of the child with disabilities on the family, and they found significant differences between the responses of parents and the predictions of the professionals. When compared to parents, professionals tended to overestimate the negative impact of the child with a disability on family relationships. They overestimated the extent to which parents reported community rejection and lack of support and the parents' ability to use appropriate teaching and behavior management techniques in the home. Professionals magnified the impact of the child with disabilities on all aspects of family functioning presented in the questionnaire: changes in marital relationships, changes in family goals, restriction of family activities, effects on other children in the family, and financial considerations. Though direct assessment of the family is necessary, Blackard and Barsch caution professionals to avoid unwarranted assumptions with regard to the negative impact of the child with disabilities on the family.

Stefans (1993) provides a tongue-in-cheek response to the findings expressed by Blackard and Barsch. She says that professionals must concentrate on moving "beyond professionalism." Stefans offers the following advice to professionals:

- Recognize that if there is a mismatch between their training and reality, they should accept reality.
- Learn from their clients and students.
- Develop clear translations of professional jargon.
- Think of clients and students as people first.
- Seek and give support to other professionals.

Perceptions of Peers

With regard to students, Condon, York, Heal, and Fortschneider (1986) found girls to be more accepting of learners with disabilities than boys. Respondents from schools in which students with disabilities were enrolled were more accepting than respondents from schools whose enrollment did not include students with disabilities. Older students were more tolerant of students with disabilities than were younger students; this was especially true in schools with students with disabilities. However, this acceptance appeared to dissipate when contact between students with and without disabilities was interrupted.

Berryman (1989) developed a picture of the general acceptance of students with disabilities in inclusive settings—that is, in the general education setting with age-peers—by measuring the attitudes of 377 adults shopping at a mall in a small city. The results of the survey suggest a positive attitude concerning the general concept of inclusion and the inclusion of learners with disabilities with a normal potential for learning. The respondents had a less favorable attitude toward students who were likely to have difficulty functioning in the general classroom setting; they were the most positive about including students with speech disorders and chronic medical problems; and they were the least favorable of including students who exhibited disruptive behavior. An interesting finding was that the respondents who had not had a child in school since 1975 were less favorable of inclusion than respondents who did have a child in school after that year. Younger persons had a more favorable attitude toward the inclusion of students with normal learning potential than did older persons.

Though inclusive education is becoming widespread, inclusive settings may limit the interactions students with disabilities have with similarly disabled peers. Opportunities for interacting with individuals with similar disabilities are necessary for the development of positive self-identity. Stainback, Stainback, East, and Sapon-Shevin (1994) suggest that planned opportunities for persons who share common challenges be established in either school or community. They suggest that such ad hoc meetings be made available to students to share information, support, and strategies for transforming prejudice, discrimination,

Annual **Edition**

Article *2*

and practices. Schools can provide the framework necessary for the formation of such groups. However, the groups themselves need to be developed by their members if the basic rights of the participants are to be recognized. Stainback and associates, however, assert that focusing on any one of an individual's characteristics (i.e., disability) and organizing a group on that basis alone may be hazardous to inclusion.

Perceptions of Educators

In 1987, Louis Harris and Associates conducted a survey on the status of special education in the United States for the ICD and the National Council on Disability (ICD, 1989). This was the first and most recent survey designed to assess the perceptions of public school educators, students with disabilities, and parents of students with disabilities with regard to the effectiveness of special education in meeting the needs of students with disabilities. Educators, parents, and students with disabilities were interviewed by telephone and asked to assess changes in the educational system and give a "report card" on present-day educational and related services, including evaluation of the instructional quality and methodology, educational placements and mainstreaming, the impact of the integration on students without disabilities, social interaction among students with and without disabilities, the Individualized Education Plan, transition from the school to employment or further education, and future projections.

The survey population included 702 educators, 1,000 parents, and 200 youth with disabilities. The educators included four representative subsamples of special education district directors, principals, and general and special education teachers. The parent sample was weighted to be representative of the ten handicapping conditions defined in Public Law 94-142. Survey results, in general, suggest that students with disabilities are receiving better services today than they were ten or twelve years ago. Parents suggested that they had fought hard to obtain appropriate services for their children but were reasonably satisfied at the present. However, the survey results indicate that schools remain inadequately prepared to serve students with disabilities or to prepare them for employment and higher education.

Both educators and parents agreed that services in the public schools for students with disabilities had improved since the passage of Public Law 94-142 in 1975. The majority of principals and teachers, however, did not have adequate training in special education and were not confident making decisions with regard to the education of students with disabilities. Only 40 percent of general teachers had any training in special education; however, on average, they had three or four students with disabilities in their classrooms. The majority of educators reported that they had modified teaching and testing procedures to accommodate students with disabilities. Educators maintained, however, that they were less successful with persons with disabilities than with persons without disabilities.

Americans with Disabilities Act

With the passage of the **Americans with Disabilities Act (ADA)** (Public Law 101-336) in July 1990, full participation of individuals with disabilities in American society was recognized (Council for Exceptional Children, 1990). This act is patterned after Section 504 of the Rehabilitation Act of 1973, which has guaranteed the civil rights of individuals with disabilities for two decades. Among the provisions of the ADA are the modification of the definition of individuals with disabilities and requirements in the areas of transportation, telecommunications, employment, and public accommodations for persons with disabilities, as well as protection for persons with Acquired Immune Deficiency Syndrome (AIDS) or Human Immunodeficiency Virus (HIV) (Kendrick, 1990; Johns, 1990).

The ADA broadly defines a person with disabilities as someone who has a physical or mental impairment (or has a record of such an impairment or is regarded as having such an impairment) that substantially limits that person's participation in some major life activity. The definition covers three groups of individuals with disabilities: (1) persons with actual physical or mental impairment such as persons with learning disabilities, visual impairments, or mental retardation; (2) persons who are discriminated against as a consequence of their past experience with a disabling condition, persons with a record of impairment such as a previous medical disability or mental illness, for example; and (3) persons who are not actually impaired but who are regarded as impaired as a result of disfigurement.

Public, private intercity, and rail transportation are all affected by the ADA. All new public transportation buses must be accessible to individuals with disabilities; retrofitting of existing public buses is not required. Paratransit services for persons with disabilities are required unless the provision of these services causes undue financial burden. Rural and small communities must make a "good faith" effort to comply with transportation requirements. Private transit providers must make their buses accessible within a period of six or seven years, depending on the size of the company. All new rail transit vehicles must be built to be accessible, and one car per train must be accessible within five years. Key rail stations must be accessible within three years, with exceptions to twenty years in extraordinary cases. Amtrak stations must be made accessible within twenty years.

The ADA requires all common telecommunications carriers to provide intrastate and interstate relay services for telephone calls made by users of telecommunications devices for the deaf (TDDs) and users of voice telephones. Relay system requirements state that an intermediary must be available twenty-four hours a day, seven days a week at regular service rates to transmit messages to and from persons with and without a TDD.

The act also includes protection against discrimination for persons with AIDS or HIV. This protection is viewed as an essential public health tool in the fight against the increased incidence of AIDS and HIV.

The ADA employment mandates apply to all employers with fifteen or more employees. Employers may not refuse to employ a person with disabilities due to the disability if the person is qualified to perform the job. The employer is required to make reasonable accommodations in the workplace for the individual with a disability, unless such accommodations impose undue hardship on the employer. The dates on which employment provisions take effect vary according to the number of employees in the company.

According to the ADA, persons with disabilities must have access to public accommodations. Public accommodations are defined as the businesses and services that are used every day by all people, department stores and restaurants, for example. New buildings must be designed and constructed for access. Accessibility to public accommodations in existing buildings is required only if such changes are "readily achievable." Public accommodations being renovated must be made accessible. Auxiliary goods and services such as braille signs and visual signals must be available within accommodations to make them accessible to persons with disabilities.

The ADA provides various remedies for violations of the law. These are similar to those provided under the Civil Rights Act of 1964.

Society continues to present challenges to individuals with disabilities. Efforts have been made, however, to enable individuals with disabilities to access the community on a more equal basis with their peers. Language has changed to attempt to address the issue of stigma. Though underemployment remains an issue, the perceptions of employers and co-workers are becoming more positive.

Making News

Who cares how high her IQ really is?

Disabled Sandra Jensen just wants to live

By Joseph P. Shapiro

Sandra Jensen represents the dark flip side to Mickey Mantle. When the late ballplayer got a new liver after just 24 hours on a waiting list, it stirred suspicion that celebrity had brought preference. But an uglier question was raised when Jensen, a 34-year-old with Down's syndrome, recently was denied a life-sustaining heart-lung operation: In scarce times, is one's worth measured by one's intelligence?

With too few organs, hospitals must make Solomonic decisions. Last year, 71 people got heart-lung transplants, while 205 others waited. Jensen's case is notable because although California's health insurance program will pay for her $250,000 transplant, the two approved hospitals made issue of her intelligence and rejected her. First came a stinging three-sentence letter from Stanford University Medical Center saying, "We do not feel that patients with Down's syndrome are appropriate candidates for heart-lung transplantation." The University of California at San Diego Medical Center at least met her and did a thorough work-up, but in the end doubted she could follow the "stringent medical routine" of post-transplant pill taking and monitoring.

To Jensen and her supporters, the rejection was discriminatory. She is a familiar presence in the Sacramento statehouse, where she has not only bused tables in the cafeteria but also testified eloquently before committees. This year, she visited scores of parents and disabled children about to leave high school and unsure of the future. Jensen tells how doctors advised her mother to institutionalize her but how she now has her own apartment and works.

Take care. Jensen's doctor, Philip Bach, argues that she will be able to take care of herself. He notes that she already takes several medicines a day and checks her own blood pressure. And her mother, Kay DeMaio, says she would move back to California. Without the operation, Bach says, Jensen will die within a few years.

To disabled people, the case represents more thinking that intelligence determines quality of life. In their bestselling book *The Bell Curve,* Charles Murray and Richard Herrnstein argue for abandoning government programs, like affirmative action, that promote social equality because, they say, genetically determined low IQ dooms social success. More direct is ethicist Peter Singer, who in a recent book proposes a 28-day period in which parents and doctors could choose infanticide

for a "life that has begun very badly." His example: Down's syndrome. With genetic advances promising control over disease and disability, there is a rising stigma against people believed "genetically predisposed to be less competent," warns Dorothy Nelkin, co-author of *The DNA Mystique.*

The publicity has forced the hospitals to reconsider Jensen for their waiting lists. She'd like to think that when she next needs medical help, she won't have to prove first how "worthy" she is.

Update . . .

Disabled woman's transplant a first

SAN FRANCISCO - Hours after her heart-lung transplant, Sandra Jensen was already trying to speak. That wasn't surprising to those who know the 35-year-old woman with Down syndrome.

"Sandra is going to get up out of that bed—and out of her mouth are going to come the marching instructions," said Dr. William Bronston, a state rehabilitation administrator and friend who helped lead the year-long fight for Tuesday's operation •

Educational services for individuals with disabilities have improved. Equal access is approaching reality through legislation, specifically the Americans with Disabilities Act. The evolution of more specific practices with regard to individuals with disabilities is described next.

Evolution of Professional Practices

Although treatment for persons with disabilities may have occurred earlier, the first documented attempt to treat and educate persons with disabilities is the establishment of a public hospital for the blind in 1260 (Juul, 1981). During the Middle Ages, with the exception of the reports of religious orders in Switzerland that administered routine and systematic assistance to persons with disabilities, references to the treatment and education of persons with disabilities are scarce.

In 1749, accounts of educator Jacob Rodreques Pereire's (1715–1780) demonstrations before the Academy of Science in Paris were published. These reports described his success in teaching persons with severe hearing impairments to speak and read.

Objective Two

To describe the evolution of current professional practices with individuals who vary from their peers.

However, according to Juul, the real impetus for the education of persons with disabilities was generated by the social and philosophical teachings of Jean Jacques Rousseau (1712–1778). In 1762, Rousseau, a philosopher and theorist, published *Emile,* a plea for the direct study of children rather than the application of results from the study of adults to children.

Rousseau's optimism about the potential for goodness in both the individual and society inspired Jean-Marc-Gaspard Itard (1774–1838), a physician and educator, in his efforts to teach Victor, **the wild boy of Aveyron.** Victor was a young boy discovered in the woods near Aveyron, France. He was thought to be a feral child, untouched by civilization. At that time, Victor's socialization was considered by most persons to be hopeless. Itard's study of Victor, published as a report of the French Academy of Science in 1801 and supplemented in 1806, is the first systematic documentation of efforts to teach a child with disabilities.

Forness and Kavale (1984) discuss three points they believe are significant about the publication of Itard's notes. First, if the publication is carefully examined, it becomes apparent that Itard applied the rudimentary form of nearly every educational technique that is applied today in the teaching of persons with disabilities. Second, special education in the United States is a direct beneficiary of Itard's work, in that his student, physician and educator Edouard Sequin (1812–1880), was invited by Samuel Gridley Howe to lecture and work in North America during the mid-nineteenth century. Finally, Itard and Sequin, both physicians, unwittingly established a legacy of medical influence on special education practices that has, in the words of Forness and Kavale, "plagued [the profession of special education] to this day." Their emphasis on etiology (finding the cause or causes of a condition), symptomatology (identifying a cluster of symptoms or the symptoms by which a condition is recognized), exclusionary diagnosis (differential diagnosis or a diagnosis that differentiates a condition from other conditions), and hospitalization for persons with mental retardation left special education, much like medicine, with an intervention system that was usually implemented only after symptoms became sufficiently severe to necessitate referral and extensive evaluation. Because of special education's adherence to this legacy, the courts have entered into the special education decision-making processes in an effort to facilitate change. At present, special education policies are being decided largely outside the profession, by the courts and legislatures. As a result, decisions with regard to the education of learners with disabilities are often based in legal and legislative considerations rather than education and psychological theory and best practice.

A significant, but perhaps a less well recognized contributor to special education, and more specifically early childhood special education, Friedrich Wilhelm August Froebel (1782–1852), educator and founder of the kindergarten, began his work with children during the mid-nineteenth century. With the founding of the Froebel Society in 1873, **compensatory education,** that is, working with children to develop skills commensurate with their more advantaged peers, was established as a goal. This goal is apparent in the work of the Head Start and Chapter One programs established during the 1960s and 1970s. Head Start and Chapter One programs are essentially compensatory and remedial education programs for preschool and school-age children whose parents' income is at or below the federally designated poverty level. The purpose of these programs is to give these children the opportunity to compete more equally with their more affluent peers.

In the late 1880s, Alexander Graham Bell became a leading advocate for the normalization of persons with disabilities, particularly individuals with hearing impairments. In his early call for the inclusion of students with disabilities, rather than their segregation in more restrictive settings, Bell stated:

> It should be recognized as a fundamental thing, that the collection of defective children exclusively together, is a thing to be avoided as much as possible. Exclusive association with one another only aggravates and intensifies the

peculiarities that differentiate them from other people, whereas, it is our object, by instruction, to do away with these differences to the greatest possible extent . . . believing as I do, in the policy of decentralization in dealing with defective children—the policy of separating them from one another as much as practicable during the process of education—and keeping them in constant personal contact with their friends and relatives and ordinary normal people— I would say that it would be better to send the teachers to the children, than to bring the children themselves together. (in Blatt, 1985, p. 407)

During the early twentieth century, Europe was the leader in the education of children and youth with disabilities. In an effort to make schools more responsive to the needs of students, Alfred Binet, working in Paris, conducted a series of studies about children who varied from their peers in learning style and rate. During this same time, Maria Montessori, working in Italy, developed new educational principles, methods, and materials for the instruction of children with mental retardation and children who were economically disadvantaged. Also during this period, American Alfred Adler established the first "child guidance centers" in an effort to improve the treatment of children with behavioral disorders. At the onset of World War II, many prominent psychoanalysts, such as Rudolf Dreikurs and Fritz Redl, fled Europe and organized treatment centers in the United States.

Juul (1981) reports that after World War II, the United States became the undisputed leader in theory, research, and writing in the field of special education. Zirpoli, Hancox, Wieck, and Skarnulis (1989) suggest that advocacy for persons with disabilities and their families evolved from the provision of public protective services organized in the late nineteenth century to private and independent advocacy service groups to the present-day emphasis on self-advocacy.

Professional practices with regard to individuals with disabilities have evolved, yet they continue to represent the legacy of the medical doctors who first worked with individuals with disabilities. Leadership in addressing the needs of learners with disabilities has traveled from Europe to the United States, and has moved from the medical to the educational profession. Individuals with disabilities, with the development of self-advocacy, are assuming greater ownership of and participation in the development of professional practices.

Issues Related to Societal Perceptions

Several issues related to societal perceptions have an impact on an individual's development. These include membership in a minority or ethnic group, gender, stigma, and socioeconomic status. Issues specific to membership in a minority or ethnic group are described elsewhere in the text. In this chapter, issues related to gender, stigma, and socioeconomic status are discussed.

Gender

In her exploration of feminine psychology, Gilligan (1982) remarks that at this time, when efforts are being made to eradicate discrimination between the sexes in the search for social justice, the differences between the sexes are being rediscovered and examined in the social sciences. Gilligan describes the nature of relationships, which, when examined with the related issues of dependency, are experienced differently by women and men. For men, separation and individual identity are tied to gender identity, since separation from the mother is necessary for the development of masculinity. For girls and women, issues of feminine identity do not depend on the achievement of separation from the mother or on the process of individuation.

Lyons (1985) contrasts male and female perspectives in several areas. Whereas women tend to perceive others in their own terms and in context, men see others in terms of equality and reciprocity. In relationships, women are typically

Objective Three

To describe issues related to societal perceptions that have an impact on the individual's development.

interdependent, whereas men are autonomous, equal, and independent. Women attach through response and are concerned with the responsiveness and isolation of others; men attach through roles, obligation, and duty and are concerned with equality and fairness in relationships. Women tend to emphasize discussion and listening in order to understand others; men emphasize the need to maintain fairness and equality in dealing with others.

Responses to the differential treatment of males and females, such as those noted by Lyons, have been studied with regard to the teaching and learning of mathematics. In a report on classroom interactions in twenty-two geometry classes, Stallings (1985) supports the hypothesis that differential treatment of boys and girls occurs in mathematics classes. The boys in these classes exhibited a higher frequency of interactions with teachers on thirteen of the factors studied, including teacher and student questioning, teacher acknowledgement, and teacher praise, instruction, and corrective feedback. Research by Luchins and Luchins (1980) supports Stallings' findings. In their survey, large differences were found when males and females were asked if they recalled receiving different treatment as mathematics students and professionals because they were male or female. Women reported being treated by their peers as though they were strange and being told that boys did not like or were afraid of smart girls. They also reported receiving less attention from teachers who they felt had lower expectations for them than for their male peers.

These differences in classroom behavior have been supported by the findings of studies related to students' goals and aspirations. Gifted females in elementary schools report interests similar to those of gifted males. However, by secondary school, gifted females develop lower career aspirations than those of gifted males (Kerr, 1985). The "cultural underachievement" of women is described by Davis and Rimm (1985) as a result of women's needs to balance professional interests and higher education with traditional sex roles. By recognizing developmental gender issues, it is possible this "cultural underachievement" of women may be avoided by instructors and by women themselves.

Levine and Edgar (1994) analyzed gender differences in postschool outcomes for youth in three disability groups: with learning disabilities, with mild mental retardation, and without disabilities. They surveyed, one, two, six, and seven years after graduation, 549 youth who graduated from high school in 1985 and 398 youth who graduated in 1990 from three school districts. Comparisons were made between genders within disability groups on employment, post-secondary education attendance and graduation, engagement (i.e., employment, post-secondary school attendance, or both), independent living, marital status, and parenting. Few significant differences were found between the genders, except in the area of parenting. Females were affected by early parenting.

Stigma

Goffman (1983), in his classic work on the subject of **stigma,** identifies it as an attribute that is deeply discrediting. By definition, he maintains, those who do not depart from the usual expectations perceive persons with the stigma as not quite human. Acceptance is the primary problem confronting an individual with a stigma. In social situations in which an individual is perceived to have a stigma, categorizations that do not fit are usually applied and uneasiness is experienced by both parties. In addition to stigma itself, Goffman identifies the "courtesy stigma," which is attributed to persons who are related in some way to persons with stigma. Many parents and brothers and sisters of persons with disabilities suffer from the "courtesy stigma." This topic is discussed further in chapter 4, "Families and Learners with Disabilities."

Socioeconomic Status

Kozol (in Rohlk, 1990) suggests that if an upper-class student succeeds and enters college, society perceives the student as succeeding because he or she wanted to succeed. For the lower-class student, not attending college is seen as a sign of apathy and lack of motivation, rather than a result of unequal precollege education. Kozol views the educational systems as generating and maintaining a serious gap between the poorest and the richest. He presents the analogy of a baseball game in which the losing team takes the field without gloves, bats, and uniforms, and the winning team, well equipped, perceives the game as equal.

Socioeconomic status may serve as a gatekeeper for capable students in several ways. Deschamp and Robson (1984) believe that high-achieving students who attend disadvantaged schools are isolates who are limited by programs aimed at their less-capable peers. Consequently, teachers may not recognize the potential of very poor children and so fail to provide them with additional help. In school, disadvantaged students may also struggle with attitudes towards school and achievement expectations that are unlike those of their ethnic group. Culturally diverse students may be limited simply because of their membership in their cultural group. This may increase the potential for overidentification of learners from various cultures as requiring special education services. In addition, most teachers are from what is often referred to as an "advantaged" background, a perspective from which they may view children and as a result lack an understanding of the children's real socioeconomic circumstances.

Summary

In this chapter, society's values and beliefs regarding persons with disabilities were described. By contrasting the terms "disability" and "handicap," a case was made for the use of language that puts the "person first" and recognizes the uniqueness of each individual. The results of a series of studies sponsored by the International Center for the Disabled were discussed to present an overview of society's values and beliefs about individuals with disabilities. Individuals with disabilities indicated in the surveys that though their lives had improved within the past ten years, they still faced challenges to having a full social life, continuing their education, and accessing transportation and buildings. A group consciousness was felt to be emerging.

Individuals with disabilities are perceived by employers and co-workers as being capable; both groups report comfort and willingness to work with individuals with disabilities. However, two-thirds of the individuals with disabilities, according to one ICD survey, are not working. Employment remains a challenge.

Professionals may make unwarranted inferences with regard to the magnitude of the challenges that confront the families of children with disabilities. Professionals tend to overestimate the negative impact a child with a disability has on family relationships. Students from schools enrolling students with disabilities, however, appear to be accepting of their peers with disabilities.

The Americans with Disabilities Act was discussed in detail. Through this act, the right of individuals with disabilities to full participation in American society was recognized. With its broader definition of "disability"—to now include a person who has a physical or mental impairment that substantially limits that person's participation in a major life activity—individuals previously excluded from support and protection through other laws are now provided protection.

The history of professional practices in the field of special education, from the work of medical doctors such as Itard and Sequin through the use of the American legal system to establish educational practice, was discussed. The evolution from protective services to private and public advocacy to self-advocacy by individuals with disabilities was also described.

Three other issues that have a strong impact on the quality of life of individuals with disabilities were described: developmental gender issues, including the cultural underachievement of women; stigma, the assignation of a discrediting attribute; and the role of socioeconomic status as gatekeeper for capable students. The issue of a "courtesy stigma," a phenomenon attributed to persons who are related in some way to persons with stigma, was introduced.

Building Your Professional Vocabulary

Match each word or phrase to its meaning.

_____ ADA

_____ disability

_____ inclusive education

_____ the wild boy of Aveyron

_____ compensatory education

_____ handicap

_____ stigma

a. an attribute that is deeply discrediting
b. working with children to build skills commensurate with peers
c. education in the general education setting with age-peers
d. legislation guaranteeing full participation of individuals with disabilities in American society

e. first systemic effort to educate an individual with disabilities
f. reduction of function
g. disadvantage limiting or preventing fulfillment of a role

Comprehension Check

Select the most appropriate response.

1. Public Law 94-142 defined handicapped children
   a. by specific disability categories.
   b. by students' needs.
   c. by etiology of disability.
2. The ability of a person with a disability is related to
   a. the type of disability.
   b. the educational category of the disability.
   c. the opportunities provided to the individual.
3. The popular media
   a. provide a realistic image of life with a disability.
   b. must be carefully reviewed regarding disabilities.
   c. increase accurate public awareness of persons with disabilities.
4. Individuals with disabilities
   a. are presenting a group consciousness and identity.
   b. require publicly funded support.
   c. are presenting greater identification with persons without disabilities.
5. Employment for persons with disabilities is
   a. guaranteed by the ADA.
   b. discouraged by supports provided by the system.
   c. a reality for most persons with disabilities.
6. Interactions with peers without disabilities
   a. is successful for students with disabilities.
   b. is inadequate for the development of positive self-identity.
   c. is required by the ADA.
7. Initial efforts in special education emerged
   a. in western Europe.
   b. in the United States.
   c. in eastern Europe.
8. Women in schools
   a. receive the same opportunity as men for interaction with teachers.
   b. receive differential treatment in interaction with teachers.
   c. receive preferential treatment from women teachers.
9. Stigma exists
   a. in the nature of the disability.
   b. in the disability's attributes.
   c. within the individual with the disability.
10. Socioeconomic status
    a. serves as a gatekeeper for adequate students.
    b. prevents few challenges in public education.
    c. provides increasing opportunities for students.

References

Berryman, J. D. (1989). Attitudes of the public toward educational mainstreaming. *Remedial and Special Education, 10,* 44–49.

Blackard, M. K., & Barsch, E. T. (1982). Parents' and professionals' perspectives of the handicapped child's impact on the family. *The Journal of the Association of the Severely Handicapped, 76* (2), 62–70.

Blackhurst, A. E. (1985). The growth of special education. In W. H. Berdine & A. E. Blackhurst (Eds.), *An introduction to special education* (2nd ed.). Boston: Little, Brown.

Blatt, B. (1985). Friendly letters on the correspondence of Helen Keller, Anne Sullivan, and Alexander Graham Bell. *Exceptional Children, 51,* 405–410.

Bronfenbrenner, U. (1979). *The ecology of human development.* Cambridge, MA: Harvard University.

Condon, M. E., York, R., Heal, L. W., & Fortschneider, J. (1986). Acceptance of severely handicapped students by nonhandicapped peers. *Journal of the Association for Persons with Severe Handicaps, 11,* 216–219.

Council for Exceptional Children. (1990). Precis: Americans with Disabilities Act of 1990: What you should know. Supplement to *Exceptional Children, 57,* 1–2.

Davis, G. A., & Rimm, S. B. (1985). *Education of the gifted and talented.* Englewood Cliffs, NJ: Prentice Hall.

Deschamp. R., & Robson, G. (1984). Identifying gifted-disadvantaged students: Issues pertinent to system-level screening procedures for the identification of gifted children. *Gifted Education International, 2,* 91–99.

Forness, S. R., & Kavale, K. A. (1984). Education of the mentally retarded: A note on policy. *Education and Training of the Mentally Retarded, 19,* 239–245.

Gilligan, C. (1982). *In a different voice.* Cambridge, MA: Harvard University.

Goffman, E. (1983). *Stigma.* Englewood Cliffs, NJ: Prentice Hall.

Greenbaum, E. (1995). When the rubber meets the road. *Mouth: The Voice of Disability Rights. 5* (5), 26–27.

ICD. (1986). Louis Harris and Associates, Inc. (March, 1986). *The ICD survey of disabled Americans: Bringing disabled Americans into the mainstream.* (Conducted for the International Center for the Disabled, New York, and the National Council on the Handicapped, Washington, DC.)

ICD. (1987). Louis Harris and Associates, Inc. (March, 1987). *The ICD survey II: Employing disabled Americans.* (Conducted for the International Center for the Disabled, New York, the National Council on the Handicapped, and the President's Committee on Employment of the Handicapped, Washington, DC.)

ICD. (1989). Louis Harris and Associates, Inc. (June, 1989). *The ICD survey III: A report card on special education.* (Conducted for the International Center for the Disabled, New York, and the National Council on Disability, Washington, DC.)

Johns, B. (1990). Federal update. *ICEC Quarterly, 39* (3), 23–29.

Juul, K. (1981). Special education in Europe. In J. F. Kauffman & D. P. Hallahan (Eds.), *Handbook of special education.* Englewood Cliffs, NJ: Prentice Hall.

Kendrick, D. (1990). Disabled cheer as Bush signs landmark bill. *Cincinnati Enquirer* (Friday, 27 July, A1, A16).

Kerr, B. A. (1995). Smart girls, gifted women: Special guidance concerns. *Roeper Review, 8,* 30–33.

Knowlen, B. (1995). Going underground. *Mouth: The Voice of Disability Rights, 5* (5), 12–15.

Levine, P., & Edgar, E. (1994). An analysis by gender of long-term postschool outcomes for youth with and without disabilities. *Exceptional Children, 61,* 282–300.

Luchins, F., & Luchins, R. L. (1980). Women and mathematics: Fact or fiction. *American Mathematical Monthly, 88,* 413–419.

Lyons, N. (1985). *Visions and competencies: Men and women as decision-makers and conflict managers.* Cambridge, MA: Harvard University.

Marsh, D. T., Stoughton, N. L., & Williams, T. A. (1985). Effects of role, gender, age, and parental status on perception of childhood problems. *Exceptional Children, 52,* 170–179.

McCarthy, E. A. (1984). Is handicap external to the person and therefore man made? *British Journal of Mental Subnormality, 30,* 3–7.

Rankin, J. L., & Phillips, S. (1995). Learning disabilities in the popular press: Suggestions for educators. *Teaching Exceptional Children, 27* (3), 35–39.

Riegel, K. F. (1975). Toward a dialectical theory of development. *Human Development, 18,* 50–64.

Rohlk, L. (1990). Equal education for all? *Beyond Behavior, 1* (1), 2–3.

Schafer, M. S., Rice, M. L., Metzler, H. M. D., & Haring, M. (1989). A survey of nondisabled employees' attitudes towards supported employees with mental retardation. *Journal of the Association for Persons with Severe Handicaps, 14,* 137–146.

Shapiro, J. (1993). *No pity: People with disabilities forging a new civil rights movement.* New York: Random House.

Stainback, S., Stainback, W., East, K., & Sapon-Shevin, M. (1994). A commentary on inclusion and the development of a positive self-identity by people with disabilities. *Exceptional Children, 60* (6), 486–490.

Stallings, J. (1985). School, classroom, and home influences on women's decision to enroll in advanced math. In S. F. Chipman (Ed.), *Women and mathematics.* Hillsdale, NJ: Erlbaum.

Stefans, V. (1993). Professionals anonymous, In *Mouth: The Voice of Disability Rights Sampler* (pp. 18–19). New York: Free Hand Press.

Yoshida, R. K., Wasilewski, L., & Friedman, D. L. (1990). Recent newspaper coverage about persons with disabilities. *Exceptional Children, 56* (5), 418–423.

Zepf, C. (1990). Overqualified and underutilized: A career disruption. *Hearsay* (Spring–Summer), 32.

Zirpoli, T. J., Hancox, D., Wieck, C., & Skarnulis, E. R. (1989). Partners in policy making. Empowering people. *Journal of the Association for Persons with Severe Handicaps, 14,* 163–167.

Chapter

Schooling and Learners with Disabilities

Objectives

After completing this chapter, you will be able to:

1. describe the development of special education in the United States.
2. describe the implications of the social systems theory of classroom management.
3. describe the special education evaluation and placement processes.
4. describe the continuum of services and related services provided through special education.

Key Words and Phrases

appropriate education	least restrictive environment
cascade of services	norm-referenced evaluation
criterion-referenced evaluation	placement
diagnostic evaluation	prereferral activities
diagnostic evaluation team	Public Law 99-457
inclusion	Public Law 99-457
Individualized Education Program (IEP)	Public Law 101-476
Individualized Family Service Plan (IFSP)	referral
	elated services
	screening
individual-referenced evaluation	transition services

*J*uly 24, 1935. Joseph, a premature infant with poorly developed lungs, is born at home with the assistance of the neighborhood midwife. He isn't breathing normally and is blue about the face, fingertips, and toes. The midwife, alarmed, sends Joseph's father to get the doctor, who lives three blocks from the family home. The doctor comes immediately. When he enters the bedroom, he is told the baby has stopped breathing. The doctor and midwife comfort the grieving parents by stating that had he lived, Joseph would "never have been right."

July 24, 1955. Joseph, a premature infant with poorly developed lungs, is born in the hospital maternity wing. He isn't breathing normally and is blue about the face, fingertips, and toes. The doctor immediately orders the child placed in an incubator with oxygen. The oxygen content is kept at a high level with the hope that it will help Joseph. After six months in the hospital, Joseph is blind as a result of the high levels of oxygen in the incubator and is having trouble eating. His grieving parents are urged to "put him in a home" and go on with their lives. Joseph enters a nursing home at eight months of age, where he resides until his death from pneumonia at four years of age.

July 24, 1975. Joseph, a premature infant with poorly developed lungs, is born in the hospital maternity wing. He isn't breathing normally and is blue about the face, fingertips, and toes. He is immediately rushed to the neonatal unit and placed in an incubator. His parents visit him daily, and volunteers are assigned to massage and talk to him. After eight months, he is released from the hospital and goes home. A social worker from United Cerebral Palsy Association visits the family monthly to discuss Joseph's problems. At three years of age, Joseph begins physical therapy. When he is four years old, Joseph enters the United Cerebral Palsy Association program for children "excused from the public schools." At age six, he is fitted with an adapted wheelchair and enters the special education district program for students with severe and profound disabilities. Joseph travels to and from school in a van provided by the special district. His parents are thankful for the new law that allows Joseph and others with disabilities to attend the public school.

July 24, 1995. Joseph, a premature infant with poorly developed lungs, is born in the hospital maternity wing. He isn't breathing normally and is blue about the face, fingertips, and toes. He is immediately rushed to the neonatal unit and placed in an incubator. His parents visit him daily, and volunteers are assigned to massage and talk to him. He receives both physical and occupational therapy, and an early intervention coordinator is assigned to the family. When Joseph is three years old, he enters the public preschool, where he is one of three children with disabilities in a group of eight. The group is team taught by a general education teacher and a special education teacher. Joseph receives daily language therapy and weekly physical and occupational therapy. Joseph scoots about on the floor and enjoys playing and working with other children. His parents are looking forward to Joseph's fifth birthday, when he will join his brother and sister in the neighborhood school.

Introduction

The social systems perspective of human development has profound implications for the conduct of special education. From this perspective, human development is perceived as the process through which the growing person acquires a more extended, differentiated, and valid conception of the environment (Bronfenbrenner, 1979). As children develop, they become increasingly motivated and more capable of engaging in activities to change their environment. From this point of view, then, efforts to control behaviors rather than to help students develop self-regulation are inappropriate. The goal of special education should not be to control individuals but to help them develop self-management and decision-making capabilities.

Breme (1975) contends that what we teach is so fundamental and often so taken for granted that it never occurs to us, the educators, to seriously question whether or not we should be teaching it. He suggests that every human group has one curriculum—itself—and there is no way in which we can participate in any group unless we learn the ways of the group. What are the implications of this proposition for the special educator? Because students must, for better or worse, learn to survive in the school, we educators have a duty to teach them its social and organizational structure. Educators should recognize that in school students are asked to behave in ways that do not have a counterpart outside of the school, that is, in the home and community. The nature of the school itself, then, is an issue for learners with disabilities. In special education, we face the dilemma of helping students survive in school while simultaneously helping them to develop the self-management and decision-making skills they need to function during adulthood in the community.

In this chapter, the development of special education in the United States is reviewed. The theme of human development continues to be explored from the social systems perspective, by examining its implications for classroom management. Diagnostic evaluation and placement processes are examined, and the continuum of services needed to address the diverse needs of learners with disabilities, including educational environments that are the least restrictive and most inclusive, is discussed.

The Development of Special Education in the United States

From 1875 to 1914, the American public school system was the most significant socialization agent for educating a diverse student population in the "American way of life" (Hoffman, 1975). It was seen as the gatekeeper of the social order (Kauffman, 1981; Hoffman, 1975), serving to modify the behavior and beliefs of urban immigrants in ways that would assure the status quo of American society (Sarason & Doris, 1979). In the school, acceptable behaviors were explicitly defined by a strict code of conduct. Compulsory school attendance became law during this time. As a result, special programs were initiated in the schools, including ungraded classes for students considered to be mentally deficient and classes for students who were "incorrigible" in their behavior, deaf, or physically handicapped (Kauffman, 1981). Also during this period, the National Education Association formed a Department of Special Education.

Kauffman (1981) reports that several factors, such as the development of intelligence tests, the flood of immigrants, the rise of organized labor, and developments in psychological theories, affected the school system during the initial decades of the present century. Interaction among these factors led to the measuring and defining of individual differences and potential.

Objective One

To describe the development of special education in the United States.

With the economic depression of the 1930s, society became increasingly aware of the potential impact of federal intervention for education. Federal intervention increased after World War II, particularly with the implementation of the G.I. Bill, which provided funds for the education and training of millions of Americans who had served in the military service during the war. At that time, in addition to being responsible for socializing students into American society, the educational system was charged with preparing citizens to preserve the American way of life in the Cold War. In the late 1950s, largely as a result of the panic in America engendered by the launch of the Sputnik satellite by the Soviet Union, Congress mandated programs for the teaching of science and mathematics to the most able students.

The general social unrest of the 1960s resulted in many changes in special education (Kauffman, 1981). For example, the notion arose, and was encouraged by special educators, that the schools were to blame for children's failure. The social systems perspective (Mercer, 1970, 1971) suggested that many students who were seen as incompetent in school were competent in other social systems, that is, in their home, neighborhood, and frequently, after they left school either voluntarily or through age-based graduation, suspension, or expulsion. Teacher accountability and competency-based instruction emerged and reached fruition in Public Law 94-142, The Education for All Handicapped Children Act, and its commitment to the Individualized Education Program (IEP). This emphasis on meeting the needs of the individual student was endorsed and furthered in Public Law 99-457 to include individualized programs for families of young children with disabilities. This tradition continued with the enactment of Public Law 101-476, The Individuals with Disabilities Education Act (IDEA) in 1990. (These laws are discussed in detail later in this chapter.)

Progressive Inclusion in General Education

Reynolds (1989) portrays the history of special education as progressive inclusion of learners with disabilities in general education. He suggests that special education has moved from a distal (a point far from) to a proximal (a point near to) arrangement with general education. Special education programs began in residential and separate schools, which frequently required the placement of children away from their families and communities. There has been a dramatic and continuing trend from such separate programs to inclusive school programs and classes for learners with disabilities.

As it developed as a discipline, special education moved from making primarily selection or rejection decisions to making placement decisions with regard to the characteristics of individual students (Reynolds, 1989). Poor test scores, poor achievement, and disruptive behaviors were once used by special educators as criteria to select or reject children. Those selected were exiled to special education. Such removal did have some advantages for the teacher and perhaps the other students in the general education class, but it was not generally advantageous for learners with disabilities. Today, decisions are made on the criteria of placing and serving learners with disabilities where they will have the best opportunity to achieve and experience education like most of their peers.

Current emphasis on **inclusion** is an effort to continue the movement of learners with disabilities into general education settings. Inclusion received its impetus from the failure of research to demonstrate that separate programs for learners with disabilities had merit, especially for learners with mild disabilities. Inclusion gained momentum as a consequence of the recognition of the unreliability of the methods used to classify and place students in special education, the growing number of students at risk for school failure, and the stigma attached to the various labels and terminology used in special education. In his discussion of the research data, Reynolds (1989) suggests that improving general education would reduce the number of students referred to special education and that

Annual **Edition**

Article *1*

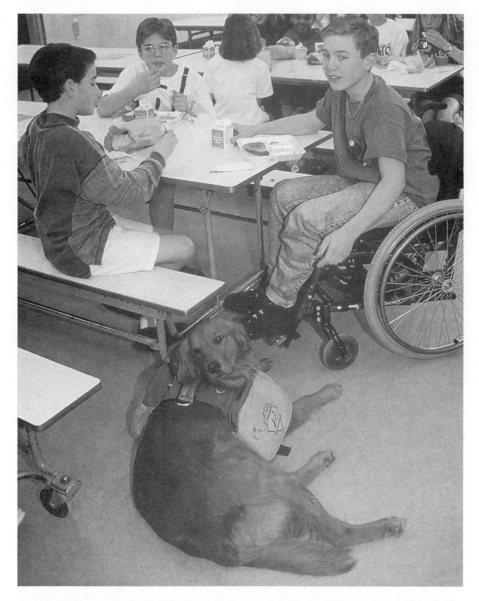

With support, learners with disabilities can be equal participants in general educational settings.

programs offered to students in several categories of disability and to at-risk students are not distinctive. In addition, he believes that there is increasing and broad interest in restructuring the schools to include all learners.

This interest in restructuring schools to include all learners is inclusion. Inclusion is the organization of a school so that all students who would usually be assigned to it are educated with their age-peers. This concept subsumes integration, in which learners with disabilities attend the same schools, but not necessarily the same classes, and mainstreaming, in which learners with disabilities are included in general education classes to increase their social interaction opportunities but not to address their educational goals.

Inclusive schools educate all students in neighborhood classrooms and schools. This shift from mainstreaming or integration to inclusion has occurred for several reasons. Stainback, Stainback, and Jackson (1992) state that

1. Inclusion accurately and clearly communicates that all children need to be included in the educational and social life of their neighborhood school.
2. Inclusion, unlike integration, means including someone from the start, rather than "putting them back in."

3.   The focus of inclusive schools is to build a system that meets everyone's needs.

4.   In inclusive schools, all children, not only those with disabilities, are provided the supports needed to be successful, secure, and welcome.

Inclusive schools assume significantly different learning outcomes than those often accepted by education. The purpose of schooling in inclusive learning communities is to enable all students to actively participate in their communities so that others care enough about what happens to them to look for a way to include them as part of that community (Ferguson, Meyer, Jeanchild, Juniper, & Zingo, 1992). This explicit value base suggests that all members of the school and community are connected and belong and that learners not only collaborate with each other in the learning process but are also empowered to make substantive decisions about the classroom process (Salisbury, Palombaro, & Hollowood, 1993).

The value base assumed by inclusive schools suggests some specific goals (Stainback & Stainback, 1990). These goals include the following:

1.   meeting the unique educational, curricular, and instructional needs of all of the students within general education classes;

2.   helping all students feel welcome and secure through the development of friendships and peer supports;

3.   challenging every student to go as fast and as far as possible to fulfilling his or her unique potential;

4.   developing and maintaining a positive classroom atmosphere conducive to learning for all students;

5.   arranging physical and organizational variables to accommodate the unique needs of each student; and

6.   providing every student any ancillary services he or she might need, such as physical, occupational, or speech therapy, instruction in Braille, sign language, English as a second language, mobility and orientation training, or such technological supports, as a computer for communication.

The Mandate to Educate All Learners with Disabilities

Public Law 94-142, The Education for All Handicapped Children Act, was passed in 1975. This law, innovative and challenging for its time, mandated that school districts provide a free, appropriate public education to all children with disabilities. It included a legal definition of special education, the specific categories of disabilities, and the related services to be provided to learners with disabilities and their families. In addition, regulations related to the law mandated that an **Individualized Education Program (IEP)** for each learner, mutually developed and agreed upon by parents and educators, be implemented in the least restrictive educational environment in which the student could function successfully. The regulations of Public Law 94-142 outlined due process procedures that ensured nondiscrimination in testing and confidentiality of records and privacy of the individual.

The most controversial provision in the law was the definition of **"appropriate education."** According to Osborne (1988), educators complained that the term *appropriate* was not clearly defined by Congress. Lower courts ruled that The Education for All Handicapped Children Act required a school to maximize the potential of each learner with disabilities commensurate with the opportunity provided to nonidentified students. The Supreme Court, in its review, known as the Rowley decision, ruled that a school district satisfied the mandate to provide a free appropriate public education if it provided personalized instruction and services that were reasonably calculated to bring about educational benefit to the child and if all the procedural provisions of the law were adhered to in the formulation of the IEP. For students who received the majority of their instruction in general education, instruction was to be sufficient to allow the student to earn

Annual **Edition**

Article 24

passing grades and to be promoted annually. The specific ruling in the Rowley decision was to deny a sign language interpreter to a high school student with a hearing impairment because the student was able to perform better than average and to easily advance from grade to grade without an interpreter. The implication of the ruling was to make the term *appropriate* less robust than originally understood: learners with disabilities should achieve commensurate with their peers, not necessarily attain their fullest potential.

The interpretation of the term *appropriate* has become an issue in the education of preschool children with disabilities as well. Edminster and Ekstrand (1987) state, in view of the Rowley decision, that programs for preschool children are appropriate if they are reasonably calculated to enable the child to progress educationally. Some parents of preschool children with disabilities, however, maintain that a full-day program would be more beneficial to their children than a half-day program. Edminister and Ekstrand, however, found that the amount of time actually engaged in learning in a full-day program was not significantly greater than in the half-day program. This was due to frequent breaks, lunch, and naps. For many preschool children with disabilities, the research appears to demonstrate that the half-day program meets the requirements for an "appropriate" education.

The appropriateness requirement was tested in an administrative hearing in the State of Maryland (Rothstein, 1990). The case involved a four-year-old child with Down syndrome whose parents requested that the child be enrolled in non-public school services five days a week for five hours each day rather than a half-day public school program. The hearing officers concluded that the half-day program did constitute an appropriate education. Edminister and Ekstrand suggest that each child's past and present progress be reviewed when determining the appropriateness of a full-day or half-day program for a preschool student. Research presently does not support the conclusion that a full-time program necessarily results in additional educational benefit to the child.

Public Law 99-457, The Education of the Handicapped Act

During the 1980s, research on early intervention with children with disabilities moved from inquiring "is early intervention effective?" to examination of which factors and interactions were most productive in early intervention programs. Kochanek, Kabacoff, and Lipsitt (1990) report that the literature and research results were so persuasive that the reauthorization of The Education of the Handicapped Act of 1986, **Public Law 99-457,** Part H, included provisions for states to initiate major program developments, underwritten by the federal government, so that by 1991 a comprehensive national early intervention system would be in place. The states were given considerable latitude in the conceptualization and implementation of their system. Essential components, however, were prescribed. Each state was required to (a) define the population to be served and develop reliable and valid procedures to promptly and accurately identify children and families to be served, (b) develop policies to ensure the identification and service of children who experience significant developmental delay or who have established conditions that result in developmental delay, and (c) consider the option of serving children at risk (Federal Register, 1986).

Kochanek and associates (1990) researched one of these state requirements, that is, defining the population to be served and developing reliable and valid procedures to promptly and accurately identify those to be served. They found that early identification models that focused on developmental delays or adverse medical events from birth to three years of age were inadequate to fully identify children eventually judged to have learning problems. They contend that screening procedures must be multivariate, focusing on both the child and the family and differentially weighing risk over time.

Parents are equal partners in the education of their children.

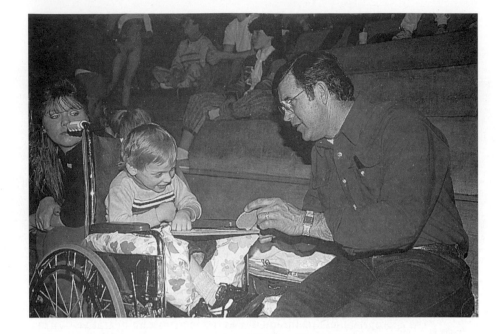

Public Law 99-457, the federal government's commitment to a free, appropriate public education for all learners with disabilities, reauthorized Public Law 94-142 and extended its rights and protections to children from three to five years of age in the 1991 school year. New state grant programs for infants and toddlers (birth through two years of age) with disabilities were also provided by the law. According to Public Law 99-457, parents were to be involved in their child's program through a written **Individualized Family Service Plan** (**IFSP**), a course of action developed by a multidisciplinary team and the parents. An IFSP, rather than an IEP, was mandated for very young children, emphasizing the importance of the family as the focus of service and its essential nature in the development and education of young children.

Public Law 101-476, The Individuals with Disabilities Education Act

Through **Public Law 101-476** (The Individuals with Disabilities Education Act, or IDEA), several shortcomings of the general and special education services for learners with disabilities were addressed. It was recognized that:

1. The special education needs of children with disabilities were not always met; more than half of these children did not receive the services they needed.
2. One million of the children with disabilities did not attend school with their peers.
3. Many children in general education continued to fail because of undetected disabilities.
4. Because of inadequate services, many children had to find services outside the public school system.

The essential purpose of IDEA was to ensure that all children with disabilities and their families received the services they needed and to support the states in the provision of these services. The significant changes in the law with regard to the learner with disabilities are described in the following paragraphs (Council for Exceptional Children, 1990).

The 1990 reauthorization and amendments to Public Law 94-142 reflected changes in the language used with regard to learners. Rather than

Table 3.1 Legislation Related to the Education of Individuals with Disabilities

Number	Title	Mandates
Public Law 94-142	The Education for All Handicapped Children Act	Free, appropriate public education for all handicapped children
		Individualized Education Program
		Due process
		Least restrictive environment
Public Law 99-457	The Education of the Handicapped Act	Provisions to initiate major program development for early intervention by 1991
		Extension of rights and protections from three to five years of age
		Individualized Family Service Plan
Public Law 101-476	The Individuals with Disabilities Education Act	"Person first" language Transition plans

"handicapped children," the law referred to "individuals with disabilities." Two new categories were added to the definition of disability: "autism" and "traumatic brain injury." Autism had been previously classified as "other health impaired." The definition of "related services" was expanded to include rehabilitation counseling and social work services. The latter was previously in the federal regulations but not in the law.

Transition services were added and defined as a coordinated set of activities for a student, designed with specific outcomes in mind. These services are to promote movement from school to post-school activities, including post-secondary education, vocational training, integrated employment (including supported employment), continuing and adult education, adult services, independent living, or community participation. Activities are to be based on the individual student's needs and should consider the student's preferences and interests. Activities may include instruction, community experiences, the development of employment and other post-school adult living objectives, and, when appropriate, acquisition of daily living skills and functional vocational evaluation.

Public Law 101-476 added two provisions to the IEP mandate: (1) a statement of the needed transition services, and (2) the requirement that the educational agency reconvene the IEP team to identify alternative strategies to meet student transition objectives when a participating agency, other than the educational agency, fails to provide agreed-upon services. The statement of needed transition services is mandated for students when they reach sixteen years of age (or earlier when appropriate). This statement lists the interagency responsibilities or linkages before the student leaves school. In addition, the Bureau of Indian Affairs of the Department of the Interior and tribally controlled schools, funded by the department, were included in the definition of "public or private nonprofit agency or organization."

Table 3.1 summarizes the legislative initiative regarding education of individuals with disabilities from 1975 through 1990. This table suggests trends towards greater participation of parents and inclusion of learners with disabilities in the community.

Annual Edition

Article 41

Mother Fights Special Classes of Autistic Son
After Years, Court May Decide Isolation of Mentally Disabled
By Brian Wallstin
Post-Dispatch Special Correspondent

Every day, Chris Atkinson, 11 years old and mildly autistic, walks from one classroom in Hallsville Elementary School to another to spend 70 minutes with mentally handicapped students.

A four-year dispute over that 70 minutes has taken the fifth-grader's mother, Nancy, and his educators, the Boone County R-IV School District from the rural mid-Missouri school to the federal district court in Jefferson City.

Nancy Atkinson says her son belongs in a regular classroom full time. The school district thinks otherwise. Atkinson says that it is costing her son a better education, not to mention nearly half his IQ.

"Before the educable mentally handicapped classroom, his IQ was 73," Nancy Atkinson said. "After, by [the school's] own testing, it was down to 39. That kind of proves my point. He's just not getting anything out of this."

Atkinson's attorney, John Murray of Missouri Protection and Advocacy Services,

said the case, which has yet to be scheduled for hearings, could affect the course taken by other parents of autistic children.

"The real issue is placement and where he will be educated," he said. "We feel he should be in a regular classroom with the help of a trained support system."

The school district maintains that Chris-the town's only autistic student-belongs in a classroom with other "educable mentally handicapped" students. The financially strapped district has paid $75,000 in legal costs on the case and recently was forced to lay off two teachers and a middle school principal because of budget problems.

At the center of the dispute is a conflict between two worthy goals: the classroom integration of regular education students and those with special needs, and an educational reform movement that stresses tougher standards and higher scores.

"The tensions seem to arise from the reform movement on one side and on the other

is the right of individuals that basically says you can't discriminate," said Michael Pullis, a professor of special education at the University of Missouri at Columbia. "Whose rights are more important? It's just a dilemma."

Kathy Boos is a psychological examiner for the Judevine Autism Project in Columbia, a pilot project for the Judevine Center for Autistic Children in St. Louis. Boos said: "It's become a philosophical thing. [The schools] want to raise the test scores, and then they see a student entering the classroom with the potential to lower the mean."

The case began four years ago when Nancy Atkinson fought to have Chris removed from a behavior disorder class. Under federal law, school districts must work with parents to develop an Individualized Education Program for special education students. The school developed a program for Chris that included daily time in a classroom for educable mentally handicapped.

Other Legal Protections

Section 504 of the Rehabilitation Act of 1973.   Students do not need to be enrolled in special education to receive related services under Section 504 of the Rehabilitation Act. The regulations pertaining to related services for persons with disabilities under Section 504 stated that "education may consist of either regular or special education and must include any related aids or services necessary to provide a free, appropriate public education designed to meet the individual student's needs" (34 D. F. R. Section 104.3 [K] [2], 1988, in National Information Center for Children and Youth with Disabilities, 1991).

Americans with Disabilities Act.   The Americans with Disabilities Act (ADA) (Public Law 101-336) passed in July 1990, recognizes the full participation of individuals with disabilities in American society. ADA provisions include the modification of the definition of individuals with disabilities and requirements in the areas of transportation, telecommunications, employment, and public accommodations for persons with disabilities, as well as protection for persons with Acquired Immune Deficiency Syndrome (AIDS) or Human Immunodeficiency Virus (HIV). Learners determined to be ineligible for special education services under The Individuals with Disabilities Education Act (IDEA) may be provided with accommodations under the Americans with Disabilities Act.

Nancy Atkinson has been fighting that program ever since. She also has found herself in a battle of wills with district superintendent Ralph Powell, who has met each challenge from Atkinson with one of his own.

"I just think it's a matter of a superintendent who is not going to have a parent telling him what to do," she said. "But if he's messing up Chris' life by making him take the EMH class, will he care in 10 years?"

Privacy laws prohibit Powell from discussing specifics of the case. But he said he has no information about a child's Individualized Education Program until it is appealed and then only to make sure the plan meets state and federal guidelines and the needs of the child.

Atkinson thought she had finally won in December 1990 when a state Department of Education review officer ruled that the school—like most schools—had no one qualified to teach Chris. The state ruled that Chris should be removed from the special class and gave the school 60 days to bring in an outside expert on autism to assess his education program.

The district appealed the state's decision, claiming that it strips the district of "its power to contract with personnel for services and hands that power to private citizens."

Powell said that Chris' full-time aides all had received training in autism through a state-sponsored program called Project Access.

Boos said Project Access was "excellent information, but it's more like an in-service presentation as opposed to hands-on practice." Chris' current aide refused the Judevine Center's offer for more practical training, she said.

"She said she wasn't making enough money," Boos said.

Because socialization and communicative skills are the main deficiencies of autistic children, many special education experts believe the best preparation for life would be exposure to non-handicapped peers.

Boos describes Chris as "mild-mannered, with no tremendous risk possibilities. He has taken on the nuances of the regular classroom in the past and tolerated it. To me it would make more sense to keep him there and train the aide."

She points to a school in Auxvasse that has a student with a much more extreme case of autism. The school has developed what Boos says is a model program to deal with the unique needs of the autistic child, without spending more money on a specialized aide.

Pullis says that, more and more, schools like the one in Auxvasse are finding benefits for all students in requiring exposure of handicapped and non-handicapped students to each other.

"There is this whole group of idealists for full inclusion that say this is how the world ought to be," Pullis said, "They're trying to get more kids integrated and not at the expense of the regular education kids."

As to why the district has fought so long and hard to keep one child from getting the education his parents believe is best for him, Boos suggests that superintendents are "between a rock and a hard place" •

Reprinted with permission of St. Louis Post–Dispatch

Social Systems Theory and Classroom Management

Objective Two

To describe the implications of the social systems theory of classroom management.

Jones (1986) suggests that in special education there is a recursive nature to the use of classroom management interventions. During the 1940s and 1950s, emphasis in classroom management was on biological causes and on interventions through routine, drill, the sequencing of instruction, and the reduction of extraneous environmental stimuli. During the 1960s, counseling and psychoeducational interventions were predominant. Emphasis was on individualized interventions, inferring the reasons for inappropriate behavior, and improving interpersonal relations. This period was followed by an emphasis on the use of behavioral interventions that focused on the principles of learning and the control or modification of student behavior. Teachers learned to state precise behavioral and instructional objectives and to persistently and consistently intervene in students' behavior. They provided individual and group reinforcement for desired behavior. Organization and management skills were emphasized. Simple, often superficial control-oriented classroom management techniques were predominant.

With the application of the social systems perspective, there is a shift from a single approach to management to an integration of the biophysical, counseling and psychoeducational, and behavioral perspectives within the systems framework. In the systems perspective, learning principles are applied (the behavioral perspective) with consideration of interpersonal relationships (the counseling and psychoeducational perspective) and with recognition of the impact of neurological and physical factors (the biophysical perspective) on children's functioning in the classroom.

The social systems perspective has significant implications for classroom management, particularly with regard to interaction between teacher and student. As Bronfenbrenner (1979) suggests, learning and development are facilitated by the participation of the developing person in progressively more complex patterns of reciprocal activity with someone with whom that person has developed a strong and enduring personal relationship. Learning occurs as the balance of power gradually shifts to the developing person. Teachers, then, must relate to students as capable persons, individuals able to make choices and manage their own behavior. More specifically, they must trust in their students' abilities.

According to Bickel and Bickel (1986), there are three characteristics associated with effective instruction: (a) teacher behavior, (b) the organization of instruction and academic learning time, and (c) instructional supports, such as class size and teacher in-service training. From the social systems perspective, appropriate teacher behavior encourages and facilitates interpersonal transactions rather than one-way communication. The appropriate organization of instruction and academic learning time involves emphasis on student choice and self-management skills whenever possible. Finally, instructional support through class size and teacher in-service training is represented in the systems perspective by limited class size, which encourages the development of relationships, and recognition of teachers as lifelong learners through frequent in-service training. Unfortunately, as Bickel and Bickel report, classroom and teacher effectiveness research, designed to judge the worth of particular instructional and management procedures, focuses primarily on basic skills achievement. There is a need for research that considers students' conceptual learning and problem-solving and interaction skills as a central outcome measure for judging teacher and classroom effectiveness.

The social systems perspective emphasizes the interaction among the setting, the student, the teacher, and all the other "actors" within the setting. Bloom, Lininger, and Charlesworth (1987) propose that disability, then, may be seen as a mismatch between the child and the environment. In this mismatch, not only is the child not able to cope with the setting as well as his or her peers are, but others are not coping with the child as well as they are coping with the child's peers. As Green and Weade (1988) believe, what occurs in classrooms, such as constructing knowledge, occurs during interaction with others. Communication that occurs in the classroom setting affects (a) what students have an opportunity to learn, (b) what they actually learn, and (c) which students have an opportunity to display their knowledge and learning.

The teaching-learning behaviors that occur in any classroom are largely a product of the interaction of the persons in that classroom with one another and the environment. Copeland (1982) contends that classrooms take on characteristics as teachers and students influence and are influenced by one another. It must be remembered that classroom events are affected by students as well as teachers.

Pinnell and Galloway (1987) summarize the developmental approach to classroom management as follows:

- Teachers recognize that students make a significant contribution to the educational process.
- Learning occurs when students feel a need to change or learn.
- Learning is holistic, rather than a series of individual pieces of information or skills.

- Teachers recognize the power of the social context of the classroom on learning.
- Teachers develop a personal understanding of learning and development.
- Teachers care about what takes place in their classrooms.

The role of the teacher, then, is to facilitate the development of each student, rather than to simply intervene in behaviors deemed inappropriate (Bauer & Sapona, 1991).

In work with students with disabilities it is important, as Hood, McDermott, and Cole (1980) suggest, to describe the social organization of situations in which abilities and disabilities are exhibited by specific individuals. In their description of one day in the educational life of a student with learning disabilities, they found that the student's disability was as much a product of interactions in the classroom as it was a product of the student's personal limitations. Though not the only setting, the classroom can serve as a "display board" for the weaknesses of the environment in which a student is functioning. When assessing a student, teachers must take into account how both the learner and the classroom are dynamically involved in behavior. If conclusions are to be made about a learner's behavior on the basis of this assessment, then classroom variables should be defined in terms of how the student is using them to organize his or her behavior and environment.

Evaluation and Placement

The evaluation and placement process in special education, structured in part by the mandates of Public Law 94-142 and its amendments, include screening, referral, diagnostic evaluation, and placement. In recent years, regular education and prereferral procedures have been implemented before initiating formal referral to special education.

Prereferral Activities

Prereferral activities are also known as "prereferral interventions" (Graden, Casey, & Christenson, 1985) and "intervention assistance," (Graden, 1989) or student support teams. The goal of prereferral activities is to provide the student with needed assistance within the general classroom. These activities are not considered to be the initial step in the special education evaluation and placement processes. Prereferral strategies are developed with general education personnel through collaborative consultation and problem-solving activities. Prereferral interventions are developed through team-based collaborative efforts. They are interventions designed to assist general educators in work with specific students who are presenting academic or behavioral problems. The intervention is implemented before the student is formally identified as at-risk for a disability and referred to special education.

Pugach and Johnson (1989) discuss several assumptions that underlie prereferral interventions. First, prereferral activities are a function of general education. The purpose of the interventions is to identify and implement strategies for working with students in the general classroom and thus avoid their classification as disabled. Second, consultation is a multidirectional activity in which all educational professionals within the school, at one time or another, serve as consultants to each other. Third, classroom teachers, given time and structure, are capable of solving many of their students' classroom problems without the direct intervention of specialists. Finally, Pugach and Johnson maintain that all problems do not require the same configuration (or group) of educators to develop interventions and that fluid membership in the prereferral teams increases schoolwide commitment and involvement. The process varies with the student's problem and personnel involved. An example of the prereferral process is presented in the "A Closer Look" box on page 46.

Objective Three

To describe the special education evaluation and placement processes.

a closer look

Prereferral Intervention

Louise was doing well in Mr. Raphael's fourth grade classroom until December, when her behavior changed. Louise no longer completed her homework, did not participate in games during recess, and had, on two occasions, pinched children who were swinging in "her" swing on the playground. After receiving no response to notes to Louise's mother regarding concerns about these behaviors, Mr. Raphael telephoned Louise's home. Louise's nineteen-year-old aunt, who was "helping out with the kids," reported that Louise's mother had entered a hospice program for terminal cancer patients. Louise's father was spending a great deal of time at the hospice, but "just couldn't bring himself to take the kids to visit."

Mr. Raphael approached Ms. Turner, the school principal, to discuss Louise's behavior; they agreed that an Intervention Assistance Team should be formed to address it. Mr. Raphael recommended that Ms. Holt, the art teacher, with whom Louise had particular rapport, be included in the team. Ms. Turner suggested that Ms. Michael, the school counselor, and Ms. Wang, who had recently worked her classroom through the death of student's mother in an automobile accident, also be included.

The intervention Assistance Team met and discussed Louise's behavior. The plan that was formulated included the following:

1. Weekly meetings for Louise with the school counselor.
2. Increased efforts to encourage Louise to participate appropriately during recess, while recognizing her feelings. Louise was to receive a cue such as the following: "I know it's hard to have fun when you're worried about someone. Would you like to talk about how you're feeling before you go join the game?" or "I know you're feeling hurt and worried right now, but the rule is to keep your hands to yourself on the playground. How could you ask [child's name] to move to another swing? Could you swing on another one?"
3. Review of materials Ms. Wang had received from the local children's hospital regarding dealing with death, separation, and loss in the classroom.
4. Continued communication attempts with the home, recognizing that the family was in crisis and all contacts should be supportive rather than reports of negative behavior.
5. Meeting again in four weeks to evaluate the plan and Louise's progress ▮

In a study by Carter and Sugai (1989), thirty-four states were found to recommend or require prereferral activities. The most common activities were instructional modifications, counseling, and behavior management strategies.

Screening and Referral

Children are identified for further study for special education services in two ways: screening and referral. **Screening** is the process of identifying students who may demonstrate a disability and so need further study. Screening may take place in the community—through private physicians and health clinics, for example—or in a more formal and systematic manner, such as when children enter preschool or kindergarten. Hearing and vision screening are usually required prior to consideration of a disability.

The second way children are identified for further study is referral. **Referral** is the process of soliciting and accepting nominations for evaluation from others. Before the child enters school, referral may originate with a parent, physician, social worker, or case manager. When the child attains school age, referral to special education may begin when the prereferral process fails to ameliorate the child's problem. At this point in the evaluation and placement processes, the

Table 3.2 Responsibilities of Special Educators During the Screening/Referral, Diagnostic Evaluation, and Placement Process

Responsibilities during referral

1. Making the initial contact positive and productive
2. Evaluating the referral
3. Providing instructional recommendations
4. Facilitating the formal referral process

Responsibilities during and following screening

1. Obtaining parent permission to screen
2. Observing the student in the current placement
3. Conducting academic screening
4. Advising whether to proceed with diagnostic evaluation
5. Conferring with the referring teacher and parents

Responsibilities during and following diagnostic evaluation

1. Coordinating activities with the school psychologist
2. Acting upon the diagnostic evaluation recommendations
3. Conferring with the referring teacher and parents
4. Collaborating on the development of the IEP

Responsibilities during the IEP conference

1. Encouraging collegial participation
2. Encouraging parent attendance
3. Obtaining parent consent for placement

special educator assumes significant responsibility. White and Calhoun (1987) interviewed experienced, "expert" special educators to determine their perceptions of their responsibilities during the evaluation and placement processes. The results of this study are presented in table 3.2.

Simply being referred to special education has an impact on the student and her or his future in the school system. Algozzine, Christenson, Ysseldyke (1982) found that 92 percent of the students referred to special education were evaluated, and of those evaluated 73 percent were placed in special education. Teachers' direct observations, it appears, are reliable criteria for referral and consequent placement.

To initiate referral, the teacher completes a referral form. This form indicates the nature of the teacher's concern and the interventions that have been attempted to improve the student's situation. Information from screening instruments and the student's records are included on the form. A sample referral form is presented in the "Guidelines for Practice" box on page 48.

The teacher usually forwards the completed referral form to the principal. If, after review, the principal determines that further action is necessary, the form is forwarded to the school referral team. A conference, attended by selected members of the referral team, the parents, the teacher, and the principal, is scheduled. During the conference, a collaborative decision is made whether or not to refer the student for diagnostic evaluation. Regardless of the decision of the majority of the team members, the parents must consent to having their child evaluated.

Diagnostic Evaluation

Diagnostic evaluation is the process of studying a learner and the learner's developmental contexts to determine the cause, nature, and circumstances of the problem if, in fact, there is a problem. Diagnostic evaluation is not an end in itself; rather, it is conducted to identify appropriate activities to assist the student in becoming more successful in school (Bender, 1988). According to Lambert

guidelines for practice

Sample School Referral Form

Student: DOB:

Address:

Telephone: Sex:

Parent or guardian:

Person initiating referral:

1. Reason for referral
2. Has an Intervention Assistance Team been involved? Summarize the efforts of the IAT.
3. Parent contacts (attach log):
4. Information from cumulative record:

    Hearing screening: Vision Screening:

    Speech & language: Medical/Health History:

    Attendance: Patterns in Grades:

    Test Scores:

       Achievement:

       Intelligence:

       Others:

5. Further information for referral:

    Social Skills Screening:

    Observations (attach)

    Anecdotal records (attach)

    Parent communication (attach)

6. Comments

    Teacher signature: Date:

    Reviewed by Principal: Date:

    Reviewed by School Referral Team:

(1988), a National Academy of Sciences panel on ability testing and the testing of persons with disabilities proposed the following guidelines for the conduct of a diagnostic evaluation:

1. Before referring children for special education diagnostic evaluation, the general education teacher should attempt several interventions and note the effects of those interventions on the child's performance.
2. Assessment specialists should demonstrate that the measurement instruments employed validly assess the student's needs and are related to the interventions.
3. Placement teams should demonstrate that different labels or classifications of disability are related to a specific prescription for intervention that is likely to lead to improved student functioning.
4. Special education staff should demonstrate, at least annually, that a child should remain in special education service.

Bender (1988) recommends that an evaluation of the learning environments in which the student is currently functioning be completed in addition to the diagnostic evaluation of the student. He contends that present procedures, which focus almost exclusively on the student, may not provide the most useful information on which to base educational decisions and may fail to provide special educators and related service personnel with the knowledge needed to

Direct observation provides information regarding children's interactions.

make meaningful intervention decisions. In addition, he suggests, the discussion of the special education placement of a student often focuses exclusively on the special education aspects of the placement and ignores the educational opportunities, or lack of them, available to the child in various general education settings. Bender contends that assessment of the student's current learning environment by the team of professionals evaluating the student would provide useful information with regard to the student's needs and how best to respond to them. This information may be obtained from self-reports from the general educators involved or through direct observation of the settings.

Public Law 94-142 required that all diagnostic evaluation instruments (a) be administered in the child's native language, (b) be valid for the purpose for which they were being administered, and (c) be administered by qualified personnel. In addition, no single instrument may be used as the basis of the decision with regard to the child's eligibility for special education services.

Tindal (1985) differentiates three types of diagnostic evaluation: **norm-referenced evaluation,** which compares learners to a specific group or sample; **criterion-reference evaluation,** which focuses on the learner's mastery of specific skills; and **individual-referenced evaluation,** which focuses on the learner's progress over time.

The evaluation of young children (infants, toddlers, and preschoolers) presents several unique challenges. Tindal (1985) believes that the reliability and validity of tests for preschool children suffer due to the limited behaviors of young children and the unevenness of the development that occurs in young children within relatively brief periods of time. Tests of developmental milestones, which are most frequently administered, pose difficulties because young children are so individualistic in the ways in which they move through developmental stages. Preschool children may demonstrate inconsistent development, which may occur in bursts, making testing even more difficult (Shepard & Smith, 1983).

Another factor that complicates diagnostic evaluation is cultural diversity. For example, although Caucasian students perform similarly with familiar and unfamiliar examiners. African American and Hispanic children score dramatically higher when evaluated by familiar examiners (Fuchs & Fuchs, 1989). This finding compels educators to ask, "Does the lack of familiarity with the examiner bias the evaluation of minority students?" An additional bias may be the standardization sample on which the norms of the test are based. More specifically, is the instrument being administered normed on a population comparable to the cultural and socioeconomic status of the student being evaluated so that if avoids a majority culture bias?

Public Law 94-142 required that a group of individuals from various disciplines be assembled and involved as a **diagnostic evaluation team.** This team has two responsibilities: to develop a child study report and to write an Individual Education Plan (IEP). Each team member contributes some information about the child so that this report and plan can be developed. The general educator provides information on the child's current functioning in the classroom. The special educator provides information from systematic observation of the child. Parents, active and contributing members of the team, provide information on the child's development, behavior in the home and community, and their perceptions of the child's strengths and weaknesses. The psychologist collects and presents diagnostic information on the child's functioning as measured by standardized tests and inventories, observations, and interviews. The social worker, serving as a liaison between home and school or school and community agencies, develops and presents the child's social history. Others who may be members of the diagnostic evaluation team, depending on the problem the child presents, are the communication specialist, audiologist, occupational therapist, physical therapist, vision specialist, and correctional personnel.

Gerken (1988) describes best practice for diagnostic evaluation teams. In order to translate information into decision making, the diagnostic evaluation team must (a) record data for each area studied; (b) determine present level of performance by describing the student's strengths and weaknesses; (c) summarize what the learner can do; (d) establish priorities; and (e) write goal statements. These activities cannot be separated from the decision-making process regarding placement. If priorities and goals are not described, services cannot be determined. The team reviews the criteria for special education services and compares the statement of the student's present level of functioning with those criteria.

Placement

During its deliberations, the diagnostic evaluation team reviews all the information gathered on the student and determines, on the basis of that information, if the student is eligible for **placement,** that is, assignment to special education services. If the student is deemed eligible, the team writes an IEP. According to the Federal Register (1977, 121a. 346), the IEP includes the following:

1. A statement of the child's present level of performance
2. Annual goals and short-term objectives
3. The specific education and related services to be provided to the child, including the amount of time to be spent with nonidentified peers
4. Projected dates for the initiation of services and anticipated duration of services
5. Criteria for determining, at least annually, progress made towards the goals and objectives

As required in Public Law 101-476, "a statement of the needed transition services" is to be included in IEPs for students beginning no later than age sixteen (in some cases earlier) and annually thereafter. A sample IEP is presented in table 3.3. A sample transition plan is presented in table 3.4. Gerber (1981) characterizes the IEP as a resource management tool. It serves as a means of allocating services and determining appropriate placement for the child.

Placement in special education has a profound impact on the remainder of the child's school career. Walker and associates (1988) studied "who leaves and who stays in special education." They found that termination of special education services was strongly associated with the child's initial primary classification of disability. Students classified as speech impaired were the most likely to be terminated (33.1 percent), followed by students classified as learning disabled (14.9 percent), behaviorally disordered (9.1 percent), and visually impaired (8.6 percent). Those classified as hearing impaired, physically/multiply handicapped, or mentally retarded were rarely, if ever, terminated from special education services.

For the infants and toddlers with disabilities, described in Public Law 99-457 as individuals from birth to their third birthday, the IFSP replaces the IEP. The IFSP is reviewed semiannually and evaluated annually. The content of the plan is similar to that of the IEP:

1. A statement of the infant's or toddler's present level of functioning
2. A statement of the family's strengths and needs as related to the development of the family's infant or toddler with disabilities
3. A statement of the major anticipated outcomes for the infant or toddler and the family, and the criteria, procedures, and timelines used to determine the degree to which progress is being made and whether revisions of the anticipated outcomes are necessary
4. A description of the specific early intervention services necessary to meet the unique needs of the infant or toddler and the family
5. The projected dates for initiation of services and the anticipated duration of the services
6. The name of the case manager from the service most relevant to the needs of the infant or toddler and family who is responsible for the implementation of the plan and coordination with other agencies and persons
7. A plan for the transition of the toddler to preschool services

A sample IFSP is presented in table 3.5. When the toddler enters preschool at three years of age, the IEP replaces the IFSP as the document used for service and placement descriptions.

Krauss (1990) suggests that unlike the IEP, the IFSP defines the service recipient as the family rather than just the child. It requires specific judgments with regard to the family's service needs and reconstitutes the decision-making team by mandating family representation. Unlike Public Law 94-142, Public Law 99-457 formally acknowledges that services to family members can and should be provided independent of the child's educational program. This, as can be readily understood, is a significant departure from the IEP process.

The Continuum of Services and Related Services

Objective Four

To describe the continuum of services and related services provided through special education.

Placement in special education services cannot occur without parental consent. Due process hearings are conducted if either party, local education agency or parent, disagrees with the placement decision. Due process hearings may be held on whether the learner may be evaluated, on the results of the evaluation, on the content of the IEP, or on the placement.

A student is placed in a special education service after the diagnostic evaluation team has determined that she or he has special educational needs and has written an IEP. The team bases its decision to place the student on the following two guidelines, mandated in Public Law 94-142:

1. To maximum extent appropriate, children with disabilities, including children in public and private institutions or other care facilities, are educated with children who are not disabled.

Table 3.3 **Sample Individual Education Program**

Metropolitan School District

INDIVIDUAL EDUCATION PROGRAM

Student's Name *Michael Riley*   Birth Date *7/6/88*

School *Metropolitan Elementary*   Date of IEP Conference *9-15-97*

Date of Initial Placement Program *9-5-95*

Summary of Present Levels of Performance – Strengths & Weaknesses

Strengths: *Enthusiastic and within grade equivalent limits of achievement, verbalizes his behavioral problems, can express steps of problem resolution*

Weaknesses: *Difficulty managing behavior in large groups; verbally aggressive when not responded to immediately; physically aggressive when children enter his personal space; difficulty playing cooperatively on playground*

Annual Goals	Description & Amount of Time in Regular Education Program	Special Consideration and Comments	Committee Members Present Signature/Position
1) Michael will work cooperatively in his classroom *2) Michael will play cooperatively on the playground*	*100%*	*Work with behavioral consultant to implement and evaluate plan*	*Sally Striker* (Chairperson) *Jo Ann Riley* (Parent) *Kathy Sanders* (Teacher)

Committee Recommendation for specific Procedures/Techniques, Materials, Etc.	Objective Evaluation Criteria for Annual Goal Statements
1) daily parent-teacher journal *2) immediate reward of praise; behavioral contracts*	*Weekly conferences with teacher and Michael — Anecdotal records and self recorded data*

Placement Recommendation:
White Copy: *Referring School*
Yellow Copy: *Director of Special Education*   *In general education classroom*
Pink Copy: *Parents*

---

2. Special classes, separate schooling, or other removal of children with disabilities from the regular educational environment occurs only when the nature or severity of the disability is such that education in regular classes with the use of supplementary aids and services cannot be achieved satisfactorily (Federal Register, 1977, 121.550).

In essence, the guidelines mandate that the student be placed in the least restrictive educational environment in which she or he can function effectively. As a consequence of the application of these guidelines, inclusion has emerged. (Inclusion is discussed in detail in the next section of this chapter.)

The application of the least restrictive environment mandate also applies to preschool programs. The **least restrictive environment** clause requires that the

Table 3.3 continued

Short Term Objectives	Specific Ed and/or Support Service	Person(s) Responsible	Amount of Time	Beginning & Ending Date	Review Date
1a) Michael will make no more than 3 verbal comments during each period with cues from teacher	BD Resource	Teacher – BD Resource	100 %	9-15-97	9-15-98
1b) Michael will self-record verbal comments	Teacher	Teacher	100 %	9-15-97	9-15-98
2a) Michael will play cooperatively with his class with his classroom aide available		Teacher – BD Resource	100 %	9-15-97	9-15-98
2b) Michael will play cooperatively with his class, meeting weekly with BD resource room teacher to discuss progress	BD Resource	BD Resource	100 %	9-15-97	9-15-98

learners be placed in the setting that provides the maximum amount of interaction with learners without disabilities while providing enough support for the learner with disabilities to be successful. Edminster and Ekstrand (1987) suggest that Public Law 99-457 mandated opportunities for preschool children with disabilities equal to those for school-age children. A problem emerges, however, in that most states that provide preschool programs for children with disabilities do not provide "general education programs" for non-identified preschool-age children. The United States Office of Education maintains that if there are programs for non-identified preschoolers available within a jurisdiction, then mainstreaming opportunities are automatically required. The Office of Education has determined that if nonidentified programs are not provided within a jurisdiction, local education agencies, if possible, must coordinate preschool special education programs with other existing public service programs, such as Head Start, and make them available for mainstreaming purposes. If, however, coordination efforts fail, school systems are not required to create preschool programs for children without disabilities or enter into contracts with private facilities for the sole purpose of implementing the mainstreaming requirement.

Due to the family intervention focus of Public Law 99-457, the least restrictive environment mandate is not an issue for infants or toddlers with disabilities. A statement of participation with peers without disabilities is not included in the IFSP.

Annual **Edition**

Article *38*

Table 3.4 **Sample Individualized Transition Plan**

Metropolitan School District
Early Childhood and Special Education

Individualized Transition Plan

Date Initiated: _9-30-97_   Review Date: _9-30-98_

Name: _Tara Trainer_   DOB: _1-5-81_   Sex: _F_ Grade: _10_

School: _Metro High School_

Placement at time of ITP: _Self Contained ; Three "out" classes_

◆ ◆ ◆ ◆ ◆ ◆ ◆ ◆ ◆ ◆ ◆ ◆ ◆ ◆ ◆ ◆ ◆

Participants:

Name:	Role:	Signature:
Sue Trainer	Parent/Guardian	_Sue Trainer_
Mark Trainer	Parent/Guardian	_Mark Trainer_
Barry Martinez	District/Rep.	_Barry Martinez_
Sandy Sharkins	Teacher	_Sandy Sharkins_
Tara Trainer	Student	_Tara Trainer_

Community Living Goals:

Objective	Activities	Responsibility
① To initiate and continue a way of managing personal finance	a) open checking account b) maintain checking account	Parent
② To use public Transportation to job and home	a) using a phone to determine schedule. b) Transportation Training	Special Ed Teacher
③ To maintain reading periodicals/newspaper for information	a) subscribe to magazine b) newspaper available daily	Parent / Spec. Ed Teacher

---

Taylor (1988) describes several "pitfalls" in the least restrictive environment principle. First, it legitimizes restrictive environments; as long as services are conceptualized with regard to the "restrictiveness of environments," some individuals will be placed in restrictive environments simply because these are available for placement. In addition, the principle equates separation of learners with disabilities from their peers with the most intensive services and integration with the least intensive services even though intensive services can be provided in inclusive or integrated settings. Taylor also argues that professionals, though allegedly following the principle of the least restrictive environment, continue to dominate decision making, emphasizing the economical provision of services rather than the provision of services in the least restrictive environment. Thus, the least restrictive environment, according to Taylor, tends to support separate programs rather than inclusion.

Table 3.4 *continued*

Employment Goals:

Objective	Activities	Responsibility
① To work two periods each day in Metro elementary Day Care Co-Op as aide	a) Bi-weekly visits	Teacher
② To complete child care course	a) attend course	Child care course instructor
③ To expand work time to 5-½ days a week	a) work with job site	Teacher

Comments:

Tara has worked as a volunteer in child care settings. She is very interested in gaining employment as a preschool aide. Her time receiving educational instruction will gradually decrease until she is working ½ day, five days a week.

Dialogue between proponents of full inclusion and those who wish to preserve the concept of the least restrictive environment is ongoing. Stainback and Stainback (1992) argue that schools should be "inclusive communities," in which each student is provided the support necessary to learn in his or her neighborhood school. Vergason and Anderegg (1992) contend that a commitment to full inclusion is tantamount to uniform placement, which violates each child's rights to an appropriate education.

Inclusion

Inclusion gained momentum through the work of Ms. Madeline Will, former assistant U.S. secretary of education. Will (1986) suggested that special educators should seriously question the effectiveness of "pull-out" services for many students with disabilities. "Pull-out" services are outside services provided to learners with disabilities that remove these students from general education classes during the school day. Gersten and Woodward (1990) discuss several factors that led Ms. Will to this recommendation and hence to the emergence of inclusion. First, there was concern that special education had become a haven for students who were difficult to teach, rather than those with disabilities. This concern was supported by the large number of students who were classified as learning disabled, though research had demonstrated a significant overlap between students classified as learning disabled and general education students in remedial programs (Jenkins, Pious, & Peterson, 1988). Second, there was concern that once placed in special education services, students were rarely terminated from them.

Annual **Edition**

Article *1*

Table 3.5 **Sample Individualized Family Service Plan**

Metropolitan School District
Early Childhood and Special Education

Individualized Family Service Plan (IFSP)

Date Completed: _10-4-97_ _____ Evaluated: _9-8-97_ _____

Reviewed: _1-4-98_   _4-4-98_   _7-4-98_   _10-4-98_

Child's Name: _Elizabeth Barrett_ _____ DOB: _5-16-96_ ____ Sex: _F_

Family Address: _214 Tampa Rd, Defiance, Ohio_ _____

Telephone: (H) _(555)555-9214_ _____ (W) _(555)555-5672_

Parent(s) or Guardian(s): _John Barrett, Marcia Hoskins_ _____

♦ ♦ ♦ ♦ ♦ ♦ ♦ ♦ ♦ ♦ ♦ ♦ ♦ ♦ ♦

IFSP Team

Name:	Role:	Signature:
Marcia Hoskins	Parent	Marcia Hoskins
John Barrett	Parent	John Barrett
Sally Schwartz	Case Manager	Sally Schwartz
Kelly Kristofer	OTR	Kelly Kristofer
Michael Brinkley	MSW	Michael Brinkley MSW
Jill Traber	Audiologist	Jill Traber
Sarah Logan	Speech/Lang	Sarah Logan

Services (Frequency, Intensity, and Duration):

Services will begin immediately and continue through 5-16-99
when Beth will be eligible for public school preschool programming.
Frequency and intensity are goal dependent.

Signatures of Parent(s) or Guardian(s):

I/we have had the opportunity to participate in the development of this IFSP. I/we understand the plan, and give permission for the implementation of this plan with my/our cooperation.

Marcia Hoskins _____ Date _October 4, 1997_
John Barrett _____ _4 Oct 97_

The assumptions regarding inclusive learning communities requires some assumptions about the responsibilities of teachers to be made. In inclusive learning communities, teachers are responsible for the following:

- Educating all the students assigned to them
- Making and monitoring instructional decisions
- Providing instruction according to the typical curriculum while adapting the particulars when children's progress is discrepant from that anticipated
- Managing instruction for diverse populations
- Seeking, using, and coordinating support for students who require more intense services than those provided to their peers (Jenkins, Pious, & Jewell, 1990)

Teachers have not always been prepared for the responsibilities generated by inclusive learning. Giangreco, Dennis, Cloninger, Edelman, and Schattman

Table 3.5 continued

Assessment Instruments and Procedures:
Receptive Expressive Language Scale (RELS)
Real Time Observation
Language Sample
Ecological Interviews

Medical Information:
Elizabeth has a bilateral profound hearing loss. Except for frequent respiratory infections, Elizabeth is physically healthy. She wears a body-aid to amplify sounds.

Developmental Levels:
Elizabeth's motor skills are developmentally appropriate. With her hearing aids, she turns to loud environmental sounds (Stereo on high); the amount of information she receives is unknown. She gives eye contact to adults and makes some gestures.

Child's Strengths and Needs:
Elizabeth's social and motor skills are clearly her strength. She needs to begin to develop a conventional communication system.

Family's Strengths and Needs:
The Hoskins-Barrett family feels that their greatest need is to have a way to communicate with Elizabeth. They are also very interested in her learning verbal language. The family is motivated, and Elizabeth's three older siblings are very supportive. The family is concerned about the effectiveness of the hearing aid.

Outcomes:

Objectives	Strategies	Duration	Responsibility
① To increase Elizabeth's expressive language.	Conversation; interaction and play	10-1-97 – 10-4-98	Speech/Lang; Parent
② To monitor Elizabeth's hearing aid and provide more effective instrument.	Contact Children's Hospital	10-97	Audiologist; Parent
③ Provide sign language instruction to family	Contact Community Service for the deaf	11-97	Parent; Caseworker

(1993) describe "transformational experiences" as teachers become inclusive teachers. These are gradual transformations and involve teachers who are willing to (a) interact with students who vary from their peers, (b) learn skills needed to teach all students, and (c) change their attitudes towards learners who vary from their peers. Teachers can take several approaches, ranging from (a) treating students with disabilities "like any other member of the class," or including them in the same activities although the learning objectives may be different, (b) engaging students in cooperative learning and group problem solving, and (c) using active and participatory strategies, such as manipulatives, games, projects, labs, or field study.

Inclusive learning communities change the role of the teacher in many ways. Lipsky and Gartner (1991) suggest that teachers become broad enablers of students' learning, working collegially with other persons across disciplines and without the artificial distinction between special and general educators. Teachers

Making News

The Goddard High School Girls Golf Team, New Mexico state champions for six of the past eight years, has Courtney Ikard as their manager. Courtney is in her junior year at Goddard. She goes to practice every day where she is able to spend time interacting with each of the girls individually. They enjoy her rolling the balls back to them while they are practicing their putting, and visiting with her about boys or dating or how they need to improve their game.

The players have truly come to know Courtney and have included her in their lives outside of golf by taking her to lunch, going shopping and going out to get ice cream or a burger. Courtney has provided a number of benefits to the team that were unexpected upon her becoming manager. Her ability to comfort them when they have had a bad game or hit a bad ball has changed the way they handle stress. They look forward to having her tell them "It's OK" and that "It is just a game," and, coming from her, they see how true that is. She encourages them and has actually been known to coach them on how they are hitting the ball. She has memorized each of their styles and has actually learned to play the game by imitating their techniques.

Having been born with developmental disabilities, Courtney began early intervention services at age ten weeks. She then spent her elementary school years in segregated classrooms. Middle school provided her with new opportunities such as changing classes and going to classes with children with far less disabilities. It has not been until now, in high school, that Courtney has had the opportunity she needed to really fit in. That opportunity has come about because of IDEA, the Individuals with Disabilities Education Act •

From "A Celebration of the Impact of the Individuals with Disabilities Educational Act" in *The ARC, 20 Years of IDEA in America.* Reprinted by permission of the publisher and the author.

engage in a variety of interactions with students so knows each child as an individual. In addition, teachers have a broader involvement with other adults, including out-of-school learning resources and parents.

In a study of inclusive preschool settings, a wide range of roles emerged for teachers (Fleming, Wolery, Weinzierl, Venn, & Schroeder, 1991). In both Head Start and other preschool programs, teachers were primarily instructors (teaching content or directing group activities) and monitors (checking on students' progress, suggesting alternatives, or encouraging persistence). Teachers also assumed the role of co-player, mutually participating in the children's activity, or observer, purposefully watching the children. Teachers were materials managers, behavior managers, and caregivers, as well as "entertainers" striving to keep children's attention. Fleming and associates suggest that rather than adapting activities, teachers in inclusive preschool settings adapt their roles.

The Cascade of Services

The concept of a **cascade of services,** first proposed by Reynolds (1962), is most widely recognized in its amended form, which was presented by Deno (1970). This cascade, or continuum, of services is presented in figure 3.1. The continuum provides a framework for tailoring services to meet the needs of individual students and remains the traditional service delivery model in many school systems. The seven levels of services in figure 3.1 range from the least restrictive services, in which most students are served (the base of the inverted triangle), to more restrictive services, in which fewer students are served (the apex of the triangle). The services in levels 1–6 are provided by the school. Level 7 services are provided by community mental health and welfare and family service agencies.

In the remainder of this section, the general functions of these traditional levels of service delivery are presented, and selected research findings regarding the efficacy of these services are reviewed.

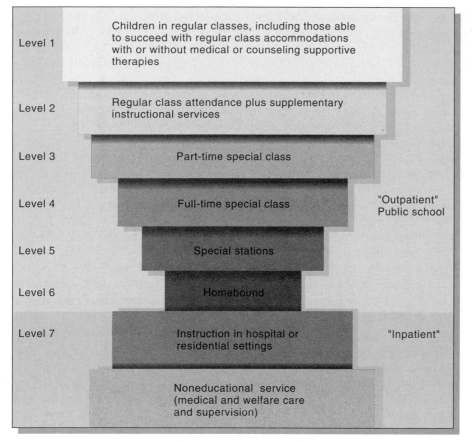

Level 1	Children in regular classes, including those able to succeed with regular class accommodations with or without medical or counseling supportive therapies
Level 2	Regular class attendance plus supplementary instructional services
Level 3	Part-time special class
Level 4	Full-time special class
Level 5	Special stations
Level 6	Homebound
Level 7	Instruction in hospital or residential settings
	Noneducational service (medical and welfare care and supervision)

"Outpatient" Public school

"Inpatient"

Figure 3.1

The cascade system of special education services

From E. Deno, "Special Education As Developmental Capital," in *Exceptional Children*, 37 (3), 1970. Copyright © 1970 The Council for Exceptional Children. Reprinted by permission.

Level 1: Students in Regular Classes　Students served at this level are in general education with or without medical and counseling support therapies. Typically, the services these students receive are provided through private and public medical, mental health, and social service agencies.

Level 2: Students in Regular Classes with Supplementary Instructional Services
Stainback, Stainback, and Harris (1989) state that the emerging role of the special educator is as a support facilitator. In this role, the special educator has three functions. First, the special educator, in consultation with the general education teacher and the student with disabilities, identifies the types of assistance and support needed. Next, the special educator collaborates with the general education teacher and the student to determine what specific assistance is most applicable in the setting in which they are functioning. In this step, general class teacher, special educator, and student jointly gather information, define the specific problem, and identify possible support interventions. Finally, the special educator assists in organizing and implementing the agreed-upon support service. This model recognizes the responsibilities of the general educator as encouraged by inclusion.

Traditionally, the most common level 2 service has been the resource room, which is a special education placement alternative in which the students receive specific support through specialized services while continuing to receive the majority of their instruction in the general education classroom. However, in an interview study of 686 students with mild disabilities, Jenkins and Heinen (1989) gave the students a choice between receiving additional assistance from their classroom teacher or from a specialist in either their classroom or a pullout program. The students overwhelmingly expressed preference for receiving the assistance in their classroom and from their general class teacher. The principal reason for the selection of the general class teacher was that the students believed their teacher knew what they needed. Embarrassment about being removed from their classroom and receiving assistance from a specialist also played a major role in the students' choice of their general teacher and classroom. Students also indicated that they wanted to remain with their classmates and that staying with their teacher was more convenient.

Level 3: Students in General Education Classes Part-Time and Special Education Classes Part-Time   In this level of service, students attend both general classes and self-contained special education classes. The transition between these two settings, however, is frequently problematic for the student with disabilities. Tymitz-Wolf (1984) found that students with mild mental retardation worried about partial placement in the general class. They reported more stress concerning social and transitional demands than academic demands.

Level 4: Students in Full-Time Special Class   At this level, students spend all of their school time in special class. Algozzine, Morsink, and Algozzine (1988) studied forty self-contained special classes for students with various disabilities. They found few differences in teacher communication patterns, learner involvement, and instructional methods among classes serving students with learning disabilities, emotional disturbances, and educable mental retardation. Teachers of the three groups were similar with regard to how they structured student time, provided feedback to students, and gave directions. The teachers worked infrequently with groups, used inquiry rather than lecture, assisted in the development of problem-solving skills, or facilitated transfer of learning. Instruction for students identified as mildly mentally retarded, learning disabled, or behaviorally disordered was more similar than different, though teachers of students who were mildly mentally retarded modified instruction to respond to individual learner needs about half as frequently as teachers of students with learning disabilities or behavioral disorders.

Level 5: Students in Special Schools   The number of special schools has decreased significantly with the trend towards the inclusion of children with disabilities into the general education system. Special schools are usually separate facilities, which severely restrict interaction between students with disabilities and students without disabilities. In most districts, a few students with severe disabilities are educated in special schools.

Level 6: Students Receiving Homebound Services   Homebound services are usually short-term interventions for students who are physically unable to attend school. Homebound placement is the most restrictive of all placements. It prohibits interaction with other students, both with and without disabilities. The hours of instruction are severely limited, in some cases one hour a day or five hours a week, and are not equivalent to the hours of instruction students attending school receive.

Exiting Special Education Services

As indicated previously, students initially classified as hearing impaired, physically/multiply handicapped, or mentally retarded rarely, if ever, exit from special education services (Walker et al., 1988). Students who remain in special education, then, must either graduate from school as a special education student or age-out of the program.

Kortering, Julnes, and Edgar (1990) describe the legal considerations involved in the graduation of special education students. They report that judicial review, though limited in scope, does provide specific guidelines to local districts. First, local districts have the discretion to restrict the awarding of a standard high school diploma—they may award either a standard or nonstandard diploma to special education students. Second, legal precedents require that procedures resulting in the differentiation of special education students be based on standards that are fair and that have been articulated to the student and his or her parents. School district procedures must give all special education students the opportunity to satisfy the standards as established or through the provisions of a reasonable accommodation. Local district personnel should keep in mind that though the court does intervene in procedural matters, it is inclined to leave the responsibility of substantive academic matters to the expertise of professional educators. Finally, the goals and objectives on each student's IEP should provide a proper means for evaluating whether or not a student can graduate. These goals and standards can be used in place of standard district requirements.

Often, if learners with disabilities are to benefit fully from the special education services discussed, they require additional support services. These "related services" are discussed in the next section.

Related Services

Public Law 94-142 defined **related services** as "transportation and such developmental, corrective, and other supportive services as are required to assist the handicapped child to benefit from special education" (Federal Register, 1977, 121.550). Related services include the following:

- Transportation—providing travel to and from school and between schools, as well as across gravel around school buildings. Special equipment that is needed, such as ramps, elevators, or lifts for buses, must be provided.
- Speech pathology—identifying, diagnosing, and appraising speech or language disorders, referral to other professionals specializing in speech and language services, and counseling and guidance of parents, children, and teachers regarding speech and language disorders.
- Audiology—identifying students with a hearing loss; determining the range, nature, and degree of that loss; providing language, auditory, and speech reading training; implementing prevention programs and counseling and guidance for students, parents, and teachers regarding hearing loss; determining the need for, selecting, fitting, and evaluating hearing aids.
- Psychological services—administering and interpreting psychological and educational tests and assessments; obtaining and interpreting information about learning styles and consulting with other staff about this data.
- Physical therapy—providing services as needed of a qualified physical therapist.
- Occupational therapy—conducting activities to improve independent functioning skills and to prevent further loss of function.
- Recreation—assessing leisure functioning and conducting therapeutic recreation, leisure education, and recreation programs.
- Early identification—creating and adhering to formal plans for identifying disabilities in children as early as possible.
- Medical services—providing services of a licensed physician to determine the child's medically related disabling condition that results in the child's need for special education and related services.
- School health services—providing services of a qualified school nurse or other qualified person.
- Counseling services—providing services of qualified social workers, psychologists, guidance counselors, or other qualified personnel.
- Social work services—preparing social or developmental histories and group and individual counseling services for children and their families.

- Parent counseling and training—helping parents understand the special needs of their child and providing them with information about child development.

As a result of Public Law 101-476, rehabilitation counseling is now included as a related service. At this time, however, the legal definition of rehabilitation counseling is undetermined in the federal regulations.

Two related services that have generated controversy are psychotherapy and school health services. Osborne (1984) suggests that if a state requires that psychotherapy be provided by a licensed psychiatrist, then it is an exempt medical service. In regard to school health services, Osborne (1988) indicates that school health and medical services must be provided if they help to ensure the child's ability to profit from the educational program. If the student, however, is already benefiting from educational services without related services, then school health and medical services do not have to be provided by the school district.

Few districts have all the professional personnel available to provide the entire range of related services. Huntze and Grosenick (1980) stress that when a service is not available within the district, the child's needs are generally either not met or are met through the purchase of services from another district or private agency.

Summary

Several topics essential to understanding special education and the relationships between special education and general education were discussed in this chapter. The development of special education and general education in the United States was reviewed, and its impact on services for children with disabilities at various times in history was emphasized. As a result of compulsory school attendance laws passed during the second half of the nineteenth century, special programs were initiated in the schools. Schools, as the primary socialization agent to "the American way of life," served to modify the behavior and beliefs of urban immigrants in ways that assured the continuation of American society. The general social unrest of the 1960s fed the interest to meet individual needs, culminating in mandated free, appropriate public education for all learners with disabilities through Public Law 94-142. Subsequent amendments to this law have increased efforts to serve students in less restrictive environments, to increase services to students at younger ages, and to support them in their transition to adult life.

The significance of social systems theory for classroom management was discussed and exemplified. Through the social systems perspective, learning principles are applied with consideration of interpersonal relationships and with recognition of the impact of neurological and physical factors on children's functioning in the classroom. Teachers must relate to students as capable persons and trust in the students' abilities. The interaction among the setting, the student, the teacher, and all the other "actors" within the setting are emphasized.

Diagnostic evaluation and placement processes were described, including screening and referral procedures. Prereferral activities were discussed, and the importance of these activities for preventing the misidentification and premature classification of children as disabled was emphasized. The Individual Education Program was characterized or described as a resource management tool. The Individual Family Service Plan which defines the family rather than the child as the service recipient for children younger than three years of age and requires specific judgments with regard to the family's service needs, was also presented.

The chapter included discussions of two concepts that are currently of great concern in special education: the least restrictive environment and inclusion. Challenges to the concept of the least restrictive environment were described. The "cascade," or continuum, of services traditionally available to students with disabilities was presented.

The chapter concluded with a section on the related services authorized by Public Law 94-142 and its amendments. These should be made available to students with disabilities as needed.

Building Your Professional Vocabulary

Match each word or phrase to its meaning.

_____ appropriate education

_____ diagnostic evaluation

_____ IEP

_____ least restrictive environment

_____ prereferral activities

_____ related services

_____ screening

_____ inclusion

_____ IFSP

_____ placement

_____ referral

_____ transition services

a. the organization of a school so that all students who would usually be assigned to it are educated with their age-peers

b. reasonably calculated to bring about educational benefit

c. Individualized Education Program

d. promote movement from school to post-school activities

e. intervention assistance in general education setting

f. Individualized Family Service Plan

g. identifying students for further study

h. nomination of a student for evaluation

i. studying a student and contexts to determine the cause, nature, and circumstances of the problem if, in fact, there is a problem

j. assignment of a student to special education services

k. placement in the setting that provides the maximum amount of interaction with learners without disabilities

l. services required to assist the student in benefiting from special education

Comprehension Check

Select the most appropriate response.

1. Prior to World War I, public schools in the United States
   a. served as the gatekeeper of the social order.
   b. served as the melting pot for urban immigrants.
   c. served as the educational system for the privileged few.

2. During the 1960s there was a shift to
   a. psychoanalytical explanations of children's behavior.
   b. blaming schools for children's failure.
   c. excluding children perceived as ineducable.

3. Special education services have moved from
   a. inclusive programs to separate programs for learners with disabilities.
   b. distal to proximal arrangement with general education.
   c. proximal to distal arrangement with general education.

4. The Individualized Education Program is
   a. a contract between parent and school system.
   b. mutually agreed upon by parent and educators.
   c. a plan for providing services for children from birth through two years of age.

5. "Appropriate education" insures that
   a. the child has the opportunity to fulfill his or her potential.
   b. learners with disabilities have the opportunity to achieve commensurate with peers.
   c. services that maximize achievement are provided.

6. The Individual Family Service Plan
   a. addresses the needs of preschoolers.
   b. addresses the needs of infants and toddlers.
   c. addresses the needs of infants and toddlers and their families.

7. As part of Public Law 101-476,
    a. transition services were required on IEPs.
    b. the mandate for free, public education was recalled.
    c. early intervention program plans were initiated.
8. From the social systems perspective, assessment and intervention must
    a. focus on the child.
    b. focus on the child and the developmental contexts of the child.
    c. focus on the family.
9. The placement instrument used in special education is
    a. the IEP.
    b. the referral.
    c. the diagnostic evaluation.
10. Though inclusion is becoming more common, many school districts retain a service delivery model referred to as
    a. mainstreaming.
    b. integration.
    c. the cascade of services.

References

Algozzine, B., Christenson, S., & Ysseldyke, J. E. (1982). Probabilities associated with the referral to placement process. *Teacher Education and Special Education, 5* (6), 15–20.

Algozzine, B., Morsink, C. V., & Algozzine, K. M. (1988). What's happening in self-contained special education classrooms. *Exceptional Children, 55,* 259–265.

Bauer, A. M., & Sapona, R. H. (1991). *Managing classrooms to facilitate learning.* Englewood Cliffs, NJ: Prentice Hall.

Bender, W. N. (1988). The other side of placement decisions: Assessment of the mainstream learning environment. *Remedial and Special Education, 9* (5), 28–33.

Bickel, W. E., & Bickel, D. D. (1986). Effective schools, classrooms, and instruction: Implications for Special Education. *Exceptional Children, 52,* 489–500.

Blom, S. D., Lininger, R. S., & Charlesworth, W. R. (1987). Ecological observation of emotionally and behaviorally disordered children: An alternative method. *American Journal of Orthopsychiatry, 57,* 49–59.

Breme, J. (1975). *A matrix for modern education.* Toronto, Canada: McClelland & Stewart.

Bronfenbrenner, U. (1979). *The ecology of human development.* Cambridge, MA: Harvard University.

Carter, J., & Sugai, G. (1989). Survey on prereferral practices: Responses from state departments of education. *Exceptional Children, 55,* 298–302.

Copeland, C. D. (1982). Teaching-learning behaviors and the demands of the classroom environment. In W. Doyle & T. L. Good (Eds.), *Focus on Teaching 1,* 83–97.

Council for Exceptional Children. (1990). Precis: Americans with Disabilities Act of 1990: What you should know. Supplement to *Exceptional Children, 57,* 1–2.

Deno, E. (1970), Special education as developmental capital. *Exceptional Children* 37, 229–237.

Edminister, P., & Ekstrand, R. E. (1987), Preschool programming: Legal and educational issues. *Exceptional Children, 54* (2), 130–136.

Federal Register, (1977). Public Law 94-142, Sec. 111–550.

Ferguson, D. L., Meyer, G., Jeanchild, L., Juniper, L., & Zingo, J. (1992). Figuring out what to do with the grownups: How teachers make inclusion "work" for students with disabilities. *Journal of the Association for Persons with Severe Handicaps, 17,* 218–226.

Fleming, L. A., Wolery, M., Weinzierl, C., Venn, M. L., & Schroeder, C. (1991). Model for assessing and adapting teachers' roles in mainstreamed preschool settings. *Topics in Early Childhood Special Education, 11* (1), 85–98.

Fuchs, D., & Fuchs, L. S. (1989). Effects of examiner familiarity on Black, Caucasian, and Hispanic children: A meta-analysis. *Exceptional Children, 55,* 303–308.

Gerber, M. M. (1981). Economic considerations of "appropriate" education for exceptional children. *Exceptional Education Quarterly, 2,* 49–58.

Gerken, K. (1988). Best practice in academic assessment. In A. Thomas & J. Grimes (Eds.), *Best Practice in School Psychology* (pp. 157–170). Washington, DC: National Association of School Psychologists.

Gersten, R., & Woodward, J. (1990). Rethinking the Regular Education Initiative: Focus on the classroom teacher. *Remedial and Special Education, 11* (3), 7–16.

Giangreco, M. F., Dennis, R., Cloninger, C., Edelman, S., & Schattman, R. (1993). I've counted Jon: Transformational experiences of teachers educating students with disabilities. *Exceptional Children, 59*, 359–372.

Graden, J. (1989). Redefining "prereferral" intervention as intervention assistance: Collaboration between general and special education. *Exceptional Children, 56*, 227–331.

Graden, J. L., Casey, A., & Christenson, S. L. (1985). Implementing a prereferral intervention system: Part I: The model. *Exceptional Children, 51*, 377–384.

Green, J. L., & Weade, R. (1988, April). Teaching as conversation and the construction of meaning in the classroom. Paper presented at the Annual Meeting of the American Educational Research Association.

Hoffman, E. (1975). The American public school and the deviant child: The origins of their involvement. *The Journal of Special Education, 9*, 414–423.

Hood, L., McDermott, R., & Cole, M. (1980). "Let's try to make it a good day"—some not so simple ways. *Discourse Processes, 3*, 155–168.

Huntze, S. L., & Grosenick, J. (1980). *National needs assessment in behavior disorders: Resource issues in behavior disorders.* Columbia, MO: University of Missouri.

Jenkins, J. R., & Heinen, A. (1989). Students' preferences for service delivery: Pull-out, in-class, or integrated models. *Exceptional Children, 55*, 516–523.

Jenkins, J., Pious, C. G., & Peterson, D. L. (1988). Categorical programs for remedial and handicapped students: Issues of validity. *Exceptional Children, 55*, 147–158.

Jenkins, J. R., Pious, C. G., & Jewell, M. (1990). Special education and the Regular Education Initiative: Basic assumptions. *Exceptional Children, 56*, 479–491.

Jones, V. (1986). Classroom management in the United States: Trends and critical issues. In D. P. Tattum (Ed.), *Management of disruptive pupil behavior in schools* (pp. 69–90). Chichester, England: John Wiley.

Kauffman, J. M. (1981). Historical trends and contemporary issues in special education in the United States. In J. M. Kauffman & D. P. Hallahan (Eds.), *Handbook of special education* (pp. 3–23), Englewood Cliffs, NJ: Prentice Hall.

Kochanek, T. T., Kabacoff, R. I., & Lipsitt, L. P. (1990). Early identification of developmentally disabled and at-risk preschool children. *Exceptional Children, 56*, 528–538.

Kortering, L., Julnes, R., & Edgar, E. (1990). An instructive review of the law pertaining to the graduation of special education students. *Remedial and Special Education, 11* (4), 7–13.

Krauss, M. W. (1990). New precedent in family policy: Individualized Family Service Plan. *Exceptional Children, 56*, 388–395.

Lambert, N. M. (1988). Perspectives on eligibility for and placement in special education programs. *Exceptional Children, 54*, 297–301.

Lipsky, D. K., & Gartner, A. (1991). Achieving full inclusion: Placing the student at the center of educational reform. In W. Stainback & S. Stainback (Eds.), *Controversial issues confronting special education: Divergent perspectives* (pp. 3–12). Boston: Allyn & Bacon.

Mercer, J. R. (1970). Sociological perspectives on mild mental retardation. In H. C. Haywood (Ed.), *Social-cultural aspects of mental retardation.* NY: Appleton-Century-Crofts.

Mercer, J. R. (1971). The meaning of mental retardation. In R. Koch & J. C. Dobson (Eds.), *The mentally retarded child and family.* NY: Brunner/Mazel.

National Information Center for Children and Youth with Disabilities. (1991). The education of children and youth with special needs: What do the laws say? *NICHCY News Digest, 1* (1), 1–15.

Osborne, A. (1984). How the courts have interpreted the related services mandate. *Exceptional Children, 51*, 249–252.

Osborne, A. (1988). The Supreme Court's interpretation of the Education for All Handicapped Children's Act. *Remedial and Special Education, 9* (3), 21–25.

Pinnell, G. S., & Galloway, C. M. (1987). Human development, language, and communication: Then and now. *Theory into Practice, 26* (Special Issue), 353–357.

Pugach, M., & Johnson, L. J. (1989). Prereferral interventions: Progress, problems, and challenges. *Exceptional Children, 56*, 217–226.

Reynolds, M. (1962). A framework for considering some issues in special education. *Exceptional Children, 28*, 367–370.

Reynolds, M. (1989). An historical perspective: The delivery of special education to mildly disabled and at risk students. *Remedial and Special Education, 10* (6), 7–11.

Rothstein, L. (1990). *Special education law.* New York: Longman.

Salisbury, C. L., Palombaro, M. M., & Hollowood, W. M. (1993). On the nature and change of an inclusive elementary school. *The Journal of the Association for Persons with Severe Handicaps, 18,* 75–84.

Sarason, S. B., & Doris, J. (1979). *Educational handicap, public policy, and social history.* New York: The Free Press.

Shepard, L. A., & Smith, M. L. (1983). An evaluation of the identification of learning disabled students in Colorado. *Learning Disabilities Quarterly, 6* (2), 115–127.

Stainback, S., & Stainback, W. (1990). Facilitating support networks. In W. Stainback & S. Stainback (Eds.), *Support networks for inclusive schooling* (pp. 25–36). Baltimore: Brookes.

Stainback, S. W., & Stainback, W. (1992). Schools as inclusive communities. In S. Stainback & W. Stainback (Eds.), *Controversial issues confronting special education* (pp. 29–44). Boston: Allyn & Bacon.

Stainback, S. B., Stainback, W. C., & Harris, K. C. (1989). Support facilitation: An emerging role for special educators. *Teacher Education and Special Education, 12,* 148–153.

Stainback, S., Stainback, W., & Jackson, H. J. (1992). Toward inclusive classrooms. In S. Stainback & W. Stainback (Eds.), *Curriculum considerations in inclusive classrooms* (pp. 3–18), Baltimore: Paul H. Brookes.

Taylor, S. (1988). Caught in the continuum: A critical analysis of the principle of the least restrictive environment. *The Journal of the Association for Persons with Severe Handicaps, 13,* 41–53.

Tindal, G. (1985). Investigating the effectiveness of special education. *Journal of Learning Disabilities, 18,* 101–117.

Tymitz-Wolf, B. (1984). An analysis of EMR children's worries about mainstreaming. *Education and Training of the Mentally Retarded, 19,* 157–168.

Vergason, G. A., & Anderegg, M. L. (1992). Preserving the least restrictive environment. In S. Stainback & W. Stainback (Eds.), *Controversial issues confronting special education* (pp. 45–54). Boston: Allyn & Bacon.

Walker, D. K., Singer, J. D., Palfrey, J. S., Orza M., Wenger, M., & Butler, J. A. (1988). Who leaves and who stays in special education: A two-year follow-up study. *Exceptional Children, 54,* 393–402.

White, R., & Calhoun, M. L. (1987). From referral to placement: Teachers' perceptions of their responsibilities. *Exceptional Children, 63* (5), 460–468.

Will, M. C. (1986). Educating children with learning problems: A shared responsibility. *Exceptional Children, 52,* 411–415.

Chapter 4

Families and Learners with Disabilities

Objectives

After completing this chapter, you will be able to:

1. describe the family as a social system.
2. discuss the adaptation of families to members with disabilities.
3. describe family collaboration in special education.

Key Words and Phrases

collaboration
collaborative support for school
   programs
criteria of the least dangerous
   assumption

information-giving activities
information-sharing activities
nonparticipation
parent training
stage theory

One dream continually haunts me. It's 'handicap family swim night' at the recreation center. My family—my husband, Tom, and I, and our sons, Tommy and Aaron, and other families are all splashing and playing in the water.

"This is a fantastic pool which is open to the public except for 'handicapped swim night.' The pool has all the latest equipment and is carefully painted with black racing lines across the bottom of the pool. On 'handicapped swim night,' between each black line is a professional person with an 'LG' (lifeguard) on his or her T-shirt. Now, this person must have courses and credentials in the various specializations, a multidisciplinary approach to lifesaving.

"As our families are swimming we notice that the pool water starts to change. Instead of calm swimming, now there are swift currents. The water keeps rising and whirlpools are pulling us under. My husband and I try to keep Aaron and Tommy above water. The rest of the families are also struggling.

"We paddle and try to go to the side of the pool, but keep getting thrown back into deep water. We cry to the lifeguards on the side of the pool, but they don't seem to hear. Every time I sink to the bottom of the pool, it seems I land on a black line. Finally, the families all gather in the middle of the pool and cry out in one loud voice, 'HELP, PLEASE HELP, WE CAN'T DO IT OURSELVES!'

"This causes the lifeguards to look at us. But there is great concern because we keep landing on the lines and they can't decide whose territory it is. Each lifeguard has specific rules and guidelines regarding who they can save. The situation gets grave. One or two of the lifeguards throw in a life preserver and shout encouragement like 'swim faster,' or 'remember the strokes we taught you,' 'we're doing all we can do, you parents just need an organized effort.' But the water is getting swifter and the families are getting weaker and weaker.

"As the situation gets desperate and we start to choke and fail, the first lifeguard turns to the second and says, 'What do you think?' the second turns to the third, and says 'What do you think?' and on down the side of the pool until finally, all eyes are on Head Lifeguard A (who is sitting high in a chair in the middle of the natatorium).

"As the families sink into unconsciousness, Head Lifeguard A is seen shaking his head and frantically . . . paging through a rule book." (Mary Ulrich, parent of a young adult with autism, regarding professional support, personal communication, 1995.)

Introduction

In recent decades, there has been a dramatic change in the complex relationship between families and schools. Coleman (1987) suggests that families at all economic levels are becoming increasingly ill-equipped to complement and augment the schools' efforts to prepare students of the next generation. Coleman contends that the following indicators demonstrate the reduced incentive of parents to assume responsibility for their children:

- Prior to the 1960s, there was a general assumption that parents would pay for their children's college education; presently, college costs are seen increasingly as a government responsibility.
- The growth of afterschool and summer school activities reflects a decrease in parents' responsibility for children and an increase in parents' concern for personal fulfillment.
- Parental authority over their college- and high school-age children has relaxed.
- Parents delegate an increasingly wide range of socialization activities to the school, including family and sexuality instruction, afterschool activities, and life-skills instructions.

These indicators appear to be paralleled in special education. For example, the cost of post-secondary special education is increasingly assumed to be the responsibility of publicly funded vocational rehabilitation agencies. The extended school year, afterschool activities, and respite-care programs are becoming more readily available at public expense. The parents of children with complex, challenging behaviors are increasingly relying on the schools and special educators to decrease these behaviors and instruct the children in socially appropriate behaviors. Special education has assumed the teaching of basic self-care, survival, and life skills to children. In recent decades, advocacy for persons with disabilities and their families has evolved from the provision of public protective services to the development of private and independent advocacy service groups and self-advocacy (Zirpoli, Hancox, Wieck, & Skarnulis, 1989).

In this chapter, we will explore the family as a social system and discuss the implications for families with members with disabilities. Using Bronfenbrenner's (1979) developmental contexts, we will summarize recent research findings with regard to families with members with disabilities. We conclude the chapter with a discussion of family collaboration in the education of children with disabilities.

The Family as a Social System

The family is not simply a collection of individuals; it is a social system. Minuchin (1974) offers several principles of social systems that apply to families:

- The family, itself, is a structured whole, a complete unit, with interdependent elements.
- As in a social system, interactions in the family are reciprocal and represent continuous give and take, accommodation and adaptation, rather than linear cause-and-effect interaction patterns.
- The family attempts to maintain stability. In the effort to maintain stability, the behavior of family members is perceived as purposeful. Resistance to change appears to be a natural occurrence.

When the family is perceived as a social system, it becomes apparent that linear cause-and-effect explanations of family members' behavior do not explain family operation (Johnston & Zemitzsch, 1988). In the family, each person's

Objective One

To describe the family as a social system.

functioning within the system helps maintain and change the behavior of other family members. Effecting change in one member provides the opportunity for effecting change in other members.

When a family member is born with or diagnosed as having disabilities, other family members assume new roles and the family system reorganizes (Bronfenbrenner, 1986). This reorganization changes the expectations and attitudes of family members. In addition, it affects other major settings, or ecological contexts, in which the individual with the disability functions, such as the school.

It must be noted that the family has changed dramatically in the latter part of this century. Families no longer typically comprise a married mother and father and two or more children. Today, most children live in one-parent families, reconstituted, or blended, families, foster homes, extended families with relatives, or in a variety of other family arrangements (Epstein, 1988).

Adaptation of Families

Objective Two

To discuss the adaptation of families to members with disabilities.

Following the birth or diagnosis of a disability in a family member, the family must adjust or adapt to the situation. There are several theories on how this adaptation occurs.

Stage Theory

Traditionally, the adaptation of families to members with disabilities has been perceived as the progression through a series of psychological stages: shock, denial, bargaining, anger, depression, and acceptance (Creekmore, 1988; Kroth & Otteni, 1985). Parents of children with disabilities are understood to experience chronic sorrow, a grieving process that persists throughout the life of the parent and child (Kroth & Otteni, 1985). Grieving is viewed by some professionals as necessary for parents in order to free themselves of the dream of the "perfect" child (Hinderliter, 1988).

Although **stage theory,** this progression through a set pattern of reactions to the birth or diagnosis of a family member with a disability, is accepted by many professionals, there is little empirical evidence to support it or the inferences drawn from it. As a result of an extensive review of the literature, Blacher (1984) concludes that the stages are a result of clinical judgments based on interviews with parents of children with disabilities, rather than analysis of objective data. Allen and Affleck (1985) report that in their analysis of the literature, they found no support for any stagelike arrangement or grouping of parents' reactions.

Kratochvil and Devereux (1988) discuss another problem with regard to the application of stage theory, which is that it presupposes a final stage: closure, with adjustment to or acceptance of the situation. In interviews with parents, however, they found that despite overall adjustment, all parents experienced "down periods." These recurring feelings of grief were triggered by unreached milestones, worries about the future, and introspection.

Alternative explanations of the adaptation of families to the birth or diagnosis of a child with disabilities have been suggested. Bauer and Shea (1987) present an integrated perspective on family adaptation in which adjustment becomes a developmental process, an effort to meet both the parents' and the child's needs. Family adaptation is seen as occurring within several personal, familial, social, and cultural ecological contexts. In her explanation, Kampfe (1989) discusses the adjustment of the family to the birth or diagnosis of a child with a disability as a transition in the family's development. These alternative explanations are discussed in the following sections.

Parents are encouraged to be active participants in their child's education.

An Integrated Perspective

In the integrated perspective (Bauer & Shea, 1987; Shea & Bauer, 1991), Bronfenbrenner's ecological contexts form a framework for the simultaneous consideration of (a) what is taking place within the immediate household, (b) the factors at work in the larger social system in which the family is functioning, (c) the interaction of these settings with one another, and (d) society's overriding cultural beliefs and values as well as personal factors for coping with disability.

Personal Factors for Coping with a Child with Disabilities Personal factors for coping include an individual's ability to deal with stress and what an individual brings to the family setting and the parenting role. In the discussion that follows, consideration is given to parent gender and personality and the characteristics of the child with the disability.

The literature suggests that the parents' stress is primarily a function of their personality and physiology and not a consequence of the nature of the disability. It appears that programs designed to relieve family stress by providing goods, services, and other resources are of questionable effectiveness (Bradshaw, 1978). Successful collaboration involves helping family members in their efforts to develop more effective ways of managing stress. The literature also reports that mothers and fathers vary in their needs and perceptions of the child with disabilities. Successful collaboration programs must, then, be designed to respond to the unique needs of both mothers and fathers.

An integrated, social systems perspective has several advantages in conceptualizing the adaptation for families. Koch (1982) suggests that when using a systems perspective, it is assumed that any event occurring within the system has an impact upon the entire system. Within the system there are both positive and negative feedback loops, which either interrupt or escalate the stress cycle.

Intrafamilial relationships As expected, a strong inverse relationship has been found between mother-reported stress and child progress; that is, mothers who observed more progress in their child's development reported less stress (Robbins, 1991). Greater stress has been reported by parents of boys with disabilities and

Individuals with disabilities participate in their family's usual activities.

parents of children with limited communication skills (Frey, Greenberg, & Fewell, 1989). Parents of children with developmental delays have reported stress related to the amount of time devoted to caregiving, concern over present and future needs, and uncertainty about the child's progress.

Several characteristics have been related to a family's positive adaptation. Well-functioning parental subsystems, with two-parent families, experienced more positive adaptation to their child with a disability (Trute & Hauch, 1988).

External family supports   External family supports are found at work, at church, within the neighborhood, at school, and in the community. Significant factors in this developmental context are the professionals who interact with the family, social interactions, and external support systems. Skillful use of family and friendship network resources also supports more positive adaptation (Trute & Hauch, 1988).

Beckman-Bell (1981) suggests that collaboration between parents and teachers on behalf of the child with disabilities is enhanced when professionals consider (a) the interaction of personal characteristics and environmental influences, (b) family characteristics that may change, and (c) family characteristics that are not likely to change. If these factors are considered in decision making, programs can be designed to respond to the individual family's issues and concerns.

Interrelationships among contexts   Families from low socioeconomic status groups tended to be very disengaged in terms of their coping skills, while families from higher income groups tended to be enmeshed, or very close-knit, families. Furthermore, these low-income families had fewer sources and resources for support available to them. Significant differences were found among the two types of families in terms of their adaptation (Lowitzer, 1989). There is, then, an interrelationship between work and adaptation.

An additional issue in the adaptation of families to children with disabilities is that of coordination of school and home. McAfee and Vergason (1979) make three recommendations to further the coordination of school and home efforts on behalf of the child with disabilities. First, a written or unwritten contract should be drawn between school and home to increase the potential that each contributes toward their common goals for the child. Second, parents must assume some responsibility for their child's education. Finally, both school and family should seek ways to regain community support for the family system.

Though the provision of appropriate services for the child is a critical issue, school (and, perhaps, social agency) personnel may oversimplify the issue of parent involvement by equating the parents' involvement in formal programs with the parents' involvement with their child. According to MacMillan and Turnbull (1983), a decision not to be involved in educational programming with their child does not mean that the parents are not involved with their child in the larger context of home and community. Parents have a right to choose not to be involved in a formal program when they feel noninvolvement is beneficial to them, their family, and their child. Decisions about the degree of involvement should grow out of the parents' individual needs and preferences rather than the generalized expectations of professionals.

Bronfenbrenner (1979) indicates that the developmental potential of a setting is enhanced if the person's initial transition into that setting is not made alone, but with one or more persons with whom he or she has participated in prior settings. For example, when Jason made the transition from his special education class to a general education class for mathematics instruction, he was placed in the fifth grade in which Michael, his peer tutor, was taking mathematics instruction. Development is enhanced if, prior to entry into a new setting, individuals are provided with appropriate information, advice, and vicarious experiences. The developmental potential of settings is enhanced to the extent that there exist direct and indirect links to power so that participants can influence the allocation of resources and make decisions that are responsive to their needs. (Transitions between developmental contexts are explored in chapter 5.)

Meeting the needs of individual parents should be the goal of any collaborative program. Strategies for intervention can be designed to respond to the family's expressed needs and concerns and to their style of adaptation. The impact of the child with disabilities on family relationships and the family itself needs to be carefully assessed if professionals are to successfully assist the family (Blackard & Barsch, 1982).

Societal Beliefs and Values about the Family and Disability   Society views marriage as a continuing union of two persons that produces healthy, perfect children (Greer, 1975). Families not producing perfect children are considered "different" (Darling, 1979). This difference creates a stigma for the parents. As a consequence, the parents may exhibit a loss of self-esteem, shame, defensiveness, aloneness, feelings of insignificance, or loss of belief in immortality, that is, the carrying on of a part of themselves in their children.

These feelings may be exacerbated by the "courtesy stigma." Parents may acquire a "courtesy stigma" by association with their child (Birenbaum, 1970). The parents' former social identity is not fully retained with the birth or diagnosis of a child with a disability. The social factors of inclusion, which will reduce intimacy with parents of similar children, may increase the parents' stress (Gallagher, Beckman, & Cross, 1983).

Voysey (1975) suggests that parents use various strategies to deal with societal expectations with regard to their child's disability and their role as parents. These strategies are characterized by the following verbalizations:

- "It could happen to anyone."
- "We take it day by day."
- "We didn't deserve this—it just happened."
- "We appreciate little successes more."
- "We understand other people's problems better."
- "Each person makes a special contribution."

Voysey also suggests that parents of children with disabilities manage the impressions they project to others. They may convey to others how successful the child is by simply mentioning the disability informally, by supplying only partial information, or by trying to "tell it like it is."

Positive and realistic changes in society's beliefs, attitudes, and values with regard to families and disabilities will provide the support parents need to help them adapt to the birth or diagnosis of a child with a disability. As professionals working with families with members with disabilities, it is essential to recognize personal presumptions and biases towards them. Open acceptance of family members as individuals rather than as a stereotypical group (for example, parents of children with mental retardation or siblings of children identified as having emotional/behavioral disorders) is essential.

Transition Model

Kampfe (1989) discusses adaptation as transition to the birth or diagnosis of a child with disabilities. The transition model assumes that the discovery of the child's deafness, mental retardation, or other disability represents a significant event or transition in the life of the family. In her model, Kampfe suggests several variables that influence the family's adaptation, including:

- the child's specific condition or disability
- the family's perceptions, or the meaning they attach to the event, including its degrees of importance, disruptiveness, manageability, and stress-creating impact
- conditioning variables, including the individual or situational factors that moderate perception, response, or outcome of the transition, including social status indicators, experiences, resources, and social supports
- responses, including the mourning process
- outcomes, which ideally are constructive actions towards the child's development

By viewing family adaptation to the birth or diagnosis of a child with a disability as transition, the complex interactions of the many variables involved become apparent. The family's adaptation is highly individualized and multivariate and includes an extremely complex set of perceptions, social status indicators, experiences, personal resources, social supports, and characteristics of the disability. According to Kampfe, the complexity and interactions of these variables account for some of the differences in parental responses to the birth and diagnosis of a child with a disability and the conflicting reports in the literature on the parents' adaptation.

ABCX Model

The ABCX model of family adaptation (Hill, 1949, cited in McCubbin & Patterson, 1981) suggests that family adaptation is based on how A (the stressor event) interacts with B (the family's crisis-meeting resources), which interacts with C (the family's interpretation of the event [X]). Using this model, McCubbin and Patterson found that families with children with disabilities who adapted well could change the power structure within the family, adapt family roles, and modify rules in response to stress. The families who were in greater stress were rigid and chaotic.

A "Double ABCX" model has also been proposed, in which family stress is defined as an imbalance in demands (the A factor: stressor event, prior challenges) and capabilities or resources (the B factor). The family's definition (C factor) of the imbalance influences its impact. When the family is unable to balance the demands and capabilities without making a change in its structure and interaction patterns, a crisis (X) occurs (Smith, 1984).

Behr (1990) uses the ABCX model to describe positive contributions of persons with disabilities to their families. In this model, families increase their coping systems and develop a way to address stressful events and even develop cognitive processes to deal with threatening events.

Family Collaboration and Special Education

According to Public Law 94-142 and its amendments, parents have the right to

- inspect and review their child's complete educational record.
- get an independent evaluation of their child.
- receive written notice of any change in the identification, evaluation, or placement of their child, or any change in the child's Individualized Education Program (IEP).
- receive an impartial due process hearing if they disagree with the school's decision.
- participate equally with school personnel in developing, reviewing, and revising their child's IEP.

Public Law 99-457, as previously discussed, reauthorized these rights and added the Individual Family Service Plan (IFSP) for children with disabilities between birth and three years of age. In the IFSP, a designated case manager is responsible for implementing the plan and coordinating services. The family, not only the child, is the client of the educational program. The philosophical position underlying the IFSP is consistent with the Syracuse University Center on Human Policy's (1987) position statement on families, which indicates that

- families should receive the supports necessary to maintain their children in the home.
- supports should serve the entire family.
- supports should maximize the family's control over the services they receive.

Donnellan and Mirenda (1984) propose several standards to serve as a foundation for all parent collaboration programs in special education. They suggest that all interventions be based on the assumption that parents are not the cause of their child's disability. They also recommend that professionals recognize the danger of blaming parents for the child's disability. In addition, professionals should be aware of their own personal and professional strengths and weaknesses. They should apply the **criteria of the least dangerous assumption,** which states that if a program is ineffective, it is because the program is ineffective and not because the family is defective or incapable. Donnellan and Mirenda further contend it is essential that a full explanation of the child's disability be given to the parents. Professionals should be sensitive to the unique emotional and practical problems of living with an individual with disabilities and ensure that support services are made readily available to parents who wish them.

Donnellan and Mirenda state that under no circumstances should parents be told by professionals that "nothing can be done" for their child. All intervention programs should involve families to the maximum extent possible and should be designed to meet the needs of the child in the broader context of the needs of the family. Parents should be recognized as the experts in all areas related to their child's unique history, behavior, and needs. They should have full access to all diagnostic and educational information.

Objective Three

To describe family collaboration in special education.

Annual **Edition**

Article 3

The unique strengths of each family should be recognized.

Dunst, Trivette, and Deal (1988) suggest the following four principles to govern assessment and intervention activities in response to the needs of families:

1. Intervention efforts should be based on family-identified needs, aspirations, and personal projects to promote positive child, parent, and family functioning.
2. The strengths and capabilities of the family should be the basis for promoting the family's ability to mobilize resources.
3. The major emphasis of programming should be on strengthening the family's personal social network, as well as untapped but potential sources of informal aid and assistance.
4. Helping behaviors should promote the family's acquisition and use of competencies and skills necessary to mobilize and secure resources.

Several researchers have described the nature of family collaboration in special education and compared special education to general education in various cultural groups. Yanok and Derubertis (1989) found comparable patterns of responses between parents of students with disabilities and nonidentified students in the areas of school involvement, quality of instruction, and equality of educational opportunity. In a comparison of parents of general education students and special education students, Salisbury and Evans (1988) found that the parents of students in special education programs were presented more opportunities for involvement, were more satisfied with their involvement, and felt more able to influence their child's education. The involvement of parents of students in general education was reported to decrease as the students grew older. The involvement of the parents of students in special education, however, remained constant throughout the child's educational career. Lynch and Stein (1987), in a study contrasting African American, Hispanic American, and majority-culture families, reported that Hispanic American families were satisfied with their children's special education programs but were less knowledgeable and less involved than were Anglo and African American families. The comments of parents from Hispanic American families with reference to their involvement seemed to convey the message "teacher knows best."

Beyond "The Room"

By Stephanie Garcia
Pueblo, Colorado

Last year when my husband's brother and his family moved to Pueblo from California, they enrolled their daughter in the same school as my son Lorenzo. Lorenzo was in the special education class at his school. During family get-togethers the kids had often played together and all was well.

During one such occasion my niece came up to me and asked what was wrong with Lorenzo. I asked what she meant. "Well," she said, "he's in that room. . . He's different." Although I tried to explain that Lorenzo was no different from other students at the school, I knew she looked at him differently now because he was in "that room."

This wake-up call by my young niece made me realize that Lorenzo's friends were made up of family members. There were no children in our neighborhood who were willing to be his friend. We had been to school on several occasions because Lorenzo had been bullied on the playground. There was also name calling like "dummy," "stupid," and the "R" word. I watched my helpless little boy accept everything his peers dished out and was determined to keep him protected in "that room."

Now, I realize that not only would my son benefit from being taught in the same environment as his peers but, it would also educate other children. I believe that the issue of self esteem along with that of acceptance should be the driving force that pushes us to include children at a very early age.

We began the new school year with an attempt to have our son educated in a more inclusive environment. We started by having his staffing with all of the teachers who would be working with him. This took some doing, but we met at 7:00 A.M. so that the entire team could be involved with his educational goals and be aware of his special needs. His success would depend on the supports that the school would be willing to provide and commitment from my husband and me.

There is no cookbook or step-by-step process on how we can make this work and make everyone happy, but we have used some great ideas and each day we see improvements and more acceptance.

Moving support personnel into the integrated classroom benefits everyone. The Special Education teacher works with the regular teacher as a consultant with aids and supports that have a spillover effect for other students.

I know that students with disabilities have a high drop-out rate and a startling 36 percent are involved with the criminal justice system within three years of leaving school. My son needs the social experiences as much as the academics.

How can we expect people with disabilities to be accepted in their communities when they are not included in their schools?

Inclusive education has the potential to reduce the fear of the unknown and promote friendship, respect, insight and cooperation. My husband and I have thought long and hard about this decision and without the Individuals with Disabilities Act (IDEA) we would not have had a choice.

Recently, it all became very clear when out of the blue the doorbell rang. When I answered the door, there stood before me a young boy on his bike. "Can I help you?" I asked, as I waited for him to ask if I wanted to buy some candy. "Hi!" he responded. "Can Lorenzo come out and play?"

As the tears streamed down our faces, we watched and realized that we had to do whatever it takes to ensure Lorenzo's place in his community and get him out of the stigma of "that room ● "

From "Beyond 'The Room' " by Stephanie Garcia, in *The ARC, 20 Years of IDEA in America*. Reprinted with permission of the publisher and the author.

A Model for Collaboration with Families

The social systems perspective recognizes that families are complex and unique social systems. Because families vary so greatly, professionals must have an understanding of the individual parent's current level of development when assisting his or her child. Olson (1988) suggests that models for working with families should consider that services and needs may range developmentally from a crisis level, in which it is difficult to address anything other than immediate needs, through a need for information and education, to the need for skill training. Throughout these stages, parents and families need emotional support and practical assistance in performing task-oriented activities, such as developing with others the child's IEP or IFSP and accessing community services in response to family and child needs.

Recognition of the uniqueness of each family necessitates the application of a model for collaboration that emphasizes individualized programming. Shea and Bauer (1991) describe such a model as a recursive system, in which the steps in the model are revisited as family collaboration develops over time. The phases

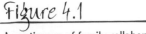

Figure 4.1

A continuum of family collaboration.

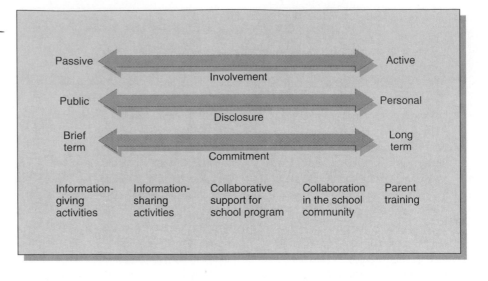

in the model for collaboration include (a) introductory activities and assessing parent/family needs, (b) selecting goals and objectives, (c) planning and implementing activities, and (d) evaluating activities.

In the recursive system model, family collaboration is an ongoing process that continues until the student leaves the school or program. In the first phase, introductory activities and assessing parent/family needs, the teacher contacts the parents, explains the program, and invites their participation. Next, assessment is conducted to ascertain the parent/family needs and priorities with regard to collaborating with others, including professionals, on behalf of their child. During the second phase, the information obtained as a result of the needs assessment is used to collaboratively select goals and objectives for collaborative parent-teacher activities. In the third phase, activities responsive to the objectives selected in the second phase are either designed or selected from those available in the classroom, school, or community. Activities should reflect the level of personal involvement the parent desires, rather than the level of involvement the professional wishes the parent to have. The final phase, evaluation, is conducted both during and at the conclusion of the collaborative activities. Both the availability of the activities and the effectiveness of the activities are evaluated. Programming should include activities and supports designed to facilitate family and child transitions between placements within a special education program, between special education programs and general education programs, and to post-secondary education programs, including higher education, employment, and independent and supervised living arrangement.

A Continuum of Activities

Collaborative activities may include information-giving activities, information-sharing activities, collaborative support for school programs activities, collaborative school community activities, and parent training activities. These activities may be viewed as a continuum based on (a) the time commitment that can be made, (b) the amount of personal disclosure the parents desire and can attain, and (c) the amount of personal involvement desired. For example, reading a classroom newsletter requires much less time, personal involvement, and personal disclosure from both parents and teacher than does participation in a discussion group on "reactions to the birth or diagnosis of a child with disabilities." A continuum of family collaboration is presented in figure 4.1.

Parent-teacher conferences provide two-way information-sharing opportunities.

Information-Giving Activities   In **information-giving activities,** the family passively receives information. Information is typically objective and the professional-parent contact is brief. Examples of activities in this area are written notes, telephone calls, periodic report cards, notices, meeting and program announcements, and newsletters.

Information-Sharing Activities   The most common of the **information-sharing activities** is the parent-teacher conference. In special education, a parent conference is conducted at least annually in the form of an IEP conference. In addition, conferences may be conducted to plan and implement collaborative activities, such as behavior management and problem-solving programs. Information also may be shared through notebooks the child carries to and from home and school and in which parents and teacher share written information about the child's performance and other common concerns. Information may be shared in the form of checklists on which the parents and teacher comment about the child's daily and weekly performance. Group meetings, either on specific topics or in the form of parent-teacher organization meetings, are also information-sharing activities.

Collaborative Support for School Programs   Activities in the area of **collaborative support for school programs** require increased activity and commitment on the part of the family members. A common activity in the area of support for the school program is a home-school intervention, in which family members work together to implement the IEP goals and objectives. In addition, parents may serve as their child's teacher or may supervise their child's home study to support the school program.

Collaboration in the School Community   **Collaboration,** that is, working together to accomplish a task, in the school community generally requires a significant time commitment on the part of family members. In school community collaboration, family members may serve as paraprofessionals, instructors, volunteers, or committee members. Other school community activities in which family members may be involved are functioning as a roomparent, tutor, instructor of mini-courses, assistant on field trips, or aide, preparing instructional materials and equipment.

A field trip is a school activity in which parents can participate.

Parent Training   **Parent training** requires both parents and professionals to make a substantial time commitment. Parent training is the most intrusive of the collaborative activities because it involves learning knowledge and skills that may require the parents to change current behaviors and interaction patterns. Both commercial and teacher-made materials may be used in parent training. Sensitivity to the parents' goals, abilities, and culture is essential to successful parent training programs.

Families Who Choose Not to Collaborate   If it is accepted that each family is a unique social system, then it is logical that the factors that influence family involvement in their child's education are also unique to each family (MacMillan & Turnbull, 1983). With the many complex problems that confront contemporary families, collaboration in the education of their child is not always a major priority.

In a study of sixty minority families and twenty-nine teachers, Leitch and Tangri (1988) reported "work" as the major reason given by working parents for **nonparticipation** in their child's education program. For the unemployed parents, poor health was the most frequent reason for not participating. In addition, many parents felt their participation would not be helpful to the child. Teachers who did not pursue active collaboration with parents most often reported their own family responsibilities as their reason for nonparticipation.

Teachers suggested that the barriers to collaboration with parents included the parents' unrealistic expectations of the school and responsibilities for a large family. Teachers suggested that parents did not collaborate because (a) parents held the attitude that school wasn't important enough to take time from work; (b) parents were unable to help with schoolwork; (c) parents were jealous of teachers' upward mobility; (d) parents felt that long-time teachers were apathetic and not responsive to them; (e) there was an absence of activities to attract parents to the schools; and (f) teachers resented and suspected the motives of parents who were involved. According to the teachers, the most frequent barrier to collaboration was the parents' attitude towards the school. Teachers indicated that the school contributed to the parents' nonparticipation by exhibiting apathy towards parents, by requiring an overabundance of paperwork, by not reducing the cumbersomeness of the system for anyone trying to initiate a program, and by intimidating parents from a position of authority.

These perceptions of parents and teachers about collaboration may increase the professional's feelings of anxiety and helplessness with regard to parent collaboration. These feelings may be exhibited by a professional through (Bloom, 1983)

- helpless anger, becoming punitive and confused when working with students.
- anger at the student's parents ("When I finally get something going he or she screws it up").
- complexity shock, becoming either anxious for more constructive efforts or angry, frustrated, and desirous of a simpler situation.
- paranoic sellout, feeling that he or she is somehow responsible for the child's problem.
- anger at a child's success and subsequent "time-warp" ("He somehow forgets how to do it between the classroom and home").
- implementation despair ("I've tried it all, nothing works").
- retreat into professional neutrality.

In work with parents with problems, Bemporad, Ratey, and O'Driscoll (1987) report that there are three sets of issues the professional must confront. First, there are the parents' innate problems, such as the physical stamina needed to live with a child with a disability. Second, there are psychological defenses parents use to cope with the exhaustion, anger, and pain experienced as a result of the disability. Finally, there are the changes in the parents' socializing experiences that result from the disability and the psychological defenses. Recognizing the complexity of the parents' personal issues may increase teacher sensitivity to the parents' needs.

There are, however, some parents whose personal difficulties are such that parent-teacher collaboration is not feasible or not adequate to meet their needs. Coleman (1987) suggests that there are times when the parents' needs are beyond the teacher's ability and training. These parents must be referred to other qualified professionals. Referral is appropriate when parents

- are experiencing financial difficulties.
- are involved in marital discord or other crisis.
- routinely express feelings of helplessness, hopelessness, and desperation.
- express the feeling that they are out of control with regard to their child.
- report that the child is habitually involved with the juvenile court system.
- appear to be constantly under high levels of stress and duress.
- consistently initiate discussions regarding personal problems rather than issues related to the student and the student's program.

Through referral to the appropriate school, community agency, or professional, the intense needs of these parents can sometimes be met.

Summary

In this chapter, attention was focused on the families of learners with disabilities. The dramatic changes that occurred in the relationships between families and schools and families and special education in recent decades were discussed.

The family as a social system was discussed and its characteristics and reorganization as a consequence of the birth or diagnosis of a member with a disability were described. Using the developmental theory of human development, we discussed the process of family adaptation to the member with a disability. We reviewed the traditional psychological stage theory, or grieving theory, of adaptation and suggested that research evidence could not be found to support their premises. Three other theories of adaptation were introduced: the integrated perspective, transition theory, and the ABCX model.

In the discussion of the integrated perspective, the empirical research evidence to support each of the ecological contexts that impact family adaptation were reported. Next, the principles and variables underlying Kampfe's transition theory of adaptation were discussed.

In the final section of the chapter, attention was given to family collaboration in special education. It was stated that Public Law 94-142, Public Law 99-457, and Public Law 101-456 all gave parents of learners with disabilities the right to collaborate with others in their child's educational program. The Donnellan and Mirenda (1984) criteria of the least dangerous assumption was discussed and recommended for application in programming.

A model for collaboration was presented and each of its four phases discussed. Using a continuum, the various collaborative activities and their impact on parents' and professionals' time, level of involvement, and degree of personal disclosure were reviewed. Five kinds of collaborative activities were discussed and exemplified: information-giving, information-sharing, program support, collaboration in the school community, and parent training. The chapter concluded with a discussion of the reasons some parents and professionals choose not to participate in collaborative-programming.

Throughout the chapter, it was emphasized that it is essential that the uniqueness of each individual family be recognized and that programs be available to respond to individual family needs and desires.

Building Your Professional Vocabulary

Match each word or phrase to its meaning.

_____ collaboration

_____ collaborative support for school programs

_____ criteria of the least dangerous assumption

_____ information-giving activities

_____ information-sharing activities

_____ nonparticipation

_____ stage theory

a. progress through a series of psychological phases
b. assumes that the program was ineffective, not that the parents were incapable
c. working together to accomplish a task

d. the family passively receives information
e. parents and teacher exchange information
f. home-school intervention
g. not engaging in school activities

Comprehension Check

Select the most appropriate response.

1. There is currently a shift in the relationship between parents and schools in that
   a. schools are becoming more open environments.
   b. parents have delegated an increasingly wide range of socialization activities to schools.
   c. parents are more actively engaged in schools.

2. In the family as a social system,
   a. family members function independently.
   b. interactions in the family are reciprocal.
   c. resistance to change is unnatural.

3. When a family member is born or diagnosed as having a disability,
   a. the family members assume new roles.
   b. the family enters an extended period of mourning.
   c. the family begins to shop for a different diagnosis.

4. Stage theory
   a. has a strong empirical base.
   b. is a necessary assumption to support families.
   c. is a result of clinical judgment rather than empirical information.

5. An integrated, systems perspective
   a. emphasizes psychological phases of adaptation.
   b. simplifies family interactions.
   c. recognizes the complexities and interactions of family interaction.

6. Society
   a. values families with members with disabilities.
   b. supports strong self-esteem among parents of children with disabilities.
   c. places a stigma on both children with disabilities and their families.

7. In the transition model,
   a. psychological phases of adaptation are apparent.
   b. Bronfenbrenner's developmental contexts provide the framework.
   c. identification of a disability is a significant event in the life of the family.

8. Due process provides that parents can
   a. request a hearing if they disagree with the school's decision.
   b. request an independent evaluation at their own expense.
   c. be involved with their child's IEP or IFSP.

9. Nonparticipation
   a. is equivalent to noninvolvement.
   b. is severely detrimental to children with disabilities.
   c. recognizes that collaboration in the education of the child may not be a family priority.

References

Allen, D. A., & Affleck, G. (1985). Are we stereotyping parents: A postscript to Blacher. *Mental Retardation, 23,* 200–202.

Bauer, A. M., & Shea, T. M. (1987). An integrative approach to parental adaptation to the birth or diagnosis of an exceptional child. *School Social Work Journal, 9,* 240–252.

Beckman-Bell, P. (1981). Child related stress in families of handicapped children. *Topics in Early Childhood Special Education, 1,* 45–52.

Behr, S. (1990). *Positive contributions of persons with disabilities to their families.* Lawrence, KA: Kansas University.

Bemporad, J. R., Ratey, J. J., & O'Driscoll, G. (1987). Autism and emotion: A theological theory. *American Journal of Orthopsychiatry, 57,* 477–484.

Birenbaum, A. (1970). On managing a courtesy stigma. *Journal of Health and Social Behavior, 11,* 196–206.

Blacher, J. (1984). Sequential stages of parental adjustment to the birth of a child with handicaps: Fact or artifact. *Mental Retardation, 22* (2), 55–68.

Blackard, M. K., & Barsch, E. T. (1982). Parents' and professionals' perspectives of the handicapped child's impact on the family. *The Journal of the Association for the Severely Handicapped, 76* (2), 62–70.

Bloom, R. B. (1983). The effects of disturbed adolescents on their teachers. *Behavioral Disorders, 8,* 209–216.

Bradshaw, J. (1978). Tracing the causes of stress in families with handicapped children. *The British Journal of Social Work, 8,* 181–192.

Bronfenbrenner, U. (1979). *The ecology of human development.* Cambridge, MA: Harvard University.

Bronfenbrenner, U. (1986). Ecology of the family as a context for human development: Research perspective. *Developmental Psychology, 22,* 723–742.

Coleman, J. (1987). Families and schools. *Educational Researcher, 16* (6), 32–38.

Creekmore, W. N. (1988). Family-classroom: A critical balance. *Academic Therapy, 24* (2), 202–207.

Darling, R. B. (1979). *Families against society.* Beverly Hills, CA: Sage.

Donnellan, A. M., & Mirenda, P. (1984). Issues related to professional involvement with families of individuals with autism and other severe handicaps. *The Journal of the Association for Persons with Severe Handicaps, 9,* 16–26.

Dunst, C. J., Trivette, C. M., & Deal, A. G. (1988). *Enabling and empowering families: Principles and guidelines for practice.* Cambridge, MA: Brookline Books.

Epstein, J. (1988). How to improve programs for parent involvement. *Education Horizons, 66* (2), 58–60.

Frey, K. S., Greenberg, M. T., & Fewell, R. R. (1989). Stress and coping among parents of handicapped children: A multidimensional approach. *American Journal of Mental Retardation, 94,* 240–249.

Gallagher, J. J., Beckman, P., & Cross, A. (1983). Families of handicapped children: Sources of stress and its amelioration. *Exceptional Children, 50,* 10–19.

Greer, B. G. (1975). On being the parent of a handicapped child. *Exceptional Children, 41,* 519.

Hinderliter, K. (1988). Death of a dream. *Exceptional Parent, 18* (1), 48–49.

Johnston, J. C., & Zemitzsch, A. (1988). Family power: An intervention beyond the classroom. *Behavioral Disorders, 14* (1), 69–79.

Kampfe, C. M. (1989). Parental reaction to a child's hearing impairment. *American Annals of the Deaf, 134,* 255–259.

Koch, A. (1982). Conceptualizing family stress: A systemic revision of Hill's ABCX model. Paper presented at the Annual Meeting of the National Council on Family Relations, Washington, DC.

Kratochvil, M. S., & Devereaux, S. A. (1988). Counseling needs of parents of handicapped children. *Social Casework, 69* (7), 420–426.

Kroth, R. L., & Otteni, H. (1985). *Communicating with parents of exceptional children: Improving parent-teacher relationships* (2nd ed.). Denver: Love.

Leitch, R. M., & Tangri, S. S. (1988). Barriers to home-school collaboration. *Educational Horizons, 66* (2), 70–75.

Lowitzer, A. C. (1989). *Family type, sources of support, and stress among families of preschool children.* Logan, UT: Early Intervention Research Institute.

Lynch, E. W., & Stein, R. C. (1987). Parent participation by ethnicity: A comparison of Hispanic, Black, and Anglo families. *Exceptional Children, 54,* 105–111.

MacMillan, D. L., & Turnbull, A. P. (1983). Parent involvement in special education: Respecting individual differences. *Education and Training of the Mentally Retarded, 18,* 4–9.

McAfee, J. K., & Vergason, G. A. (1979). Parent involvement in the process of special education: Establishing the new partnerships. *Focus on Exceptional Children, 11* (2), 1–15.

McCubbin, H. I., & Patterson, J. M. (1981). Family stress and adaptation to crises: A double ABCX model of family behavior. Paper presented at the Annual Meeting of the National Council for Family Relations, Milwaukee, WI.

Minuchin, S. (1974). *Families and family therapy.* Cambridge, MA: Harvard University Press.

Olson, D. G. (1988). A developmental approach to family support: A conceptual framework. *Focal Point, 2* (3), 3–6.

Robbins, F. (1991). Family characteristics, family training, and the progress of young children with autism. *Journal of Early Intervention, 15* (2), 173–184.

Salisbury, C., & Evans, I. M. (1988). Comparison of parent involvement in regular and special education. *The Journal of the Association for Persons with Severe Handicaps, 13,* 268–272.

Shea, T. M., & Bauer, A. M. (1991). *Parents and teachers of children with exceptionalities: A handbook for collaboration* (2nd ed.). Boston: Allyn & Bacon.

Smith, S. (1984). Family stress theory: Review and critique. Paper presented at the Annual Meeting of the National Council on Family Relations, San Francisco, CA.

Syracuse University Center on Human Policy (1987). *A statement in support of families and their children.* Syracuse, NY: Author.

Trute, B., & Hauch, C. (1988). Building on family strength: A study of families with positive adjustment to the birth of a developmentally disabled child. *Journal of Marital and Family Therapy, 14* (2), 185–193.

Voysey, M. (1975). *A constant burden: The reconstitution of family life.* London: Routledge and Keagan Paul.

Yanok, J., & Derubertis, D. (1989). Comparative study of parental participation in regular and special education programs. *Exceptional Children, 56,* 195–199.

Zirpoli, T. J., Hancox, D., Wieck, C., & Skarnulis, E. R. (1989). Partners in policymaking: Empowering people. *The Journal of the Association for Persons with Severe Handicaps, 14* (2), 163–167.

Objectives

After completing this chapter, you will be able to:

1. describe the transitions confronting individuals who vary from their peers.
2. describe strategies for facilitating transitions.

Key Words and Phrases

Civil Rights Act of 1964
The Education of the Handicapped
    Act of 1983
generalization
The Individuals with Disabilities
    Education Act of 1990

Perkins Vocational Education Act
    of 1973
transition
Vocational Education Act of 1963

In 1988, 7 percent of first-time, full-time college freshmen were students with identified disabilities; by 1991, 8.18 percent of first-time, full-time college freshmen were students with identified disabilities (Henderson, 1992).

Fifty-seven percent of youth with identified disabilities who had been out of school three to five years were competitively employed, as compared to 69 percent of the general population (Wagner, D'Amico, Marder, Newman, & Blackorby, 1992).

Thirty-seven percent of youth with identified disabilities who had been out of high school for three to five years were living independently, as compared to 60 percent of the general population (Wagner et al., 1992).

The median hourly wage for youth with identified disabilities was $5.72, less than $12,000 per year for full time, year-round employment (Wagner et al., 1992).

Introduction

In the social systems perspective, the relationships between settings represents the interaction among the subsystems in which an individual functions. In special education, these interactions generally involve the transitions (a) from early childhood intervention programs to school-age programs, (b) between educational settings, usually from a more-restrictive to a less-restrictive setting, such as from special class to resource room and regular class, and (c) from school to work, vocational training, or higher education and independent or supported living arrangements. Social systems theory suggests that an individual's developmental potential is enhanced if that individual's initial transition into a new setting is not made alone, that is, if the individual enters the new setting in the company of one or more persons with whom he or she has participated in prior settings.

In this chapter, we explore the transitions that occur during the educational career of individuals with disabilities. The implications of the social systems approach for enhancing the developmental potential of transitions for individuals with disabilities are discussed.

Bronfenbrenner (1986) suggests that there are three steps in the **transition,** or movement, of a child from one setting to another. The first step involves the intersetting relationships that exist prior to the actual transition. Preexisting relationships are powerful factors in forming attitudes and expectations about the child's anticipated performance in the new environment. During the second step, which follows the transition into the new setting, the family system reorganizes. Reorganization involves changes in the family members' expectations and attitudes towards the child. The final step occurs after the transition and results in changes in the relationship between the family and school, or the child, school, and family.

To facilitate the transition process, Bronfenbrenner suggests focusing efforts on enhancing the interrelationship between each of the child's present environments and the environment into which the child is making the transition. For example, if a child was to make a transition between a preschool program and a school-based special education program, an effort would be made to enhance the interrelationships among persons from the preschool program, the school-based program, and the family. The child either actively participates or will actively participate in each of these environments.

The Transition Process

A transition is not an event; it is a process. Lazzari and Kilgo (1989) write that for families with a member with a disability, the transition process includes three phases: preparation, implementation, and follow-up. Professionals should recognize that, consistent with the social systems perspective, both the child and the family are making the transition and, as a consequence, feel the stress of change. This stress is exacerbated by the fact that subsystems, or environments, that are unfamiliar to the parents and child are involved in the process.

During the transition process, parents may have to interact with unfamiliar private and public agencies that vary with regard to eligibility criteria and quality of available services (Smith & Strain, 1988). In addition, the focus of the interventions to be implemented with child and family often changes from program to program. These and similar issues arise whether the transition is between an early childhood intervention or preschool program to a school-based program, between various school programs, or between a school program and adult life in the community.

Objective One

To describe the transitions confronting individuals who vary from their peers.

Annual **Edition**

Article *41*

Ferguson, Ferguson, and Jones (1988) state that transitions are socially constructed processes and therefore are responsive to planning. When planning a transition, the professional must assess the family's historical and cultural contexts as these relate to the transition. Though the study by Ferguson and associates was conducted with the parents of individuals with disabilities who were entering adulthood, their findings are relevant to the transitions of students during their school careers.

Rather than a single transition process, the parents studied by Ferguson and associates reported three distinct, simultaneous transition processes associated with their child's movement into adulthood. The processes included (a) a bureaucratic transition, (b) a family life transition, and (c) a status transition.

Bureaucratic transition is the process whereby agencies and professionals become involved with the child and family. The specific agencies and professionals involved in a transition vary with the particular transition being made by the child and family. These may include, among others, representatives of agencies delivering early childhood or preschool services, representatives of various school-based programs, and representatives of the special education district and adult service agencies.

The absence of planned bureaucratic transition processes can be a disruptive force and lead to unsatisfactory outcomes. With regard to their bureaucratic transitions, some parents reported that they "surrendered to professionals." By "surrendered to professionals," the parents meant that they deferred to the opinions and explanations of professionals with regard to services for their child even though these services appeared to them to be inadequate. Other parents reported "abandonment by professionals." They received little assistance from professionals who chose not to help or who gave up on the child and family. A third group of parents felt they were forced to assume the role of "pseudo-professionals" in order to obtain the services their child needed. Finally, some parents reported they could interact with some professionals in a positive and constructive manner, but with others they had to assume a negative and adversarial stance.

The second type of transition, as reported by Ferguson and associates, is the family-life transition. Some parents reported that they met this transition with both passive resignation and self-reliance. They perceived the problems related to the transition into the new setting and the problems encountered in the new setting itself as just one more phase in their never-ending isolated struggle to obtain appropriate services for their child. They had to rely on their own ability to obtain stable and secure services. Another group of parents felt they were forced to rely on personal resources and resented being put in such a position by professionals. They reported active feelings of being unjustly treated when they found it necessary to assume the added responsibilities of ensuring that their child received appropriate services. Finally, the parents reported a natural, collective sense of self-reliance, that is, a strong sense of social support from and mutual reliance on other parents of children with disabilities.

The third form of transition reported by the parents was related to changes in the status of the child. In some of the families Ferguson and associates studied, for example, the issue of the adult status of the individual with the disability became an issue of control of the individual rather than the independence of the individual. To be more specific, the issue of the individual's independence, which is a child-or-adult question, became a parent-or-professional question of who would control the individual.

Ferguson and associates urge professionals to understand that transition is not a single process, but several simultaneous processes that the child and family must negotiate successfully. Throughout these processes communication is essential. Communication, and thus transition, is facilitated by family collaboration in decision making and the use of appropriate services in a timely manner.

Transition from Early Intervention and Preschool to School

Several issues surrounding the transition from early childhood intervention and preschool programs to school-based programs became apparent with the implementation of the mandates of Public Law 99-457. Diamond, Spiegel-McGill, and Hanrahan (1988) remind us that the transition from an early childhood intervention or preschool program to a public school program sometimes involves considerable upheaval for the child and the family. The familiar faces of the preschool program are replaced by the more "businesslike" affect of public school. They suggest that separation from the preschool experience may be the most abrupt and permanent break with past experiences that the child makes before leaving home as an adult. Turnbull and Turnbull (1986) note that early childhood transitions are important because they set the stage for all future transitions.

Diamond and associates report that there are several changes that occur during the transition to a school-based environment. The demands of school differ greatly from the demands of the preschool. The skills needed to function successfully in kindergarten include social skills, self-help skills, and the ability to function independently. In addition, the transition to a school-based program has a direct effect on the family in the areas of personal and family schedules, transportation, family support services, and communication strategies between the home and the school.

In a survey of parents of young children with disabilities, Hanline (1988) found the parents had informational needs, service needs, and concerns about the child's transition into the public school special education program. Parents stated that they needed information about services offered by the school district, felt discomfort in working with unfamiliar individuals with regard to the child, and experienced concern about whether their child would actually receive needed services. The parents were also concerned about being excluded from the decision-making process and losing control over their child's daily activities. Hanline suggests that a major goal for professionals working with parents during a transition should be to help them to identify actual and potential problems and assist them in carrying out the task of solving or mitigating those problems.

Transition Between School-Age Programs

As inclusion becomes a reality for more learners with disabilities, the challenges of transition between school-age programs will become less frequent. Indeed, one of the arguments for inclusion is that it is far easier to function in an environment if you have consistently been educated in that environment. Special education services that remove the student from the general education environment and then require reentry add a time-consuming, challenging process to the learner's education. The transition between school-age programs, as with all transitions, impacts on both the child and the family. The secure, protected environment of the segregated classroom is difficult to leave behind. Hanline and Halvorsen (1989) interviewed the parents of fourteen children with disabilities in an effort to evaluate the support they received during the child's transition to an integrated educational placement from a segregated special education setting. Prior to the transition, the parents reported concerns about their child's safety, the nonaccepting attitudes of the general education teachers and students, a decrease in program quality, transportation problems, lack of district commitment to the integration of students with disabilities, and the child's potential failure in the new environment. After the child's integration into the less-restrictive program, however, the parents reported several positive changes. The primary benefit they cited was the child's skill enhancement, including their child's demonstration of more appropriate social skills. Parents were pleased that their child was developing friendships with nonidentified peers, which often extended beyond school hours. In addition, the parents reported that their personal expectations for their child had risen. The brothers and sisters of the children with disabilities reported that they were less concerned about their responsibilities for the long-term care of their brother or sister with the disability.

According to the parents interviewed by Hanline and Halvorsen, the transition to the less restrictive environment was facilitated by parent representation on planning teams and observations of model integrated school settings. Parents reported that it was helpful to link up with other parents and consistently communicate with special and regular education personnel involved with the child and family.

Another strategy for easing the transition to less-restrictive settings is referred to by its developers as "exit assistance" (George & Lewis, 1991). This strategy involves four stages that allow special educators and parents to make data-based decisions about readiness to move to less-restrictive settings. In the first phase, long-range planning must take place. George and Lewis contend that at the initial IEP meeting, in which the child enters special educational services, goals and objectives that address the reasons for the student's placement into special education should be discussed. Academic and behavioral issues that must be addressed for the child to be successful in less restrictive placements should serve as long-range student goals.

When the student begins to achieve the goals that address issues related to the restrictiveness of his or her placement, pre-exit activities may begin. In this phase, three steps should be completed. First, the materials, setting, schedule, student evaluation, behavioral management, and student responsibilities of the less restrictive setting should be assessed. In the next step of this phase, the special educator approximates the requirements of the new, less-restrictive setting in the student's current, supported placement. As the student becomes successful, the third step, the assessment of the student's readiness, takes place. In this step, the academic and behavioral skills the student is demonstrating should be compared with those of his or her peers in the less-restrictive setting.

The third phase, the transition itself, involves final preparations for the student, staff, and parents to deal successfully with the change. During the IEP meeting, decisions should be made about the types of accommodations, adaptations, and support services needed. George and Lewis suggest an "exit coordinator" be appointed to ensure that the required activities and services take place.

Finally, in the follow-up and evaluation phase, information is gathered on the student's performance in the new setting. Consultative services are delivered as necessary, and a gradual reduction of teacher support takes place.

Generalization   One issue that has emerged with regard to the transition of students between school-based programs is the generalization of skills and behaviors from one environment to another. **Generalization** refers to the individual's ability to apply a skill learned in one setting to another setting. The value of interventions in more restrictive environments is lost if the skills and behaviors learned in that environment are not generalized to the new environment (Brown, Kiraly, & McKinnon, 1979). Skills and behaviors learned in special education settings are frequently highly individualized and completed independently. Skills learned in this manner may not transfer to group instructional settings such as the general classroom (Bauer & Shea, 1989). To be successful in the less-restrictive environment of the general classroom, students need to learn to interact positively with others, obey class rules, and display proper work habits (Salend & Lutz, 1984). The lack of these behaviors, less evident in the more-restrictive environment of the special education classroom with fewer children and vigilant special education teachers, may be very apparent in the less-restrictive setting of the general classroom. Plans should be implemented to facilitate the generalization of skills learned in the more restrictive environment to the less restrictive environment.

The challenge of generalization is addressed through the inclusion of learners with disabilities in the general education environment from the onset. Through placement in inclusive classrooms, the difficulties of transition and generalization are mitigated.

Transition from School to Community

In the transition from school life to adult life in the community, there are many challenges that confront young adults with disabilities. According to Rusch and Phelps (1987), the general public first became aware of the challenges confronting these young adults following World War I, when thousands of American veterans with physical disabilities were found to require assistance in their effort to return to the work force. In 1918, the first vocational rehabilitation act became law. This law provided assistance to veterans with disabilities and translation services for individuals with visual impairments. During the 1920s and 1930s, programs such as the Civilian Conservation Corps (CCC) were implemented to provide employment opportunities to youth, many of whom were mildly disabled. In the 1950s, work-study programs were instituted to assist individuals with mild disabilities.

A major event in the history of the United States was the **Civil Rights Act of 1964,** which banned discrimination in education on the grounds of race, ethnic origin, or religion. During the 1970s, nondiscrimination assurances were extended to individuals with disabilities. The **Vocational Education Act of 1963,** as amended in 1968 and 1976, set aside 10 percent of the funds allocated to vocational education for programs for persons with disabilities. The **Perkins Vocational Education Act of 1973** included a major emphasis on services for individuals with severe disabilities. In addition, the Perkins act mandated that the states improve services by requiring client involvement in the design and delivery of vocational rehabilitation services.

In **The Education of the Handicapped Act of 1983** (Public Law 98-199), Congress sought to address directly the major educational and employment transition difficulties confronting young adults in special education services. The United States Office of Special Education and Rehabilitation Services was authorized to spend $6.6 million annually in grants and contracts to strengthen and coordinate education, training, and related services to assist youth with disabilities in the transition to post-secondary education, competitive employment, or adult services.

In Public Law 101-476, **The Individuals with Disabilities Education Act (IDEA)** "transition services" were mandated for the movement of individuals with disabilities from school to post-school, including post-secondary education, vocational training, integrated employment (including supported employment), continuing and adult education, adult services, and independent living or community participation. Transition services were based on individual needs, preferences, and interests. Individualized Education Programs prepared for individuals sixteen years of age, and in some cases, younger, were to include a transition service plan. The transition place was to be designed to include instruction, community experiences, the development of employment and other post-school adult living objectives, and, when appropriate, acquisition of daily living skills and functional vocational evaluation (see chapter 3 for an example of a transition plan). The law authorized "rehabilitation counseling" and "social work services" to facilitate the transition process. Finally, the law provided for and authorized interagency responsibilities or linkages with appropriate community and adult services before the individual with disabilities leaves school.

Secondary School Programming and the Least Restrictive Environment Edgar (1987) reports on two trends that have prompted criticism of current secondary school programs for individuals with mild disabilities. First, salary data indicate that only 18 percent of the individuals with mild disabilities who were studied

Increased academic standards for graduation from high school challenges inclusion.

earned more than minimum wage, and if individuals with learning disabilities and emotional/behavioral disorders were removed from the sample, only 5 percent of this population made more than the minimum wage. Second, special education students were more likely to drop out of school than were their regular class peers. In addition, students with learning disabilities and emotional/behavioral disorders dropped out of school more frequently and made poorer use of post-secondary school educational opportunities than did their disabled peers.

Edgar suggests that the least restrictive environment concept, currently in broad use in special education, has translated into inclusion in secondary education programs. Though inclusion was questioned when originally suggested, it appears to be effective because academic education is the core of most secondary special education programs.

The current "excellence in education" movement in the United States has resulted in increased academic standards and consideration of proficiency tests for graduation from high school. Even a cursory glance at a secondary special education curriculum indicates the curriculum is nonfunctional as it relates to the goals of secondary special education. Edgar suggests that a radical shift in curriculum is needed if it is to serve the needs of secondary special education students. The curriculum must focus on functional, vocational, and independent living skills.

In addition to the content of the secondary curriculum for individuals with disabilities, concern has been expressed regarding the manner in which functional activities are conducted. Chadsey-Rusch (1990), in her observational study, found that students with disabilities typically (a) were more involved in task-related than nontask-related interactions; (b) engaged in more interactions with teachers than with peers; (c) engaged in interactions that were similar across contexts, rather than in a wide range of social contacts characteristic of those that occur in the community; and (d) were dependent on contrived or extra cues and feedback from the teachers or trainers in their vocational settings to facilitate performance. Chadsey-Rusch argues that teachers need to increase the frequency of nontask interactions among secondary school students and consciously decrease the frequency of directions and praise. More interactions are needed with nondisabled peers to encourage interactions with nonidentified individuals after leaving the special education setting.

The Transition from School to Work   The emphasis in intervention programs for youth in transition from school to adult life is frequently on "finding a job." Neubert, Tilson, and Iancone (1989), however, argue that transition outcomes should be viewed in terms of economic self-sufficiency, not simply as an individual's ability to access an initial job. In their study, Neubert and associates found that during the first three months of employment, 74 percent of the individuals experienced problems that necessitated the intervention of a staff member. During the first year of employment, over one-half of the participants changed jobs and requested additional assistance. It is evident that the outcome of the transition from school to adult life should be viewed in terms of obtaining a job, keeping a job, and becoming a self-sufficient adult member of the community.

In interviews with the parents or guardians of high school special education graduates, Haring, Lovett, and Saren (1991) found a wide range of opinions, concerns, and beliefs regarding these adult children with disabilities. Though 60 percent of the parents indicated that they encouraged their child to be as independent as possible, 22 percent expressed their desire to keep their child at home with them. Though 59 percent indicated that they encouraged as much independence as possible, 22 percent believed supervision was necessary and 20 percent did not desire independent mobility for their child. Thirty percent of the parents expressed a concern that if their child had a job, he or she

Effective transitions for young children require careful planning.

would lose Supplementary Security Income and/or Medicaid. Special educators are confronted with the challenge of alleviating parents' concerns while providing opportunities for the children.

The need for quality transition services is supported by a qualitative study by Gallivan-Fenlon (1994). In this study of family and service provider perspectives, challenges to transition became apparent when there were differing future expectations for the youth with disabilities and inconsistent implementation of special education curricula. In view of the problems generated by "reentry," the lack of inclusion in general education was perceived as a problem. In addition, a lack of knowledge about transition and hastily and poorly coordinated transition plans were a serious problem for the young adults with disabilities and their families.

Strategies to Facilitate Transitions

Transition from Early Intervention and Preschool Programs

The goal of transition for infants and children is to provide a program that meets their needs more effectively and efficiently and minimizes the adjustment difficulties during the transition (Wolery, 1989). Transition planning for a move from an early intervention or preschool program to a school-based program should be initiated six to twelve months prior to the anticipated change in placement (McDonald, Kysela, Siebert, McDonald, & Chambers, 1989). Parents should be informed of the projected transitions and consulted as to how they would like to be involved in the process. In addition, the family should be assisted in planning for future environments and transitions beyond the change in placement presently under consideration. Finally, follow-up support services should be provided to the parents. McDonald and associates suggest a four-step process to facilitate the transition process. These steps are presented in the "Guidelines for Practice" box on page 94.

An alternative transition process begins in the fall prior to the child's entrance into kindergarten and continues throughout the first term of kindergarten year (Diamond, Spiegel-McGill, & Hanrahan, 1988). This process is summarized in the "Guidelines for Practice" box on page 94. During the preliminary planning

Objective Two

To describe strategies for facilitating transitions.

Annual **Edition**

Article *38*

guidelines for practice

Transition Facilitation Process

Step 1   Determine the time frame in collaboration with parents (minimum of six months prior to anticipated transition).

Step 2   Add specific transition goals and activities to the Individualized Family Service Plan or Individualized Education Program.

Step 3   Establish a time line that includes activities for both parents and staff, such as visitations, observations, and reviewing program descriptions.

Step 4   Provide follow-up services ▌

*Adapted from McDonald, Kysela, Siebert, McDonald, and Chambers (1989).

guidelines for practice

Phases in Preschool to Kindergarten Transition

Phase	Time
Preliminary planning	One year prior to kindergarten entry
Initial contacts with accepting school district	November through February
Exploring placement options	February through June
Implementing the transition process	June through August
Follow-up in school district	First term in receiving kindergarten ▌

*Adapted from Diamond, Spiegel-McGill, and Hanrahan (1988).

phase, the child's IEP is written to reflect goals and objectives that will enable the child to enter the least restrictive environment during the upcoming kindergarten school year. During this phase, the parents are encouraged to observe kindergarten and preschool programs for nondisabled children. The observations will facilitate their development of a frame of reference for the discussions of their child's placement. A liaison person from the preschool who will monitor the transition process is identified. This liaison person is responsible for assisting the parents in efforts to gain information about placement options, accessing services in the community, and the transition process itself.

The second phase in the transition process involves making the initial contact with the school district in which the child will be served. The contact is made through a referral to the school district's child study team. At this time, it is helpful to conduct a parent conference to discuss the child's current functioning and the parents' expectations for school placement. This conference may evolve into a series of meetings to help the parents develop realistic expectations for their child and the placement. Members of the child study team may begin informal contact with the preschool or early intervention program to familiarize themselves with the child and the environment. Assessment information appropriate for planning the transition are provided to both child study team members and parents.

The third phase of the transition planning process suggested by Diamond and associates involves the exploration of placement options. A meeting is conducted with a member of the child study team; this person recommends various programs for the parents' consideration. Parents are encouraged to visit the

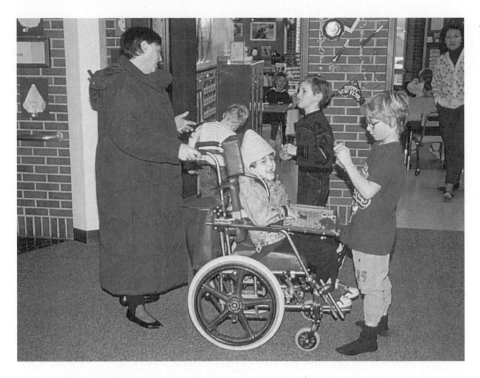

A visit to the school the child will attend supports the transition for parents and student.

recommended programs. At this time, if not prior to it, the parents must be informed of their legal rights under both state and federal law, and these rights must be explained to them. Finally, in this phase, the child study team meets to recommend an appropriate placement by developing and then writing an IEP.

Before the end of the child's final preschool year and during the following summer, the public school teacher makes visits to the preschool and the child visits the school and program he or she will attend. Preschool records and parent information are provided to the receiving program so that the child will be "ready to go" as soon as the school year begins.

The final phase, follow-up, takes place throughout the first term of the school year. Through follow-up, early intervention or preschool program personnel demonstrate a continuing commitment to the child and the family. During the follow-up, the parents are provided assistance if needed.

Transition from School to Post-Secondary Education and Training

Youth with disabilities participate in post-secondary education and training programs at only one-fourth the rate of their nonidentified peers and at only one-third the rate of economically disadvantaged youth (Fairweather & Shaver, 1991), yet a major factor in the transition from high school to adulthood is access to and success in post-secondary training. Only a small proportion of youth with disabilities—those with speech, visual, hearing, or health impairments—are more likely than their nonidentified peers to receive additional training after high school. Even among those who receive a high school diploma (in contrast to a certificate of attendance or other indicator of participation in but not completion of high school content area units required for graduation), participation remains far less likely than that of nonidentified peers.

It is evident from this discussion that there is a need for a plan or strategy to enhance an individual's transition to a new environment. For children moving from an early intervention or preschool program to a school-based program, a transition plan is required as a part of the Individualized Family Service Plan mandated in Public Law 99-457. As previously discussed, the Individuals with Disabilities Education Act (Public Law 101-476) mandates "transition services," and a transition plan must be included in the IEP for learners sixteen years of age, and in some cases, as young as fourteen years of age. According to Wolery (1989), the literature indicates that carefully planned transitions are essential to (a) ensure continuity of services; (b) minimize disruptions to the family system by facilitating the family's adjustment to the changes that occur; and (c) ensure that children are prepared to function in the receiving program.

In a national survey of 1,549 local educational agencies, stratified by enrollment, geographic region, and socioeconomic status, Fairweather (1989) found that more than 50 percent of the agencies provided at least one of four vocational programs: counseling, vocational education, occupational/physical therapy, or vocational rehabilitation. Less than 1 percent of the agencies, however, had some type of transition program, and only one-third had a staff member whose main function was to help students find employment. Fairweather found that the size of the local educational agency was strongly related to the likelihood that secondary-age students with disabilities would have vocational preparation programs available to them. Students in large districts were more likely to have access to vocational preparation programs than were students in smaller districts. Transition-oriented programs directed essentially at assisting students with disabilities to find employment, enroll in post-secondary educational programs, and live independently in the community were uncommon.

In a follow-up report, Fairweather, Sterns, and Wagner (1990) write that the opportunities for special education students in transition-related programs are influenced by the size of the district and wealth of the community. These findings may have significance because transition-oriented programs tested on a few students in a limited number of locations may not be replicable in other settings. The writers suggest that program requirements should take into account variations in opportunities by type of district in which the student resides.

White and Bond (1992) have suggestions to address the complexities of transition planning for large school districts. They suggest that large districts may develop programs based on their own community needs and philosophy but must accept that transition is a priority. They recommend full-time transition specialists to support students. In addition, extensive collaboration with principals, district administrators, and the community regarding the delivery of services is advised. They also suggest the extensive use of paraprofessionals to maximize the effectiveness of community programming.

There are several roles special educators and parents fulfill in order to optimize the transition process (Everson & Moon, 1987). Special educators should be responsible for

- organizing and attending meetings related to planning the transition.
- coordinating the development and implementation of the transition plan.
- identifying the need to refer and ensuring referral to other appropriate agencies and services.
- ensuring parent, family, and student participation in transition planning and implementation processes.

To optimize the process, parents should be responsible for

- attending meetings related to planning the transition.
- providing information on the needs of the family and the individual as well as the responsibilities the family is able and willing to assume.
- focusing the team's planning on individual student and family needs.
- providing informal home and community skill training and behavioral interventions that support the student's development.

Several barriers to effective planning and coordination of services may emerge, including service fragmentation and duplication, unsystematic transition planning, and limited parent involvement (Johnson, Bruininks, & Thurlow, 1987). Johnson and associates contend that each educational system needs a coherent policy framework that incorporates greater consistency across programs in philosophy, goals, standards, and practices to guide the ongoing management of planning for transition.

Transition Between School-Based Settings

When addressing the issues of transition between school-based programs, two factors must be considered: (a) the transition decision, which must match the student's needs to the new environment, and (b) obtaining services needed to facilitate the transition.

Making the Transition Decision   Students entering new, less-restrictive educational settings generally confront increased class size, less individual attention, a more rapid instructional pace, and different evaluation standards from those they experienced in the special education setting. Wood and Miederhoff (1989) explain that there is a need to compare the characteristics of the original setting with the setting into which the student is moving. To facilitate this comparison, they developed a transition checklist, which includes three subsections: (a) requirements for functioning successfully in the classroom, (b) requirements for successful interpersonal and social relations, and (c) requirements for functioning in related environments. The classroom subsection includes consideration of physical and instructional variables, dominant teaching techniques, materials, content, and evaluation strategies. In the interpersonal and social relations subsection, consideration is given to student interactions, dress and appearance, and attitudes. In the section on related environments, the student's ability to self-manage in the cafeteria, during physical education, and in specialized classes such as art and music are assessed. The characteristics of the more-inclusive setting are compared with the student's present functioning to determine in which areas the student needs assistance and instruction to function successfully in the new setting.

Services to Facilitate the Transition   Adamson, Matthews, and Schuller (1990) propose five procedures to bridge the gap between special education services and the general education classroom program. These services are consultation, collaborative teaching/co-teaching, structured recess, work completion groups, and contract checkouts.

During consultation, the special educator assists the general educator in the selection of methods and techniques designed to assist the student. The special educator models the methods or techniques and facilitates and monitors their implementation by the general educator. In addition, the special educator assists the general educator in obtaining, adapting, and supplementing instructional materials, evaluating selected methods or techniques, developing other techniques if the selected ones are ineffective, and providing positive reinforcement to the general educator.

In collaborative teaching/co-teaching, the special educator serves as a model for the general educator, engaging in collaborative planning for implementation of specific strategies that may have been used previously by either of the educators. The teachers may choose to team teach, divide the class into two groups for instruction, teach small groups, or engage in individual instruction.

The third strategy, structured recess, is implemented to help students to learn appropriate game playing, self-structuring—that is, the skills needed to organize themselves for play—the use of time, skills for coping with difficulties, and

And Baby Makes Controversy

A couple breaks new ground for disabled parents

Natalie Earl is only 5 weeks old, but one day, like most kids, she'll probably ask her parents how they met. It was 1978, Leigh and Bill Earl might tell her, at a nursing home in Grand Rapids, Mich. They were 15. They had cerebral palsy and they lived there.

In recent years, through advances in technology, changing social attitudes and new legislation, people with severe handicaps have achieved independence unimaginable a generation ago. Both the Earls went to college. In 1988, they moved to an East Lansing apartment, assisted 17 hours a week by social-service aides. Though unemployed (Bill is looking for a job), they were a model, mainstream couple.

All that changed last year, when Leigh got pregnant and decided not to have an abortion. Who, concerned friends asked, would care for the child? The Earls were convinced that, with some extra help from the aides, they could. "All we're asking for," says Bill, "is a chance to have a family." As soon as she became pregnant, Leigh says, she started asking Ingham County Department of Social Services (DSS) exactly what they would provide but never got an answer. It took Mark Cody, an attorney from a nonprofit advocacy agency, to discover that, since the Earls didn't work outside the home, they didn't qualify for state-funded child care. (By then, Leigh was in her seventh month.) Since Leigh delivered a healthy daughter on May 5, volunteer nannies have moved in to help. The DSS aides who come to the Earls' home aren't permitted to help at all, even to pick the baby up. Natalie's parents cannot lift or bathe her, but Leigh is able, with assistance, to breast-feed. "The system has not been set up to handle this kind of a case that is so different," says DSS spokesman Chuck Peller. "It's just not equipped."

Many Americans with disabilities are deciding that if they can live and work in the mainstream, they can also have children. But if they need extra child care, who pays? If the state does, says Janet Strope, DSS director for Ingham County, there are bound to be problems. Any parents with some sort of impairment, as well as parents who abuse drugs or their kids, "could keep their children if we would provide someone in the home 24 hours a day. That carries it to an extreme, but we would then have to draw a line as to when we would provide [help] and when we wouldn't. That would be very, very difficult to do." The Earls are willing to challenge the state. "What Bill and Leigh are doing is really breaking new ground for people with severe disabilities to be parents," says Marsha Morse, a project coordinator at United Cerebral Palsy of Michigan. "There currently are no programs that support people with disabilities to do parenting." She thinks Bill and Leigh "deserve the opportunity to try. They can be parents, but not in the traditional role." In the last 20 years, the definition of family has changed radically, Clearly, it's also time to rethink the definition of parent •

Katrine Ames with Frank Washington and Nichole Christian in East Lansing

appropriate interaction with peers. As the structured recess program progresses over time, the external supports, provided by the teacher, are faded as the students increase their skills and ability to play independently.

The next strategy, work completion groups, is a daily thirty-minute work period used to monitor student performance. During the work completion period, the general educator sends the special student to the resource room to work on incomplete classroom assignments. Students who have completed their assignments may be sent to the resource room for a reinforcement period.

The final strategy, the daily checkout, is implemented to monitor student-teacher contingency contracts or agreements. For example, the student may have an agreement (a contract) with the teacher to complete an assignment during reading class. The teacher checks the assignment and provides an agreed-upon reward. The checkout period is used to evaluate progress on the contract and distribute reinforcers for appropriate work and behavior. A daily checkout form may be used to report performance to parents and concerned teachers.

Transition to Work and Community

Individual transition planning is necessary to increase the access of students enrolled in high school programs to community services (McDonnell, Wilcox, & Boles, 1986). Planning for the transition into the community must begin early in the student's high school career and focus on the development of the skills, opportunities, and services that will be necessary to support the individual in the community. The writers suggest that transition activities should be a part of the IEP and should culminate during the last year of high school with a formal plan that identifies and establishes the specific services required to meet the individual's needs upon graduation.

Goals of the transition plan for the move from school to community should be very broad, such as (a) to learn what transition is and why it is important to the family; (b) to identify the information and skills needed by the family for transition into the new program; (c) to identify the transitions that will take place during the next five years (Lazzari & Kilgo, 1989). Planning for transition from school to work must occur three to five years prior to the time at which the student leaves school.

D'Alonzo, Owen, and Hartwell (1985) suggest several goals appropriate for the transition of young adults as they approach departure from school programs. First, the educational plans should address the development of appropriate life-skill educational goals and objectives. Second, employment-seeking and maintenance skills should be emphasized, as well as community survival skills training. In addition, transition plans should provide for supervised on-site employment training. Support should be provided to special and general educators as they address transition issues with students. Finally, the plan should address increased collaboration between community agencies and special education as well as vocational education and special education.

Three transition preparation stages may be designed to meet goals, such as those suggested by D'Alonzo and associates (Wehman, Kregal, & Barcus, 1985). First, school instruction is presented to the student; second, the transition plan is developed; and third, the student is placed in meaningful employment which is the desired outcome of the transition.

In the transition to adult life, individuals with disabilities must learn self-advocacy (Martin, 1993). Barretti (1993) describes a practicum for students with learning disabilities that supports the development of self-advocacy. Instruction is provided in (a) understanding one's disability and finding strategies necessary to compensate for it; (b) understanding one's learning style, promoting self-advocacy, and enhancing study skills, and (c) dealing with frustration and low self-esteem. Students who had experienced the practicum reported increased academic and social skills.

Independent living is a goal for many individuals with disabilities.

Summary

In this chapter, the transitions learners with disabilities make during their educational careers were discussed. Bronfenbrenner's three steps in the transition process—intersetting relationships, family system reorganization, and changes among the learners' various environments—were reviewed.

The literature and research on transitions from early childhood intervention and preschool programs to school-based programs, between school-based programs, and from school programs to adult life in the community were presented. We noted, in agreement with Ferguson and associates, that a typical transition is more appropriately described as three distinct, simultaneous transitions: a bureaucratic transition, a family life transition, and a status transition.

Transitions between early intervention and preschool programs to school-based programs may be the most abrupt and permanent break with past experiences that the child makes before leaving home as an adult. This transition has a direct effect on the family in terms of schedules, transportation, support services, and communication strategies between home and school. The transition between school-age programs can be facilitated by parent observations and participation in planning. Generalization of skills plays an important role in transitions between programs.

The transition from school to community presents unique challenges to the learner and family. Tension exists between academic and functional curricula for learners in secondary programs. The transition from school to work should be viewed as a transition towards self-sufficiency, not merely "finding a job."

In the final section of the chapter, attention was focused on specific strategies for facilitating transitions between various environments. Emphasis was placed on the need for long-range planning and collaboration among the student with disabilities, parents, family members, special educators, and social agency personnel. The role of the special educator and the parents in transition planning and implementation were discussed. Specific strategies for planning and implementing transitions from early childhood intervention and preschool programs to school-based programs, between school programs, and from school programs to adult life in the community were presented. As inclusion becomes more pervasive, the challenges confronting learners with disabilities in making the transition between school environments will be less frequent.

Building Your Professional Vocabulary

Match each word or phrase to its meaning.

_____ Civil Rights Act of 1964

_____ The Education of the Handicapped Act of 1983

_____ generalization

_____ The Individuals with Disabilities Education Act of 1990

_____ Perkins Vocational Education Act of 1973

_____ transition

_____ Vocational Education Act of 1963

a. movement from one setting to another
b. an individual's ability to apply a skill learned in one setting to another setting
c. banned discrimination in education on grounds of race, ethnic origin, or religion
d. set aside 10 percent of funds allocated to vocational education for programs for persons with disabilities

e. emphasized services for individuals with severe disabilities
f. mandated transition services
g. funded grants and contracts to strengthen and coordinate education, training, and related services for transition

Comprehension Check

Select the most appropriate response.

1. Social systems theory suggests that transition is enhanced if
   a. the skills needed in the new setting are mastered.
   b. generalization has taken place.
   c. the transition is not made alone.
2. The transition process
   a. affects the student and future environments.
   b. affects the family.
   c. affects both the student and family.
3. In the "bureaucratic transition," parents reported
   a. either surrendering to or feeling abandoned by professionals.
   b. support from professionals who sought to understand the student's developmental context.
   c. support from positive, constructive professionals.

4. Transitions to a school-based environment are challenging because
   a. parents distrust teachers.
   b. the demands of school are very different from the demands of preschool.
   c. young children are developmentally more challenged by transitions.
5. Planning for transitions between school-age programs
   a. is facilitated by parent representation on the planning team.
   b. is facilitated by allowing the child to visit the new program setting.
   c. is facilitated by the receiving educator observing the student.
6. The Individuals with Disabilities Education Act (IDEA) requires
   a. a transition plan for students leaving a secondary program.
   b. a transition plan for students sixteen years of age, and in some cases, younger.
   c. a transition plan guaranteeing vocational support.

7. Transition programs should be viewed in terms of
   a. getting a job for the student.
   b. securing post-secondary education for the student.
   c. economic self-sufficiency.

8. Transition planning from an early intervention program should begin
   a. up to one year before the transition.
   b. when requested by the family.
   c. as early as three months before the transition.

References

Adamson, D. R., Matthews, P., & Schuller, J. (1990). Five ways to bridge the resource-room-to-regular-classroom gap. *Teaching Exceptional Children, 22* (2), 74–78.

Barretti, M. R. (1993). *Increasing the success of learning disabled high school students in their transition to the community college through the use of support services.* (ERIC No. 365075)

Bauer, A. M., & Shea, T. M. (1989). *Teaching exceptional students in your classroom.* Boston: Allyn & Bacon.

Bronfenbrenner, U. (1986). Ecology of the family as a context for human development: Research perspectives. *Developmental Psychology, 22,* 723–742.

Brown, L., Kiraly, Jr., J., & McKinnon, A. (1979). Resource rooms: Some aspects for special educators to ponder. *Journal of Learning Disabilities, 12,* 56–58.

Chadsey-Rusch, J. (1990). Social interactions of secondary-aged students with severe handicaps: Implications for facilitating the transition from school to work. *The Journal of the Association for Persons with Severe Handicaps, 15* (2), 69–78.

D'Alonzo, B. J., Owen, S. D., & Hartwell, L. K. (1985). Transition models: An overview of the current state of the art. *Techniques, 1* (6), 429–436.

Diamond, K. E., Spiegel-McGill, P., Hanrahan, P. (1988). Planning for school transition: An ecological-developmental approach. *Journal for the Division of Early Childhood, 11,* 245–253.

Edgar, E. (1987). Secondary programs in special education: Are many of them justifiable? *Exceptional Children, 53,* 555–561.

Everson, J. M., & Moon, M. S. (1987). Transition services for young adults with severe disabilities: Defining professional and parental roles and responsibilities. *The Journal of the Association for Persons with Severe Handicaps, 12* (2), 87–95.

Fairweather, J. S. (1989). Transition and other services for handicapped students in local education agencies. *Exceptional Children, 55,* 315–320.

Fairweather, J. S., & Shaver, D. M. (1991). Making the transition to postsecondary education and training. *Exceptional Children, 57* (3), 264–270.

Fairweather, J. S., Stearns, M. S., & Wagner, M. M. (1990). Resources available in school districts serving secondary special education students: Implications for transition. *The Journal of Special Education, 22* (4), 419–432.

Ferguson, P. H., Ferguson, D., & Jones, D. (1988). Generalizations of hope: Parental perspectives on the transitions of their children with severe retardation from school to adult life. *The Journal of the Association for Persons with Severe Handicaps, 13* (3), 177–187.

Gallivan-Fenlon, A. (1994). "Their senior year": Family and service provider perspectives on the transition from school to adult life for young adults with disabilities. *Journal of the Association for Persons with Severe Handicaps, 19* (1), 11–23.

George, N. L., & Lewis, T. J. (1991). EASE: Exit assistance for special educators—helping students make the transition. *Teaching Exceptional Children, 23* (2), 34–39.

Hanline, M. F. (1988). Making the transition to preschool: Identification of parent needs. *Journal of the Division for Early Childhood, 12,* 98–107.

Hanline, M. F., & Halvorsen, A. (1989). Parent perceptions of the integration transition process: Overcoming artificial barriers. *Exceptional Children, 55* (6), 487–492.

Haring, K. A., Lovett, D. L., & Saren, D. (1991). Parent perceptions of their adult offspring with disabilities. *Teaching Exceptional Children, 23* (2), 6–11.

Henderson, C. (1992). *College freshmen with disabilities: A statistical profile.* Washington, DC: American Council on Education, HEATH Resource Center. (ERIC No. ED354792)

ICD. (1986). *Survey of disabled Americans: Bringing disabled Americans into the mainstream: A nationwide survey of 1,000 disabled people.* New York: International Center for the Disabled.

Johnson, D. R., Bruininks, R. H., & Thurlow, M. L. (1987). Meeting the challenge of transition service planning through improved interagency cooperation. *Exceptional Children, 543,* 522–530.

Lazzari, A. M., & Kilgo, J. L. (1989). Practical methods for supporting parents in early transitions. *Teaching Exceptional Children, 22* (1), 40–43.

Martin, J. E. (1993). Transition policy: Infusing self-determination and self-advocacy into transition programs. *Career-Development for Exceptional Individuals, 16* (1), 53–61.

McDonald, L., Kysela, G. M., Siebert, P., McDonald, S., & Chambers, J. (1989). Parent perspectives: Transition to preschool. *Teaching Exceptional Children, 22* (1), 4–9.

McDonnell, J., Wilcox, B., & Boles, S. M. (1986). Do we know enough to plan for transition? A national survey of state agencies responsible for services to persons with severe handicaps. *The Journal of the Association of Persons with Severe Handicaps, 11* (1), 53–60.

Mithaug, D., Horiuchi, C., & Fanning, P. (1985). A report on the Colorado statewide follow-up survey of special education students. *Exceptional Children, 51,* 397–404.

National Council on the Handicapped. (1986). *Towards independence.* Washington, DC: Author.

Neubert, D. A., Tilson, G. P., & Iancone, R. N. (1989). Postsecondary transition needs and employment patterns of individuals with mild disabilities. *Exceptional Children, 55,* 494–500.

Rusch, F. R., & Phelps, L. A. (1987). Secondary special education and transition from school to work: A national priority. *Exceptional Children, 53,* 487–492.

Salend, S. J., & Lutz, G. L. (1984). Mainstreaming or mainlining: A competency based approach to mainstreaming. *Journal of Learning Disabilities, 17* (1), 27–29.

Smith, B. J., & Strain, P. (1988). Early childhood special education in the next decade: Implementing and expanding PL 99-457. *Topics in Early Childhood Special Education, 8* (1), 37–47.

Turnbull, A., & Turnbull, R. (1986). *Families, professionals and exceptionality: A special partnership.* Columbus, OH: Merrill.

U.S. Department of Education. (1983). SSA publishes major work disability survey. *Programs for the Handicapped, 1,* 7–8.

Wagner, M., D'Amico, R., Marder, C., Newman, L., & Blackorby, J. (1992). *Trends in postschool outcomes of youth with disabilities.* Menlo Park, CA: SRI International.

Wehman, P. H., Kregel, J., & Barcus, J. M. (1985). School to work: Vocational transition for handicapped youth. In P. Wehman & J. H. Hewitt (Eds.), *Competitive employment for persons with mental retardation: From research to practice.* Richmond, VA: Commonwealth.

White, S., & Bond, M. R. (1992). Transition services in large school districts: Practical solutions to complex problems. *Teaching Exceptional Children, 24* (4), 44–46.

Wolery, M. (1989). Transitions in early childhood special education: Issues and procedures. *Focus on Exceptional Children, 22* (2), 1–15.

Wood, J. W., & Miederhoff, J. W. (1989). Bridging the gap. *Teaching Exceptional Children, 21* (2), 66–68.

Family and Community Issues in Contemporary Society

Objectives

After completing this chapter, you will be able to:

1. describe the impact of divorce on the learner's development.
2. describe the impact of child abuse, neglect, and maltreatment on the learner's development.
3. describe the impact of substitute care on the learner's development.
4. describe the issue of learners raised in poverty.
5. describe the effects of prenatal drug and alcohol exposure on the learner's development.

Key Words and Phrases

Adoption Assistance and Child
   Welfare Act of 1980
child abuse
Child Abuse Prevention and
   Treatment Act of 1974
child maltreatment

child neglect
fetal alcohol syndrome
foster care
possible fetal alcohol effect
prenatal drug and alcohol exposure
substitute care

etween 1980 and 1986, the number of children reported as maltreated in the United States rose from 1,154,000 to 2,086,000, representing an increase from 18.1 per 1,000 children to 32.8 per 1,000 children (U.S. Bureau of the Census, 1990).

For every ten Caucasian children in a classroom, at least half have experienced life in a single-parent family, and one or two are currently living in a stepfamily. As many as six of their first eighteen years may be spent in a single-parent home (Carlson, 1992).

For children of color, eight or nine out of ten children have resided in a single-parent home and have spent, on average, eleven of their first eighteen years of life with a single parent (Hernandez, 1988).

Family income is overwhelmingly the factor that is most related to being at risk for child maltreatment, with families income under $15,000 having the highest rates of maltreatment (Brassard & Apellanz, 1992).

Introduction

The American family no longer comprises "mom, dad, and two children." During the past several decades, there have been significant and dramatic changes in family style and structure in America. These changes continue at the present and will continue into the foreseeable future. As a result of these changes and changes in contemporary society, many children are developing in environments that place them at risk for varying from their less-challenged peers and thus in need of special education services.

Dubowitz, Newberger, Melnicoe, and Newberger (1988) discuss several factors that have caused changes in the American family: high incidence of divorce, adolescent parenthood, single-parent families, formation of stepfamilies, maternal employment outside of the home, lack of child-care services, and poverty. The frequency of divorce has increased to approximately one in every two marriages. It is generally agreed that divorce generates considerable stress for children. The increase in adolescent parenthood has increased the number of low-birth-weight infants, this condition frequently results in medical and developmental complications. In addition, adolescent parenthood is related to higher infant mortality rates and family instability.

Dubowitz and associates also discuss the single-parent family. If the current trend in single-parent families continues, nearly 60 percent of all children born in 1982 will spend at least one year of their life living in a single-parent home before they reach the age of eighteen. Single-parent households, particularly those headed by a female, are at a significant economic disadvantage. Families headed by women are likely to be poor. In addition, children living in single-parent families have been found to be at greater risk for maltreatment than children from two-parent families. Being raised in a single-parent household places the children at risk for stress and may impact the children's future educational accomplishments and economic status.

Concurrent with the increase in divorce is an increase in the number of stepfamilies. Dubowitz and associates report that each year one-half million adults become stepparents. Researchers have reported conflicting results in studies of children raised in these stepfamilies. This family arrangement is not necessarily negative, especially if an absent parent is replaced and the remaining

Young mothers are more likely to have low-birth-weight infants with the potential for medical and developmental complications.

A Village of Hope

By Michael Ryan
Page B June 4, 1995 Parade Magazine

I went to a small village up the road from my house the other day and suddenly found myself surrounded by art, creativity and happiness, "This is my home," said Wendy Stark, 48, a weaver. "It's the best place in the world to live." As I wandered around, I began to understand why she felt that way. Camphill Village covers only 680 acres in Copake, N.Y., in the foothills of the Berkshires, near the border with Massachusetts. It has about 220 residents, 26 houses and a smattering of other buildings. Yet, as I went from building to building, I found residents making stained-glass windows, binding books, manufacturing candles, milking cows, tending gardens and practicing a chorale from Bach's Cantata No. 4. Poems were inscribed on the wall of a barn, and paintings hung everywhere.

If you get the impression that Camphill Village is a special place, you are right. About half of the people who live here are challenged—the kind of people we used to call "mentally handicapped" or "physically handicapped" or "retarded," who not long ago might have been locked up in state institutions. At Camphill, they are simply called "villagers." All of the villagers are mentally challenged, but some are physically challenged as well. The other half who live here are called "co-workers"—people who raise their families in homes they share with the mentally challenged villagers. About half of the co-workers are young volunteers, usually high school seniors or college graduates, who stay for a year or two.

I imagined that some of the villagers might be able to do a few simple tasks, but I doubted they could be self-sufficient. I thought that professional care-takers would perform all but the most elementary jobs in the village. Nothing prepared me for what I discovered.

"This village was founded in 1961," said Wanda Root, one of the co-workers. "It was the first Camphill Village in North America." The Camphill Movement, she explained, was started in 1939 by an Austrian doctor named Karl König, who had lived on an estate called Camphill in Aberdeen, Scotland. He and his associates practiced his belief that many children labeled "retarded" could in fact develop significant abilities.

"In the beginning, the main therapeutic aspect was just sharing life and work," Root said. "Then it was realized that these children had a right to an education." Working intensively with each student, König and his colleagues were able to teach some to read, write, express themselves clearly and learn about arts and crafts and music too. Almost all of them gained at least some rudimentary work skills.

The Camphill Movement grew quickly. There are now 68 centers worldwide. Like most nonprofit institutions, the Camphill Village in Copake struggles to meet its annual $2 million budget. About half of that comes from monthly disability payments to the villagers. "They get $825. The state hasn't raised it in 12 years," said Ron Admiral, who handles the fund-raising for the village. To make up the shortfall, the village sells bread, cookies and crafts made in its small stores, and runs a gift shop and cafe. Anne Ratner, the grandmother of a villager, has arranged dozens of concerts to raise money for the village, in venues that range from her living room in New York City to Lincoln Center.

The village also supports itself by growing vegetables and fruits, putting up preserves, making cheese and butter, and raising a dairy herd, some pigs and sheep, as well as beef cattle. One day, I walked through the barn and found Chris Rivinus,

biological parent gains the love and support he or she needs and if the family's economic difficulties are alleviated. However, in all probability, the children's loyalty will remain divided between the biological parent and the stepparent.

Due to financial need, increased societal pressure to attain career satisfaction and achievement in the workplace, and desire by women for greater involvement with and autonomy in the world at large, maternal employment outside of the home has increased significantly in recent decades. No direct causal relationship between the mother working outside of the home and particular child problems has been established. The quality and consistency of child care during infancy and early childhood may be a more valid predictor of the child's development than whether or not the mother works outside of the home. Children of mothers employed outside of the home have a less-rigid stereotypic perception of the female sex role. This is true, particularly, if their mother performs work that has not been traditionally associated with the female sex role. In addition, maternal employment has been shown to be beneficial for adolescent sons and daughters because it provides a positive model for them.

Dubowitz and associates report several other factors that consistently confront families in contemporary society. There is a shortage of quality and affordable child-care services and uncertainty surrounding the effects of raising

29, rhythmically milking a Jersey cow. "This is my favorite job," he said. As I watched him work alongside other villagers and co-workers, I marveled at how Chris and his friends had learned to make their way in life.

Camphill Village is a community in which graduates of the Camphill schools can find permanent housing when they become adults. "We're not thinking, 'What can we do to help them?'" said Deborah Admiral, a co-worker. "We think, 'How can we help them to find their particular gifts and make a contribution to our common life?' That approach allows them to be givers, rather than just receivers, and we all need that."

I found out what she meant when I browsed through some of the village's shops. Ricky Hauptman, 41, was in the wood shop when I met him. "I've been here almost 21 years," he boasted. "I've run the spindle sander, the disc sander, the band saw and the drill press."

Not all Camphill residents come from its schools. The average villager is between 35 and 45; the youngest are in their early 20s, the oldest is 81. For some newcomers, the transition can be daunting at first. "It took me six months before I'd come here." said Linda Lang, 46, who helped to prepare

dinner for the others in her house. "It took me more than a month to get used to it. Now it's going on my 25th year in the village."

The eloquence of many of the villagers (not all can speak, or speak clearly) surprised me, so I sought out an expert—Martin Lyden, a psychologist who performed New York State-mandated assessments of all the villagers several years ago. Lyden, who specializes in mental retardation, admitted that he too was startled by his findings. "The social skills, the articulateness, the conversational and interpersonal skills, and the ways they express themselves are well beyond what I would have expected from their I.Q. numbers," said Lyden.

All seven Camphill centers in North America, both schools and villages, are at or near their capacity. A group of parents in California is trying to raise funds to build a village there. For a village to thrive, though, it needs not just villagers but also co-workers.

The daily life of Camphill is sustained by the adult co-workers who choose to devote their lives to the village. They receive no salary, although their food, clothing and shelter are provided within the village budget. They work side-by-side with the villagers. Most are married and have children who live with them and the villagers.

"I came to Camphill for three months when I was in college," said Wanda Root. "I was astonished to find a place where you could have great ideals and realize them in your daily life." After working at other jobs for several years, Root came back to Camphill, where she has worked for 24 years in three villages and schools, has married and raised a son.

When I asked Deborah Admiral if her life with the disabled was ever a burden, she replied candidly: "Yes, but it can sometimes also be a burden to live with your husband, or your children, or even with yourself. The village is no different."

And what is it like to grow up as the child of co-workers? I asked Ellen Roberts, 21, who had just finished a stint as a co-worker before she left for Reed College in Oregon last year. "I think everyone might have a little resentment about sharing your parents with others," she said, "but I've enjoyed the feeling of helping people when they needed me and having people there to help me." For more information, write: Camphill Village U.S.A., Inc., Dept. P, Copake, N.Y. 12516 ●

First Published in *Parade.* Copyright © 1995 by Michael Ryan. Reprinted by permission of the author and the author's agents, Scovil Chichak Galen Literary Agency, Inc., 381 Park Avenue South, New York, NY 10016.

children in substitute-care settings, such as an infant- or child-care center. The nation's low birthrate and the increase in the child mortality rate are significantly correlated with poverty. There is a dramatic increase in the number of homeless families in America, and homelessness generates enormous stress and special health and psychological vulnerabilities in children.

The Impact of Divorce

Objective One

To describe the impact of divorce on the learner's development.

When individuals end a marriage through divorce, they do so in the hope of improving the quality of life for themselves and their children. Wallerstein and Blakeslee (1989), in a report based on an extensive study of families ten years following a divorce, state that several issues have an impact on child development. They describe several differences between the impact of divorce and other life crises, such as death, illness, and unemployment. Divorce more often involves anger, which may be expressed physically or verbally or both. Rather than striving to ensure their children's safety and emotional security, parents in the process of seeking a divorce frequently give priority to their adult problems. This diminishes their capacity to parent. In addition, during the process of divorce, the usual social supports are less available to parents and children because relatives and friends tend to withdraw from the conflict occurring within the family.

According to Guidubaldi and Perry (1985), divorce is the most pervasive severe psychological stressor for children. Wiehe (1984) compared sixty-two children, nine to fourteen years of age, who had experienced divorce in their families with sixty matched children who had not experienced divorce. He found that the children from divorced families had poorer social and academic skills and lower self-esteem, more negative attitudes towards both of their parents, and a more external locus of control—that is, they viewed personal life events as occurring outside of their control.

The effects of divorce on the learner's development endures over time. In one study, children from divorced families were found, two years after the divorce, to perform more poorly on a multifactored mental health index than their intact-family peers. This effect was more evident among boys than girls (Guidubaldi & Perry, 1985). Six years following divorce, children in divorced families encountered more negative life changes than did children from intact families. The boys demonstrated externalizing behavior problems, such as fighting or inappropriate language; the girls demonstrated internalizing behavior problems, such as withdrawal and depression. In addition, girls experienced more disruption than the boys when their parents remarried (Hetherington, Cox, & Cox, 1985). After ten years, a significant number of adolescent and young adults remained burdened by vivid memories of the parents' divorce, feelings of sadness, resentment towards their parents, and a sense of being deprived of their childhood (Wallerstein, 1985).

Though divorce is common in contemporary society, social sanctions and the stereotyping of children of divorce continue to affect the children's development. Guttman, Geva, and Gefen (1988) found that the knowledge that a child's parents were divorced had an adverse effect on evaluations of the child's academic, social, and emotional functioning. The "child of divorce" stereotype was present in both teachers' and students' perceptions and became an organized theme in their perceptions of the child. The strongest effect was in the area of emotional disturbance; teachers assumed the child's problems arose from the parents' unfriendly divorce.

Wallerstein and Blakeslee (1989) describe a series of dilemmas present in contemporary society with regard to the frequency of divorce. Just because the parents are divorced does not necessarily mean that the child's psychological needs change. Family structures have become asynchronous with emotional needs. Rather than serving as an "oasis," a place where the individual can relax and repair, the home has become a place of significant stress. In addition, the economic burden of divorce is falling on women and children, with women with minor children experiencing, on the average, a 73 percent decline in their standard of living in the first year of divorce. Following a divorce, parent-child relationships are permanently altered.

As a result of their ten-year study of families and divorce, Wallerstein and Blakeslee conclude that divorce does affect the children's development. Cooperative parenting by both parents, which is vital to the child's proper development, is difficult in adoptive families. The process of divorce results in a diminished capacity to parent, which continues and permanently disrupts the children's developmental processes. New, unfamiliar parent-child relationships may develop in which the child is overburdened by responsibility for a parent's psychological welfare or serves as an instrument of parental rage. Frequently, the children bear the psychological, economic, and moral brunt of the divorce.

Teachers can play an important role in mitigating the negative effects of divorce on the development of their students. Berger, Shoul, and Warschauer (1992) suggest that teachers can provide children with a sense of stability in the classroom that they may not be experiencing in the home. In addition, teachers may provide kindness and understanding coupled with firm and realistic expectations, as well as extra support and recognition of learning accomplishments. They contend that throughout the divorce process, the learner needs to experience school as a stable, nonchanging aspect of his or her life.

The Impact of Maltreatment

Objective Two

To describe the impact of child abuse, neglect, and maltreatment on the learner's development.

Annual  **Edition**

Article *30*

In 1986, the U.S. Department of Health and Human Services (1988) reported 1.5 million cases of maltreatment or endangerment. However, the report noted that the "vast majority" of cases remained unreported and/or uninvestigated. Teachers have a legal, moral, and professional responsibility to report suspected and actual child abuse and neglect to the appropriate authorities. All educators should know the reporting procedures in their school, community, and state.

Child maltreatment, a term used to describe both abuse and neglect as well as their complex interactions, from a developmental organizational perspective is not a single or fixed incident, but rather ongoing transactions or patterns of behavior wherein the individuals involved reciprocally influence one another to cause disturbances in the caretaking process (Cicchetti, Toth, & Hennessy, 1989). Public Law 93-247, the **Child Abuse Prevention and Treatment Act,** which became law in 1974, uses the terms **child abuse** and **child neglect** to refer to physical or mental injury, sexual abuse, or neglect of a child under the age of eighteen by a person responsible for the child's welfare under circumstances that indicate that the child's health or welfare is harmed or threatened.

Though child abuse and neglect have different definitions, Ney, Fung, and Wickett (1994) report that less than 5 percent of the reports of maltreatment are of one type of mistreatment occurring in isolation. The vast majority of children are subjected to more than one kind of abuse or neglect. The combination of physical neglect, physical abuse, and verbal abuse occurs most frequently. In addition, neglect appears to be a precursor to abuse in many cases.

In an extensive review of the literature on the effects of child maltreatment on child development. Youngblade and Belsky (1989) conclude that child maltreatment is associated with dysfunctional parent-child relations, as evidenced by the child's increased likelihood of forming an insecure attachment for the maltreating parent during infancy. In addition, they conclude that the effects of child maltreatment are not limited to familial relations, as there are repeated indications that maltreatment is associated with dysfunctional peer relations.

In a detailed description of the effects of child maltreatment on children's development, Cicchetti, Toth, and Hennessy (1989) report that the formation of a secure attachment relationship with the primary caregiver(s) during the first year of life is one of the most important developmental tasks of infancy. During this critical period, children who have sensitive caregivers come to view themselves as acceptable and lovable, whereas children with insensitive and/or irresponsible caregivers learn to see themselves as unacceptable and unlovable. Children who have not developed an attachment with a primary caregiver may display a preoccupation with attachment concerns, which interferes with their ability to adapt to the preschool environment.

Cicchetti and associates found that as early as thirty months of age, maltreated children use proportionately fewer words to describe their internal psychological states than their nonmaltreated peers. In older elementary-school students, maltreatment is reflected in a negative self-image, which leaves students feeling less competent and less academically motivated than their peers. Children who have been maltreated exhibit more avoidance and aggressive behavior towards peers. They exhibit limited social skills and a greater frequency of withdrawal. As a group, these children are more anxious, inattentive, and apathetic than other children and rely more heavily on teachers for encouragement and approval.

Home should be a place where children can be safe, not a stressful setting that will damage them physically and mentally.

Crittenden (1989) discusses a combination of deficits and distortions in the development of maltreated children that can be expected to affect both their classroom behavior and academic achievement. Maltreated children often exhibit disruptive, defiant, bullying aggression, which results in interpersonal confrontations with peers and teachers. Defiant abused children appear to spend too much time fighting to learn well. Other maltreated children may become so compliant and overly concerned with meeting others' standards that they rarely experience the joy of discovery or the satisfaction of achievement. Overcompliant abused children are so concerned with finding the right answer that they are frequently unable to attend to and manipulate ideas and concepts.

The underlying issues for all maltreated children are predictability and control in their life. It is generally agreed that most maltreated children have experienced unpredictable and uncontrollable environments (Crittenden, 1989). Crittenden describes the following hierarchy of needs of maltreated children. These children need to learn

1. to predict events in their environment; without this skill they cannot organize their behavior.
2. to achieve their desired objectives in socially appropriate ways.
3. to communicate openly with others and use developmentally appropriate cognitive and language skills.
4. to develop trust through carefully regulated, unambiguous, and consistent affective experiences.
5. to develop the self-confidence, self-motivation, and self-control necessary to enjoy and benefit from the intellectual stimulation of education programs.

A broad range of transaction patterns occur among parents and children. In their work at the Marlborough Family Service Agency, Asen, George, Piper, and Stevens (1989) found that the identification of the typical pattern of abuse was a helpful first step in planning the management of families engaged in physical abuse. They found a broad range of transaction patterns that occur among abusing parents and abused children: helpless and help-recruiting, professional, transgenerational, stand-in, distance-regulating, transferred, cultural, and denied. These patterns, which are described in detail in the remainder of this section, are not separate entities, and in many families more than one pattern can be identified. Those administering treatment, however, are encouraged to assume that one pattern predominates, and treatment should focus on that pattern.

The first pattern Asen and associates describe is helpless and help-recruiting abuse. Families exhibiting this form of abuse appear to have a limited range of skills for dealing with everyday issues and thus resort to abuse. To help resolve the problems of abuse, those in the family's extended social systems contexts—for example, school personnel, relatives, and therapists—attempt to help the inexperienced family develop more appropriate ways of behaving. Repeated offers of help and its acceptance by the family may lead to a situation wherein the helper, knowingly or unknowingly, becomes involved in the problem of abuse to a point of assuming parenting responsibilities. As a consequence, the outside help becomes a problem in itself. Such families then require additional help to decrease their dependency on the helping relationship.

The second pattern of abuse described by Asen and associates is professional abuse. In this pattern, the professional becomes overinvolved in the family's problem and assumes parenting duties. As a general rule in helping relationships, professionals work with an individual or family only as long as they have a problem, and service is terminated when the problem is resolved. In the professional abuse pattern, the family demonstrates just enough progress to keep the professional motivated, engaged, and interested in maintaining a relationship with the family. To resolve this situation, the professional must separate from the family situation sufficiently to conduct an objective evaluation of the relationship.

Transgenerational abuse can occur when the grandparents become involved in raising their grandchildren, by accepting the caretaking role or as a consequence of sharing a residence with their son's or daughter's family. In some cases, transgenerational abuse results in a repetition of the cycle of poor parenting and abuse that occurred when the grandparents were raising their children. In other cases, the fact that the child's biological parents remain dependent on the grandparents gives the grandparents a second opportunity to parent. In this situation, unresolved problems related to the parent's own childhood may be reactivated. To assist these families, authority and responsibility within the family must be shifted from the grandparents to the child's biological parents.

The fourth pattern is stand-in abuse. If one parent has a close relationship with the child and the relationship between the parents is distant, then maltreatment of the child may represent a means of punishing the partner without undermining the marriage. The family may adopt a pattern of behavior in which, at times of crisis, one child is singled out and punished or the child learns to behave in a manner that elicits abuse. In this situation, the child serves as a conflict regulator between the parents. Stand-in abuse may also occur in situations where one parent is "overengaged" with the child and the other is "disengaged." The primary issue for the professional working with these families is to find a way to help the parents resolve their conflicts without using the child as the focus of anger.

In some families, there is a pattern of distance-regulating abuse. The child learns that the only way to achieve close physical contact with mother or father is to behave in such a way as to evoke punishment. In these cases, closeness is experienced in the act of punishment and the subsequent hugs and comforting that are a consequence of the parent's feelings of guilt about the abuse of the child. In other families who regulate personal distance through child abuse, there is a predictable sequence of outbursts of violence. The violence serves the purpose of stabilizing the family at a point where there is neither too much closeness nor too much distance between the members. In working with these families, enjoyable experiences that enhance cohesion among the family members are essential.

Transferred abuse is another pattern found among families. It is difficult to understand the processes underlying this particular pattern of abuse. It appears that intense experiences from the parent's past are transferred to the present, and the child becomes the target of the feelings associated with these past experiences. These families need help differentiating between the past and the present and understanding that they are superimposing the past on the present.

Cultural abuse occurs in some families. When these families are challenged with regard to their disciplinary practices, they state that their behavior towards their children is appropriate from the perspective of their cultural origins, even though their behavior is not accepted in the culture in which they presently live or by authorities within that culture. The parent may state that a particular way of disciplining their child is an inherited family practice. To assist these families, it is often necessary to involve other families with the same cultural background who manage their children without abusing them. The essential message to be communicated to families involved in cultural abuse is "We recognize that your culture may have different disciplinary practices, but in this community the law and the authorities take a firm stand against those practices." The parents are urged to rethink their interactions with their children because they risk losing their child if the abuse continues.

The traditional family unit has been changed by adoption and fostering.

The final pattern, which may include any of the previously discussed patterns, is denied abuse. In this situation, the child is injured but the cause of the injury is denied by the abusing parent. In order to work effectively with these families, the focus of intervention must shift from "Who did this?" to an analysis of the pattern of interaction within the family. The family must demonstrate that their parenting is "good enough" to keep their child rather than children's service authorities demonstrating that the parenting is "bad enough" to remove the child from the family's custody.

These various patterns of abuse emphasize the functions of abuse within the child's family and extended social systems context. The teacher's primary role in child abuse is to refer any evidence or suspicion of abuse to the proper authorities and to cooperate with professionals working with the family, not to treat abusive families or to attempt the interventions suggested for each type of abuse.

Perhaps of greatest importance in the discussion of child maltreatment is the topic of prevention. However, prevention is a complex issue. Melton and Flood (1994) contend that child maltreatment is correlated to a broad range of personal and social problems. As such, child maltreatment not only causes personal and social problems, it may also be an indicator of negative social momentum. Knowledge about interventions and preventions remains scant, though the need is great.

The Impact of Substitute Care

Objective Three

To describe the impact of substitute care on the learner's development.

Children are described as being in **substitute care** when their primary caregivers are individuals other than their biological parents. Substitute caregivers include relatives, informal foster parents, licensed foster parents, adoptive families, or group residential facility personnel.

Schor (1988), in a detailed discussion of **foster care** (care in foster homes), reports that since 1983 the foster-care population in the United States has grown in absolute size and contains higher proportions of older children and children with disabilities. Today, foster children have more serious physical and emotional problems than in the past.

According to Schor, foster-care placement is intended to be a planned, temporary service implemented for the purpose of strengthening families. Ideally, if after studying the family and providing appropriate services, reuniting the child and the family is not deemed possible or is considered not to be in the best interest of the child, parental rights are terminated and the child is placed with an adoptive family. There are, however, some children for whom neither reunion with their family nor adoption is feasible. Frequently, these children remain with foster-care families, in various settings and on a temporary basis, until they reach their majority.

According to the Schor report, the current foster-care population is composed of approximately equal numbers of males and females. Forty percent of the population are children from minority cultures. Twenty-five percent of the population are disabled. Approximately three-quarters of the children are in foster placement because of maltreatment; most of these children return to their biological family within one year. Twenty percent of the children reenter foster care within a year of discharge. Twenty-five percent of the children are likely to remain in foster care after a two-year placement. The number of children entering foster care and the severity of their physical, emotional, and social problems are increasing. Social service agencies are having increasing difficulties recruiting and retaining foster-care parents.

Children in foster care have been found to demonstrate more frequent and serious health-care problems than children living with their biological families. Schor reports that these children may have chronic medical disorders, dental needs, prenatal exposure to drugs, and congenital infections. The children demonstrate variations from their peers in growth, decreased visual and auditory acuity, elevated rates of developmental delays and educational problems, and serious emotional problems. Hochstadt, Jaudes, Zimo, and Schachter (1987) found in their study of learners in foster care ranging in age from ten days to seventeen years of age that these subjects had significantly greater delays and major deficits in adaptive behavior. In addition, these learners demonstrated behavioral problems often associated with psychiatric disorders.

Substitute care is a challenge to both child and family. Normal developmental family processes are challenged by a distortion in the family cycle (Elbow, 1986). Whereas biological families begin with dependent relationships and progress towards individuation as the children assume more and more responsibility for their personal lives, the members of the substitute family begin as independent individuals and progress towards attachments. The process is further limited by the temporary nature of the placement.

The **Adoption Assistance and Child Welfare Act of 1980** (Public Law 96-272) was a consequence of national concern for children who were "adrift in foster care" (Seltzer & Blocksberg, 1987). The law emphasized the need to develop plans for the permanent placement of children in need of out-of-home placement for either a short or extended period of time. Maluccio and Fein (1983) describe permanency planning as the process of designing and implementing a set of goal-directed activities aimed at helping children live in families that offer ongoing relationships with nurturing individuals and at giving children the opportunity to establish lifetime relationships. The process of permanency planning is intended to (a) protect the child, (b) support stable relationships between the child and the caregivers, (c) preserve the biological family, and (d) enhance the psychosocial and behavioral adjustment of the child. Seltzer and Blocksberg (1987) report a higher rate of adoption from foster care when social service workers and agencies accept the philosophy of permanency planning.

Brodzinsky, Schechter, and Brodzinsky (1986) summarize the behavior of older adopted children in a manner that is perhaps applicable to all foster and biological families. They suggest that attempts by school-age children to understand the basis of their relinquishment by their parents, usually through sadness and anger, are actually normal, age-appropriate, inevitable components of the experience. The children's reactions are similar to those associated with a parent's death or divorce; they represent children's grief and mourning in response to parental loss. Unlike children of divorce, however, many children in substitute care are struggling with the loss of parents for whom they may have only vague, distorted memories. Their loss is more pervasive and potentially more problematic as they enter adolescence and begin to struggle with the issues of personal identity.

An additional group of children in substitute care live in group homes and residential treatment centers, which, essentially, are the institutional descendants of orphanages. Weisman (1994) reports that these children are far more likely to be mentally ill, distrustful of adults (especially parents), and intolerant of the intensity of family life. Most are between the ages of five and eighteen. Though the goal of residential placement is to return a healthier child to his or her home, the reality is that in many cases, return to the biological parents may not be in the best interest of the child.

The Impact of Poverty

Objective Four

To describe the issue of learners raised in poverty.

Baumeister, Kupstas, and Klindworth (1990) report on the significant reversals that are occurring in the specific and general health indicators that affect children. They contend that a new, multifactored model is needed to explain the increased prevalence of children's health disorders. The model takes into consideration the wide array of contemporary psychosocial problems, such as adolescent pregnancy, suicide, substance abuse, and developmental disorders. Without specific prevention efforts, they suggest that a "biologic underclass" of children will emerge whose problems will be related to poverty, lack of adequate and timely prenatal care, and prevalence of human immunodeficiency virus (HIV) and other chronic illnesses.

The impact of poverty on children's development has been referred to as "double jeopardy," since the factors of biologic vulnerability—secondary to prematurity, maternal depression, temperamental passivity, and inadequate environmental stimulation—and the insufficient social support available to the poor serve to potentiate each other (Parker, Greer, & Zuckerman, 1988). This increased biologic vulnerability is related to teenage pregnancy, limited prenatal care, poor maternal nutrition, and maternal depression.

Parker and associates state that the interaction of biological factors and poor social support put children at serious risk. They argue that intervention should involve strengthening relationships and social supports for children in poverty, suggesting that even in stressed families, the presence of a good relationship with one parent reduces the risk for children. For older children, the presence of a close, enduring relationship with an external support figure (for example, a schoolteacher) may likewise serve a protective function. One goal of social support and therapeutic interventions must be to establish environments and relationships for the child that promote a positive self-concept.

Early intervention for children living in poverty is essential; the House Select Committee on Children, Youth, and Families estimates that every $1.00 spent on preschool education saves at least $4.75 in later educational and social costs. Chapter One programs, designed during the mid-1960s as a part of the "War on Poverty," annually serve approximately five million students identified as living in poverty (Wang, Reynolds, & Walberg, 1995). However, Wang and associates suggest that the efforts of Chapter One, frequently delivered to students as a program that removes them from their classrooms for help, contribute to the disjointed nature of their education. Pugach (1995) concurs, suggesting that though Chapter One programs may appear to address the individual problems of students, these services are only a brief respite from the overcrowded classrooms, inflexible bureaucracies, test-driven curricula, and age-graded organizational structure that challenge urban education. In addition, the structure of Chapter One services may alienate children, providing too little services at too late a time to have a real impact on the students' learning.

The Impact of Parental Substance Abuse

When a family is involved in substance abuse, two things happen to the children. First, the interactions that usually occur between parents and young children may not occur because the parents are preoccupied with obtaining and using drugs. Second, parents involved in substance abuse frequently do not have the same priorities as other parents. Their primary concern is to acquire and use their substance of choice, not to care for their children. As a result, the children's needs are neglected. Children living with parents who are substance abusers live in unstable, often dangerous environments and are cared for inconsistently by parents who frequently have psychological and physical complaints.

When discussing children from families in which there is substance abuse, Weston, Ivins, Zuckerman, and Lopez (1989) stress the importance of carefully considering the mother's behavior. Maternal behaviors associated with drug-induced organic mental disorders, such as seizures, paranoid and suicidal ideations, violent or aggressive behavior, harming self and others as a consequence of delusions, and impaired motor coordination, present significant dangers to children. In addition, the effects of the mother's drug of choice are frequently intensified by the use of other health-impairing substances, such as alcohol, tobacco, alternate drugs, and drug substitutes.

Conducting research with families who engage in substance abuse is problematic. Research subjects are difficult to locate, largely due to the nature of substance abuse, which is illegal and frequently requires abusers to participate in illicit activity to sustain their habit. It is difficult to collect research data because the subjects typically lead disorganized daily lives and are preoccupied with activities associated with their addiction (Howard, Beckwith, Rodning, & Kropenske, 1989).

Two groups of children associated with substance abuse in families are of great significance to educators and the educational system. Due to the potentially serious effects of *any* maternal use during pregnancy, children whose mothers used any drugs or alcohol of any kind at any time during the pregnancy have experienced what is termed **prenatal drug and alcohol exposure.** This includes far more children than those born addicted to a controlled substance. The first group is composed of children prenatally exposed to cocaine, usually in the form of alkaloidal cocaine (crack). The second group is composed of children prenatally exposed to alcohol.

Children Prenatally Exposed to Cocaine

There are several reasons why cocaine has become known as the "first substance of abuse." First, it is readily available and thus does not require the user to seek drugs in the so-called "underclass" society. Second, it does not require injection for use and effect; in the form of crack, it can be smoked. Finally, it is cost-competitive with similar quantities of alcohol purchased in public establishments (Keith et al., 1989). Crack cocaine is sold in the form of small, cream-colored chunks that resemble rock salt. Its use leads to a five- to fifteen-minute reaction, or "high," within less than ten seconds, and it has a far more powerful effect than that of powdered cocaine (Gold, 1987). The use of crack results in an intense but fleeting feeling of competence, which is quickly replaced with feelings of irritability, restlessness, and depression. Cocaine use is frequently part of a multidrug or polydrug abuse syndrome. Its use is not restricted to those persons usually perceived as "drug addicts." Farrar and Kearns

Objective Five

To describe the effects of prenatal drug and alcohol exposure on the learner's development.

Annual **Edition**

Article *11*

Infants who have been exposed to drugs and alcohol may be of low birth weight.

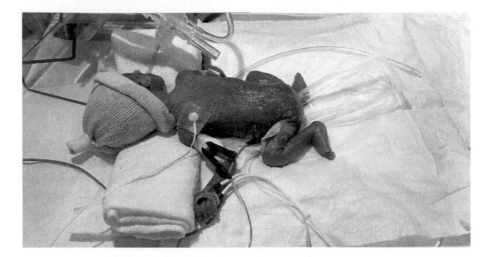

(1989) urge medical personnel not to dismiss the possibility of cocaine use solely on the basis of a patient's appearance, age, and socioeconomic status. In fact, in one study, 25 percent of cocaine users denied use at the time of their hospital admission interview. Cocaine use is reported to be associated with a greater risk for sexually transmitted diseases and increased use of alcohol, to-bacco, marijuana, opiates, and illicit drugs during pregnancy (Frank and asso-ciates, 1988).

When a woman uses cocaine one or two days prior to delivery, it can be detected in the urine of the newborn child for as long as ninety-six hours after the birth. In contrast, in adults, cocaine is apparent in the urine for approximately sixty hours. The slower metabolism of the cocaine by the newborn is due to the relative immaturity of the infant's liver (Van de Bor, Walther, & Sims, 1990). Al-though the exact risk of cocaine exposure during human pregnancy is unknown, physicians are urged to counsel patients with regard to possible risks to the fetus and to carefully monitor their patients (Hoyme et al., 1990).

The most frequently reported characteristic of cocaine-exposed infants is low birth weight, also known as prenatal growth retardation (Bingol, Fuchs, Diaz, Stone, & Gromisch, 1987; Chasnoff, 1988a; Farrar & Kearns, 1989; Frank et al., 1988). In a follow-up study of three- to seven-year-old children who as infants were exposed to cocaine, growth retardation was found to be related to delayed cognitive, motor, and perceptual performance (Harvey, Prince, Burton, Parkin-son, & Campbell, 1982).

Neurobehavioral abnormalities are well documented in cocaine-exposed infants (Chasnoff, 1988a). According to Hadeed and Siegel (1989), 10 percent of babies exposed to cocaine exhibit unexplained jitteriness. Using the Brazelton Neonatal Behavioral Assessment Scale, Chasnoff, Burns, Schnoll, & Burns (1985) found that infants exposed to cocaine exhibited serious depression in interactive behaviors and poor organizational responses to environmental stimuli. In a com-parison of the motor development of cocaine-exposed infants to non-drug-exposed infants, Schneider and Chasnoff (1987) found infants exposed to cocaine to feel stiff when their limbs were moved and to exhibit excessively extreme pos-tures. They exhibited tremors, especially in their arms and hands when reaching for objects. As they grow older, the primitive reflexes must be replaced by more mature movement patterns if the children are to develop a normal body image.

Children who have been prenatally exposed to cocaine may demonstrate various physical abnormalities, for example, extremely small head size (Hadeed & Siegel, 1989) and malformations of limbs (Bingol et al., 1987). In a study by Hoyme and associates (1990), seven of ten cocaine-exposed infants had limb defects, such as the absence of arms below the elbow, missing digits, or missing forearm bones. Due to an increase in cerebral blood flow, infants exposed to cocaine are at risk for intracranial hemorrhaging after birth (Van de Bor, Walther, & Sims, 1990).

When interacting with their environment, Howard and associates (1989) found infants exposed to cocaine to be disorganized. They were less responsive to their mothers and more difficult to both engage in interaction and to console. In addition, they exhibited unpredictable fluctuations in emotional responses (Chasnoff, 1988b). These infants did not experience the normal processes of mother-child attachment, which are essential to the early relationship between mother and infant.

Children prenatally exposed to cocaine have developmental scale scores that are in the low average range (Howard et al., 1989). Their most striking deficits are in unstructured free play situations, which require self-organization, self-initiation, and independent follow-through in play activities. For their age, the children demonstrate significantly less representational play than expected. Their play activities are characterized by scattering, batting, and picking up and putting down toys.

Dixon and Bejar (1989) report what is, to date, the most alarming results of research on infants exposed to cocaine. Using cranial ultrasonography, they contrasted cocaine-exposed and drug-free yet clinically ill children. They found that the type, location, and distribution of brain lesions in cocaine-exposed infants suggest that neural damage may not be clinically evident during infancy or early childhood. Rather, such neural damage may become evident only after the child's first year of life, when more complex visual-motor and social cognition tasks are required, such as during preschool and school activities. Dixon and Bejar suggest that even among drug-exposed "normal neonates," there is grave concern for abnormal neurologic, cognitive, and behavioral development as they approach school age.

In a study of the status of cocaine-exposed infants in the social welfare and juvenile justice system, Sagatin-Edwards, Saylor, and Shifflett (1995) report that among infants who tested positive for drugs at birth, a petition to juvenile court for protective custody was filed in almost half of the cases. Of these cases, about 80 percent of the babies were removed from their mothers. Approximately one-third of these babies were eventually returned to their mothers, while two-thirds were placed in foster and adoptive homes. In this study, African American and Hispanic babies were overrepresented in the group removed from the custody of the mother.

Teachers are cautioned concerning their personal perceptions and generalizations regarding children who have been prenatally exposed to cocaine. Thurman, Brobeil, Ducette, and Hurt (1994) found that telling early intervention personnel that a baby had been prenatally exposed to cocaine evoked a more-negative evaluation using a rating scale. They caution that labeling children as "cocaine exposed" or "crack babies" may set the stage for lowered expectations and additional risk.

Children Prenatally Exposed to Alcohol

The effects of the unborn child's exposure to alcohol were first described by Jones and Smith in 1973. They suggested that in utero exposure to alcohol could be the primary cause of children's growth deficiencies, birth defects, and mental retardation. Streissguth (1977) reported that prior to 1973, most health-care professionals attributed the learning and developmental problems of children from alcoholic families to chaotic home life and poor parenting. However, children from alcoholic families raised in foster homes characterized by a consistent and nurturing environment were found to demonstrate similar problems (Streissguth, 1976).

Making News

The following is an essay written by a
classmate of **Matt Byra** as a writing sample for
college admissions:

It is quite difficult to narrow down any one single person or event that has had the most influence on me. My seventeen years of life have provided me with an abundance of influences. Recently, however, there is one person who has changed my outlook. His name is Matt and society has labeled him severely disabled.

Matt is an 18 year old who has just enrolled in Hunterdon Central High School. Most of his life has been spent in an institution specializing in educating the disabled. Matt can not speak or hear.

At first, I did not understand how his being enrolled in a public school and a "normal" environment would help him. Now I do. His parents wanted him to be in an environment that would have a positive impact on him. He was not able, nor given the chance to feed himself, drink from water fountains or simply walk.

After two years, Matt has accomplished all of this—abilities that "abled" people take for granted.

I think some of the limits placed on handicapped people can be blamed on ourselves. Things such as feeding ourselves, walking or laughing are things we learn as babies. We forget that these people need our help and without the ability to communicate, their needs are not met. As a result, we do for them what they probably could do for themselves.

Matt is in our class only twice a week, but when he is there, he always puts a smile on our faces. Going to the right college, being popular, winning titles and awards, making the most points or driving the right car are wonderful goals to strive for, but when we understand what is truly important in our lives, then our priorities are in the right order.

Society still treats the handicapped as second class citizens—yet they always find it in their hearts to laugh or smile. It makes me wonder who the disabled people really are •

From "A Celebration of the Impact of the Individuals with Disabilities Educational Act" in *The ARC, 20 Years of IDEA in America*. Reprinted by permission of the publisher and the author, Sarah Koenig.

Discussions and research led professionals to the conclusion that in affected children of alcoholic mothers, the primary damage may have occurred in utero. This condition is called the **fetal alcohol syndrome.**

In 1980, the Fetal Alcohol Study Group of the Research Society on Alcoholism (Rossett & Weiner, 1984) presented minimal criteria for the diagnosis of fetal alcohol syndrome. The diagnosis of the syndrome is recommended when the child has symptoms in each of the following categories:

1.   Prenatal and/or postnatal growth retardations: weight, length, and/or head circumference below the tenth percentile when corrected for gestational age.
2.   Central nervous system involvement: signs of neurologic abnormality, developmental delay, or intellectual impairment.
3.   Common facial characteristics with at least two of these three symptoms: (a) microcephaly, (b) microophthalmia and/or widely spaced eyes, (c) poorly developed median groove between the upper lip and the nose, thin upper lip, or flattening of the upper jaw.

Abel (1984) suggests that if only one or two of these symptoms are evident and if the mother is suspected of alcohol use during pregnancy, then diagnosis of **possible fetal alcohol effect** may be made. Cooper (1987) suggests that the option of diagnosing possible fetal alcohol effect broadens the view of alcohol effects on the fetus, emphasizing that alcohol may not only cause the fetal alcohol syndrome but may be associated with a wide range of adverse outcomes. Fetal-alcohol-effect children, who are far more numerous than fetal-alcohol-syndrome

children, represent a significant challenge to teachers and health-care professionals (Rossett & Weiner, 1984). Nadle (1985) suggests that three to five children per
one thousand have fetal alcohol effect.

Children with fetal alcohol effect or fetal alcohol syndrome present a
broad range of intelligence test scores. A significant relationship has been found
between intellectual functioning and the physical symptoms of these syndromes:
children with more predominant facial characteristics and slower skeletal growth
demonstrate more severe brain dysfunction (Streissguth, Herman, & Smith,
1978). Infants as young as eight months of age with prenatal alcohol exposure exhibit lower weight, shorter length, smaller head circumference than normal,
minor physical anomalies, and feeding problems (Day et al., 1990).

The most common anomaly associated with prenatal exposure to alcohol
is growth retardation, with the child's length being more severely affected than
weight (Rossett & Weiner, 1984). Of perhaps greater concern, however, is that
most of these children demonstrate persistent hyperactivity and distractibility,
which contributes significantly to poor educational performance (Spohr & Steinhausen, 1987). Cooper (1987) contends that these children display a variety of
school problems that are characteristic of central nervous system impairment.

In a series of carefully controlled empirical studies, Streissguth and associates (1984, 1987, 1989) and Sampson, Streissguth, Barr, and Bookstein (1989) documented the neurobehavioral effects of prenatal alcohol exposure. They found that
as little as 1.5 ounces of alcohol per day is significantly related to an average intelligence quotient decrement of almost five points. In longitudinal studies controlled
for birth order and maternal education, nutrition, and use of caffeine, alcohol, and
nicotine, Sampson and associates found that their four-year-old subjects had significantly poorer attention spans and orientation and longer reaction times than did
nonexposed children. By school age, analysis revealed a pattern of neurobehavioral
deficits in the areas of memory, problem solving, focusing and maintaining attention, and regulating impulsivity across three settings: (a) on standardized intelligence and achievement tests, (b) on laboratory vigilance tasks, and (c) in the
classroom, as reported by teachers. Though the children exhibited auditory, spatial,
and verbal memory deficits, impulsivity was found to be the most significant characteristic in the laboratory and classroom.

In a sample of primarily middle-class, majority-culture mothers who reported occasional multiple drinks in the period prior to realizing they were pregnant, Sampson and associates (1989) found alcohol use significantly correlated
with a lowered intelligence quotient, poor academic achievement, school behavior
problems, and deficits in attention and vigilance. The children's fetal alcohol effects included poor short-term memory, impulsivity, problems with quantitative
functioning, and difficulties with sustaining attention. In a study by Streissguth
(1976), alcohol-effect children demonstrated hyperactivity and fine-motor problems, such as tremulousness, weak and primitive grasp, poor finger articulation,
and delay in establishing hand dominance. As Van Dyke and Fox (1990) report, a
significant number of children who were diagnosed with fetal alcohol exposure in
the 1970s exhibited learning problems, behavioral problems, and attention
deficits in the 1980s.

Shaywitz, Caparulo, and Hodgson (1981) describe the behavior and language disorders among their patients with prenatal exposure to alcohol. These
children had adequate nonverbal skills, yet had difficulty in verbally expressing
themselves. They were found to perseverate—that is, repeat beyond the usual end
point of a behavior—on familiar routines and play themes and topics, as well as
apparently blocking some concepts their teachers reported they knew. The children were anxious, had poor peer relationships, and played immaturely or inappropriately. The language of these children was unusual; they used adequate

articulation but displayed poor knowledge of the rules of dialogue, reduced sentence length, a failure to appreciate the communicative functions of language, and diminished or inappropriate spontaneous language. The children were hypervigilant, distractible even in normal levels of auditory and visual stimulation, and behaviorally disorganized.

Streissguth, Herman, and Smith (1978) report that school was a particular challenge to the alcohol-exposed children they studied. Their most significant problem appeared to be hyperactivity. None of the children was described as rebellious, anti-social, or negative. Considerable difficulty, however, was noted in regard to both learning and classroom management. Younger alcohol-exposed children were found to be generally cooperative and friendly, yet difficult to work with due to their hyperactivity. In some cases, hyperactivity decreased as the children grew older, but they continued to have difficulties focusing their attention (Streissguth, Clarren, & Jones, 1985).

Shaywitz, Cohen, and Shaywitz (1980) suggest that behavioral and learning problems may be the most significant, yet most frequently overlooked, deficits of children exposed to alcohol. Though the children in their sample had intelligence quotients well within the normal range, all experienced school failure. Hyperactivity, usually controlled with medication, was found to be present in all but one of the students. The students were described as being unable to function without one-to-one or small-group instruction. Statements by school personnel such as "cannot sit still" and "seems to have the skills yet is not learning" were noted in all of the students' records. By third grade, all the students were recommended for special education services.

Other medical disorders are also apparent in alcohol-exposed children. In a ten-year follow-up study, Streissguth, Clarren, and Jones (1985) reported intra-oral problems, including poor dental alignment, malocclusions, and cleft palate; eye problems, ranging from strabismus to severe myopia; heart murmurs; and skeletal problems, such as scoliosis and dislocated hips. Chronic otitis media and permanent hearing loss, which also have a serious impact on language learning, were noted in over half of the children.

Summary

In this chapter we described various family and community factors that place children at risk for disabilities. The impact of divorce, child abuse, neglect and maltreatment, and prenatal drug and alcohol exposure were explored. In addition, issues related to children growing up in substitute care or poverty were presented.

Divorce is perhaps the most pervasive psychological stressor for children. The process of divorce diminishes the parents' ability to provide for the child's emotional needs; the child's developmental process is disrupted.

Child maltreatment is associated with problematic parent-child interactions and insecure attachment. Children who have been maltreated are more inattentive and anxious than are their peers. The underlying issues for these children are predictability and control in their life. The children may be removed from their biological families and placed in substitute care. Though foster care is ideally a temporary, planned service, some children cannot be reunited with their families, and they may either remain in foster care or be placed in adoptive homes.

Poverty places the child's development in "double jeopardy"; there are both biologic vulnerability and limited resources for children living in poverty. Prenatal drug and alcohol exposure places children at even greater risk. These children are low in birth weight and may demonstrate a pattern of physical and behavioral challenges.

Though the complex interaction of these factors does have a serious impact on children's development, the teacher's role in assisting in the mitigation of their effects cannot be overemphasized. Even in stressed families, the presence of one close, enduring relationship with an external support figure (such as a schoolteacher) may serve as a protective function. Through this relationship children may develop a positive self-concept, and children with positive self-concepts seek, establish, and maintain the kind of supportive relationships and experiences that promote successful outcomes.

Building Your Professional Vocabulary

Match each word or phrase to its meaning.

_____ child abuse

_____ child maltreatment

_____ child neglect

_____ fetal alcohol syndrome

_____ foster care

_____ possible fetal alcohol effect

_____ prenatal drug and alcohol exposure

_____ substitute care

a. physical or mental injury or sexual abuse by a person responsible for the child's welfare

b. neglect of a child by a person responsible for the child's welfare

c. abuse and neglect and their complex interactions

d. primary caregivers are individuals other than the child's biological parent

e. care in foster homes

f. children of alcoholic mothers with growth retardation, central nervous system involvement, and common facial characteristics

g. one or two symptoms of fetal alcohol exposure and suspicion that there was maternal use of alcohol during pregnancy

h. mother used any drugs or alcohol of any kind during pregnancy

Comprehension Check

Select the most appropriate response.

1. The American family
   a. represents the traditional nuclear family.
   b. has changed dramatically from the nuclear family.
   c. has experienced a resurgence in two-parent families.

2. Divorce differs from other life crises in that
   a. anger is more frequently expressed verbally and physically.
   b. resolution is more forthcoming.
   c. the effects on child development are less devastating.

3. The effects of divorce on learner's development
   a. are mitigated after two years.
   b. are mitigated within a year after the divorce.
   c. endure over time.

4. Child maltreatment
   a. is an ongoing pattern of behavior.
   b. is usually an isolated incident.
   c. is usually related to the child's disability.

5. The impact of child maltreatment on development is evident in that the most important developmental task of infancy is
   a. developing an understanding of limits.
   b. developing an understanding of contingencies and behavior.
   c. developing a secure attachment with the primary caregiver.

6. The underlying issues for all maltreated children are
   a. safety and understanding.
   b. nurturing and limits.
   c. predictability and control.

7. The teacher's role with families engaged in abuse is
   a. attempting interventions.
   b. protecting the child.
   c. reporting any suspicion of abuse to the proper authorities.

8. Children in foster care are likely to
   a. rebound developmentally when placed in nurturing environments.
   b. successfully return to their biological families.
   c. demonstrate frequent health and behavioral problems.

9. Chapter One programs
   a. can serve as a substitute for special education.
   b. may further alienate children from school.
   c. can provide services to children based on need, not income.

10. "Prenatally exposed to drugs and alcohol" means
    a. a positive test on a drug screening at birth.
    b. evidence of drugs and/or alcohol in the amniotic fluid.
    c. maternal use of drugs and/or alcohol at any time during pregnancy.

11. Fetal-alcohol-effect children
    a. are far more numerous than fetal-alcohol-syndrome children.
    b. are far more seriously impaired than fetal-alcohol-syndrome children.
    c. are easier to identify than fetal-alcohol-syndrome children.

References

Abel, E. L. (1984). Prenatal effects of alcohol. *Drug and Alcohol Dependence, 14,* 1–10.

Asen, K., George, E., Piper, R., & Stevens, A. (1989). A systems approach to child abuse: Management and treatment issues. *Child Abuse and Neglect, 13,* 45–57.

Baumeister, A. A., Kupstas, F., & Klindworth, L. M. (1990). New morbidity: Implications for prevention of children's disabilities. *Exceptionality, 1,* 1–16.

Berger, S. R., Shoul, R., & Warschauer, S. (1992). A school-based divorce intervention program. In M. J. Fine & C. Carlson (Eds.), *The handbook of family-school intervention* (pp. 386–399). Boston: Allyn & Bacon.

Bingol, N., Fuchs, M., Diaz, V., Stone, R. K., & Gromisch, D. S. (1987). Teratogenicity of cocaine in humans. *Journal of Pediatrics, 110,* 93–96.

Brassard, M. R., & Apellaniz, I. M. (1992). The abusive family: Theory and intervention. In M. J. Fine & C. Carlson (Eds.), *The handbook of family-school intervention* (pp. 215–230). Boston: Allyn & Bacon.

Brodzinsky, D. M., Schechter, D., & Brodzinsky, A. B. (1986). Children's knowledge of adoption: Developmental changes and implication for adjustment. In R. D. Ashmore & D. M. Brodzinsky (Eds.), *Thinking about the family: Views of parents and children* (pp. 205–232). Hillsdale, NJ: Lawrence Erlbaum.

Carlson, C. (1992). Single parenting and stepparenting: Problems, issues, and interventions. In M. J. Fine & C. Carlson (Eds.), *The handbook of family-school intervention* (pp. 188–214). Boston: Allyn & Bacon.

Chasnoff, I. J. (1988a). Drug use in pregnancy: Parameters of risk. *The Pediatric Clinics of North America, 35,* 1403–1412.

Chasnoff, I. J. (1988b). Newborn infants with drug withdrawal symptoms. *Pediatrics in Review, 9,* 273–277.

Chasnoff, I. J., Burns, N. J., Schnoll, S. H., & Burns, K. A. (1985). Cocaine use in pregnancy. *New England Journal of Medicine, 313,* 666–669.

Cicchetti, D., Toth, S., & Hennessy, K. (1989). Research on the consequences of child maltreatment and its application to educational settings. *Topics in Early Childhood and Special Education, 9* (2), 33–55.

Cooper, S. (1987). The fetal alcohol syndrome. *The Journal of Child Psychology and Psychiatry and Allied Professionals, 28,* 233–227.

Crittenden, P. M. (1989). Teaching maltreated children in the preschool. *Topics in Early Childhood Special Education, 9* (2), 16–32.

Day, N. L., Richardson, G., Robles, N., Sambamoorthi, U., Taylor, P., Scher, M., Stoffer, D., Jasperse, D., & Cornelius, M. (1990). Effect of prenatal alcohol exposure on growth and morphology of offspring at eight months of age. *Pediatrics, 85,* 748–752.

Dixon, S. D., & Bejar, R. (1989). Echoencephalographic findings in neonates associated with maternal cocaine and methamphetamine use: Incidence and clinical correlates. *Journal of Pediatrics, 115,* 770–778.

Dubowitz, H., Newberger, C. M., Melnicoe, L. H., & Newberger, E. H. (1988). The changing American family. *The Pediatric Clinics of North America, 35,* 1291–1311.

Elbow, M. (1986). From caregiving to parenting: Family formation with adopted older children. *Social Work, 31,* 366–370.

Farrar, H. C., & Kearns, G. L. (1989). Cocaine: Clinical pharmacology and toxicology. *The Journal of Pediatrics, 115,* 665–675.

Frank, D. A., Zuckerman, B. S., Amaro, H., Aboagye, K., Baucher, H., Cabral, H., Fried, L., Hingson, R., Kayne, H., Levenson, S., Parken, S., Reece, H., & Vinci, R. (1988). Cocaine use during pregnancy: Prevalence and correlates. *Pediatrics, 82,* 888–895.

Gold, M. S. (1987). Crack abuse: Its implications and outcomes. *Resident and Staff Physician, 33* (8), 3–6.

Guidubaldi, J., & Perry, J. D. (1985). Divorce and mental health sequelae for children: A two-year follow-up of a nationwide sample. *Journal of the American Academy of Child Psychiatry, 24,* 531–537.

Guttman, J., Geva, N., & Gefen, S. (1988). Teachers' and school children's stereotypic perception of "the child of divorce." *American Educational Researcher Journal, 25,* 555–571.

Hadeed, A. J., & Siegel, S. R. (1989). Maternal cocaine use during pregnancy: Effect on the newborn infant. *Pediatrics, 84,* 205–210.

Harvey, D., Prince, J., Burton, J., Parkinson, D., & Campbell, S. (1982). Abilities of children who were small for gestational age babies. *Pediatrics, 69,* 296–300.

Hernandez, D. J. (1988). Demographic trends and the living arrangements of children. In E. M. Hetherington & J. D. Aratesh (Eds.), *Impact of divorce, single parenting, and stepparenting on children* (pp. 3–20). Hillsdale, NJ: Erlbaum.

Hetherington, E. M., Cox, M., & Cox, R. (1985). Long-term effects of divorce and remarriage on the adjustment of children. *Journal of the American Academy of Child Psychiatry, 24,* 518–530.

Hochstadt, N. J., Jaudes, P. K., Zimo, D. A., & Schachter, J. (1987). The medical and psychosocial needs of children entering foster care. *Child Abuse and Neglect, 11* (1), 53–62.

Howard, J., Beckwith, L., Rodning, C., & Kropenske, V. (1989). The development of young children of substance abusing parents: Insights from seven years of intervention and research. *Zero to Three, 9* (5), 8–12.

Hoyme, H. E., Jones, K. L., Dixon, S., Jewett, T., Hanson, J. W., Robinson, L. K., Msall, M. E., & Allanson, J. E. (1990). Prenatal cocaine exposure and fetal vascular disruption. *Pediatrics, 85,* 743–747.

Jones, K. L., & Smith, D. W. (1973). Recognition of the fetal alcohol syndrome in early infancy. *Lancet, 2,* 999–1001.

Keith, L. G., MacGregor, S., Friedell, S., Rosner, M., Chasnoff, I. J., & Sciarra, J. J. (1989). Substance abuse in pregnant women: Recent experience at the perinatal center for chemical dependence of Northwestern Memorial Hospital. *Obstetrics and Gynecology, 73,* 715–723.

Maluccio, A. N., & Fein, E. (1983). Permanency planning: A redefinition. *Child Welfare, 63,* 197.

Melton, G. B., & Flood, M. R. (1994). Research policy and child maltreatment: Developing the scientific foundations for effective protection of children. *Child Abuse and Neglect, 18* (Supplement 1).

Nadle, M. (1985). Offspring with fetal alcohol effects: Intervention and identification. *Alcoholism Treatment Quarterly, 2* (1), 105–116.

Ney, P. G., Fung, T., & Wickett, A. R. (1994). The worst combinations of child abuse and neglect. *Child Abuse and Neglect, 18* (9), 705–714.

Parker, S., Greer, S., & Zuckerman, B. (1988). Double jeopardy: The impact of poverty on early child development. *The Pediatric Clinics of North America, 35,* 1227–1240.

Pugach, M. (1995). Twice victims: The struggle to educate children in urban schools and the reform of special education and Chapter 1. In M. C. Wang & M. C. Reynolds, (Eds.), *Making a difference for students at risk* (pp. 27–52). Thousand Oaks, CA: Corwin.

Rossett, H. L., & Weiner, L. (1984). *Alcohol and the fetus.* New York: Oxford Press.

Sagatun-Edwards, I. J., Saylor, C., & Shifflett, B. (1995). Drug exposed infants in the social-welfare system and juvenile court. *Child Abuse and Neglect, 19* (1), 83–91.

Sampson, P. D., Streissguth, A. P., Barr, H. M., & Bookstein, F. L. (1989). Neurobehavioral effects of prenatal alcohol. Part II: Partial least squares analysis. *Neurotoxicology and Teratology, 11,* 477–491.

Schneider, J., & Chasnoff, I. J. (1987). Cocaine abuse during pregnancy: Its effects on infant motor development: A clinical perspective. *Topics in Acute Care and Trauma Rehabilitation, 2,* 59–73.

Schor, E. L. (1988). Foster care. *The Pediatric Clinics of North America, 35* (6), 1241–1252.

Seltzer, M. M., & Blocksberg, L. M. (1987). Permanency planning and its effects on foster children: A review of the literature. *Social Work, 37,* 65–68.

Shaywitz, S. E., Caparulo, B. K., & Hodgson, E. S. (1981). Developmental language disability as a consequence of prenatal exposure to ethanol. *Pediatrics, 96,* 978–982.

Shaywitz, S. E., Cohen, D. J., & Shaywitz, B. A. (1980). Behavior and learning difficulties in children of normal intelligence born to alcoholic mothers. *The Journal of Pediatrics, 96,* 978–982.

Spohr, H. L., & Steinhausen, H. C. (1987). Follow-up studies of children with fetal alcohol syndrome. *Neuropediatrics, 18,* 13–17.

Streissguth, A. P. (1976). Psychologic handicaps in children with the fetal alcohol syndrome. *Annals of the New York Academy of Sciences, 273,* 140–145.

Streissguth, A. P. (1977). Maternal drinking and the outcome of pregnancy: Implications for child mental health. *American Journal of Orthopsychiatry, 47,* 422–431.

Streissguth, A. P., Barr, H. M., Sampson, P. D., Darby, B. L., & Martin, D. C. (1989). IQ at age four in relation to maternal alcohol use and smoking during pregnancy. *Developmental Psychology, 25,* 3–11.

Streissguth, A. P., Bookstein, F. L., Sampson, P. D., & Barr, H. M. (1987). Neurobehavioral effects of prenatal alcohol: PLS analysis of neuropsychologic tests. *Neurotoxicology and Teratology, 11,* 492–507.

Streissguth, A. P., Clarren, S. K., & Jones, K. L. (1985). Natural history of the fetal alcohol syndrome: A ten-year follow-up of eleven patients. *Lancet* (Part 2), *47,* 422–431.

Streissguth, A. P., Herman, C. S., & Smith, D. W. (1978). Intelligence, behavior, and dysmorphogenesis in the fetal alcohol syndrome: A report on 20 patients. *Journal of Pediatrics, 92,* 262–267.

Streissguth, A. P., Martin, C. D., Barr, H. M., Sandman, B. M., Kirchner, G. L., & Darby, B. L. (1984). Intrauterine alcohol and nicotine exposure: Attention and reaction time in four-year-old children. *Developmental Psychology, 20,* 533–541.

Thurman, S. K., Brobeil, R. A., Ducette, J. P., & Hurt, H. (1994). Prenatally exposed to cocaine: Does the label matter? *Journal of Early Intervention, 18* (2), 119–130.

U.S. Bureau of the Census. (1990). *Statistical abstract of the United States* (110th ed.). Washington, DC: Author.

U.S. Department of Health and Human Services. (1988). 1 *Study findings: Study of national incidence and prevalence of child abuse and neglect: 1988.* Washington, DC: National Clearinghouse on Child Abuse and Neglect.

Van de Bor, M., Walther, F. J., & Sims, M. E. (1990). Increased cerebral blood flow velocity in infants of mothers who abuse cocaine. *Pediatrics, 85,* 733–736.

Van Dyke, D. C., & Fox, A. A. (1990). Fetal drug exposure and its possible implications for learning in the preschool and school-age population. *Journal of Learning Disabilities, 23* (3), 160–163.

Wallerstein, J. (1985). Children of divorce: Preliminary report of a ten-year follow-up of older children and adolescents. *Journal of the American Academy of Child Psychiatry, 24,* 545–553.

Wallerstein, J., & Blakeslee, S. (1989). *Second changes: Men, women and children a decade after divorce.* New York: Ticknor & Fields.

Wang, M. C., Reynolds, M. C., & Walberg, H. J. (1995). Introduction: Inner city students at the margins. In M. C. Wang & M. C. Reynolds (Eds.), *Making a difference for students at risk* (pp. 1–26). Thousand Oaks, CA: Corwin Press.

Weisman, M. L. (1994). When parents are not in the best interests of the child. *The Atlantic Monthly, 274* (1), 42–65.

Weston, D. R., Ivins, B., Zuckerman, B., & Lopez, R. (1989). Drug-exposed babies: Research and clinical issues. *Zero to Three, 9* (5), 1–7.

Wiehe, V. R. (1984). Self-esteem, attitude towards parents, and locus of control in children of divorced and nondivorced families. *Journal of Social Service Research, 8* (1), 17–28.

Youngblade, L. M., & Belsky, J. (1989). Child maltreatment, infant-parent attachment security, and dysfunctional peer relationships in toddlerhood. *Topics in Early Childhood Special Education, 9* (2), 1–15.

Learners Who Vary in Their Interactions

2

*P*erhaps no group of learners greater reflects the systems perspective of human development than those who vary in their interaction patterns. In this section, both learners identified as emotionally/behaviorally disordered and learners from various ethnic, cultural, and linguistic groups are discussed. These learners vary from the behavioral expectations of school, yet they frequently are competent in other social systems.

Since the turn of the century, the American public school has emerged as the main socialization agent for learning the "American way of life." Appropriate behavior and normalcy have been explicitly defined by the schools through the expected and accepted behaviors and interactions (Hoffman, 1975). The social systems perspective assumes that as social beings, students in schools are socialized to act in specific ways (Kugelmass, 1987). Conflicts occur when the values and expectations of the school contradict those the child has learned or when the same behavior has different meanings to the child and those in authority. Mercer (1965, 1973) argues that in regard to applying the social systems perspective to the educational system, it is primarily the expectations of the teacher that determine who will be identified and referred as possible candidates for special education. In public school, students are considered "normal" if not visibly defective, and they remain there until they fail to meet the role expectations of teachers.

Students identified as different represent a discordance with the general education system, demonstrating a lack of fit with expectations (Hobbs, 1980). Due to this lack of fit, the general education system assumes that the "problem" lies exclusively within the child. Mehan, Hertweek, and Meihls (1986) suggest that it is not the students' characteristics or behavior that leads to success or failure, but the expectations that teachers have for students' behavior that causes these academic outcomes. The reasons students are successful or unsuccessful is not because of the inherent characteristics of their actions, but because they are labeled successful or unsuccessful. What is "normal," then, is socially constructed by the educational system and is a consequence of educators' and students' interactions. These interactions generate an original designation such as "problem student," and the student's actions are taken into account as different.

One model of the interactions that generate the student's identification is presented by Wood (1981). In this model, a teacher's attention is drawn to the behavior of a student. The teacher then judges whether the behavior is pleasing or disturbing. If the teacher is disturbed by the behavior, he or she must decide whether some action should be taken. Depending on an appraisal of social and political factors, the teacher may decide not to react, to respond immediately, to seek support in acting to change the student's behavior, or to escape from the setting. If action is taken, the teacher puts in motion the system to label the student disordered, disruptive, or problematic. If the teacher infers that the disturbing behavior has been learned and is maintained by the environment, the student is then labeled behaviorally disordered. If the behavior is inferred to be a function of past experiences and the student's inner emotional state, the student is then labeled emotionally disturbed.

The social systems perspective attempts to view the definition of the individual's behavior as a function of the values of the social system within which he or she is being evaluated (Mercer, 1965). In this view, no clear consensus regarding which behaviors represent a norm violation exists; behaviors that may be considered appropriate in one setting may be perceived as deviant in another. Kugelmass (1987) asserts that majority-culture, middle-class children may, in fact, have less difficulty in conforming to their behavioral expectations of school than other children, not because they are never disobedient, aggressive, or overtly defiant, but because they have been exposed to a variety of social situations and have learned a fact of life essential for survival: different social situations demand different behaviors.

Learners Identified as Emotionally/Behaviorally Disordered

Kugelmass (1987) suggests that the procedure by which students are referred and placed in special programs for emotional/behavioral disorders is generally thought of as an event that assures that students with special needs will receive an education that is appropriate. The outcome of this procedure is believed to be a proper educational response. Yet, Kugelmass found that more than the students' condition was responsible for placement. The school district's definition of deviant behavior contributed significantly. Psychologists presented an official and sanctioned definition of students' behaviors. Their perspective and the power attached to their professional role identity caused the school district to remove difficult-to-manage students without questioning any prior assumptions about how the classrooms in which they were attempting to function were being operated.

Developmental Contexts of Learners Identified as Emotionally/Behaviorally Disordered and from Various Ethnic, Cultural, and Linguistic Groups

According to Sarason and Doris (1979), the public school system in the past served as a means to mold successive groups of urban immigrants in a manner that would propagate the existing control of society. The educational system continues to be responsible for this function in our society.

As social beings, children in schools are socialized to act in a specific way. A conflict occurs when the values and expectations of the school contradict those the child has learned or when the same behavior has different meanings to the child and those in authority. Labeling children depends on the conformity of the child's behavior and school achievement to some criteria. However, the subjectivity of these criteria impacts students' opportunities. Many of these learners may function competently outside of the school and may be indistinguishable from the general population once they leave the educational system.

Competencies emerge not as the properties of persons, but as the properties of situations presented in the educational system (Mehan et al., 1986). In these two chapters, the focus is on learners who, as suggested by the school system perspective, challenge the general educational system, yet may be seen as competent in other settings.

References

Hobbs, N. (1980). *The futures of children*. San Francisco: Jossey Bass.

Hoffman, E. (1975). The American public school and the deviant child: The origins of their involvement. *The Journal of Special Education, 9,* 414–423.

Kugelmass, J. W. (1987). *Behavior, bias, and handicaps*. New Brunswick, NJ: Transaction, Inc.

Mehan, H., Hertweck, A., & Meihls, J. L. (1986). *Handicapping the handicapped*. Stanford, CA: Stanford University.

Mercer, J. (1965). Social system perspective and clinical perspective: Frames of reference for understanding career patterns of persons labeled as mentally retarded. *Social Problems, 13,* 18–34.

Mercer, J. (1973). *Labeling the mentally retarded.* Berkeley: University of California Press.

Sarason, S. B., & Doris, J. (1979). *Educational handicap, public policy, and social history.* New York: The Free Press.

Wood, F. (1981). *Perspective for a new decade.* Reston, VA: Council for Exceptional Children.

Learners
Identified as
Emotionally/
Behaviorally
Disordered

Objectives

After completing this chapter, you will be able to:

1. describe the personal characteristics of learners identified as emotionally/behaviorally disordered.
2. describe the identification and evaluation of learners identified as emotionally/behaviorally disordered.
3. describe the impact of emotional/behavioral disorders on interactions in the home and school.
4. describe ways to mediate the environment for learners identified as emotionally/behaviorally disordered.
5. describe the impact of emotional/behavioral disorders on participation in larger social systems—the school, community, and society.

Key Words and Phrases

aggression
depression
Diagnostic and Statistical Manual of
    Mental Disorders
disturbed behaviors
disturbing behaviors
emotional/behavioral disorders

externalizing behaviors
internalizing behaviors
levels systems
life space interview
seriously emotionally disturbed
suicidal ideation
token economy

ave you ever felt weird, but couldn't figure out why? Sometimes I feel like that. Maybe it's a part of growing up. I don't know, but I keep moving anyway. Things have been smooth sailing. I have nothing to think about or worry over. That's for grownups, and my parents do that well. All I have to do is make sure my room is cleaned, put my bike away, stay out of trouble and get fair grades. Fair grades, sometimes that's hard to do, but I keep moving.

"One day something happened and things began to change. I began to feel really weird, like a yo-yo, swirling around and round. I didn't get it, but I keep moving anyway. At times the swirling would be strong like a swift wind passing by, but I keep moving anyway. Some days the swirling would be smooth as the flowing sea, but I keep moving anyway. Ask me how I feel. Fine, I guess. How should a kid my age feel? I have nothing to worry about. Besides, that's for grownups.

"As time went on, things really got rough. Remember the swirls, remember the wind, I found myself within, being tossed to and fro, feeling like I had no place to go. I have parents, what did they care, I found myself alone. My life seemed to drag, there was no hope. My only thought was to give up the ghost, but I keep moving. Now, what will I do? Where will I go?"

(Excerpted with permission from *Patrick* by J. A. Johnson. Copyright © 1991 J. A. Johnson.)

Introduction

Rhodes (1967) states that emotional/behavioral disorders are as much a function of where and with whom a child interacts as the child's behavior itself. Algozzine (1980) reaffirms this position when he states:

> . . . it is not simply the level and type of behavior that the child exhibits which may result in being identified as "disturbed," but the fact that that particular set of characteristics which make him/her an individual results in differential reactions (or degrees of disturbingness and intolerance) from others within the child's ecosystem. (p. 112)

A systems perspective of programming for learners identified as emotionally/behaviorally disordered within schools can serve to assist staff in understanding the various subsystems that have interactive effects upon an individual learner (Johnston & Zemitzsch, 1988). Though an extremely heterogeneous group, learners identified as having emotional/behavioral disorders challenge the school systems and professionals who serve them in their interactions.

During the 1993–1994 school year, .89 percent of the students between six and seventeen years of age were identified as emotionally/behaviorally disordered (U.S. Department of Education, 1995). The actual prevalence of emotional/behavioral disorders, though, varies greatly from the number of students served. Estimates of between 3–6 percent (Kauffman, 1989) and 20 percent (Whitaker et al., 1990) are proposed as to the actual prevalence of emotional/behavioral disorders. This group of learners may be the most underserved of all of those with disabilities.

Personal Characteristics

Cognitive Functioning and Academic Achievement

Morse, Cutler, and Fink's (1964) early work suggested that learners identified as behaviorally disordered had above-average cognitive ability. More recent studies, however, suggest that these learners exhibit average or lower-than-average measured cognitive abilities when compared to their typical peers (Coleman, 1986). Learners with more-severe behavioral disorders exhibit intelligence quotients in the mentally retarded range (Freeman & Ritvo, 1984).

During the 1989–1990 school year, 44.6 percent of the learners identified as emotionally/behaviorally disordered in the United States failed one or more courses in their most recent year of high school, far more than students in the other closest disability areas (speech impaired—35.0 percent, learning disabilities—34.8 percent). The average grade point of learners identified as behaviorally disordered was the lowest among students in all disability areas, 1.7 of a possible 4.0; in addition, these students were integrated into the fewest general education courses in high school (an average of 1.9). Learners identified as emotionally/behaviorally disordered were also the most likely to drop out of high school: 40.14 percent of these learners dropped out nationally, and, in New York, 66.4 percent dropped out (U.S. Office of Education, 1992).

In a study exploring the concomitance of learning disabilities and behavioral disorders, Fessler, Rosenberg, and Rosenberg (1991) found the proportion of learners identified as emotionally/behaviorally disordered who also had learning difficulty to be surprisingly large. Over 37 percent of the learners were identified as learning disabled, and an additional 17.8 percent were found to have learning problems and academic deficiencies sufficient enough to impede normal rates of achievement.

Objective One

To describe the personal characteristic of learners identified as emotionally/behaviorally disordered.

A primary characteristic of these learners is difficulty in demonstrating changes through academic instruction (Epstein, Kinder, & Bursuck, 1989). In comparing reading performance of learners identified as emotionally/behaviorally disordered to that of their peers, reading achievement was significantly below (about 1.5 to 2 grade levels) that of their peers in elementary school; by secondary school the discrepancy was about 3.5 grade levels (Coutinho, 1986).

A challenging set of data are presented by Scruggs and Mastropieri (1986), who found that there was no real difference between the academic achievement of learners identified as emotionally/behaviorally disordered and learners with learning disabilities. In a later study that used teacher ratings, learners identified as emotionally/behaviorally disordered and learners with learning disabilities were rated as equally, significantly below normal levels in academic achievement (Luebke, Epstein, & Cullinan, 1989). In this study, no difference was found in subject area or by gender.

Social Skills, Interaction, and Behavior

Schloss, Schloss, Wood, and Kiehl (1986), in a critical review of social skills research with learners identified as emotionally/behaviorally disordered, find that research has failed to build a comprehensive body of knowledge due to the absence of theory base. In addition, social skills training has not been individualized in response to learners' needs or characteristics. The social significance of social skills training has not been studied.

In a role-playing test of social competence that focused on positive and negative statements, learners identified as emotionally/behaviorally disordered and their nonidentified peers demonstrated significantly different responses (Hughes & Hall, 1985). Both the content and voice quality of the learners' responses to role-play scenes of positive and negative assertions differentiated the two groups.

The general education classroom behaviors of learners identified as emotionally/behaviorally disordered and their peers have also been explored. In a study of male third, fourth, and fifth graders, ten behaviors accounted for over 80 percent of the variance in group measurement, including social interaction with teacher, following directions, out-of-seat behavior, teacher-group approach to schoolwork, seeking approvals, responding to disapprovals, attending to schoolwork, raising of hands for attention, teacher-group approach to other activity, and calling out in class without raising a hand. Only teacher and child behaviors combined produced these significant results, again calling to mind the need to assess the context in which behaviors occur (Slate & Saudargas, 1986).

More than half the referrals for learners demonstrating potential emotional/behavioral disorders are enrolled in third grade through sixth grade, and almost three-fourths of these are male (Hutton, 1985). The most frequently stated reasons for referral are in the area of conduct disorders: (a) poor peer relationships, (b) frustration, (c) below academic expectations, (d) shy and withdrawn behavior, (e) disruptive behavior, (f) fighting, (g) refusing to work, and (h) short attention span. Poor peer relationships was the most frequent reason for referral among both boys and girls.

Caseau, Luckasson, and Kroth (1994) suggest a gender bias against the identification of girls with emotional/behavioral disorders. In their study, boys far outnumbered girls in students identified and served in public schools and students identified in public school who received other mental health services. Girls, however, outnumbered boys among students who were not identified by the public schools but received mental health services independently. Girls were more likely than boys to have serious problems of depression, family conflict, suicidal ideation, and suicide attempts. Caseau and associates contend that girls had emotional/behavioral problems serious enough to warrant identification, but not of the type that would cause them to be identified in public schools. The small number of girls who did receive services in the public schools exhibited external behaviors similar to those demonstrated by boys.

Edelbrock (1984), in an analysis of data from the Child Behavior Checklist he developed with his associates, found two broad clusters of behaviors among learners identified as behaviorally disordered: internalizing and externalizing. **Externalizing behaviors** included stealing, lying, disobedience, and fighting, for example, and **internalizing behaviors** included physical complaints, phobias, worrying, social withdrawal, and fearfulness, among others. The clusters of behavior by sex and age, as derived by Edelbrock, are presented in table 7.1.

Language There is a significant difference in the expressive language characteristics in conversations of learners identified as emotionally/behaviorally disordered and their nonidentified peers (McDonough, 1989). The learners identified as emotionally/behaviorally disordered use shorter utterances than do their peers. In their discourse, learners identified as emotionally/behaviorally disordered make errors in relations, failing to identify new information or repair responses when there are communication breakdowns. For example, a learner identified as emotionally/behaviorally disordered may approach a teacher and state, "Man, he's going to get busted for doing that," failing to recognize the need to identify both the individual or the activity for the teacher. These learners demonstrate poor topic maintenance, inappropriate responses, situational inappropriateness, and inappropriate speech style.

In a study of learners identified as demonstrating mild to moderate emotional/behavioral disorders, Camarata, Hughes, and Ruhl (1988) found that 97 percent of the children fell a minimum of one standard deviation before the normative mean on an individually administered test of language. The pattern of language problems these learners demonstrated was consistent with the pattern of learners identified as learning disabled.

Adolescents placed in a psychiatric hospital were found to be significantly less informative and less effective in their communication than were nonidentified peers (Rosenthal & Simeonsson, 1991). In yet another study, 54 percent of a group of learners identified as emotionally/behaviorally disordered were found to demonstrate speech or language difficulty (Trautman, Giddan, & Jurs, 1990).

Depression The diagnostic criteria for **depression** are the same for adults and children. These criteria require that there be a dysphoric mood—that is, a loss of interest or pleasure—for at least two weeks. At least four of the following symptoms must also be present: appetite disturbance, sleep disturbance, psychomotor agitation (excitability, hyperactivity) or retardation, loss of energy, feelings of worthlessness or guilt, diminished ability to think, and thoughts of suicide or death. Depression in children is not a rare occurrence; from 30 percent to 60 percent of child psychiatry outpatients fulfill the criteria for depression. This depression, without intervention, can last for months and lead to impaired school performance, poor peer and family interaction, and even suicide (Weller & Weller, 1986).

Though the symptoms of depression are similar among adults and children, the ways in which these symptoms are expressed vary (Weller & Weller, 1986). Some depressed children present behaviors such as a conduct disorder, which often is mistaken for the problem rather than a symptom. In addition, difference in cognitive and language functioning make assessment of depression in children difficult.

Table 7.1   Emotional/Behavioral Problem Syndromes Derived for Boys and Girls Ages 4–5, 6–11, and 12–16

Internalizing	Mixed	Externalizing
Boys 4–5		
1. Social Withdrawal	5. Sex Problems	6. Schizoid
2. Depressed		7. Aggressive
3. Immature		8. Delinquent
4. Somatic Complaints		
Girls 4–5		
1. Somatic Complaints	5. Obese	6. Aggressive
2. Depressed		7. Sex Problems
3. Schizoid		8. Hyperactive
4. Social Withdrawal		
Boys 6–11		
1. Schizoid	6. Social Withdrawal	7. Hyperactive
2. Depressed		8. Aggressive
3. Uncommunicative		9. Delinquent
4. Obsessive-Compulsive		
5. Somatic Complaints		
Girls 6–11		
1. Depressed		6. Sex Problems
2. Social Withdrawal		7. Delinquent
3. Somatic Complaints		8. Aggressive
4. Schizoid-Obsessive		9. Cruel
5. Hyperactive		
Boys 12–16		
1. Somatic Complaints	6. Hostile-Withdrawal	7. Delinquent
2. Schizoid		8. Aggressive
3. Uncommunicative		9. Hyperactive
4. Immature		
5. Obsessive-Compulsive		
Girls 12–16		
1. Anxious-Obsessive	5. Immature-Hyperactive	6. Delinquent
2. Somatic Complaints		7. Aggressive
3. Schizoid		8. Cruel
4. Depressed, Withdrawal		

From Thomas H. Ollendick and Michel Hersen, *Child Behavioral Assessment: Principles and Behaviors.* Copyright © 1984. Reprinted by permission of Allyn & Bacon.

Learners identified as emotionally/behaviorally disordered can be distinguished from their nonidentified peers in terms of characteristics associated with depression (Cullinan, Schloss, & Epstein, 1987). Depression among these learners is only related to lack of acceptance by peers, unlike the nonidentified children, in whom depression is also related to educational performance. Females are significantly at greater risk for falling into severe depression than are their male counterparts identified as behaviorally disordered (Maag & Behrens, 1989).

Working with families of depressed children is essential (Cytryn & McKnew, 1986). Individual psychotherapy for the child should be used after parent counseling and family therapy have not made a change in the child's behavior. The use of medication is justified only when a depressive illness has been reliably diagnosed and the child has failed to respond to psychotherapy and

Aggression is fairly pervasive among learners identified as emotionally/behaviorally disordered.

environmental manipulation. Side effects, blood pressure, and electrocardiograms must be screened at regular intervals, as careful monitoring of medication for children is essential.

An issue often associated with depression is that of suicide. Miller (1994) studied suicidal behavior, including **suicidal ideation** (thoughts about suicide), reported attempts, and rationales for such behavior among learners identified as emotionally/behaviorally disordered and those with no identified disabilities. Alarmingly, students who were not identified as emotionally/behaviorally disordered or depressed still thought about or attempted suicide. Female adolescents with behavioral/emotional disorders reported a higher frequency of suicide ideation and attempts than did male adolescents with or without emotional/behavioral disorders. Miller urges the education of teachers and other service providers in the public schools regarding suicide, as well as teaching adolescents alternative problem-solving strategies and facilitating the belief among adolescents that they can construct their futures.

Aggression **Aggression,** behavior intended to dominate others, has been found to be fairly pervasive among learners identified as emotionally/behaviorally disordered. In Ruhl and Hughes's (1985) study using teacher surveys, 84 percent reported having encountered extreme physical aggression among their students; 64 percent indicated that students, teachers, and aides had all been targets of these actions. Over half indicated that severe aggressive acts, such as choking or hitting, occurred at least once a month, and 29 percent reported weekly occurrences. Most commonly, between one and three times a month, mild physical aggression occurs. Learners' physical aggression towards themselves was reported by 73 percent of the teachers, and 94 percent noted destruction of property. This pervasiveness of aggression and disruption was also found by Epstein, Kauffman, and Cullinan (1985) in their study of behavior patterns among learners identified as emotionally/behaviorally disordered. The most consistent, persistent pattern they found among the learners they assessed was that of aggression, demonstrated as disobedience, negativism, boisterousness, temper tantrums, disruptiveness, fighting, profane language, jealousy, irresponsibility, attention seeking, uncooperativeness, irritability, and impertinence.

Aggressive behaviors have been found to follow interactions in which the students identified as emotionally/behaviorally disordered initiated greetings or made requests of peers and the peers ignored the greetings, denied the requests, or made a derogatory comment to the students. Knapczyk (1988) used videotape exemplars of social situations to model, rehearse, and provide directed feedback of appropriate alternatives. The intervention was effective, and peers were more willing to interact with students identified as behaviorally disordered.

In their study of the nature of classroom aggression among learners identified as emotionally/behaviorally disordered, Wehby, Symons, and Shores (1995) found that students who were aggressive had low overall rates of positive social interactions. These students engaged in negative verbal aggression and verbal behavior approximately ten times as often as their peers. However, Wehby and associates contend that the entire classroom ecology must be taken into account. Rates of teacher praise towards highly aggressive students were very low and accounted for only a small proportion of the antecedents and consequences for the students' aggression. They suggest that aggressive behaviors may actually be induced by the intermittent reinforcement they receive in classrooms or simply occur when no programmed reinforcement schedules are operating.

Identification and Evaluation

Objective Two

To describe the identification and evaluation of learners identified as emotionally/behaviorally disordered.

Since the term "seriously emotionally disturbed" was first defined in Public Law 94-142, there has been controversy relating to the terminology used with these learners, the definition itself, and the assessment of learners identified as having emotional/behavioral disorders.

In a general sense, learners identified as having **emotional/behavioral disorders** are those whose behavior varies in frequency, intensity, and duration from their general education peers to such an extent that it comes to the attention of authority figures, usually teachers, and results in their being labeled as emotionally/behaviorally disordered. Kauffman (1985) suggests that identifying learners as emotionally/behaviorally disordered is the process of comparing them to the nebulous standard of "normal," which is in itself difficult, if not impossible, to define. Shea and Bauer (1987) contend that it is normal for all learners to have periods during their lives that are characterized by ineffective decision-making, inadequate learning of accepted behavior, crisis, conflict, depression, and stress. At such times, behaviors similar to those exhibited by learners identified as emotionally/behaviorally disordered are not uncommon.

Kauffman (1981) discusses another difficulty when defining behavioral disorders. He states that some behavior may be deemed inappropriate in one setting and not in another simply due to differences in expectations in the settings. This means that there are both "disturbed" and "disturbing" behaviors. **Disturbing behaviors** are those that occur at a certain place and time and in the presence of certain individuals. **Disturbed behaviors** are those that occur in many settings and are a part of the individual's habitual behavior pattern. Disturbing behaviors, though difficult to accept under specific circumstances, are not indicative of a behavioral disorder.

Public Law 94-142 used the term **seriously emotionally disturbed** to identify the learners referred to in this chapter as "identified as emotionally/behaviorally disordered." According to the definition in the law, this term means:

(i) . . . a condition exhibiting one or more of the following characteristics over a long period of time and to a marked degree, which adversely affects educational performance:
  (a) an inability to learn which cannot be explained by intellectual, sensory, and health factors;

(b) an inability to build or maintain satisfactory interpersonal relationships with peers and teachers;

(c) inappropriate types of behavior or feelings under normal circumstances;

(d) a general pervasive mood of unhappiness or depression; or

(e) a tendency to develop physical symptoms or fears associated with personal or school problems.

(ii) The term includes children who are schizophrenic or autistic. The term does not include children who are socially maladjusted unless it is determined that they are seriously emotionally disturbed (Federal Register, 1977, 42, 162).

Children classified as autistic were excluded from the federal definition of "seriously emotionally disturbed" in the 1981 regulations and reclassified as "other health impaired." In 1990, through Public Law 101-456 (The Individuals with Disabilities Education Act), learners with autism were again reclassified, and a separate category of disability was delineated.

In 1985, the Council for Children with Behavioral Disorders (Huntze, 1985) argued that the term *behaviorally disordered* should replace the term *seriously emotionally disturbed* because (a) the term is not associated exclusively with any particular theory of causation or intervention techniques, (b) the term would afford a more-comprehensive assessment of the population, (c) "behaviorally disordered" is far less stigmatizing, (d) the term is more representative of the students who are disabled by their behavior, and (e) the change in terminology is representative of a focus on the educational responsibility delineated in the law.

In 1987, the Executive Committee of the Council for Children with Behavioral Disorders urged the following:

1. The federal definition of "seriously emotionally disturbed" be revised, with a functional *educational* definition taking its place.

2. "Socially maladjusted" children and youth should not be excluded from the definition.

3. Any new definition should focus on the sources of data collection necessary to determine whether a student is behaviorally disordered.

4. Any new definition should require documentation of prior attempts to modify a targeted student's deviant behavior within the regular education setting and the use of intervention models that exemplify the least restrictive alternative.

5. Priorities within the field of behavioral disorders include leadership training on a national basis, teacher training, research, and training for general education personnel.

The task force on definition of the National Mental Health and Special Education Coalition (Council for Children with Behavioral Disorders, 1990) completed its work on the draft definition that it is promoting as a substitute for the current definition of seriously emotionally disturbed in the Education for All Handicapped Children Act. The definition includes the following points:

• Emotional or behavioral disorder refers to a condition in which behavioral or emotional responses of an individual in school are so different from his/her generally accepted, age-appropriate, ethnic, or cultural norms as to result in significant impairment in self-care, social relationships, educational progress, classroom behavior, or work adjustment. This category may include children or youth with schizophrenia, depression, anxiety disorders, attention deficit disorders, or with other sustained disturbances of conduct or adjustment.

Some behavior may be deemed inappropriate in one setting and not in another due to differences in expectations.

Annual **Edition**

Article *16*

- Emotional or behavior disorder is more than a transient, expected response to stressors in the individual's environment and persists despite individualized interventions, such as feedback to the individual, consultation with parents or families, and/or modifications of the educational environment.
- The eligibility decision must be based on multiple sources of data about the individual's behaviors or emotional function. Emotional or behavioral disorder must be exhibited in at least two different settings, at least one of which is educational.

Public Law 98-199, the Education of the Handicapped Act Amendments of 1983, mandated a study to determine the potential impact that changing the terminology and definition used with learners identified as emotionally/behaviorally disordered would have. Arguments were that the federal label of "seriously emotionally disturbed" was stigmatizing and educationally irrelevant; others argued that any change would cause an incredible influx of students with purely behavioral problems into the category, which would strain states' financial resources.

The federal definition and the definition proposed by the Task Force on Definition of the Mental Health and Special Education Coalition, discussed above, are but two of the many definitions that have been applied to differentiate learners identified as emotionally/behaviorally disordered from other learners. Definitions tend to vary with the purpose of their authors. In the literature, there are definitions written by authorities in the field based on their experience and theoretical point of view, by researchers to delineate a specific population for study, and by administrators for the purpose of planning and managing programs.

In their 1985 study, Talmadge, Gamel, Munson, and Hanley (1985) found considerable variation from state to state in the numbers of learners identified as behaviorally disordered who were served. Differences in definition from state to state account for 35 percent of the variation among the numbers of students served (Wright, Pillard, & Cleven, 1990). Roughly two-thirds of the variation among the numbers of students served remained unaccounted for. Wright and associates propose that this variation could be accounted for at three levels: (a) state definitions and identification procedures, which are not directed by federal guidelines, (b) school district procedures, which, depending on the state, may not be directed by state guidelines, and (c) the training and practices of prereferral intervention teams, evaluation teams, and team members.

Issues Related to Assessment of Learners Identified as Emotionally/Behaviorally Disordered

The most widely used classification system for learners identified as emotionally/behaviorally disordered is the fourth edition of *Diagnostic and Statistical Manual of Mental Disorders* (American Psychiatric Association, 1994). This is a classification system based on the clinical expertise of hundreds of mental-health practitioners. The DSM-IV includes nineteen major diagnostic categories, including one specifically for infants, children, and adolescents. The major syndromes and subsyndromes of this category are presented in table 7.2. In the manual, each diagnostic syndrome is described in detail, much as the attention-deficit/hyperactivity disorder shown in table 7.3.

The Revised Problem Behavior Checklist (Quay & Peterson, 1987) as part of the screening process is a good example of issues of reliability and validity in identifying learners as emotionally/behaviorally disordered. Simpson (1989), in a comparison of two groups of teachers' ratings of the same ninety-five children, found little agreement between the two groups of teachers in identifying children who were described as either mildly or highly deviant. He concludes that the rating of the behavior of children is extremely subjective. The issue of the context is

Table 7.2   DSM-IV Classification System: Disorders Usually First Diagnosed in Infancy, Childhood, or Adolescence

A. Mental Retardation
        Mild mental retardation
        Moderate mental retardation
        Severe mental retardation
        Profound mental retardation
        Mental retardation, severity unspecified
B. Learning Disorders
        Reading disorders
        Mathematics disorders
        Disorders of written expression
        Learning disorders, not otherwise specified
C. Motor Skills Disorder
        Developmental coordination disorder
D. Communication Disorders
        Expressive language disorder
        Receptive language disorder
        Mixed receptive-expressive language disorder
        Phonological disorder
        Stuttering
        Communication disorder, not otherwise specified
E. Pervasive Developmental Disorders
        Autistic disorder
        Rett's disorder
        Childhood disintegration disorder
        Asperger's disorder
        Pervasive developmental disorder, not otherwise specified
F. Attention-Deficit and Disruptive Behavior Disorders
        Attention-deficit/hyperactivity disorder
            Combined type
            Predominantly inattentive type
            Predominantly hyperactive-impulsive type
        Attention-deficit/hyperactivity disorder not otherwise specified
        Conduct disorder (Childhood onset or adolescent onset)
        Oppositional defiant disorder
        Disruptive behavior disorder, not otherwise specified
G. Feeding and Eating Disorders of Infancy or Early Childhood
        Pica
        Rumination disorder
        Feeding disorder of infancy or early childhood
H. Tic Disorders
        Tourette's disorder
        Chronic motor and vocal tic disorder
        Transient tic disorder (single episode or recurrent)
        Tic disorder, not otherwise specified
I. Elimination Disorders
        Encopresis
            With constipation and overflow incontinence
            Without constipation and overflow incontinence
        Enuresis (not due to general medical condition) (Nocturnal only, diurnal only, or nocturnal
            and diurnal)
J. Other Disorders of Infancy, Childhood, or Adolescence
        Separation anxiety disorder (specify if early onset)
        Selective mutism
        Reactive attachment disorder of infancy or early childhood (inhibited type or disinhibited type)
        Stereotype movement disorder (specify it with self-injurious behavior)
        Disorder of infancy, childhood, or adolescence, not otherwise specified

American Psychiatric Association: *Diagnostic and Statistical Manual of Mental Disorders, Fourth Edition.* Washington DC, American Psychiatric Association, 1994.

Table 7.3   **Diagnostic Criteria for Attention-Deficit/Hyperactivity Disorder**

A. Either (1) or (2):

  (1) Six (or more) of the following symptoms of inattention have persisted for at least six months to a degree that is maladaptive and inconsistent with developmental level:

    (a) often fails to give close attention to details or makes careless mistakes in schoolwork, work, or other activities

    (b) often has difficulty sustaining attention in tasks or play activities

    (c) often does not seem to listen when spoken to directly

    (d) often does not follow through on instructions and fails to finish schoolwork, chores, or duties in the workplace (not due to oppositional behavior or failure to understand instructions)

    (e) often has difficulty organizing tasks and activities

    (f) often avoids, dislikes, or is reluctant to engage in tasks that require sustained mental effort (such as schoolwork or homework)

    (g) often loses things necessary for tasks or activities (e.g., toys, school assignments, pencils, books, or tools)

    (h) is often easily distracted by extraneous stimuli

    (i) is often forgetful in daily activities

  (2) Six (or more) of the following symptoms of hyperactivity-impulsivity have persisted for at least six months to a degree that is maladaptive and inconsistent with developmental level:

    (a) often fidgets with hands or feet or squirms in seat

    (b) often leaves seat in classroom or in other situations in which remaining seated is expected

    (c) often runs about or climbs excessively in situations in which it is inappropriate (in adolescents or adults, may be limited to subjective feelings of restlessness)

    (d) often has difficulty playing or engaging in leisure activities quietly

    (e) is often "on the go" or often acts as if "driven by a motor"

    (f) often talks excessively

    (g) often blurts out answers before questions have been completed

    (h) often has difficulty awaiting turn

    (i) often interrupts or intrudes on others (e.g., butts into conversations or games)

B. Some hyperactive-impulsive or inattentive symptoms that caused impairment were present before age seven years.

C. Some impairment from the symptoms is present in two or more settings (e.g., at school [or work] and at home).

D. There must be clear evidence of clinically significant impairment in social, academic, or occupational functioning.

E. The symptoms do not occur exclusively during the course of a pervasive developmental disorder, schizophrenia, or other psychotic disorder and are not better accounted for by another mental disorder (e.g., mood disorder, anxiety disorder, dissociated disorder, or personality disorder).

American Psychiatric Association: *Diagnostic and Statistical Manual of Mental Disorders, Fourth Edition.* Washington DC, American Psychiatric Association, 1994.

very relevant in these findings; situations may differ markedly from one general education class to another, and raters may vary markedly, even when attempting to identify learners whose behavior is very different from their peers.

Skiba (1989) reviewed eighty-nine correlations between classroom observations and behavioral ratings drawn from sixteen studies. He found very low correlations between what was actually observed and what was rated by teachers using formal rating scales. He suggests that there are serious problems with the validity of assessments that look for the problems within the students themselves. He maintains that the recognition of the "problem situation" rather than the "problem student" should be used to identify and describe behavior problems in schools.

The lack of consensus regarding designation and description of learners identified as emotionally/behaviorally disordered extends to researchers in the field. Kavale, Forness, and Alper (1986) found in their survey of 323 research studies in behavioral disorders and emotional disturbance that the literature presents a divergent picture in regards to the nature and prevalence of behavioral disorders and reflects a lack of consensus regarding standard identification criteria. The

Executive Committee of the Council for Children with Behavioral Disorders (1989) argues that until definition, classification, and measurement criteria for learners identified as emotionally/behaviorally disordered are made more objective and verifiable, assessment of behavioral disorders will continue to be highly subjective and open to multiple sources of bias.

Cultural Diversity and Assessment

Many factors may contribute to the misclassification of learners from diverse cultures as emotionally/behaviorally disordered. Some of these factors include:

1. Language, which affects how the educational community interacts and perceives the learner's behavior.
2. Faulty teacher perceptions and lowered expectations.
3. The higher rates at which learners from cultural minorities enter the referral-to-placement process, which increases their likelihood of identification. (Executive Committee of the Council for Children with Behavioral Disorders, 1989)

In order to address these issues and reduce the overrepresentation of learners from minority cultures in programs for learners identified as emotionally/behaviorally disordered, the Executive Committee of the Council for Children with Behavioral Disorders recommends that assessment include a recognition of the context in which the behavior occurs. This more functional means of assessment assumes that learning is an interactive process that occurs within a context. In addition, it assumes that learners from minority cultures will respond to "good teaching" and that this programming may be provided without labeling or classifying the child. Finally, this functional assessment assumes that early collaborative intervention is preferred to entering the referral-to-placement process.

Carlson and Stephens (1986), in their study of the Social Behavior Assessment Scale, conclude that bias is not found in the instrument itself; rather, differential scores on the rating forms are either an indication of teacher bias or of real cultural differences.

The Impact of Emotional/Behavioral Disorders on the Home and School

Ramsey and Walker (1988) studied the family management practices of male fourth-grade learners identified as antisocial. Though they found no differences between these learners and their nonidentified peers in the area of involvement, significant differences were found in discipline, monitoring, positive reinforcement, and problem solving. They concluded that learners identified as antisocial were exposed to far more negative and less-competent family management practices than were their peers.

Parent Involvement in Interventions

Reimers and Wacker (1988) find that though the amount of disruption an intervention causes and the willingness of parents to participate in the intervention initially has an affect on its acceptability, once the treatment is in place, the effectiveness of the treatment as rated by the parents has the largest influence on acceptability.

Parents' Needs   Simpson (1988), in his exploration of parents' needs, finds that the most widely used and/or requested service by parents is that of information exchange, through informal feedback, progress reports, conferences, and program information. Parents also request parent-coordinated service programs; counseling, therapy, and consultation; consumer and advocacy training; and home

Annual **Edition**

Article 17

Objective Three

To describe the impact of emotional/behavioral disorders on interactions in the home and school.

Annual **Edition**

Article 15

Parents are equal partners in their child's education.

program training. Teachers perceive parents as needing parent-coordinated service programs; home program training; consumer and advocacy training; and counseling, therapy, and consultation. According to Simpson, there is a significant difference between teachers' perceptions of parents' needs and parents' expressed needs.

Relationships in the Classroom

As indicated earlier, one of the most pervasive indicators of identification as emotionally/behaviorally disordered is poor peer relationships. In addition, relationships with teachers are challenging for these learners. Teachers rated extreme social withdrawal (lack of communication) and deficiencies in specific academic learning strategies and skills as the most difficult to manage in the classroom (Safran, Safran, & Barcikowski, 1988).

In a recent study, Farmer and Hallowell (1994) found that students identified as having emotional/behavioral disorders did indeed affiliate with their peers in inclusive classrooms. However, they tended to affiliate with peers who, like themselves, had fewer prosocial behaviors and higher levels of problematic behavior. The individuals with whom students identified as having emotional/behavioral disorders interacted demonstrated significantly lower levels of cooperation, leadership, and academic abilities when assessed by their peers. Nevertheless, learners identified as emotionally/behaviorally disordered did form friendships and close associations in inclusive classrooms. The students tended to sort themselves into peer clusters with classmates who shared their social characteristics.

Objective Four

To describe ways to mediate the environment for learners identified as emotionally/behaviorally disordered.

Mediating the Environment

In mediating the environment for learners identified as having emotional/behavioral disorders, strategies and interventions have been historically tied to several competing perspectives. The psychodynamic perspective maintains that the cause of behavior is within the individual, and thus interventions must deal with the learners' dynamic, intrapsychic life. The biophysical perspective postulates a relationship between physical conditions and the behavior the learner exhibits. The behavioral perspective defines behaviors as all human acts that are observable and measurable and maintained by variables in

guidelines for practice

$\mathcal{S}$econdary students identified as emotionally/behaviorally disordered who are in inclusive settings take the same tests as their peers. However, they may not have successful test-taking strategies. Hughes, Deshler, Ruhl, and Schumaker (1993) describe the following test-taking strategy for students identified as emotionally/behaviorally disordered.

P – Prepare to succeed. Put name on test and write PIRATES (the name of the strategy) on the test as a cue.

I – Inspect the instructions. Read the instructions and underline key words.

R – Read the first item, remember what was studied, reduce the number of responses by ruling out the ones that are clearly inappropriate.

A – Answer the question if known, abandon if not sure, and come back to it later.

T – Turn back and answer abandoned questions.

E – Estimate or make a wise guess.

S – Survey to make sure all items are answered ▮

the environment. The systems or ecological perspective, such as that in which this text is grounded, focuses on the reciprocal relationship between the learner or group of learners and the contexts in which they are interacting.

A test-taking strategy for students identified as emotionally/behaviorally disordered is shown in the "Guidelines for Practice" box above.

Though these perceptual fields argue strongly for significantly different strategies, very few comprehensive program descriptions for learners identified as emotionally/behaviorally disordered are available in the literature (Grosenick, George, & George, 1988). McConnell (1987) suggests a reemphasis on the careful selection of which behaviors should be addressed. She argues that to maximize the likelihood that the behaviors and skills will be "entrapped"—that is, kept under the control of naturally occurring reinforcement—those selected should (a) be maintained after the intervention is terminated, (b) generalize across other settings or other behaviors, and (c) co-vary with specific social behaviors of peers. When behaviors such as these are selected, it is likely that newly acquired social behaviors will continue at high rates and generalize to new settings after the specific intervention stops.

In their three-year study of programs and policies regarding learners identified as emotionally/behaviorally disordered, Knitzer, Steinberg, and Fleisch (1990) sought to explore the scope of policy, program possibilities, and the experiences of parents with children identified as emotionally/behaviorally disordered and to review current information to underscore the data gathered. Knitzer and associates describe seven typical placement possibilities for learners identified as emotionally/behaviorally disordered. These include regular classrooms, resource rooms in the regular school, self-contained classrooms in regular schools, special schools and day schools, day-treatment programs, residential treatment centers, in-patient psychiatric hospitals, and homebound instruction. Enormous variation was found in placement. For example, in seven states, between 10 percent and 20 percent of all learners identified as emotionally/behaviorally disordered were in residential placements; in seven others, under 1 percent were in residential placements. In seven states, more than half of all learners identified as emotionally/behaviorally disordered were served in resource rooms, whereas eleven states relied heavily on self-contained classrooms or separate facilities.

The placement that emerged as most problematic was residential placement. Evidence suggested that decisions for residential placement were driven by factors other than student needs, such as a lack of services in the school or the family's need for respite. Children were often placed far from their homes, making case monitoring and parent contact difficult. In some states, parents were required to relinquish custody in order to obtain residential treatment for their child. Rather than supporting the child's development, residential placement further isolated the child from family and peers.

In their observations of programs throughout the nation, Knitzer and associates found several pervasive themes in the educational programs of learners identified as emotionally/behaviorally disordered.

- Control of learners served as a central part of the nature of the learners' school experience.
- Academics—what was being taught and how it was being taught—were secondary to behavior control. The authors suggested a haphazard nature of curricula activities.
- Social skills curricula were held to be important, but classrooms were structured so that no social interaction could take place.
- Physical activity was rare; students were sometimes expected to sit at their desks without talking or interacting for hours on end. Physical activity was sometimes regarded as a reward rather than a right for the children.
- In many programs, access to therapy for the children and consultation and support for teachers was limited.
- Parents often experienced difficulties in ensuring appropriate placements, and teachers often experienced a sense of isolation and lack of support.
- Transitions were frequently ignored, in particular transitions from one placement to another.

In a study of how students perceived their educational environments, Leone, Luttig, Zlotlow, and Trickett (1990) describe data that support the work of Knitzer and her associates. They found that students in special schools for learners identified as behaviorally disordered perceived order and organization lower and teacher control higher than did students in traditional school programs. Student satisfaction, however, was related to greater levels of perceived involvement, affiliation, and teacher support for learners with special needs.

Preschool   Beare and Lynch (1986) contend that there are substantial numbers of preschool children who demonstrate behaviors indicative of behavioral disorders but who are not being served by mandated public school programs or consultative programming. Public schools are apparently unaware of these children, despite screening efforts. Scruggs, Mastropieri, Cook, and Escobar (1986) performed a metanalysis of single-subject research conducted on young children. They found that reinforcement produced the most positive outcomes, followed by punishment/time-out, and then differential attention, and that learners' characteristics, such as sex, disability, and target behavior, generally bore little relation to treatment outcome. They concluded that positive results were found for home-based interventions and for younger subjects, though these findings were somewhat inconsistent.

Impact of Placement Options   During the 1992–1993 school year, the largest percentage of learners identified as emotionally/behaviorally disordered were served in separate classes (35.2 percent), with fewer in resource rooms (26.7 percent), and far fewer in general classes (19.6 percent), separate schools (13.7 percent), residential settings (3.5 percent), and homes or hospitals (1.3 percent). Only two categories of disability have more students served in separate facilities: learners with multiple handicaps and learners who are deaf and blind (U.S. Department of Education, 1995).

It comes as no surprise that learners identified as emotionally/behaviorally disordered exhibited more problem behaviors than did their peers with learning disabilities, and secondary students exhibited more rule-breaking than did elementary students (Sindelar, King, Gantland, Wilson, & Meisel, 1985). More-anxious, fearful behavior and rule breaking were exhibited in special classes than in resource rooms.

In an intensive interview study, Martin, Lloyd, Kauffman, and Coyne (1995) explored teachers' perceptions of educational placement decisions for learners identified as emotionally/behaviorally disordered. They found that teachers had a wide range of opinions about the benefits and drawbacks of various placement options. Teachers agreed, however, that schools were encountering problems that they did not have the capacity to handle. The teachers also expressed frustration about administrative procedures and structures they saw as impediments to providing appropriate services and a lack of collaboration and support among the various participants in placement decisions. On the whole, teachers reported that they had little influence in placement decisions.

Referral of Learners Identified as Emotionally/Behaviorally Disordered   Sevcik and Ysseldyke (1986) found that prior to referral for evaluation for identification as emotionally/behaviorally disordered, teachers proposed and actually used interventions that involved teacher-directed actions, such as specific behavioral methods, nonspecific methods, structure change, and grouping change. When teachers employed specific interventions, however, it was found that just slightly over one-third involved positive reinforcement, while punishment and unspecified interventions made up slightly under two-thirds of the interventions. When given a choice, teachers selected using the services of a consultant almost as readily as teacher-directed actions, but consultative options were actually used in only 10 percent of the cases.

In another study of prereferral intervention, Noll, Kamps, and Seaborn (1993) report that over a three-year span, from 43 percent to 64 percent of the students referred remained in the general education classroom, from 14 percent to 22 percent were identified as having other disabilities, and from 23 percent to 39 percent were identified as having emotional/behavioral disorders. The prereferral process utilized an itinerant teacher and included collaborative agreements with the teacher, pupils, and parents. Contracts, with goals, criteria for progress evaluation, and built-in consequences and loss of privileges for noncompliance, were used. In addition, self-monitoring, which encouraged self-management and intrinsic control, were employed. Each prereferral intervention included procedures for fading supports and gradually delaying reinforcement strategies.

Classroom Management

The selection of techniques and strategies for classroom management is viewed through the lens of the individual implementing the strategy. A practitioner who views the learner from a psychodynamic perspective will focus on counseling techniques, expressive media, and bibliotherapy, and surface-management techniques to deal with the "here and now" of behaviors. An example of bibliotherapy is shown in the "Guidelines for Practice" box on page 147. The behaviorist will manipulate the immediate environment and apply social learning theory, including modeling, desensitization, and various self-management and self-instruction interventions. Biophysical interventions may include diet or medication. In the systems perspective, however, each of the wide range of interventions available may be applied after careful consideration of the learners and the context in which the behavior is occurring.

Learners who choose to cooperate are granted more and more privileges, such as field trips.

Bauer and Sapona (1988) argue that with the increasing recognition of child development within context, behavioral models of behavior management will be used as only one part of comprehensive management frameworks. With the emphasis on control implicit in the behavioral model of management, learners identified as behaviorally disordered may be limited in their ability to achieve by the restrictive classroom environment. The emerging concept of schooling is to "bring to students the skills that will widen for each of them the spectrum of learning environments in which they can relate" (Joyce, 1987, p. 427). With an emphasis on controlling behaviors, many incidental opportunities for learning may be lost. Bauer and Sapona (1988) suggest that instead the teacher should be a proactive facilitator. This stance supports co-learning in a meaningful context, with mutual negotiation between teacher and student and greater opportunities to interact.

When working with learners identified as emotionally/behaviorally disordered, the student's interaction pattern is usually viewed as a problem in itself. Brooks (1991) relates some of these behavior patterns, however, to the power relationship that is evident in classroom or treatment settings. Hubbell (1981) describes first- and second-order changes in addressing these behavior problems. Hubbell describes first-order changes as management strategies that change the environment, such as putting contingencies in place, providing a rationale for rules and rewards, or modifying attitude and activity. All of these strategies occur with the teacher remaining in charge. These first-order changes may, however, fail among learners for whom behavior represents the relationship tactic of challenging the power and authority of adults. When the student's problem is with authority itself, any action taken by the teacher will be met with opposition.

In second-order changes, the teacher needs to relinquish authority. The learner is allowed to choose among several alternatives. Brooks (1991) describes the ultimate choice: participating or doing nothing. He indicates, however, that several conditions are necessary for the successful use of this approach. For example, activities must be inherently appealing, and they must be accompanied by materials reinforcing to those who choose to cooperate. If the learner spontaneously joins in the activity at any point, he or she should be included without comment as long as behavior is appropriate.

guidelines for practice

$\mathcal{B}$ibliotherapy is the use of reading materials to help students learn about social and emotional issues and to promote their mental health. Bauer and Balius (1995) suggest the use of several questions following a reading to support learners identified as emotionally/behaviorally disordered. Questions for discussion include the following:

- What was the lesson in the story?
- What feelings did the characters have at different points in the story?
- What was the main problem in the story?
- How did the characters try to solve the problem?
- Have you had a similar problem, or do you know someone who has?
- How did you react in a similar situation?
- How are you like or unlike the character?

The use of stories can provide a safe way for students with emotional/behavioral disorders to discuss feelings and experiences ▌

Levels systems, organizational frameworks within which various behavior management interventions are applied to shape students' social, communicative, and academic behaviors to preestablished levels, are frequently used with learners identified as behaviorally disordered. A levels system includes (a) a description of each level, (b) criteria for movement from one level to another, and (c) behavioral expectations, restrictions, and privileges for each level. As students proceed through each of the levels, the behavioral responsibilities and privileges increase (Bauer, Shea, & Keppler, 1986). Levels systems may vary in many ways, such as

1. how a student proceeds through the levels. Options include student negotiation of level, moving lock-step through the system, group consensus on each student's level, or teacher designation of level, depending on an assessment of the student's behavior.
2. the amount of time a student remains on each level. A specific amount of time may be designated as a minimum stay.
3. who reviews the student's status and monitors the learner's behavior. Students, peers, teacher, or any combination of these may be involved in the evaluation process. Self-monitoring or teacher monitoring may be used.

The advantages of a well-developed, individualized levels system include security, structure, and routine. Teachers are delivered from the "me against them" position, and structures and procedures enhance self-management. An example of a levels system is shown in table 7.4.

Students' survey responses suggest that they attribute positive behavior change to the implementation of levels systems (Mastropieri, Jenne, & Scruggs, 1988). However, this finding in itself is of concern when the use of such systems is only to provide a framework for students. If students attribute the change to the system rather than themselves, they remain externally controlled instead of attributing change to enhanced self-management.

Rosenberg (1986) reports that structured classroom managements systems such as token economies and level systems are common, yet they may not achieve maximum effectiveness. In his study, daily review of classroom rules resulted in an overall time-on-task improvement and a reduction in disruption.

Table 7.4 Sample Levels System

Behavior Management System
Severe Behavior Handicap Class
Aiken Senior High School (Murphy, 1991)

Level I

Responsibilities

1. Follow classroom rules.
2. Earn at least 53 points daily.
3. Goal set by staff.
4. Supervised by staff at all times.
5. Attend group meetings.

Consequences

1. Points are earned when responsibilities are met.
2. If 53 points are not earned for three days in a row, you drop to the beginning of Level I.

Privileges

1. Participate in goal activity.
2. 50 bonus points are given for earning all 70 daily points.

Level II

Responsibilities

1. Follow classroom rules.
2. Earn at least 56 points daily.
3. Participate in group meetings.
4. Set own goal.

Consequences

1. Points are earned when responsibilities are met.
2. If 56 points are not earned for three days in a row, you drop to the beginning of Level II.
3. Three more consecutive days of minimum points not earned will result in a drop to the beginning of Level I.

Privileges

1. Participate in goal activity.
2. Buying time.*
3. Participate in field trips.
4. 75 bonus points for earning all 70 daily points.
5. Self-escort.

Level III

Responsibilities

1. Follow classroom rules.
2. Earn at least 59 points daily.
3. Participate in group meetings.
4. Make honest "I" statements.

Consequences

1. Points are earned when responsibilities are met.
2. If 59 points are not earned for three days in a row, you drop to the beginning of Level III.
3. Three more consecutive days of minimum points not earned will result in a drop to the beginning of Level II.
4. If you are unable to be honest about your behavior and continue to blame others for your actions, you will be required to go to Level II.

Privileges

1. Lead group meetings.
2. Keep own point record.
3. 100 bonus points for earning maximum points.
4. Buying time.
5. Participate in field trips.

*A time to purchase items such as pencils, tablets, chewing gum, and hygiene items with points earned. Buying time takes place at a designated time each week.

continued

Table 7.4 *continued*

Level IV

Responsibilities

1. Follow classroom rules.
2. Earn at least 63 points daily.
3. Make honest "I" statements.
4. Turn in homework.
5. Complete class assignments.
6. Participate in all assigned general education classes.
7. Come to school with supplies.

Consequences

1. Points are earned when responsibilities are met.
2. If 63 points are not earned for three days in a row, you drop to the beginning of Level IV.
3. Three more consecutive days of not earning 63 points will result in a level drop to the beginning of Level III.
4. If you are unable to meet the responsibilities of this level, you will be required to move to Level III.

Privileges

1. Set goal activity in collaboration with other students.
2. Earn a "no homework pass" (1 per week if all days count).
3. Run buying time.
4. 125 bonus points for earning all 70 points.
5. Lead group meetings.

Level V

Responsibilities

1. Follow classroom rules.
2. Earn at least 66 out of the possible 70 daily points.
3. Put forth effort and maintain passing grades in all classes.
4. Turn in homework.
5. Make honest statements about your behavior and put forth effort to change areas needing improvement.
6. Successfully participate in all assigned general education classes.
7. Come to school with supplies.

Consequences

1. Points are earned when responsibilities are met.
2. If 66 points are not earned for three days in a row, you will drop to the beginning of Level V.
3. Three more consecutive days of minimum points not earned will result in a level drop to the beginning of Level IV.
4. If you are unable to meet the responsibilities of this level, you will be required to move to Level IV.

Privileges

1. Lunch with a staff member once a month at the Overlook or a restaurant.
2. Earn a free period once a month if all days are counted.
3. Earn 175 bonus points for earning all 70 points daily.
4. Lead group meetings.
5. Keep own point record.
6. Run buying time.
7. Participate in field trips.

Maintenance

Responsibilities

1. Follow school and classroom rules.
2. Put forth effort in all classes and maintain passing grades.

Privileges

1. No point chart will be maintained for maintenance-level students; however, a student on maintenance is given all of the above privileges.
2. 200 bonus points daily for meeting all the required responsibilities.

Note: A referral to an administrator or skipping a class will result in a drop to the beginning of the level you are on. A suspension or expulsion will result in a drop to the beginning of the previous level.

Courtesy E. Susanne Murphy, Aiken Senior High School, Cincinnati, Ohio.

guidelines for practice

Class Meetings

*C*lass meetings are frequently used in programs serving learners identified as behaviorally disordered. The purpose of the meeting is for teachers and students to collaboratively discuss behavioral, personal, and academic problems. Meetings can assist students in developing their own goals, thinking about their own behavior in contexts, and becoming more attentive to the class environment (Morris, 1982). A typical class meeting agenda follows (Bauer, personal observation, 1993):

1. Meeting called to order.
2. Rules for class meeting read (for example, statements should be positive; listen while others talk; everyone has a say).
3. Goals stated (students state their weekly goals and progress made towards those goals, other students may assist the student in evaluating his or her behavior).
4. Group business attended to (any issues affecting the group may be discussed).
5. Personal business attended to (personal issues may be discussed).
6. Gripes aired (concerns about situations, events, or interpersonal problems may be discussed; gripes must be stated as an issue, and problem-solving strategies are applied to support the individual presenting the gripe).
7. Positives stated (each individual makes a positive statement about himself or herself or another).
8. Meeting adjourned ❚

Courtesy E. Susanne Murphy, Aiken Senior High School, Cincinnati, Ohio.

A **token economy** is an exchange system that provides individuals or groups whose behavior is being changed with nearly immediate feedback cues of the appropriateness of their behavior. These cues (tokens) are exchanged for backup reinforcers (items and activities) at a later time. Tokens are usually valueless to the students initially. However, their value becomes apparent when the students learn that the tokens can be exchanged (traded) for backup reinforcers.

When developing a token economy, the educator must first select the specific behavior or behaviors to be changed. These behaviors, referred to as target behaviors, must be discussed and clarified with the individual or group whose behavior is to be changed. Next, a token is selected. Then, a menu, or list of backup reinforcers, is developed and posted in the classroom. Finally, the economy is implemented.

During the course of the intervention, time must be provided during the school day for the exchange of tokens. As the school year progresses, the teacher must revise the reward menu and backup reinforcers to avoid satiation.

The properly managed token economy is effective because individuals are only competing among themselves and the reinforcer menu provides a variety of desirable items and activities.

Self-Management Programs   Self-management through self-evaluation has been demonstrated to reduce students' off-task and disruptive behaviors in a resource room. However, even when trained to make judgments about their own behavior and to solve social problems, students had difficulty applying these skills in the general education classroom (Smith, Young, West, Morgan, & Rhode, 1988). In an attempt to increase generalization, strategies such as the group meeting (See the "Guidelines for Practice" box above) and "Think Aloud" (See the "Guidelines for Practice" box on page 151) have been used.

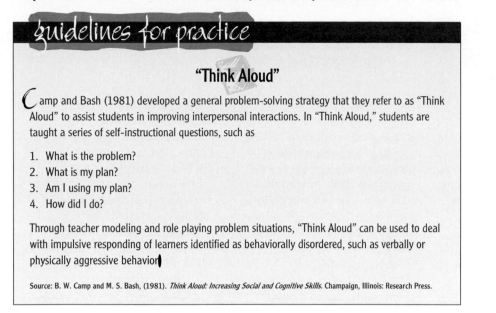

guidelines for practice

"Think Aloud"

Camp and Bash (1981) developed a general problem-solving strategy that they refer to as "Think Aloud" to assist students in improving interpersonal interactions. In "Think Aloud," students are taught a series of self-instructional questions, such as

1. What is the problem?
2. What is my plan?
3. Am I using my plan?
4. How did I do?

Through teacher modeling and role playing problem situations, "Think Aloud" can be used to deal with impulsive responding of learners identified as behaviorally disordered, such as verbally or physically aggressive behavior.

Source: B. W. Camp and M. S. Bash, (1981). *Think Aloud: Increasing Social and Cognitive Skills.* Champaign, Illinois: Research Press.

In a review of self-management outcome research with learners identified as behaviorally disordered, Nelson, Smith, Young, and Dodd (1991) report that the procedures did indeed promote productive social and academic behaviors among learners identified as behaviorally disordered. In addition, the procedures appeared to be durable. Spontaneous generalization, however, was not noted, although treatment effects were found to generalize if the generalization was part of the systematic program.

Transition The issue of transition frequently emerges in discussion of programs for learners identified as behaviorally disordered. Swan, Brown, and Jacob (1987) found that over one-half of the preschool group and over one-third of the elementary, middle, and high school groups were reintegrated directly into general education. Of those reintegrated into less-restrictive special education settings, over half continued as learners identified as behaviorally disordered, suggesting that most students are not reclassified when they are reintegrated into less-restrictive settings.

Medical Intervention Medication is the most common medical intervention for behavioral disorders (Cullinan, Epstein, & Lloyd, 1983). In their review of the use of medication with learners identified as behaviorally disordered, Epstein and Ollinger (1987) concluded that (a) school personnel should be well informed about the drug therapy, (b) teachers should follow school policy for the administration and management of prescribed medications, (c) the school should ensure that a physician-school-parent communication link is established in every case where medications have been prescribed, and (d) teachers should collect data on target behaviors during and after the use of medication. Through direct observation, more-careful and profitable use of medication may emerge.

Life Space Interviews The **life space interview** is a technique developed by Redl (1966) in which the teacher and student interact in a guided interview, allowing the learner to describe an incident that occurred and the feelings related to the incident and discuss how to respond more effectively in the future. Though the literature on life space interviewing is "fragmented, out of date, and lacks any conclusive evidence about the efficacy of this strategy" (Long, 1990), the strategy is one which very aptly fits a systems or contextual model of

Making News

Phils' 'Oddball' Eisenreich Remains On Even Keel

St Louis Post Dispatch
© 1993, Los Angeles Times

They treated Jimmy Eisenreich like a freak. They laughed. They taunted. Kids refused to stop until he ran home crying.

Now, on a chilly Sunday night in St. Cloud, Minn., it was Ann Eisenreich who was sitting in front of her TV set, crying her eyes out.

Jim Eisenreich had become a genuine World Series hero, leading Philadelphia to a 6–4 victory over Toronto in Game 2.

The man who long ago had given up ever playing professional baseball again, sleeping in late each day wondering why life had dealt him such a rotten hand, has helped give the Phillies new life.

Eisenreich's three-run homer in the third inning helped even the series at a game apiece, and made his proud mother weep with joy.

"I just started yelling when it went over the fence," Ann Eisenreich said, "and then, I started to cry. To know what Jimmy has overcome, knowing everything he's gone through, and to see something like this happen . . .

"I don't think any mother could be prouder of her son than I am tonight."

Eisenreich, his eyes moist in the Phillies clubhouse, could hardly believe it himself. He spoke in front of a packed room of reporters, then stood in front of his locker answering wave after wave of questions.

This became a story about a guy trying again, and again and again. Eisenreich has Tourette's syndrome, a long-misunderstood neurological disorder that causes individuals to behave erratically.

The disease manifests itself in jerky, uncontrollable tics, sudden eruption of profanities and even occasional barking. It can tyrannize and traumatize the person who suffers from it.

"I know it might sound funny coming from this clubhouse," Eisenreich said, "but because of that, I'm the oddball of the team.

"I guess I've been an oddball all of my life."

Eisenreich was only 22 when Minnesota Twins owner Calvin Griffith called him a "a future All-Star." He never made it. Instead, he became a center fielder suddenly twitching and gasping for breath, bending at the waist, not sure he would ever find air again.

It could happen at any time. In the middle of the game. He would call time out and run off the field, scared and embarrassed. He was suffering from Tourette's, but he didn't know it then— and the Twins didn't believe it.

The Twins put him in the hospital, sent him to psychiatrists, and then came the medication, the hypnotists, the faith healers and the headlines.

"I felt like an idiot," Eisenreich said. He quit in 1984, and the game forgot him. But he never forgot the game.

Three seasons passed until the Kansas City Royals picked him up for $1 off the voluntarily retired list. It wasn't until 1989 when he made the major leagues for good, and at the end of last season, the Royals were the next team to give up on him.

The Phillies, who spent the winter picking up players who nobody wanted, determined that Eisenreich could still play. They gave him another chance, and Sunday night, he became yet the latest castoff to turn into a hero •

From *Phils' 'Oddball' Eisenreich Remains On Even Keel,* by Bob Nightengale. Published October 19, 1993 in the St. Louis Post Dispatch. Copyright © 1993 Los Angeles Times. Reprinted by permission.

development: teachers need to understand a crisis from the student's point of view, while also promoting the student's active choice and responsibility for the behavior. The "Guidelines for Practice" box on page 153 provides descriptive information about life space interviews.

Psychiatric Hospitalization   Feinstein and Uribe (1986) contend that hospitalization should be considered for learners identified as behaviorally disordered only after all out-patient alternatives have been ineffective or refused, or when the problem is severe enough to necessitate a comprehensive inpatient program. Problems judged severe include being overtly or potentially dangerous to self, family, or others; self-destructive behavior through drug or alcohol abuse or self-inflicted injuries; or repetitive running away, violence, truancy, promiscuity, social isolation, extreme mood swings, or a psychotic disorder. Hospitalization is reasonable when there are problems in all life support areas (family, community, and school) and efforts to mobilize the individual to change have failed.

In a study of the characteristics of children and adolescents who entered psychiatric hospitalization, Singth, Landrum, Donatelli, Hampton, and Ellis (1994) found that 46 percent of the total sample in one large public university-affiliated

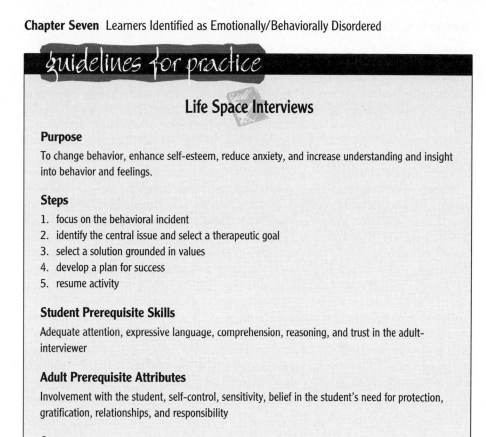

guidelines for practice

Life Space Interviews

Purpose

To change behavior, enhance self-esteem, reduce anxiety, and increase understanding and insight into behavior and feelings.

Steps

1. focus on the behavioral incident
2. identify the central issue and select a therapeutic goal
3. select a solution grounded in values
4. develop a plan for success
5. resume activity

Student Prerequisite Skills

Adequate attention, expressive language, comprehension, reasoning, and trust in the adult-interviewer

Adult Prerequisite Attributes

Involvement with the student, self-control, sensitivity, belief in the student's need for protection, gratification, relationships, and responsibility

Outcomes

Resolution of the incident, as well as increased student understanding, problem-solving ability, and self-esteem ▌

From M. M. Wood and N. J. Long, *Life Space Intervention: Talking with Children and Youth in Crisis.* Copyright © 1991 Pro-Ed, Austin, TX. Reprinted by permission.

---

child and adolescent psychiatric hospital were not identified as having disabilities and were served in general education classrooms. Thirty-six percent of the students were identified as emotionally/behaviorally disordered, and 18 percent had other disabilities. Over half of the students had previously been admitted to the psychiatric hospital. The most frequent reason for the hospitalization of students identified as emotionally/behaviorally disordered was that they were felt to be a threat to themselves or others.

The use of short-term hospitalization (periods up to three months) has been abused by some programs since short-term care fits many insurance plans (Feinstein & Uribe, 1986). Problems with short-term hospitalization occur when individuals are rapidly discharged back to families, special education programs, or loosely organized programs when the learner shows evidence of superficial compliance but has not resolved problems.

The Impact on the School, Community, and Society

Individuals identified as emotionally/behaviorally disordered demonstrate difficulties in interacting with their peers in positive ways. These difficulties present challenges to these learners throughout their school careers and as they enter the community.

In data generated from 145 special education administrators in twenty-seven states, Grosenick, George, George, and Lewis (1991) found that the identification of students as emotionally/behaviorally disordered seemed fairly well

Objective Five

To describe the impact of emotional/behavioral disorders on participation in larger social systems—the school, community, and society.

developed. The ways in which students exited programs and the ways in which these programs were evaluated were less formalized. In this study, teachers continued to play the central role in program implementation, with general education teachers considerably less involved. The self-contained classroom remained the most prevalent setting for these students, but a great deal of variability among programs was noted. The behavioral perspective continued to dominate, with the primary focus on determining eligibility, curriculum and programming, and exit criteria based on the tenets of the behavioral perspective. A lack of communication and collaboration with agencies external to the schools continued to be evident.

Learners identified as emotionally/behaviorally disordered had lower status in the classroom, though they were known as well by their peers as were their nonidentified peers (Sabornie & Kauffman, 1985). The learners identified as emotionally/behaviorally disordered rated their fellow learners identified as behaviorally disordered in the same class higher than their peers in social status. Learners identified as emotionally/behaviorally disordered, in comparison with matched nonidentified peers, assigned higher social rejection to their nonidentified peers and received far less acceptance and more rejection from them (Sabornie, 1987). No differences in assigned acceptance or assigned and received familiarity among same- and opposite-gender classmates were found between learners identified as emotionally/behaviorally disordered and their nonidentified peers.

Grade-level differences in degrees of behavioral tolerance occurred; children demonstrated increased tolerance as they progressed into upper elementary grades (Safran & Safran, 1985). The total group of learners studied, however, agreed that the most disturbing behaviors were outer-directed—negative aggressive, and poor peer cooperation—which held definite interpersonal consequences. Consistent with Voeltz's (1980) study of peer acceptance, learners felt justified in rejecting rule breakers when social rules were violated. The learner identified as behaviorally disordered, with limited strategies for approaching peers in positive ways, was rejected when his or her efforts resulted in breaking socially accepted rules.

Leone (1984) assessed adolescents who had been judged to have successfully left a residential day-treatment program for students identified as behaviorally disordered two to four years earlier. These students were found to be seriously deficient in reading, spelling, mathematics, and written language. The students were, for the most part, living with their families. In a later study of more specific characteristics, Leone, Fitzmartin, Stetson, and Foster (1986) found that the more-successful adolescents were those who were enrolled in day- rather than residential-treatment programs and who had lower rates of absenteeism. The most successful learners were also able to name specific characteristics that others liked about them and were likely to be working and/or attending school. Both successful and unsuccessful former students held generally positive attitudes towards the program in which they had been enrolled, though more successful students tended to disassociate themselves from enrollment in the program.

In a day-treatment program, the younger, nontruant and less-disturbed child's functioning at entry was found to be the best predictor of the family's ability to work well as a unit (Baenen, Glenwick, Stephens, Neuhaus, & Mowrey, 1986). Children with behavioral problems such as poor concentration, passivity, and daydreaming tended to have comparatively positive outcomes, though research has demonstrated that children with such problems progress with no intervention. Children with conduct disorders had more severe problems and more changes in family structure during treatment, such as moves in foster care.

Positive perceptions were also reported in a study that used telephone interviews. Nearly two-thirds of emotionally/behaviorally disordered students contacted reported that they had a job and that their parents were satisfied with their adjustment (Neel, Meadows, Levine, & Edgar, 1988). However, fewer than one in five were involved in post-secondary programs, whereas about 50 percent of their nonidentified peers were in post-secondary programs; their rate of unemployment was nearly three times as high as that of national figures; and about one-third were not engaged in structured activities outside the home and were not receiving the training and support necessary to enable them to participate in the adult world.

In their survey of emotionally/behaviorally disordered students one year after their class was scheduled to be graduated, Frank, Sitlington, and Carson (1991) found that of those who had graduated, about two-thirds of the males and one-third of the females were living with parents or relatives. Only slightly over half (58 percent) of the graduates were currently employed full- or part-time. Only an additional 14 percent of the graduates were "otherwise meaningfully engaged" (as homemakers or students or in on-the-job training). Among the dropouts, 81 percent reported their marital status as single, and 30 percent were employed at least part-time. An additional 14 percent were "otherwise meaningfully engaged." Only a small proportion of these individuals were receiving help from a community agency or school personnel.

Carson, Sitlington, and Frank (1995) interviewed students who had graduated or dropped out of programs for students identified as emotionally/behaviorally disordered one and three years after their class exited high school. Interview questions addressed living arrangements, employment status, and financial situation. A high percentage of graduates (almost three-fourths) were working as laborers and service workers. This underemployment may be due to a lack of post-secondary education or training; only half of these students received any. Less than half of the students were receiving any type of fringe benefits in their employment settings. Three years after their class had exited from high school, only 25 percent were deemed successful, that is, they had a job in the community and were earning at least minimum wage; they were either buying a home, living independently, or living with a friend; they were paying for more than half of their living expenses; and they were involved in more than three leisure activities.

Summary

Identification of a learner as emotionally/behaviorally disordered depends on the context in which the learner is participating. There is great variation in the numbers of learners identified from school system to school system and from state to state. Nationally, it is generally felt that learners identified as emotionally/behaviorally disordered are underidentified.

Learners identified as emotionally/behaviorally disordered demonstrate lower academic achievement than do their nonidentified peers. In addition, they frequently have poorer communication skills and as a consequence have greater difficulty in social settings.

The definition of emotional/behavioral disorders and the identification of learners as emotionally/behaviorally disordered are controversial. The need to assess behavior in the context in which it occurs has emerged as an essential part of the identification of emotional/behavioral disorders.

There is also great controversy related to the provision of programs for learners identified as emotionally/behaviorally disordered. Recent studies have demonstrated that most programming emphasizes control rather than the development of social interaction and communication skills, often to the neglect of other curriculum areas. Learners who leave programs for learners identified as emotionally/behaviorally disordered are frequently behind their peers in academic skills and are underemployed.

Building Your Professional Vocabulary

Match each word or phrase to its meaning.

_____ aggression

_____ emotional/behavioral disorders

_____ depression

_____ disturbed behaviors

_____ disturbing behaviors

_____ externalizing behaviors

_____ internalizing behaviors

_____ levels systems

_____ life space interview

_____ seriously emotionally disturbed

_____ suicidal ideation

_____ token economy

a. thoughts about suicide
b. stealing, lying, disobedience, and fighting
c. physical complaints, phobias, worrying
d. dysphoric mood for at least two weeks
e. behavior intended to dominate others
f. increased frequency, intensity, or duration of behavior
g. behaviors related to a certain place and time
h. behaviors seen across settings

i. federal term for emotional/behavioral disorders
j. organizational frameworks within which behavior management interventions are applied
k. an exchange system
l. a guided interview to discuss how to respond more effectively in the future

Comprehension Check

Select the most appropriate response.

1. The number of students served in programs for learners identified as emotionally/behaviorally disordered
   a. is equivalent to estimates of prevalence.
   b. is far greater than estimates of prevalence.
   c. is far less than estimates of prevalence.
2. Emotional/behavioral disorders
   a. often occur concomitantly with other disorders.
   b. often occur concomitantly with mental retardation.
   c. usually occur independently.
3. Most of the referrals for learners as potentially demonstrating emotional/behavioral disorders are
   a. males between first grade and third grade.
   b. males between third grade and sixth grade.
   c. females between sixth grade and ninth grade.
4. The diagnostic criteria for depression
   a. are very different for children and adults.
   b. apply for both children and adults.
   c. are not applied prior to adolescence.
5. Aggression is
   a. pervasive among learners identified as emotionally/behaviorally disordered.
   b. often apparent among males identified as emotionally/behaviorally disordered.
   c. rarely reported among learners who internalize.

6. Identification of learners as having emotional/behavioral disorders
   a. is objective when using the DSM-IV.
   b. is subjective.
   c. is objective when using federal definitions.
7. Learners from diverse cultural, ethnic, and linguistic groups
   a. are seldom identified as emotionally/behaviorally disordered.
   b. are overidentified as emotionally/behaviorally disordered.
   c. are as likely as Anglo children to be identified as emotionally/behaviorally disordered.
8. Teachers perceive the most difficult behavior to manage in the classroom as
   a. extreme social withdrawal.
   b. verbal aggression.
   c. physical aggression.
9. Programs for learners identified as emotionally/behaviorally disordered are
   a. dominated by a curriculum of control.
   b. dominated by psychoanalytic perspectives.
   c. dominated by psychoeducational perspectives.
10. Token economies
    a. are considered self-management programs.
    b. provide a cue that is exchanged at a later time for a backup reinforcer.
    c. are difficult to manage in classrooms.

References

Algozzine, B. (1980). The disturbing child: A matter of opinion. *Behavioral Disorders, 5* (2), 112–115.

American Psychiatric Association (1994). *Diagnostic and statistical manual of mental disorders* (4th ed.). Washington, DC: American Psychiatric Association.

Baenen, R. S., Glenwick, D. S., Stephens, M. A. S., Neuhaus, S. M., & Mowrey, J. D. (1986). Predictors of child and family outcome in a psychoeducational day school program. *Behavioral Disorders, 11,* 272–279.

Bauer, A. M. (1993). Personal observation: Aiken Senior High School, E. S. Murphy, teacher.

Bauer, A. S., & Balius, F. A. (1995). Storytelling: Integrating therapy and curriculum for students with serious emotional disturbance. *Teaching Exceptional Children, 27* (2), 24–28.

Bauer, A. M., & Sapona, R. H. (1988). Facilitating communication as a basis for intervention for students with severe behavioral disorders. *Behavioral Disorders, 13,* 280–287.

Bauer, A. M., Shea, T. M., & Keppler, R. (1986). Levels systems: A framework for the individualization of behavior management. *Behavioral Disorders, 12,* 28–35.

Beare, P. L., & Lynch, E. C. (1986). Underidentification of preschool children at risk for behavioral disorders. *Behavioral Disorders, 11,* 177–183.

Brooks, A. P. (1991). Behavior problems and the power relationship. *Language, Speech and Hearing Services in the Schools, 22,* 89–91.

Camarata, S. M., Hughes, C. A., & Ruhl, K. L. (1988). Mild/moderately behaviorally disordered students: A population at risk for language disorders. *Language, Speech, and Hearing Services in the Schools, 19* (2), 191–200.

Camp, B. W., & Bash, M. S. (1981). *Think aloud: Increasing social and cognitive skills.* Champaign, IL: Research Press.

Carlson, P. E., & Stephens, T. M. (1986). Cultural bias and identification of behaviorally disordered children. *Behavioral Disorders, 11,* 191–199.

Carson, R. R., Sitlington, P. L., & Frank, A. R. (1995). Young adulthood for individuals with behavioral disorders: What does it hold? *Behavioral Disorders, 20,* 127–135.

Caseau, D. L., Luckasson, R., & Kroth, R. L. (1994). Special education services for girls with serious emotional disturbance: A case of gender bias? *Behavioral Disorders, 20,* 51–60.

Coleman, M. C. (1986). *Behavior disorders: Theory and practice.* Englewood Cliffs, NJ: Prentice Hall.

Council for Children with Behavioral Disorders (1990, August). Coalition finalizes definition. *CCBD Newsletter,* August, p. 1.

Coutinho, M. J. (1986). Reading achievement of students identified as behaviorally disordered at the secondary level. *Behavioral Disorders, 11,* 200–207.

Cullinan, D., Epstein, M. H., & Lloyd, J. W. (1983). *Behavior disorders of children and adolescents.* Englewood Cliffs, NJ: Prentice Hall.

Cullinan, D., Schloss, P. J., & Epstein, M. H. (1987). Relative prevalence and correlates of depressive characteristics among seriously emotionally disturbed and nonhandicapped students. *Behavioral Disorders, 12,* 90–98.

Cytryn, L., & McKnew, D. H. (1986). Treatment issues in childhood depression. *Pediatric Annals, 15* (12), 856–860.

Edelbrock, C. (1984). Developmental considerations. In T. H. Ollendick & M. Hersen (Eds.), *Child behavioral assessment principles and procedures* (pp. 230–237). New York: Pergamon.

Epstein, M. H., Kauffman, J. M., & Cullinan, D. (1985). Patterns of maladjustment among the behaviorally disordered. II: Boys aged 6–11, Boys aged 12–18, Girls aged 6–11, Girls aged 12–18. *Behavioral Disorders, 10,* 125–135.

Epstein, M. H., Kinder, D., & Bursuck, B. (1989). The academic status of adolescents with behavioral disorders. *Behavioral Disorders, 14,* 157–165.

Epstein, M. H., & Ollinger, E. (1987). Use of medication in school programs for behaviorally disordered pupils. *Behavioral Disorders, 12,* 138–145.

Executive Committee of the Council for Children with Behavioral Disorders (1987). Position paper on definition and identification of students with behavioral disorders. *Behavioral Disorders, 13,* 9–19.

Executive Committee of the Council for Children with Behavioral Disorders (1989). White paper on best assessment practices for students with behavioral disorders: Accommodation to cultural and individual differences. *Behavioral Disorders, 14,* 263–278.

Farmer, T. W., & Hallowell, J. H. (1994). Social networks in mainstream classrooms: Social affiliations with behavioral characteristics of students with EBD. *Journal of Emotional and Behavioral Disorders, 2,* (3), 143–155.

Federal Register. (August 23, 1977). *42* (162), 478.

Feinstein, S. C., & Uribe, V. (1986). Hospitalization of the young: Rationale and criteria. *Pediatric Annals, 15* (12), 861–866.

Fessler, M. A., Rosenberg, M. S., & Rosenberg, L. A. (1991). Concomitant learning disabilities and learning problems among students with behavioral/emotional disorders. *Behavioral Disorders, 16* (2), 97–106.

Frank, A. R., Sitlington, P. L., & Carson, R. (1991). Transition of adolescents with behavioral disorders: Is it successful? *Behavioral Disorders, 16,* 180–191.

Freeman, B. M., & Ritvo, E. R. (1984). The syndrome of autism: Establishing the diagnosis and principles of management. *Pediatric Annals, 13,* 284–296.

Grosenick, J. K., George, N. L., & George, M. P. (1988). The availability of program descriptions among programs for seriously emotionally disturbed students. *Behavioral Disorders, 13,* 108–115.

Grosenick, J. K., George, N. L., George, M. P., & Lewis, T. J. (1991). Public school services for behaviorally disordered students: Program practices in the 1980s. *Behavioral Disorders, 16,* 87–96.

Hubbell, R. (1981). *Children's language disorders: An integrated approach.* Englewood Cliffs, NJ: Prentice Hall.

Hughes, C. A., Deshler, D. D., Ruhl, K. L., & Schumaker, J. B. (1993). Test-taking strategy instruction for adolescents with emotional and behavioral disorders. *Journal of Emotional and Behavioral Disorders, 1,* 189–198.

Hughes, J. N., & Hall, D. M. (1985). Performance of disturbed and nondisturbed boys on a role play test of social competence. *Behavioral Disorders, 11,* 24–29.

Huntze, S. L. (1985). A position paper of the Council for Children with Behavioral Disorders. *Behavioral Disorders, 10,* 167–174.

Hutton, J. B. (1985). What reasons are given by teachers who refer problem behavior students? *Psychology in the Schools, 22,* 79–82.

Johnson, J. A. (1991). *Patrick.*

Johnston, J. C., & Zemitzsch, A. (1988). Family power: An intervention beyond the classroom. *Behavioral Disorders, 14* (1), 69–79.

Joyce, B. R. (1987). Learning how to learn. *Theory into Practice, 26,* 416–428.

Kauffman, J. M. (1981). *Characteristics of children's behavior disorders* (2nd ed.) Columbus, OH: Merrill.

Kauffman, J. M. (1985). *Characteristics of children's behavior disorders* (3rd ed.). Columbus, OH: Merrill.

Kauffman, J. M. (1989). *Characteristics of behavioral disorders of children and youth* (4th ed.). Columbus, OH: Charles E. Merrill.

Kavale, K. A., Forness, S. R., & Alper, A. E. (1986). Research in behavioral disorders/emotional disturbance: A survey of subject identification criteria. *Behavioral Disorders, 11,* 159–167.

Knapczyk, D. R. (1988). Reducing aggressive behaviors in special and regular class settings by training alternative social responses. *Behavioral Disorders, 14* (1), 27–39.

Knitzer, J., Steinberg, Z., & Fleisch, B. (1990). *At the schoolhouse door: An examination of problems and policies for children with behavioral and emotional problems.* New York: Bank Street College of Education.

Leone, P. (1984). A descriptive follow-up of behaviorally disordered adolescents. *Behavioral Disorders, 9,* 207–214.

Leone, P., Fitzmartin, R., Stetson, F., & Foster, J. (1986). A retrospective follow-up of behaviorally disordered adolescents: Identifying predictors of treatment outcome. *Behavioral Disorders, 11,* 87–97.

Leone, P. E., Luttig, P. G., Zlotlow, S., & Trickett, E. J. (1990). Understanding the social ecology of classrooms for adolescents with behavioral disorders: A preliminary study of differences in perceived environments. *Behavioral Disorders, 16,* 55–65.

Long, N. J. (1990). Comments on Ralph Gardner's article "Life space interviewing: It can be effective, but don't . . ." *Behavioral Disorders, 15,* 119–124.

Luebke, J., Epstein, M. H., & Cullinan, D. (1989). Comparison of teacher-rated achievement levels of behaviorally disordered, learning disabled, and nonhandicapped adolescents. *Behavioral Disorders, 15,* 1–8.

Maag, J. W., & Behrens, J. T. (1989). Epidemiologic data on seriously emotionally disturbed and learning disabled adolescents: Reporting extreme depressive symptomatology. *Behavioral Disorders, 15,* 21–27.

Martin, K. F., Lloyd, J. W., Kauffman, J. M., & Coyne, M. (1995). Teacher's perception of educational placement decisions for pupils with emotional and behavioral disorders. *Behavioral Disorders, 20* (2), 106–117.

Mastropieri, M. A., Jenne, T., & Scruggs, T. E. (1988). A level system for managing problem behaviors in a high school resource program. *Behavioral Disorders, 13,* 202–208.

McConnell, S. R. (1987). Entrapment effects and the generalization and maintenance of social skills training for elementary school students with behavioral disorders. *Behavioral Disorders, 12,* 252–263.

McDonough, K. M. (1989). Analysis of the expressive language characteristics of emotionally handicapped students in social interactions. *Behavioral Disorders, 14,* 127–139.

Miller, D. (1994). Suicidal behavior of adolescents with behavior disorders and their peers without disabilities. *Behavioral Disorders, 20,* 61–68.

Morris, S. M. (1982). A classroom process for behavior change. *The Pointer, 26* (3), 25–28.

Morse, W. C., Cutler, R. L., & Fink, A. H. (1964). *Public school classes for the emotionally handicapped.* Washington, DC: Council for Exceptional Children.

Murphy, E. S. (1991). *Behavior management systems.* Cincinnati, OH: Aiken Senior High School.

Neel, R. S., Meadows, N., Levine, P., & Edgar, E. G. (1988). *Behavioral Disorders, 13,* 209–216.

Nelson, J. R., Smith, D. J., Young, R. K., & Dodd, J. (1991). A review of self-management outcome research conducted with students who exhibit behavioral disorders. *Behavioral Disorders, 16,* 169–179.

Noll, M. B., Kamps, D., & Seaborn, C. F. (1993). Prereferral interventions for students with emotional or behavioral risks: Use of a behavioral consultation model. *Journal of Emotional and Behavioral Disorders, 1,* 203–214.

Ollendick, T. H., & Hersen, M. (1984). *Child behavioral assessment: Principles and behaviors.* Boston: Allyn & Bacon.

Quay, H. C., & Peterson, D. R. (1987). *Manual for the revised behavior problem checklist.* Unpublished manuscript available from H. C. Quay, Box 248704, University of Miami, Coral Gables, FL 33124.

Ramsey, E., & Walker, H. M. (1988). Family management correlates of antisocial behavior among middle school boys. *Behavioral Disorders, 13,* 187–201.

Redl, F. (1966). The life space interview: Strategy and techniques. In F. Redl, *When we deal with children* (pp. 35–67). New York: Free Press.

Reimers, T. M., & Wacker, D. P. (1988). Parents' ratings of the acceptability of behavioral treatment made in an outpatient clinic: A preliminary analysis of the influence of treatment effectiveness. *Behavioral Disorders, 14* (1), 7–15.

Rhodes, W. C. (1967). The disturbing child: A problem of ecological management. *Exceptional Children, 33,* 449–455.

Rosenberg, M. S. (1986). Maximizing the effectiveness of structured classroom management programs: Implementing rule-review procedures with disruptive and destructible students. *Behavioral Disorders, 11,* 239–248.

Rosenthal, S. L., & Simeonsson, R. J. (1991). Communication skills in emotionally disturbed and nondisturbed adolescents. *Behavioral Disorders, 16,* 192–199.

Ruhl, K. L., & Hughes, C. A. (1985). The nature and extent of aggression in special education settings serving behaviorally disordered students. *Behavioral Disorders, 10,* 95–104.

Sabornie, E. J. (1987). Bidirectional social status of behaviorally disordered and nonhandicapped elementary school pupils. *Behavioral Disorders, 13,* 45–57.

Sabornie, E. J., & Kauffman, J. M. (1985). Regular classroom sociometric status of behaviorally disordered adolescents. *Behavioral Disorders, 10,* 191–197.

Safran, J. S., & Safran, S. P. (1985). A developmental view of children's behavioral tolerance. *Behavioral Disorders, 10,* 87–94.

Safran, S. P., Safran, J. S., & Barcikowski, R. S. (1988). Assessing teacher manageability: A factor analytic approach. *Behavioral Disorders, 13,* 245–252.

Schloss, P. J., Schloss, C. N., Wood, C. E., & Kiehl, W. S. (1986). A critical review of social skills research with behaviorally disordered students. *Behavioral Disorders, 12,* 1–14.

Scruggs, T. E., & Mastropieri, M. A. (1986). Academic characteristics of behaviorally disordered and learning disabled students. *Behavioral Disorders, 11,* 184–190.

Scruggs, T. E., Mastropieri, M. A., Cook, S. B., & Escobar, C. (1986). Early intervention for children with conduct disorders: A quantitative synthesis of single-subject research. *Behavioral Disorders, 11,* 260–271.

Sevcik, B. M., & Ysseldyke, J. E. (1986). An analysis of teachers' prereferral interventions for students exhibiting behavioral problems. *Behavioral Disorders, 11,* 109–117.

Shea, T. M., & Bauer, A. M. (1987). *Teaching children and youth with behavior disorders.* Englewood Cliffs, NJ: Prentice Hall.

Simpson, R. L. (1988). Needs of parents and families whose children have learning and behavior problems. *Behavioral Disorders, 14* (1), 40–47.

Simpson, R. L. (1989). Agreement among teachers in using the Revised Behavior Problem Checklist to identify deviant behavior in children. *Behavioral Disorders, 14,* 151–156.

Sindelar, P. T., King, M. C., Gartland, D., Wilson, R. J., & Meisel, C. J. (1985). Deviant behavior in learning disabled and behaviorally disordered students as a function of level and placement. *Behavioral Disorders, 10* (2), 105–112.

Singth, N. N., Landrum, T. J., Donatelli, L. S., Hampton, C., & Ellis, C. R. (1994). Characteristics of children and adolescents with serious emotional disturbance in systems of care. Part I: Partial hospitalization and inpatient psychiatric services. *Journal of Emotional and Behavioral Disorders, 2,* 13–20.

Skiba, R. J. (1989). The importance of construct validity: Alternative models for the assessment of behavioral disorder. *Behavioral Disorders, 14,* 175–185.

Slate, J. R., & Saudargas, R. A. (1986). Differences in the classroom behaviors of behaviorally disordered and regular class students. *Behavioral Disorders, 12,* 45–53.

Smith, D. J., Young, K. R., West, R. P., Morgan, D. P., & Rhode, G. (1988). Reducing the disruptive behavior of junior high students: A classroom self-management procedure. *Behavioral Disorders, 13,* 231–239.

Swan, W. W., Brown, C. L., & Jacob, R. T. (1987). Types of service delivery models used in the reintegration of seriously emotionally disturbed/behaviorally disordered students. *Behavioral Disorders, 12,* 99–103.

Talmadge, D. K., Gamel, N. M., Munson, R. G., & Hanley, T. M. (1985). *Special study on terminology: Comprehensive review and evaluation report.* (Contract No. 300–84–0144). Mountain View, CA: SRA Technologies.

Trautman, R. C., Giddan, J. J., & Jurs, S. G. (1990). Language risk factor in emotionally disturbed children within a school and day treatment program. *Journal of Childhood Communication Disorders, 13* (2), 123–133.

U.S. Department of Education. (1995). *Seventeenth annual report to Congress on the implementation of the Individuals with Disabilities Education Act.* Washington, DC: Author.

Voeltz, L. M. (1980). Children's attitudes toward handicapped peers. *American Journal of Mental Deficiency, 84,* 455–464.

Wehby, J. H., Symons, F. J., & Shores, R. E. (1995). A descriptive analysis of aggressive behavior in classrooms for children with emotional and behavioral disorders. *Behavioral Disorders, 20,* 87–105.

Weller, E. B., & Weller, R. A. (1986). Clinical aspects of childhood depression. *Pediatric Annals, 15* (12), 843–850.

Whitaker, A., Johnson, J., Shaffer, D., Rapoport, J. L., Kalinkow, K., Walsh, B. T., Davies, M., Braiman, S., & Dolinsky, A. (1990). Uncommon troubles in young people: Prevalence estimates of selected psychiatric disorders in a nonreferred adolescent population. *Archives of General Psychiatry, 47,* 487–496.

Wood, M. M., & Long, N. J. (1991). *Life space intervention: Talking with children and youth in crisis.* Austin, TX: Pro-ed.

Wright, D., Pillard, E. D., & Cleven, C. A. (1990). The influence of state definitions of behavior disorders on the number of children served under PL 94-142. *Remedial and Special Education, 11* (5), 17–22.

Objectives

After completing this chapter, you will be able to:

1. describe the largest minority cultural and ethnic groups and the behavioral patterns generally attributed to each.
2. describe issues related to the assessment of learners from various cultural and ethnic groups.
3. describe the impact of various cultural and ethnic groups on classroom interactions.
4. describe ways to mediate the environment for learners from various cultural and ethnic groups.
5. describe the impact of membership in various cultural and ethnic groups in the larger social systems of the community and society.

Key Words and Phrases

African American	Hispanic
Anglo	migrant
Appalachian	minority
Asian American	Native American
ethnicity	Puerto Rican

8

Chapter

Learners from Diverse Ethnic, Cultural, and Linguistic Groups

s an experienced first-grade teacher, I am convinced that a child needs to be familiar with a significant number of these concepts [standard English, print as communication] to be able to assimilate so much new knowledge in one sitting . . . I do not advocate a simplistic 'basic skills' approach for children outside of the culture of power . . . Rather, I suggest that schools provide these children the content that other families from a different cultural orientation provide at home [e.g., experience with books, visits to museums, trips to the library]. This does not mean separating children according to family background, but instead, ensuring that each classroom incorporates strategies appropriate for all the children in its confines." (Delpit, 1988, p. 286) [Comments made with reference to teaching learners representing minority cultures and ethnic groups by a professional who represents a minority culture.]

Introduction

Mindel and Habenstein (1981) define **ethnicity** as membership in a group of people who share a unique social and cultural heritage that is transmitted from one generation to the next. In North America, race and ethnicity may overlap (as with Chinese Americans or African Americans) or be independent of each other (Hispanics may be white, black, native American, or all three). Ethnic identity is a particular challenge when individuals also represent a racial minority. These individuals are generally easily distinguishable from the members of the mainstream of society. Many Caucasian ethnic groups may practice their cultural customs in their homes and places of worship but blend into the mainstream of society at their pleasure. This is often not possible for racially distinguishable groups.

Minority groups are those groups who have unequal access to power and who are for the most part considered by the majority group to be inferior or less worthy of sharing power in some way (Mindel & Habenstein, 1981). However, by the year 2000, one in three Americans will be African American, Hispanic, or Asian American (Yates, 1987). Applying this prediction to practice, Hodgkinson (1985) suggests that the motive for addressing diversity can no longer be liberalism or obligation, but a question of societal self-interest. Society must recognize the contributions of various minority groups and implement procedures to permit them equal access to power within society.

Changes in society and a new kind of pluralism also support the need to address diversity. Pluralism suggests that members of diverse ethnic, cultural, and linguistic groups continue their participation in their customs while participating in society on the whole. Kochman (1991) contrasts the old "melting pot" pluralism with the new "salad bowl" pluralism. Whereas in the past, individuals were expected to assimilate into society, individuals are now expected to demonstrate their uniqueness.

In this chapter, an effort is made to represent the unique experiences of the many children in our schools from various cultural and ethnic groups. In this effort, five significant minority and ethnic groups will be discussed: Asian Americans, Hispanics, African Americans, Native Americans, and Appalachians. As Gibbs and Huang (1989) suggest, the discussion of cultural and ethnic groups must be done within the frame of reference of the great diversity of the individuals within these groups. However, individuals within a cultural and ethnic group typically share some history, cultural tradition, and social experiences when compared with the Anglo or majority, culture. It is this shared cultural experience that is discussed in this chapter, while recognizing the uniqueness of each individual within each group. At no time is it suggested that all members of a cultural or ethnic group demonstrate the characteristics or behaviors described. Rather, it is the impact of the context in which the learner develops and the impact of the interpersonal differences on the development of each learner that are important.

Though it is recognized that each child is unique, several trends have been identified in persons from the different cultural groups, these may help in understanding members of culturally diverse groups (Olion & Gillis-Olion, 1984). In addition to cultural and ethnic identity, the issues of class and poverty frequently impact the individual values and behaviors of members of minority cultures.

An additional issue for students from diverse ethnic, cultural, and linguistic groups is a lack of congruence between what happens in and out of school. Resnick (1987) suggests that school learning is discontinuous with daily life of learners from various cultural and ethnic groups in several important ways. First, in schools individual rather than shared cognition is valued. Students ultimately are judged by what they can do themselves. Work, personal life, and recreation, on the other hand, take place within social systems, and each person's ability to function successfully depends on what others do and how several individuals' mental and physical performances mesh. Schools also vary from personal life in that in school pure mentation (mental activity) rather than tool manipulation is emphasized. School is an institution that values thought that proceeds independently. In schools, symbols are manipulated rather than the contextualized reasoning that takes place outside of school. Some of the key issues related to learners from diverse ethnic, cultural, and linguistic groups are shown in the "Guidelines for Practice" box on page 165. Finally, in schools all children are required to be generalists; outside of school specific competencies and skills are emphasized.

Cultural and Ethnic Minorities

Objective One

To describe the largest minority cultural and ethnic groups and the behavioral patterns generally attributed to each.

In this discussion of Hispanics, African Americans, Native Americans, Asian Americans, and Appalachians it is important to keep in mind that the developmental context, experience, and personal characteristics of each learner are unique. To suggest that all learners represent all the characteristics presented is racial, cultural, or ethnic stereotyping. This section and those that follow describe potentially common threads through the cultural or ethnic experience of these learners. Throughout this discussion the term **Anglo** is used to describe the mainstream Caucasian, male, middle-class ways of knowing and being.

Hispanic Americans

Hispanics are those learners of all races whose cultural heritage is tied to the use of the Spanish language and Latino culture (Fradd, Figueroa, & Correa, 1989). Hispanic students may belong to any of a large number of ethnic subgroups: Mexican American, Chicano, Puerto Rican, Cuban, or Central or South American.

The Hispanic population has entered a tremendous period of growth, which may result in an American demographic picture composed of 47 million Hispanics out of 265 million Americans by the year 2000 (Hodgkinson, 1985). The poverty rate among Hispanic families in 1986 was about 2.5 times greater than that of non-Hispanic families (Buenning, Tollefson, & Rodriguez, 1992).

Hyland (1989) describes the American Hispanic population as highly concentrated in urban areas and highly isolated in housing and schooling. This isolation is reputedly related to linguistic skills, in that Hispanic children are usually placed in classrooms or schools where children of limited English proficiency are in the majority.

Mexican Americans   Mexican Americans tend to be the youngest among Hispanic groups, with a median age of 23.3 years. In 1984 the reported median income of Mexican American families was $19,200. Besides being young and poor, Mexican Americans live in large families while confronting problems of illiteracy and lack of facility in English (Ramirez, 1990).

The contemporary Mexican American family is a mixture of traditional and contemporary patterns. Traditional values such as the primacy of the family and extended kinship remain strong. The kinship system is highly integrated, including *compadres* (godparents), for emotional and social support, help with child rearing, financial support, and assistance in problem solving (Ramirez & Arce, 1981).

The concept of *machismo* (male dominance) continues to influence the role of the male in Mexican American culture. Trankina (1983) indicates that this concept traditionally requires men to be forceful and strong and to be without tender emotions. This traditional masculine aggressiveness also encompasses a strong sense of personal honor and belief in the importance of the family and the need to care for children. Ramirez and Arce (1981) found that the concept of machismo and absolute patriarchy have diminished, with joint decision making and greater equality apparent.

guidelines for practice

*W*hat are some of the key issues related to learners from diverse ethnic, cultural, and linguistic groups?

Ethnicity, culture, and language may have a significant impact on learners in five ways (Gibbs & Huang, 1989).

1. Individual adjustment: ways of looking, acting, and attitudes
2. Family relationships: roles and patterns of interaction among family members
3. School adjustment and achievement: both in academic areas and in relationships to teachers and peers
4. Relationship with peers: students may feel that they live in two worlds, the world of school and the world of their peers
5. Adaptation to the community: ranging from being a scapegoat to a token member

It is important to celebrate everyone's cultural and ethnic identity.

Ramirez (1990) indicates that the parent-child relationship overshadows the marital relationship in Mexican American culture. The home is usually child centered, with parents being indulgent and passive with younger children. Parents are nurturing and protective, and they accept the child's individuality. As children grow older, they are often assigned greater tasks and responsibilities. The father's role with older children is that of strict disciplinarian; he serves as authoritarian while the mother often serves as mediator between father and children.

In comparison with Anglo culture, Mexican Americans expect less physical distance in personal interactions and are accustomed to frequent physical contact. These interaction patterns often create discomfort in others not of the Mexican American culture.

In Mexican American culture, there is an emphasis on cooperation and respect for authority (Ramirez, 1990). A Mexican American student may appear to accept the teacher's directions and suggestions even though they are covertly resistant. Guinn (1977) suggests that Mexican Americans are more oriented to the here and now, rather than the future, than are Anglo students. In addition, Mexican American learners emphasize "doing" rather than "being" and depend on group cooperation. Whereas members of the Anglo culture assume that an individual can master adversity, Mexican Americans are more fatalistic and accommodate themselves to problems.

Puerto Rican Americans The majority of mainland **Puerto Ricans** reside in the greater metropolitan New York area (Inclan & Herron, 1989). As American citizens, Puerto Ricans have voting privileges as well as ease of travel between the mainland and the island. However, Puerto Ricans have no congressional representatives, speak Spanish, maintain a Hispanic culture, and experience racial and political discrimination. This juxtaposition of cultures makes self-definition of Puerto Ricans residing on the mainland particularly challenging (Inclan & Herron, 1989).

Mass migration from Puerto Rico to the United States did not begin until after World War II (Sowell, 1981). By 1970, the mainland Puerto Rican population was 1.5 million, about one-half of the island population. Typical of Hispanic cultures, machismo is considered a virtue, and personalism calls for the development of inner qualities to attain self-respect and the respect of others. Catholicism, with an emphasis on a personal relationship with God, is the predominant religion. In addition, Puerto Ricans often demonstrate spiritism, which is a belief in good and evil spirits that can affect one's life (Garcia-Preto, 1982).

Generational change is apparent in Puerto Ricans. First-generation migrants exhibit predominantly traditional values, with *barrios,* Hispanic neighborhoods, serving to recreate and preserve the native culture. Second and third generations cope with and adapt to the language and values of the mainstream culture, which sometimes generates personal stress and feelings of failure due to the tension between cultures (Inclan, 1985).

African Americans

Since 1900, the **African American** population (individuals whose ancestry can be traced to Africa) of the United States has remained between 10 percent and 12 percent of the total population. By the year 2000, there will be approximately 35 million African Americans in the United States (Allen & Majidi-Ahi, 1989). According to McAdoo (1978), the lifestyles, values, and experiences of African Americans vary, but as a group, they share the common experience of economic isolation, prejudice, and legally reinforced racism. Long-established cultural patterns and a high level of maternal employment have led to shared decision-making processes in many African American families.

An important socialization issue for African American learners is coping with racism. African American parents, in efforts to combat racism, emphasize the development of achievement motivation, self-confidence, and high self-esteem (Peters, 1981). In addition, there may be a cultural difference in attitudes towards time, which may be perceived as resistance or apathy by Anglo individuals.

Communication styles among African Americans vary from that of Anglo culture in that it is possible to converse without constant eye contact (Allen & Majidi-Ahi, 1989). In addition, Smith (1981) indicates that African Americans are less likely to verbally reinforce one another in conversation.

According to Steward and Logan (1992), traditional research on African American family life has perpetuated the notion of a lower-class subculture. The strengths and resilience of African American families, as described in *Growing Up Literate* (Taylor & Dorsey-Gaines, 1988), suggest that African American families "spent time together, that there was a rhythm to their lives, and that they enjoyed each other's company" (p. 191). Taylor and Dorsey-Gaines report that parents shared a sense of conviction in their own abilities and were determined to raise healthy children. To the best of their abilities and resources, they provided loving, structured home environments with climates of cooperation and participation. Parents were concerned with the safety and well-being of their children. In their efforts to combat racism, African American parents emphasized the development of achievement motivation, self-confidence, and high self-esteem (Peters, 1981).

In regard to African American communities, Steward and Logan assume that African American communities and neighborhoods are, like the families that they comprise, not homogeneous entities. The communities reflect a variety of lifestyles and experiences for the inhabitants based on the availability or lack of resources. Cohesiveness in these communities is demonstrated by the tendency to informally adopt children and to incorporate nonfamily members into the family household. In addition, there is a pervasive assumption that people are doing the best they can. The African American community is a valuable source of support for children and families.

Native Americans

Once estimated at 10 million, the population of **Native Americans** (any member of the indigenous peoples of North America and South America) has been reduced through "cultural genocide" to between 1.5 million and 1.8 million (LaFrombroise & Low, 1989). Native Americans were victims of war with the majority culture. Those who survived were then systematically deprived of access to their way of life.

The family remains the center of many Native American tribal cultures.

In further efforts to dilute the Native American culture, rather than accepting tribally defined memberships or community consensus, federal programs require one-quarter genealogically derived Native American ancestry to be legally recognized as Native American and therefore eligible for many federal, state, and Indian nation benefits. There are, in the United States, 517 federally recognized native entities (196 of which are in Alaska) and thirty-six state-recognized Native American tribes. Each of these tribes maintains unique customs, traditions, social organizations, and ecological relationships (Leap, 1981).

Economic and educational challenges for Native Americans are pervasive. The median income of Native Americans living on reservations is $9,942, approximately one-third of the median income of Caucasian American households and far below the median income of $17,786 for African American families (U.S. Bureau of Census, 1986). About one-third of adult Native Americans are illiterate, and only 20 percent have a high school education (Brod & McQuiston, 1983). An overriding problem for Native American youth is alcohol and substance abuse. The use of alcohol among Native American teenagers is three times that of adolescents in the population at large (Bobo, 1985).

Native American cultures are complex and diverse. One common thread among the various Native American cultures is the collective interdependence of tribes and nations, with family members responsible to each other, to the clan, and to the tribe (LaFrombroise & Low, 1989). Relationships between family members and the community are complex. Some nations, such as the Navaho, are matriarchal, with women taking primary responsibility for the children, while others are patriarchal. The family, however, has remained the forum for problem solving and support in Native American communities.

As a consequence of efforts first to eliminate them and then to assimilate them, many Native Americans experience a sense of alienation from Anglos (LaFrombroise & Low, 1989). Responses of Native Americans to this sense of alienation are described by Spindler and Spindler (1994), who worked with the Menominee tribe. These responses include reaffirmation, withdrawal, constructive marginality, biculturalism, and assimilation.

Among the Menominee, reaffirmation was represented by a group of cultural "survivors" from the past and a larger number of younger people who had met Euro-American culture in school and work and who were trying to recreate and sustain a recognizable Native American way of life. Another group of Native Americans was so torn by conflict that they could identify with neither the traditional nor Euro-American cultural symbols or groups and withdrew either into self-destruction through substance abuse or by doing nothing.

"Constructive marginality" is defined by the Spindlers as forming a personal culture that is instrumentally productive but is usually constituted of several different segments, some of which are Euro-American.

Among those Menominee who assimilated, two groups emerged: (1) those who were more "respectable" than most Euro-Americans and denigrated Native Americans who did not conform, and (2) those who were undifferentiated culturally from Euro-Americans but who were interested in Native American traditions in a more distant way.

Bicultural Native Americans were equally at home in the traditional and mainstream context.

Spindler and Spindler describe these strategies as defensive because the self-esteem of the people is threatened.

Grimm (1992) reports that several issues challenge the identity of learners who are Native Americans. These issues include removal from the family to boarding schools and foster placements, high dropout rates (60 percent among children attending boarding school), overidentification as special education students, high incidence of alcohol and drug abuse, high suicide rates, chronic health problems, and low income.

Brendtro, Brokenleg, and Bockern (1990) present a holistic Native American philosophy of child development, which, they suggest, emerges from the wisdom of the people. They contend this philosophy is appropriate for all children in our complex society. The basic premise underlying this Native American philosophy is that to develop successfully, children must have or feel the spirit of belonging (trust, attachment, love, friendship), mastery (success, achievement, motivation, creativity), independence (autonomy, confidence, responsibility, self-discipline, inner control), and generosity (self-sacrifice, caring, sharing, loyalty). Examples of the characteristics of Native American child development are presented in the "A Closer Look" box on page 169. The authors believe that all children should be reared in an environment that encourages and supports these basic philosophical principles.

Asian Americans

Asian Americans have roots in Asia, including China, Japan, and the Southeast Asian nations.

Chinese Americans   The Chinese Exclusion Act of 1882 was the first legislation to ban a particular race from entering the United States. This law was followed sixty years later by the Oriental Exclusion Act, which banned all immigration from Asia. These acts came about largely due to economic depression and the fear that Chinese immigrants would take jobs from majority-culture individuals. During the period from 1890 to 1945, more Chinese left than entered the United States, with the remaining living under the constraints of the exclusion laws (Huang & Ying, 1989).

Chinese family structure, Huang and Ying report, is based on Confucian ethics. Sons are more highly valued than daughters, with the firstborn son perceived as the most valued child. Fathers, removed from the everyday tasks of the family, are often the figurative heads of families, while the mothers may in fact be the driving force in the family.

The expression of emotion is highly frowned upon in Chinese American families, and the ability to suppress undesirable thoughts or emotions is highly valued. These communication patterns sharply contrast with mainstream American values of expression (Shon & Ja, 1982). In addition, Shon and Ja describe the

a closer look

Characteristics of Native American Child Development

In their discussion of the characteristics of Native American child development, Brendtro, Brokenleg, and Bockern (1990) provide excellent examples of the spirits of belonging, mastery, independence, and generosity.

Belonging: "The days of my infanthood and childhood were spent in surroundings of love and care. In manner, gentleness was my mother's outstanding characteristic. Never did she, nor any of my caretakers, ever speak crossly to me or scold me for failures or shortcomings." (Standing Bear, 1933)

Mastery: "There was always one, or a few in every band, who swam the best, who shot the truest arrow, or who ran the fastest, and I at once set their accomplishments as the mark for me to attain. In spite of all this striving, there was no sense of rivalry. We never disliked the boy who did better than the others. On the contrary, we praised him. All through our society, the individual who excelled was praised and honored." (Standing Bear, 1933)

Independence: "I can remember . . . a toddler trying to open a door to a cabin. He could not make it. This was a big, heavy door, and he was shoving and shoving. Well, Americans would get up and open the door for him. The Blackfoot Indians sat for half an hour while the baby struggled with that door, until he was able to get it open himself. He had to grunt and sweat, and then everyone praised him because he was able to do it himself." (Hoffman, 1988)

Generosity: "A high school boy will spend his last coins in buying a pack of cigarettes, walk into a crowded recreation room, take one cigarette for himself and pass out the rest to the eager hands around him. . . . Another high school boy will receive a new coat in the mail and wear it proudly to the next school dance. For the next three months the same coat will appear on cousins and friends at the weekly dances, and it may be several months before the original owner wears his new coat again." (Bryde, 1971) ∎

essential need to avoid shame and loss of face. The ability to place the group's or family's wishes above individual desires is held as a virtue. In this way, everything an individual does is viewed as a reflection on the family. In light of this desire to save face, Chinese Americans rarely approach formal psychological helpers except as a last resort (Huang & Ying, 1989).

Japanese Americans Specific Japanese terms are usually applied to identify the various generations of Japanese Americans. The *issei* are the first generation of Japanese to come to the United States; the *nisei,* second-generation Japanese Americans, are born here. The third generation are often called the *sansei,* while the fourth and fifth generations are referred to as *yonsei* and *gosei.*

The second generation of Japanese Americans (the nisei) are typically raised with a mixture of Japanese and American values. In the early 1900s the nisei associated primarily with other Japanese Americans and were exposed to pressures to conform to the issei experience. Laws preventing Japanese from marrying Caucasians existed in most states, and until 1952 the issei were not allowed to apply for citizenship. During World War II all persons of Japanese ancestry were forcibly removed from their homes, businesses, and communities on the West Coast of the United States and placed in internment camps in the interior of the country. In recent years, the federal government has apologized for this act and has remunerated members of the Japanese American population for the injustice of internment.

Asian family culture holds that an individual's behavior reflects on the family.

Yamamoto and Kubota (1989) describe the Japanese American family structure as one that emphasizes the family over the individual, hierarchical relationships, conformity, and social control based on shame, guilt, and duty. Japanese culture values being "reserved," that is, not expressing one's wishes or preferences, deferring to those in authority, and repressing or internalizing emotion.

Southeast Asian Refugees   Today's Southeast Asian refugee children and youth have spent a large part of their lives amid violence, experiencing great personal loss, anxiety, and discontinuous education and health care. The extended family, so vital in Asian cultures, is not accessible to these children and youth. In addition to relocation, families have undergone sociocultural changes, in which children view their parents as changing from previously competent, independent individuals into persons who acculturate more slowly than they do. Yet, as in other Asian cultural groups, self-control and repression of emotions are highly valued. Post-traumatic stress disorder, marked by night terrors, numbing of the emotions, and flashbacks to violent incidents, may be apparent in Southeast Asian refugees (Huang, 1989).

Appalachians

Sullivan and Miller (1990) suggest that Appalachians in urban areas are a distinct cultural group who are not easily identifiable as a minority, since race, sex, or surname do not identify them as such. **Appalachians** are those individuals who were born, or whose ancestors were born, in the federally defined Appalachian region of 397 counties and five independent cities in portions of thirteen states, including New York, Pennsylvania, Maryland, Ohio, Virginia, West Virginia, Kentucky, Tennessee, North Carolina, South Carolina, Georgia, Alabama, and Mississippi (McCoy & Watkins, 1980). The challenge confronting these individuals is exemplified by Appalachians living in Cincinnati. In the Cincinnati area, first- and second-generation Appalachian migrants constitute about one-fourth of the population (Obermiller, Borman, & Kroger, 1988). Of the ten neighborhoods in Cincinnati with the highest school dropout rates, eight are predominantly Appalachian. Urban Appalachian students perform poorly on the standardized tests used to classify students throughout their academic careers (Borman, Mueninghoff, & Piazza, 1989). Berlowitz and Durand (1977) identify high absenteeism, high suspension, and low reading and math achievement as variables linked with high dropout rates of Appalachian students enrolled in public secondary schools. The use of Appalachian dialect and the cultural emphasis on individuation are in conflict with Standard English and the conformity emphasized in many public schools.

Appalachian migration to urban areas began before World War II and peaked during the 1950s. Borman and Obermiller (1994) describe several stages in the process during which Appalachians have become "urban Appalachians." First, the newcomers were obviously migrants, with the Appalachian individual viewed as transient and adults perceived as undependable because of absenteeism related to visits "back home." During the next stage, Appalachians were not regarded as transients but were seen as a social problem, a perception that was heightened by federal and state social welfare programs. As social advocacy organizations developed in urban Appalachian neighborhoods, a third stage of identity began to emerge, a movement to establish an ethnic identity for urban Appalachians. In the current stage of identity formation for urban Appalachians, an ecological point of view has emerged, keeping in mind the existence of a distinctive, positive Appalachian culture. The term *urban Appalachian* itself was coined in the early 1970s by Appalachians living in midwestern cities to describe themselves after realizing that, due to their permanence, the term *Appalachian migrant* was no longer appropriate (Obermiller & Maloney, 1994).

Migrant Families

One of the most seriously underserved and inappropriately served groups of learners with disabilities are the children of migrant families (Interstate Migrant Council, 1984). **Migrants** are individuals or groups who move frequently to find work. In the United States, there are an estimated 800,000 migrant students. Of this number, 8,000 (1 percent) are receiving special education services, compared to approximately 10 percent of students in the general student populations (Perry, 1982). According to Salend (1990), California and Oregon, among the states employing the largest number of migrant workers, serve 1.37 percent and 3 percent of their migrant students, respectively, in special education. These percentages may be compared to 8.33 percent (California) and 10 percent (Oregon) of the general student population receiving special education services (Bird, 1985; McCoy, 1986).

Among the factors that place this group of learners at risk for disabilities are the following (Baca & Harris, 1988):

- High mobility: Migrant families change residence frequently, moving from state to state with the harvest seasons and availability of employment.
- Low socioeconomic status: Migrant families are generally employed in low-wage, unskilled jobs. Most frequently these jobs do not provide adequate housing and employee benefits, such as health care.
- Language and cultural differences: The vast majority of migrant families are members of cultural and ethnic minorities, especially Spanish-speaking minorities. Because they move in groups, they often lack the opportunity for exposure to the English language and majority American culture.
- Poor general health and nutrition: Due to mobility, low wages, lack of health insurance, lack of an understanding of how to use community medical and social services, and the hazards of their employment, migrant families frequently are in poor health and lack proper nutrition. The fact that children begin working in the field with parents at a young age contributes to the general lack of health and nutrition.

Objective Two

To describe issues related to the assessment of learners from various cultural and ethnic groups.

Annual **Edition**

Article *4*

Assessment of Learners from Diverse Cultural and Ethnic Groups

An overrepresentation of learners from various cultural and ethnic groups in the special education population often leads to discussions of assessment of these learners. In 1968, Dunn described the "six-hour mentally retarded child." "Six-hour mentally retarded children" were those who were only considered to be "different" in school during the school day and year. At other times and in other settings, such as at home, in the community, at church, and at work, these children could not be differentiated from their peers without disabilities. Using U.S. Office of Education statistics, Dunn reported that one-third of all special educators were teachers of students with mental retardation, and between 60 percent and 80 percent of their students were minority children from low socioeconomic status homes. Mercer (1973) reported similar overrepresentation in her study of special education classes in California, with Hispanics constituting only 11 percent of the school population yet 45.3 percent of the students in classes for individuals with mild mental retardation. In her findings, white students constituted 81 percent of the public school population but only 32.1 percent of the individuals placed in classes for students with mental retardation.

In a review of the Office of Civil Rights Elementary and Secondary Schools Civil Rights surveys published between 1980 and 1986, Chinn and Hughes (1987) confirm that representation of some minority groups continues to be disproportionately high in certain categories. They find that the overrepresentation of African Americans in classes for students who are mentally retarded or who have behavioral disorders remains at twice the level that would be expected from the percentage of Africa Americans in the school population. Dramatically fewer Hispanics are now being placed in classes for students who are mentally retarded than Mercer reported in 1973—an indication of recognition that Hispanic representation was disproportionately high and that many learners were misdiagnosed. Disproportionately low numbers of African Americans, Hispanics, and Native Americans were found in classes for the gifted and talented. When the intelligence quotient was the same across groups, African American children were found to perform better on visual spatial tasks of the Wechsler Intelligence Scale for Children (revised), while Caucasian children performed better on tasks of abstract thinking and general knowledge (Taylor & Richards, 1991). These findings offer some insight into the disproportionately high numbers of referrals and placements from diverse cultural and ethnic groups.

The U.S. Department of Education (1992) reports that African American youth are more highly represented in every disability category. This overrepresentation is most evident in the categories of speech and language disorders, mental retardation, and behavioral disorders. Though 12 percent of the school-age population are African American, 24 percent of all individuals with disabilities are African American.

In a migrant population, Barresi (1984) found that (a) approximately 10.7 percent of migrant students with mild disabilities were identified; (b) the identification of these students' disabilities occurred late in their school career; (c) there were significant delays in the transfer of students' special education records from jurisdiction to jurisdiction; (d) students' assessment data were duplicated in the various districts; (e) there were significant gaps in the services provided to the students due to the differences in services provided by the various schools the learners attended; (f) placements were often inappropriate due to language barriers that also appeared to delay the referral process; and (g) services were impeded by a lack of awareness and consistent and purposeful coordination between migrant education service personnel and special education service personnel.

In a discussion of the assessment of individuals from various cultural and ethnic groups, Gibbs and Huang (1989) suggest that culture may have a significant impact on five major domains of functioning. These include (a) individual psychological adjustment, (b) family relationships, (c) school adjustment and achievement, (d) relationships with peers, and (e) adaptation to the community.

During the assessment process, consideration must be given to *individual psychosocial adjustment.* Physical appearance, particularly variations from the Anglo norms in height, weight, or physique, should be considered. Culturally appropriate ways of expressing emotion or participating in social interaction can be confused with lack of affect or depressed affect. For example, eye contact, which is discouraged in some ethnic groups, is demanded in mainstream cultural communication. In order to assess self-concept and self-esteem, which are grounded in self-evaluation, the examiner should understand cultural standards. Other issues that emerge with regard to individual assessment include the cultural or ethnic group's perceptions of interpersonal competence, attitudes towards autonomy, attitudes toward achievement, management of aggression and impulse control, and coping and defense mechanisms.

When assessing *family relationships,* professionals should recognize that role and functions vary according to families. Subtle issues, such as who is addressed first, mother or father, and to whom correspondence should be addressed, may have an impact on the teacher's relationship with the family. Male children may have culturally based difficulties complying with the requests of a female teacher. In some cultural and ethnic groups, age and sex-role hierarchies emerge, and traditional family interaction patterns may not be compatible with the demands of the American educational system, which stresses verbal fluency and competition.

During the assessment of *school adjustment and achievement,* professionals should recognize that there may be a significant transition for the student between home and school. In dealing with achievement, minority-culture individuals rarely achieve as well as majority-culture students on tests. Relationships with peers in school become more difficult as the student matures; as students grow older they are more likely to become aware of their particular ethnic or minority status and its associated degree of desirability.

In *relationships with peers,* minority students frequently have two distinct sets of peer relationships and interaction patterns. One set is used in school, the other outside school.

In viewing and understanding their *adaptation to the community,* professionals should recognize that minority children are sometimes token members of groups or the group's scapegoat. Children from minority cultures may view the world of work quite differently than do children from the majority culture. These perceptions may affect the way in which children of minority cultures view education, the purpose of education, preparation for work, and work as a significant factor in their lives.

Alternative instructional strategies must be used prior to referring learners from diverse ethnic, cultural, and linguistic groups to special education services in order to eliminate the unnecessary assessment of children challenged by cultural mismatch with a teacher or other professional (Olion & Gillis-Olion, 1984). Olion and Gillis-Olion emphasize that all professionals should recognize that assessment should document assets as well as deficits. In addition, the collection of multisource data is especially important, and gathering this data in assessment should be an ongoing process. The active involvement of the parents and teachers is emphasized.

Olion and Gillis-Olion also argue that professionals must be culturally aware. Cultural awareness can indeed impact the interpretation of results. Dana (1988), in his study of the Minnesota Multiphasic Personality Inventory, found

guidelines for practice

Recommendations for Nonbiased, Functional Assessment

The Executive Committee for the Council for Children with Behavioral Disorders (1989) offers the following recommendations for the conduct of a nonbiased, functional assessment of learners from diverse ethnic, cultural, and linguistic groups.

1. Attention should be focused on classroom and school learning environments rather than medical- or mental health-based models.
2. Learner, teacher, and administrator culture, expectations, tolerance, learning and reinforcement history, and family situations should be considered.
3. Attention should be focused on student and teacher behaviors and the contexts in which they occur.
4. The conditions under which behaviors are observed, taught, and required should be studied.
5. Specific, measurable, instructionally based standards for academic and social behaviors should be established.
6. An assessment of the student's current learning environment, with documentation of prereferral interventions, should be implemented prior to referral.
7. Effective and efficient instructional procedures should be applied.
8. Teaching behaviors, instructional organization, and instructional supports should be assessed.
9. The responsibility for learning or performance failure should not be placed on the student.
10. Teachers should be prepared in a functional assessment perspective that focuses on children at risk for academic and/or behavioral difficulties.
11. Professionals should be realigned towards a functional assessment perspective ∎

culturally distinct patterns in results, which may then be misidentified as problems. For example, African Americans demonstrate symptoms of alienation, which, rather than demonstrating a problem, reflect a cultural variance. Annis and Corenblum (1988) report that among Canadian Native American children, who are fluent in both English and their native language (Ojibwa), significant differences occur in self-identification depending on the language used in assessment.

In a position paper on the assessment of children from various cultural and ethnic groups, the Executive Committee for the Council for Children with Behavioral Disorders (1989) states that misdiagnosis often occurs as a result of (a) language differences, (b) teachers' faulty perceptions and low expectations of the academic and social competence of learners from various cultural and ethnic groups, and (c) the fact that more learners from various cultural and ethnic groups are classified as behaviorally disordered because a disproportionate number of students from these groups are referred for assessment. Further recommendations for nonbiased assessment of learners from diverse ethnic, cultural, and linguistic groups appear in the "Guidelines for Practice" above.

The Impact of Various Cultural and Ethnic Groups on Classroom Interactions

Objective Three

To describe the impact of various cultural and ethnic groups on classroom interactions.

Though considerable variation exists within and across cultures, the interactions that many of the cultural or linguistic minority children engage in prior to entering school are context-embedded situations in which children have been able to negotiate meaningfully. However, when they enter the classroom, they find that the context is very different. They are provided with limited feedback from their efforts to learn and understand the Anglo school culture.

Hispanic Americans

According to Hyland (1989), Hispanic learners are significantly behind the general population in academic attainment. They enter school with a significantly different social, economic, and cultural background than do their peers who understand Anglo culture. Delgado-Gaitan and Trueba (1985) found, by carefully observing and recording the classroom interactions of seven Mexican American students under four different participation structures (group response, individual called response, silent work, and instructional group work), that copying was a legitimate activity among the students. This behavior appeared to be based on home socialization patterns that stress collectivity and social cohesiveness. Rather than representing low ability and lack of motivation, copying is considered by Mexican students to be a constructive approach to intellectual exchanges and the acquisition of new knowledge in a social unit composed of peers.

Commins and Miramontes (1989) report the results of an ethnographic study that explored the relationship of Mexican American students' achievement and language abilities. Students were perceived by teachers to have limited language abilities in Spanish and English; yet, across all settings, students displayed strengths in both languages. The organization of instruction in the classroom tended to limit the students' abilities to demonstrate their full range of competence in two languages. The students' lack of English structural proficiency and lack of vocabulary in Spanish were interpreted by teachers as a lack of conceptual ability; over a variety of contexts, however, students showed the ability to use language as a vehicle for effective self-expression both socially and cognitively.

African Americans

Hanna (1988) suggests that individuals belong to both speech and movement communities. As a consequence of the differences between the African American children's and Anglo teachers' speech and movement communities, six important areas of potential problems emerge: achievement, disruption, family cooperation, interpersonal negotiation of relationships, motor movement, and the expression of anger.

In the area of achievement, Hanna reports that many African American inner-city children consider academic book learning to be "white." She states that African American children who operate in a dual system of Standard English dialect and Black English Vernacular carry a more demanding cognitive burden than individuals operating in a single system in which fewer translations are necessary.

In reference to disruption, Hanna suggests that students may set into motion forces to eliminate poor self-image. These students may play to a peer audience for recognition when they do not receive recognition from the teacher. Hanna speaks of a culture of disruption rather than cooperation among some young, frustrated learners.

Other cultural variations emerge as problems for Anglo teachers. The African American practice of family cooperation is interpreted by some teachers as cheating. New children in the classroom negotiate interpersonal relationships, and participants probe for common experiences with their peers. They seek cues in how to act or what to expect from the teacher. These behaviors are problematic if they differ from the teacher's expectations of behavior, if the teacher does not understand that these are cultural ways of behaving. African American children demonstrate more motor activity and wear clothing that accent body movement. Touch is initiated sooner and is more common among black children.

Lower socioeconomic status African American learners appear to be socialized to greater aggression and expression of anger. Aggression or acting out is related to the development and maintenance of friendships and personal defenses. These friendships exist on several levels and emerge into kinships. In defending these ties, African American learners strike out with less restraint.

Native Americans

Perhaps most difficult to Native American learners is a conflict between cooperative learning styles and the competitive setting of the school. Native American children often learn by observation rather than displays of curiosity and verbal questioning, and they prefer cooperation and harmony. In school, these behaviors are perceived to be a general lack of individual competition and reliance on peer structure (Brod & McQuiston, 1983).

According to Gilliland and Rehner (1988), professionals teaching Native Americans have two major areas of concern: (a) understanding the Native American culture, which varies from the Anglo culture with regard to self-image, learning styles, discipline, and motivation, and (b) making the subject matter presented in schools, such as language arts, social studies, mathematics, science, and art, culturally relevant.

Asian Americans

Asian Americans, unlike other cultural, ethnic, and linguistic groups, have a positive stereotype as related to school achievement. Dao (1991) contends, however, that changes have occurred in the Asian American population and that many of these children are now at risk for school failure. Children from families with disrupted life and educational experiences differ vastly from children from established Asian American families. Recent immigrant or refugee children face the triple burden of learning English and the new school curriculum, adjusting to a new culture, and surviving an impoverished environment. In addition, recent refugees may have had traumatic experiences, including death, piracy, and extreme violence, and may not be emotionally ready to benefit from instruction.

Appalachians

Lewis, Messner, and McDowell (1985) describe Appalachian culture (especially the isolation and reliance on folk remedies) as unchanging. There are two particular segments of this culture: those who remain in the Appalachian region and Appalachian migrants who have moved to urban areas seeking employment.

Appalachians in the Region   In Heath's (1983) ethnographic study of two working-class Appalachian communities, the contrast of school and home play and communication patterns became evident as a mismatch challenging for teachers. She observed these patterns as early as preschool. One group of children found the concept of play centers in which specific toys were used for designated time periods puzzling; teachers' attempts to maintain schedules and encourage play activities were met with student frustration.

In terms of communication style, Heath found that the use of indirect questions rather than commands (for example, "could we have some air in here?" rather than "open the window") was difficult for the children to understand. When gathered for group story time, one group of children interrupted and spoke with other children while the teacher was reading.

Hensen and Resick (1990) believe that even Appalachians who have remained in the region are in a cultural transition. The traditional remedies appropriate to the care and prevention of health problems have been lost, and new ways of the mainstream culture have not yet been learned by the surviving generation, creating a void in knowledge.

In terms of the relationship with their children, Appalachian mothers were found to have unrealistically high expectations of their infants. They were restrictive of their older children's activities and used physical punishments, paired with reasoning and rewards, as discipline (Kennedy, 1985). Though low-income Appalachian Caucasian mothers valued self-direction and internalization, they acknowledged the need for conformity as an adaptive mechanism and maintained a desire for their children to rise above their current status (Peterson & Peters, 1985).

Urban Appalachians   Relocated Appalachian families have been described as suffering from "existential depression," reactive to separation from the meanings found in both nature and the family's extended network "back home" (Lantz & Harper, 1989). Those families who left the Appalachian region were more highly motivated to follow the goals set by mainstream society, whereas those who stayed behind placed greater importance on their continued association with family and familiar surroundings and the lifestyle of the region (Daniel, 1985).

A study exploring a Caucasian mainstream-culture female teacher and her interactions with three first graders—a Caucasian mainstream-culture male, an Appalachian male, and an African American male found that, in terms of recognition of discourse differences, the Appalachian student was the most challenged; he finished the year in the lowest reading group (Pepinsky & DeStefano, 1983).

Migrant Families

Migrant children with disabilities have several unique educational needs in addition to their need for special education services. These include the following (Baca & Harris, 1988):

- native-language development and instruction. These services must be provided either by a bilingual educator in consultation with a special educator or by a bilingual special educator.
- English as a second language (ESL) instruction, provided by the special educator or in cooperation with an ESL teacher. Instruction should be meaningful and appropriate to the child's age and level of development. Caution must be taken to assure that the child's culture is not denigrated.
- self-concept enhancement. Mobility, poverty, and the general lifestyle of the migrant child appear to have a negative impact on self-concept (Henggeler & Tavormina, 1979). Self-concept enhancement is an important part of the curriculum for migrant students.
- acculturation enhancement. Migrant learners can be helped greatly through instruction and experiences that familiarize them with the majority culture. Caution must be taken to assure that the child's culture is not denigrated.
- family and community involvement. The family appears to be the one constant social unit in the life of the migrant student. It is important that the family be involved to the extent possible in the learner's educational program. Family involvement is enhanced through home visits and the use of the family's primary language.
- coordination of services. The special educator or other service provider should assume the role of consultant to the family.
- use of the Individualized Education Program. The migrant educator, ESL educator, and other community and school service providers should be involved in the development of the comprehensive IEP. In addition, available services for the transfer of information from jurisdiction to jurisdiction should be used.

The classroom teacher has made obvious efforts to recognize and integrate the students' cultures (bulletin boards, etc.) into the environment.

Objective Four

To describe ways to mediate the environment for learners from various cultural and ethnic groups.

Mediating the Environment

Cummins (1989) suggests that learners from minority cultural and ethnic groups are disempowered educationally in much the same way that their communities are disempowered by interactions in society. In short, these learners are either "empowered" or "disabled" as a direct result of their interactions with educators in the schools. He links empowerment to the extent to which the following occur:

1. Language and culture are a part of the school program.
2. Community participation is an integral component of the children's education.
3. Instruction promotes intrinsic motivation on the part of students to use language and generate their own knowledge.
4. Assessment focuses on the ways in which academic difficulties are a function of interactions within the school context rather than problems within the students.

In working with learners from different cultures, Au (1980) suggests developing a social context that is comfortable for the teacher and for the learners. Through interweaving text-derived content and personal experience, a more comfortable social context should evolve. In addition, a level of comfort must be negotiated between teachers and parents of the learners whom they teach. Lightfoot (1981) contends that territoriality exists between parents and teachers because of stereotypes about minority parents and teachers. Schools, she argues, organize public "rites," such as PTA meetings, open houses, or newsletters, which delineate rather than explore collaboration. These interactions are institutionalized means of establishing boundaries under the guise of "partnership."

Cross (1988) proposes a five-part framework for providing culturally competent services that would enhance true collaboration. The following elements are essential to the framework:

1. An awareness and acceptance of ethnic difference. Celebrating diversity, rather than arguing that everyone is really the same, enhances collaboration.

2. Awareness of one's personal culture. Teachers must examine their own values and beliefs regarding family, goals, and schooling.
3. Recognition of the dynamics of differences. The culturally transmitted patterns of communication, etiquette, and problem solving should be recognized.
4. Knowledge of the family's culture.
5. Adaptation of skills, that is, modification of the teacher-child interaction and teaching/learning process to support cultural differences.

Beyond academic competence there is a need for students to demonstrate interactional competence in social settings in order to do well in school; the major identified literacy/achievement problem was called an "attitude" problem. Gilmore (1987) found that students who frequently displayed stylized "sulking and stepping" were usually described by teachers as having a "bad attitude."

For effective learning, the role of the culture must be recognized and used in the activity settings during the actual learning process (Trueba, 1988a). Culture appears to be at the heart of academic success regardless of the learner's ethnicity or culture. An effective learning environment must be constructed in which the learner is assisted through meaningful and culturally appropriate relationships in the internalization of the Anglo values embedded in the school system. Trueba (1988b) believes that at the heart of academic failure may be a profound cultural conflict and that there are ways to socialize minority children for academic success. Culturally based instructional models can help in the acquisition of English literacy for academic success.

Annual Edition

Article *17*

Language

As suggested by the quotation that opened this chapter, Delpit (1988) believes that students must be taught the language codes needed to participate fully in the mainstream of American life, not by being forced to attend to low, inane subskills, but rather within the context of meaningful communicative endeavors. Learners must be allowed the resource of the teacher's expert knowledge while being helped to acknowledge their own "expertness." An appropriate education for poor children and children of color can only be devised in consultation with adults who share their culture. Teachers need to not only "help students to establish their own voices, but to coach those voices to produce notes that will be heard clearly in the larger society" (p. 296).

Dialects serve to identify speakers in either geographical or social space (Farr, 1986). Different rules distinguish different dialects. Learners who have rules in their linguistic competence that produce nonstandard features have difficulty editing their writing so that it reflects written grammatical standards. Bidialectalism is based on the assumption that nonstandard dialects are as valid as Standard English; if a second dialect is acquired, two linguistic systems are available for oral and written communication.

In his study of English language learning among Hispanic children, Trueba (1988b) followed twelve children across school and home settings. Trueba found that cultural conflict may help explain problems in the acquisition of English literacy. English literacy school activities presuppose cultural knowledge and values that the children and their families have not acquired. To address these challenges, he recommends that

1. students should be placed in learning environments in which there are opportunities for educators to evaluate and analyze incidents of failure and degradation related to academic performance.
2. learning skills and levels students have achieved in specific subjects should be identified.

Making News

Head Start gets a fresh start—at night

By Anne Carothers-Kay
Register Staff Writer

It's sundown, and the fading light downtown has a reddish hue from all the taillights of cars streaming out of the city's center. Thousands of workers are ending their day, but for preschooler Tabatha Eddins, the best part of the day is just beginning.

At 6 p.m., in a small glass room tucked under a downtown Des Moines parking garage, Tabatha scribbles back and forth on a paper with her name on it and "signs in" to the first nighttime Head Start class in the country.

For the next 3½ hours, she and six other children will sing songs, learn to count with a puppet called "the Count," and play with Play-Doh, blocks and a host of other toys that promote learning through play. They'll eat dinner and a snack. They'll wash their hands and brush their teeth.

And at 9:30 p.m., when most of their peers are sound asleep, they're just getting out of school.

Head Start—the 30-year success story for poor children—meets the swing shift.

About Time

And it's about time, said Anne Bardwell, director of the Drake Head Start program that operates 28 Head Start centers in central Iowa.

Head Start is a free preschool program designed to give poor children an educational and social boost toward kindergarten.

"And poor people are the people who tend to work the second shift," said Bardwell.

They are the maids at the Marriott Hotel, the data entry operators at insurance companies, the admitting clerks and nursing aides at the hospitals. They are the factory workers. And they are the single mothers who are taking night classes to get off of welfare.

Few child-care centers keep their hours.

A federal Department of Labor study earlier this year reported that nearly one in five full-time workers worked non-standard hours in 1991, a trend that child-care agencies have not kept pace with.

The study was prompted by reports that workers at a food-processing plant in Idaho were leaving sleeping children in cars in the plant's parking lot.

But Bardwell said the evening class wasn't created as part of some grand national plan to expand Head Start. Instead, it was prompted by a desire to maximize the use of the downtown building that Head Start uses.

Joyce Wisby, Head Start program coordinator, said the city suggested adding an evening program, given the number of people who work downtown at night.

3. learning experiences should be constructed that are more congruent with a child's cultural and linguistic backgrounds and in which children play a major role in determining or negotiating the level and content of what they want to learn.
4. learning experiences should be expressed in clear goals, well understood and internalized by the children and supported by a creative reward system.

Trueba states that two factors must be addressed simultaneously: (1) the school system should be sensitized to develop culturally based instructional models that are effective for minorities, and (2) children representing minorities should be socialized to achieve academically.

Migrant Families

Through the states, the federal government provides migrant education services. The migrant educator is the primary service provider. She or he has a diverse role, which includes the following (Salend, 1990):

- certification of the migrant family as eligible for service
- assisting parents in enrolling their children in school and serving as parent advocate
- identifying and contacting community agencies, organizations, and other resources that can offer assistance to the family, such as medical and dental services
- providing supplemental instruction to the student, including bilingual instruction, ESL instruction, and career education
- consulting with special and general educators

"We look at the downtown as a community within itself, and that we are there to serve that community to become a part of that community," she said.

Wisby said it was originally thought that the program would appeal to parents searching for nighttime child care. But parents of several children in the evening Head Start program said they were looking for more than just baby-sitting.

Ardenia Lee works the overnight shift at Hardees—11 p.m. to 7 a.m. The evening Head Start program doesn't replace her child care, but Lee said after she saw how much Head Start helped her kindergartner, Jasmine, she wanted her 4-year-old, Ray, to benefit from it.

Tracy Moats works from 3 p.m. to 11 p.m. in the admitting office of Iowa Methodist Medical Center. Her mother helps by caring for her three children at night, but Moats said

she knew her son, Deric, needed a preschool environment. She had tried a daytime preschool, but the cost was prohibitive. The waiting list for daytime Head Start was too long for Deric, who just turned 5.

The evening Head Start solved two problems for Moats. It eased the burden on her mother and provided Deric with a challenging learning environment for 3½ hours a day.

Eventually, Moats noticed another benefit. Evenings were actually the best time for learning for her son.

Deric takes Ritalin to control his hyperactivity. The drug wears off about 8 p.m., and those evening hours often were difficult at home because he gets hyperactive. Then he can't calm down to go to sleep, she said.

At Head Start, his teachers found that the program's structure helped Deric focus his energy into learning. And by the time he gets

home at 10 p.m., he's tired and goes right to sleep, his mother said.

It's a benefit that the program's coordinators confess they had not anticipated.

Several children with hyperactivity or attention disorders in the class reacted similarly, said Grace Pirello-Towne, who runs the evening program. She said they seem to learn more intensely as their medications are wearing off, and none of the children in the class are too sleepy or tired to learn at night.

"They are very calm, very relaxed," said Wisby. "You have to remember that these children are on a different schedule than the rest of us. They don't get up until 10 or 11 in the morning • "

From The Des Moines Register, *Head Start Gets A Fresh Start — At Night* by Anne Carothers-Kay, January 26, 1996. Reprinted with permission of The Des Moines Register.

- providing parent training
- serving as interpreter
- providing transportation for families

Migrant students should be entered into the Migrant Student Record Transfer System (MSRTS) as soon after school enrollment as possible. MSRTS is a computerized communications system that collects, maintains, and transfers the academic and health records of migrant children throughout the United States. The system includes information about special education services required by individual children entered into the program. It lists information on the child's disability, assessment, related services, and IEP. Information is provided on how to contact the child's previous school.

The Impact of Larger Social Systems on Diverse Cultural and Ethnic Groups

Objective Five

To describe the impact of membership in various ethnic and cultural groups in the larger social systems of the community and society.

Ogbu (1985) explores why cultural and language dissonance appears temporary for some minority groups and more persistent for others. He suggests that minorities are characterized by at least two types of cultural/language differences. One is a primary cultural difference which existed before the group became a minority. The other is a secondary difference, which arose after the group became subordinate to others, as cultural ways of behaving in order to cope with their subordination and exploitation, protect their identity, and maintain their boundary. Ogbu describes three kinds of minority groups: (1) autonomous minorities, who are not usually victims of stratification, (2) immigrant minorities, who have not had time to internalize the effects of discrimination, and (3) castelike or subordinate minorities, who are denied true assimilation into the mainstream. Castelike minorities may demonstrate school difficulties due to their forced incorporation and subordination, the cumulative effects of being denied access to a good education, early discrimination experienced in white schools, limited opportunities, and school behavior of accommodation and assimilation being seen as "buying out."

Another issue in the discussion of cultural diversity is social class. Turner (1973) reports clear evidence of the relevance of social class to the child's definition of the control situation and his or her own choice of control. In discussing control, working-class children mention control by threats. Control in the schools seems to maintain social differences, in that middle-class children may have an orientation to an elaborated code, such as that found in schools, while other children may be less comfortable with such codes.

In an analysis of lower-track classes in a secondary school, Page (1987) found that these classes were neither specific to the individual needs of the students nor were they determined by social order. Teachers made explicit references to the children's socioeconomic class concurrently with academic and behavioral characteristics to form a constellation of traits by which they identified the students. The curricula used in these "terminal education classes" recreated the educational norm of each institution and translated teachers' perceptions of students' social class characteristics and made them visible in the classroom. Being "low class" emerged as a culture in itself in the school, cutting across race and ethnicity.

Self-Perception and Society's Perceptions of Racial and Ethnic Differences

In the earliest studies of racial preference, Clark and Clark (1939) found that racial identification occurs between the third and fourth year of the child's life. Yet in terms of racial preference (in the selection and description of dolls representing different races as "pretty" or "nice"), African American children typically chose to play with the Caucasian doll. These findings have been confirmed in more recent studies with not only African American children, but Native Americans, Asian Americans, Hispanics, and New Zealand Moaris. What is called a "white bias" was consistently demonstrated (Aboud & Skerry, 1984).

Clark and Clark (1939), in their explanation of the "white bias," write that learners are distressed by the conflict between personal racial identity and the perceived value of that race in society. The selection of Caucasian dolls or pictures indicates an attempt to identify with the dominant group. Williams and Morland (1976) contend that what is actually in place is a "light-color bias" with children acting according to learned behavior that light is good, clean, and nice, while dark is bad, dirty, or mean.

Though these are probably not the only possible theories for the so-called "white bias," this bias can also be viewed in terms of the context of the assessment. Trent (1964) found that African American assessors elicited different preferences for pictures of Caucasian and African American persons from children who were African American or Caucasian. Corenblum and Wilson (1982) found that Native American children were more likely to select a Native American doll as looking like themselves when dolls were presented by a Native American. In addition to race, the language used may also impact preferences children report. Gibbons (1983) believes that language acts as another contextual cue that enhances personal group identification and helps learners define the situation.

Several independent variables contribute to the "white bias." Its very existence raises some questions about racial and ethnic minorities in North American society. Aboud and Skerry (1984) suggest that when the power or status of a minority group is low, preferences emerge for the majority group. Dana (1988)

Schools should recognize that learners from minority cultural and ethnic groups are often challenged by the Anglo culture of schools.

states that group consciousness—the restoration of an original cultural identity as a means of making sense out of life experiences and dealing with the effects of racism—emerges in situations such as the "white bias" to increase positive self-affirmation and cultural identity. Learners from various cultural and ethnic groups are simultaneously and in various degrees dealing with the social and economic reality of Anglo culture.

Perceptions Regarding Family

Chavkin (1989) argues that although minority parents want to be involved in their children's education, appropriate structures and strategies do not exist for involving them. Communication does not occur because of lack of resources and time. Professionals must, however, debunk the myth that minority parents do not care about their children's education.

In their survey of 1,118 black and Hispanic parents, Williams and Chavkin (1985) demonstrated that these parents, regardless of ethnicity or minority status, were concerned about their children's education. Parents expressed strong interest in a variety of roles and activities and were interested in being involved in school decisions, going to school performances, helping their children at home, and assisting at school events.

The results of the Metropolitan Life Survey of the American Teacher (1987) indicated that parents in inner-city districts were less satisfied than were suburban parents with the frequency of their contacts with the teacher. Minority parents reported that they were intimidated by the staff and institutional structures of the school.

Impact of Segregation

Coleman and associates (1966) conducted an extensive series of national studies regarding the impact of segregated facilities on the education life of learners. Predominantly African American schools were found to have lower quality and quantity of facilities and curricular choices for students. These learners were found to score as much as one standard deviation below Anglo pupils' scores at first grade. Coleman and associates found that the most important variable in improving the education of African American learners who had been educated in segregated settings was the educational backgrounds and aspirations of their school peers.

As Coleman and his associates were studying segregated facilities, Rosenberg (1965) presented the concept of contextual dissonance, which he described as a sense of not belonging with the people or to the environment in which one finds oneself. He reported that African American learners in integrated schools had lower self-esteem than those in primarily African American schools. When a group of African American students who had not been dislocated for purposes of integration was examined, they held higher self-esteem than Caucasians.

While de facto segregation continues to exist, some means of creating heterogeneous groups to prepare learners to exist in a pluralistic society remains necessary (Streitmatter, 1988). Schools have, in Streitmatter's opinion, been deemed the primary means of implementing this goal. He argues that care must be taken to consider all of the ramifications of implementing this goal; the individual learner's self esteem and healthy progression through the identity development process is an important consideration for policymakers working toward more effective and positive school integration.

Summary

In this chapter, five major ethnic, cultural, and linguistic groups were discussed: Asian American, African American, Hispanic, Native American, and Appalachian. The material in this chapter was written with the recognition that within each ethnic and cultural group there is vast diversity and individuality.

By the year 2000, one in every three Americans will be African American, Hispanic, or Asian American. This change in population requires that the school be reorganized to respond to the individual and group needs of learners from diverse ethnic and cultural groups and at the same time respect and protect the uniqueness of the members of these groups as individuals and groups having common history, traditions, and experiences. In addition, attention should be given to the unique challenges presented to the children of migrant families.

Ethnic and minority groups are overrepresented in special education. Assessment is not sensitive to the cultural uniqueness of the members of these minorities.

A greater emphasis on assessment within cultural context was suggested in this chapter. Assessment must be responsive to individual psychological adjustment, family relationships, school adjustment and achievement, and relationships with peers.

Learners from various cultures and ethnic groups must be helped to adjust to a difficult transition from their familiar cultural context to the unfamiliar context of the classroom and school. This may be accomplished through educator sensitivity to learners' culture and language, the integration of minority community leaders and parents into the educational process, and the use of learners' personal experiences and perceptions in the educational process.

Finally, society and especially educators must develop an awareness of and sensitivity to diverse cultural and ethnic backgrounds.

Building Your Professional Vocabulary

Match each word or phrase to its meaning.

_____ Anglo

_____ Hispanic

_____ ethnicity

a. membership in a group of people who share a unique social and cultural heritage
b. groups that have unequal access to power
c. mainstream middle-class male Caucasian

_____ migrant

_____ minority

d. learners whose cultural heritage is tied to the use of Spanish
e. individuals who move frequently, following employment

Comprehension Check

Select the most appropriate response.

1. Ethnicity
   a. is usually race specific.
   b. may be independent of race.
   c. overlaps with race.

2. Minority groups
   a. have fewer members than the majority culture.
   b. have equal access to power and legal protection.
   c. are considered by the majority group to be less worthy of sharing power.

3. American society is now best depicted as
   a. a melting pot.
   b. ethnically bound.
   c. a salad bowl.

4. Students from diverse ethnic, cultural, and linguistic groups
   a. experience a lack of congruence between what happens in and out of school.
   b. generalize school behaviors to their culture.
   c. are socialized to American culture by public schools and assimilate Anglo culture.

5. The fastest growing cultural group in America is
   a. African American.
   b. Asian American.
   c. Hispanic.

6. Unlike other cultural, ethnic, and linguistic groups, Native Americans
   a. have been assimilated through boarding schools and reservations.
   b. have been victims of genocide.
   c. have embraced Standard English due to the diversity of languages.

7. Appalachians
   a. experience less discrimination in that they are usually Caucasian.

b. experience challenges in school due to dialect.
   c. experience and succeed at efforts at assimilation.

8. Learners from diverse cultural, linguistic, and ethnic groups
   a. often experience low expectations for social and academic competence from teachers.
   b. often experience high expectations for social and academic competence from teachers.
   c. often are equally competent regarding social and academic areas as their Anglo peers.

9. Assessment of learners from diverse cultural, linguistic, and ethnic groups must
   a. apply standardized measures to gather objective information.
   b. include an assessment of the current learning environment.
   c. apply measures with large norming samples.

10. In mediating the environment for learners from diverse ethnic, cultural, and linguistic groups, the teacher should
    a. aim for assimilation of students into Anglo culture.
    b. emphasize basic skills in order to build leadership in the culture.
    c. incorporate the learners' language and culture into the school program.

11. A challenge in involving parents from diverse cultural, linguistic, and ethnic groups in their children's education is
    a. lack of interest.
    b. lack of time on the part of parents and teachers.
    c. lack of appropriate structures and strategies for involving them.

References

Aboud, F. E., & Skerry, S. A. (1984). The development of ethnic attitudes: A critical review. *Journal of Cross-Cultural Psychology, 15,* 3–34.

Allen, L., & Majidi-Ahi, S. (1989). Black American children. In J. Gibbs & L. Huang (Eds.), *Children of color* (pp. 148–178). San Francisco: Jossey Bass.

Annis, R. C., & Corenblum, B. (1988). Effect of test language and experimenter race on Canadian Indian children's racial and self-identity. *The Journal of Social Psychology, 126,* 761–773.

Au, H. K. (1980). Participation structures in a reading lesson with Hawaiian children: Analysis of a culturally appropriate instructional event. *Anthropology and Education Quarterly, 11,* 91–115.

Baca, L., & Harris, K. C. (1988). Teaching migrant exceptional children. *Teaching Exceptional Children, 20* (4), 32–35.

Barresi, J. (1984). *Interstate Migrant Council: National workshop on special education needs of migrant handicapped students. Proceedings report.* Denver: Education Commission of the States.

Berlowitz, M. J., & Durand, H. (1977). School dropout or school pushout? A case study of the possible violation of property rights and liberties by the de facto exclusion of students from the public schools. Working Paper #8. Cincinnati: Urban Appalachian Council.

Bird, B. (1985). Comparisons of the total school population with migrant students in special education. Unpublished manuscript, California Task Force on Migrant Education, Sacramento.

Bobo, J. K. (1985). Preventing drug abuse among American Indian adolescents. In L. D. Gilchrist and & S. P. Schinke (Eds.), *Preventing social and health problems through life skills training.* Seattle: University of Washington School of Social Work.

Borman, K. M., Mueninghoff, E., & Piazza, S. (1989). Urban Appalachian girls and young women: Bowing to no one. In L. Weis (Ed.), *Class, race, and gender in U.S. schools* (pp. 230–248). Albany, NY: Sage.

Borman, K., & Obermiller, P. (1994). Introduction. In K. Borman & P. Obermiller (Eds.), *From mountain to metropolis: Appalachian migrants in American cities* (xvii–xxi). Westport, CT: Bergin & Garvey.

Brendtro, L. K., Brokenleg, M., & Bockern, S. V. (1990). *Reclaiming youth at risk: Our hope for the future.* Bloomington, IN: National Education Service.

Brod, R. L., & McQuiston, J. M. (1983). American Indian adult education and literacy: The first national survey. *Journal of American Indian Education, 1,* 1–16.

Bryde, J. (1971). *Indian students and guidance.* Boston: Houghton Mifflin Company.

Buenning, M., Tollefson, N., & Rodriguez, F. (1992). Hispanic culture and the schools. In M. J. Fine and C. Carlson (Eds.), *The handbook of family-school intervention: A systems perspective* (pp. 86–101). Boston: Allyn & Bacon.

Chavkin, N. F. (1989). Debunking the myth about minority parents. *Educational Horizons, 67* (4), 119–123.

Chinn, P. C., & Hughes, S. (1987). Representation of minority students in special education classes. *Remedial and Special Education, 8,* 41–46.

Clark, K., & Clark, M. (1939). The development of consciousness of self and the emergence of racial identification in Negro preschool children. *Journal of Social Psychology, 10,* 591–599.

Coleman, J. S., Campbell, E. Q., Hobson, C. J., McPartland, J., Mood, A. M., Weinfeld, F. D., & York, R. L. (1966). *Quality of educational opportunity.* Washington, DC: Government Printing Office.

Commins, N. L., & Miramontes, O. B. (1989). Perceived and actual linguistic competence: A descriptive study of four low-achieving Hispanic bilingual students. *American Educational Research Journal, 26,* 443–472.

Corenblum, B., & Wilson, A. E. (1982). Ethnic preferences and identification among Canadian Indian and white children: Replication and extension. *Canadian Journal of Behavioral Science, 14,* 50–59.

Cross, T. (1988). Services to minority populations: What does it mean to be a culturally competent professional? *Focal Point, 2* (4), 1–3.

Cummins, J. (1989). A theoretical framework for bilingual special education. *Exceptional children, 56* (2), 111–119.

Dana, R. H. (1988). Culturally diverse groups and MMPI interpretation. *Professional Psychology: Research and Practice, 19,* 490–495.

Daniel, B. P. (1985). Cultural influences on moving or staying: An Appalachian case study. *Journal of Applied Social Sciences, 10* (1), 51–61.

Dao, M. (1991). Designing assessment procedures for educationally at-risk Southeast Asian American students. *Journal of Learning Disabilities, 24,* 594–601, 629.

Delgado-Gaitan, C., & Trueba, H. T. (1985). Ethnographic study of participant structures in task completion: Reinterpretation of "handicaps" in Mexican children. *Learning Disability Quarterly, 8,* 67–75.

Delpit, L. D. (1988). The silenced dialogue: Power and pedagogy in educating other people's children. *Harvard Educational Review, 58,* 280–298.

Dunn, L. (1968). Special education for the mildly retarded: Is much of it justifiable? *Exceptional Children, 7,* 5–24.

Executive Committee for the Council for Children with Behavioral Disorders (1989). White paper: Best assessment practices for students with behavioral disorders: Accommodation to cultural diversity and individual differences. *Behavioral Disorders, 14,* 263–278.

Farr, M. (1986). Language, culture, and writing: Sociolinguistic foundations of research on writing. In E. Z. Rothkopf (Ed.), *Review of research in education,* (Vol. 13, pp. 195–223). Washington, DC: American Educational Research Association.

Fradd, S., Figueroa R. A., & Correa, V. I. (1989). Meeting the multicultural needs of Hispanic students in special education. *Exceptional Children, 56,* 102–104.

Garcia-Preto, N. (1982). Puerto-Rican families. In M. Goldriek, J. K. Pierce, & J. Gordano (Eds.), *Ethnicity and family therapy.* New York: Guilford.

Gibbons, J. P. (1983). Attitudes towards languages and code-mixing in Hong Kong. *Journal of Multilingual and Multicultural Development, 4,* 129–147.

Gibbs, J. T., & Huang, L. N. (1989). A conceptual framework for assessing and treating minority youth. In J. T. Gibbs & L. N. Huang (Eds.), *Children of color.* San Francisco: Jossey Bass.

Gilliland, H., & Rehner, J. (1988). *Teaching the Native American.* Dubuque, IA: Kendall/Hunt.

Gilmore, P. (1987). Sulking, stepping, and tracking: The effects of attitude assessment on access to literacy. In D. Bloome (Ed.), *Literacy and schooling* (pp. 98–119). Norwood, NJ: Ablex.

Grimm, L. L. (1992). The Native American child in school: An ecological perspective. In M. J. Fine and C. Carlson (Eds.), *The handbook of family-school intervention: A systems perspective* (pp. 102–118). Boston: Allyn & Bacon.

Guinn, R. (1977). Value clarification in the bicultural classroom. *Journal of Teacher Education, 28,* 46–47.

Hanna, J. (1988). *Disruptive school behavior: Class, race, and culture.* New York: Holmes and Meyer.

Heath, S. B. (1983). *Ways with words.* New York: Cambridge University Press.

Henggeler, S. W., & Tavormina, J. B. (1979). The children of Mexican-American migrant workers: A population at risk? *Journal of Abnormal Child Psychology, 6* (1), 1–10.

Hensen, M. M., & Resick, L. (1990). Health beliefs, health care, and rural Appalachian subcultures from an ethnographic perspective. *Family and Community Health, 13* (1), 1–10.

Hodgkinson, H. (1985). *All one system.* Washington, DC: Institute for Educational Leadership.

Hoffman, E. (1988). *The right to be human: A biography of Abraham Maslow.* Los Angeles: Jeremy P. Tarcher, Inc.

Huang, L. N. (1989). Southeast Asian refugee children and adolescents. In J. T. Gibbs & L. N. Huang (Eds.), *Children of color: Psychological interventions with minority youth* (pp. 278–321). San Francisco: Jossey Bass.

Huang, L. N., & Ying, Y. (1989). Chinese American children and adolescents. In J. T. Gibbs & L. N. Huang (Eds.), *Children of color* (pp. 30–66). San Francisco: Jossey Bass.

Hyland, C. R. (1989). What we know about the fastest growing minority population: Hispanic Americans. *Educational Horizons, 67* (4), 124–130.

Inclan, J. (1985). Variations in value orientations in mental health work with Puerto Ricans. *Psychotherapy, 33* (2S), 324–334.

Inclan, J. E., & Herron, D. G. (1989). Puerto Rican adolescents. In J. T. Gibbs & L. N. Huang (Eds.), *Children of color* (pp. 251–277). San Francisco: Jossey Bass.

Interstate Migrant Council (1984). *National policy workshop on special education needs of migrant handicapped students. Proceedings report.* Denver: Education Commission of the States.

Kennedy, J. H. (1985). Childrearing attitudes in Appalachia today: A preliminary look. *Psychological Reports, 56,* 677–678.

Kochman, T. (1991). Culturally based patterns of difference. Paper presented at the University of Cincinnati.

LaFrombroise, T. D., & Low, K. G. (1989). American Indian children and adolescents. In J. Gibbs & L. Huang (Eds.), *Children of color* (pp. 114–147). San Francisco: Jossey Bass.

Lantz, J. E., & Harper, K. (1989). Network intervention, existential depression, and the relocated Appalachian family. *Contemporary Family Therapy: An International Journal, 11,* 213–223.

Leap, W. L. (1981). American Indian language maintenance. *Annual Review of Anthropology, 10,* 271–280.

Lewis, S., Messner, R., & McDowell, W. A. (1985). An unchanging culture. *Journal of Gerontological Nursing, 11* (8), 20–25.

Lightfoot, S. (1981). Toward conflict resolution: Relationships between families and schools. *Theory into Practice, 20* (2), 97–104.

McAdoo, H. P. (1978). Minority families. In J. H. Stevens & M. Matthers (Eds.), *Mother-child, father-child relationships.* Washington, DC: The National Association for the Education of Young Children.

McCoy, C. B., & Watkins, V. M. (1980). Drug use among urban ethnic youth. *Youth and Society, 11,* 83–106.

McCoy, J. L. (1986). The migrant handicapped student: Strategies for involving the migrant parent in the IEP process. Salem, OR: COPE Project.

Mercer, J. (1973). *Labeling the mentally retarded.* Los Angeles: University of California Press.

The Metropolitan Life Survey of the American Teacher—Strengthening links between home and school (1987). New York: Louis Harris and Associates.

Mindel, C. H., & Habenstein, R. W. (Eds.) (1981). *Ethnic families in America: Patterns and variations* (2nd ed.). New York: Elseview.

Obermiller, P., Borman, K., & Kroger, J. (1988). The Lower Price Hill Community School. *Urban Education, 23,* 123–132.

Obermiller, P. J., & Maloney, M. (1994). Living city, feeling country: The current status and future prospects of urban Appalachians. In K. Borman & P. Obermiller (Eds.), *From mountain to metropolis: Appalachian migrants in American cities* (3–12). Westport, CT: Bergin & Garvey.

Ogbu, J. U. (1985). Research currents: Cultural-ecological influences on minority school learning. *Language Arts, 62,* 860–869.

Olion, L., & Gillis-Olion, M. (1984). Assessing culturally diverse exceptional children. *Early Child Development and Care, 15,* 203–232.

Page, R. (1987). Teachers' perceptions of students: A link between classrooms, school cultures, and the social order. *Anthropology and Education Quarterly, 18,* 77–99.

Pepinsky, H. B., & DeStefano, J. S. (1983). Interactive discourse in the classroom as organizational behavior. *Advances in Reading/Language Research, 2,* 107–137.

Perry, J. (1982). The ECS interstate migrant education project. *Exceptional Children, 48,* 496–500.

Peters, M. (1981). Parenting in Black families with young children. In H. McAdoo (Ed.), *Black families.* Newbury Park, CA: Sage.

Peterson, G. W., & Peters, D. F. (1985). The socialization values of low-income Appalachian white and rural black mothers: A comparative study. *Journal of Comparative Family Studies, 16* (1), 75–91.

Ramirez, O. (1990). Mexican American children and adolescents. In J. T. Gibbs & L. N. Huang (Eds.), *Children of color* (pp. 224--250). San Francisco: Jossey Bass.

Ramirez, O., & Arce, C. H. (1981). The contemporary Chicano family: An empirically based review. In A. Baron, Jr. (Ed.), *Explorations in Chicano psychology.* New York: Praeger.

Resnick, L. B. (1987). Learning in school and out. *Educational Researcher, 16* (9), 13–20.

Rosenberg, M. (1965). *Society and the adolescent self-image.* Princeton, NJ: Princeton University Press.

Salend, S. J. (1990). A migrant education guide for special educators. *Teaching Exceptional Children, 22* (2), 18–21.

Shon, S., & Ja, D. (1982). Asian families. In M. McGodrick, J. K. Pearce, & J. Giordano (Eds.), *Ethnicity and family therapy.* New York: Guilford Press.

Smith, E. (1981). Cultural and historical perspectives in counseling Blacks. In D. W. Sue (Ed.), *Counseling the culturally different: Theory and practice.* New York: Wiley.

Sowell, T. (1981). *Ethnic America.* New York: Basic Books.

Spindler, G., and Spindler, L. (1994). What is cultural therapy? In G. Spindler and L. Spindler (Eds.), *Pathways to cultural awareness: Cultural therapy with teachers and students* (pp. 1–35). Thousand Oaks: CA: Sage.

Standing Bear, L. (1933). *Land of the spotted eagle.* New York: Houghton Mifflin.

Steward, R. J., & Logan, S. L. (1992). Understanding the Black family and child in the school context. In M. J. Fine and C. Carlson (Eds.), *The handbook of family-school intervention: A systems perspective* (pp. 57–74). Boston: Allyn & Bacon.

Streitmatter, J. L. (1988). School desegregation and identity development. *Urban Education, 23,* 280–293.

Sullivan, M., & Miller, D. (1990). Cincinnati's Urban Appalachian Council and Appalachian identity. *Harvard Educational Review, 60* (1), 106–124.

Taylor, D., & Dorsey-Gaines, C. (1988). *Growing up literate: Learning from inner city families.* Portsmouth, NH: Heinemann.

Taylor, R. L., & Richards, S. B. (1991). Patterns of intellectual differences of Black, Hispanic, and white children. *Psychology in the Schools, 28,* 5–9.

Trankina, F. (1983). Clinical issues and techniques in working with Hispanic children and their families. In G. J. Powell, J. Yamamoto, A. Romero, & A. Morales (Eds.), *The psychosocial development of minority group children.* New York: Brunner/Mazel.

Trent, R. (1964). The colour of the investigator as a variable in experimental research with Negro subjects. *Journal of Social Psychology, 40,* 280–284.

Trueba, H. T. (1988a). Culturally based explanations of minority students' academic achievement. *Anthropology and Education Quarterly, 19,* 270–287.

Trueba, H. T. (1988b). English literacy acquisition: From cultural trauma to learning disabilities in minority students. *Linguistics and Education, 1,* 125–152.

Turner, G. J. (1973). Social class and children's language of control at age five and age seven. In B. Bernstein (Ed.), *Class, codes, and control* (pp. 135–201). London: Routledge & Kegan Paul.

U.S. Bureau of Census (1986). *Money income and poverty status of families and persons in the United States—1985.* Washington, DC: U.S. Government Printing Office.

U.S. Department of Education. (1992). *Fourteenth annual report to Congress on the implementation of the Individuals with Disabilities Act.* Washington, DC: Author.

Williams, Jr., D. L., & Chavkin, N. F. (1985). *Final report of the parent involvement in education project.* Washington, DC: National Institute of Education.

Williams, J. E., & Morland, J. K. (1976). *Race, color, and self-concept.* College Hill, NC: University of North Carolina Press.

Yamamoto, J., & Kubota, M. (1989). The Japanese American family. In G. Powell, J. Yamamoto, & A. Morales (Eds.), *The psychosocial development of minority group children.* New York: Brunner-Mazel.

Yates, J. R. (1987). Current and emerging forces. *Counterpoint, 7* (4), 4–5.

Learners Who Vary in Accessing the Environment

Teaching and learning in classrooms is a communicative process (Puro & Bloome, 1987). Spoken language is the medium for most teaching and the way most students demonstrate what they have learned (Cazden, 1986). For learners whose communication, physical, and sensory systems are intact, the communicative process that occurs in teaching is automatic. For those who vary in these ways, the communicative process is a challenge.

Learners who vary in their communication, physical, and sensory systems are confronted with the challenge of accessing the vast amount of information and interactions that occur in the environment. Those with communication disorders have difficulty in either comprehension or expression of language, the primary mode of communication. Those with orthopedic handicaps or health impairments are challenged in accessing the physical environment and are limited in the experiences common to others in their interactions with objects, places, and positions or in their mobility. Learners with visual impairments are challenged in their acquisition of concepts that others learn vicariously through observation. Learners with hearing impairments are challenged in their acquisition of verbal language, an essential mode of instruction and interaction.

Though these challenges have a serious impact on all interactions within the learner's developmental context, technology is emerging that assists in mediating them. However, this technology does not give these learners the equivalent experience of their peers. Rather, this technology provides an even further challenge of sense-making to individuals whose developmental contexts have varied due to their inability to access the environment.

In this section, we explore learners with communication disorders, with an emphasis on the issue of language and its impact on exploiting the developmental context. We discuss learners with orthopedic and health impairments, and the variations in their experiences. Finally, we explore the experiences of learners with visual and hearing impairments. In these discussions, it is important to recognize that the impairment itself must be viewed in terms of the impact it has on the learner's ability to gain access to the information, interactions, and options available to their peers.

References

Cazden, C. B. (1986). Classroom discourse. In M. C. Wittrock (Ed.), *Handbook of research on teaching* (3rd ed., pp. 432–463). New York: Macmillan.

Puro, P., & Bloome, D. (1987). Understanding classroom communication. *Theory into Practice, 26* (Special Issue), 26–31.

9 Chapter

Learners with Communication Disorders

Objectives

After completing this chapter, you will be able to:

1. describe the personal characteristics of learners with communication disorders.
2. describe the identification and evaluation of learners with communication disorders.
3. describe the impact of communication disorders in the home and classroom.
4. describe ways to mediate the environment for learners with communication disorders.
5. describe the impact of communication disorders on participation in the larger social systems—the school, community, and society.

Key Words and Phrases

articulation disorders	phonology
augmentative systems	pragmatics
cluttering	receptive language
cognition	semantics
communication	speech
disfluency	speech disorders
expressive language	stuttering
language	symbols
language disorders	syntax
morphology	transactional model
phonemes	voice disorders

In consequence of an attack of apoplexy a soldier found it impossible to express in spoken language his feelings and ideas. His face bore no signs of a deranged intellect. His mind (espirit) found the answer to questions addressed to him and he carried out all he was told to do. . . . He could not articulate on the spot a word pronounced for him to repeat. . . . It was not his tongue which was embarrassed, for he moved it with great agility and could pronounce quite well a large number of isolated words. His memory was not at fault, for he signified his anger at being unable to express himself concerning many things which he wished to communicate (Head, 1926, p. 11).

Introduction

Language is the ability to communicate complex ideas through an organized system of meaning (Sameroff & Fiese, 1988). This ability to communicate not only supports every social interaction that takes place throughout the day, but it plays a major role in the learner's cognitive development. Sameroff and Fiese state that language is best described in a developmental context, where performance is viewed as the outcome of a learner interacting within human social environments.

Language develops from the learner's need to be understood and to understand. The learner's system relies on rules that are generated out of social interaction and the need to maintain contact and shared understanding (Sameroff & Fiese, 1988). This is known as the **transactional model** of language development. Within this model, the development of the child is seen as the product of the continuous interactions of the learner and the experiences provided by the caregivers in the social context (Sameroff & Chandler, 1975). There is, in this model, an equal emphasis placed on the effect of the child on the environment and that of the environment on the child. Sameroff and Fiese provide the example of a complicated childbirth, which may have made an otherwise calm mother anxious. The mother's anxiety may have caused her to be uncertain and to interact inappropriately with the child. The infant, in response to this inconsistency, may develop difficulties in feeding and sleeping patterns that give the appearance of a difficult temperament. This apparent difficult temperament decreases the pleasure that the mother obtains from being with the child, and thus she spends less time with the child. Less time with the child again alters the mother's interaction with the child, making early language development even more difficult. This transactional development of a communication difficulty is depicted in figure 9.1.

Communication is the verbal and nonverbal means of transmitting and decoding messages from one individual with the intention of stimulating meaning in the mind of another. **Symbols** are the media through which communication occurs. They are the tools with which we think. Symbols, which make up language, serve as internal representations of the external world (Richards & Richards, 1988). Kaiser and Warren (1988) describe a series of assumptions related to the development of the symbols system we call language. First, language is behavior, which both affects and is affected by the environment. Second, the meaning of language is not only in the words themselves, but in how they are used; that is, language cannot be understood outside of its particular context. Finally, form usually follows function. Form develops as the learner's needs, wants, and intentions become more specific and require a more sophisticated system of communication. Language, voice, and hearing, then, are used to influence others.

Language is described as **expressive** (developing and sending messages) and **receptive** (receiving and interpreting messages). **Speech** is the vocal response mode of language (Schiefelbush & McCormick, 1981). Speech integrates breathing, producing sounds, and controlling the quality and articulation of those sounds to form words.

The mechanism involved in speech production is illustrated in figure 9.2. When an individual wishes to speak, the brain sends a message to activate the speech mechanism, which includes respiratory, vocal, vibrating, resonating, and articulation mechanisms. The primary function of the respiratory system (diaphragm, lungs, chest, and throat muscles) is to inhale oxygen and expel gases. When air is expelled, the voice mechanism is activated. Voice or sound is produced by the larynx, which is located at the top of the trachea and contains the vocal folds, or cords. The larynx and vocal cords form the vibrating system. As air is pushed from the lungs, its flow causes the vocal cords to vibrate and produce sound. As the sound passes through the throat, mouth, and nasal cavities (the resonating system), it is shaped into speech sounds by

Annual **Edition**

Article *20*

Figure 9.1

Transactional development of a communication problem.

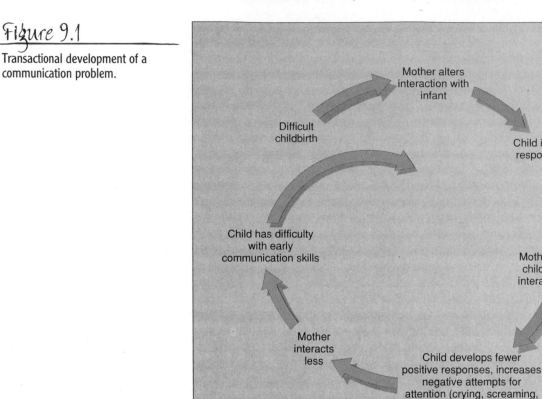

the articulation system (tongue, soft and hard palate, teeth, lips, and jaw). All of these systems must be intact and functioning effectively for the proper production of speech.

Language and Speech Development

The cries, coos, and gurgles of the infant are the beginnings of language and speech development and production. Both the sounds of comfort and distress provide the infant with the exercise needed to develop the complex muscles necessary for speech. The child's babbling gradually begins to take form, as if the child is practicing consonants and vowel sounds.

At approximately the sixth month, the child begins to use sounds to gain the attention of others and appears to make an effort to respond to others as if in conversation. Vocal play, which contains inflection and apparent syllables, becomes evident. The child begins to imitate the sounds of others and to make new sounds.

As early as eight to nine months of age, children use prelinguistic gestures and vocalizations to communicate for a variety of reasons. Bruner (1981) suggests that in the first year of life, children use gestures and vocalizations for three communicative intentions: (a) regulating another's behavior for obtaining or restricting environmental goals; (b) social interaction; and (c) joint attention, which is directing another's attention for purposes of sharing the focus on some thing or event. Even before words, children use signals intentionally to communicate (Wetherby, Cain, Yonclas, & Walker, 1988).

At about nine months of age, children use gestures to give an object, show an object, or push an adult's hands, and by eleven months, they begin to reach, point, and wave. At about thirteen months, children begin using a small number of

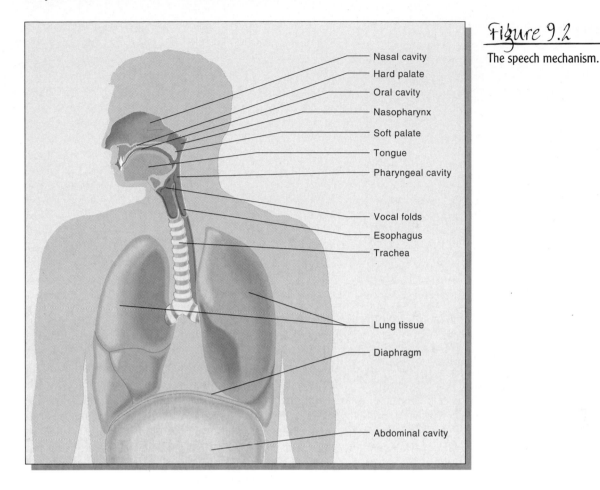

Figure 9.2
The speech mechanism.

Nasal cavity
Hard palate
Oral cavity
Nasopharynx
Soft palate
Tongue
Pharyngeal cavity
Vocal folds
Esophagus
Trachea
Lung tissue
Diaphragm
Abdominal cavity

words that are truly symbolic, referring to objects, events, or classes of objects or events. Between twelve and eighteen months, new words are acquired at a slow rate, but children steadily increase their rate of communicating, using sounds in coordination with gestures and using consonants in utterances comprising many syllables (Kent & Bauer, 1985). Around eighteen months of age, children experience a surge in vocabulary growth, and rather than learning one new word a week, they learn several words in a day (Ingram, 1978). Children begin to request information, talk about events, and maintain topics over several turns (Prutting, 1979).

Communication Disorders

Students with communication disorders account for the second largest group of learners served under the special education services mandate of Public Law 94-142 (U.S. Department of Education, 1995). According to the U.S. Department of Education (1995), 1,009,379 children and youth ages six to twenty-one were served as speech or language impaired during the 1993–1994 school year. This represents a 14.68 percent decrease since the 1976–1977 school year. Across states, a low of .44 percent of the school population was served in the District of Columbia to a high of 4.06 percent of the school population in New Jersey. Over three-fourths of these learners were served in general education classes, and about 11 percent received resource room services. Approximately 7.36 percent attended separate classes or schools, and very few were in other placements (U.S. Department of Education, 1995). The provision of services for learners with communication disorders is the largest service function of special education (Casby, 1989). Unlike all other disability categories, there is an

Infants use gestures to communicate.

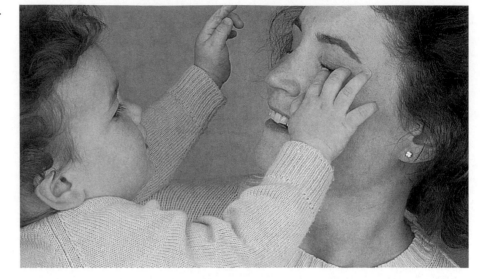

overrepresentation of Caucasian students (73 percent of those served) as compared to learners representing diverse ethnic, cultural, and linguistic groups (Office for Civil Rights, 1992).

In addition to those learners served as primarily communication disordered, it is estimated that approximately one-fourth of learners with other disabilities (for example, mental retardation, learning disabilities, behavioral disorders) receive speech and language services as a related service. In addition, there is frequent association between communication disorders and psychiatric disorders in children (Kotsopoulos & Boodoosingh, 1987). A significant interrelationship has also been found between behavioral disorders and attention deficit disorders and communication disorders (Love & Thompson, 1988).

Personal Characteristics

Objective One

To describe the personal characteristics of learners with communication disorders.

Kretschmer and Kretschmer (1988) report that the consensus of the literature produced in the last decade is that the learner's development and the use of communication (spoken, signed, or written) must be seen in a socially interactive context. In other words, learners must have both communication models and opportunities to communicate to construct their own communication competence. Some call this shift in emphasis in the study of language the pragmatics revolution. **Pragmatics** are those rules a learner knows and uses in determining who says what to whom, how, why, when, and in what setting (Muma, 1978). Kaiser and Warren (1988) assert that pragmatics assume the following:

1. Communicative language is grounded in other behaviors, specifically cognitive skills and social interaction patterns of the learner.
2. Utterances are given contextually relevant meanings by their intentions.
3. There are rules for the use of intention in conversational intercourse.
4. Meaning is determined by function in context.

Pragmatics, however essential, are but one component of language. In addition, there are several other components that contribute to the communication of meaning. Smith (1991) defines these components as follows:

1. **Phonology,** which is the study of the individual speech sounds, or **phonemes,** characteristic of a language and the rules governing the distribution and sequence of phonemes within a language. Phonemes (there are forty-three in American English) do not have meaning unto themselves.

Practicing routines helps students develop communicative competence.

2. **Morphology,** which is the study of the smallest units of meaning, or morphemes. Free morphemes can stand alone, such as "cat," "dog," "out." Bound morphemes contribute to the meaning of free morphemes, and include tense, plurality, possession, or ways of deriving new words (as in the use of prefixes and suffixes).
3. **Syntax,** which is the rule system for constructing sentences. Rather than words randomly strung together, English is characterized by a subject-verb-object sentence order.
4. **Semantics,** which is the meaning of individual words, words in relationship to each other, and the network of meaning.

There are two general categories of communication disorders: speech disorders and language disorders. **Speech disorders** are impairments in the production of oral or spoken language. Disfluency, voice disorders, and articulation disorders are classified as speech disorders. **Language disorders** involve deviant or delayed development of comprehension and/or the use of the signs or symbols applied to express or receive ideas in a spoken, written, or other symbol system. The absence of language, delayed language, deviant and interrupted development of language, and post-language development disorders are examples of language disorders. Learners may demonstrate receptive (receiving and interpreting), expressive (developing and sending), or mixed (both receiving and sending) language disorders.

Speech Disorders

Learners Who Are Disfluent   Fluency refers to the smooth flow and rhythm of speech. **Disfluency** includes repetitions or prolongations of sounds, words, or phrases; hesitations or long pauses; and struggle behaviors, such as distortions of lips and mouth, facial grimaces, eye blinks, and extraneous body movements (Rice, 1988). Stuttering and cluttering are examples of disfluency. **Stuttering** is a disruption in the timing of speaking; **cluttering** is running together sounds, words, and phrases, producing rapid, jumbled speech. According to Van Riper and Emerick (1984), two million persons in the United States exhibit disfluency.

Nippold (1990) reviewed the literature concerning concomitant speech and language disorders in learners who are disfluent that has been published since 1920. He suggests that, though the evidence is not convincing, these learners, as a group, are more likely than those who are not disfluent to have other problems in speech and language. Some may have problems that bear relationship to their stuttering. Byrd and Cooper (1989) found that five- to nine-year-old learners who were disfluent were not delayed in their receptive language skills but were delayed in their expressive language skills. They suggest that young children who are disfluent appear to have expressive language delays because they attempt to simplify verbal responses as a means of coping with their stuttering. St. Louis and Hinzman (1988), however, found that learners who were disfluent were more likely to have difficulty in articulation.

Disfluency has also been related to the learner's personal perception of control. Madison, Budd, and Itzkowitz (1986) found that as learners increased ability to manage their disfluency, they gained a sense of internal rather than external control.

Learners with Voice Disorders   **Voice disorders** are present when a learner has difficulty modulating the resonant quality of speech. Voices vary widely in pitch, volume, and timbre. The listener can identify moods, emotional states, and attitudes by the speaker's voice quality. Great variations in voice quality are tolerable. However, some voice qualities interfere with effective communication. Learners may have too much nasality in the voice (hypernasal) or too little nasality (denasal), or they may use an unnaturally high pitch (falsetto) or be harsh, breathy, or throaty (Van Riper, 1978).

Voice disorders appear to persist. Powell, Filter, and Williams (1989) found that almost 40 percent of the learners identified as showing a voice disorder retained that disorder after one year. Four years later, of the learners available in the same school system, 38 percent still demonstrated a voice disorder. They contend that without intervention, voice disorders persist in children.

Learners with Articulation Disorders   **Articulation disorders,** or phonologic disorders, occur when the learner has difficulty with the sound system of oral language or speech. There are four types of articulation disorders, which are a consequence of the faulty production of phonemes. These four types are (Van Riper & Emerick, 1984) (a) substitution of one phoneme for another, as "mudder" for mother, (b) disorder of a phoneme, as "shoup" for soup, (c) omission of a sound, as in "mik" for milk, and (d) addition, placement of an extra sound within a word, as "warsh" for "wash."

Articulation disorders are the most common of speech disorders served by communication specialists in the schools. Among learners with articulation disorders, voice disorders, deficits in expressive language, and hearing problems have been found to occur more frequently than in their typical peers.

Language Disorders

A broad range of language disorders interfere with a learner's development and communication. Among the most common are the absence of language, delayed language, deviations and interruptions in language development, and language disorders acquired after language has developed. Learners with language disorders typically have academic difficulties throughout their school careers, resulting from the challenges they face acquiring language, learning with language, and applying language knowledge for academic learning and social development (Bashir & Scavuzzo, 1992). The "Guidelines for Practice" box on page 201 suggests several techniques to help students with language disorders.

guidelines for practice

Students with language disorders frequently have difficulty in reading comprehension and vocabulary development. Leverett and Diefendort (1992) present several techniques to help students in independent language activities. Some of their suggestions include the following:

- Write notes to students in the margins of reading materials. Underline and circle key concepts and vocabulary.
- Develop vocabulary guides, which provide definitions of the key words, the page on which the word occurs, and space on which to copy the sentence in which the word occurs.
- Cue the student to the nouns and to the pronouns that refer to the nouns. For example, the first time a noun occurs, place a letter above it. Then write that letter over the pronouns that refer to the noun.
- Provide a structured overview of the reading, identifying key vocabulary words or concepts.
- Visually demonstrate the relationships among key components of stories by placing the component on a web or diagram.

Leverett, R. G., & Diefendort, A. O. (1992). Students with language deficiencies: Suggestions for frustrated teachers. *Teaching Exceptional Children, 24* (4), 30–33.

Cognition **Cognition** is the process of knowing and thinking. Several studies have been conducted to determine potential patterns in cognitive skills among learners with language disorders. Condino, Im-Humber, and Stark (1990) suggest that learners with language disorders have significantly more problems in coding, memory, hypothesis generation, hypothesis evaluation, and deduction than their typical peers. Difficulty in encoding information is also found in solving discrimination-learning problems (Nelson, Kamhi, & Apel, 1987). Learners with language disorders may have difficulty in sustaining and manipulating nonlinguistic symbols as well as linguistic symbols (Snyder, 1987).

Language Not surprisingly, the most broadly researched characteristic of learners with language disorders is language itself. Learners with language disorders have difficulty with syntactic comprehension (Adams, 1990) and do not monitor their own comprehension as well as do their peers with typical language skills (Dollaghan, 1987). Conversations may be interrupted because of an inappropriate response by a learner with language disorders, which may, in fact, occur because the learner with language disorders misunderstands the literal or implicit meaning of the utterances of the person with whom they are conversing (Bishop & Adams, 1989). Learners with language disorders have been found to rely heavily on semantic expectations or the sequence of content words in comprehending sentences (Van der Ley & Deward, 1986).

When a breakdown in communication occurs, learners with language disorders are more likely to blame the listener than are their peers, who are more likely to blame the speaker (Meline & Brackin, 1987). Significantly more communication breakdowns are found in the conversation and narration of learners with language disorders than that of their age-matched peers (MacLachlan & Chapman, 1988). Learners with language disorders have significantly more unrepaired sentences in their conversation, and they tend to overlap on their own speech, beginning a new thought before completing the first one (Fujiki, Brinton, & Sonnenberg, 1990). The number of errors in taking turns while having a conversation, interruptions, turn switch times, and poorly timed responses is significantly greater among learners with language disorders (Craig & Evans, 1989). Learners with language disorders are less able to identify the errors in word order in sentences than are their age-matched peers (Fujiki, Brinton, & Dunton, 1987).

Social and Emotional Characteristics   Language disorders affect social behaviors as well as the more commonly recognized area of academic achievement (Goldman, 1987). Learners with language disorders demonstrate a high prevalence of anxiety disorders, as described in the Diagnostic Statistical Manual of Mental Disorders (DSM-III) (Cantwell & Baker, 1987). Learners with language disorders demonstrate significantly poorer understanding of humor, due to their inability to grasp the nature of multimeaning words. These learners tend to segment and redefine phrases involved, losing meaning of that which is perceived as funny (Spector, 1990). Learners with language disorders demonstrate significant problems in symbolic, adaptive, and integrative play as compared to their peers (Roth & Clark, 1987).

Windsor (1995) suggests that language skills and social skills may be perceived as "different views of the same animal" (p. 214). Language disorders and social skills problems follow the transactional model of development described earlier in this chapter. Children with language disorders have problems successfully entering social interactions and are likely to be ignored and excluded from interactions with their peers. These children may then develop ways to compensate for being socially rebuffed, which may then limit their opportunities to take advantage of socialization to support their language learning.

Fine-Motor Skills   Learners with language disorders have been found to have difficulty copying simple figures when compared to their age-peers (Moore & Law, 1990). In a study examining the relationships between fine-motor skills and linguistic abilities of developmentally delayed learners, Sommers (1988) found that language disorders were strongly associated with poor fine-motor skills.

Medical Issues   Localized brain damage has been posited as one potential cause of language disorders (Bishop, 1987). Otitis media (middle-ear infection) has been suggested as interacting with risk factors occurring at the time of birth in the etiology of language disorders (Bishop & Edmundson, 1986).

Identification and Evaluation

Objective Two

To describe the identification and evaluation of learners with communication disorders.

Public Law 94-142 defined students with communication disorders as "speech impaired." The definition included communication disorders such as impaired articulation, language or voice disorders, and fluency disorders (such as stuttering), which adversely affect a child's educational performance. The American Speech-Language-Hearing Association (ASHA) described communicative disorders as impairments in the ability to perceive and/or process a symbol system, represent concepts, and/or transmit and use symbols systems (National Joint Committee for Learning Disabilities, 1982).

ASHA described both communication disorders and communication variations (1982).* In communication disorders, ASHA included the following:

1.   Speech disorders, which are impairments of voice, articulation of speech sounds, and/or fluency, observed in the transmission and use of the oral symbol system. Included in speech disorders are voice disorders (the absence or abnormal production of voice quality, pitch, loudness, resonance, and/or duration), articulation disorders (abnormal production of speech sounds), and fluency disorders (impaired rate and rhythm).

*Reprinted by permission of the American Speech-Language-Hearing Association.

Augmentative communication systems provide learners with disabilities with a way to communicate.

2. Language disorders, which are impairments or atypical development of comprehension and/or use of spoken and/or written symbol system. Included are disorders of the form, content, or function of language.

In communication variations, ASHA included the following:

1. Communicative differences or dialects, which are variations of a symbol system used by a group of individuals. This symbol system reflects and is determined by shared regional, social, or cultural and ethnic factors.
2. **Augmentative systems**—sign language, gestures, or technological devices—which are used to supplement the communicative skills of individuals for whom speech is temporarily or permanently inadequate to meet communicative needs.

As can be understood from the previous discussion of communication disorders, the number and intricacy of these disorders make the process of identification and assessment complex. Learners with obvious speech and language disorders are readily identified by parents, physicians, and day care and preschool professionals. These children are generally referred to the communication specialist prior to entering kindergarten and the primary grades. Learners with more subtle speech and language disorders are not as readily identified.

The assessment of communication disorders is conducted through a comprehensive diagnostic evaluation, appropriate to the learner's age and overall level of development. The evaluation is conducted by the communication specialist in cooperation with other professionals and the parents. It may include the administration of formal standardized instruments to measure intelligence, language, behavior, and achievement. During the initial phase of the assessment process, the presence of a physical problem or hearing impairment is ruled out as the cause of the communication disorder. If a physical or hearing impairment is discovered, it is the primary target of intervention. Also during this initial phase of assessment, the learner's primary language and the language used in the home are determined.

In general, standardized language tests have been found to have limited value in the task of developing an individualized therapeutic program for the learner. To augment standardized tests, language samples are obtained and analyzed with regard to the learner's use, content, and form of expressive and receptive language. Such samples are most useful if obtained in the various contexts in which the learner is functioning. The learner is observed in interaction with peers and teachers. Information is obtained from the parents and teachers about the learner's schoolwork, developmental history, and use of free time (Wood, 1982). The purpose of the diagnostic evaluation is to obtain a comprehensive picture of the learner and his or her communicative strengths and deficits and to write and implement a remedial or therapeutic program. What the child is doing or not doing and what the environment is doing or not doing must be analyzed before intervening with children (Calvert & Murray, 1985). The child's current functional language and the events that stimulate language use must be documented.

Assessment is an attempt to understand the performance of an individual in the environments in which that individual functions (Broen, 1988). Craig (1991) proposes that the best professional practice of assessment includes the following:

1. Examination of the child's conversational knowledge while controlling the linguistic demands of the task, and conversely, linguistic knowledge while controlling the conversational demands of the task
2. Examination of the child's ability to integrate conversational and linguistic skills
3. Examination of both expressive and receptive language

A model for the evaluation of communication disorders is presented in the "Guidelines for Practice" box on page 205. The "Guidelines for Practice" box on page 206 presents a contextual analysis of classroom behaviors as related to communication disorders.

Learners with Articulation Disorders   Of all the forms of communications disorders, articulation disorders are the problem for which children are most frequently referred for assessment and service (Edwards, Cape, & Brown, 1989). Care must be taken in assessing the articulation of learners representing various ethnic, cultural, and linguistic groups. In a study of working-class African American children who use Black English Vernacular, Cole and Taylor (1990) found that African American children performed differently on standardized tests of articulation as a function of the linguistic norms used to score items. Failure to consider dialect substantially increased the likelihood of mislabeling normally speaking African American children as having articulation disorders. More naturalistic strategies, such as that proposed by Shriberg and Kwiatowski (1980), may be useful. In the Natural Process Analysis Test, one such strategy, conversational samples of the child's language are gathered. At least one hundred of these utterances are then used to identify and note changes in the individual's sound system.

Assessing Very Young Learners   Several issues emerge in the assessment of very young children. Crais and Roberts (1991) state that there are a limited number of standardized instruments for the birth to five-year-old population, with even fewer standardized instruments for learners from birth to three years of age. In addition, the available standardized instruments tend to be narrow in scope and omit important assessment areas. They suggest that using a series of decision trees may be helpful for providing a nonstandard assessment method for collecting and organizing information. A decision tree is a sequenced set of questions posed by the examiner either to the child directly or to an informant such as a parent or teacher. Responses to the questions may also be obtained by the examiner through observation of the child. For example, if the child does not imitate three-word combinations (a negative response to an assessment question), intervention in increasing word combinations is suggested.

guidelines for practice

Areas for a Model for Communication Assessment

Form

Does the student demonstrate:

- a flexible vocabulary (varies with person or setting)?
- regular grammar?
- tense and subject/verb agreement?
- clear use of referents?
- appropriate use of subordinators?

Function

Does the student:

- sustain topics?
- phrase for intent?
- support points of view?
- use elaborated codes (school, peer, and home language codes)?
- use social and cognitive language?
- use varied functions and intents of language?
- use tactful deviousness?
- modify his or her utterance when needed?

Style

Does the student:

- take into account the listener's needs?
- plan the content of responses?
- have adequate word finding?
- express himself or herself fluently?
- speak intelligibly?
- use distinct speech?
- speak at a comfortable rate?
- speak audibly?

(Based on Simon, 1985)

Communication in the Home and Classroom

Learners Who Are Disfluent

Mothers of five- to nine-year-old learners who were disfluent made significantly more demands, commands, and requests when talking with their children than mothers of fluent children (Langlois, Hanrahan, & Inouye, 1986). Langlois and associates also found that learners who were disfluent were more verbal. They contend that parent-child interactions may be critical to the onset, development, and maintenance of stuttering. In another study, mothers of learners who were disfluent were found to talk significantly faster than mothers of fluent children, though their disfluent children spoke more slowly than their peers (Meyers & Freeman, 1985). In fact, Meyers and Freeman's correlational analysis indicated that the more the child stuttered, the more slowly he or she talked during fluent speech, and the

Objective Three

To describe the impact of communication disorders in the home and classroom.

guidelines for practice

Observation Guide for Classroom Interactions and Communication

Knowledge about the school routine:

- knows routine for activities (starting the day, going to lunch, ending the day)
- knows routine for participating in activities (where to go for reading group, setting up paper for spelling tests)
- deviates from the routine when appropriate (adapts to reading group in a different area of the room, different-sized papers)
- reads the teacher's strategies for cuing a given routine (anticipates transitions from the teacher's cues)
- participates effectively in peer routines (playing games in and out of the classroom, sitting with someone at lunch or on the bus)

Knowledge about communicative routines:

- knows when to raise hand, when to join in
- takes turns appropriately, doesn't interrupt
- initiates conversation
- has more than one style of interaction (interacts with formal language with teacher, peer or "in group" language with classmates)
- uses appropriate greetings and closings

Giving and following directions:

- specifies locations and objects adequately, doesn't use pronouns until the listener knows the topic (e.g., walking up to the teacher and saying, "it's broken" rather than "my pencil is broken")
- watches listener to check communication, responds to puzzled looks
- revises directions when necessary
- takes responsibility when directions do not work

Comprehension and use of figurative language:

- restates figurative meaning of idioms
- uses idiomatic expressions that are used by peers
- uses idiomatic expressions appropriately for context and listener
- comprehends material containing figurative language

(Adapted from Creaghead and Tattershall, 1985)

more slowly the child talked during fluent speech, the faster the mother interacting with him or her talked. Meyers and Freeman believe that there is an interactive and complex relationship between mother and child speech rates.

Learners with Language Disorders

Strong evidence has been found that language disorders are not randomly distributed across families but tend to concentrate within families (Tomblin, 1989). All family members of learners with language disorders are more likely to have language disorders than are members of families in which there are no members with language disorders. Though birth order was at one time presumed to make a difference, neither firstborns nor last borns are now considered to be more at risk for language disorders (Tomblin, 1990).

Bishop (1987) states that familial variables may affect the presence of language disorders in either auditory-verbal deprivation (due to home environment or hearing loss) or genetic influences. Two family patterns have been related to language disorders. Learners with fetal alcohol syndrome have been found to vary from their peers in grammatical, semantic, language, articulation, and language structuring abilities (Becker, Warr-Leeper, & Leeper, 1990). Learners who have been maltreated or severely physically abused are also at risk for language disorders.

Though the speech and language of parents of learners with expressive language delays have been found to be less complex, Whitehurst, Fischel, Lonigan, and Valdez-Manchaca (1988) believe that this is due to the sensitivity of parents to their child's level of expressive ability rather than a cause of the problem itself. These mothers have been found to recast their children's utterances more often than the mothers of learners with typical language in an effort to clarify and give information (Conti-Ramsden, 1990).

In a study of parents' attitudes towards family involvement in speech and language services, Andrews, Andrews, and Shearer (1989) found that over half of the parents desired family involvement in their child's therapy. Twenty-eight percent, however, were satisfied without family involvement.

Learners with Articulation Disorders

Learners with articulation disorders are judged more negatively by their peers with regard to both intelligence and personality. Among the raters, girls were more positive in their ratings of others than were boys. Girls with articulation disorders were judged more positively than were boys (Freeby & Madison, 1989). In a study of the attitudes of university students, learners with speech disorders were perceived as less mentally healthy than learners with clear speech and were felt to be unable to monitor or change their speech patterns (Bebout & Arthur, 1992).

Learners with Voice Disorders

In a study in which college undergraduate students reviewed audiotapes of normal-speaking individuals and individuals with voice disorders, the listeners were found to form negative attitudes towards speakers with voice disorders. Listeners' perceptions of characteristics such as kindness, cleanliness, honesty, and pleasantness were adversely affected by the presence of voice disorders (Ruscello, Lass, & Podbesek, 1988).

Mediating the Environment

Objective Four

To describe ways to mediate the environment for learners with communication disorders.

Traditionally, learners with speech and language disorders were removed from the classroom for individual and small group intervention with a communication specialist. The specialist assessed the learner's communication disability, established objectives for intervention, and planned and implemented the intervention. The communication specialist determined whether the learner's language problem was a primary or secondary disability.

Currently, emphasis is placed on the remediation of the learner's communication disorder in the general and special education classrooms in collaboration with the teacher, whenever possible. Schiefelbush and McCormick (1981) propose that the best place to learn and practice communication skills is in the context in which those skills naturally occur. The generalization of remedial techniques should improve both the learner's speaking performance and social interaction.

There are several placement options available for learners with communication disorders. These options include indirect service through consultation with teacher or parent, itinerant services, resource room, and self-contained class.

Consultation is the provision of indirect services to the learner by the communication specialist through the learner's teacher. This option is also used when the communication specialist works indirectly with the learner through the parents.

One of the more traditional options for learners with communication disorders is the provision of therapy by an itinerant communication specialist. In an itinerant program, the communication specialist travels from school to school during the day or week to serve the learners on his or her case load. Although this option is minimally disruptive to the classroom program, it creates scheduling problems and reduces the probability of teacher-specialist consultation.

In the resource room program, the communication specialist is located in a single school. This service is especially valuable in a school with large numbers of learners with multiple disabilities.

The final placement option is the self-contained program. This is useful and appropriate for learners with severe communication disorders, very young children, and children making a transition from one program to another, such as day care or preschool to kindergarten. The self-contained program is frequently a half day and involves parents.

The emphasis on remediating learners with communication disorders in the classroom places demands on general and special education teachers. According to Seibert and Oller (1981), a positive, responsive relationship between learner and teacher is needed so that the learner can risk engagement in the communication process. The learner's willingness to communicate is enhanced when the teacher uses a facilitative style, such as that described by Peck and Schuler (1983) and Peck (1985). In this style, the facilitative teacher

- allows the learner to control and initiate conversation topics
- allows the learner to assume the lead in conversation
- encourages the learner to contribute to the ongoing conversation in many ways
- investigates the communicative environment of the learner and identifies language that is useful to the learner
- develops communicative competence within the context of social interaction
- provides frequent opportunities for learner initiation and control of social interaction
- provides choices and other communicative opportunities to the learner
- responds to learner-initiated social/communicative behavior
- imitates and elaborates on the learner's social/communicative behavior

Annual **Edition**

Article *18*

Very Young Learners

Jones and Warren (1991) state that current knowledge about language learning can be used to increase the engagement of young children in intervention concerning their language. They suggest following the child's attentional lead in topic and content, as well as providing novelty. They emphasize that with very young children, activity-based therapy is essential. The communication specialist should avoid asking too many questions, giving too many instructions, and giving the child too little time to respond.

Learners Who Are Disfluent

Starkweather (1990) describes several trends in therapy for learners who are disfluent. Children are now receiving treatment at earlier ages, and the communicative environments in which the child is developing are being assessed as is the child himself or herself. Additional emphasis is being placed on the parents in the treatment process and on environmental and behavioral management. The role of language and the relationship between language skill or language use and the development of disfluency, as well as the emotional components of disfluency, are also being addressed.

Technology   For learners for whom verbal communication does not emerge to a point of being strategically effective and communicative, augmentative systems may be devised to facilitate communication. The purpose of such systems is to promote and facilitate, not replace, the communication modes available to the learner (Russel, 1984). As discussed later in the section concerning learners with hearing impairments, there are several manual systems, such as signing and finger spelling, to facilitate communication. In addition, there are technological aids, which are generally dependent on the computer and other electronic hardware, that help facilitate communication.

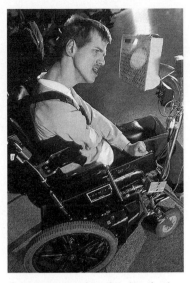

Though microcomputer applications are in their infancy with regard to providing assistance to those with communication disorders, they can be helpful to both the learner and the communication specialist. The specialist can use the computer to manage records, store and analyze speech samples, and make therapeutic programs available to the learner. The microcomputer, as the basis of various kinds of talking machines, can be used to facilitate the learner's communication. Augmentative communication systems can provide visual, printed, and verbal messages to the individuals with whom the learner is interacting.

Great care must be taken in selecting any technological device to respond to the needs of the learners with communication disorders.

Television, the videocassette recorder, and the videodisc can be used to facilitate the learning of communication skills. These devices can be used to collect assessment information and to record and analyze speech samples and for the presentation of instructional programs and interventions for learners and parents. Other devices, though less technically complex, such as the voice light and delayed feedback devices, can be of assistance to learner and communication specialist. The voice light, controlled by voice intensity, provides the learner feedback on voice control. The delayed feedback device provides the learner with delayed feedback through earphones and thus facilitates the control of disfluency.

The communication specialist must give great care to individualize any technological device so that it responds to the specific needs and desires of the learner with communication disorders.

With the emergence of technology, several new issues regarding "providing a voice" for learners with severe disabilities have emerged. Gorenflo (1994) found that when using an augmentative communication voice, the clarity of the synthetic voice was more important to listeners than gender appropriateness. In some cases, however, listeners required training in order to understand the communicative efforts of a learner with severe disabilities who was using a synthetic voice (Rounsefell, 1993).

Learners from Diverse Cultural, Ethnic, and Linguistic Groups

Working with learners from diverse cultural, ethnic, and linguistic groups who have communication disorders poses additional challenges to teachers. Kayser (1995) reports that using language-intervention techniques known to be effective with Anglo children has not been effective with learners from diverse cultural, ethnic, and linguistic groups. She suggests that the content of intervention programs, as well as the methods for instruction, may be affected by the child's cultural understanding of how learning and teaching should be accomplished. Kayser contends that in working with these learners, teachers and specialists should consider the child's culture, teacher-child interactions, the language of intervention (in contrast to the child's native language), and parent involvement.

Annual **Edition**

Article *19*

Emphasis in working with learners from diverse cultural, ethnic, and linguistic groups should be on the development of communicative competence (Volker, 1992). Common classroom routines, such as "morning circle" or "sharing time," may have complex requirements for participation, including topic development, turn taking, and social demands, which may be difficult for learners with limited experience in Anglo culture (Ernst, 1994). A renewed emphasis on using the learner's native language to facilitate the development of competence in the second language has emerged (Belander, 1994). Teachers must remember that the acculturation of learners from culturally and linguistically diverse backgrounds is achieved primarily through language socialization (Damico & Damico, 1993).

The Impact on Participation in Larger Social Systems

Objective Five

To describe the impact of communication disorders on participation in the larger social systems—the school, community, and society.

Horsley and FitzGibbon (1987) investigated the stereotype applied to learners who were disfluent. In their study, a negative stereotype was found to exist towards individuals who stuttered, particularly towards school-age boys. Boone (1987) believes that adult stutterers frequently determine the kinds of activities they participate in and the occupations they select on the basis of their stuttering. In another study, unsophisticated listeners judged individuals from speech samples in which there were adult articulation problems as "dumb," less likely to be hired, and slow, and in other negative ways (Langhans & Boone, 1975). Though the articulation distortions of a preschool child may be seen as amusing, the persistence of articulation problems in adulthood is not tolerated well in society (Boone, 1987).

Adolescents with communication disorders are confronted with many new challenges as they begin to participate in larger social systems. Montgomery and Levine (1995) present several ways in which adolescent learners with communication disorders have more challenges and differ from their younger peers. Adolescents with communication disorders are more likely to be additionally challenged by a loss of motivation and poor social skills. They are also less likely to be appropriately identified, and they have interrelated problems (such as communication disorders and difficulties in problem solving). Affected adolescents also improve their reading and advanced oral language knowledge abilities (such as vocabulary) less readily. Montgomery and Levine suggest that while working with instructors, adolescents with communication disorders are more likely to deny their problems and may be unwilling to accept help. Due to their difficulties in school, adolescents with communication disorders may seek out peers who are also having trouble in school, further limiting their attempts to achieve.

Summary

Communication not only supports every social interaction that takes place throughout the day, but it plays a major role in the learner's cognitive development. Learners with communication disorders account for the largest single group of learners served under the special education services mandate of Public Law 94-142. In addition to those learners served as primarily communication disordered, it is estimated that approximately one-fourth of learners with other disabilities (e.g., mental retardation, learning disabilities, behavioral disorders) demonstrate communication disorders.

Communication disorders may involve speech, language, or voice. Assessment and evaluation of learners with communication disorders must include examination of (a) the child's conversational knowledge, (b) the child's ability to integrate conversational and linguistic skills, and (c) both expressive and receptive language skills. Family variables may have an impact on the presence of communication disorders.

There are several placement options available for learners with communication disorders. Consultation or indirect services for the learner through teacher or parents, and itinerant, resource room, and self-contained programs are all options for learners with communication disorders.

During the 1980s, there was a decrease in the number of learners identified with communication disorders. This decrease is attributed to several factors, including (a) a current trend to identify students with language disorders as having specific learning disabilities, rather than having speech and language impairments; (b) increased availability of speech and language services within general education; and (c) more accurate identification of learners with communication disorders.

Building Your Professional Vocabulary

Match each word or phrase to its meaning.

_____ augmentative systems

_____ cognition

_____ communication

_____ expressive language

_____ language

_____ pragmatics

_____ receptive language

_____ speech

_____ speech disorders

_____ transactional model

a. the verbal and nonverbal means of transmitting and decoding messages
b. the vocal response mode of language
c. development is the product of continuous interactions of the learner and experiences in the social context
d. the ability to communicate complex ideas through an organized system of meaning
e. sending messages

f. receiving messages
g. rules about who says what to whom, how, why, when
h. the process of knowing and thinking
i. sign language, gestures, technological devices
j. impairments in the production of oral, or spoken, language

Comprehension Check

Select the most appropriate response.

1. Children use prelinguistic gestures and vocalizations to communicate
   a. at eight or nine months of age.
   b. from birth.
   c. at about one year of age.
2. Learners with communication disorders
   a. are uncommon in schools.
   b. are second only to learners with learning disabilities in the number of individuals served.
   c. are the largest group of individuals served.
3. The "pragmatics revolution" was generated by a shift to
   a. the study of individual speech sounds.
   b. the study of the smallest units of meaning.
   c. the study of the rules a learner uses in communicating.
4. Voice disorders
   a. include difficulties in modulating the resonant quality of speech.

   b. include running together sounds, words, and phrases, producing rapid, jumbled speech.
   c. are impairments in the production of oral language.
5. Social competence
   a. is caused by lack of communicative competence.
   b. is engaged in a transactional relationship with communicative competence.
   c. improves with increased communicative competence.
6. Standardized language tests
   a. are the basis for developing individualized therapeutic programs regarding communication disorders.
   b. are of limited value in developing individualized therapeutic programs regarding communication disorders.
   c. are clear measures of the individual's communicative competence.

7. Learners with articulation disorders
    a. are supported by individuals in their developmental contexts in transactional relationships.
    b. are judged to be immature by their peers.
    c. are judged negatively by their peers regarding both intelligence and personality.
8. Facilitative teachers
    a. take the lead in teacher-learner interactions.
    b. allow the learners to control and initiate topics.
    c. provide directive instruction in communicative competence.
9. Learners from diverse cultural, ethnic, and linguistic groups
    a. rarely demonstrate communication disorders.
    b. require supports in learning basic classroom routines and structures.
    c. require individualized instruction in Standard English.
10. In working with adolescents,
    a. communication disorders tend to decrease as students mature.
    b. communicative competence increases with academic achievement.
    c. a loss of motivation is common.

References

Adams, C. (1990). Syntactic comprehension in children with expressive language impairment. *British Journal of Communication, 25,* 149–171.

American Speech-Language-Hearing Association. (1982). Definitions: Communication disorders and variations. *Journal of the American Speech-Language-Hearing Association, 24,* 949–950.

Andrews, J. R., Andrews, M. A., & Shearer, W. M. (1989). Parents' attitudes toward family involvement in speech-language services. *Language, Speech, and Hearing Services in the Schools, 20,* 391–399.

Bashir, A. S., & Scavuzzo, A. (1992). Children with language disorders: Natural history and academic success. *Journal of Learning Disabilities, 25* (1), 53–65.

Bebout, L., & Arthur, B. (1992). Cross-cultural attitudes toward speech disorders. *Journal of Speech and Hearing Research, 35,* 45–52.

Becker, M., Warr-Leeper, G. A., & Leeper, H. A. (1990). Fetal alcohol syndrome: A description of oral motor, articulatory, short-term memory, grammatical, and semantic abilities. *Journal of Communication Disorders, 23* (2), 97–124.

Belander, P. (1994). Literacy and literacies: Continuity and discontinuity. *Language and Education, 8,* 87–94.

Bishop, D. V. (1987). The causes of specific developmental language disorder. *Journal of Child Psychology and Psychiatry and Allied Disciplines, 28* (1), 1–8.

Bishop, D. V., & Adams, C. (1989). Conversational characteristics of children with semantic-pragmatic disorder: II. What features lead to inappropriacy? *British Journal of Disorders of Communication, 24,* 241–263.

Bishop, D. V., & Edmundson, A. (1986). Is otitis media a major cause of specific developmental language disorders? *British Journal of Disorders of Communication, 21,* 321–338.

Boone, D. R. (1987). *Human communication and its disorders.* Englewood Cliffs, NJ: Prentice Hall.

Broen, P. A. (1988). Plotting a course: The ongoing assessment of language. In R. L. Schiefelbusch & L. L. Lloyd (Eds.), *Language perspectives* (2nd ed., pp. 299–320). Austin, TX: Pro-Ed.

Bruner, J. (1981). The social context of language acquisition. *Language and Communication, 1,* 155–178.

Byrd, K., & Cooper, E. B. (1989). Expressive and receptive language skills in stuttering children. *Journal of Fluency Disorders, 14,* 121–126.

Calvert, M. B., & Murray, S. L. (1985). Environmental communication profile: An assessment procedure. In C. S. Simon (Ed.), *Communication skills and classroom success* (pp. 135–164). San Diego: College Hill Press.

Cantwell, D. P., & Baker, L. (1987). The prevalence of anxiety in children with communication disorders. *Journal of Anxiety Disorders, 1* (3), 239–248.

Casby, M. W. (1989). National data concerning communication disorders and special education. *Language, Speech and Hearing Services in the Schools, 20,* 22–30.

Cole, P. A., & Taylor, O. L. (1990). Performance of working class African American children on three tests of articulation. *Language, Speech, and Hearing Services in the Schools, 21* (3), 171–176.

Condino, R., Im-Humber, K., & Stark, R. E. (1990). Cognitive processing in specifically language impaired children. *Journal of Psychology, 124,* 465–478.

Conti-Ramsden, G. (1990). Maternal recasts and other contingent replies to language-impaired children. *Journal of Speech and Hearing Disorders, 55* (2), 262–274.

Craig, H. K. (1991). Pragmatic characteristics of the child with specific language impairment: An interactionist perspective. In T. M. Gallagher (Ed.), *Pragmatics of language: Clinical practice issues* (pp. 163–198). San Diego, CA: Singular.

Craig, H. K., & Evans, J. L. (1989). Turn exchange characteristics of SLI children's simultaneous and nonsimultaneous speech. *Journal of Speech and Hearing Disorders, 54,* 334–347.

Crais, E. R., & Roberts, J. E. (1991). Decision making in assessment and early intervention planning. *Language, Speech and Hearing Services in the Schools, 22,* 19–30.

Creaghead, N., & Tattershall, S. S. (1985). Observation and assessment of classroom pragmatic skills. In C. S. Simon (Ed.), *Communication skills and classroom success* (pp. 105–134). San Diego: College Hill.

Damico, J. S., & Damico, S. K. (1993). Language and social skills from a diversity perspective: Considerations for the speech-language pathologist. *Language, Speech and Hearing Services in Schools, 24,* 236–243.

Dollaghan, C. A. (1987). Comprehension monitoring in normal and language-impaired children. *Topics in Language Disorders, 7,* 45–60.

Edwards, M., Cape, J., & Brown, D. (1989). Patterns of referral for children with speech disorders. *Child Care, Health, and Development, 15,* 417–424.

Ernst, G. (1994). "Talking Circle": Conversation and negotiation in the ESL classroom. *TESOL Quarterly, 28,* 293–322.

Freeby, N., & Madison, C. L. (1989). Children's perceptions of peers with articulation disorders. *Child Study Journal, 19,* 133–144.

Fujiki, M., Brinton, B., & Dunton, S. (1987). The ability of normal and language-impaired children to produce grammatical corrections. *Journal of Communication Disorders, 20,* 413–424.

Fujiki, M., Brinton, B., & Sonnenberg, E. A. (1990). Repair of overlapping speech in the conversations of specifically language impaired and normally developing children. *Applied Psycholinguistics, 11,* 201–215.

Goldman, L. G. (1987). Social implications of language disorders. *Journal of Reading, Writing, and Learning Disabilities International, 3,* 119–130.

Gorenflo, C. W. (1994). Effects of synthetic voice output on attitudes toward the augmented communicator. *Journal of Speech and Hearing Research, 37,* 64–68.

Head, H. (1926). *Aphasia and kindred disorders of speech.* London: Cambridge University Press.

Horsley, I. A., & FitzGibbon, C. T. (1987). Stuttering children: Investigation of a stereotype. *British Journal of Disorders of Communication, 22,* 19–35.

Ingram, D. (1978). *Phonological disability in children.* New York: Elsevier.

Jones, H. A., & Warren, S. F. (1991). Enhancing engagement in early language teaching. *Teaching Exceptional Children, 23* (4), 48–50.

Kaiser, A. P., & Warren, S. F. (1988). Pragmatics and generalization. In R. L. Schiefelbusch & L. L. Lloyd (Eds.), *Language perspectives* (2nd ed., pp. 393–442). Austin, TX: Pro-Ed.

Kayser, H. (1995). Intervention with children from linguistically and culturally diverse backgrounds. In M. E. Fey, J. Windsor, & S. F. Warren (Eds.), *Language intervention: Preschool through the elementary years* (pp. 315–332). Baltimore: Paul H. Brookes.

Kent, R., & Bauer, H. (1985). Vocalizations of one-year-olds. *Journal of Child Language, 12,* 491–526.

Kotsopoulos, A., & Boodoosingh, L. (1987). Language and speech disorders in children attending a day psychiatric programme. *British Journal of Disorders of Communication, 22* (3), 227–236.

Kretschmer, R. R., & Kretschmer, L. W. (1988). Communication competence and assessment. *Journal of the Academy of Rehabilitative Audiology, 21,* 5–17.

Langhans, J., & Boone, D. R. (1975). *Attitudes towards the communicatively handicapped.* Tucson: University of Arizona.

Langlois, A., Hanrahan, L. L., & Inouye, L. L. (1986). A comparison of interactions between stuttering children, nonstuttering children, and their mothers. *Journal of fluency disorders, 11,* 263–273.

Leverett, R. G., & Diefendort, A. O. (1992). Students with language deficiencies: Suggestions for frustrated teachers. *Teaching Exceptional Children, 24* (4), 30–33.

Love, A. J., and Thompson, M. G. (1988). Language disorders and attention deficit disorders in young children referred for psychiatric services. *American Journal of Orthopsychiatry, 58* (1), 52–64.

MacLachlan, B. G., & Chapman, R. S. (1988). Communication breakdowns in normal and language learning-disabled children's conversation and narration. *Journal of Speech and Hearing Disorders, 53,* 2–7.

Madison, L. S., Budd, K. S., & Itzkowitz, J. S. (1986). Changes in stuttering in relation to children's locus of control. *Journal of Genetic Psychology, 147,* 233–240.

Meline, T. J., & Brackin, S. R. (1987). Language-impaired children's awareness of inadequate messages. *Journal of Speech and Hearing Disorders, 52,* 263–270.

Meyers, S. C., & Freeman, F. J. (1985). Mother and child speech rates as a variable in stuttering and disfluency. *Journal of Speech and Hearing Research, 28,* 436–444.

Montgomery, J. W., & Levine, M. D. (1995). Developmental language impairments: Their transactions with other neurodevelopmental factors during the adolescent years. *Seminars in Speech and Language, 16* (1), 1–15.

Moore, V., & Law, J. (1990). Copying ability of preschool children with delayed language development. *Developmental Medicine and Child Neurology, 32,* 249–257.

Muma, J. (1978). *Language handbook, concepts, assessment, intervention.* Englewood Cliffs, NJ: Prentice Hall.

National Joint Committee for Learning Disabilities. (1982). Learning disabilities: Issues on definition. *American Speech and Hearing Association, 24,* 945–949.

Nelson, L. K., Kahmi, A. G., & Apel, K. (1987). Cognitive strengths and weaknesses in language-impaired children: One more look. *Journal of Speech and Hearing Disorders, 52,* 36–43.

Nippold, M. A. (1990). Concomitant speech and language disorders in stuttering children: A critique of the literature. *Journal of Speech and Hearing Disorders, 55,* 61–70.

Office for Civil Rights, U.S. Department of Education. (1992). *National and state summaries of data from the 1990 elementary and secondary civil rights survey.* Washington, DC: Authors.

Peck, C. A. (1985). Increasing opportunities for social control by children with autism and severe behavior handicaps: Effects on student behavior and perceived classroom climate. *Journal of the Association for Persons with Severe Handicaps, 10,* 182–193.

Peck, C. A., & Schuler, A. L. (1983). Classroom-based language interventions for children with autism: Theoretical and practical considerations for the speech and language specialist. *Seminars in Speech and Language, 4,* 93–103.

Powell, M., Filter, M. D., & Williams, B. (1989). A longitudinal study of the prevalence of voice disorders in children from a rural school division. *Journal of Communication Disorders, 22,* 375–382.

Prutting, C. (1979). Process: The action of moving forward progressively from one point to another on the way to completion. *Journal of Speech and Hearing Disorders, 47,* 123–134.

Rice, M. L. (1988). Speech and language impairments. In E. L. Meyen & T. M. Skrtic (Eds.), *Exceptional children and youth: An introduction* (3rd ed., pp. 233–261). Denver: Love.

Richards, M. M., & Richards, L. G. (1988). The development of language and imagery as symbolic processes. In R. L. Schiefelbusch & L. L. Lloyd (Eds.), *Language perspectives* (2nd ed., pp. 35–68). Austin, TX: Pro-Ed.

Roth, F. P., & Clark, D. M. (1987). Symbolic play and social participation abilities of language-impaired and normally developing children. *Journal of Speech and Hearing Disorders, 52,* 17–29.

Rounsefell, S. (1993). Effects of listener training on intelligibility of augmentative and alternative speech in the secondary classroom. *Education and Training in Mental Retardation, 28,* 296–308.

Ruscello, D. M., Lass, N. J., & Podbesek, J. (1988). Listeners' perceptions of normal and voice disordered children. *Folia Phoniatrica, 40,* 290–296.

Russel, M. (1984). Assessment and intervention issues with nonspeaking children. *Exceptional Children, 51,* 64–71.

St. Louis, K. O., & Hinzman, A. R. (1988). A descriptive study of speech, language, and hearing characteristics of school-aged stutterers. *Journal of Fluency Disorders, 13,* 331–355.

Sameroff, A. J., & Chandler, M. J. (1975). Reproductive risk and the continuum of caretaking casualty. In F. D. Horowitz, M. Hetherington, S. Scarr-Salapatek, & G. Siegel (Eds.), *Review of child development research* (Vol. 4). Chicago: University of Chicago.

Sameroff, A. J., & Fiese, B. H. (1988). The context of language development. In R. L. Schiefelbusch & L. L. Lloyd (Eds.), *Language perspectives* (2nd ed., pp. 3–19). Austin, TX: Pro-Ed.

Schiefelbush, R. L., & McCormick, L. (1981). Language and speech disorders. In J. Kauffman & D. Hallahan (Eds.), *Handbook of special education.* Englewood Cliffs, NJ: Prentice Hall.

Seibert, J. M., & Oller, D. K. (1981). Linguistic pragmatics and language intervention strategies. *Journal of Autism and Developmental Disorders, 11,* 75–88.

Shriberg, L., & Kwiatowski, J. (1980). *Natural process analysis.* New York: Wiley.

Simon, C. S. (1985). Presentation of communication evaluation information. In C. S. Simon (Ed.), *Communication skills and classroom success* (pp. 255–317). San Diego: College Hill.

Smith, C. (1991). What's in a word? On our acquisition of the term "language learning disability." *Teacher Education and Special Education, 14,* 103–109.

Snyder, L. S. (1987). Symbolization in language impaired children. *New Directions for Child Development, 36,* 87–108.

Sommers, R. C. (1988). Prediction of fine motor skills of children having language and speech disorders. *Perceptual and Motor Skills, 67,* 63–72.

Spector, C. C. (1990). Linguist humor comprehension of normal and language impaired adolescents. *Journal of Speech and Hearing Disorders, 55,* 533–541.

Starkweather, C. W. (1990). Current trends in therapy for stuttering children and suggestions for future research. *ASHA Reports Series,* (No. 18, pp. 82–90).

Tomblin, J. B. (1989). Familial concentration of developmental language impairment. *Journal of Speech and Hearing Disorders, 54,* 287–295.

Tomblin, J. B. (1990). The effect of birth order on the occurrence of developmental language impairment. *British Journal of Disorders of Communication, 25,* 77–84.

U.S. Department of Education. (1995). *Seventeenth annual report to Congress on the implementation of the Education of the Handicapped Act.* Washington, DC: Author.

U.S. Department of Education, Office of Special Education Programs. (1993). *Fifteenth annual report to Congress on the implementation of the Individuals with Disabilities Education Act.* Washington, DC: Author.

Van der Ley, H., & Deward, H. (1986). Sentence comprehension strategies in specifically language impaired children. *British Journal of Disorders of Communication, 21,* 291–306.

Van Riper, C. (1978). *Speech correction: Principles and methods.* Englewood Cliffs, NJ: Prentice Hall.

Van Riper, C., & Emerick, L. (1984). *Speech correction: An introduction to speech pathology and audiology.* Englewood Cliffs, NJ: Prentice Hall.

Volker, J. A. (1992). Communicative competence in the multicultural classroom. *Journal of the Middle States Council for the Social Studies, 13,* 30–37.

Wetherby, A., Cain, D., Yonclas, D., & Walker, V. (1988). Analysis of intentional communication of normal children from the prelinguistic to the multi-word stage. *Journal of Speech and Hearing Research, 31,* 240–252.

Whitehurst, G. J., Fischel, J. E., Lonigan, C. J., & Valdez-Manchaca, M. C. (1988). Verbal interaction in families of normal and expressive language delayed children. *Developmental Psychology, 24,* 690–699.

Windsor, J. (1995). Language impairment and social competence. In M. E. Fey, J. Windsor, & S. F. Warren (Eds.), *Language intervention: Preschool through the elementary years* (pp. 213–240). Baltimore: Paul H. Brookes.

Wood, L. M. (1982). *Language disorders in school-age children.* Englewood Cliffs, NJ: Prentice Hall.

Learners with Physical Disabilities and Health Impairments

Objectives

After completing this chapter, you will be able to:

1. describe the personal characteristics of learners with physical disabilities and health impairments.
2. describe the identification and evaluation of learners with physical disabilities and health impairments.
3. describe the impact of physical disabilities and health impairments on interactions in the home and classroom.
4. describe ways to mediate the environment for learners with physical disabilities and health impairments.
5. describe the impact of physical disabilities and health impairments on participation in the larger social systems—the school, community, and society.

Key Words and Phrases

acquired immune deficiency
    syndrome (AIDS)
adapted physical education
allergies
amputations
asthma
cancer
catheterization
cerebral palsy
cystic fibrosis
epilepsy (seizure disorders)
heart conditions
hemophilia
HIV (human immunodeficiency virus)
hydrocephaly
juvenile diabetes

juvenile rheumatoid arthritis
lead poisoning
muscular dystrophy
occupational therapy
orthopedic disability
orthotic device
health impairments
physical disabilities
physical therapy
prostheses
scoliosis
sickle cell disease
spina bifida (neural tube defect)
spinal cord injuries
talipes
traumatic brain injuries

"inety-six percent of the population does not think that I have anything to communicate that is worth their time. I can't talk; I drool; my teeth protrude; I make inappropriate facial expressions. People range from being generally uncomfortable to scared stupid by my disabilities. Before I had a voice with which to speak, I had no direct means of telling those people, 'Hey, before you show your ignorance and treat me like a person without cognition, talk with me.'" (Rick Creech, an individual with cerebral palsy, describing reactions of individuals without disabilities and the impact of his electronic communication, 1995)

Introduction

Learners with **physical disabilities** involving physical functioning and health impairments number 139,895, or approximately 2.9 percent of the population of students served under the Individuals with Disabilities Education Act (U.S. Department of Education, 1995). Learners with health impairments demonstrated an increase in students served between 1992–1993 and 1993–1994 with a 26.1 percent increase (U.S. Department of Education, 1995). Both learners with orthopedic disabilities and health impairments were most likely to be served in the general education classroom, though almost 9.1 percent of those identified as health impaired were served in hospitals or at home.

With the number and variety of physical disabilities and health impairments identified, it is impossible to thoroughly discuss them all in a single chapter of an introductory text. For this reason, the physical disabilities and health impairments reviewed in this chapter were selected on the basis of those most frequently encountered by general and special education teachers.

Personal Characteristics

Orthopedic Disabilities

As in all the categories of disability, environmental interaction and the developmental context influence the development of learners with orthopedic disabilities (Sigmon, 1986). **Orthopedic disabilities** include a wide range of disabilities that are severe enough to challenge the learner's participation in daily activities. Lawrence (1991) argues that physical ability is crucial to self-concept development. As a consequence, persons with orthopedic impairments may be challenged through difficulties in mobility, managing body functions, social interaction, and achieving life goals (Lawrence, 1991).

Cerebral palsy is the most frequently occurring orthopedic disability among young learners, present in between 1.5 and 5 of every 1,000 births (Verhaaven & Connor, 1981). Cerebral palsy refers to a dysfunction of the neurological motor system resulting from a nonprogressive brain abnormality that occurred before, during, or shortly after birth (Hardy, 1983). Any condition that adversely impacts the brain may result in cerebral palsy, including maternal infection, chronic disease, fetal infection, and birth injury. Cerebral palsy is, in fact, several conditions, which are grouped into seven categories (see table 10.1).

The impact of cerebral palsy on the individual varies with the extent to which the individual is affected. In addition to difficulties in the area of motor functioning, learners with cerebral palsy may have mild to severe communication disorders, hearing impairments, visual impairments, intellectual deficits, seizure disorders, and perceptual difficulties. Many learners with cerebral palsy have multiple disabilities.

Another orthopedic disability is **spina bifida,** or **neural tube defect,** which occurs in approximately .3 to .9 of every 1,000 births in the United States and has a female-to-male ratio of occurrence of approximately 3:1. Spina bifida is a defect of the spinal column in which the spine fails to close properly around the column of nerves it is designed to protect. Figure 10.1 differentiates between the normal spine and the spine of an individual with spina bifida.

Spina bifida results in varying degrees of paralysis, a loss of sensation in the legs, and various degrees of bowel and bladder incontinence (Pieper, 1983). This defect may also cause

a.   weakness or diminished sensation in the feet, ankles, and/or legs.

b.   incontinence.

Objective One

To describe the personal characteristics of learners with physical disabilities and health impairments.

Figure 10.1

Neural tube defects (spina bifida).

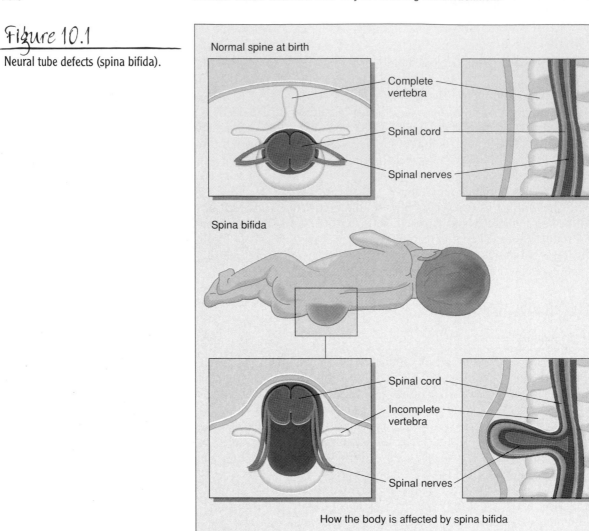

Normal spine at birth

Complete vertebra

Spinal cord

Spinal nerves

Spina bifida

Spinal cord

Incomplete vertebra

Spinal nerves

How the body is affected by spina bifida

Table 10.1 Categories of Cerebral Palsy

Category	Neuromuscular Characteristics
Spasticity	Excessive muscle tone; involuntary contractions; difficulties in movement and motion
Athetosis	Continual involuntary, slow, writhing movements that occur during voluntary actions; contortions in wrists, fingers, and face that prevent well-controlled motion
Ataxia	Poor balance and equilibrium; poor control of gross and fine-motor functions; coordinated movement difficult to impossible
Rigidity	Rigid, essentially immobile limbs; movement extremely difficult
Tremor	Repetitive, rhythmic contractions of muscles; constant, uncontrollable involuntary motion
Atonicity	Decreased muscle tone
Mixed	Combinations of the above categories

The disabilities presented by cerebral palsy vary from learner to learner.

c.   **hydrocephaly** (fluid accumulated in the ventricles of the brain: a surgically implanted valve may be needed to divert excess fluid from the brain cavities).

d.   learning disabilities and perceptual difficulties.

e.   motor difficulties in the arms and hands.

f.   seizure disorders.

Due to complications that affect bladder control, individuals with neural tube defect may require **catheterization,** or the insertion of a tube into the bladder for the withdrawal of urine.

Traumatic brain injuries and **spinal cord injuries** may present a variety of symptoms, depending on the extent and location of the injury. Learners with traumatic brain injuries may need to relearn in areas as simple as focusing or as sophisticated as formulating concepts. The effects of spinal cord injuries, depending on the extent and location of the injury, are similar to the effects of neural tube defect. Traumatic brain injuries and spinal cord injuries may be caused by disease or as a result of accidents or injuries. According to Yashon (1986), the prevalence of spinal cord injuries is 3 in 100,000 individuals. Both traumatic brain injuries and spinal cord injuries are most frequently caused by falls, automobile accidents, and sports injuries.

Traumatic brain injury is a category of disability in Public Law 101-476 (The Individuals with Disabilities Education Act of 1990). It is defined as severe trauma to the head that impairs learning, behavior, and motor functioning. During the 1993–1994 school year, 5,295 students ages six to twenty-one were served in special education programs (U.S. Department of Education, 1995). The National Head Injury Foundation estimates that there are 500,000 cases of traumatic brain injury annually that require hospital admission. Of this group, 100,000 of the victims die and 100,000 of the victims have permanent disabilities. Traumatic brain injury is the number-one killer of people under thirty-four years of age (Smith & Luckasson, 1992).

Scoliosis, a lateral curve in the spine, is characterized by a prominent shoulder (usually on the right), unlevel shoulders and hips, poor posture, and a flattening of the back. Scoliosis rarely affects the learner's educational functioning. A back brace may be used or surgery may be performed to stabilize the spine (Boos, Garlonsky, MacEwen, & Steg, 1984).

Talipes, or clubfoot, involves one or both feet. The foot or feet are turned at an incorrect angle at the ankle.

Other physical disabilities include Legg-Calvé-Perthes disease, a hip disorder, and osteomyelitis, a bacterial bone infection. Also included under the general heading of physical disabilities are arthrogryposis, in which the muscles are smaller and weaker than normal or missing completely, and osteogenesis imperfecta, in which the bones are improperly formed and brittle (Hallahan & Kauffman, 1986).

Amputations, either congenital or acquired, may require accommodations in the classroom and school. Congenital amputations involve the partial or total absence of limbs. Acquired amputations occur as a consequence of trauma (approximately 70 percent) and malignancy (approximately 30 percent) (Verhaaven & Connor, 1981). Learners with amputations may be fitted with prostheses or receive training that allows other parts of the body to assume the functions of the missing part. These children usually attend general education classes.

Gon, Boyce, and Advani (1983) found no significant differences between learners with orthopedic disabilities and their peers. Variations have been found, however, in the defense mechanisms used by learners with or without orthopedic disabilities. When frustrated or confronted with a problem, male learners without orthopedic disabilities turn against the object involved more frequently than learners with orthopedic handicaps, who more frequently turn against themselves. Significantly more anxiety and introversion has been reported among persons with orthopedic disabilities than among those without disabilities (Bandyopadhyay, Roy, Basum, & Chattopadhyay, 1987).

Chronic Illnesses

Learners who are chronically ill or medically fragile are concerned about their autonomy, their ability to explore the environment, and the effects of the intrusion of treatments on their bodies and their activities (Ritchie, Caty, & Ellerton, 1984). In a study of learners with various health issues, similar emotional functioning for empathy, emotional responsiveness, and depression was found in children with and without chronic illness. Children who were actively ill demonstrated higher levels in each of these areas than did children who were well (Nelms, 1989). Learners with chronic illness are at risk for academic failure, even in the absence of a known cognitive problem (Schlieper, 1985).

Human Immunodeficiency Virus (HIV) and Acquired Immune Deficiency Syndrome (AIDS)   **Human immunodeficiency virus (HIV),** is a virus that affects the immune system and impairs the individual's ability to fight infection. There are no treatments or preventative interventions, such as vaccination, for HIV, though some medications are available that appear to delay the development of HIV into **acquired immune deficiency syndrome (AIDS).** AIDS is characterized by the body's inability to fight infection and is fatal. The Centers for Disease Control (1993) reports that there are approximately 3,605 children with AIDS under the age of five and 875 between the ages of five and twelve.

There are four stages in the development of HIV infections (SUNY Research Foundation, 1994). First, shortly after infection, the immune system develops an antibody response to the infection. In the second stage, the virus remains asymptomatic. During the third stage, persons who are HIV positive develop symptoms of common illness, with swollen glands and fever. The average age that this stage occurs in infants infected before or during birth is nine months (Indacochea & Scott, 1992). The fourth stage represents the actual diagnosis of AIDS and the onset of opportunistic infections.

Table 10.2 Types of Seizures and Appropriate Action

Type of Seizure	Appearance	Appropriate Action
Generalized tonic-clonic (grand mal)	Sudden cry, fall, rigidity, and muscle twitching and jerking; frothy saliva from lips; irregular breathing; possible loss of bladder and/or bowel control; confusion or fatigue may follow when individual regains consciousness	Look for medical identification; protect from hazards. Loosen clothing; pad head if possible; turn on side to keep airway clear; place nothing in the mouth. If seizure lasts longer than five minutes, or if multiple seizures occur, call for emergency assistance.
Absence (petit mal)	Blank stare; begins and ends abruptly; may be accompanied by chewing movements or blinking	None apart from reassurance if the individual is under medical supervision for seizures.
Simple partial (Jacksonian)	Individual remains aware; jerking begins in toes or fingers; may proceed to hand, arm; may become convulsive	None apart from reassurance if the individual is under medical supervision for seizures.
Complex partial	Blank stare, followed by chewing and random activity; movement undirected; may pick at clothing; may run or appear afraid; may struggle at restraint; usually follows a typical pattern; no memory of event afterwards	Reassure the individual; gently guide from hazards; stay with the individual until completely recovered.
Atonic	Seen in children or adults; sudden collapse; recovery after about ten seconds to a minute	None apart from reassurance if the individual is under medical supervision and was not injured in a fall.
Myoclonic	Sudden, brief, massive muscle movements that may involve all or part of the body	None apart from reassurance if the individual is under medical supervision.

© Epilepsy Foundation of America, 1991—Adapted with permission.

In addition to the medical problems associated with AIDS, children with AIDS may have changes in muscle tone as well as visual or hearing impairments (Bruder, 1995). In addition, they may experience repeated hospitalizations and poor nutrition, which again contribute to developmental delays.

Seizure Disorders **Epilepsy,** or **seizure disorders,** marked by recurrent, unprovoked seizures, occurs in approximately 4 percent of schoolchildren. Seizures, which may involve only parts of the body or be generalized throughout the individual's system, are sudden, brief, temporary states of abnormal brain functioning due to uncontrolled electrical discharges in the brain (Chee & Clancy, 1984). A description of the types of seizures, their appearance, and immediate treatment is provided in table 10.2.

Though usually mainstreamed, learners with seizure disorders often have special physical and emotional needs that challenge learning and socialization (Frank, 1985). Learners with epilepsy were found to vary from their peers in higher anxiety levels and higher dissatisfaction in their self-concept (Margalit & Heiman, 1983). Those learners with seizure disorders with abnormalities in their electroencephalograms and/or complex partial seizures were found to demonstrate significantly more psychiatric disorders than did other school children

(Hoare, 1984b). These psychiatric disorders were frequently found to be related to the learner's inappropriate dependency on parents and other adults (Hoare, 1984a). Children with epilepsy were more likely than their peers to attribute the success or failure of their school performance to unknown sources of control. They held less-positive feelings about school and about their personal worth (Matthews, Barabas, & Ferrari, 1983). It is essential that persons working with learners with seizure disorders project a positive attitude and avoid becoming a "terrified observer." The teacher must have reliable information about the learner and his or her seizures and treatment.

Sickle Cell Disease   **Sickle cell disease,** an inherited blood disorder, affects one in every 650 African Americans. Sickle cell disease causes chronic anemia because red blood cells are unable to survive in circulation in the bloodstream for the usual period of time. These red blood cells become rigid and deformed and are not sufficiently pliable to circulate through small blood vessels. Painful crisis periods of bleeding can lead to extended absences, interrupting the educational experience of learners with sickle cell disease (Kim, Gaston, & Fithian, 1984).

Learners with sickle cell disease were not found to vary from their matched peers in self-concept or depression. Rather, consistent patterns of behavior were linked to socioeconomic status rather than presence of the disease (Lemanek, 1986). Variations in personal adjustment and behavioral problems were not found to be related to illness severity (Hurtig, Koepke, & Park, 1989). In a study related to satisfaction with their bodies, adolescents with sickle cell disease were found to be less satisfied than were their healthy peers and to experience less social involvement (Morgan & Jackson, 1986). In addition, sickle cell disease may be related to subtle neuropsychological and learning problems that may contribute to decreased school performance.

Annual **Edition**

Article *29*

Health Impairments

Health impairments is a generic term used to refer to several physical conditions or diseases that have an impact on the individual's functioning. Descriptions of several of the conditions follow. Learners with these health impairments are disabled only to the extent that the health condition restricts their participation at home, in the school, and in the community.

Heart conditions, congenital or acquired through bacterial or viral infection, occur in as many as 8 in 1,000 learners. The degree of impairment ranges from mild to severe. These learners typically engage in general education curricula and participate in activities within the limits prescribed by their physical condition (Woolf, 1984).

Hemophilia, a sex-linked inherited condition, occurs in approximately 1 in 10,000 male children. Children with this condition, due to problems with coagulation of the blood, may be frequently absent from school. They may have difficulties with mobility and participation in physical education (Gill & Butler, 1984).

Cancer, a group of diseases of unknown cause that produce abnormal cell growth, is diagnosed in approximately 7,000 children each year. The two most frequently diagnosed cancers in children are leukemia and brain tumors. These learners may be frequently absent from school (Ross, 1984).

Acute lymphoblastic leukemia accounts for one-third of all the cases of cancer among children. It occurs when abnormal immature white blood cells multiply and eventually overtake the bone marrow, preventing formation of normal blood cells (Poplack, 1989). Acute lymphoblastic leukemia is curable in 50 percent to 60 percent of all cases.

When diagnosed, the child with acute lymphoblastic leukemia typically has symptoms of unexplained fevers, abdominal pain, fatigue, and excessive bruising. A complete blood count shows an increased number of lymphoblasts and a decreased number of normal red blood cells and platelets. A bone marrow biopsy is done to confirm the diagnosis, and a spinal tap is performed to detect any leukemic cells in the central nervous system. The child is then assigned to a treatment plan, which usually involves two to three years of chemotherapy (Coniglio & Blackman, 1995).

Allergies, abnormal reactions to specific substances, occur in approximately 20 percent of the general population. The most common allergy among children is seasonal allergic rhinitis, which is caused by inhaled pollen. Learners may experience a variety of symptoms, including nasal obstruction; discharge of clear, thin mucus; sneezing; eye and nose itching; and tearing. They may experience swelling of the nasal tissues, which blocks drainage of the nasal passages and results in fluid in the ears. This fluid may cause hearing impairments (Kolski & Burg, 1984). Symptoms of allergies are treated with antihistamines, decongestants, eyedrops, and injections.

A small number of children are diagnosed with chronic perennial allergic rhinitis. The symptoms of this disorder are similar to the symptoms of seasonal rhinitis noted above.

Other common allergies include reactions to insect stings and gastrointestinal reactions. Students with allergies may have difficulties attending and concentrating in school.

Juvenile diabetes is a metabolic disorder caused by the inadequate production of insulin by the body. It occurs in about 1 in every 500 to 1,000 children. Though the specific cause of juvenile diabetes is unknown, an inherited predisposition is suspected. The symptoms of juvenile diabetes include frequent urination and thirst. These children are often tired, irritable, and moody, and they may have achievement problems.

Diabetes is treated with insulin, diet, and exercise. The type, timing, and quantities of food these children ingest is essential to controlling diabetes. The delay or omission of a snack or meal can be dangerous for the student and result in hypoglycemia (an overdose of insulin). These students must avoid prolonged and strenuous exertion, which lowers their blood sugar levels. Fluctuations in blood sugar levels result in hypoglycemia and ketoacidosis (an elevation of blood sugar).

Cystic fibrosis occurs in 1 in 2,000 Caucasian Americans and 1 in 17,000 African Americans. Persons with cystic fibrosis have abnormally thick and sticky mucus and highly concentrated glandular secretions. The disorder is terminal and is often complicated with secondary respiratory infections. These learners have a persistent cough. Frequent urination and thirst are common.

Muscular dystrophy is the most frequent cause of progressive muscular weakness in children. Muscular dystrophy is a group of disorders characterized by the wasting and progressive weakness of skeletal muscles. This disorder is inherited and usually shortens the individual's life span.

The four most frequently identified types of muscular dystrophy are

- Duchenne, which develops rapidly between the ages of two and six. Students require the use of a wheelchair by age twelve. They often die from heart failure or pneumonia in their late teens or early adulthood.
- Facioscapulohumeral, which progresses slowly beginning in the teens. There are long periods during which symptoms do not progress. This form of the disorder begins in the muscles of the face, shoulders, and upper arms.
- Limb-girdle, which is diagnosed in late childhood or early adolescence. Its variable progression begins in either the muscles of the lower trunk or upper legs.
- Myotonic, which progresses steadily, beginning in early adulthood. Initially, weakness is noted in the fingers, hands, forearms, feet, and legs.

Juvenile rheumatoid arthritis, a joint inflammation, is a chronic disorder that affects between 50,000 and 250,000 children. According to the Arthritis Foundation (1983) approximately 36 million children and adults in the United States are affected by arthritis. Systemic juvenile rheumatoid arthritis is one of the major types of arthritis. It affects children of any age and accounts for 20 percent of all cases (Athreya & Ingall, 1984). Symptoms vary from day to day; sore and stiff joints in the late afternoon is the most common problem for learners with juvenile rheumatoid arthritis. Learners appear to be most comfortable from midmorning to early afternoon.

Lead poisoning is a consequence of the ingestion of lead (usually from lead-based paints), which produces neurological damage. In an extensive review of the literature, Marlowe (1985) concludes that lead, at levels far below those accepted for clinical lead poisoning, is associated with a wide range of behavioral symptoms, including reduced scores on measures of intellectual ability; decreased efficiency in auditory, visual, and language processing; reduced fine-motor performance; attention problems; and inappropriate classroom behavior.

Asthma is a chronic lung disease characterized by inflammation, obstruction, and increased sensitivity of the airways (National Institutes of Health, 1991). Asthma is the most common chronic illness of childhood, affecting 5 percent to 7 percent of all children (National Institutes of Health, 1993). Asthma is not reversible; rather, individuals with asthma have hyperresponsive airways that react to environmental stimuli, called triggers. This results in increased mucus production, inflammation, and bronchospasm (Simeonsson, Lorimer, & Sturtz, 1995).

Simeonsson and associates (1995) report that the classic signs of asthma include wheezing, coughing, and shortness of breath or rapid breathing. Children with a family history of asthma or eczema (an allergic skin condition) are more likely to develop asthma than others. With proper diagnosis and management, asthma can be controlled but not cured. The goals of asthma management are to allow the learner to participate fully without symptoms, to prevent acute episodes of asthma, to permit uninterrupted sleep, and to have little or no side effects from medication.

Learners' Understanding of Their Disabilities

Young children develop from having a general understanding of their limitations at about age six to realizing the implications of their disability at around age eight (Minde, Hackett, Killon, & Silver, 1972). Teplin, Howard, and O'Connor (1981), based on their study of learners with cerebral palsy, report that children vary in their willingness to discuss their disabilities. Though all of the four- to eight-year-old children they interviewed were aware that their arms and legs were different from those of their peers, all of the younger children and about half of the older children denied their difficulty in running. The age of the learner is significantly related to the child's awareness of differences and disability (Dunn, McCartan, & Fuqua, 1988). Children whose orthopedic disabilities were openly discussed at home were significantly more aware of their disability and its implications. Discussion at school about disabilities has not been statistically related to a child's knowledge about being different or about his or her specific disability.

Objective Two

To describe the identification and evaluation of learners with physical disabilities and health impairments.

Identification and Evaluation

Three groups of learners with physical disabilities and health impairments were included in Public Law 94-142: those who were orthopedically impaired, those with other health impairments, and those with multiple disabilities.

Public Law 94-142 identified learners who were orthopedically impaired as those with a severe skeletal deformity that adversely affects their educational performance. These learners may have congenital anomalies (such as clubfoot, hip displacement, or neural tube defects), disabilities attributed to disease processes (such as poliomyelitis or bone tuberculosis), or impairments from other causes (such as cerebral palsy, amputations, and fractures or burns that cause contractures).

Learners who have other health impairments may have limited strength, vitality, or alertness due to chronic or acute health problems such as heart conditions, tuberculosis, rheumatic fever, nephritis, asthma, sickle cell disease, hemophilia, seizure disorders, lead poisoning, leukemia, or diabetes, any of which could adversely affect a child's educational performance. Of these, heart conditions, asthma, sickle cell disease, seizure disorders, and lead poisoning are the most common. Under the amendments of Public Law 94-142, learners with autism were classified as "other health impaired" from 1981 to 1990. In 1990, under Public Law 101-476 (The Individuals with Disabilities Education Act), learners with autism were classified in a separate category of disability. Prior to 1981, these learners were classified as "seriously emotionally disturbed." These learners, however, are frequently served in programs for learners with multiple disabilities (see chap. 16). Efforts to include learners with attention deficit disorders in this category failed with the passing of Public Law 101-476. However, notice to solicit public comment regarding the appropriate components of an operational definition of "attention deficit disorder" was given in Public Law 101-476. (These learners are discussed in chapter 15.)

"Multihandicapped," or having multiple disabilities, as described in Public Law 94-142, means experiencing concomitant impairments (such as being mentally retarded and visually impaired, or mentally retarded and orthopedically impaired). The combination causes such severe educational problems that these learners cannot be accommodated in special education programs soley for one of the disabilities. (These learners are discussed in chapter 17.)

The identification of learners with physical disabilities and health impairments is typically completed by medical professionals. Depending on the particular physical disability or health impairment, the learner is given a series of general and specialized medical examinations. Evaluation is conducted by a variety of general and specialized medical personnel and allied health professionals.

Though the vast majority of learners with physical disabilities and health impairments are served in the general education classroom and study the typical curriculum, it is frequently necessary to make some educational accommodations to effectively respond to these learners' individual needs. Due to a learner's disability, it may be difficult to obtain valid educational assessment information from standardized measurement instruments. For example, learners with motor involvement or communication disorders may not be effectively evaluated on instruments requiring motor coordination or verbal communication. For effective educational evaluation or assessment of learners with physical disabilities and health impairments, criterion-referenced instruments, task analysis, and direct observation of functioning are recommended. Sirvis (1988) and Gleckel and Lee (1990) recommend assessment of the following areas of functioning: (a) daily living activities, (b) mobility, (c) physical abilities and limitations, (d) psychosocial development, (e) communication, (f) academic potential, (g) adaptations for learning, and (h) transition skills.

The Impact on Interactions in the Home and Classroom

Interactions in the Home

Objective Three

To describe the impact of physical disabilities and health impairments on interactions in the home and classroom.

Chronic Illness Kazak (1989) emphasizes the need to view children's chronic illness through a family systems approach. The interactions among the various family contexts must be recognized in working with children who have a chronic illness. This concept is particularly evident in Williams, Williams, and Landa's (1989) work regarding the developmental performance of children with chronic illness. They found that family composition (including higher levels of maternal and paternal education, residing in an urban area, and having fewer children) and being an only child contributed to children's resilience to the challenges of chronic illness.

Among children with sickle cell anemia, diabetes, and leukemia, those whose general functioning was relatively good were found to come from families that had more resources to cope with the condition (Jessop & Stein, 1985). In addition, the children's mothers reported that the conditions had less impact on the family. Though mothers of children with chronic illness reported greater stress than mothers of children with no known medical problems, no differences were found between the two groups in marital satisfaction (Kazak, 1987, 1989). Mothers of children with chronic illness who had greater social support demonstrated less psychological distress (Hobfoil & Lerman, 1988). In addition, Hobfoil and Lerman report that mothers who experienced greater distress received greater social support at the time of crisis, and intimacy with spouse was related to better stress resistance. Social support, however, has been shown to decrease over time (Kazak & Meadows, 1989). Mothers of children with chronic diseases, such as sickle cell disease, diabetes, and leukemia, who had more resources judged their functioning more positively and tended to have children with better psychological adjustment than did families with fewer resources (Jessop & Stein, 1985).

The children with fewer previous surgeries and whose parents exhibited the extremes of parenting stress and an overinvolvement with their child were found more likely to become disturbed by hospitalization and surgery. When compared with their typical peers, however, children with chronic illness responded much the same when confronted with hospitalization and surgery (Wells & Schwebel, 1987). Poor social functioning of children with chronic illnesses has been related to parental overprotection, while in children with no known illnesses, poor social functioning has been related to a lack of parental care (Cappelli, McGrath, McDonald, & Katsanis, 1989).

Fathers of children who are ill are less likely to perceive social support in their environment than are fathers of children with no known medical problems or disabilities (Ferrari, 1986). Fathers of children with chronic illnesses are less likely than mothers to report that they feel the challenges strengthen them and their understanding of the medical situation (Powers, Gaudet, & Powers, 1986).

No consistent relationship has been found between the presence of a chronic illness and risk for psychological problems among siblings; rather, the quality of family functioning and relationships has both direct and indirect effects on siblings (Drotar & Crawford, 1985). Wood, Boyle, Watkins, and Noqueira (1988) explored the relationship between disease type, disease activity, and the psychological status of school-age siblings of children with chronic illnesses. The more psychologically healthy siblings displayed more externalizing than internalizing behaviors.

Young children are able to understand information about another child's illness. However, this information base does not necessarily facilitate acceptance of the child with the illness (Potter & Roberts, 1984).

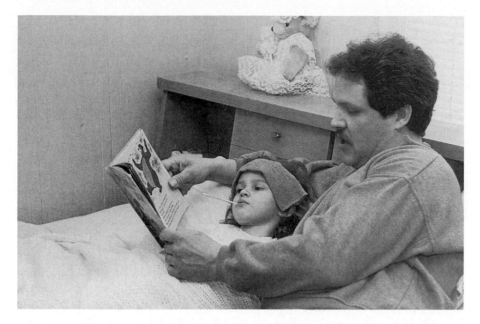

Illness increases family stress.

Seizure Disorders   Parents of children with seizure disorders varied from those of healthy children in their perceptions of epilepsy. Parents of children with epilepsy, though far more knowledgeable about the educational and behavioral problems of children with epilepsy, often regarded epilepsy as a sign of serious disease (Hoare, 1986). Mothers of children with seizure disorders were found to use fewer verbal directions and fewer positive responses with the children, using, instead, more negative feedback (Chavez & Buriel, 1988).

Sickle Cell Disease   The presence of a child with sickle cell disease presents stress in a family. Single mothers of children with sickle cell disease estimated their child's behavior traits and their relationship with the child less positively than did two-parent families, who also reported stress (Evans, Burlow, & Oler, 1988). Dilworth-Anderson (1989), finding varied family structure and overlapping systems of functioning among families of children with sickle cell disease, suggests that families need both broad-based and problem-specific interventions. Self-help groups for individuals with sickle cell disease and their families have been found valuable and capable of enhancing family and learner personal goals (Nash, 1989).

The healthy siblings of learners with sickle cell disease, when compared with their ill siblings, were found to be at increased risk of psychological adjustment problems. Treiber, Mabe, and Wilson (1987) report that these distress levels were associated with reports of problems in the home and maternal depression and anxiety.

Learners Who Are HIV Positive   As indicated earlier, most babies born to women with HIV infection, though they test positive for the virus, do not develop AIDS (Levine & Dubler, 1990). An estimated one-third of the children who are HIV positive are currently in foster or adoptive placements. For these children, specialized foster homes with specific training and medical support systems have evolved (Gurdin & Anderson, 1987).

Interactions in the Classroom

When asked who they would rather help first, why, and how much, young schoolage children selected persons with orthopedic impairments most frequently over children with either Down syndrome or those with no known disability (Kennedy & Thurman, 1982). In a study in which they were asked to rank "who they liked best," learners with visible orthopedic disabilities and learners with no disabilities ranked wheelchair users and nonidentified persons high and persons with facial marks and obese persons low (Giancoli & Neimeyer, 1983). de Apodaca, Watson, Mueller, and Isaacson-Kailes (1985) offer three possible explanations for significantly higher ratings in some areas of peer rating scales: (a) the persons were truly liked, (b) the children were admired because of their ability to deal with their disability, or (c) peers have a defensive inability to express negative feelings towards persons with disabilities.

Teachers were found to hold negative attitudes (as indicated by placements in more-restrictive environments) towards learners with orthopedic disabilities only when the level of achievement was low (Pliner & Hannah, 1985). Johnson (1986) indicates that teachers may require a broad range of supports and resources when working with learners with chronic illnesses, including in-service training sessions, classroom visits by health professionals, programs for parents, contact with national organizations, and use of computer, local, and regional networks.

A particularly challenging group of learners are those who are medically dependent on technology. Educational placements for these learners range from homebound tutoring, to segregated special education classes, to inclusive general education. Taylor and Walker (1991) indicate that when these learners are in the public school system, they are typically provided the assistance of either a private-duty nurse or other trained individual. Court decisions related to technology-assisted learners indicate that because some services are truly medical and not related to the learner's education, and therefore not covered by Public Law 94-142, such services may be covered by Medicaid. Services required by the learner's individualized education program must be provided by Medicaid (Taylor & Walker, 1991).

Bennett-Levy and Stores (1984) explored teachers' perceptions of classroom behavior relevant to learning difficulties of learners with epilepsy. Four variables—concentration, processing, confidence, and alertness—were found to identify these learners. Teachers were found to perceive learners with epilepsy as having poorer concentration and mental processing ability, as well as being less alert than their peers. Even when matched for educational attainment, teachers perceived learners with epilepsy to be less alert. Bennett-Levy and Stores suggest that the effects of drugs on the learner may explain these findings and may be related to teachers' perceptions.

Mediating the Environment

The effect of a learner's disability in the environment and the accommodations needed to help the learner mediate the environment are highly individualized. Accommodations needed to mediate the environment are determined by the individual's age and degree of the disability, the visibility of the disability, the availability of family and other support systems, the attitude of the learner toward the disability, the individual's social status among peers, the presence of architectural barriers, and the need for and availability of transportation (Lewandowski & Cruickshank, 1980; Hardman, Drew, Egan, & Wolf, 1990).

Learners with physical disabilities and health impairments seldom need variations in the curriculum itself; however, the learner's physical condition may require the presence of medical equipment. Mediating the environment, then, in addition to collaborating with medical professionals, may involve administering medication or using assistive devices and equipment. A teacher's role with learners taking medication includes documenting changes in behavior and, in some cases, the severity of symptoms. The most common medications used by learners and their potential side effects are included in table 10.3.

Objective Four

To describe ways to mediate the environment for learners with physical disabilities and health impairments.

Annual **Edition**

Articles *31 & 32*

Accommodations needed to mediate the environment are highly individualized for learners medically dependent on technology.

Table 10.3 Common Medications Used by Learners with Physical Disabilities or Health Impairments

Medication	Condition	Possible side effects
Imipramine (Tofranil)	Enuresis	Sedation, dry mouth, constipation
Dextroamphetamine (Dexadrine)	Attention deficit hyperactivity disorder	Insomnia, behavioral rebound
Methylphenidate (Ritalin)	Attention deficit hyperactivity disorder	Loss of appetite, weight loss, or failure to gain
Clonidine (Catepress)	Attention deficit hyperactivity disorder	Sedation
Diphenhydramine (Benedryl)	Allergies	Dizziness, oversedation, agitation
Diazepam (Valium)	Seizures	Substance abuse
Phenobarbital	Seizures	Memory and attention problems; hyperactivity
Diphenylhydamotoin (Dilantin)	Seizures	Irritability, aggression, depressed mood
Carbamazepine (Tegretol)	Seizures	Drowsiness, nausea, rash, eye problems
Valproic acid (Depakene)	Seizures	Nausea, gastrointestinal distress, weight gain, tremor

Information from Brown, Dingle, and Landau (1994).

A physical therapist focuses on increasing the individual's strength, endurance, and range of motion.

With some learners, diet control is important. For example, the timing, type, and quantity of food is essential to the continued functioning of learners with diabetes. Learners with seizure disorders may also be on a specialized diet (Scherer, 1983).

Three related services frequently required by learners with physical disabilities and health impairments are (a) occupational therapy, (b) physical therapy, and (c) adapted physical education. The occupational therapist's role is to assist learners, infants through adults, in the development of needed work, recreation, and self-care skills. Concern may be for the initial learning or the restoration, or relearning, of skills related to everyday life. The focus of **occupational therapy** is on functional outcomes and practical solutions to problems challenging the individual. The therapist may use various tools, toys, appliances, and utensils to help learners with physical disabilities use their body more effectively. The learner may have difficulty in such areas as balance, posture, tactile discrimination, motor planning, coordination, and eye-hand coordination. Assistance may also be given with the social-emotional concerns related to physical disabilities. Services provided by the occupational therapist may range from consultation with teacher and parents to direct service and may be provided in the home, private office, school, or hospital.

The physical therapist focuses on increasing the learner's strength, endurance, and range of motion. **Physical therapy** is used to prevent, correct, and relieve physical conditions. The physical therapist uses various forms of therapy, including heat, cold, massage, and exercise. Physical therapy may be provided directly or through consultation with teacher and parents and in the home, private office, school, or hospital.

The teacher of **adapted physical education** is concerned primarily with the learner's successful participation in physical education. Attention is focused on the physical education curriculum and activities. Consideration is given to the learner's strength, endurance, and coordination, as well as the learner's safety. Services are generally delivered at school and usually in a small-group setting. Services may be offered either directly or through consultation with the learner's teacher.

For very young children with chronic illnesses, medically supervised early intervention programs in either health-care settings or in settings closely associated with a medical center or hospital may be necessary (Kahn & Battle, 1987). In these settings, the philosophy of care should develop the children's trust in caregivers and consistency in caregivers, with a goal of increasing interaction with the environment (Jansen, DeWitt, Meshul, & Krasnoff, 1989).

Learners with Seizure Disorders

Colandra, Dominguez-Granados, Gomez-Rubio, and Molina-Font (1990) found that learners with seizure disorders who were on therapeutic levels of phenobarbital demonstrated greater differences between their medicated and nonmedicated verbal, performance, and total intelligence quotient scores. These differences were not noted among children receiving valproic acid, another common medication for epilepsy. The "Guidelines for Practice" box on page 233 provides guidelines for those persons unfamiliar with but confronted with seizures.

Learners Who Are Positive for HIV

Wetterau and Stegelin (1991) report that the likelihood of HIV positive learners being in educational settings increases annually. In their study of the knowledge and attitudes of licensed day-care workers with regard to HIV and AIDS, they found that care providers had a generally strong knowledge base related to the virus and the disease. However, there seemed to be little relationship between an

guidelines for practice

Seizures: When to Seek Immediate Assistance

- if you are unaware of the individual ever having had a seizure (persons with seizure disorders frequently wear a medical warning necklace or bracelet)
- if the individual's seizure lasts longer than ten minutes
- if the individual experiences a series of seizures without regaining consciousness
- if the individual is injured during the seizure
- if normal breathing does not resume
- if the individual requests medical assistance ▌

individual's knowledge and his or her attitudes about AIDS. Professionals reported that they felt ill-prepared in helping to control infection and a lack of confidence in their ability to work with individuals who had tested positively for HIV.

The recommendations of the American Academy of Pediatrics (Newschwander, 1987) concerning students who test positive for HIV include unrestricted school attendance and strict maintenance of the child's confidentiality. Teachers and other learners are not at risk by working and learning in close proximity to these children.

The health status and increased vulnerability for illness of children with AIDS may limit their participation in school (Kelker, Hecimovic, & LeRoy, 1994). For their safety, then, as well, Bruder (1995) recommends following universal precautions against infection, including the following:

- Wear disposable gloves for diapering.
- Wash hands frequently.
- Use gloves and bleach for cleanup of bodily fluids.
- Wash toys and surfaces with bleach after sessions.
- Prevent spread from runny noses and other conditions that result in loss of bodily fluids.
- Dispose of waste materials in a systematic way.

The "Guidelines for Practice" box on page 234 lists additional recommendations for teachers who have a student with AIDS.

Transitional Services

Care must be taken when learners with physical disabilities or health impairments make transitions between programs in the school system (day care or preschool to the primary grades, elementary to secondary school) and from school to independent living in the community, higher education, or work. Transition planning should begin well in advance of the time when the transition is to occur and should be a team effort, involving the learner and the learner's parents as well as the sending and receiving professionals.

Assistive Equipment, Prostheses, and Orthotic Devices

There are three categories of devices that may be used to facilitate the effective functioning of learners with physical disabilities and health impairments: assistive equipment, prostheses, and orthotics. Assistive equipment includes ordinary devices that are specially designed or modified and applied to facilitate the daily living of learners with disabilities in the home, classroom, school, and office. Among the devices that may be of assistance are uniquely designed cups, spoons, plates,

Prosthetic devices enhance independence.

guidelines for practice

When You have a Child with AIDS in Your Classroom

There is no justification for excluding children with AIDS from schooling with their peers. However, several issues may emerge when a child with AIDS is placed in the classroom. Kelker, Hecimovic, and LeRoy (1994) suggest that teachers review the following items when a child with AIDS is placed in their classroom:

- Maintain confidentiality of the child.
- Request state and local policies regarding inclusion of students with AIDS.
- Gather information about AIDS and its potential effects on learning.
- Design ways for the child to participate in classroom activities.
- Allow for flexibility related to hospitalizations and frequent absences.
- Request training in infection-control procedures, frequently referred to as "universal precautions" (i.e., disposing of items that come in contact with bodily fluids in a safe way; wearing gloves when treating bleeding injuries; covering wounds; cleaning surfaces with a bleach solution).
- Become knowledgeable so that you can answer students' questions

Kelker, K., Hecimovic, A., & LeRoy, C. H. (1994). Designing a classroom and school environment for students with AIDS. *Teaching Exceptional Children, 26,* 52–55.

bookholders, pencils, positioning devices, chairs, tables, computer keyboards, and computer screens. These devices must be individually modified to respond to the needs of each learner.

In many ways, the use of technology has forced the redefinition of disability. The Alliance for Technology Access (1994) argues that the "unrealistic" expectations for persons with disabilities regarding the potential of technology are actually achievable. For example, voice-recognition software allows individuals to access computer programs by speaking. Environmental control units, which turn on lights and appliances and secure doors with a gentle-pressure switch, puff on a

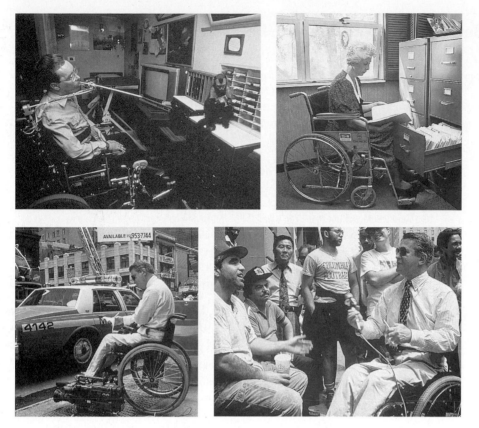

Adults with physical disabilities are confronted with greater challenges in both employment and societal perception of their usefulness and ability to contribute.

straw-switch, eyeblink, or gaze, are available and support independence. Augmentative communication devices provide a voice to many individuals who previously were considered nonverbal.

Prostheses are artificial replacements for missing body parts such as an artificial arm, hand, or leg. Though the effective use of a prosthesis is dependent on residual functioning, it is essential that the prosthesis not interfere with this residual functioning and be acceptable for use by the individual. Some individuals with disabilities prefer not to use prostheses.

An **orthotic device** is an assistive device designed to enhance the partial functioning of a part of an individual's body. Examples of such devices include braces, crutches, canes, and walkers.

Section 504 of the Rehabilitation Act of 1973 mandated that facilities be accessible to individuals with disabilities. During the past two decades, great progress has been made in making buildings and transportation accessible. In 1990, Public Law 101-336 (the Americans with Disabilities Act) required that accommodations be made for individuals with disabilities, even in the private sector (see chap. 3).

The Impact on Participation in the School, Community, and Society

Bohan and Humes (1986) interviewed adults with orthopedic disabilities, all of whom used a wheelchair as either their primary or only means of mobility. These adults felt that able-bodied individuals abridged their social rights through continual staring, intrusive questioning, unsolicited assistance, or public humiliation. Those interviewed also indicated that they were dissatisfied with the way they responded to public encounters. They felt that they did not respond appropriately for the circumstances. University students using wheelchairs reported that they

Objective Five

To describe the impact of physical disabilities and health impairments on participation in the larger social systems—the school, community, and society.

John Hockenberry: Journalist First, Disabled Second

By Roxanne Roberts

National Public Radio correspondent John Hockenberry, soon to join ABC, is determined not to become solely known as the "disabled" journalist, although it's a role in which he is becoming increasingly comfortable and visible.

At age 19, Hockenberry was in a car accident in which his spinal cord was damaged and he was paralyzed from the chest down. In 1980, he began working as a volunteer at NPR affiliate KLCC-FM in Eugene, Ore. Within a year, he was filing reports for NPR and was in the middle of the biggest story of the year—the eruption of Mount St. Helens.

His bosses in Washington didn't realize he used a wheelchair until he missed a deadline—because he couldn't fit his wheelchair into a phone booth to file his story. He didn't discuss his disability with listeners until years later when he returned from two years based in Jerusalem.

"In the Middle East, I was expecting architectural barriers, but I found psychological access," he said. "I found incredible openness about physical helplessness in the Third World that doesn't exist in the United States."

He returned to the Middle East during the Persian Gulf War. Hockenberry left his wheelchair at a Kurdish outpost and spent eight hours on the back of a donkey to get to a story on the thousands of refugees pouring into the mountains.

"Kurds would come by and say, 'Why are we wasting a perfectly good donkey with a journalist on top?' I would explain or a Kurd would explain that I can't walk. Then these starving, dying Kurds would say, 'Then why are you here? You could die up there'—which was the story I was trying to get."

Hockenberry went into journalism thinking he and the chair were two separate entities; today he is one of the leading spokesmen for the disabled and an active proponent of enforcement of the Americans With Disabilities Act, which went into effect this year. As host of the Peabody Award-winning show "Heat," he explored the issues with other disabled people and took his audience through the New York subway system—in a wheelchair.

"I've gone through a very personal transformation on that," he said. "From 'Leave me alone. I have a real job'—which

is a bitter, awful way to be—to really understanding that I have a role."

In June, Hockenberry filed a lawsuit against Jujamcym Theaters in New York after being denied access to "Jelly's Last Jam" at the Virginia Theatre. He had purchased a $60 ticket the previous day and was told the house manager would seat him. But at curtain time, the manager allegedly refused to help and turned him away.

He wrote an essay for The New York Times about the incident. But, he said, don't look for him to use his television job primarily to report on the disabled. The fact is, he said, he's "too close" to do those stories effectively.

"The fact that he's in a wheelchair made us ask, 'Can he do the job?'" said ABC executive producer Tom Yellin. "I asked around. When I heard about him being dragged across Turkey on a camel, I figured the guy could get from one place to another reasonably efficiently. The real issue is what you do when you get there. What he does is very exciting. Nothing gets in John's way, as far as I know." •

participated less in extracurricular activities than their peers (Bohan & Humes, 1986). Though social interactions posed few problems, the physical environment often challenged university students with orthopedic disabilities (Burbach & Babbitt, 1988). Such items as automatic doors, elevators, and desks at the proper height were not available.

Pfeiffer (1991) reports that although a physical disability may have an impact on an individual's employability, the social class structure that enables Caucasian males in the United States to have access to education, jobs, and higher income is in place within the disabled community. Caucasian males are far more likely to be employed and to receive higher income than their peers who are female or from minority cultures. Hanna and Rogovsky (1991) suggest that women with disabilities have "two handicaps plus," and are confronted with greater challenges in both employment and in society's perception of their usefulness and ability to contribute.

In their study of the post-secondary experiences of learners with physical disabilities, Liebert, Lutsky, and Gottlieb (1990) found that about two-thirds of the individuals were employed at least part-time. The majority of jobs were in competitive employment, though about one-half could be classified as semiskilled. Personal networks, such as families and friends, were the ways in which individuals found employment, rather than through rehabilitation or other placement agencies. Almost all of the individuals were single, and most were living with their parents.

Often lack of accessibility limits even simple social interactions for individuals with physical disabilities. Smith (1994) describes a "segregation imposed by architectures." She contends that unless each home has one safe no-step entrance and thirty-two-inch door openings (including the door opening to the bathroom), houses are consistently constructed with built-in barriers. In Atlanta, Georgia, an ordinance was passed requiring this minimal accessibility in new housing units.

Summary

With the number and variety of physical disabilities and health impairments identified, it is impossible to thoroughly discuss each in a single chapter of an introductory text. For this reason, the physical disabilities and health impairments reviewed in this chapter were selected on the basis of those most frequently encountered by general and special education teachers. This chapter provided an overview of the nature of accommodations for these learners. In most cases, learners with orthopedic disabilities and health impairments are most likely to be served in the general education classroom.

Learners with physical disabilities and health impairments vary with the symptoms and intensity of their impairments. These learners are at risk for academic failure, even in the absence of a known cognitive problem.

The identification of learners as physically disabled or health impaired is typically a medical task. Standardized instruments may not provide an accurate picture of the learner. Because of the problems standardized instruments present to these learners, criterion-referenced measures provide a more accurate picture of what they are able to achieve.

In the home, parents of learners with physical disabilities or health impairments may experience more stress. No consistent relationship has been found between the presence of a chronic illness and risk for psychological problems among siblings. In the classroom, the teacher's negative attitude has been linked to the learner's achievement rather than his or her impairment itself. A particular challenge for teachers and school systems are learners who are dependent on medical technology.

The accommodations necessary for learners with physical disabilities and health impairments are highly individualized. Seldom do these learners require changes in the curriculum itself. Mediating the environment, in addition to collaborating with medical professionals, may involve administering medication or using assistive devices and equipment. Learners may require related services, such as occupational therapy, physical therapy, or adapted physical education.

In the community, adults with physical disabilities who used wheelchairs reported that others abridged their social rights by staring and questioning. Although social interactions may pose few problems, the opportunity for social interactions and employment may be hindered by the lack of accessibility.

Building Your Professional Vocabulary

Match each word or phrase to its correct meaning.

_____ catheterization

_____ cerebral palsy

_____ epilepsy

_____ health impairments

_____ hydrocephaly

_____ orthotic device

_____ prostheses

_____ scoliosis

_____ spina bifida

_____ talipes

a. dysfunction of the neurological motor system due to a nonprogressive brain abnormality
b. a defect of the spinal column in which the spine fails to close properly around the neural column
c. insertion of a tube into the bladder for the withdrawal of urine
d. fluid accumulated in the ventricles of the brain

e. marked by recurrent, unprovoked seizures
f. commonly referred to as clubfoot
g. artificial replacements for missing body parts
h. an assistive device to enhance the partial functioning of a body part
i. a lateral curve of the spine
j. a generic term used to refer to physical conditions or diseases that have an impact on the individual's functioning

Comprehension Check

Select the most appropriate response.

1. Cerebral palsy
   a. has a similar impact on functioning in all affected individuals.
   b. varies in its impact with the extent to which the individual is affected.
   c. requires the affected individual to use a wheelchair.
2. Learners with neural tube defects
   a. suffer only from paralysis of some degree.
   b. frequently have learning disabilities and perceptual difficulties.
   c. have little difficulty with mobility.
3. Learners with orthopedic disabilities
   a. do not vary from their peers in interactions.
   b. vary significantly from their peers in interactions.
   c. vary from their peers in the use of defense mechanisms.
4. Learners with human immunodeficiency virus
   a. are a risk to their teachers and peers due to contagion.
   b. do not demonstrate disabilities.
   c. are limited in their participation due to illness and their vulnerability to infection.
5. Cancer
   a. is rare among children.
   b. has no effect on the schooling of children.
   c. is most commonly seen in children in the form of leukemia.

6. General functioning of children with chronic illness is related to
   a. the nature of the illness.
   b. the potential for remission.
   c. the resources available to the family.
7. Teachers' perceptions of learners with orthopedic disabilities
   a. reflect concern and anxiety.
   b. are generally negative.
   c. are negative only when related to poor achievement.
8. The focus of occupational therapy is on
   a. range of motion and mobility.
   b. vocational training.
   c. functional outcomes.
9. When present at a learner's seizure, the teacher should
   a. force something into the learner's mouth so the child does not swallow his or her tongue.
   b. seek assistance when the seizure lasts longer than ten minutes.
   c. call for emergency medical assistance.
10. The use of technology
    a. is required by the Americans with Disabilities Act.
    b. is forcing a redefinition of the term *disability*.
    c. reduces the number of individuals with disabilities.

References

Alliance for Technology Access. (1994). *Computer resources for people with disabilities*. New York: Hunter House.

Arthritis Foundation. (1983). *Arthritis: Basic Facts*. Atlanta, GA: Author.

Athreya, B. H., and Ingall, C. G. (1984). Juvenile rheumatoid arthritis. In J. Fithian (Ed.), *Understanding the child with a chronic illness in the classroom*. Phoenix, AZ: Oryx.

Bandyopadhyay, S., Roy, D., Basum, A., & Chattopadhyay, P. (1987). Emotional status of orthopedically handicapped subjects and neurotic patients. *Indian Psychological Review, 32* (8–9), 1–6.

Bennett-Levy, J., & Stores, G. (1984). The nature of cognitive dysfunction in schoolchildren with epilepsy. *Acta Neurologica Scandinavica, 59*, 79 –82.

Bohan, D., & Humes, C. W. (1986). Assessment of the integration of physically handicapped college students into extracurricular activities. *Journal of College Student Personnel, 27* (1), 55–57.

Boos, M., Garlonsky, R. M., MacEwen, G. D., & Steg, N. (1984). Orthopedic problems. In J. Fithian (Ed.), *Understanding children with a chronic illness in the classroom*. Phoenix, AZ: Oryx.

Brown, R. T., Dingle, A., & Landau, S. (1994). Overview of psychopharmacology in children and adolescents. *School Psychology Quarterly, 9*, 4–25.

Bruder, M. B. (1995). The challenge of pediatric AIDS: A framework for early childhood special education. *Topics in Early Childhood Special Education, 15*, 83–99.

Burbach, H. J., & Babbitt, C. E. (1988). Physically disabled students on the college campus. *Remedial and Special Education, 5* (2), 12–15.

Cappelli, M., McGrath, P. J., McDonald, N. E., & Katsanis, J. (1989). Parental care and overprotection of children with cystic fibrosis. *British Journal of Medical Psychology, 62* (3), 281–289.

Centers for Disease Control. (1993, April). *HIV/AIDS surveillance report.* Atlanta, GA: Author.

Chavez, J. M., & Buriel, R. (1988). Mother-child interactions involving a child with epilepsy. *Journal of Pediatric Psychology, 13,* 349–351.

Chee, C. M., & Clancy, R. R. (1984). Epilepsy. In J. Fithian (Ed.), *Understanding the child with a chronic illness in the classroom.* Phoenix, AZ: Oryx.

Colandra, E. P., Dominguez-Granados, R., Gomez-Rubio, M., & Molina-Font, J. A. (1990). Cognitive effects of long-term treatment with pentobarbital and valproic acid in school children. *Acta Neurologica Scandinavica, 81,* 504–505.

Coniglio, S. J., & Blackman, J. A. (1995). Developmental outcome of childhood leukemia. *Topics in Early Childhood Special Education, 15,* 19–31.

Creech, R. (1995). In the beginning was the word. *Mainstream, 19* (4), 22–26.

de Apodaca, R. F., Watson, J. D., Mueller, J., & Isaacson-Kailes, J. (1985). A sociometric comparison of mainstreamed, orthopedically handicapped high school students and nonhandicapped classmates. *Psychology in the Schools, 22* (1), 95–101.

Dilworth-Anderson, P. (1989). Family structure and intervention strategies: Beyond empirical research. *Annals of the New York Academy of Sciences, 565,* 183–188.

Drotar, D., & Crawford, P. (1985). Psychological adaptation of siblings of chronically ill children: Research and practice implications. *Journal of Developmental and Behavioral Pediatrics, 6* (6), 355–362.

Dunn, N. L., McCartan, K. W., & Fuqua, R. W. (1988). Young children with orthopedic handicaps: Self-knowledge about their disability. *Exceptional Children, 55,* 249–252.

Epilepsy Foundation of America. (1991). *Epilepsy: Recognition and first aid.* Landover, MD: Author.

Evans, R. C., Burlow, A., & Oler, C. H. (1988). Children with sickle cell anemia. *Social Work, 33,* 127–130.

Ferrari, M. (1986). Perceptions of social support by parents of chronically ill versus healthy children. *Children's Health Care, 15* (1), 26–31.

Frank, B. B. (1985). Psychosocial aspects of educating epileptic children: Roles for school psychologists. *School Psychology Review, 14,* 196–203.

Giancoli, D. I., & Neimeyer, G. J. (1983). Liking preferences toward handicapped persons. *Perceptual and Motor Skills, 57* (3), 1005–1006.

Gill, F. M., & Butler, R. (1984). Hemophilia. In J. Fithian (Ed.), *Understanding the child with a chronic illness in the classroom.* Phoenix, AZ: Oryx.

Gleckel, L. K., & Lee, R. J. (1990). Physical disabilities. In E. L. Meyen (Ed.), *Exceptional children in today's schools* (2nd ed., pp. 359–393). Denver: Love.

Gon, M., Boyce, B., & Advani, K. (1983). Locus of control in orthopedically handicapped and nonhandicapped persons. *Journal of Psychological Research, 27* (2), 75–80.

Gurdin, P., & Anderson, G. R. (1987). Quality care for ill children: AIDS specialized foster family homes. *Child Welfare, 66,* 291–302.

Hallahan, D. P., & Kauffman, J. M. (1986). *Exceptional children* (3rd ed.). Englewood Cliffs, NJ: Prentice Hall.

Hanna, W. J., & Rogovsky, B. (1991). Women with disabilities: Two handicaps plus. *Disability in America, 6* (2), 312–325.

Hardman, M. L., Drew, C. J., Egan, M. W., & Wolf, B. (1990). *Human exceptionality: Society, school, and family* (3rd ed.). Boston: Allyn & Bacon.

Hardy, J. C. (1983). *Cerebral palsy.* Englewood Cliffs, NJ: Prentice Hall.

Hoare, P. (1984a). Does illness foster dependency? A study of epileptic and diabetic children. *Developmental Medicine and Child Neurology, 26,* 20–24.

Hoare, P. (1984b). The development of psychiatric disorder among school children with epilepsy. *Developmental Medicine and Child Neurology, 26,* 3–13.

Hoare, P. (1986). Adults' attitudes to children with epilepsy: The use of visual analogue scale questionnaire. *Journal of Psychosomatic Research, 30,* 471–479.

Hobfoil, S. E., & Lerman, M. (1988). Personal relationships, personal attributes, and stress resistance: Mothers' reactions to the child's illness. *American Journal of Community Psychology, 16,* 565–589.

Hurtig, A. L., Koepke, D., & Park, K. (1989). Relation between severity of chronic illness and adjustment in children and adolescents with sickle cell disease. *Journal of Pediatric Psychology, 14* (1), 117–132.

Indacochea, F. J., & Scott, G. B. (1992). HIV infection the acquired immunodeficiency syndrome in children. *Current Problems in Pediatrics, 22,* 166–204.

Jansen, M. T., DeWitt, P. K., Meshul, R. J., & Krasnoff, J. B. (1989). Meeting psychosocial and developmental needs of children during prolonged intensive care unit hospitalization. *Children's Health Care, 18* (2), 91–95.

Jessop, D. J., & Stein, R. E. (1985). Uncertainty and its relation to the psychological and social correlates of chronic illness in children. *Social Science and Medicine, 20,* 993–999.

Johnson, B. H. (1986). Resources available to teachers working with chronically ill children and their families. *Topics in Early Childhood Special Education, 5* (4), 92–104.

Kahn, N. A., & Battle, C. U. (1987). Chronic illness: Implications for development and education. *Topics in Early Childhood Special Education, 6* (4), 25–32.

Kazak, A. E. (1987). Families with disabled children: Stress and social networks in three samples. *Journal of Abnormal Child Psychology, 15* (1), 137–146.

Kazak, A. E. (1989). Families of chronically ill children: A systems and social-ecological model of adaptation and challenge. *Journal of Consulting and Clinical Psychology, 57* (1), 25–30.

Kazak, A. E., & Meadows, A. T. (1989). Families of young adolescents who have survived cancer: Social-emotional adjustment, adaptability, and social support. *Journal of Pediatric Psychology, 14* (2), 175–191.

Kelker, K., Hecimovic, A., & LeRoy, C. H. (1994). Designing a classroom and school environment for students with AIDS: A checklist for teachers. *Teaching Exceptional Children, 26,* (4), 52–55.

Kennedy, A. B., & Thurman, S. K. (1982). Inclinations of nonhandicapped children to help their handicapped peers. *Journal of Special Education, 16,* 319–327.

Kim, H. C., Gaston, G., & Fithian, J. (1984). Sickle cell anemia. In J. Fithian (Ed.), *Understanding the child with a chronic illness in the classroom.* Phoenix, AZ: Oryx.

Kolski, G., & Burg, I. (1984). Allergies. In J. Fithian (Ed.), *Understanding the child with a chronic illness in the classroom.* Phoenix, AZ: Oryx.

Lawrence, B. (1991). Self-concept formation and physical handicap: Some educational implications for integration. *Disability, 6* (2), 240–245.

Liebert, D., Lutsky, L., & Gottlieb, A. (1990). Postsecondary experience of young adults with severe physical disabilities. *Exceptional Children, 57,* 56–63.

Lemanek, K. L. (1986). Psychological adjustment of children with sickle cell anemia. *Journal of Pediatric Psychology, 11,* 397–410.

Levine, C., & Dubler, N. N. (1990). HIV and childbearing. *Milbank Quarterly, 68,* 321–351.

Lewandowski, L. J., & Cruickshank, W. M. (1980). *Psychological development of crippled children and youth.* Englewood Cliffs, NJ: Prentice Hall.

Margalit, M., & Heiman, T. (1983). Anxiety and self-dissatisfaction in epileptic children. *International Journal of Social Psychiatry, 29,* 220–224.

Marlowe, M. (1985). Low lead exposure and learning disabilities. *Research Communications in Psychology, Psychiatry, and Behavior, 10,* 153–169.

Matthews, W. S., Barabas, G., & Ferrari, M. (1983). Achievement and school behavior among children with epilepsy. *Psychology in the Schools, 20,* 10–12.

Minde, K. K., Hackett, J. D., Killon, D., & Silver, S. (1972). How they grow up: Physically handicapped children and their families. *American Journal of Rehabilitation Research, 5,* 235–237.

Morgan, S. A., & Jackson, J. (1986). Psychological and social concomitants of sickle cell anemia in adolescents. *Journal of Pediatric Psychology, 11,* 429–440.

Nash, K. B. (1989). Self-help groups: An empowerment vehicle for sickle cell disease patients and their families. *Social Work with Groups, 12,* 81–97.

National Institutes of Health. (1991). *Guidelines for the diagnosis and management of asthma* (NIH Publication No. 91-3042). Bethesda, MD: National Heart, Lung, and Blood Institute.

National Institutes of Health. (1993). *Asthma awareness: Curriculum for the elementary classroom* (NIH Publication No. 93-2894). Bethesda, MD: National Heart, Lung, and Blood Institute.

Nelms, B. C. (1989). Emotional behaviors in chronically ill children. *Journal of Abnormal Child Psychology, 17,* 657–668.

Newschwander, G. E. (1987). Update on AIDS for teachers and policy makers. *Educational Horizons, 65,* 110–113.

Pfeiffer, D. (1991). The influences of the socio-economic characteristics of disabled people on their employment status and income. *Disability in America, 6* (2), 210–215.

Pieper, E. (1983). The teacher and the child with spina bifida (2nd ed.). Rockville, MD: Spina Bifida Association of America.

Pliner, S., & Hannah, M. E. (1985). The role of achievement in teachers' attitudes towards handicapped children. *Academic Psychology Bulletin, 7* (3), 327–335.

Poplack, D. (1989). Acute lymphoblastic leukemia. In P. Pizzo & D. Poplack (Eds.), *Principles and practice of pediatric oncology* (2nd ed., pp. 323–366). Philadelphia: Lippincott.

Potter, P. C., & Roberts, M. C. (1984). Children's perceptions of chronic illness: The roles of disease symptoms, cognitive development, and information. *Journal of Pediatric Psychology, 9* (1), 13–27.

Powers, G. M., Gaudet, L. M., & Powers, S. (1986). Coping patterns of parents of chronically ill children. *Psychological Reports, 59* (2), 519–522.

Ritchie, J. A., Caty, S., & Ellerton, M. L. (1984). Concerns of acutely ill, chronically ill, and healthy preschool children. *Research in Nursing and Health, 7* (4), 265–274.

Ross, J. W. (1984). The child with cancer in school. In J. Fithian (Ed.), *Understanding the child with a chronic illness in the classroom.* Phoenix, AZ: Oryx.

Scherer, A. (1983). *Epilepsy: You and your child.* Landover, MD: Epilepsy Foundation of America.

Schlieper, A. (1985). Chronic illness and school achievement. *Developmental Medicine and Child Neurology, 27* (1), 75–79.

Sigmon, S. B. (1986). The orthopedically disabled child: Psychological implications with an individual basis. *Individual Psychology: Journal of Adlerian Theory, Research, and Practice, 42* (2), 274–278.

Simeonsson, N., Lorimer, M., & Sturtz, J. L. (1995). Asthma: New information for the early interventionist. *Topics in Early Childhood Special Education, 15,* 32–43.

Sirvis, B. (1988). Physical disabilities. In E. L. Meyer & T. M. Skrtic (Eds.), *Exceptional children and youth: An introduction* (3rd ed., pp. 387–411). Denver: Love.

Smith, D. D., & Luckasson, R. (1992). *Introduction to special education: Teaching in an age of challenge.* Boston: Allyn & Bacon.

Smith, E. (1994). America the unvisitable. *Mouth, 5* (2), 20–23.

SUNY Research Foundation. (1994). *HIV/AIDS and children: Answers for caregivers.* Buffalo, NY: Author.

Taylor, S., & Walker, P. (1991). Where there is a will, there is not always a way: Psychology, public policy, and the school programming of children who are technology assisted. *Children's Health Care, 20,* 115–120.

Teplin, S. W., Howard, J. A., & O'Connor, M. J. (1981). Self-concept of young children with cerebral palsy. *Developmental Medicine and Child Neurology, 23,* 730–738.

Treiber, F. A., Mabe, P., & Wilson, G. (1987). Psychological adjustment of sickle cell children and their siblings. *Children's Health Care, 18,* 82–88.

U.S. Department of Education. (1995). *Seventeenth annual report to Congress on the implementation of the Individuals with Disabilities Education Act.* Washington, DC: Author.

Verhaaven, P. R., & Connor, F. P. (1981). Physical disabilities. In J. Kauffman & D. Hallahan (Eds.), *Handbook of special education* (pp. 248–290). Englewood Cliffs, NJ: Prentice Hall.

Wells, R. D., & Schwebel, A. I. (1987). Chronically ill children and their mothers. *Journal of Developmental and Behavioral Pediatrics, 8* (2), 83–89.

Wetterau, P., & Stegelin, D. (1991). Child care professionals' knowledge and attitudes towards AIDS: A needs assessment. *Children's Health Care, 20,* 21–25.

Williams, P. D., Williams, A. R., & Landa, A. R. (1989). Factors influencing performance of chronically ill children on a developmental screening test. *International Journal of Nursing Studies, 26* (2), 163–172.

Wood, B., Boyle, J. T., Watkins, J. B., & Noqueira, J. (1988). Sibling psychological status and style as related to the disease of their chronically ill brothers and sisters: Implications for models of biopsychosocial interaction. *Journal of Developmental and Behavioral Pediatrics, 9* (2), 66–72.

Woolf, P. K. (1984). Cardiac disease. In J. Fithian (Ed.), *Understanding the child with a chronic illness in the classroom.* Phoenix, AZ: Oryx.

Yashon, D. (1986). *Spinal injury* (2nd ed.). NY: Appleton-Century-Crofts.

11

Chapter

Learners with Visual Impairments

Objectives

After completing this chapter, you will be able to:

1. describe the personal characteristics of learners with visual impairments.
2. describe the identification and evaluation of learners with visual impairments.
3. describe the impact of visual impairments on interactions in the home and classroom.
4. describe ways to mediate the environment for learners with visual impairments.
5. describe the impact of visual impairments on participation in the larger social systems—the school, community, and society.

Key Words and Phrases

amblyopia
astigmatism
blind
cataracts
diabetic retinopathy
glaucoma
hyperopia
macular degeneration
myopia
nystagmus

partially sighted
peripheral vision
presbyopia
retinitis pigmentosa
retinopathy of prematurity
stereotypies
strabismus
visual acuity
visual impairment
visually handicapped

Many of history's greatest artists were known to have vision impairments. These include Monet, Pissarro, Degas, Daumier, Renoir, Goya, Cassatt, and others. It is no paradox that artists with little or no vision can actually create works of art in visual media which are rich and varied, and which tell of a continued participation in a visual world. For each artist, including those with no light perception who work in purely tactile media, inner vision becomes activated and is fueled by necessity and translated into shape, form, and color by drawing upon visual and spatial memory, imagination, and dreams. (From the catalog for the art exhibit "Art of the Eye," a collection of works by artists with visual impairments. Delta Gamma Foundation, 1991.)

Introduction

Learners with **visual impairment** include those whose sight is limited in any way to the extent that special services are required. Many of these persons have sight that is useful for some purposes (Finkelstein, 1989). Others are **blind,** or have profound visual impairment that prohibits the use of vision as an educational tool. Finkelstein suggests that public misinformation about the impact of blindness is evident in surveys conducted on visual impairment: for example, the public fears blindness more than any condition except cancer; children fear only the death of a parent more than they fear becoming blind.

Visual impairment is a low-incidence disability—during the 1993–1994 school year, only 24,935 learners with disabilities served had visual impairments (U.S. Department of Education, 1995). Only the category of individuals who are deaf-blind had fewer learners receiving services. The largest number of these individuals were educated in general education classrooms (45.5 percent), yet 9.4 percent were served in residential facilities. The only categories of individuals served in residential facilities larger than the category of individuals with visual impairments are individuals who are hearing impaired and those who are deaf-blind (U.S. Department of Education, 1995).

Personal Characteristics

Objective One

To describe the personal characteristics of learners with visual impairments.

Finkelstein (1989) contends that because as much as 85 percent or 90 percent of what we learn comes through our vision, it is often presumed that learners with visual impairments are less capable or have less potential than those who see. However, vision is only one source of information, and learners with visual impairments are as varied as any other group of individuals. These learners' visual impairments have equally varied effects on their personal characteristics.

The mannerisms of learners who are visually impaired have been studied fairly extensively. Stereotypic behaviors, or **stereotypies**—repetitive behaviors with no apparent effect on the environment—and "blindisms"—behaviors apparent in learners who are visually impaired—cover a broad range of verbal and motor behavior. Leonhardt (1990) found that stereotypies occur more frequently in conditions under which the learner has little or no control, in demanding situations, in situations that refer to the visual world, or in situations of loneliness or isolation. Eye and head movements have been related to the onset and severity of the visual impairment, with the more severely and congenitally visually impaired individuals demonstrating more of these stereotypies (Jan, Farrell, Wong, & McCormick, 1986). These behaviors can have a significant impact on learners. Raver-Lampman (1990) found that when individuals with visual impairments used gaze direction, or positioning the face and eyes toward the questioner, they were evaluated as being more intelligent and more socially competent than those who did not use gaze direction.

Language Development

Though studies have been conducted on the language development of learners with visual impairments, findings only reemphasize the heterogeneous nature of these learners. Bigelow (1987) notes that the early vocabulary of learners with visual impairments parallels that of their sighted peers in age and speed of acquisition and in the underlying characteristics of what the children selected to label. Their early words differ, however, and are a function of a combination of the lack of vision and the learner's particular language learning context. In a longitudinal study of the development of function of language in learners with congenital visual impairments, Orwin (1984) found that learners demonstrated limited use of object names and requests, relied heavily on routine phrases and people's names, imitated a great deal, and infrequently referred to objects and events beyond their reach or touch. She feels, however, that given the fact that their language development followed that of peers in other ways, it is unlikely that the children had any general cognitive delay or impairment in representation processes. Anderson and Fisher (1985) report that young learners with visual impairments tend to cling to nominal realism (assigning animistic qualities to objects and concretely using labels) longer than their sighted peers do, possibly due to the limitations the visual impairment imposes on children's interactions with objects.

McConachie (1990) reports that though some learners with visual impairments show an early facility with expressive language, greater even than their true level of comprehension, many show a lag in expressive speech relative to comprehension, with first words appearing as late as four years of age. Erin (1990) generated language samples from learners who were both blind and partially sighted, using common household objects. She found that partially sighted learners had slightly greater complexity of utterances. The learners who were visually impaired had a higher frequency of inappropriate pronoun use than did those who were partially sighted, and they employed less variation in sentence types. However, Erin states that there was a greater variation in the level of language maturity among learners with visual impairments than among those who were partially sighted, suggesting that the developmental context of the learners may influence language development.

In a study of thirteen- to seventeen-year-old adolescents with visual impairments and their sighted peers, Civelli (1983) asked the subjects to define twenty words representing objects, movements, animals, and expressions. He found that the learners with visual impairments performed better than the sighted group on all categories except material objects. Persons with more severe visual impairments were found to ask more frequent questions about objects and events (Erin, 1986).

Children with visual impairments engage in as much emotional facial display as do individuals who are sighted. They are less likely, however, to refer spontaneously to their facial expression in explaining how the examiner knew how they felt (Cole, Jenkins, & Shott, 1985).

Cognitive Development

Research studies of cognitive development have generally demonstrated variations of development in learners with visual impairments when compared to their peers who are sighted. Ittyerah and Samarapungavan (1989) report that though the cognitive development of individuals who are visually impaired and those who are sighted is not identical, the differences in performance between groups are content or task specific and do not take the form of global deficits across groups of tasks. They hypothesize that these variations in performance are a function of absence of experience and absence of visual information. The development of object permanence in children with visual impairments parallels that of children who are sighted; however, the modalities (touch, sound) used to organize information are necessarily different (Bigelow, 1986). The mental images or concepts of objects that children with visual impairments develop through nonvisual experiences are not significantly different from those acquired by children who are sighted (Anderson, 1984).

The development of spatial concepts by learners with visual impairment has received a great deal of attention. These concepts are of particular importance to learners with visual impairments because of their relationship to personal mobility. In terms of their own bodies in space, learners with visual impairments have been found to vary from their sighted peers in that they had a poorer ability to balance (Mereira, 1990). Though learners with visual impairments are as able as learners who are sighted to discriminate right and left in tasks related to themselves, they have difficulty relating right and left to others. Learners with visual impairments have difficulty projecting positions in space, including recognition of shapes, construction of a projective straight line, and conceptualization of right and left in absolute- and mirror-image orientation (Birns, 1986).

Learners with visual impairments have the ability to reproduce the extent of movements accurately. They have difficulty, however, reproducing movements in their orientation to space or a specific reference point (Dodds & Carter, 1983). Differences have also been found between learners with visual impairments and their sighted peers, with the former demonstrating poorer posture and cardiovascular endurance. In tests of obstacle perception, learners with visual impairments were able to, at above-chance levels, demonstrate distal perception of objects. As a consequence, Ashmead, Hill, and Talor (1989) hypothesize that children with little or no visual experience or formal training use nonvisual information, presumably auditory, to perceive objects.

Social-Emotional Development and Behavior

The social adaptation of learners with visual impairments has been found to be a consistent challenge throughout their development. Van Hasselt (1983) reports consistent patterns of problems in social adaptation in children, adolescents, and adults with visual impairments. He attributes some of these problems to inadequately formed attachments as early as infancy. The most marked problems in social adaptation have been reported among learners who attend residential schools (Hirshoren & Schnittjer, 1983). In addition, problem behavior has been found to be most marked among learners in residential placements (Van Hasselt, Kazdin, & Hersen, 1986). Specific problems have been reported in verbal and nonverbal social skills, but the broad measures of social adaptation have not demonstrated serious problems (Van Hasselt, 1985). If learners with visual impairments have had significant verbal interaction with others, such as participating in games and friendships, they do not differ from their sighted peers in social cognitive tasks (Schwartz, 1983). Learners with visual impairments have been found to be more externally controlled, though social adaptation improved with age and intellectual achievement (Parsons, 1987).

The self-concept of learners with visual impairments has not been found to be less sound than that of their sighted peers (Ubiakor & Otile, 1990). In addition, though specific fears related to concern for bodily injury have been noted, the fears and anxiety levels of learners with visual impairments have not been found to vary from those of their sighted peers (Wilhelm, 1989). Even young learners with visual impairments, however, realize that they see differently than do sighted persons and that they need to feel objects to gain a sense of them while sighted individuals do not.

Identification and Evaluation

Objective Two

To describe the identification and evaluation of learners with visual impairments.

Public Law 94-142 defined **visually handicapped** as having "a visual impairment which, even with correction, adversely affects a child's educational performance. The term includes both partially seeing and blind children" (Federal Register, 1977, 300.05). Public Law 101-476 (passed in 1990) modified the term to reflect changes in language, referring to these learners as "visually impaired."

Educational and legal definitions for visual impairment vary. Educationally, students considered blind require alternatives to print and visual materials, and **partially sighted** students may use print and visual materials with the help of large print, optical aids, technological aids, and education in using their residual vision (Orlansky & Rhyne, 1981).

How well an individual can see, or visual efficiency, is measured by acuity and peripheral vision. **Visual acuity** is a measure of how well the individual can see at various distances. **Peripheral vision** is a measure of the width of the individual's field of vision, or the ability to see outside a direct line of vision. Learners are legally blind if central vision acuity does not exceed 20/200 in the better eye with corrective lenses or if the visual field is less than an angle of 20 degrees (normal vision acuity is defined as 20/20). Learners with 20/200 vision see at 20 feet that which the learner with normal vision sees at 200 feet. Partially sighted individuals are those whose visual acuity is between 20/70 and 20/200 in the better eye with the best correction possible (Finkelstein, 1989). Learners whose impairment is in the angle of vision have a restricted visual field, which makes participation in such activities as reading and driving difficult. Problems in the angle of vision are known as tunnel vision, pinhole vision, and tubular vision.

In 1986, Barrage proposed the following educationally relevant classification of visual impairments.

- Profound: Most gross visual tasks are very difficult; vision generally not used for detail tasks.
- Severe: Visual tasks demand considerable time and energy; performance less accurate than that of learners with normal vision even with visual aids and other modifications.
- Moderate: Tasks performed with the use of aids and lighting; performance comparable to learners with normal vision.

Visual impairments may be the consequences of various factors. The most frequent causes are prenatal influences and heredity, injuries, poisoning, tumors, infectious diseases such as rubella and German measles, and general systemic disorders such as central nervous system disorders.

The Vision System

The discussion of the various visual impairments and their impact on the learner's development is best understood with some comprehension of the way in which the vision system functions. The vision system is composed of three parts: (a) the eye (fig. 11.1), (b) the optic nerve, and (c) the vision center of the brain.

What we see begins as light reflected on the external covering of the eye, or the cornea. The light reflected by the cornea passes through the pupil, an opening in the iris, the colored part of the eye. As the pupil expands and contracts, it controls the amount of light entering the eye. Rays of light pass through the lens, which focuses the light through the transparent, gel-like vitreous humor onto the retina. As light passes through the lens, it is reversed, much like light passing through the lens of a camera. The retina, like the film in a camera, receives the upside-down light "picture," which, to use Finkelstein's (1989) analogy, is then developed by the brain. The photoreceptors of the retina are rods and cones: the rods are responsible for vision in darkness and for peripheral vision and the cones are responsible for color vision, vision in bright light, and central vision.

The outer coat, or "white of the eye," is the sclera, a strip of tendon. Just below the cornea is a chamber containing a continuously flowing clear fluid called the aqueous humor, which is contained by the front and back chambers between the cornea and the lens and separated by the iris. Since the lens and the cornea have no blood vessels, they receive their nourishment from the aqueous humor, which flows through small channels located at the angle where the iris and cornea meet. If this outlet of aqueous humor is impeded in any way, the pressure of the eye rises, and a condition known as **glaucoma** may result.

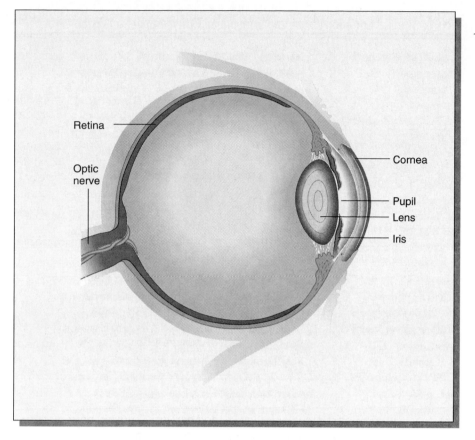

Figure 11.1

Diagram of the eye.

Muscles on the outside of the eye "aim" the eye at an object. When looking at close objects, the eyes converge and the lens focuses. By the time most individuals reach about forty-five years of age, this ability to focus for close work is usually lost or impaired, a condition called **presbyopia.**

When we see something clearly, our eyes are aimed in such a way as to place the object's image onto a depression in the central portion of the retina, known as the fovea, which is surrounded by the macula lutea. The concentration of cones in this part of the eye makes it the area of the most acute vision. The retina, however, has both the visual property of resolution (central vision) and detection (peripheral vision). Each of these properties comes into play when discussing visual impairments.

Though the most common visual problems confronting children are those of visual acuity, there is a broad range of visual impairments, each of which varies in degree of impact on the individual. The most common of these visual problems and their impact on the individual are presented in table 11.1.

The major refractive visual impairments include myopia, hyperopia, and astigmatism. Each of these impairments is the result of refractive errors due to the shape of the eye and can be corrected with glasses or contact lenses. **Myopia** is nearsightedness. The individual has difficulty seeing distant objects but near or close vision is unaffected. **Hyperopia,** or farsightedness, impairs the individual's ability to see close objects but does not affect seeing distant objects. **Astigmatism** is a refractive error that prevents the light rays from coming to a sharp focus on the retina, causing blurred or distorted vision at any distance.

Cataracts, a clouding of the lens, block the passage of light through the eye, causing blurred vision. Although some cataracts are congenital, their likelihood increases with age. Surgical removal and replacement of the lens results in regained sight in as high as 95 percent of cases (Finkelstein, 1989).

Table 11.1   **Common Visual Impairments and Their Impact on Vision**

Visual Impairment	Impact on Vision
Amblyopia	"Lazy eye"; may report poor vision in one or both eyes
Astigmatism	Refractive error that prevents light rays from coming to a sharp focus on the retina; blurred vision
Cataracts	Lens of the eye becomes cloudy or opaque, obstructing vision
Diabetic retinopathy	Blood vessels of the retina hemorrhage, causing blurred or distorted vision
Glaucoma	Increased pressure in the eye; gradual vision loss, beginning with peripheral vision
Hyperopia (Farsightedness)	Blurry near vision; headaches after close work; discomfort
Macular degeneration	Deterioration of the central part of the retina; peripheral vision retained
Myopia (Nearsightedness)	Blurry far vision; missing distant details
Nystagmus	Involuntary rapid movement of the eyes
Retinitis pigmentosa	Dark pigment layer of the retina is slowly lost, causing a gradual reduction of the visual field
Retinopathy of prematurity	Deterioration of the retina, formerly caused by high levels of oxygen administered to premature infants
Strabismus	Inability to focus on the same object with both eyes

Sources: Grayson, 1984; Rouse & Ryan, 1984; Scott, 1982; National Association for the Visually Handicapped, 1978.

Three visual impairments affecting the muscle functioning of the eyes are strabismus, amblyopia, and nystagmus. These impairments make it difficult for individuals to use their eyes efficiently and effectively. **Strabismus** is the inability to focus on the same object with both eyes. This is a result of the inward or outward deviation of one or both eyes. **Amblyopia** is the reduction or loss of vision in an individual's weaker eye. This loss is due to a lack of use of the eye—a "lazy eye"; no disease is present. **Nystagmus** is the involuntary rapid movement of the eyes. This impairment may be a result of an inner ear disorder or a malfunction of the brain.

Several conditions causing visual impairment involve the retina. **Diabetic retinopathy** is a leading cause of visual impairments in diabetics, and it has had increased incidence as a result of their increased life span. Long-term diabetes changes the tiny blood vessels in the retina. These changes may cause aneurysms in the retinal capillary blood vessels or they may cause the blood vessels to become engorged with blood and burst, or detach the retina. Laser treatment to seal broken vessels or a detached portion of the retina can often slow the course of this impairment.

Macular degeneration, or breakdown, another retinal problem, may result from many causes. Some cases are hereditary, and others are caused by viruses (such as histoplasmosis) or arteriosclerosis. Usually the individual keeps good peripheral vision, though central vision is blurred. Retinal breaks and detachment may occur as part of the aging process or from other causes, with noticeable symptoms such as "floaters," haziness or smokiness, or light flashes in the eye.

Retinitis pigmentosa, a hereditary disease characterized by degeneration of the retina, involves an abnormal development of excess pigment. With this disorder, the learner's visual field begins to narrow, with a progressive visual loss. The field of vision decreases to the extent that the individual usually becomes legally blind by young adulthood and gradually loses residual vision thereafter.

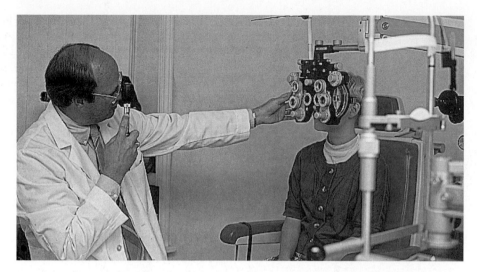

An optometrist measures an individual's visual acuity.

Retinopathy of prematurity, which at times advances to a condition known as retrolental fibroplasia, was thought for a long time to be caused by exposing the newborn (and frequently premature) infant to a high concentration of oxygen in an incubator. Presently, researchers disagree regarding the cause of the impairment. An abnormal proliferation of blood vessels in the eye occurs, with the potential for subsequent development of scar tissue and bleeding and detachment of the retina. Blindness may result. Strabismus and myopia are commonly associated with cases in which the blood vessels partially heal. In the large majority of retinopathy of prematurity cases (about 80 percent) the abnormal blood vessels heal completely in the first year of life. In other cases, scarring results in either mild or severe retrolental fibroplasia (Finkelstein, 1989).

Corneal problems may result in either blurred vision or blindness. Scarring or perforation due to corneal ulceration is a major cause of visual impairment throughout the world (Finkelstein, 1989). Ulceration may be caused by streptococcus bacteria, herpes virus, vitamin A deficiency, or other disorders. The cornea may degenerate due to age. When the cornea becomes scarred, hazy, or opaque, or when there is danger of perforation of a corneal ulcer, an ophthalmic surgeon may remove the affected cornea and replace it with a healthy one taken from a donor. Probabilities of rejecting the new cornea are rated by most authorities at 1 percent to 5 percent (Finkelstein, 1989).

Visual impairments affect adults, especially older adults, with greater frequency than children. According to the National Society to Prevent Blindness (1983), vision problems impact 25 percent of the school-age population and one in every twenty children between the ages of three and five years. Scott (1982) states that 1 in 500 students is sufficiently visually impaired to affect school functioning. In 1984, Grayson reported the following data on the prevalence of visual impairments: 11.4 million persons in the United States were visually impaired, and 1.4 million persons were severely visually impaired.

Screening and Assessment

Screening for visual impairments usually begins with a measure of visual acuity using the Snellen chart. This chart, presented in figure 11.2, consists of rows of letters or symbols (Es). The use of letters or symbols is largely dependent on the child's developmental level. The size of the letters on the chart corresponds to normal vision at various distances (15, 20, 30, 40, 50, 70, 100, and 200 feet). The learner, seated twenty feet from the chart, is directed to read the letters in the various rows, and visual acuity is calculated by the examiner. It is important to remember that the Snellen chart is only a measure of visual acuity.

LETTER CHART FOR 20 FEET

E — 200

H N — 120

D F N — 100

P T X Z — 80

U Z D T F — 60

D F N P T H — 40

P H U N T D Z — 30

N P X T Z F H — 20

Eye problems are often identified by parents and teachers through observation. Table 11.2 lists several common symptoms to alert parents and teachers about possible visual impairments. Persons observing these symptoms should refer the child for examination by a vision specialist.

Learners with visual impairments are assessed in four general areas: medical, psychological, social, and educational. Medical assessment is conducted by a vision specialist, primarily an ophthalmologist or an optometrist. The ophthalmologist, a medical doctor specializing in disorders of the eye, conducts a physical examination of the eye, prescribes medication and corrective lenses, and performs surgery. The optometrist measures vision and prescribes corrective lenses.

The assessment used for educational placement or instructional decision-making purposes includes the evaluation of (a) functional vision; (b) intelligence and cognitive development; (c) psychomotor skills; and (d) academic achievement. The assessment of academic achievement should include an evaluation of concept development, braille and print reading, listening skills, social interaction and leisure skills, and functional living skills, including daily living skills, orientation and mobility, and community and vocational skills (Scholl, 1986).

Due to the relatively small number of children with visual impairments and the variability in their characteristics, examiners find few norm-referenced assessment instruments specifically for this population. In addition, the norms of most existing standardized measures were not developed including samples of learners with visual impairments. However, selected subtests and items that are not visually dependent may be useful for prescriptive purposes. Criterion-referenced instruments are appropriate for use with learners with visual impairments, as are teacher-made checklists, interviews, and direct observation.

Table 11.2 **Signs of Possible Eye Trouble in Children**

Appearance

Crossed eyes
Red-rimmed, encrusted, or swollen eyelids
Inflamed or watery eyes
Recurring styles (infections) on eyelids

Behavior

Rubs eyes excessively
Shuts or covers one eye
Tilts head or thrusts head forward
Has difficulty with reading or other close-up work; holds objects close to eyes
Blinks more than usual or is irritable when doing close-up work
Is unable to see distant things clearly
Squints eyelids together or frowns

Complaints

Eyes itch, burn, or feel scratchy
Cannot see well
Dizziness, headaches, or nausea following close-up work
Blurred or double vision

Copyrighted by the National Society to Prevent Blindness. Reprinted with permission.

Barrage and Morris (1980) developed the Program to Develop Efficiency in Visual Functioning. This instrument assesses visual functioning and offers 150 instructional programs to train functional visual skills. In the area of concept development and readiness skills, several tests are available for application with learners who have visual impairments. Among these is the tactile version of the Boehm Test of Basic Concepts (Caton, 1976). The Peabody Mobility Scales (Harley, Wood, & Merbler, 1981) assesses concept development in body image, spatial relations, left-right discrimination, sound location, and tactile and olfactory discrimination. Mangold's Development Program of Tactile Perception and Braille Letter Recognition (1977) assess braille readiness skills.

Some achievement and diagnostic instruments are available in braille or large print. Among these are the Stanford Reading Achievement Test, the Stanford Diagnostic Reading Test, the Iowa Test of Basic Skills, and the Key Math Diagnostic Arithmetic Test. There are no adaptive behavior scales specifically designed for learners with visual impairment, but portions of the Vineland Adaptive Behavioral Scales and the AAMD Adaptive Behavior Scales are of assistance.

The accurate assessment of learners with visual impairments is a collaborative venture including medical and educational professionals. As with all learners, emphasis must be placed on the learner's abilities and ways to accommodate the learner so that he or she has educational opportunities similar to those of his or her sighted peers.

Annual **Edition**

Article 26

The Impact on Interactions in the Home and Classroom

In the Home

One of the contextual factors related to young children with visual impairments that impacts on their development is that of early relationships with caregivers. Simmons and Davidson (1985a) believe that the ways in which the primary caregiver mediates the environment with the child has a direct influence on

Objective Three

To describe the impact of visual impairments on interactions in the home and classroom.

Providing a stimulating yet safe environment is a challenge for parents of learners with visual impairments.

how the child with a visual impairment learns about the world and thus develops. Problems in mediating the environment with children born with visual impairments challenge parents and affect the emotional relationship that the baby forms with the primary caregivers. Problems may occur in early bonding between the caregiver and child, in contact with professionals, and in the child's early exploring (Simmons & Davidson, 1985b). The primary caregivers of toddlers with visual impairments were found to provide highly directive input, offer relatively few descriptions, and initiate a greater proportion of discussion topics than the children, focusing almost exclusively on child-centered topics (Kekelis & Anderson, 1984).

Providing a stimulating yet safe home environment for young learners with visual impairments is a consistent challenge for families. Lang and Sullivan (1986) suggest that the environment should be designed to promote greater perception through vision or other senses, be safe, have decreased barriers to movement and integration, and promote increased interactions with various spatial elements, forms, and configurations.

Parents of learners with visual impairments have been found to be weak encouragers, mere tolerators, or outright discouragers of sports-related experiences for their children. This, perhaps, explains the limited participation of children with visual impairments in such activities (Nixon, 1988a).

The nature of the home environments of young children with visual impairments has not been significantly related to developmental scores (Dote-Kwan & Hughes, 1994). However, when mothers were verbally and emotionally responsive, the children developed better expressive pragmatic language abilities.

Both social-emotional support and support related to the care and education of the child with visual impairment should be provided to families of learners with visual impairments. Successful support groups have been found to demonstrate three themes (Nixon, 1988b): (a) the support needs of different parents are met in different ways; (b) parents' perceived need for a support group varies at different stages in a child's life; and (c) professionals play a role in facilitating social support, organizational issues, and professional intervention.

In the Classroom

The placement of learners with visual impairments in the general education classroom may cause increased anxiety on the part of the teacher. The National Federation of the Blind (1991) provides the following guidelines and suggestions:

guidelines for practice

Interacting with Learners With Visual Impairments

- When you initiate an interaction with the student, tell him or her your name. Tell the student when you are walking away.
- Ask the student if she or he needs help. If the student says yes, ask the nature of help needed.
- Serve as a "sighted guide" in new situations: Have the student grasp your arm above the elbow, walk half a step ahead with the student's left shoulder behind your right shoulder. In narrow areas, drop the guiding arm and tell the student to follow behind.
- Use "clock directions" as necessary (objects directly ahead are 12 o'clock, slightly to the right 1 o'clock, etc.).
- When an object is closer or farther away than usual, or if an object may be knocked over, guide the student's hand towards it and describe where it has been placed.
- Point out landmarks when the student first enters a room (i.e., teacher's desk, student's desk, shelves, windows, pencil sharpener). If something has been rearranged, report the new position to the student▌

Sources: American Foundation for the Blind, 1984; Corn & Martinez, 1985.

1. Learners with visual impairments can learn the same concepts that are taught other learners; the only difference is the method of learning.
2. Parents are used to helping their child get accustomed to new places and can provide guidance to the teacher in regards to orienting the child to the environment.
3. Children should be encouraged to join in active play; bumps and bruises last a few days, the negative effects of sheltering last a lifetime.
4. With few verbal additions, the soundtracks of movies and videos are sufficient in communicating information.
5. Knowledge of braille is not essential; a specially trained teacher provides that instruction.
6. Additional hands-on direction may be necessary, but providing an individualized aide for the child is not necessary.
7. Learners with visual impairments should be disciplined in the same manner as their peers.

The "Guidelines for Practice" above provides a list of specific guidelines for teachers, students, and others interacting with learners with visual impairments in the classroom and school.

Mediating the Environment

Preschool

Researchers have suggested some specific ways to mediate the environment for preschoolers. With these strategies, preschoolers with visual impairment can experience many of the same activities as their peers with vision. When working with infants and toddlers with visual impairments, educators should focus on interventions to create, improve, or facilitate connections between children and some aspects of their environment. Davidson and Simmons (1984) describe three stages of each interaction: (a) providing access; (b) stimulating or guiding exploration; and (c) encouraging interpretation of the interaction. Proficiency in major motor areas, such as posture, balance, locomotion, coordination, and

Objective Four

To describe ways to mediate the environment for learners with visual impairments.

Thurber Remembered

**Legally blind humorist James Thurber was born one hundred years ago.
His writing and cartoons continue to amuse.**

By Kathi Wolfe

I've gotten into scrapes with the best of them; but only once have I been expelled for my sins.

A few years ago, I went one evening to a meeting of a feminist writers group. The gathering was uneventful, until a woman asked us to name the author whose books we would take along if we were marooned on a desert island. When my turn came, I quickly responded, "American humorist James Thurber." Just as swiftly the discussion leader asked me to leave, saying, "we can't have anyone here who reads such a male-oriented writer."

This request pleased me. If you're legally blind, I thought to myself as I left the meeting, it's not so easy to get a citation from the "political correctness police;" this is as close as I'll ever get to being on The Most Wanted List. I went home and listened to the first Thurber book on Talking Books that I could get my hands on.

This month is the centennial of Thurber's birth. (He was born in Columbus, Ohio on December 8, 1894 and was buried there on November 4, 1961.) To mark the event, Harcourt Brace & Company has published *People Have More Fun Than Anybody*—a new collection of Thurber's writings and drawings, edited by Michael J. Rosen.

I have been reading Thurber all my life: his stories and drawings hooked me, like so many others, on books, humor, and writing. But as a legally blind writer, Thurber's work has a special hold on me. This, I believe, is true for other writers who are blind.

When I was in elementary school in a small New Jersey town, I'd stay awake at night because I was afraid to face the taunts of non-disabled students the next day. My parents would comfort me by reading Thurber. I came to know "The Thirteen Clocks" and about "The Night the Bed Fell." School wouldn't seem so hard compared to the trials and tribulations of Walter Mitty or "The Scotty Who Knew Too Much."

As a teenager struggling to survive P.E., I felt the way Thurber did as a student during gym class at Ohio State University. He writes in *My Life and Hard Times,* "They wouldn't let you play games or join in the exercises with your glasses on and I couldn't see with mine off. I bumped into professors, horizontal bars, agricultural students and swinging iron rings. Not being able to see, I could take it but I couldn't dish it out."

When I visited New York as a college student, the trip seemed to spring from a Thurber story. Some friends and I looked up at a sign in Penn Station. I thought, through my blurred vision and racing mind, that the sign said BEER PARTIES ON SKID ROW. "Come on," I said to my companions, "it must be what artists do here." My friends gently informed me that the sign really said BEEF PATTIES TO GO.

Some years later, I felt like Walter Mitty, when I saw several judges (dressed in judicial robes) in the middle of the lobby of a state building in Trenton, New Jersey. I was upset when they wouldn't greet me or shake my outstretched hand. Later, I learned that these rude people were actually life-sized statues.

What does Thurber have to say to those of us who are blind or visually impaired?

Before answering this question, one must first say that Thurber's work is of interest because of his wonderful writing, humor, imagination, and drawings: not because of his blindness. His work made Thurber, who wrote pieces and drew cartoons for *The New Yorker* magazine for some two decades, popular during his lifetime: his blindness didn't endear him to his thousands of readers.

Second, Thurber, who underwent many eye operations, became progressively blind over many years. From the present vantage point, his personal life doesn't stand as a "model" for those of us who are blind or sighted.

basic concepts (such as position in space) are necessary to facilitate orientation and mobility training as the child grows older (Palazesi, 1986). The use of social routines and language play can assist children in language development and independently initiating play activities (Rogow, 1983). Taped books with sound illustrations (that is, accurate narrative descriptions of graphics and photos) and tactile books stimulate learners with visual impairments (Larsen & Jorgensen, 1989). In addition, technological aids, such as sonar-sensory devices, can be used with infants and toddlers to help them avoid objects, increase reach, and explore near space (Humphrey, Dodwell, Muir, & Humphrey, 1988).

One particular area of concern when working with toddlers and preschoolers with visual impairments in the least restrictive environment involves problems perceived by the agency or center that in fact may be appropriate behaviors when the visual impairment is considered. Tait and Wolfgang (1984) give the example of mouthing objects, as children with visual impairments do to

Thurber, according to Rosen, had physical and emotional illnesses related to his blindness. Rosen says, "Thurber wasn't happy about being blind." He drank too much and took out his frustration by lashing out at those around him. His wife never varied the arrangement of the furniture so that Thurber wouldn't ever have to relearn how to get around his house. Thurber didn't travel with a white cane or guide dog; people assisted him when he went anywhere.

I don't know of anyone who'd want to model his or her life on Thurber's. However, in fairness to Thurber, it must be said that he was blind during a different era—during a time when there was no adaptive equipment (such as computers with voice-synthesizer programs) for blind people—when few who were blind travelled, lived or worked independently. In such a context, it's astounding that Thurber completed some 30 volumes of work—many of them after he began losing his vision.

Thurber, who possessed total recall—he could remember the birthdays of friends he hadn't seen in over 40 years—was able to compose from 500 to 1,500 words in his mind. He would then dictate to his wife or secretaries, who would read what he had dictated back to him. For a time Thurber was able to keep drawing with the aid of his "Zeiss loop" (a magnifying device) but eventually he had to give up drawing.

Despite the unhappiness in his personal life, Thurber's work is filled with insights and humor about the world and people as well as blindness.

It's impossible to be depressed when reading Thurber. How can you despair when you see a Thurber drawing of a seance where the medium says, "I can't get in touch with your uncle, but there's a horse here that wants to say hello."

Thurber is candid, humorous and without self-pity about his blindness in his work and interviews.

On giving up drawing, Thurber said in an 1958 interview in the New Republic, "You mustn't think I grieve about not being able to draw. If I couldn't write, I couldn't live, but drawing to me was a little bit more than tossing cards in a hat."

Thurber believed that his writing changed after he became blind. In **Collecting Himself**—a collection of his articles and interviews edited by Michael J. Rosen—Thurber says:

"I used to be a writer who thought on the typewriter . . . I have shifted from being an eye to being an ear writer.

"I often tell them (works in progress) at parties and places and I write them there too. I never quite know when I'm not writing."

Thurber thought that his blindness kept him from being distracted by visual details while he was writing. In *Collecting Himself,* Thurber tells this story about eating lunch with New Yorker editor and founder Harold Ross:

"He (Ross) picked up a bottle of Worcestershire sauce and then threw it down saying, 'Goddam it, that's the tenth-thousandth time I've read the label on this bottle.' I told him, 'Goddam it, Harold, that's because you're handicapped by vision.'"

In *The Years with Ross,* Thurber recalls how Ross told his New Yorker colleagues, "Thurber's over at the Algonquin lacing 'em in. He's the only *drinking* blind man I know." He tells how Ross came to visit him in the hospital after an eye operation in 1940 (while England was going through the German blitz). Ross growled at Thurber, "Goddam it, Thurber, I worry about you and England."

So many self-pitying memoirs on vision loss are published, that reading what Thurber writes about blindness is like a day at the races or a drink at the Algonquin.

To celebrate Thurber's birthday, have some cake or a drink and dip into his work. You'll find it to be a real eye-opener ●

Kathi Wolfe is a regular contributor to MAINSTREAM.

Copyright 1994, MAINSTREAM, Magazine of the Able-Disabled, 2973 Beech Street, San Diego, CA 92102.

gain information, which is usually deemed unacceptable behavior for a three-year-old child. Tait and Wolfgang recommend that personnel be instructed in behaviors to be expected in children with visual impairments, ways to overcome passivity, and ways of establishing effective communication. A concern when working with toddlers and preschoolers with visual impairments in the least restrictive environment, that is, in general education classrooms, is staff misperceptions of how children with visual impairments interact with the environment and learn.

School-Age Children

The most frequent services provided to learners with visual impairments in the public schools include professional development services, special intervention services, summer school programs, and books, equipment, and supplies (Harley & English, 1988). Matien and Curry (1987) report three sets of needs that must be addressed if schools are to provide services for learners with visual impairments.

James Thurber

Annual Edition

Article 27

1. Needs that can be met by adapting the curriculum
2. Needs that require changes in teaching method but not curriculum or objective
3. Needs that are the direct result of visual impairments that cause a lack of incidental learning

Specific educational interventions may be needed in the areas of communication, social skills, recreation, and career-oriented skills. In addition, with the growing emphasis on using computers for instruction, teachers should be sensitive to the increased graphical applications that may not be practical for learners with visual impairments (Wilson, 1994).

To facilitate the instruction of learners with visual impairments, the school may provide nonoptical aids, tactual aids, and auditory aids. Nonoptical aids include large-print texts, bookstands to reduce postural fatigue, yellow acetate to improve the contrast between print and its background, broad-tip marking pens and pencils to increase the readability of print, and dimmer switches to increase or decrease light intensity. Among the tactual aids that can be provided in the classroom for learners with visual impairments are braille books, braillewriters, braille computers, slate and stylus sets, tactual globes and maps, abacus and similar counting frames, measuring devices, and various templates and writing guides. Two of the more essential auditory aids are the cassette tape recorder and recorded books. The tape recorder can be used for taking notes, recording home assignments, and listening to assignments. Recorded or talking

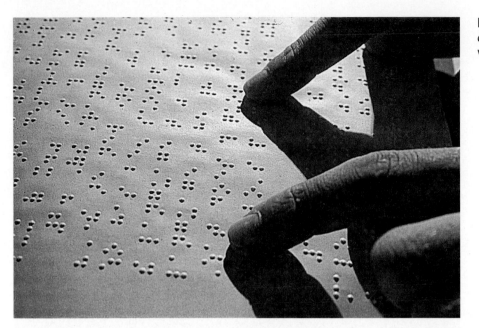

Braille is a private mode of communication for individuals with visual impairments.

books can be used for study and leisure. A number and variety of recorded books are available through the Library of Congress and other institutions and organizations serving learners who are visually impaired.

Braille

Braille is a tactile system for reading and writing. The braille system is generally used by those whose vision limits their ability to read print. The braille letter is based on six cells, or potential positions for raised points (fig. 11.3). There are various levels of braille writing, and in its simplest form each letter of each word is spelled out, much like the print on this page. In its more complex form, various letters and letter combinations are used to represent whole words. Braille is introduced to students with visual impairments at the same time that sighted students are introduced to reading and writing.

The use of braille has steadily decreased with the introduction of technological aids and alternative materials (Orlansky & Rhyne, 1981). Ferrante (1986) contends that braille remains an extremely useful tool for learners who are blind because (a) learners can make and read their own notes, giving them a private mode of communication, (b) personal and household objects can be labeled and identified, and (c) it is concrete and can be reviewed, whereas audio materials cannot.

Wittenstein (1993) found that teachers who attended teacher preparation programs that emphasized the development of tactual perception tended to have positive attitudes toward braille and felt competent in teaching braille to children. He suggests that teachers' feelings against the use of braille may be related to their own discomfort with writing in this mode. Using braille has been related to increased phonological awareness and reading ability similar to that of sighted children (Pring, 1994).

Braille is written with the aid of a braillewriter or a slate and stylus. The slate is a simple metal frame through which braille dots are punched with a stylus. The learner works from right to left, embossing the paper in the slate. When the paper is turned over, the message can be read by feeling the embossed dots from left to right. The slate and stylus are presented in figure 11.4.

Figure 11.3

The braille alphabet.

The braillewriter is used to type braille on paper. The braillewriter has six keys, which correspond to the six braille cells. The keys are punched to emboss the paper. The braillewriter also has a space bar, back spacer, and line spacer. The braillewriter is presented in figure 11.5.

Mobility and Orientation Training

Both orientation and mobility training are essential to learners with visual impairments and should be integrated throughout the curriculum. The purpose of mobility training is to teach learners to safely move from one location to another. Orientation training teaches an individual about his or her position in the environment and that position relative to other objects in the environment. Both of these skills are essential to the independence of learners with visual impairments. Spatial-orientation training should be introduced no later than the primary grades (Feoktistove, 1987). Through discussion, modeling, physical prompting, and feedback, children can be taught to increase their gaze direction and sitting behavior, increasing positive perceptions of others towards them (Raver, 1987a, 1987b).

There are several aids available to facilitate orientation and mobility training, including sighted guides, the long cane, guide dogs, and electronic travel aids. Electronic aids are becoming increasingly common as their cost decreases and availability increases. The laser cane sends out three beams ahead of the traveler and allows the detection of obstacles straight ahead, at head height, and downward. The Sonicguide is used with the long cane. It sends out ultrasonic impulses from a transmitter mounted in an eyeglass frame and provides the traveler with information about direction, distance, and surface characteristics of objects. The Mowat sensor is a hand-held device that sends out a narrow beam of ultrasound. The beam reflects back, and the device vibrates and alerts the traveler to obstacles.

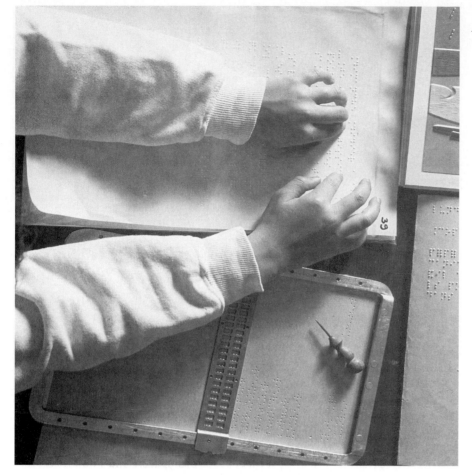

Figure 11.4

A child using a slate and stylus.

Annual **Edition**

Article 26

Technological Aids

In recent years there have been several technological advances, in addition to those previously discussed in this chapter, that are of great assistance to learners with visual impairments. Among these are the Kurzweil Reader, the Opticon, devices that incorporate synthesized speech, the braille printer, the braille computer, and closed circuit television.

The Kurzweil Reader converts print directly into synthetic speech. When an open book is placed over a glass surface on the reader, a high-resolution camera scans the lines of print. The camera image is processed by a computer, which identifies the words and activates a speech synthesizer. Large community and university libraries frequently have readers available, and a new model for personal use is now available.

The Opticon (Optical to Tactile Converter) translates an image from a small camera into a vibrating image of the same shape that can be felt with the index finger. As the reader moves the camera along the line of print, words are read by feeling the letters.

Synthesized speech has been incorporated into many common items of great value to learners with visual impairments. Synthetic speech is available in watches, clocks, calculators, thermometers, and scales. Synthetic speech incorporated into computers provides the learner with visual impairments with valuable feedback.

Figure 11.5

Examples of students using braillewriters.

The braille printer converts the printed word into braille. Closed circuit television allows for the enlargement of printed materials for learners with visual impairments.

The National Library Service for the Blind and Physically Handicapped (NLS), Library of Congress, is a free national library program offering recorded materials. Anyone who is unable to read or use standard printed materials as a result of temporary or permanent visual or physical limitations may receive service. A survey sponsored by NLS found that two million persons with some type of visual impairment may be eligible for the service. Playback equipment is loaned free to readers for as long as recorded materials provided by NLS and its cooperating libraries are being borrowed. Talking-book machines play disc books and magazines recorded at 8 rpm and 16 rpm; cassettes, which play up to six hours, are also available. Similar materials are available through the Recording for the Blind Program, a private organization that lends free recorded textbooks and other educational materials to learners who are visually impaired. Recording for the Blind, however, does not provide playback equipment to its patrons (National Library Service for the Blind and Physically Handicapped, 1994).

Though strategies to mediate the environment for learners with visual impairments are many and frequently specialized, teachers are typically supported through resource teachers, occupational therapists, and medical professionals. An effort should be made to present accommodations in as matter-of-fact a way as possible.

The Impact on Participation in the School, Community, and Society

Objective Five

To describe the impact of visual impairments on participation in the larger social systems—the school, community, and society.

Children with visual impairments have lower educational aspirations than do children with sight. They also tend to have occupational expectations that are highly related to the type of training they receive at school (Kahn, 1986).

According to Willis, Groves, and Fuhrman (1979) visual impairments are among the most difficult disabilities for a person without visual impairment to accept. In a review of literature on public attitudes toward people who are blind,

Technological aids make print more accessible for some learners. Adaptive devices such as "beep balls" enable learners with visual impairments to participate in sports.

Lowenfeld (1980) concludes that the general attitude that individuals who are blind are helpless and dependent persists. However, he suggests that this attitude is changing.

Society as a whole has responded to the unique needs of learners with visual impairments. Every state has free library services for those who, because of a physical or visual defect, cannot read ordinary print books. Special cassette machines and record players to use in listening to the taped or recorded reading materials are also loaned without cost. Recorded, braille, and large-print reading matter can be mailed to and from learners with visual impairments free of charge if "Free Matter for the Blind" is written or stamped on the envelope or package (Finkelstein, 1989). With the passage of the Americans with Disabilities Act, other accommodations, such as tactual maps of the subway system (Luxton, 1994), have also become available, increasing the mobility of individuals with visual impairments.

Summary

Because of the large amount of information most people gather through vision, it is often presumed that learners with visual impairments are less capable or have less potential than those who see. However, vision is only one source of information, and learners with visual impairments are as varied as any other group of individuals. Among learners with visual impairments, two large groups emerge: (a) those who are blind and require alternatives to print and visual materials, and (b) those who are partially sighted and may use print and visual materials with the help of large print, optical aids, technological aids, and education in the use of residual vision.

Problems in mediating the environment for children born with visual impairments challenge parents as well as teachers. The placement of learners with visual impairments in the general education classroom may cause increased anxiety on the part of the teacher. To facilitate the instruction of learners with visual impairments, the school may provide nonoptical aids, tactual aids, and auditory aids. In addition, both orientation and mobility training are essential to learners with visual impairments and should be integrated throughout the curriculum.

Society has responded positively to the unique needs of learners with visual impairments. Every state has free library services for those who, because of a physical or visual defect, cannot read ordinary print books. Special cassette machines and record players for listening to the taped or recorded reading materials are also loaned without cost.

Building Your Professional Vocabulary

Match each word or phrase to its meaning.

_____ amblyopia

_____ astigmatism

_____ blindness

_____ cataracts

_____ hyperopia

_____ myopia

_____ nystagmus

_____ presbyopia

_____ stereotypies

_____ strabismus

a. repetitive behaviors with no apparent effect on the environment
b. visual impairment that prohibits the use of vision as an educational tool
c. loss or impairment of the ability to focus on close work
d. nearsightedness

e. farsightedness
f. blurred or distorted vision at any distance
g. reduction or loss of vision in the weaker eye
h. clouding of the lens
i. involuntary rapid movement of the eyes
j. inability to focus on the same object with both eyes

Comprehension Check

Select the most appropriate response.

1. Learners who are blind
   a. are those whose sight is limited in any way.
   b. are those whose visual impairment prohibits the use of vision as an educational tool.
   c. are able to use print with technological support.
2. "Blindisms"
   a. are related to the neurological damage of the visual impairment.
   b. are apparent to the same extent in most learners with visual impairments.
   c. have a negative impact on the perceptions of persons interacting with the learner with a visual impairment.
3. The social adaptation of learners with visual impairments
   a. are similar to those of their sighted peers.
   b. are mitigated with the use of technological aids.
   c. remains a consistent challenge throughout the learner's development.
4. Educationally, persons who are partially sighted
   a. use braille.
   b. require special education services.
   c. use print, with supports.
5. The most common visual problems confronting children are
   a. those involving visual acuity.
   b. those involving strabismus.
   c. those involving retinopathy of prematurity.

6. There are few norm-referenced assessments for learners with visual impairments because
   a. standard norm-referenced assessment may be readily adapted.
   b. there are so few learners with visual impairments and great variability in their characteristics.
   c. norm-referenced assessment cannot be administered to learners with visual impairments.
7. A consistent challenge for families of learners with visual impairments includes
   a. providing adequate prebraille reading experiences.
   b. providing adequate tactile input.
   c. providing safe yet stimulating experiences.
8. In inclusive classrooms for learners with visual impairments,
   a. the general education teacher must learn braille.
   b. braille instruction is provided by a specially trained teacher.
   c. an instructional assistant is required to provide adequate safety monitoring.
9. The use of braille
   a. is no longer needed with the advent of technological aides.
   b. puts learners with visual impairments at a disadvantage.
   c. provides a private mode of communication.
10. In general, the public perceives learners with visual impairments
    a. as capable and inspirational.
    b. as helpless and dependent.
    c. as adaptable and independent.

References

American Foundation for the Blind. (1984). *What do you do when you meet a blind person?* New York: Author.

Anderson, D. W. (1984). Mental imagery in congenitally blind children. *Journal of Visual Impairment and Blindness, 76,* 200–210.

Anderson, D., & Fisher, K. F. (1985). Nominal realism in congenitally blind children. *Journal of Visual Impairment and Blindness, 80,* 555–560.

Ashmead, D., Hill, E. W., & Talor, C. A. (1989). Obstacle perception by congenitally blind children. *Perception and Psychophysics, 46,* 425–433.

Barrage, N. C. (1986). Sensory perceptual development. In G. Scholl (Ed.), *Foundations of education for blind and visually handicapped children and youth.* New York: American Foundation for the Blind.

Barrage, N. C., & Morris, J. (1980). *Program to develop efficiency in visual functioning.* Louisville, KY: American Printing House for the Blind.

Bigelow, A. C. (1968). Blind children's concepts of how people see. *Journal of Visual Impairment and Blindness, 82,* 65–68.

Bigelow, A. C. (1987). Early words of blind children. *Journal of Child Language, 14,* 47–55.

Birns, S. L. (1986). Age at onset of blindness and development of space concepts: From topological to projective space. *Journal of Visual Impairment and Blindness, 82,* 577–582.

Caton, H. (1976). *Tactile test of basic concepts.* Louisville, KY: American Printing House for the Blind.

Civelli, L. (1983). Verbalism in young blind children. *Journal of Visual Impairment and Blindness, 77,* 61–63.

Cole, P., Jenkins, P., & Shott, C. T. (1985). Spontaneous expressive control in blind and sighted children. *Child Development, 60,* 683–688.

Corn, A. L., & Martinez, I. (1985). *When you have a visually handicapped child in your classroom: Suggestions for teachers.* New York: American Foundation for the Blind.

Davidson, I. F., & Simmons, J. N. (1984). Mediating the environment for young blind children: A conceptualization. *Journal of Visual Impairment and Blindness, 74,* 251–255.

Delta Gamma Foundation. (1991). *Art of the eye: An exhibition on vision.* St. Louis, MO: Author.

Dodds, A. C., & Carter, D. D. (1983). Memory for movement in blind children: The role of previous visual experience. *Journal of Motor Behavior, 14,* 343–352.

Dote-Kwan, J., & Hughes, M. (1994). The home environments of young blind children. *Journal of Visual Impairment and Blindness, 88,* 31–42.

Erin, J. N. (1986). Frequencies and types of questions in the language of visually impaired children. *Journal of Visual Impairment and Blindness, 80,* 670–674.

Erin, J. N. (1990). Language samples from visually impaired four-and five-year-olds. *Journal of Childhood Communication Disorders, 13,* 181–191.

Federal Register. (1977). 42 (163), 42659–42688.

Feoktistove, V. (1987). Improvement of space orientation training of junior blind school-children. *Defektologiya,* No. 4, 60–64.

Ferrante, O. (1986). Why blind children should learn braille. *Journal of Visual Impairment and Blindness, 80,* 594.

Finkelstein, D. (1989). *Blindness and disorders of the eye.* Baltimore, MD: The National Federation for the Blind.

Grayson, D. (1984). *Facts about blindness and visual impairment.* New York: American Foundation for the Blind.

Harley, R. R., & English, W. H. (1988). Support services for visually impaired children in local day schools: Residential schools as a resource. *Journal of Visual Impairment and Blindness, 83,* 405–410.

Harley, R. K., Wood, T. A., & Merbler, J. B. (1981). *Peabody mobility scales.* Chicago: Stoelting.

Hirshoren, H., & Schnittjer, C. J. (1983). Behavior problems in blind children and youth: A prevalence study. *Psychology in the Schools, 20,* 197–210.

Humphrey, S., Dodwell, P., Muir, D. W., & Humphrey, D. E. (1988). Can blind infants and children use sonar sensory aids? *Canadian Journal of Psychology, 42* (2), 94–119.

Ittyerah, M., & Samarapungaven, A. (1989). The performance of congenitally blind children in cognitive developmental tasks. *British Journal of Developmental Psychology, 7* (2), 125–139.

Jan, J., Farrell, K., Wong, P. K., & McCormick, A. W. (1986). Eye and head movements of visually impaired children. *Developmental Medicine and Child Neurology, 28,* 286–293.

Kahn, M. N. (1986). Educational aspirations and occupational expectations of blind and normal children. *Perspectives in Psychological Research, 5* (2), 25–27.

Kekelis, L., & Anderson, E. (1984). Family communication styles and language development. *Journal of Visual Impairment and Blindness, 78,* 54–55.

Lang, M. A., & Sullivan, C. (1986). Adapting home environments for visually impaired and blind children. *Children's Environments Quarterly, 3* (1), 50–54.

Larsen, S., & Jorgensen, N. (1989). Talking books for preschool children. *Journal of Visual Impairment and Blindness, 83,* 118–119.

Leonhardt, M. (1990). Stereotypies: A preliminary report on mannerisms and blindisms. *Journal of Visual Impairment and Blindness, 84,* 216–218.

Lowenfeld, B. (1980). Psychological problems of children with severely impaired vision. In W. M. Cruickshank (Ed.), *Psychology of exceptional children and youth* (4th ed.). Englewood Cliffs, NJ: Prentice Hall.

Luxton, K. (1994). The usefulness of tactual maps of the New York City Subway System. *Journal of Visual Impairment and Blindness, 88* (1), 75–84.

Mangold, S. S. (1977). *The Mangold developmental program of tactile perception and Braille letter recognition.* Castro Valley, CA: Exceptional Teaching Aids.

Matien, P., & Curry, S. (1987). In support of specialized programs for blind and visually impaired children. *Journal of Visual Impairment and Blindness, 81,* 7–13.

McConachie, H. (1990). Early language development and severe visual impairment. *Child Care, Health, and Development, 10,* 55–61.

Mereira, L. (1990). Spatial concepts and balance performance: Motor learning in blind and visually impaired children. *Journal of Visual Impairment and Blindness, 84,* 100–114.

National Association for the Visually Handicapped. (1978). *The eye and your vision.* New York: Author.

National Federation of the Blind. (1991). *The blind child in the regular preschool program.* Baltimore, MD: Author.

National Library Service for the Blind and Physically Handicapped. (1994). *Books for blind and physically handicapped individuals.* Washington, DC: Library of Congress.

National Society to Prevent Blindness. (1983). Home eye test gets a rousing send off. *Prevent Blindness News, 8* (1), 3.

Nixon, H. L. (1988a). Getting over the worry hurdle: Parental encouragement and the sports involvement of visually impaired children and youth. *Adapted Physical Activity Quarterly, 5,* 26–43.

Nixon, H. L. (1988b). Reassessing support groups for parents of visually impaired children. *Journal of Visual Impairment and Blindness, 82,* 271–278.

Orlansky, M. D., & Rhyne, J. M. (1981). Special adaptations necessitated by visual impairments. In J. M. Kauffman & D. Hallahan (Eds.), *Handbook of special education* (pp. 552–575). Englewood Cliffs, NJ: Prentice Hall.

Orwin, L. (1984). Language for absent things: Learning from visually handicapped children. *Topics in Language Disorders, 4* (4), 24–37.

Palazesi, M. A. (1986). The need for motor development programs for visually impaired preschoolers. *Journal of Visual Impairment and Blindness, 80,* 573–576.

Parsons, S. (1987). Locus of control and adaptive behavior in visually impaired children. *Journal of Visual Impairment and Blindness, 81,* 420–432.

Pring, L. (1994). Touch and go: Learning to read braille. *Reading Research Quarterly, 29,* 66–74.

Raver, S. (1987a). Training blind children to employ appropriate gaze direction and sitting behavior during conversation. *Education and Treatment of Children, 10,* 237–246.

Raver, S. (1987b). Training gaze direction in blind children: Attitude effects on the sighted. *Remedial and Special Education, 3* (5), 40–45.

Raver-Lampman, S. (1990). Effect of gaze direction on evaluation of visually impaired children by informed respondents. *Journal of Visual Impairment and Blindness, 84,* 87–90.

Rogow, S. (1983). Social routines and language play: Developing communication responses in developmentally delayed blind children. *Journal of Visual Impairment and Blindness, 77,* 1–4.

Rouse, M. W., & Ryan, J. B. (1984). Teacher's guide to vision problems. *The Reading Teacher, 38,* 306–317.

Scholl, G. T. (1986). What does it mean to be blind? In G. T. Scholl (Ed.), *Foundations of education for the blind and visually handicapped children and youth* (pp. 23–34). New York: American Foundation for the Blind.

Schwartz, T. (1983). Social cognition in visually impaired and sighted children. *Journal of Visual Impairment and Blindness, 77,* 377–381.

Scott, E. P. (1982). *Your visually impaired student: A guide for teachers.* Baltimore, MD: University Park Press.

Simmons, J. N., & Davidson, I. F. (1985a). Mediating the environment: A case study approach. *Child Care, Health, and Development, 11,* 185–207.

Simmons, J. N., & Davidson, I. F. (1985b). Perspectives on intervention with young blind children. *Child Care, Health, and Development, 11,* 183–185.

Tait, M. C., & Wolfgang, C. (1984). Mainstreaming a blind child: Problems perceived in a preschool day care program. *Early Child Development and Care, 13,* 135–137.

Ubiakor, F., & Otile, S. (1990). The self-concepts of visually impaired and normally sighted middle school children. *Journal of Psychology, 124,* 190–200.

U.S. Department of Education (1995). *Seventeenth annual report to congress on the implementation of the Education of the Handicapped Act.* Washington, DC: Author.

Van Hasselt, V. (1983). Social adaptation in the blind. *Clinical Psychology Review, 3,* 87–102.

Van Hasselt, V. (1985). A behavioral analytic model for assessing social skills in blind adolescents. *Behavior Research and Therapy, 23,* 355–405.

Van Hasselt, V., Kazdin, A., & Hersen, M. (1986). Assessment of problem behavior in visually handicapped adolescents. *Journal of Clinical Child Psychology, 15,* 134–141.

Wilhelm, J. G. (1989). Fear and anxiety in low vision and totally blind children. *Education of the Visually Handicapped, 20,* 163–172.

Willis, D. J., Groves, C., & Fuhrman, W. (1979). Visually disabled children and youth. In B. M. Swanson & D. J. Willis (Eds.), *Understanding exceptional children and youth: An introduction to special education.* Chicago: Rand McNally.

Wilson, D. L. (1994). Assuring access for the disabled. *Chronicle of Higher Education, 40,* A25, A28.

Wittenstein, S. (1993). Braille training and teacher attitudes: Implications for personnel preparation. *RE: view, 25,* 103–111.

12

Chapter

Learners with Hearing Impairments

Shobha Chachie Joseph and Sally Ann Zwicker Contributing Authors

Objectives

After completing this chapter, you will be able to:

1. describe the personal characteristics of persons with hearing impairments.
2. describe the identification and evaluation of learners with hearing impairments.
3. describe the impact of hearing impairment on interactions in the home and classroom.
4. describe ways to mediate the environment for learners with hearing impairments.
5. describe the impact of hearing impairment on participation in larger social systems—the school, community, and society.

Key Words and Phrases

American Sign Language (ASL)	immitance testing
amplification	interpreters
behind-the-ear (BTE) hearing aids	in-the-ear (ITE) hearing aids
bilingual-bicultural (Bi-Bi) education	otitis media
conductive loss	postlingual hearing impairment
cued speech	pragmatics
deaf	prelingual hearing impairment
Deaf	sensorineural loss
fluctuating conductive hearing impairment	speech audiometry
	speechreading
FM systems	TDD
hard of hearing	TTY
hearing impairment	tympanogram

deafness, a hearing loss, is invisible. Almost nothing about me alerts the hearing world that something is amiss in my communication system. I say "almost" because there are actually two noticeable differences about me: I wear two hearing aids and I am always accompanied by a dog . . . I am not—and there are many like me—one of the aggressive militant disabled. I did not fight for my right to each job. I slunk away, eventually selecting a solitary style of employment based on another skill, writing. My selection is suitable to my temperament and my life as a writer, but such selectivity is hardly every disabled person's wish or choice. Most want to be out there, in there, involved, with people, part of the normality, that nine-to-five life that is sometimes a complaint but *always* the prerogative of anyone else.*

"I come from a Deaf family and I have been Deaf from birth. I am proud of my deafness and I take pride in being a part of the Deaf Community, with its culture and traditions. I see myself as a motivated, driven, Deaf person, who can accomplish anything. As I, King Jordan, the president of the world's only liberal arts university for the deaf, Gallaudet University, once said, 'Deaf people can do anything, except hear.' In light of the larger society I am disabled, insofar that I require assistive devices and interpreters in some situations.

"I have spent the last twenty-six years of my life in the deaf and hard-of-hearing community. A year ago I joined a 'hearing' university and, for the first time in my life, I have been forced to confront all of the deficit characteristics associated with a hearing loss. These perceptions, I believe, come largely from society's pathological perspective of deafness. In seeking to 'fix' deaf and hard-of-hearing individuals, precious years of learning are lost, and the deficits are further accentuated. When I am in the company of people who do not understand deafness, expect me to be oral or fit into their preferred communications styles, and to not respect the diversity of needs of deaf and hard-of-hearing people, I feel dependent, incapable, restricted, and truly disabled. On the other hand, when I am in the company of friends, both deaf and hearing, who can sign, respect my culture and my deafness, and see me for who I am, I feel relaxed, uninhibited and capable.

"I hope that some day, the well-meaning people who try to fix us will realize that with all the current technology and modern medicine, we will never be able to hear and speak like hearing people. Individual priorities, as in the hearing world, are different. I earnestly propose that we bear in mind at all times the great diversity of the deaf and hard-of-hearing population, respect these differences, and accommodate them on the basis of individual needs." (Sally Ann Zwicker, who provided technical assistance for this chapter, is the deaf child of deaf parents whose primary language is American sign. 1995)

*From "Who Is Handicapped? Employees or Employers?" by Hannah Merker. Copyright © 1990 Hannah Merker. Excerpted by permission.

Introduction

Approximately eight million of the 39.5 million school children in the United States have some degree of hearing impairment (Berg, 1987). In describing this group of children, Wray, Flexer, and Ireland (1988) caution that hearing impairment is not an either/or proposition; rather, hearing impairment occurs along a continuum ranging from being mildly hard of hearing to profoundly deaf. Ross and Calvert (1984) argue that 92 percent to 94 percent of the entire population of individuals with hearing impairment are functionally hard of hearing and not deaf. In general, it is estimated that in every one thousand children, one is deaf, three or four are severely hard of hearing, and thirty have an educationally significant hearing loss (Ross, 1982).

The generic term **hearing impairment** includes both "deaf" and "hard of hearing." Individuals who are **deaf** have a hearing impairment that precludes successful processing of linguistic information through hearing with or without amplification. **Hard of hearing** individuals have hearing that is adequate for successful processing of linguistic information through hearing with amplification (Report of the Ad Hoc Committee to Define Deaf and Hard of Hearing, 1975). In addition, there is a cultural definition of deafness related to the use of American Sign Language and self-identification of a cultural group comprising individuals who use American Sign Language as their primary language (Henwood & Pope-Davis, 1994).

During the 1993–1994 school year, 64,249 learners with hearing impairments were served under the Individuals with Disabilities Education Act (U.S. Department of Education, 1995). Of these, about 29.5 percent were served in the regular classroom, 19.7 percent in the resource room, 28.1 percent in separate classes, 8.3 percent in separate schools, and 14.0 percent in residential facilities. Only children who were visually impaired and deaf-blind children were served more often in residential facilities (U.S. Department of Education, 1995). Over half of the learners with hearing impairments completed secondary school with a diploma (U.S. Department of Education, 1990).

Personal Characteristics

The groups of learners identified as hearing impaired are quite diverse. Any aspect of the personal characteristics of these learners involves the variations in their hearing mechanisms. An understanding of these variations can provide further insight into the personal characteristics of these learners.

A report of the Conference of Educational Administrators Serving the Deaf (Brill, MacNeil, & Newman, 1986) provided clarification of two important terms associated with the education of the deaf: prelingual hearing impairment and postlingual hearing impairment. **Prelingual hearing impairment** is present at birth or occurs before the individual develops speech or language, which is generally at about two years of age. These learners require specialized services, which, as discussed later in this chapter, require special curriculum and equipment. An ever-increasing number of educational programs serve children with prelingual hearing impairment from birth to three years of age.

Postlingual hearing impairment occurs after the child has developed speech or language. Due to medical advances, the number of children with postlingual deafness is relatively small—approximately 5 percent to 10 percent of the hearing-impaired population. These learners have educational needs that differ significantly from children with prelingual hearing impairment. They need assistance to maintain voice variations and idioms and to develop visual communication strategies.

Objective One

To describe the personal characteristics of learners with hearing impairments.

Davis (1988) proposes several assumptions regarding the personal characteristics of learners with hearing impairments. First, students' hearing losses result in speech and language challenges of varying degrees, which in turn affect either academic achievement, social adjustment, or both. Second, schools present communicative demands that are particularly difficult for learners with hearing impairments. Communication is primarily verbal, persons speaking frequently do not face the person with whom they wish to communicate, schedules are maintained by bells, and audio and audiovisual aids are used frequently. In addition, if the unique needs of these students are not met, poor self-esteem and social isolation may occur.

Kretschmer and Kretschmer (1978) remind us that variations in communication development among learners with hearing impairments may be due to the restrictions placed on these individuals by their environments rather than the cognitive functions that result from their hearing impairments. Kretschmer and Kretschmer pose several possible scenarios regarding the communication development of an auditory language of persons with hearing impairments.

1. Language may be delayed because of a lack of cognitive experiences due to the hearing impairment.
2. The hearing impairment and the use of other means of communication (gestures, signs, finger spelling) may cause differences in development between learners who hear and those whose hearing is limited.
3. The language of learners with hearing impairments may be dialectical in nature because English is a second language.
4. Any combination of the essentials of the three preceding scenarios may occur.

Any description of the characteristics of learners with hearing impairments must address the two groups of children involved: those who are hard of hearing and those who are deaf. In reference to communication, learners who are deaf have difficulties with the sound system of language, articulation, changes in pitch, and voicing. The speech of hard-of-hearing children is less affected in these areas. Though voice problems are less frequent, learners with mild hearing impairments have many misarticulations, consisting generally of consonant substitutions and distortions of sounds. Unlike learners who are deaf, hard-of-hearing learners do not misarticulate vowels, and their speech is typically intelligible.

In a study by Wolk and Schildroth (1986), teachers reported that 23 percent of the students with hearing impairments had unintelligible speech, 22 percent had speech that was marginally intelligible, and 10 percent were unwilling to speak in public. According to the teachers, 75 percent of the learners who were profoundly deaf did not have intelligible speech, and 14 percent of the learners with less-severe hearing impairments had nonintelligible speech. Musselman (1990) found that most children with losses of 70–89 decibels developed some intelligible speech, those with losses of 90–104 decibels varied in the intelligibility of their speech, and few learners with losses greater than 105 decibels developed intelligible speech.

Vocabulary skills also differentiate learners with hearing impairments from individuals who can hear (Davis, 1988). On the average, children with hearing impairments seem to be delayed two to three years in vocabulary development. This may occur because learners with hearing impairments do not learn as much incidental vocabulary as do individuals without hearing impairments. In addition, they do not learn the slang use of words necessary for conversations among classmates and friends. Learners with hearing impairments, because they do not hear or do not hear well, are unable to use verbal models effectively and are frequently unable to profit from feedback provided by others in the environment.

We must recognize that social adjustment is communication dependent. Social adjustment is grounded in interpersonal interactions, such as talking, laughing, joking, and discussing. Learners with hearing impairments are challenged in environments such as their classroom, school, and community, all of which make a variety of communicative demands.

The communicative disability related to deafness is present predominantly when interacting in "hearing" settings. In other settings, the communicative disability may not be present. The term *Deaf culture* is used to identify the beliefs and practices of individuals who are deaf and share a common signed language (Padden & Ramsey, 1993). Members of this culture refer to themselves as "Deaf." The use of the term *Deaf culture,* Padden and Ramsey suggest, reflects changing ideas about how to describe people who are deaf. Rather than judgments regarding an individual's ability to use speech, which is essential when interacting with those who speak, individuals in Deaf culture make judgments regarding hearing impairment on use of American Sign Language. Individuals who are Deaf (as members of Deaf culture identify themselves) are able to engage in unimpaired social interaction with others who use sign language and through the use of an interpreter.

Some young children with hearing impairments have been reported by their mothers to have more difficult temperaments, but no more behavior problems than young children who hear. Teachers in general education settings also rated learners with hearing impairments as less well adjusted and more anxious than their peers without hearing impairments (Prior, Glazner, Sanson, & Debelle, 1988).

Some children with hearing impairments have been found to be generally less assertive than their hearing peers (Macklin & Matson, 1985). They have been found to be more fearful of the unknown, injury, and small animals than are their hearing peers (King, Mulhall, & Gullone, 1989). Using a self-report procedure, Maxon, Brackett, and van der Berg (1991) found that learners with hearing impairments perceived themselves differently than did their hearing peers in verbal expression of emotions, verbal aggression, physical aggression, and interpersonal interaction. They suggested that these differences may be addressed through specific programming that emphasizes the language involved in appropriate interactions, as well as strategies for coping with anger and frustration through language.

Research findings on the self-concept of learners with hearing impairments are difficult to interpret because of the use of assessment instruments or procedures designed for hearing learners, which are inappropriate for those who are hearing impaired (Garrison & Tesch, 1978). The language demands in tests of self-esteem tend to lower the scores of learners who are hearing impaired. However, in one commonly used measure of self-esteem, Koelle and Convey (1982) found the scores of learners with hearing impairments to be inflated. Oblowitz, Green, and Heyns (1991) responded by developing a self-concept scale specific to learners with hearing impairments, which appears sufficiently reliable and valid for further research. Nonverbal measures, such as drawing of the human figure, demonstrate comparable projective drawings between learners with hearing impairment and learners without hearing impairment (Cates, 1991).

Identification and Evaluation

Objective Two

To describe the identification and evaluation of learners with hearing impairments.

Public Law 94-142 defined deaf as "having a hearing impairment which is so severe that the child is impaired in processing linguistics information through hearing, with or without amplification, which adversely affects educational performance." Hard of hearing means "a hearing impairment, whether permanent or fluctuating, which adversely affects a child's educational performance but which is not included under the definition of deaf" (Federal Register, 1977, 300.5).

Making News

Deaf Pianist Sets Example For Others

By Roger Signor
Post-Dispatch Science-Medicine Editor

Boudi Foley, 11, began playing the first notes of Bach's "Minuet in G." His tempo was too quick, so his piano teacher stopped him.

Boudi looked up sheepishly from under the bill of his Majic 108 cap. His teacher, Sona Haydon, told him to slow down. Pushing aside thoughts of playing ball, he focused on the music that he was preparing for the group recital that takes place at 1:30 p.m. Saturday in Washington University's Graham Chapel.

Boudi plays so well that no one knows he's been profoundly deaf since birth.

What Boudi "hears" in a given piece of music is a mystery. But it's pleasing enough to make him want to play. He feels the pulse of rhythm and hears some of the frequencies, especially those at the very bottom of the sound spectrum. Then his brain puts it together in a way that's unique to him. One thing is certain: Very rarely do profoundly deaf children play the piano at Boudi's level.

His success spells hope for many thousands of other deaf children who would like to play—but think it's beyond them.

In Haydon's 20 years of teaching piano at Washington University, she's never had a deaf student. So she and Boudi have developed their own language: a blend of his lip-reading and her back-tapping.

A skillful lip-reader, Boudi knows what Haydon says. But he can't watch her all the time. When he's playing, for example, he must keep a sharp watch on his keyboard. Otherwise, he isn't sure his hands are in the correct position to begin a new section of the music. To communicate while he's playing, she sits next to him, resting her hand on his back.

Fastest Fingers In The West

"This is *my* keyboard," Haydon explains, patting Boudi on his back. They have an elaborate code of communicating by touch. A quick succession of finger-taps means the rhythm's wrong. A firm pressure means "Stop!"

"Boudi knows exactly how I want him to play," she said. "After 2 1/2 years of teaching him, I have the fastest fingers this side of the West Coast!"

Boudi's repertory and skills match that of Haydon's other young "hearing" students, she says. He loves Mozart and plays many of his shorter pieces. He also plays simple compositions by Beethoven, Schubert and Handel, among others.

He's told his parents he wants to become as well-known as Beethoven—to heighten public awareness of what deaf people can do. Beethoven became deaf later in life but kept on writing superb music.

In fact—when Boudi was 7—it was a Beethoven symphony that made his parents aware that their son actually heard music and enjoyed it.

Types and Degrees of Hearing Impairment

The primary types of hearing impairment are described by the location of the problem in the hearing mechanism. The ear is composed of three parts: the outer ear, the middle ear, and the inner ear. The outer ear includes the auricle (that part of the ear that protrudes from the side of the head, the only part of the hearing mechanism that is visible) and the external auditory canal. The auricle collects sound waves from the environment and channels them into the external auditory canal. The external auditory canal carries the sounds from the auricle to the tympanic membrane (the eardrum), which marks the beginning of the inner ear (fig. 12.1).

Besides the tympanic membrane, the middle ear is composed of three small bones within an air-filled chamber. These bones, or ossicles, are called the hammer (malleus), anvil (incus), and stirrup (stapes). These bones conduct vibrations from the eardrum to the oval window, which connects the middle ear to the inner ear. **Conductive loss** is caused by impairment of the outer ear and middle ear that prevents the transfer of sound to the inner ear.

The two major components of the inner ear are the vestibule and the cochlea. The vestibular mechanism is concerned with the sense of balance and is extremely sensitive to movement. The function of the vestibular mechanism is to transmit information to the brain that enables an individual to determine his or her position in space and sense of balance, as well as acceleration and deceleration.

The cochlea is a crucial element of the ear. It is responsible for converting the mechanical energy received from the middle ear into electrical signals that are transmitted to the brain. The movement of the fluid in the cochlea stimulates hairlike cells. These cells are part of the auditory nerve. **Sensorineural loss** is associated with damage to the auditory nerve or the inner ear.

He's Really Hearing Music!

His parents, Drs. Suma Khalil and Ahmed Foley, had tickets to hear the St. Louis Symphony in 1991, but their baby sitter didn't show up. So they took Boudi with them to Powell Hall.

"We thought he'd fall asleep," Foley said. "To our surprise, his fingers were tapping to the beat of the symphony." His parents looked at one another in joy. Boudi was absorbed in the program.

Khalil, who plays the piano, then taught Boudi to play scales at home. After eight months or so, he could play simple pieces, so they tried to find a piano teacher.

But teachers were hesitant to take a profoundly deaf pupil. "So we asked Sona (Haydon) if she'd teach *us* to teach Boudi," said Foley. When Haydon learned that Boudi was deaf, she was eager to take on the challenge.

After working out their communications, Haydon said, he progressed steadily in learning technique and playing harder pieces. After a year, he held his first recital. Then they locked horns over homework assignments. Boudi wanted more time to perfect his skills at karate and swimming, so Haydon backed off a little. "He got through that stage six months ago, and disciplines himself well."

In fact, they never exceed her normal one-hour lessons. "I'm constantly amazed how he continues to learn. He wanted daily lessons this week, but I told him 'No!' "

Haydon says the devotion of Boudi's parents is the main reason for his achievements. They were reared in Alexandria, Egypt, and both took medical degrees: his in radiology, hers in pediatrics. They moved to Kuwait, where they had large practices.

After learning that Boudi was deaf, his parents searched for the best schools for him, and then moved to St. Louis so Boudi could attend the Central Institute for the Deaf. After six years of study there, he transferred to St. Joseph Institute for the Deaf—near their new home in St. Louis County.

His parents both earned master's degrees in speech and hearing here to better understand how to help their son. To pay for his education—and theirs—they worked part time and spent their savings.

Foley has returned to medicine, but Khalil has nearly completed a doctorate in speech and hearing.

"We have much less income than in Kuwait, but when we look at Boudi and see how much he's doing, we have no second thoughts," Khalil said ●

When the hearing mechanism is working efficiently, it converts sound waves to mechanical energy, then to fluid or hydraulic energy, and, finally, to electrical energy that stimulates the brain and thus permits the individual to hear.

To understand the evaluation of hearing, it is necessary to understand the concepts of sound, frequency, and loudness. Sound is produced by vibrations of molecules through air, water, or another medium.

Frequency is the number of variations of the medium per second. High frequencies are perceived through the hearing mechanism as high pitch, low frequencies as low pitch. Hertz (Hz) is the accepted unit of measurement for frequency. Individuals with normal hearing perceive sounds in the range of 20 Hz to 20,000 Hz.

Loudness, or the intensity of sound, is measured in decibels (dB). Loud sounds have a high dB measurement; soft sounds have a low dB measurement. A dB range of 0 to 120 is used to measure how well an individual hears at different frequencies. A dB level of 125 or louder is generally painful to a human being. A normal hearing individual should hear sounds at the 0dB level.

Determining the type and degree of hearing loss is the first goal of audiologic evaluation (Maddell, 1990a). A basic audiologic evaluation includes air and bone conduction testing. Air conduction testing (the tones are presented through the regular channels that sound waves use to enter the hearing system) reveals the degree of hearing loss. Thresholds of decibel hearing level and designations for the severity of hearing loss are presented in table 12.1.

The type of hearing loss is determined by the relationship between test results obtained with earphones (air conduction) and with a vibrator placed on the mastoid bone outside the ear (bone conduction). If there is a match between the bone conduction and air conduction measures, the hearing loss is considered

Figure 12.1

Internal and external structure of the ear.

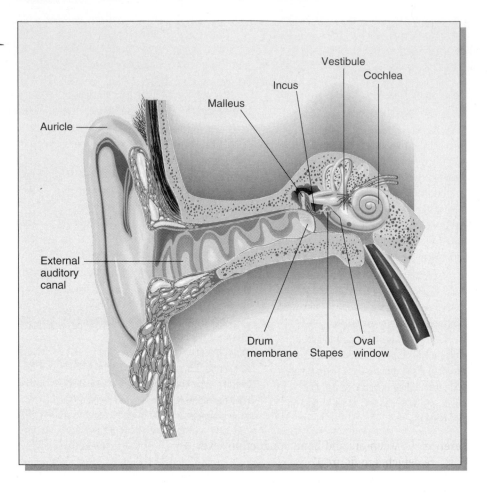

Table 12.1 **Hearing Levels and Severity of Hearing Loss**

Decibel Hearing Level	Type of Hearing Loss
25–50 decibels	Mild
40–55 decibels	Moderate
55–70 decibels	Moderate-Severe
70–90 decibels	Severe
>90 decibels	Profound

to be sensorineural, that is, caused by damage to the inner ear. If the bone conduction test is normal and the air conduction test indicates a hearing loss, then the loss is conductive, that is, caused by damage to or blockage of the outer or middle ear. A mixed hearing loss, with both conductive and sensorineural losses, is also possible.

Many conductive hearing losses are treatable medically; most sensorineural losses are not. For this reason, medical evaluation is an important component of a comprehensive hearing evaluation (Maddell, 1990a).

Hearing levels are depicted on a chart called an audiogram. There are several conventions used in audiograms. For example, an "x" is used to depict air conduction levels in the left ear and an "o" is used to depict air conduction levels

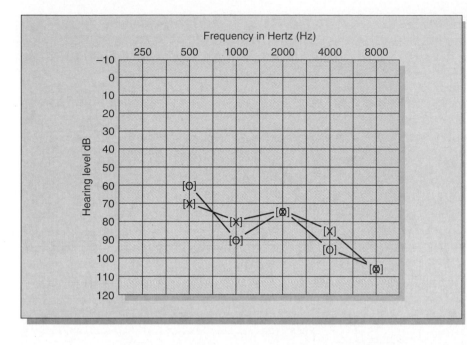

Figure 12.2

An audiogram for sensorineural hearing loss.

in the right ear. The intensity of sound is designated by decibels on one axis, and the pitch or frequency of the sounds, measured in Hertz, is along the horizontal axis. Levels that an individual hears with bone conduction are indicated with a "<" for the left ear and a ">" for the right ear. Air and bone conduction measures at the same level indicate a sensorineural loss, as depicted in figure 12.2. The differences between air and bone conduction levels representative of a conductive loss are depicted in figure 12.3.

One particularly challenging group of children to teach are those with **fluctuating conductive hearing impairment.** The most common fluctuating conductive hearing loss is caused by **otitis media,** or middle-ear infections (Webster, Saunders, & Bamford, 1984). Webster and associates report that fluctuating conductive hearing impairments have a serious effect on verbal-process and language-dependent skills. Persistent otitis media has been related to underachievement in school. Webster and associates urge educators to give middle-ear infection careful consideration as a contributing factor in children's developmental and learning difficulties.

Two additional assessments that are frequently used during an audiologic evaluation include (a) immitance, and (b) speech audiometry tests. **Immitance testing** includes the administering of a **tympanogram,** which measures the mobility of the eardrum, and acoustic reflex testing, which is used to confirm pure tone test results. Essentially, immitance testing provides information about the way in which the middle ear is working. **Speech audiometry,** the second test, determines how much speech an individual is able to understand. Maddell (1990b) suggests obtaining speech audiometry test results (a) at a low conversational level in a quiet environment, and (b) in an environment with competing noise. These test results are useful for educational programming and determining how well a learner may function in the classroom.

Communication Assessment

The second area of evaluation for learners with hearing impairments is communication skills. In 1978, Kretschmer and Kretschmer advocated the use of informal grammatical samplings as a component of the language evaluation for children with hearing impairments. Since that time, evidence has accumulated for the

AUDIOLOGIC EVALUATION REPORT

Name _Ian Joseph_   Date Seen _10-29-97_   Birthdate _8-21-92_   Age _5_

Address _729 Terrace, Park Place, OH 45376_   Phone _555-7896_

Audiologist _Truman_   Audiometer _2701_   Referred by _S. Richards_

Frequency in Hertz (Hz)

Hearing Level dB re: ANSI — audiogram grid, Frequency 250–8000 Hz, Hearing Level −10 to 120 dB

Legend:					
UNMASKED	R	L	MASKED	R	L
Air Conduction	O	X	Air Conduction	△	□
Bone Conduction	<	>	Bone Conduction	[	]
No Response	↓	↓	Did Not Test	DNT	
Soundfield	S		Aided	A	

Test Reliability ✓ Good   ____ Questionable

TYMPANOMETRY

	Right	Left
Middle Ear Pressure mm H₂O	−400 rounded	−250 rounded
Compliance	.5 stiff	1.0 stiff
Volume	.5	.5

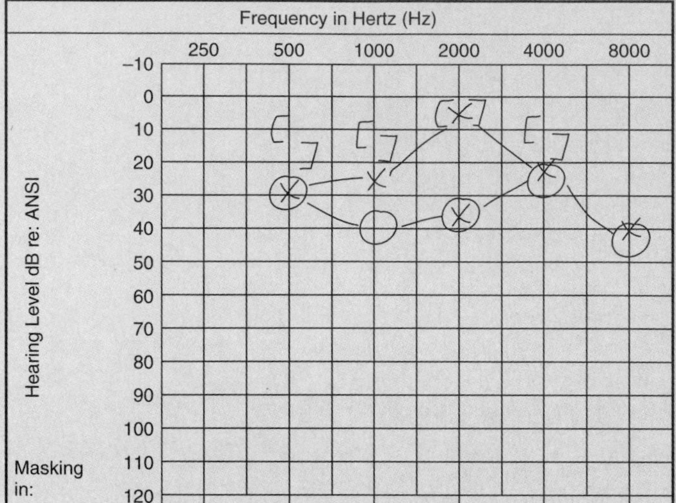

Masking in:

Right	Air		
	Bone	55 ——————→	
Left	Air		
	Bone	50 ——————→	

Weber Lateralization

Hearing Aid:

ACOUSTIC REFLEX

Stim. Ear	Probe Ear	Acoustic Reflex	Eliciting Frequency (Hz)			
			500	1000	2000	4000
L	R	Threshold dB HL	NR ————→			
R	L	Threshold dB HL	NR ————→			
		Threshold dB HL				
		Threshold dB HL				

Reflex Decay in 10 sec:

SPEECH AUDIOMETRY

	SRT				SPEECH RECOGNITION (DISCRIMINATION)							NOISE		
					QUIET									
	dB	Mask	MCL	LDL	1 %/HL	Mask	2 %/HL	Mask	3 %/HL	Mask		%/HL	S/N	Type
Right	30	—			96/55	—								
Left	20	—			100/50	—								
Sound Field (Unaided)														
Sound Field (Aided)														

Speech Recognition: ✓ Boothroyd   ____ WIPI   ____ Sentences   ____ Rec
____ Campbell   ____ PBK's   ____ Informal   ✓ MLV

Figure 12.3

An audiologic evaluation report for conductive hearing loss.

inclusion of all aspects of communication in context during assessment (Kretschmer & Kretschmer, 1988). This application of **pragmatics,** defined by Duchan (1988) as "the study of how linguistic, situational, or social contexts affect language use," has significantly changed the assessment process for learners with hearing impairments. According to Duchan, the evaluation of pragmatics includes (a) functional analysis (the intent of the communication); (b) conversational assessment (conversational turn taking, topic maintenance, and repairing communicative breakdowns); (c) conversational fine tuning (the style of communication); and (d) the nature of the individual's discourse.

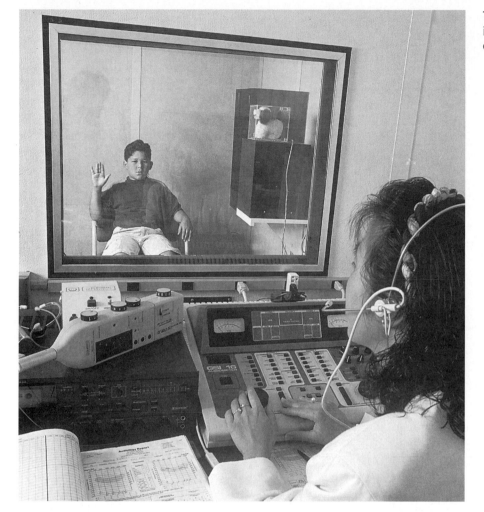

The goal of audiological evaluation is to determine the type and degree of hearing loss.

Both formal and informal strategies may be used to assess an individual's language. Many agencies and schools may designate specific tests for use in evaluation. These tests, however, may not provide a comprehensive sampling of the child's language skills, may not be well standardized, may have very few items in each area to be used for teaching applications, or may not reflect current theoretical models of language (Moeller, 1988). Any individual conducting an assessment of a learner with a hearing impairment must accomplish it with the communication system used by the learner, be it American Sign Language, manually coded English, or speech.

Ying (1990) argues that the ultimate purpose of evaluating the communication of learners with hearing impairments is to determine the learner's appropriate educational placement. For this reason, assessment must be made of the communicative demands placed on students in each potential placement. Individualizing, she argues, is necessary in selecting appropriate testing modifications, in interpreting the results obtained, and in designing programs.

The assessment of children with hearing impairments is a particular challenge. The pragmatic errors these children make bias assessment to such an extent that Ray (1989) urges that a multidisciplinary team approach should be in place during all assessment and evaluation activities with children with hearing impairments.

The Impact on Interactions in the Home and Classroom

Objective Three

To describe the impact of hearing impairment on interactions in the home and classroom.

Interactions in the Home

The learner's hearing impairment may have a significant impact on parent-child communication. Kenworthy (1986) found that the presence of a hearing impairment in a learner substantially alters the linguistic input the parent provides both at the interaction and the conversational level. Nienhuys, Horsborough, and Cross (1985) also found differences in the interactions of mothers and their preschool children with hearing impairments. Mothers of children with hearing impairments were found to address their children with verbalizations with lower cognitive complexity issues, and the mothers had more than twice the initiations as their children. All of the communication between parent and child, in one study, was embedded in activities, with very little purely social communication observed (Brown, Maxwell, & Browning, 1990).

Further research has shown that these findings regarding mother-child interactions may, in some cases, be related to the contexts in which they occur. Plapinger and Kretschmer (1991) reaffirm the didactic style of mother-child interaction as reported by other researchers in a clinic. In the home, however, mothers were very interactive and used dialogue more similar to that of mothers of hearing children. They suggest that without viewing interactions in a variety of contexts, parents of learners with hearing impairments may be viewed as nonfacilitative of their child's language development. Viewing interactions in a variety of contexts and over an extended period of time may demonstrate that parents use a wide range of interaction styles with their children.

Parents of learners who are hearing impaired feel that their counseling needs regarding their child's hearing loss are not met (Martin, George, O'Neal, & Daly, 1987). Parents report the need for greater communication and support from the audiologist. This need for communication was also reported by McNeil and Chabessol (1984), who found that both mothers and fathers felt ignored during the diagnostic period and wanted greater and deeper communication with the professionals involved.

Some mothers of children with hearing impairments were found to have elevated levels of anxiety, depression, and overall problem scores when compared with mothers of children with normal hearing (Prior, Glazner, Sanson, & Debelle, 1988).

In her study of the siblings of students with hearing impairment, Israelite (1985) found a mixed pattern of sibling reaction. The siblings were divided in their opinions as to the effects of the child with hearing impairments on relationships with their parents and in feelings of jealousy. The siblings who expressed positive feelings about their brother or sister with a hearing impairment tended to express positive opinions with regard to family relationships and social relationships. Conversely, siblings who were negative remained negative in all topics explored throughout the interview.

Interactions in the Classroom

Students spend at least 45 percent of the school day engaged in listening activities (Berg, 1987). Hearing is essential to classroom performance. The visual cues in the environment are not sufficient to allow learners with hearing impairments to compensate for their inability to hear. Though learners with hearing impairments may learn to speechread, many words look alike on the lips and cannot be discriminated without some kind of auditory information (Boothroyd, 1978).

The development of speechreading requires learners to follow the cues related to the message.

Though children with hearing impairments may recognize that hearing loss is the cause of their problems in communicating in the classroom, they tend to not want other children to know they are hearing impaired (Davis, 1988). To avoid recognition, they may not ask for clarification, request changes in the classroom setting such as a better seat, or discuss adjustments in requirements with the teacher. In some situations, social isolation occurs because other children may find the communication attempts made by the learner with a hearing impairment either difficult to understand or slightly embarrassing.

Mediating the Environment

There appears to be no consensus in the field as to where and how to educate individuals with hearing impairments. The Council on the Education of the Deaf (1976) has formally stated that no single method of instruction or communication can best meet the needs of all students with hearing impairments. In a national survey of 576 programs, King (1984) found that many educators combined different parts of various language instruction approaches rather than adhering closely to any single method. The type of symbol system used and the way the symbol systems were used varied greatly among the programs. The three most common methods of instruction and communication included (a) oral communication, (b) total communication, which involves simultaneous signing and oral communication, and (c) American Sign Language.

Northcott (1980b) states that the priority in the education of learners with hearing impairments is to ensure that all learners with usable hearing have the maximum opportunity to develop listening and oral skills, with the maximum

Objective Four

To describe ways to mediate the environment for learners with hearing impairments.

Figure 12.4

Cued speech (vowels).

From *Speaking the Language of Sign* by Jerome D. Schein.
Copyright © 1984 by Jerome D. Schein. Used by permission
of Doubleday, a division of Bantam Doubleday Dell
Publishing Group, Inc.

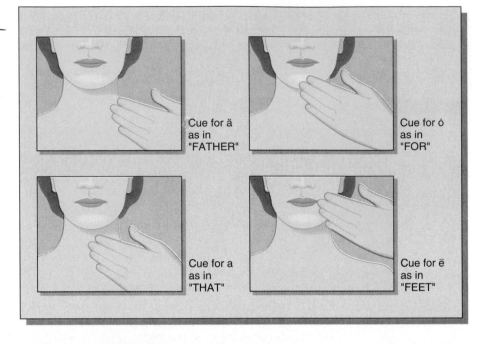

opportunity to speak for themselves, to be understood, and to participate actively in decisions regarding their own lives and goals. It is important to support students in the use of their residual hearing. Children typically begin wearing hearing aids as early as possible to increase an awareness of environmental sounds (Sanders, 1982) and to facilitate language development.

The development of **speechreading** requires learners to follow all the cues, both environmental and those produced by the speech movements of another related to the message. Not only do many sounds vary in their visibility when spoken, but speech movements vary from individual to individual, making speechreading an extremely complex skill.

Cued speech is sometimes used to augment speechreading, helping the student to differentiate sounds that appear similar on the speaker's face when spoken (Nicholls & Ling, 1982). **Cued speech** is the use of hand cues that, together with speechreading, permit the visual identification of sounds. Consonants are represented by eight hand configurations, vowels by four configurations, and diphthongs by gliding from beginning to ending vowels (fig. 12.4). Cued speech is not a language, but rather a teaching tool that transmits a visual form of spoken sound patterns. Accuracy rates in reception of greater than 95 percent can be achieved by adding cued speech to speechreading.

Most parents initially select oral communication programs for their children (Northcott, 1980a). Before the mid-1960s, oral programs were the most prevalent programs, and in many cases signing was prohibited (Moores & Maestas y Moores, 1981). During this time, total communication programs emerged, with the development of a system called "signed English," or manually coded English. In the signed English communication systems, the individual signs an equivalent for each word and diacritical marking. Though sometimes referred to as sign language, signed English is actually manually coded forms of English itself.

American Sign Language (ASL) is a unique language that is the most common native language of deaf adults (Wilbur, 1979). ASL is not signed English, nor is it derived from spoken language, nor is it the same as the British sign language system. ASL word order is dissimilar from that of spoken English, and frequently signs are used that indicate concepts or groups of words rather than individual words. Variations in ASL, fingerspelling, divergent signs, and

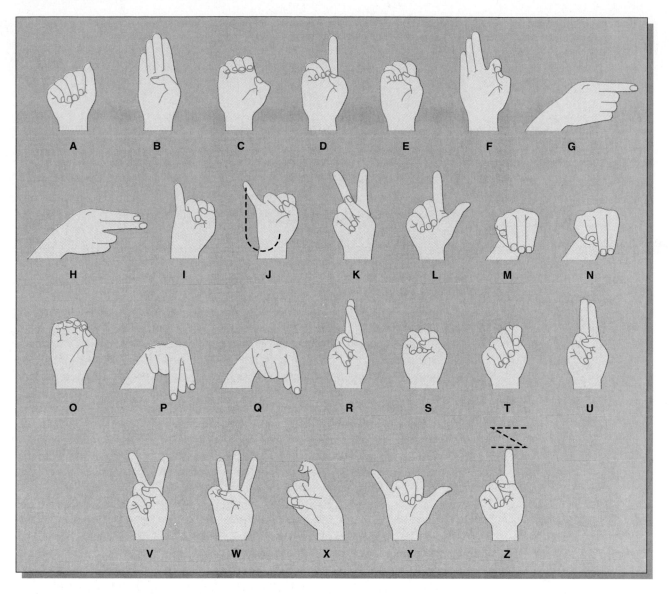

Figure 12.5

The American manual alphabet.

"homemade" signs are used when the appropriate ASL sign is unknown, difficult to form, or nonexistent (Lewis, 1986). The American manual alphabet, which allows individuals to "finger spell" words, is depicted in figure 12.5.

In the middle of the manual communication continuum is what is commonly called Pidgin Sign English (PSE), which uses ASL signs in an English word order. PSE may have more English characteristics in some settings and more ASL characteristics in others. Typically, more fingerspelling is used in PSE than in ASL (Kyle & Woll, 1988).

With the continuum of communication strategies for learners with hearing impairment ranging from spoken English to ASL, another issue emerges. Depending on the context, learners with hearing impairments may "code switch," or change from one form of communication to another and back again (Kluwin, 1981). Code switching is a complex and pervasive part of the daily communication of individuals with hearing impairments. Kluwin suggests that code switching by teachers can serve to help children understand more complex concepts by moving into whatever mode of communication is most readily understood.

Children may communicate
through signing.

In an effort to evaluate the various forms of communication, Crittenden, Ritterman, and Wilcox (1986) found that in isolated tasks, such as a standardized receptive vocabulary test, communication modes using manual communication, including manual communication without mouth movement, total communication with audio, and total communication without audio, yielded performances significantly superior to those of oral communication with or without audio.

The use of signed English, or manually coded English, in classrooms is based on the premise that by exposing learners who are deaf to English in various modalities, they will have more opportunities to become proficient in English. However, this premise has not been supported; the reading levels of children who are deaf are about the same today as they were thirty years ago, when oral education was most common (Stewart, 1993).

Nelson, Loncke, and Camarata (1993) used implications of language learning among deaf and hard-of-hearing children to generate recommendations regarding educational practice. They suggest that like children who can hear, children who are deaf learn from only a small number of the learning opportunities presented to them—those which they are most able to process. Sign language is the most processable form of language for many children who are deaf, but these children may not become fluent unless sign is used at communication rates equal to speech. However, most children who are deaf do not have regular conversations with fluent users of sign language. Learners who are deaf will not achieve high mastery of sign language unless they have concentrated opportunities for interacting with or observing fully fluent communicators. If they are unable to receive concentrated experiences in fluent conversational language, their progress in most educational achievement areas will also be slowed.

The prime directive for the education of learners who are deaf, Nelson and associates contend, is that the actual conversational exchanges the learner enters must be monitored for fluency. In addition, they believe that

- the learner's current conversational partners should be taught how to facilitate communication.
- new conversational partners should be identified who both understand how to facilitate communication and who have higher levels of sign language fluency and total communication fluency than most of the learner's current partners.

- videotapes of fluent communicators, including both adults and children, should be used to provide additional models for the learner.
- language teaching in all modes should be combined with a new emphasis on teaching higher order thinking skills.
- targets for mastery for deaf children should be set very high, in most areas equal to that of hearing children.

Nelson and associates contend that until recently educators assumed that the best use of sign language was support in learning speech, reading, and writing. Now, however, it is evident that for some learners, sign language is a full and fluent language central to their self-concept, thinking, relationships, life goals, and creativity. It is also evident that most learners who are deaf encounter low-to-moderate levels of fluency in simultaneous communication from their teachers. Nelson and associates urge filling the gaps through multiple, fluent communication partners.

This new approach in both signed and spoken language, which builds upon the linguistic skills of learners who are deaf, is referred to as **bilingual-bicultural (Bi-Bi) education.** Bi-Bi does not refer to a single instructional strategy, but encourages a number of communication strategies, including immersion in American Sign Language and viewing English as a second language. With American Sign Language assuming a more-prominent role in classroom instruction, it is hoped that children who are deaf will learn more about themselves and their disability (Stewart, 1993).

The courts, in attempts to define an appropriate public education, have also entered into decisions regarding the mode of communication to be used with learners who are hearing impaired (Katsiyannis, 1991). In one case in which parents desired placement in an oral program for their children, the hearing officer appointed under PL 94-142 procedures stated that the dominant view among scholars and practitioners in the profession was that total communication was an appropriate approach. This does not mean that the oral approach is inappropriate or comment on whether it might be more beneficial for a particular child, but that total communication is *one* appropriate approach (*In re* Jean Marie & Michelle Lyn H., 1979).

In an attempt to investigate the criteria used for placement of children with hearing impairments, Spear and Kretschmer (1987) found that among the team members involved—that is, administrators, psychologists, special education teachers, and audiologists—relatively different importance was given to different variables for placements (degree of impairment, learner and parent wishes, availability of services, etc.). A tendency towards placements with less inclusion occurred among all teams.

Ross (1982) contends that hearing loss and other demographic variables aside, the more fully included the average learner with hearing impairments, the better his or her academic achievements. Northcott (1980b) also suggests that less-restrictive settings have the advantages of increased learning of coping skills, increased motivation, fewer unusual behaviors stemming from social isolation, and an enhanced understanding on the part of parents regarding their child's abilities. However, she suggests that daily competition and social problems may be difficult and, at times, challenging for some learners with hearing impairments.

In terms of social adjustment, Aplin (1987) found that children with sensorineural hearing losses who attended ordinary schools had significantly better levels of social adjustment and behavior than did their peers with hearing impairments who attended special schools. Yet, with an emerging emphasis for the recognition of a Deaf culture, residential settings are gaining more attention.

guidelines for practice

What do you do when meeting a student and his or her interpreter for the first time?

Students who use interpreters should meet with the interpreter and teacher prior to the beginning of the school year to establish guidelines for their interactions. During that meeting, several questions should be asked.

- What communication system is used?
- Will the interpreter also voice for the student?
- What role will the interpreter assume with the student's peers?
- Is the interpreter available after class?
- How will the interpreter deal with personal information about the student?

During this initial meeting, student, interpreter, parents, and teachers should establish a consensus on roles and develop policies for situations such as absences.

Salend, S. J., & Longo, M. (1994). The roles of the educational interpreter in mainstreaming. *Teaching Exceptional Children, 26,* 22–27

There has been a trend in the last decade towards more naturalistic interventions with children with hearing impairments. Wood and Wood (1984) investigated the relationship between teacher control of conversations and children's initiative and fluency in communication. As teachers changed their conversational style to increase personal contributions, students responded with increased initiative and mean length of turn. When teachers refrained from questioning them, children had more opportunities for spontaneous contributions and were more willing to take advantage of them.

Fisher, Monen, Moore, and Twiss (1989) posited a reverse mainstreaming approach to increase the social integration of children with and without hearing impairments. Three interventions were in place with hearing students: signing class, novel play equipment, and a buddy system. These interventions significantly increased the interaction among the children with and without hearing impairments.

Interpreters

Interpreters may support learners with hearing impairments in the general education setting. **Interpreters** are hearing individuals who communicate spoken language, usually through one of the manual or signed systems, to the learner who is hearing impaired. Quigley and Paul (1984) contrast interpreting with translating, which is providing the verbatim signed equivalent of the speaker's oral communication.

Since 1964, the National Registry of Interpreters for the Deaf has maintained a list of certified interpreters (Levine, 1981). These interpreters may communicate what has been said in some form of sign language or finger spelling or may inaudibly repeat the message more slowly and with clearer enunciation so that speechreading is facilitated (Northcott, 1984). Interpreters may also convert the signs of the learner who is hearing impaired into English for hearing listeners.

The interpreter should be positioned so that the learner with hearing impairments can see both the speaker and the interpreter. In addition, teachers frequently provide educational interpreters with vocabulary lists, lesson outlines, study guides, and other materials to provide a context for them as they interpret. In the "Guidelines for Practice" box above there are some suggestions for the initial meeting of student, teacher, and interpreter.

FM broadcast hearing aids are commonly worn by children with hearing impairments.

Annual **Edition**

Article 23

Each learner has his or her own preferred mode of communication, so there are many variations in educational interpreting. An interpreter may translate spoken language into American Sign Language or manually coded English. An oral interpreter may facilitate the student's understanding by silently mouthing the verbal message or paraphrased equivalent.

Salend and Longo (1994) offer several suggestions for the effective use of interpreters. First, they suggest that the interpreter and the student should meet prior to the beginning of the year and develop clear guidelines regarding their interactions, including when and where to intervene. Ground rules should be developed, including that (a) the student will direct all classroom communication to the teacher and peers; (b) the interpreter will not redirect the student's attention during class; and (c) the interpreter will only assist the student with peers outside the classroom at the student's request. In order to provide a context for the interpreter's efforts, he or she should be provided with information about the curriculum, class routines, projects, and long-term assignments. Interpreters should be seated in glare-free, well-lit locations with a solid background. Interpreters usually sit slightly in front of the student without blocking his or her vision..

When an interpreter is being used, it is important to remember that there could be processing delays. Teachers and peers should talk to the student and not to the interpreter. The interpreter should be free to ask for clarification. Teachers should make it clear to the other students in the classroom that the interpreter is not available to assist with assignments and tests; the role is interpreter, not tutor (Salend & Longo, 1994).

Amplification and Other Technological Ways to Mediate the Environment

Amplification is not a cure for a hearing impairment; it simply increases the intensity, or loudness, of some sounds, augmenting the individual's residual hearing while the amplification device is in place. The selection and use of appropriate amplification may be the single most important tool available for the learner with hearing impairment (Ling, 1984). Maddell (1990b) indicates that the main purpose of amplification is to permit the learner to use her or his residual hearing to

Figure 12.6

Amplification devices.

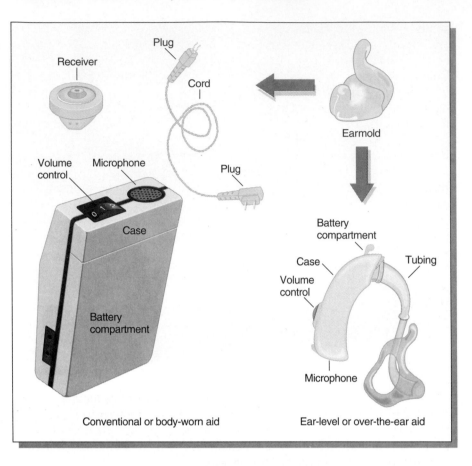

perceive speech. She contends that the characteristics of the learner and the communication environment are the basis of choice regarding the amplification system, but that nearly all children with hearing impairments benefit from classroom use of FM amplification in addition to personal amplification, because even the best classroom is not a good acoustic environment.

An **FM** (frequency modulated) **system** is a wireless amplification system in which speech is transmitted from a microphone worn by a teacher to an FM receiver worn by the student via FM radio signals (Maddell, 1990b). In the classroom, there are several advantages of FM systems over individual hearing aids.

1. Problems that emerge as a result of distance from the speaker, noise in the classroom, and poor classroom acoustics are managed.
2. The signal is more intense than that arriving directly at the child's ear through a hearing aid.
3. Significantly more auditory information is available.

Maddell believes that an FM system may benefit many learners with a hearing impairment.

In addition to FM systems, individual amplification systems, or hearing aids, are used by some learners with hearing impairments. Maddell (1990a) describes several types of individual amplification systems. These personal amplification systems are presented in figure 12.6. **Behind-the-ear (BTE) hearing aids** are the most common for children because they can be easily adjusted and are compatible with FM systems. **In-the-ear (ITE) hearing aids,** popular with adults, are not good choices for children because children grow rapidly and several expensive remakes may be necessary. Body-worn amplification, with the microphone on the chest, makes it possible to amplify sound with less interference, which is useful for children with severe and profound losses. Contralateral routing of offside sound (CROS) aids include a microphone behind both ears, making the wearer aware of sounds from either side, although the signals are routed to the better ear.

A recent technological option for some persons with profound hearing impairments is the cochlear implant. This implant requires a surgical procedure during which an internal electromagnetic coil, with an electrode that extends to the cochlea of the inner ear, is placed in the mastoid bone, behind the external ear. Another coil is fitted to the skull over the internal coil. A microphone worn on the clothing transmits sounds from the environment to the cochlear nerve through the implant. The implant does not enable the person to understand speech but the individual is able to distinguish some environmental sounds. In addition, with therapy the learner may learn to differentiate some speech sounds and thus facilitate speechreading and communication (Schein, 1984; Brill, MacNeil, & Newman, 1986).

The Impact on Participation in the School, Community, and Society

Learners with Hearing Impairments in School

In a review of research related to the language of learning of children with hearing impairments in classrooms, though much remains unknown, the ways in which students with hearing impairments cope with educational demands is very similar to that of their peers with learning disabilities (Weiss, 1986).

The strategies used by learners with hearing impairments are similar to those of their hearing peers. For example, Andrews and Mason (1991) found that when "reading between the lines," that is, understanding the multiple meanings of words and idioms, learners with hearing impairments described ways of understanding reading material from the context similar to those strategies used by their peers. However, learners with hearing impairments used some strategies, such as rereading and background knowledge, more frequently than students who could hear.

Learners with Hearing Impairments in the Community

There are several societal myths regarding hearing loss (Trychin, 1994). These include the following:

1) The "hearing aid myth"—People believe that hearing aids work like eyeglasses, eliminating the hearing problem. Rather, hearing aids are helpful in some situations and not helpful in others, particularly noisy environments. In addition, some individuals are unable to effectively use hearing aids.
2) The "lipreading myth"—There is a pervasive notion that all individuals with hearing impairments are good lip-readers. Speechreading is helpful, but there is variability both in personal proficiency and when speechreading can be effectively used.
3) The "mild hearing losses are no big deal" myth—The impact of hearing loss on the individual's life cannot be judged simply by its severity.

Objective Five

To describe the impact of hearing impairment on participation in larger social systems—the school, community, and society.

Annual **Edition**

Article 25

Making News

Sound Advice
Cochlear Implants Improve Learning For Deaf Children

By Roger Signor
Post-Dispatch Science-Medicine Editor

Kayla Hall, 7, knows that both of her sisters need all the help they can get. All three of the girls are profoundly deaf.

Kayla got a cochlear implant last year and is learning to hear and speak. Her 2½-year old twin sisters—Megan and Jenna—got implants in March.

At their home in south St. Louis last week, the twins were studying flash cards with words. Their mother, Kelly Hall, 34, was trying to get them to speak the words.

Finally, Jenna said, "Up!"

Kayla triumphantly raised her thumbs over her head.

"Kayla knows what it takes to teach a deaf child—it really perks the twins up," Kelly Hall said.

Cochlear implants are mechanical devices that let people who are severely deaf read lips better by deciphering speech patterns, vowels and consonants. Kayla is already hearing words without the benefit of lip-reading. Her lip-reading has improved, and she's added hundreds of words to her vocabulary.

Experts say her success shows the importance of speech therapy, special classes and help from parents and siblings. Without such help, cochlear implants aren't of much use to children, says Dr. James E. Benecke, a west St. Louis County otolaryngologist who did the implant surgery on the Hall sisters.

Only five years ago, cochlear implants for children were still experimental. But a study published in May by St. Louis researchers shows that profoundly deaf children with implants learn to talk and understand speech better and quicker than severely deaf youngsters who use hearing aids.

Hearing aids, which amplify sound, usually are sufficient for children with less than severe deafness. Cochlear implants give severely deaf children a chance to hear by turning sound waves into electrical impulses and sending them to the brain.

The implant study was done at the Central Institute for the Deaf, which provides Kayla with most of her therapy and training. Megan and Jenna attend nursery school there. All three girls, especially the twins, need extensive tutoring at home.

The Halls moved to St. Louis last summer from San Antonio, Texas. They wanted their daughters' implants done here so they could get the all-important follow-up training at the Central Institute.

The girls' father, Maj. Lee Hall, was unable to join his family full time. The Air Force assigned Hall to Fort Leavenworth, Kan., for advanced military training. Usually Lee Hall flies F-16 fighters. But in the last year he's put 35,000 miles on his Nissan, going back and forth between Kansas and St. Louis on weekends.

Meanwhile, his wife has done most of their daughters' home tutoring. She also tries to give their son, David, 4, all the attention he needs. He was born with normal hearing. The four children play together and are very close.

The girls' deafness is probably inherited, but no defective gene for their type of deafness has been identified.

About half of all deaf people are born deaf; the rest lose their hearing from infections or injuries. Of the 7,000 deaf residents of the St. Louis area, only 10 percent might be candidates for implants because of their profound deafness. Nationwide, about 1,000 implants are done annually in children and adults.

In a study that assessed the independent behavior of children with hearing impairments, those children, as well as children with normal hearing, demonstrated equivalent independent social behaviors in areas of motor development, personal living, and community living. Significant discrepancies were identified between expected skills and the students' abilities to independently deal with money and its value, and social and communication skills (Klansek-Kyllo & Rose, 1985).

In recent years, technology has facilitated the community functioning of learners with hearing impairments. Among these supports are closed-caption television, computer-assisted instruction, videodiscs, the telecommunication device for the deaf **(TDD),** and the teletypewriter **(TTY)** and printer.

Closed-caption television allows the learner with hearing impairments to see in subtitles the dialogue being presented verbally through the television's sound system. Closed-caption films for instruction and entertainment are available through many libraries in the United States. Converters that allow the television set to receive closed-caption programs are available and all television sets with a 13″ screen or larger will have a converter built into the set.

Both computer-assisted instruction and instructional videodiscs allow learners with hearing impairments to interact in a learning setting without auditory

The cost of an implant, including two years of follow-up therapy and care, ranges from $45,000 to $50,000. Now that the procedure is approved by the Food and Drug Administration, most insurance plans pay for the procedure.

Shortly after moving to St. Louis, the outgoing Kayla had no trouble befriending children with normal hearing. But one afternoon she could not make friends understand that she wanted to play hide-and-seek.

Until then, it really hadn't fully hit her that she was different. She ran home, tears on her face.

"I don't want to be deaf—I want to go to heaven to make my ears work!" she told her mother.

Those words gave Kelly Hall heartache—and made her determined to succeed.

"I never want anyone to think that implants are a miracle, or a quick fix," she said in an interview at her home last week. "You just keep plugging away."

She points out objects and asks the girls many simple questions about the objects. "Then, just maybe, they'll try to name the object," she said.

The effort has paid off, she said. After a few months of classes at the Central

Institute for the Deaf, Kayla became a star pupil. Her teachers say she has a very sharp, inquisitive mind.

But Kelly Hall wasn't prepared for a surprise she got during a parent-teacher conference in November.

During a speech therapy class, a teacher concealed her lips so Kayla had to rely on her ability to hear and interpret what was said.

Small dolls and toy cars and furniture were scattered on top of a table. "The teacher told Kayla to pick up a little girl and place her under a car—and Kayla did just that," Kelly Hall said.

"I thought, for the first time, Kayla's *really* learning to hear and understand!" she said. "I was so happy that tears came to my eyes."

When the girls reach their early teens, they should be able to attend school with children who have normal hearing. They will understand virtually all that is said in class, and their classmates and teachers will understand them about 90 percent of the time, experts at the Central Institute say.

Next year, the Halls will move to Ogden, Utah. Lee Hall has been assigned to Hill Air Force Base to resume flying F-16s.

The family had hoped he'd be transferred to Scott Air Force Base.

Then the girls could have finished their post-implant schooling at the Central Institute.

"CID's one of the best schools for the deaf in the world," Lee Hall said. In five years, he'll retire from the Air Force and pursue a second career. Without the health insurance provided by the military, he said, the family would be financially strapped. The insurance has covered the $150,000 in costs for the girls' implants, testing, therapy and schooling.

The Halls are reluctant to take their daughters out of CID.

But Ogden's public school system is among a handful of school systems nationwide that teach speech and lip-reading to deaf children.

"We'll do everything we can to make it work," said Kelly Hall.

"Our family's been split up for a year. That's long enough." •

demands. The TDD system facilitates the sending, receiving, and printing of written messages by persons with hearing impairments through thousands of stations in the United States.

The use of the telephone communication remains a major obstacle for learners who are hearing impaired; even with the use of amplification, many hearing-aid users report difficulty understanding speech over the telephone (Rodriguez, Meyers, & Holmes, 1991). The TTY allows a person with a hearing impairment to communicate by telephone. Typed letters are converted to electric signals through a modem. The signal is transmitted through the telephone line and reconverted to a typed message by the receiver's telephone.

The Americans with Disabilities Act of 1990 (Public Law 101-336) mandated that communications companies providing telephone services to the general public must offer intrastate and interstate telephone relay services to individuals who use telecommunications devices for the deaf (TDDs), voice telephones, or similar devices twenty-four hours a day, seven days a week, at regular rates. This legislation had a significant impact on the ability of individuals with hearing impairments and speech impairments to communicate for social, family, and business purposes.

Closed-caption television allows the learner with hearing impairments to read the dialogue being presented verbally.

Learners with Hearing Impairments in Society

Luetke-Stahlman and Luckner (1991) describe "ethnic Deaf adults" as those who view themselves as members of the Deaf community. Capitalizing the word deaf signifies membership in the Deaf community. Padden and Humphries (1988) argue that the Deaf culture is not simply a support system among persons with a similar physical condition, but that it is a historically created and actively transmitted culture. It has its own humor, heroes, clubs, publications, fraternal organizations, churches, and theater groups. The primary identifying characteristic of the group, they argue, is its language, or manual communication. Persons who are members of the Deaf culture tend to associate with other members of the culture both in personal and business activities (Walker, 1986). In the bilingual-bicultural educational program philosophy, it is anticipated that greater awareness of Deaf culture will lead to greater self-esteem, which will translate into higher academic achievement (Stewart, 1993).

Summary

There are approximately eight million children with hearing impairments in the United States. Learners with hearing impairments are generally classified into two groups: hard of hearing and deaf. Learners who are deaf do not access the sound system of language, which has a significant impact on interaction and functioning in a hearing society. They also may have difficulties in the areas of articulation, changes in pitch, and voicing. Learners who are hard of hearing are less affected in these areas but do have voice problems. This group exhibits misarticulations, substitutions, and distortions of sound. Learners who are hard of hearing have difficulties with the sound system of language and, as a consequence, vocabulary. The learner who is deaf has great difficulty learning voiced language. In a social context, learners with hearing impairments may be less assertive and more fearful than are their peers with normal hearing.

The learner with hearing impairments has difficulty in social interaction and communication. In that approximately one-half of the typical learner's school day is devoted to listening activities, it is extremely difficult for the learner with a hearing impairment to understand all of the information being communicated in the environment. Considerable controversy exists as to how to mediate the environment for learners with hearing impairments, and the Council on the Education of the Deaf has formally stated that no single method of instruction or communication can best meet the needs of all students with hearing impairments. Programming must be individualized in response to the needs of the individual within the context in which the learner is functioning or will function.

Building Your Professional Vocabulary

Match each word or phrase to its meaning.

_____ American Sign Language

_____ cued speech

_____ Deaf culture

_____ FM system

_____ hard of hearing

_____ hearing impairment

_____ postlingual hearing impairment

_____ speechreading

_____ TDD

_____ tympanogram

a. a hearing loss occurring after language has developed
b. any decrease in hearing efficacy
c. able to successfully process verbal language with amplification
d. using American Sign Language and support from Deaf culture
e. the common language of Deaf adults

f. measures the mobility of the eardrum
g. wireless amplification system
h. telecommunication device
i. use of hand signals to clarify which sounds are produced
j. observing cues and speech movements for communication

Comprehension Check

Select the most appropriate response.

1. The term *Deaf* refers to
   a. individuals who use total communication and speechreading.
   b. members of a specific culture who use American Sign Language.
   c. individuals who cannot process linguistic information.
2. Sensorineural hearing impairments are
   a. related to profound hearing loss.
   b. related to middle-ear infections.
   c. related to damage to the auditory nerve or the inner ear.
3. Hearing levels are depicted on
   a. TTYs.
   b. tympanograms.
   c. audiograms.
4. Speech audiometry measures
   a. an individual's pure-tone thresholds of hearing.
   b. mobility of the eardrum.
   c. an individual's ability to understand speech.
5. The priority of education for learners with hearing impairments is
   a. providing them with skills to participate in Deaf culture.
   b. providing the maximum opportunity to speak for themselves and be understood.
   c. providing adequate skills in English.

6. American Sign Language
   a. is a signed form of English.
   b. decreases the ability to learn English.
   c. is a unique language.
7. Interpreters
   a. communicate what is said to the learner.
   b. provide instructional support to the learner.
   c. work with the teacher to ensure that the learner is completing the material presented in class.
8. Amplification
   a. works much as eyeglasses and eliminates hearing problems.
   b. is appropriate for most individuals with hearing impairments.
   c. simply increases the loudness of some sounds.
9. Cochlear implants
   a. cure deafness.
   b. enable the person to understand speech.
   c. enable the individual to distinguish some environmental sounds.
10. Loudness, or intensity of sound, is measured by
   a. decibels.
   b. Hertz.
   c. audiograms.

References

Andrews, J. F., & Mason, J. M. (1991). Strategy usage among deaf and hearing readers. *Exceptional Children, 57,* 536–545.

Aplin, D. Y. (1987). Social and emotional adjustment of hearing-impaired children in ordinary and special schools. *Educational Research, 29,* 56–64.

Berg, F. S. (1987). *Facilitating classroom listening: A handbook for teachers of normal and hard-of-hearing students.* Boston: College-Hill Press/Little, Brown.

Boothroyd, A. (1978). Speech perception and severe hearing loss. In M. Ross & T. G. Giolas (Eds.), *Auditory management of hearing-impaired children* (pp. 117–144). Baltimore, MD: University Park Press.

Brill, R. G., MacNeil, B., & Newman, L. R. (1986). Framework for appropriate programs for deaf children: Conference of Educational Administrators Serving the Deaf. *American Annals of the Deaf, 131,* (2), 65–76.

Brown, S. H., Maxwell, M., & Browning, L. D. (1990). Relations in public: Hearing parents and hearing impaired children. *Journal of Childhood Communication Disorders, 13,* (1), 43–61.

Cates, J. A. (1991). Comparison of human figure drawings by hearing and hearing impaired children. *The Volta Review, 93,* 31–39.

Council on the Education of the Deaf. (1976). *Resolution on individualized educational programming for the hearing impaired.* Washington, DC: CED.

Crittenden, J. B., Ritterman, S I., & Wilcox, E. W. (1986). Communication mode as a factor in the performance of hearing-impaired children on a standardized receptive vocabulary test. *American Annals of the Deaf, 131,* 356–360.

Davis, J. (1988). Management of the school age child: A psychosocial perspective. In F. H. Bess (Ed.), *Hearing Impairment in Children* (pp. 401–416). Parkton, MD: York Press.

Duchan, J. (1988). Assessing communication of hearing-impaired children: Influences from pragmatics. *Journal of Rehabilitative Audiology* (Monograph Supplement), *21,* 19–40.

Federal Register. (1977). 42 (163), 42478.

Fisher, A., Monen, J., Moore, D. W., & Twiss, D. (1989). Increasing the social integration of hearing-impaired children in a mainstream school setting. *New Zealand Journal of Educational Studies, 24,* 189–204.

Garrison, W. M., & Tesch, S. (1978). Self-concept and deafness: A review of the research literature. *The Volta Review, 80,* 457–466.

Henwood, P. G., & Pope-Davis, D. B. (1994). Disability as cultural diversity: Counseling the hearing impaired. *Counseling Psychologist, 22,* 489–503.

In re Jean Marie and Michelle Lyn H., (1979). *EHLR, 401,* 330.

Israelite, N. K. (1985). Sibling reaction to a hearing impaired child in the family. *Journal of Rehabilitation of the Deaf, 18,* 1–5.

Katsiyannis, A. (1991). Communication methods for hearing-impaired students: The role of the judiciary. *The Volta Review, 93,* 97–101.

Kenworthy, O. T. (1986). Caregiver-child interaction and language acquisition of hearing-impaired children. *Topics in Language Disorders, 6,* (3), 1–11.

King, C. (1984). National survey of language methods used with hearing impaired students in the United States. *American Annals of the Deaf, 129,* 311–316.

King, N., Mulhall, J., & Gullone, E. (1989). Fears in hearing impaired and normally hearing children and adolescents. *Behavior Research and Therapy, 27,* (5), 577–580.

Klansek-Kyllo, V., & Rose, S. (1985). Using the scale of independent behavior with hearing-impaired students. *American Annals of the Deaf, 130,* 533–537.

Kluwin, T. (1981). The grammaticality of manual representations of English in classroom settings. *American Annals of the Deaf, 127,* 417–421.

Koelle, H. W., & Convey, J. J. (1982). The prediction of the achievement of deaf adolescents from self-concept and locus of control measures. *American Annals of the Deaf, 127,* 769–778.

Kretschmer, R. R., & Kretschmer, L. W. (1978). *Language development and intervention with the hearing impaired.* Baltimore, MD: University Park Press.

Kretschmer, R. R., & Kretschmer, L. W. (1988). Communication competence and assessment. *Journal of Rehabilitatitve Audiology* (Monograph Supplement), *21*, 5–17.

Kyle, J. G., & Woll, B. (1988). *Sign language: The study of deaf people and their language.* New York: Cambridge.

Levine, E. (1981). *The ecology of deafness.* New York: Columbia University Press.

Lewis, M. A. (1986). South Carolina develops reference manual of preferred instructional signs. *Counterpoint, 6* (1), 16.

Ling, D. (1984). *Early intervention for hearing impaired children: Oral options.* San Diego: College Hill Press.

Luetke-Stahlman, B., & Luckner, J. (1991). *Effectively educating students with hearing impairments.* New York: Longman.

Macklin, G. F., & Matson, J. L. (1985). A comparison of social behaviors among nonhandicapped and hearing impaired children. *Behavioral Disorders, 11* (1), 60–65.

Maddell, J. R. (1990a). Audiological evaluation of the mainstreamed hearing-impaired child. In M. Ross (Ed.), *Hearing-impaired children in the classroom* (pp. 27–44). Parkton, MD: York Press.

Maddell, J. R. (1990b). Managing classroom amplification. In M. Ross (Ed.), *Hearing-impaired children in the classroom* (pp. 95–118). Parkton, MD: York Press.

Martin, F. N., George, K. A., O'Neal, J., & Daly, J. A. (1987). Audiologists' and parents' attitudes regarding counseling of families of hearing-impaired children. *ASHA Reports Series, 29* (2), 27–33.

Maxon, A. B., Brackett, D., & van der Berg, S. A. (1991). Self perception of socialization. The effects of hearing status, age, and gender. *The Volta Review, 93*, 7–17.

McNeil, M., & Chabessol, D. J. (1984). Paternal involvement in the programs of hearing-impaired children: An exploratory study. *Family Relations Journal of Applied Family and Child Studies, 33* (1), 119–125.

Merker, H. (1990). Who is handicapped? Employees or employers? *Shhh, 11* (4), 3–4.

Moeller, M. P. (1988). Combining formal and informal strategies for language assessment of hearing-impaired children. *Journal of Rehabilitative Audiology* (Monograph Supplement), *21*, 73–100.

Moores, D. G., & Maestas y Moores, J. (1981). Special adaptations necessitated by hearing impairments. In J. Kauffman & D. Hallahan (Eds.), *Handbook of special education.* Englewood Cliffs, NJ: Prentice Hall.

Musselman, C. R. (1990). The relationship between measures of hearing loss and speech intelligibility in young deaf children. *Journal of Childhood Communication Disorders, 13* (2), 193–205.

Nelson, K. E., Loncke, F., & Camarata, S. (1993). Implications of research on deaf and hearing children's language learning. In M. Marschark & M. D. Clark (Eds.). *Pyschological perspectives on deafness* (pp. 123–151). Hillsdale, NJ: Lawrence Erlbaum.

Nicholls, G. H., & Ling, D. (1982). Cued speech and the reception of spoken language. *Journal of Speech and Hearing Research, 25*, 262–269.

Nienhuys, T. G., Horsborough, K. M., & Cross, T. G. (1985). A dialogic analysis of interaction between mothers and their deaf or hearing preschoolers. *Applied Psycholinguistics, 5* (2), 131–139.

Northcott, W. (1980a). Freedom through speech: Every child's right. *The Volta Review, 83*, 162–181.

Northcott, W. (1980b). *Implications of mainstreaming for the education of hearing impaired children in the 1980s.* Washington, DC: Alexander Graham Bell Association for the Deaf.

Northcott, W. (1984). *Oral interpreting: Principles and practices.* Baltimore,.MD: University Park Press.

Oblowitz, N., Green, L., & Heyns, I. de V. (1991). A self-concept scale for the hearing-impaired. *The Volta Review, 93*, 19–29.

Padden, C., & Humphries, T. (1988). *Deaf in America: Voices from a culture.* Cambridge, MA: Harvard University Press.

Padden, C., & Ramsey, C. (1993). Deaf culture and literacy. *American Annals of the Deaf, 138*, 96–104.

Plapinger, D., & Kretschmer, R. (1991). The effect of context on the interactions between a normally-hearing mother and her hearing-impaired child. *The Volta Review, 93*, 75–85.

Prior, M. R., Glazner, J., Sanson, A., & Debelle, G. (1988). Research note: Temperament and behavioral adjustment to hearing impaired children. *Journal of Child Psychology and Psychiatry and Allied Disciplines, 29* (2), 209–216.

Quigley, S., & Paul, P. (1984). *Language and deafness.* San Diego, CA: College Hill Press.

Ray, S. (1989). Context and the psychoeducational assessment of hearing impaired children. *Topics in Language Disorders, 9* (4), 33–44.

Report of the Ad Hoc Committee to Define Deaf and Hard of Hearing. (1975). *American Annals of the Deaf, 120,* 509–512.

Rodriguez, G., Meyers, C., & Holmes, A. (1991). Hearing aid performance under acoustic and electromagnetic coupling conditions. *The Volta Review, 93,* 89–95.

Ross, M. (1982). *Hard of hearing children in the regular classroom.* Englewood Cliffs, NJ: Prentice Hall.

Ross, M., & Calvert, D. R. (1984). Semantics of deafness revisited: Total communication and the use and misuse of residual hearing. *Audiology, 9,* 127–145.

Salend, S. J., & Longo, M. (1994). The roles of educational interpreter in mainstreaming. *Teaching Exceptional Children, 26,* 22–28.

Sanders, D. A. (1982). *Aural rehabilitation* (2nd ed.). Englewood Cliffs, NJ: Prentice Hall.

Schein, J. D. (1984). Cochlear implants and the education of deaf children. *American Annals of the Deaf, 129,* 325–332.

Spear, B., & Kretschmer, R. E. (1987). The use of criteria in decision making regarding the placement of hearing impaired children. *Special Services in the Schools, 4* (1–2), 107–122.

Stewart, D. A. (1993). Bi-Bi to MCE? *American Annals of the Deaf, 138,* 331–337.

Trychin, S. (1994). Getting beyond hearing loss: A guide for families. *SHHH Journal, 15* (4), 7–10.

U.S. Department of Education. (1990). *Twelfth annual report to Congress on the implementation of the Education of the Handicapped Act.* Washington, DC: Author.

U.S. Department of Education. (1995). *Seventeenth annual report to Congress on the implementation of the Individuals with Disabilities Education Act.* Washington, DC: Author.

Walker, L. A. (1986). *A loss for words: The story of deafness in a family.* New York: Harper & Row.

Webster, A., Saunders, E., & Bamford, J. M. (1984). Fluctuating conductive hearing impairment. *AEP: Association of Educational Psychologists Journal, 6* (5), 6–19.

Weiss, A. L. (1986). Classroom discourse and the hearing impaired child. *Topics in Language Disorders, 6* (3), 60–70.

Wilbur, R. B. (1979). *American Sign Language and sign systems.* Baltimore, MD: University Park Press.

Wolk, S., & Schildroth, A. N. (1986). Deaf children and speech intelligibility: A national survey. In A. N. Schildroth & M. A. Karchmer (Eds.), *Deaf children in America* (pp. 139–159). San Diego, CA: College Hill Press.

Wood, H. A., & Wood, D. J. (1984). An experimental evaluation of the effects of five styles of teacher conversation on the language of hearing impaired children. *Journal of Child Psychology and Psychiatry and Allied Disciplines, 25* (1), 45–62.

Wray, D., Flexer, C., & Ireland, J. (1988). Mainstreaming hearing-impaired children: Typical questions posed by classroom teachers. *Hearsay* (Fall, 1988), 76–79.

Ying, E. (1990). Speech and language assessment: Communication evaluation. In M. Ross (Ed.), *Hearing-impaired children in the classroom* (pp. 45–60). Parkton, MD: York Press.

Learners Who Vary in Their Learning Styles and Rates

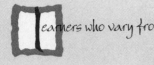earners who vary from peers' learning styles and rates are generally identified as a result of the mismatch between expectations and demands in classrooms and the cognitive abilities and styles they demonstrate. Carnine (1994) suggests that rather than learning disabilities, these learners are confronted with "curriculum disabilities," an emphasis on what students should learn rather than an emphasis on how students should be taught in a way that they succeed.

Sapona and Phillips (1993), in a description of ideal schools for learners who vary in their styles and rates, discuss a classroom environment in which there is a community of learners. In this community, each member is encouraged to be actively involved and engaged in the learning process. Variations in students' learning styles and developmental levels are not seen as "problems." Such variations are seen to provide opportunities for sharing diverse means of working through complex difficulties and exploring a variety of interest areas and perspectives. In recognition of the wide range of developmental levels demonstrated even by learners who are not identified as disabled, it is suggested that rather than making the learner fit the system, the system should fit the learner.

In this section, the various developmental contexts of learners identified as learning disabled and those with mild or moderate mental retardation are explored. Learners with both mild and severe disabilities are discussed. The section concludes with a discussion of learners who challenge the system in a unique way, with their unusual talents and abilities. Throughout these discussions, it is important to keep in mind the similarities of these learners to their peers rather than the variations.

References

Carnine, D. (1994). Introduction to the mini-series: Diverse learners and prevailing, emerging, and research based educational approaches and their tools. *School Psychology Review, 23,* 341–350.

Sapona, R. H., & Phillips, L. J. (1993). Classrooms as communities of learners: Sharing responsibility for learning. In A. M. Bauer (Ed.), *Children who challenge the system* (pp. 63–88). Norwood, NJ: Ablex.

Learners Identified as Learning Disabled

Objectives

After completing this chapter, you will be able to:

1. describe the personal characteristics of learners identified as learning disabled.
2. describe the identification and evaluation of learners identified as learning disabled.
3. describe the impact of learning disabilities on interactions in the home and classroom.
4. describe ways to mediate the environment for learners identified as learning disabled.
5. describe the impact of learning disabilities on participation in larger social systems—the community and society.

Key Words and Phrases

attention-deficit/hyperactivity disorder (ADHD)
cognitive behavior modification
curriculum-based assessment
d-amphetamine (Dexedrine)
holistic communication-based approaches

learning disabilities
methylphenidate (Ritalin)
social skills training
strategies training
tutoring

The purpose of education is to develop talents, not to reinforce weaknesses. As teachers, you should not waste precious instructional time in an attempt to identify the academic shortcomings of your students. Some problems that are burdensome in childhood may be sidestepped in adulthood. For example, the learning disabled child who does not do well in physical education classes may choose to forsake athletic pursuits as an adult. However, no individual may ignore his or her talents. Consequently you should not discount the abilities of your students (David Quinn, an adult identified as a child as learning disabled, describing the implications of his experiences in special education, 1984, p. 297).

Introduction

Working with learners identified as having learning disabilities represents the largest and fastest growing field in special education (Torgesen, 1991). During the 1993–1994 school year, learners identified as learning disabled accounted for 51.1 percent of the learners in special education. Between the 1992–1993 and 1993–1994 school years, the number of six- to twenty-one-year-old individuals identified as learning disabled increased 3.3 percent. Between the 1976–1977 and 1993–1994 school years, the number of learners identified as learning disabled increased over 207.63 percent (U.S. Department of Education, 1995). During the 1993–1994 school year, 2,444,020 learners were served as learning disabled; this number represents approximately 4.1 percent of all the learners between six and twenty-one years of age. Approximately 34.8 percent of these students were served in regular classes, approximately 43.9 percent were served in resource rooms, and 20.1 percent were served in separate classes within the public schools (U.S. Department of Education, 1995).

Although the field of learning disabilities has a relatively brief history, emerging in the early 1960s, learners who demonstrated "congenital word blindness" were identified as early as 1917 (Hinshelwood, 1917). Over the past three decades, a learning disability has been described in many ways, ranging from a "dysfunction of the brain" (Johnson & Mykelbust, 1967), to a way to explain the growing number of reading failures (Sleeter, 1984), to an issue related to the curriculum and desired outcomes of education (Carnine, 1994). Though questions emerged related to the validity of identifying large numbers of learners as learning disabled, a large number of learners were identified, and the preponderance of programs seems to demonstrate that the concept of learning disabilities has been socially accepted, politically protected, clinically assumed, and educationally endorsed.

Wood (1991) suggests that problems related to the identification of learners as learning disabled occur in part through a lack of consonance between definitions of learning disabilities and identification criteria. She contends that a total picture of the student's functioning is necessary, rather than simply identifying a discrepancy between achievement and abilities or school failures. Yet as Ysseldyke and Algozzine (1983) argue, discussions over what to call these students and who they are sidetracks educators from the question of how to serve this large group of children who need support.

Poplin (1988) argues strongly for a holistic or constructivist perception of learning disabilities, suggesting that the context must be considered in all interventions. She contends that applying a reductionist perspective can put limits on learners who are already challenged by an insensitive system. Considering the learner in the context of a community of learners in the area of reading, for example, would emphasize developing a strategic concept of reading rather than to decode the sound-symbol relationship. In mathematics, rather than completing a speed drill, instruction would emphasize applying computation to daily situations from the beginning of the instructional process.

Learners identified as learning disabled bring many challenges to the instructional setting, including variations in the way in which they learn to read, write, use language, and engage in mathematics. These challenges and variations, however, are highly individualized.

Personal Characteristics

In a clinical-psychological investigation of the characteristics of learners identified as having **learning disabilities,** Cohen (1986) argues that these learners are more heterogeneous than homogeneous. However, several common characteristics emerge: (a) problems in working and learning; (b) chronic, low-level depression

Objective One

To describe the personal characteristics of learners identified as learning disabled.

and relatively high, free-floating anxiety; and (c) unconscious concerns about self and others. In addition to higher anxiety, Rodriguez and Routh (1989) report greater peer-nominated depression among learners identified as learning disabled when compared to their peers.

Social and Behavioral Competence

McConaughy (1986) studied parent reports of social competence and behavior problems among learners identified as learning disabled. Among boys twelve to sixteen years of age, there were significantly more behavior problems among learners identified as learning disabled than among their nonidentified peers. Boys identified as having learning disabilities received significantly lower scores on all social competence scales, including participation in activities, social contact with organizations and friends, school performance, and total social competence. In a longitudinal study of a cohort of learners from their kindergarten year through fifth grade, Vaughn and Haager (1994) explored peer relations, social cognition, behavior problems, and social skills of learners identified as learning disabled and their unidentified peers. The students who were identified as learning disabled did not differ significantly from low-achieving nonidentified students in any of these areas. However, the learners identified as learning disabled were significantly different from average and high-achieving nonidentified students on social skills and behavior problems.

Using teacher reports, learners identified as learning disabled have been found to demonstrate more acting out, distractibility, and problems with peer relationships (Bender & Golden, 1988). These students may not "tune in" to learning situations (Reiff & Gerber, 1990). Teachers suggested that problems in physical competence may also contribute to the peer acceptance of learners identified as learning disabled (Margalit, Raviv, & Pahn-Steinmetz, 1988).

The self-concept of learners identified as learning disabled has been related to the setting in which they receive services (Beltempo & Achille, 1990). Learners identified as learning disabled in restrictive placements, such as the special classroom, demonstrated and retained the lowest self-concepts throughout the school year. Those in partial placement with inclusion demonstrated higher self-concepts at the beginning and end of the academic year. Girls were found to demonstrate poorer self-concepts than boys.

In a longitudinal three-year study, McKinney (1989) found that learners identified as learning disabled demonstrated a persistent pattern of classroom behavior that distinguished them from nonidentified peers. These problems included attention problems, conduct and classroom management problems, and withdrawn-dependent behavior. Identified learners with attention and conduct problems demonstrated poorer academic outcomes than those of their nonidentified peers. When compared with their classmates, learners identified as learning disabled were more likely to be off-task and to be interacting with teachers (McKinney & Speece, 1983).

As with all learners, generalizations related to social skills must be viewed with caution. Not all learners identified as learning disabled experience peer difficulties, and girls may be as much at risk as boys for peer problems (laGreca, 1987).

Language

In a study of 242 eight- to twelve-year-old children with learning disabilities, Gibbs and Cooper (1989) found that a speech, language, or hearing problem was exhibited by 96.2 percent of the students. Among the students exhibiting difficulties, language problems were found in 90.5 percent, articulation disorders in 23.5 percent, and voice disorders in 12 percent. However, only 6 percent of the students were receiving the services of a speech-language pathologist.

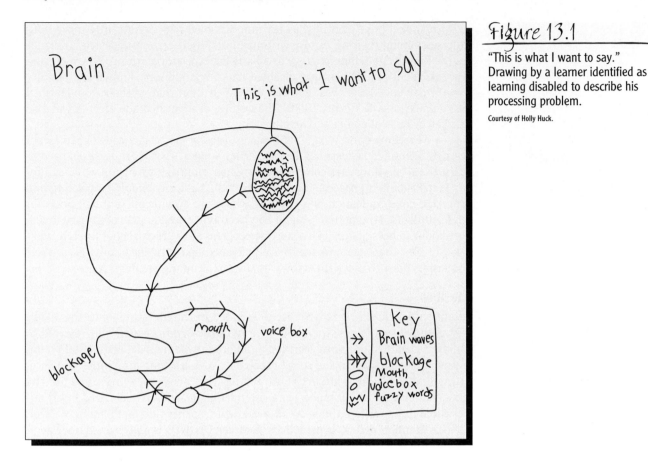

Figure 13.1
"This is what I want to say."
Drawing by a learner identified as learning disabled to describe his processing problem.
Courtesy of Holly Huck.

Terrell (1990) reports that in preschool, children are frequently labeled as "language disordered"; however, in school, these same children are labeled "learning disabled." He contends that though their language issues remain, the language disorders "go underground" because of the issue of reading and overriding concern for academic problems.

Language problems frequently associated with learning disabilities include (a) trouble with word meanings; (b) off-target responding; (c) inaccurate word selection; (d) difficulty with word finding; (e) neologisms (invented words); (f) topic closure; (g) use of immature grammatical structures; and (h) disorganization (Candler & Hildreth, 1990). Olson, Wong, and Marx (1983) found that in a situation in which students were taught a board game, learners identified as learning disabled demonstrated communication patterns that varied from their nonidentified peers. Learners identified as learning disabled used fewer adjectives and prepositions and asked fewer questions than their peers. In addition, learners identified as learning disabled used fewer organizational strategies and planned ahead less than normal-achieving learners during communication in a semistructured task. Learners identified as learning disabled performed more poorly than did their peers on tasks that involved the use of metaphoric language (Lee & Kamhi, 1990). In conversation, learners identified as learning disabled demonstrated a greater rate of communication breakdowns than that of their peers (MacLachlan & Chapman, 1988). Figure 13.1 shows one learner's expression of what it's like to communicate in ways different from one's peers.

In written language, those identified as learning disabled differ from their peers in syntax and number of grammatical errors (Johnson & Grant, 1989). Thomas, Englert, and Gregg (1987) found both quantitative and qualitative differences between learners identified as learning disabled and their peers in writing

Children with short attention spans find the classroom a challenging learning environment.

Annual **Edition**

Article *8*

performance. Those identified as learning disabled had significantly more difficulty sustaining their expository writing efforts; their errors suggested a reliance on the knowledge-telling strategy as a basis for expository writing. Although adolescents identified as learning disabled had a rudimentary knowledge of story form, their knowledge was less well developed than that of their nonidentified peers (Vallecorsa & Garris, 1990). The writing of identified adolescents was also marked by less coherence and less fluency.

Freedman and Wiig (1995) suggest several language needs of adolescent learners identified as learning disabled. They suggest that these learners need to learn to self-monitor and compensate for their language problems while assuming responsibility to become more self-directed. A priority should be given to oral language communication and reading, which are significant problem areas for these students. An emphasis should be placed on concepts and vocabulary fundamental for understanding and academic progress at the high school level. In addition, in that these learners may have plateaued and remained concrete in their thinking, efforts to move them towards abstract thinking are necessary.

Attention

Attention-deficit disorders have been described in the literature since the 1930s. Using current concepts, the early term *minimal brain dysfunction* referred to children identified as having learning disabilities, hyperactivity, distractibility, impulsivity, and emotional and social problems. Now, learning disabilities are a presumed neurological disorder affecting the processes involved in the understanding or use of spoken or written language and characterized by an imperfect ability to listen, think, speak, read, write, spell, or do mathematics (Silver, 1990). **Attention deficit/hyperactivity disorder (ADHD)** is a presumed neurological disorder that impacts the ability to control motor activity level, to determine which external stimuli are relevant or not relevant, and to reflect before acting (Shaywitz & Shaywitz, 1988).

The fourth edition of *Diagnostic and Statistical Manual of Mental Disorders* (American Psychiatric Association, 1994) describes three types of attention-deficit/hyperactivity disorder, including the following:

1. Attention-deficit/hyperactivity disorder, combined type, in which individuals demonstrate symptoms related to both inattention and hyperactivity/impulsivity.
2. Attention-deficit/hyperactivity disorder, predominantly inattentive type, in which the individual demonstrates symptoms related to inattention.
3. Attention-deficit/hyperactivity disorder, predominantly hyperactive-impulsive type, in which the individual demonstrates symptoms related to hyperactivity and impulsivity.

Symptoms must persist for at least six months to a degree inconsistent with developmental level for an individual to be identified with ADHD. In addition, adolescents and adults who have symptoms that no longer meet the full criteria may be identified as "in partial remission."

Studies of the relationship between learning disabilities and attention-deficit disorders demonstrate that between 15 percent and 20 percent of children and adolescents with learning disabilities also have ADHD (Silver, 1980; Halperin, Gittelman, Klein, & Rudel, 1984). Other researchers maintain, however, that the majority of learners identified as learning disabled demonstrate attention problems (Epstein, Bursuck, & Cullinan, 1985).

Using the current federal definition of learning disabilities, ADHD is an associated disorder but not a learning disability. As a consequence, children identified as having ADHD who are not learning disabled are not served in school programs for learners with learning disabilities (Silver, 1990). Yet, Eliason and Richman (1988) found that attention problems account for 30 percent of the behavior problems among these learners. If a student demonstrates ADHD to the extent that school performance suffers, the student may be identified as having a disability under Section 504 and must be provided accommodations even though he or she is not eligible for special education under Public Law 94-142 (U.S. Department of Education, 1992).

Though children were originally felt to outgrow ADHD, current evidence suggests that the impulsivity and concentration problems related to the disorder persist into adulthood. Wender (1987) indicates that the primary symptoms that persist include attention problems, impulsivity, mood swings, disorganization and inability to complete tasks, and low stress tolerance.

A "notice of inquiry" was included in Public Law 101-476 (The Individuals with Disabilities Education Act of 1990), which requires the secretary of education to solicit public comment regarding the appropriate components of an operational definition of attention-deficit disorder. This appears to be an initial step in clarifying the concerns of parents and professionals with regard to this disorder and its place within services for individuals with disabilities.

Achievement

Learning disabilities are typically recognized as a discrepancy between ability and achievement (Rhodes & Dudley-Marling, 1988). However, judgments with regard to underachievement are difficult, and they may not discriminate between those students with learning disabilities and those who are underachieving or demonstrating low achievement. Identification as learning disabled tends to be limited to learners performing significantly below grade level. Though some exceptionally bright students with learning disabilities may be functioning at grade level, the effort and energy they apply to this "typical" level of achievement may be great and stressful.

Results of studies indicate that school psychologists may have difficulty discriminating reliably between students in the lowest quartile of academic achievement and children identified as learning disabled (Epps, Ysseldyke, & McGue, 1984). Rhodes and Dudley-Marling (1988) suggest that the only characteristic that separates groups of learners with learning disabilities from learners who are underachieving is the degree of underachievement. McLeod (1983) goes as far as suggesting that students with learning disabilities are a subset of underachievers.

Identification and Evaluation

The federal definition of learners with learning disabilities, which appears in guidelines published in the Federal Register (1977), is as follows:

> ". . . children with learning disabilities" means those children who have a disorder in one or more of the basic psychological processes involved in understanding or in using language, spoken or written, which disorder may manifest itself in imperfect ability to listen, think, speak, read, write, spell, or to do mathematical calculations. Such disorders include such conditions as perceptual handicaps, brain injury, minimal brain dysfunction, dyslexia, and developmental aphasia. Such terms do not include children who have learning problems which are primarily the result of visual, hearing, or motor handicaps, of mental retardation, of emotional disturbance, or of environmental, cultural, or economic disadvantage. (p. 65083)

Many professionals consider this definition to be exclusionary; it defines what a learning disability is *not* rather than what it is.

Objective Two

To describe the identification and evaluation of learners identified as learning disabled.

According to the Federal Register, learners could be determined by a mutidisciplinary team to have a learning disability if

    a. the child does not achieve commensurate with his or her age and ability levels in one or more of the following areas when provided with learning experiences appropriate for the child's age and ability levels: oral expression, listening comprehension, written expression, basic reading skill, reading comprehension, mathematics calculation, or mathematics reasoning.

    b. the team finds that a child has a severe discrepancy between achievement and intellectual ability in one or more of the same areas listed in the preceding statement. (p. 65083)

Learners could not be identified as learning disabled if the discrepancy between ability and achievement is the result of a hearing, visual, or motor disability, mental retardation, emotional disturbance, or environmental, cultural, or economic disadvantage.

The Interagency Committee on Learning Disabilities (1987) presented a report to Congress that identified four basic concerns related to the federal definition:

1. Learning disabilities are not clearly described as a heterogeneous group of disorders.
2. The persistence of learning disabilities through adulthood is not recognized.
3. The definition does not clearly indicate that there are inherent alterations in the way information is processed.
4. The potential for other disabling or environmental conditions to co-occur with learning disabilities is not recognized.

Hammill (1990) argues that the National Joint Council on Learning Disabilities (NJCLD) definition represents the broadest current consensus on definition in the field. The NJCLD definition states that

> Learning disabilities is a general term that refers to a heterogeneous group of disorders manifested by significant difficulties in the acquisition and use of listening, speaking, reading, writing, reasoning, or mathematical abilities. These disorders are intrinsic to the individual, presumed to be due to central nervous system dysfunction, and may occur across the life span.
>
> Problems in self-regulatory behaviors, social perception, and social interaction may exist with learning disabilities but do not in themselves constitute a learning disability.
>
> Although learning disabilities may occur concomitantly with other handicapping conditions (for example, sensory impairment, mental retardation, serious emotional disturbance) or with extrinsic influences (such as cultural differences, insufficient or inappropriate instruction), they are not the result of those conditions or influences. (NJCLD Memorandum, 1987)

Though many states use a formula to describe the discrepancy between aptitude and achievement, Dangel and Ensminger (1988) found that about half of the learners assessed who did not demonstrate a discrepancy adequate for state eligibility were placed in special education classes on the basis of the judgment of the multidisciplinary team.

As a result of their study of the perception of successful adults with learning disabilities, Reiff, Gerber, and Ginsberg (1994) suggest that future attempts to arrive at a uniform definition of learning disabilities should include or at least consider input from adults with learning disabilities. Many of the adults interviewed believed that their problems with learning were caused by some processing dysfunction in the brain. The adults suggested that learning disabilities affect each individual uniquely. For some, problems were global in nature; for others, certain areas were limited compared to other areas. They emphasized that learning disabilities do not preclude achievement, but do necessitate alternative approaches to achieve vocational success.

Assessment

The assessment of learners identified as learning disabled remains as problematic as the definition itself. Gelzheiser (1987), for example, argues for an emphasis on support for all challenging students on the basis of classroom needs, rather than on numbers of students identified as learning disabled. Early identification of learning disabilities remains a serious challenge. Preschool screening instruments lack rigor and generally have not been validated (Satz & Fletcher, 1988).

Ysseldyke and associates (1983) summarized several issues related to learners identified as learning disabled. In five years of research, they could find no reliable psychometric differences between students labeled learning disabled and those who were perceived to be low achievers. In addition, identification as learning disabled depended on the criteria used, with different children being identified depending on the definition applied. If a child moved to a different school district, she or he may no longer be identified as learning disabled.

Algozzine (1991) argues that problems related to the identification of learners as learning disabled begin at the point of referral. The first problem, he suggests, is teachers' reasons for referral. For example, the new move towards "excellence" in education increases the likelihood that low-performing students will be referred as potentially disabled and appropriate for special education services. The second problem includes the high rate of referral, with a shortage of individuals well prepared and certified to conduct the necessary evaluations. The third problem is that over 90 percent of students referred are tested, and over 70 percent of those tested are then placed in special education programs.

Though current practice seems to involve searching for discrepancy between measured ability and performance, Algozzine (1991) proposes alternative means of assessment to guide the instruction of learners identified as learning disabled. He suggests **curriculum-based assessment.** This assessment approach includes direct observation and analysis of the learning environment, analysis of the processes used by students in approaching tasks, examination of students' products, and control and arrangement of tasks for the student. In his emphasis on curriculum-based instruction, Algozzine reminds us that "time spent looking for definitions, tests, or criteria is not time spent teaching students" (p. 53).

The Impact on Interactions in the Home and Classroom

Interactions in the Home

In an exploration of parents' perceptions of their children's adjustment problems, Konstantereas and Homatidis (1989) found that parents of learners identified as learning disabled reported externalizing behavior, such as fighting and acting out, as more stressful than internalizing behaviors, such as withdrawal and daydreaming. Boys were rated by both parents as significantly more problematic and stressful than girls. Mothers who were younger and fathers with a lower self-concept were found to report greater child adjustment problems. Although mothers did not differ from fathers in rating children's behavior, they reported greater stress in response to them.

Annual **Edition**

Article 7

Objective Three

To describe the impact of learning disabilities on interactions in the home and classroom.

Annual **Edition**

Article 9

The academic and occupational outcome of learners identified as learning disabled has been related to the socioeconomic status of the family. O'Connor and Spreen (1988) found that 28 percent of the variance among learners' outcomes was related to the fathers' socioeconomic status. This relationship held across groups of children with learning disabilities, whether hard and soft neurological or no neurological findings were reported.

In addition to socioeconomic status, Switzer (1990) reports four commonly observed factors in families with learners identified as having learning disabilities who were perceived to be high functioning: the families of these children accepted the learning problems, engaged with the child around achievement, and were consistent and explicit in their discipline. The child's role in the family was related to the child's success.

The teachers of learners identified as learning disabled perceived the parents of these children to have needs in excess of those they used or requested (Simpson, 1988). Parents' greatest reported need was that of information exchange. Participation in parent group sessions has been found to increase parents' acceptance of their child being identified as learning disabled and to increase their awareness of the potential impact of their behavior on the child (Omizo, Williams, & Omizo, 1986).

Annual **Edition**

Article *9*

Interactions in the Classroom

The classroom status of learners identified as learning disabled has often been judged to be low. However, as Wiener (1987) urges, peer status must not be viewed as a unidirectional relationship between peer status and social skills. Peer status of these learners must be seen as an outcome of reciprocal interactions between learners identified as learning disabled and their teachers and peers. The source of peer relationship problems must be viewed as problems of both partners (Forman, 1987), and learners identified as learning disabled cannot be assumed to earn low esteem because of their limited social strategies.

The peer acceptance of learners identified as learning disabled has not been related to achievement or intelligence; rather, ratings by peers reveal that most learners identified as learning disabled are accepted by their classmates and that acting out and withdrawn behaviors are related to peer rejection (Kistner & Gatlin, 1989). Wiener, Harris, and Shirer (1990), however, found that learners identified as having learning disabilities were less popular due to difficulties with prosocial skills rather than because they exhibited negative social behavior.

Zigmond, Kerr, and Schaeffer (1988), using observational data, depicted the student identified as learning disabled as a passive learner who comes to class ill-equipped for the lesson, goofs off during about 40 percent of class time, fails to follow teachers' procedural directions, avoids giving information, and seldom volunteers. Though this seems to focus on negative classroom behaviors, Zigmond, Kerr, and Schaeffer also found that in one-task behaviors, compliance rates to procedural requests, response rates to informational requests, asking questions, and making unsolicited, content-appropriate comments, learners identified as learning disabled did not significantly differ from their nonidentified peers.

Teachers, in rating the "teachability" of learners identified as learning disabled and of nonidentified peers, report less-positive ratings on identified students' school-appropriate behavior (Bender, 1986). In addition, they report a greater frequency of classroom problem behaviors (acting out, distractibility, and immaturity) among identified learners. Teachers also appear to view the problem behaviors of students identified as having learning disabilities as a major determinant of adaptive behavior in the classroom (Bender & Golden, 1989). Teachers rate learners identified as learning disabled as having significantly more difficulty than their peers in terms of frustration tolerance, adaptive assertiveness, and global adjustment (Toro, Weissberg, Guare, & Liebenstein, 1990).

guidelines for practice

Students with learning disabilities often have difficulty in reading comprehension. Dixon and Rossi (1995) describe a process, taught through teacher modeling, that can assist students with learning disabilities in reading and critical thinking. In teaching this strategy, the teacher follows these steps:

1. Help students ask and label the level of question being asked. In this phase, the teacher chooses a fairy tale and asks students to develop questions about it. Working with the teacher, the students then sort the questions into categories, such as fact, inference, or opinion. The teacher and students then label the questions.
2. Demonstrate the role of discussion leader. In this phase, the teacher reads a story and labels the comprehension questions as described in step 1. The teacher then models a discussion group, emphasizing rules related to listening and talking about responses, not the people giving them.
3. Students become leaders. After the teacher has served as a model for several weeks, student teams are assigned a story or short reading. The student teams then work together to generate and label questions. After the teams share their responses, the group members evaluate their teamwork.

Using this three-step strategy has been successful with students with learning disabilities and has been adapted for secondary students, students who are gifted, creative or talented, and other students with mild disabilities **I**

Source: Dixon, M. E., & Rossi, J. C. (1995). Directors of their own learning: A reading strategy for students with learning disabilities. *Teaching Exceptional Children, 27* (2), 10–14.

Mediating the Environment

The majority of learners identified as learning disabled are served in resource rooms (McNutt, 1986). Thurlow, Ysseldyke, Graden, and Algozzine (1983) found that more opportunities for differentiated instruction, particularly in reading, occurred in resource rooms, though no real differences were noted in the amount of time students were actively engaged in instruction when comparing resource rooms with general education classrooms. In a critical analysis of resource rooms, Wiederholt and Chamberlain (1989) report great variability in terms of what occurs in these settings.

As indicated earlier, most learners identified as learning disabled are educated to some extent within general education. In one study, the extent to which students remained in general education, however, was determined one-third of the time by the data generated by the battery of assessment instruments rather than by observational or behavioral data (Vance, Bahr, Hubert, & Ewer-Jones, 1988).

Cognitive behavior modification (also called metacognitive training or cognitive behavior management) has been used to alleviate social skill problems of learners identified as learning disabled. In cognitive behavior modification, learners are taught (a) to recognize and define the problem that exists, (b) to identify alternative courses of action and likely consequences, (c) to select an adequate problem solution, (d) to carry out the solution through instructions, modeling, reinforcement, peer feedback, and other ways, and (e) to evaluate the effectiveness of the solution attempted (Cullinan, Epstein, & Lloyd, 1991). Cognitive behavior

Objective Four

To describe ways to mediate the environment for learners identified as learning disabled.

Annual **Edition**

Article *7*

Table 13.1   **Strategy for Maintaining Attention in Class**

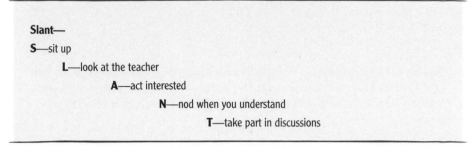

Slant—

S—sit up

  L—look at the teacher

    A—act interested

      N—nod when you understand

        T—take part in discussions

modification has been used successfully in content-area instruction as well as in improving social skills (Ross & Braden, 1991). The "Guidelines for Practice" box on page 309 details a process to assist students with learning disabilities in reading and critical thinking.

Most research applying cognitive strategies with learners identified as learning disabled has focused on self-monitoring (Rooney & Hallahan, 1985). This approach is useful in that it stresses self-initiative, engages the learner, and seems appropriate in managing distractibility and impulsivity (Hallahan & Kauffman, 1988).

Learning strategies are one form of cognitive behavior modification frequently used with learners identified as learning disabled. These approaches focus on helping the learner acquire content through **strategies training** (Mercer, 1988). Derry (1990) describes a learning strategy as the complete plan one formulates for accomplishing a learning goal, whereas a learning tactic is described as any individual processing technique one uses in service of the plan. Strategies build on mental processes, such as focusing attention, building schema (developing a mental outline or plan), comprehension monitoring, and idea elaboration.

Strategy instruction involves selecting a strategy, such as paraphrasing reading material, and teaching it directly to the learner to increase his or her comprehension. The strategy in itself is taught, but the application is restricted to the task for which it is applied. In this way, content and strategy are learned at the same time (Mercer, 1988). A sample strategy for maintaining attention in class is presented in table 13.1.

Larson and Gerber (1987) found that among adjudicated delinquent adolescents identified as learning disabled, those given metacognitive training showed significant improvements in quantity of negative behavior reports, staff ratings on rehabilitation achievement, and institutional living unit phase level promotions.

Metacognitive programming is an educational program structured to assist learners in planning, implementing, and evaluating approaches to learning and problem solving. Although both those identified as learning disabled and those not identified who received cognitive training significantly improved their behavior, on every variable the learners identified as learning disabled had a greater proportion of learners improve. Parallel improvement in metacognitive skills and significant correlations between social metacognitive scores and indicators of effective behavior supported the notion that social metacognition was the "mechanism" of change and that social metacognition mediated over social behavior in novel contexts without specific cuing from the environment.

Social skills training also uses cognitive behavior modification techniques. One of the most widely used social skills training techniques typically involves five steps: (1) instruction; (2) demonstration (self or using

Small group instruction allows for social skills to be introduced.

others); (3) imitation; (4) feedback; and (5) practice (Cartledge & Milburn, 1986). Role playing is frequently used to assist students in learning and practicing the technique.

School survival skills and classroom survival skills are often taught through structured learning experiences, much in the same way as social skills training is implemented. However, the focus of these group training sessions is on those skills needed to survive in school. McGinnis, Goldstein, Sprafkin, & Gershaw (1984) describe thirteen classroom survival skills, including listening, asking for help, saying "thank you," bringing materials to class, following instructions, completing assignments, contributing to discussions, offering to help adults, asking questions, ignoring distractions, making corrections, finding something to occupy time, and setting goals. Silverman, Zigmond, & Sansone (1981) describe three groups of school survival skills, including behavior control, teacher-pleasing behaviors, and study skills. Small-group instruction, role playing, and challenge activities are used to practice the skills. Four methods of instruction are utilized: presentation, practice, mastery in isolation, and mastery in context.

Tutoring

In a review of empirical studies of **tutoring,** or one-on-one instruction, involving learners identified as learning disabled, Scruggs and Richter (1988) found that these learners can and do learn in tutoring situations. However, there was little data to support social benefits to the tutors or tutees. Though tutoring supports learners in passing their classes, remaining in school, and addressing immediate problems, it generally serves as a short-term solution (Alley & Deshler, 1979). The use of tutoring also may increase the learner's dependence on the resource room. Special education teachers, particularly at the secondary level, may not be adequately trained in content areas to support learners in tutoring sessions.

Peer tutoring has also been explored for learners identified as learning disabled. Mathes and Fuchs (1994) report that peer-tutoring programs in which students with disabilities are paired with achieving peers and that allow students with disabilities to serve in the role of the tutor, at least some of the time, consistently produce improvement in the learners' skills.

Annual **Edition**

Article 5

Adaptations in the Inclusive Classroom

There are, essentially, two types of adaptations that occur in inclusive classrooms: (a) routine adaptations, in which the teacher establishes initial routines that facilitate ongoing adaptation or varied goals, and (b) specialized adaptation, in which teachers modify their planned instruction in light of specific student problems (Fuchs, Fuchs, Hamlett, Phillips, & Karns, 1995). Fuchs and associates report that when general educators were specifically prompted and supported to engage in specialized adaptation, they did so. Some teachers, they reported, were dedicated, modifying student programs repeatedly in a variety of ways to support student learning. Three of four adaptations teachers put in place were implemented either for the entire class or simultaneously for both poorly progressing students and learners identified as having learning disabilities. This suggests that all of the learners in an inclusive setting may profit from adaptations designed for learners identified as learning disabled.

Freedman and Wiig (1995) describe several classroom adaptations to support learners identified as learning disabled in inclusive settings. In regards to learners who have difficulty reading, they suggest giving the student the passage he or she will be asked to read ahead of time so there is time to practice. To support learners who have difficulty understanding, they suggest adapting the oral language, using both age-appropriate and simpler vocabulary. Elaboration on the context and asking students to paraphrase also supports comprehension. For learners who have difficulty with memory tasks, Freedman and Wiig suggest encouraging students to use visual images, asking the student to repeat what was said or to paraphrase it, and reducing the complexity of the task to aid memory (e.g., have someone else read so that the student can focus on remembering).

Medication

Medication is helpful to many children identified as demonstrating ADHD (Wender, 1987). Medication is prescribed by a physician with specific knowledge about children and youth with such behavioral issues and psychogenic medication, usually a psychiatrist. Wender suggests that parents and professionals may be hesitant to use medication because (a) it indicates a physical, and therefore perhaps persistent rather than developmental, problem; (b) treatment seems artificial, controlling rather than addressing the behavior; and (c) parents fear the child will become dependent on the medication both physically and psychologically.

The most commonly used medication for learners identified as having ADHD are stimulants, including **methylphenidate (Ritalin)** and **d-amphetamine (Dexedrine).** Approximately two-thirds of the children and youth identified as having ADHD respond to these medications by becoming calmer, less active, more attentive, and easier to manage. The duration of these medications is short-lived (about four hours for Ritalin, six hours for Dexedrine). Side effects include loss of appetite and sleeplessness. Medication must be carefully monitored by the physician, with teachers and parents documenting the learner's behaviors.

According to Wender (1987), when medication is effective, it produces a dramatically effective response. The effects of stimulant medication on children identified as having ADHD have been reported as (a) improved peer perceptions of the child (Henker & Buhrmester, 1989), (b) increased academic performance (Tannock, Schacher, & Carr, 1989), and (c) improved task performance (Milich & Lichet, 1989).

Though medical strategies for the treatment of ADHD have been criticized, efforts to increase the attention of individuals through alternative strategies have not been particularly successful. However, Gordon, Thomason, Cooper, and Ivers (1991) did find a response-cost program (that is, a loss of the reinforcer occurs as a result of inappropriate behavior) for increasing attention temporarily effective, but results dissipated when the program was not enforced.

Practicing the writing process may improve the quality of students' writing.

Holistic Communication-Based Approaches

Holistic communication-based approaches emerged in response to the failure of traditional, mechanics-driven direct teaching strategies to increase the writing skills of learners identified as learning disabled. Holistic approaches are those in which persons and processes are seen as a whole and treated in such a manner rather than the parts being treated separately. Vallecorsa, Ledford, and Parnell (1991) describe the use of the process approach to writing, as originally defined by Graves (1983), for learners identified as learning disabled. In this approach, writing is presented as an activity in which errors are to be expected and serve as ways to learn. Writing is seen as a process involving planning, multiple drafts, editing, and revising. Rules of grammar, punctuation, capitalization, and spelling are taught as needed within the context of composing. Students are given extensive opportunities to write so that they will have multiple means of practicing the writing process.

Teaching writing as a process appears to help learners identified as learning disabled improve the maturity of their writing and their vocabulary level (Bos, 1988). It has been demonstrated to have a positive impact on the length and overall quality of students' compositions (Roit & McKenzie, 1985).

In addition to compositions, dialogue journals have been used to increase the writing fluency of learners identified as learning disabled (Gaustad & Messenheimer-Young, 1991). In this process, the student writes in his or her journal and the teacher reads and responds. This written conversation reinforces the tenet that written work is in itself communication, rather than merely a mechanical skill.

Table 13.2 Procedures for Reciprocal Teaching

1. Teacher and learner begin by discussing why a task may be difficult, the importance of strategies, and the conditions for using strategies.
2. Teacher introduces, defines, and provides the rationale for the strategy.
3. Teacher and learner practice the strategy in family situations.
4. Teacher checks the learners' use of the strategy before the dialogue begins.
5. Learners apply the strategy to increasingly difficult aspects of the tasks and are supported by the teacher.
6. Teacher engages in dialogue with students and models the use of strategies by thinking out loud.
7. Learners comment on the model, clarify, make predictions, and answer questions.
8. Learner assumes responsibility for the dialogue from the teacher through guided practice.
9. Teacher monitors performance and provides additional instruction and modeling when necessary.

(Palincsar & Brown, 1984; 1986).

A well-documented holistic approach to reading instruction is presented by Palincsar and Brown (1986). This "reciprocal teaching" approach engages students in a dialogue between the teacher and students. Instruction begins at the point where it is required to support the learner in the next step needed to complete the task and faded so that learners are challenged to apply the strategy. The steps involved in using reciprocal teaching are summarized in table 13.2. Learners have been found to generalize this strategy over time and settings (Brown & Palincsar, 1987).

Annual **Edition**

Article 6

Technological Aids

Recent advances in technology may assist in the instruction of learners identified as learning disabled. Such technologies, in all probability, will have a greater impact on instruction in the future. Of greatest assistance to learners identified as learning disabled, at present, appears to be computer-assisted instruction. Kneedler (1984) suggests that computer-assisted instruction can be used for drill and practice and learning-style modification. Ellis and Sabornie (1986) find that educational software may take any of the following formats: (a) drill and practice, (b) tutorials, in which the computer serves as teacher, (c) games, to promote problem solving, (d) simulations, (e) problem solving, and (f) word processing. They report good results when computer-assisted instruction supplements rather than replaces teacher instruction.

The Impact on Participation in the Community and Society

Objective Five

To describe the impact of learning disabilities on participation in larger social systems—the community and society.

Learners identified as learning disabled appear to retain their learning patterns through adulthood (Kroll, 1984). These learning problems have a continued impact on their lives, demonstrated through lower employment rates and income than the general population, difficulties in locating and holding jobs, and remaining home far beyond the teenage years. The persistence and pervasiveness of learning disabilities throughout an individual's life and inappropriate adult diagnostic procedures are emerging as such essential issues that the National Joint Committee on Learning Disabilities has issued a position paper with a "call to action" in response to the problem (National Joint Committee on Learning Disabilities, 1987).

Vocational education prepares adults for the working world.

        In a survey of adults identified as learning disabled, the results describe individuals with ongoing specific problems in education, employment, and psychosocial functioning who aspire to learn more about themselves and their learning disabilities (Malcolm, Polatajko, & Simons, 1990). In another study, many of the characteristics of learning disabilities, including low motivation, distractibility, self-concept problems, emotional instability, and lack of organization, were found to persist through adulthood (Buchanan & Wolf, 1986). While many of the adults in this study described themselves as lacking motivation, they tended to be unusually persistent in efforts to achieve their goals.

Employment

Adults identified as learning disabled, though generally optimistic about future career success, voiced frustration regarding previous jobs and admitted employment-associated anxieties (Kokaska & Skolnik, 1986). In a large-scale national needs assessment, a comparison across all need areas indicated that service providers and consumers identified vocational needs involving securing an appropriate job and vocational rehabilitation services as the most critical need areas of adults identified as learning disabled, with secondary areas of concern including poor self-concept, lack of self-understanding, and lack of self-acceptance (Hoffman, Shelton, Minskoff, & Sautter, 1987). Michaels (1989) notes that employers may need to become more flexible in supervisory styles when working with these adults.

        Social competence is viewed as the most serious vocational adjustment of adults identified as learning disabled (Cartledge, 1987). Due to persistent vocational problems, Smith (1988) believes that educational interventions should be targeted on the demands of adulthood and adaptation to adult roles, that is, work. DeBettencourt, Zigmond, and Thornton (1989), however, found that in comparison with their same-age peers who also dropped out of secondary education, learners identified as learning disabled did not vary in how they fared in their employment. However, identified learners were more likely to drop out of school and demonstrated lower age-competency levels.

Adults identified as learning disabled, Weller, Watteyne, Herbert, and Crelly (1994) report, often attempt to ignore and hide their weaknesses. They found, however, that this strategy generally fails because it does not take the individual's strengths into account and assumes that learning difficulties are the responsibility of the individual. Weller and associates urge adults identified as learning disabled to empower themselves to set appropriate goals and engage in self-directed behavior. They contend that these adults should accept responsibility for (a) gaining equal opportunity under the Americans with Disabilities Act; (b) openly sharing information about their disability with those around them; (c) understanding how their own strengths, weaknesses, preferences, and requirements affect their adaptation to new settings; (d) identifying accommodations they require to succeed, and (e) learning how they can apply the skills they learn in multiple environments.

Post-Secondary Education

Involvement in extracurricular activities while in high school, the use of community resources, intelligence, and reading and mathematic grade equivalent scores were found to be important factors that differentiated learners identified as learning disabled who chose to participate in post-secondary education during the year after high school from those who did not (Miller, Snider, & Rzonca, 1990). Bursuck, Rose, Cowen, and Yahaya (1989) explored the nature of services available for learners identified as learning disabled who engaged in post-secondary education. Ninety percent of the responding members of the Association of Handicapped Student Service Programs institutions indicated that they provided taped textbooks, tape recordings of lectures, note takers, and modified exam procedures. Most of the institutions also had special services, including academic advisement, tutoring, counseling, advocacy, and progress monitoring. Seventy-seven percent had reading remediation, 82 percent offered written language remediation, 78 percent offered remedial math, and 86 percent offered remedial study skills. Few schools monitored whether or not their students identified as learning disabled were graduated.

Three factors have been associated with how services are provided to post-secondary learners identified as learning disabled (Nelson & Lignugaris-Kraft, 1989). First, differences in program emphasis and service delivery reflected differences in program objectives, from supporting students in classes to remediating basic skills. The provision of remedial services or support services often reflected differences in the expected entry-level skills of students. Second, the mission of the college influenced services, by providing opportunities ranging from preparation for high school equivalency to noncredit courses. Finally, the amount of funding allocated was associated with how services were delivered.

According to McGuire and Shaw (1987), the learner identified as learning disabled who chooses to pursue college work should identify the post-secondary program that best meets his or her needs. Three major components should be explored, including (a) the characteristics of the students, (b) the characteristics of the institution, and (c) the characteristics of the support program available for individuals identified as learning disabled. They state, however, that the proper gathering of information to make appropriate decisions takes time, and that both students and parents should be actively involved throughout high school in planning for the most appropriate educational program to prepare the student for post-secondary study.

Forty-nine adults identified as learning disabled who were interviewed by Greenbaum, Graham, and Scales (1995) reported that, despite their learning disabilities, most adjusted well to the demands and complexities of college. The participants involved took approximately 5.5 years to complete their college education. Several factors were related to success in college:

- Mild-to-moderate rather than severe learning disabilities
- Self-knowledge about the disabilities, acceptance, and self-awareness
- Determination and perseverance
- Support, guidance, and encouragement from significant others
- A strong relationship with an advisor or faculty member in the university support program for students with disabilities

Summary

Over the past three decades, learning disabilities have been conceived in many ways, ranging from a "dysfunction of the brain" to a category of disability derived to explain the growing number of reading failures, to a developmental lag in movement through the preoperational and concrete operational stages, to the formal operational stages of Piagetian development. In this chapter, questions related to the validity of identifying large numbers of learners as learning disabled were explored, as was the impact of learning disabilities in the school and home. The constructivist view was presented and discussed as consistent with systems theory.

Learners identified as learning disabled are the largest and fastest growing group of learners with disabilities. However, these learners are far more heterogeneous than homogeneous. These learners have common problems in (a) working and learning; (b) chronic, low-level depression and relatively high, free-floating anxiety; and (c) unconscious concerns about self and others. In terms of social and behavioral abilities, learners identified as learning disabled may have difficulty in peer relationships. These learners often have a speech, language, or hearing problem, manifested both in oral and written communication.

The definition of learning disabilities has long been controversial. Early identification of learning disabilities remains a serious challenge. The use of standardized measures is giving way to curriculum-based assessment and an emphasis on what the learner knows.

The progress demonstrated by learners identified as learning disabled has been related to socioeconomic status. In the classroom, peer status is usually poor. Teachers' acceptance of the learners is related to their perception of how difficult the learner is to teach.

Most learners identified as learning disabled are served in resource rooms. Cognitive behavior management, tutoring, and medication are all used to mediate the environment. Two emerging trends in intervention include holistic communication-based approaches and technological aids.

Learners identified as learning disabled retain their learning patterns through adulthood. Difficulties in employment may result from their challenges in the area of social competence.

Building Your Professional Vocabulary

Match each word or phrase to its meaning.

_____ ADD

_____ cognitive behavior modification

_____ curriculum-based assessment

_____ social skills training

_____ strategies training

_____ tutoring

a. one-on-one instruction
b. programs designed to increase social competence
c. metacognitive training
d. a presumed neurological disorder involving attention, impulsivity, and distraction
e. a learning tactic for accomplishing a specific task
f. grounded in curriculum and materials in which the learner receives instruction

Comprehension Check

Select the most appropriate response.

1. The number of learners described as learning disabled
   a. has steadily increased.
   b. has steadily decreased.
   c. has remained stable.
2. Learners identified as learning disabled often
   a. achieve at the same level as their peers.
   b. are identified as mentally retarded.
   c. have speech, language, or hearing problems.
3. Attention-deficit/hyperactivity disorder is presumed to be
   a. faulty learning in the area of attention and impulse control.
   b. a neurological disorder.
   c. a behavioral disorder.
4. Learners identified as having attention-deficit/hyperactivity disorder
   a. usually outgrow the disability during adolescence.
   b. have problems with impulsivity and concentration into adulthood.
   c. usually outgrow the need for medication during adolescence.
5. The identification of learning disabilities
   a. is problematic.
   b. is based on standardized assessment.
   c. is based on neurological assessment.
6. Cognitive behavior modification
   a. involves the use of tokens for reinforcement.
   b. involves learning a problem-solving strategy.
   c. involves the use of medication.
7. Ritalin is
   a. a stimulant with an approximately four-hour effect.
   b. a depressant with a short-term effect.
   c. a stimulant that builds up to a specific blood level.
8. Holistic communication-based approaches
   a. provide direct instruction in specific skills.
   b. emphasize a prescriptive teaching approach.
   c. emphasize writing as a process rather than separate skills.
9. The use of computer-assisted instruction
   a. supplements rather than replaces teacher instruction.
   b. provides appropriate intervention for learners identified as learning disabled.
   c. successfully remediates reading difficulties.
10. Adults with learning disabilities
    a. rarely complete post-secondary education programs.
    b. complete post-secondary education programs in a longer period of time.
    c. find vocational rather than academic settings more appropriate for their needs.

References

Algozzine, B. (1991). Decision-making and curriculum-based assessment. In B. Y. L. Wong (Ed.), *Learning about learning disabilities* (pp. 40–55). San Diego, CA: Academic Press.

Alley, G., & Deshler, D. (1979). *Teaching the learning disabled adolescent: Strategies and methods.* Denver, CO: Love.

American Psychiatric Association. (1990). *Diagnostic and statistical manual of mental disorders* (4th ed.). Washington, DC: Author.

Beltempo, J., & Achille, P. A. (1990). The effect of special class placement on the self-concept of children with learning disabilities. *Child Study Journal, 20* (2), 81–103.

Bender, W. N. (1986). Teachability and behavior of learning disabled children. *Psychological Reports, 59* (2, Pt. 1), 471–476.

Bender, W. N., & Golden, L. B. (1988). Adaptive behavior of learning disabled and non-learning disabled children. *Learning Disability Quarterly, 11* (1), 55–61.

Bender, W. N., & Golden, L. B. (1989). Prediction of adaptive behavior of learning disabled students in self-contained and resource classes. *Learning Disabilities Research, 5,* 45–50.

Bos, C. (1988). Process-oriented writing: Instructional implications for mildly handicapped students. *Exceptional Children, 54,* 523–527.

Brown, A. L., & Palincsar, A. S. (1987). Reciprocal teaching of comprehension strategies. In J. Borkowski & J. D. Day (Eds.), *Intelligence and cognition in special children: Comparative studies of giftedness, mental retardation, and learning disabilities.* New York: Ablex.

Buchanan, M., & Wolf, J. S. (1986). A comprehensive study of learning disabled adults. *Journal of Learning Disabilities, 19* (1), 34–38.

Bursuck, W. D., Rose, E., Cowen, S., & Yahaya, M. A. (1989). Nationwide survey of postsecondary education services for students with learning disabilities. *Exceptional Children, 56,* 236–245.

Candler, A. C., & Hildreth, B. L. (1990). Characteristics of language disorders in learning disabled students. *Academic Therapy, 25,* 333–343.

Carnine, D. (1994). Introduction to the mini-series: Diverse learners and prevailing, emerging, and research-based educational approaches and their tools. *School Psychology Review, 23,* 341–350.

Cartledge, G. (1987). Social skills, learning disabilities, and occupational success. *Journal of Reading, Writing, and Learning Disabilities, 3* (3), 223–239.

Cartledge, G., & Milburn, J. F. (1986). *Teaching social skills to children* (2nd ed). New York: Pergamon.

Cohen, J. (1986). Learning disabilities and psychological development in childhood and adolescence. *Annals of Dyslexia, 36,* 287–300.

Cullinan, D., Epstein, M. H., & Lloyd, J. W. (1991). Evaluation of conceptual models of behavioral disorders. *Behavioral Disorders, 16* (2), 148–157.

Dangel, H. L., & Ensminger, E. E. (1988). The use of a discrepancy formula with LD students. *Learning Disabilities Focus, 4,* 24–31.

DeBettencourt, L. U., Zigmond, N., & Thornton, H. (1989). Follow-up of postsecondary-age rural learning disabled graduates and dropouts. *Exceptional Children, 56,* 40–49.

Derry, S. J. (1990). Remediating academic difficulties through strategy training: The acquisition of useful knowledge. *Remedial and Special Education, 11,* (6), 19–31.

Dixon, M. E., & Rossi, J. C. (1995). Directors of their own learning: A reading strategy for students with learning disabilities. *Teaching Exceptional Children, 27,* (2), 10–14.

Eliason, M. J., & Richman, L. C. (1988). Behavior and attention in LD children. *Learning Disability Quarterly, 11,* 360–369.

Ellis, E. S., & Sabornie, E. J. (1988). Effective instruction with microcomputers: Promises, practices and preliminary findings. In E. L. Meyer, G. A. Vergason, & R. J. Whelan (Eds.). *Effective instructional strategies for exceptional children* (pp. 355–379). Denver: Love.

Epps, D., Ysseldyke, J. E., & McGue, M. (1984). "I know one when I see one"—Differentiating LD and non-LD students. *Learning Disability Quarterly, 7,* 89–101.

Epstein, M. H., Bursuck, W., & Cullinan, D. (1985). Patterns of behavior problems among the learning disabled: Boys aged 12–18, girls aged 6–11, and girls aged 12–18. *Learning Disability Quarterly, 9,* 43–54.

Federal Register. (1977). 42, 65082–65085.

Forman, E. A. (1987). Peer relationships of learning disabled children: A contextualist perspective. *Learning Disabilities Research, 2* (2), 80–90.

Freedman, E., & Wiig, E. H. (1995). Classroom management and instruction for adolescents with language disabilities. *Seminars in Speech and Language, 16* (1), 46–60.

Fuchs, L. S., Fuchs, D., Hamlett, C. L., Phillips, N. B., & Karns, K. (1995). General educator's specialized adaptation for students with learning disabilities. *Exceptional Children, 61,* 440–459.

Gaustad, M. G., & Messenheimer-Young, T. (1991). Dialogue journals for students with learning disabilities. *Teaching Exceptional Children, 23* (Spring), 28–30.

Gelzheiser, L. M. (1987). Reducing the number of students identified as learning disabled: A question of practice, philosophy, or policy? *Exceptional Children, 54,* 145–150.

Gibbs, D. P., & Cooper, E. B. (1989). Prevalence of communication disorders in students with learning disabilities. *Journal of Learning Disabilities, 22* (1), 60–63.

Gordon, M., Thomason, D., Cooper, S., & Ivers, C. L. (1991). Nonmedical treatment of ADHD/hyperactivity. *Journal of School Psychology, 29,* 151–159.

Graves, D. (1983). *Writing: Teachers and children at work.* Exeter, NH: Heineman.

Greenbaum, B., Graham, S., & Scales, W. (1995). Adults with learning disabilities: Educational and social experiences during college. *Exceptional Children, 61,* 460–471.

Hallahan, D. P., & Kauffman, J, M. (1988). *Exceptional children: Introduction to special education* (4th ed.). Englewood Cliffs, NJ: Prentice Hall.

Halperin, J. M., Gittelman, R., Klein, D. F., & Rudel, R. G. (1984). Reading disabled hyperactive children: A distinct subgroup of attention deficit disorder with hyperactivity. *Journal of Abnormal Child Psychology, 12,* 1–14.

Hammill, D. D. (1990). On defining learning disabilities: An emerging consensus. *Journal of Learning Disabilities, 23,* 74–84.

Henker, B., & Buhrmester, D. (1989). Does stimulant medication improve the peer status of hyperactive children? *Journal of Consulting and Clinical Psychology, 57,* 545.

Hinshelwood, J. (1917). *Congenital word blindness.* London: Lewis.

Hoffman, F., Shelton, K. L., Minskoff, E. H., & Sautter, S. W. (1987). Needs of learning disabled adults. *Journal of Learning Disabilities, 20* (1), 43–52.

Interagency Committee on Learning Disabilities. (1987). Learning disabilities: A report to the U.S. Congress. Bethesda, MD: National Institutes of Health.

Johnson, D. J., & Grant, J. O. (1989). Written narratives of normal and learning disabled children. *Annals of Dyslexia, 39,* 140–158.

Johnson, D., & Myklebust, H. R. (1967). *Learning disabilities: Educational principles and practices.* New York: Grune and Stratton.

Kistner, J. A., & Gatlin, D. (1989). Correlates of peer rejection among children with learning disabilities. *Learning Disability Quarterly, 13,* 133–140.

Kneedler, R. D. (1984). *Special education for today.* Englewood Cliffs, NJ: Prentice Hall.

Kokaska, C. J., & Skolnik, J. (1986). Employment suggestions from LD adults. *Academic Therapy, 21,* (5), 573–577.

Konstantereas, M. M., & Homatidis, S. (1989). Parental perception of learning-disabled children's adjustment problems and related stress. *Journal of Abnormal Child Psychology, 17,* 177–186.

Kroll, L. G. (1984). LD's: What happens when they are no longer children? *Academic Therapy, 20* (2), 133–148.

laGreca, A. M. (1987). Children with learning disabilities: Interpersonal skills and social competence. *Journal of Reading, Writing, and Learning Disabilities International, 3* (2), 167–185.

Larson, K. A., & Gerber, M. M. (1987). Effects of social metacognitive training for enhancing overt behavior in learning disabled and low achieving delinquents. *Exceptional Children, 54,* 201–211.

Lee, R. F., & Kamhi, A. G. (1990). Metaphoric competence in children with learning disabilities. *Journal of Learning Disabilities, 23,* 476–482.

MacLachlan, B. G., & Chapman, R. S. (1988). Communication breakdowns in normal and language learning disabled children's conversation and narration. *Journal of Speech and Hearing Disorders, 53* (1), 2–7.

Malcolm, C. B., Polatajko, H. J., & Simons, J. (1990). A descriptive study of adults with suspected learning disabilities. *Journal of Learning Disabilities, 23* (8), 518–520.

Margalit, M., Raviv, A., & Pahn-Steinmetz, N. (1988). Social competence of learning disabled children: Cognitive and emotional aspects. *Exceptional Children, 35* (3), 179–189.

Mathes, P. G., & Fuchs, L. S. (1994). The efficacy of peer tutoring in reading for students with mild disabilities: A best-evidence synthesis. *School Psychology Review, 23,* 59–80.

McConaughy, S. H. (1986). Social competence and behavioral problems of learning disabled boys aged 12–16. *Journal of Learning Disabilities, 19,* 101–106.

McGinnis, E., Goldstein, R. P., Sprafkin, R. P., & Gershaw, N. J. (1984). *Skillstreaming the elementary school child.* Champaign, IL: Research Press.

McGuire, J. M., & Shaw, S. F. (1987). A decision making process for the college-bound student: Matching learner, institution, and support program. *Learning Disabilities Quarterly, 10,* 106–111.

McKinney, J. D. (1989). Longitudinal research on the behavioral characteristics of children with learning disabilities. *Journal of Learning Disabilities, 22* (3), 141–150.

McKinney, J. D., & Speece, D. L. (1983). Classroom behavior and the academic progress of learning disabled students. *Journal of Applied Developmental Psychology, 4* (2), 149–161.

McLeod, J. (1983). Learning disability is for educators. *Journal of Learning Disabilities, 16,* 23–24.

McNutt, G. (1986). The status of learning disabilities in the states: Consensus or controversy. *Journal of Learning Disabilities, 19,* 291–293.

Mercer, C. D. (1988). *Students with learning disabilities.* Columbus, OH: Merrill.

Michaels, C. A. (1989). Employment: The final frontier. *Rehabilitation Counseling Bulletin, 33* (1), 67–73.

Milich, R., & Lichet, B. G. (1989). Attention deficit hyperactivity disordered boys' evaluations of and attributions for task performance on medication versus placebo. *Journal of Abnormal Child Psychology, 98,* 280.

Miller, R. J., Snider, B., & Rzonca, C. (1990). Variables related to the decision of young adults with learning disabilities to participate in postsecondary education. *Journal of Learning Disabilities, 23,* 349–354.

National Joint Committee on Learning Disabilities. (1987). Adults with learning disabilities: A call to action. *Journal of Learning Disabilities, 20,* 172–175.

Nelson, R., & Lignugaris-Kraft, B. (1989). Postsecondary education for students with learning disabilities. *Exceptional Children, 56,* 246–265.

O'Connor, S. C., & Spreen, O. (1988). The relationship between parents' socioeconomic status and education level, and adult occupational and educational achievement of children with learning disabilities. *Journal of Learning Disabilities, 21,* 148–153.

Olson, J. L., Wong, B. Y. L., & Marx, R. W. (1983). Linguistic and metacognitive aspects of normally achieving and learning disabled children's communication process. *Learning Disabilities Quarterly, 6,* 289–304.

Omizo, M. M., Williams, R. E., & Omizo, S. A. (1986). The effects of participation in parent group sessions on child-rearing attitudes among parents of learning disabled children. *Exceptional Children, 33,* 134–139.

Palincsar, A. S., & Brown, A. L. (1984). Reciprocal teaching of comprehension fostering and comprehension monitoring activities. *Cognition and Instruction, 1,* 117–175.

Palincsar, A. S., & Brown, A. L. (1986). Interactive teaching to promote independent reading from text. *Reading Teacher, 39,* 771–777.

Poplin, M. S. (1988). The reductionist fallacy in learning disabilities: Replicating the past by reducing the present. *Journal of Learning Disabilities, 21,* 389–400.

Quinn, D. (1984). Perspective from the other side: A message of hope for learning disability teachers and students. *Learning Disability Quarterly, 7,* 295–298.

Reiff, H. B., & Gerber, P. (1990). Cognitive correlates of social perception in students with learning disabilities. *Journal of Learning Disabilities, 23,* 260–262.

Reiff, H. B., Gerber, P. J., & Ginsberg, R. (1994). Definitions of learning disabilities from adults with learning disabilities: The insiders' perspective. *Learning Disability Quarterly, 17,* 114–125.

Rhodes, L. K., & Dudley-Marling, C. (1988). *Readers and writers with a difference.* Portsmouth, NH: Heinemann.

Rodriguez, C. M., & Routh, D. K. (1989). Depression, anxiety, and attributional style in learning disabled and nonlearning disabled children. *Journal of Clinical Child Psychology, 18,* 299–304.

Roit, M., & McKenzie, R. (1985). Disorders of written communication: An instructional priority for LD students. *Journal of Learning Disabilities, 18,* 258–260.

Rooney, K. J., & Hallahan, D. P. (1985). Future directions for cognitive behavior modification research. *Remedial and Special Education, 6,* 46–51.

Ross, P. A., & Braden, J. P. (1991). The effects of token reinforcement versus cognitive behavior modification on learning-disabled students' math skills. *Pyschology in the Schools, 28,* 247–256.

Satz, P., & Fletcher, J. M. (1988). Early identification of learning disabled children. *Journal of Consulting and Clinical Psychology, 56,* 824–829.

Scruggs, T. E., & Richter, L. (1988). Tutoring learning disabled students: A critical review. *Learning Disability Quarterly, 11,* 274–286.

Shaywitz, S. E., & Shaywitz, B. E. (1988). Attention deficit disorder: Current perspectives. In J. F. Kavanagh & T. J. Truss, Jr. (Eds.), *Learning disabilities: Proceedings of the national conference* (pp. 369–423). Parktown, MD: York Press.

Silver, L. B. (1980). The relationship between learning disabilities, hyperactivity, distractibility, and behavior problems. *Journal of the American Academy of Child Psychiatry, 20,* 385–397.

Silver, L. B. (1990). Attention deficit-hyperactivity disorder: Is it a learning disability or related disorder? *Journal of Learning Disabilities, 23,* 394–397.

Silverman, R., Zigmond, N., & Sansone, J. (1981). Teaching coping skills to adolescents with learning problems. *Focus on Exceptional Children, 13* (6), 1–20.

Simpson, R. L. (1988). Needs of parents and families whose children have learning and behavior problems. *Behavioral Disorders, 14,* 40–47.

Sleeter, C. (1984). Why is there learning disabilities? A critical analysis of the birth of the field in its social context. Paper presented at the annual meeting of the American Educational Research Association, Chicago, IL.

Smith, J. O. (1988). Social and vocational problems of adults with learning disabilities: A review of the literature. *Learning Disabilities Focus, 4,* 46–58.

Switzer, L. B. (1990). Family factors associated with academic progress for children with learning disabilities. *Elementary School Guidance and Counseling, 24,* 200–206.

Tannock, R., Schacher, R. J., & Carr, R. P. (1989). Dose-response effects of methylphenidate on academic performance and overt behavior in hyperactive children. *Pediatrics, 84,* 648.

Terrell, B. Y. (1990). Some thoughts on language-learning disabilities and the preschool child. *Hearsay* (Spring-Summer), 58–59.

Thomas, C. C., Englert, C. S., & Gregg, S. (1987). An analysis of errors and strategies in the expository writing of learning disabled students. *Remedial and Special Education, 8* (1), 21–30.

Thurlow, M. L., Ysseldyke, J. E., Graden, J., & Algozzine, B. (1983). What's special about the special education resource room for learning disabled adolescents? *Learning Disability Quarterly, 6* (3), 283–288.

Torgesen, J. K. (1991). Learning disabilities: Historical and conceptual issues. In B. L. Wong (Ed.), *Learning about learning disabilities* (pp. 3–31). San Diego, CA: Academic Press.

Toro, P. A., Weissberg, R. P., Guare, J., & Liebenstein, N. L. (1990). A comparison of children with and without learning disabilities on social problem solving skill, school behavior, and family background. *Journal of Learning Disabilities 23,* 115–120.

U.S. Department of Education. (1992). Memo regarding services for learners with ADHD. Washington, DC: Author.

U.S. Department of Education. (1995). *Seventeenth annual report to Congress on the implementation of the Individuals with Disabilities Education Act.* Washington, DC: Author.

Vallecorsa, A. L., & Garris, E. (1990). Story composition skills of middle-grade students with learning disabilities. *Exceptional Children, 57,* 48–54.

Vallecorsa, A. L., Ledford, R. R., & Parnell, G. G. (1991). Strategies for teaching composition skills to students with learning disabilities. *Teaching Exceptional Children, 23* (2), 52–54.

Vance, L. K., Bahr, C. M., Hubert, T. J., & Ewer-Jones, B. (1988). An analysis of variables that affect special education placement decisions. *Journal of Learning Disabilities, 21,* 444–447.

Vaughn, S., & Haager, D. (1994). Social competence as a multifaceted construct: How do students with learning disabilities fare? *Learning Disability Quarterly, 17,* 53–267.

Weller, C., Watteyne, L., Herbert, M., & Crelly, C. (1994). Adaptive behavior of adults and young adults with learning disabilities. *Learning Disability Quarterly, 17,* 282–295.

Wender, P. (1987). *The hyperactive child, adolescent, and adult.* New York: Oxford University Press.

Wiederholt, J. L., & Chamberlain, S. P. (1989). A critical analysis of resource programs. *Remedial and Special Education, 11* (1), 22–31.

Wiener, J. (1987). Peer status of learning disabled children and adolescents. *Learning Disabilities Research, 2,* 62–79.

Wiener, J., Harris, P. J., & Shirer, C. (1990). Achievement and social-behavioral correlates of peer status in LD children. *Learning Disability Quarterly, 13,* 114–127.

Wood, D. M. (1991). Discrepancy formulas and classification and identification issues that affect diagnoses of learning disabilities. *Psychology in the Schools, 28,* 219–225.

Ysseldyke, J. E., & Algozzine, B. (1983). LD or not LD: That's not the question! *Journal of Learning Disabilities, 16,* 29–31.

Ysseldyke, J. E., Thurlow, M. L., Graden, J. L., Wesson, C., Algozzine, B., & Deno, S. L. (1983). Generalizations from five years of research on assessment and decision making: The University of Minnesota Institute. *Exceptional Education Quarterly, 4* (1), 75–93.

Zigmond, N., Kerr, M. M., & Schaeffer, A. (1988). Behavior patterns of learning disabled and non-learning disabled adolescents in high school academic classes. *Remedial and Special Education, 9* (2), 6–12.

Learners with
Mild or
Moderate
Mental
Retardation

Objectives

After completing this chapter, you will be able to:

1. describe the personal characteristics of learners with mild or moderate mental retardation.
2. describe the identification and evaluation of learners with mild or moderate mental retardation.
3. describe the impact of mild or moderate mental retardation on interactions in the home and classroom.
4. describe ways to mediate the environment for learners with mild or moderate mental retardation.
5. describe the impact of mild or moderate mental retardation on participation in the larger social systems of the community and society.

Key Words and Phrases

deviance disavowal	moderate mental retardation
mental retardation	normalcy fabrication
mild mental retardation	severe mental retardation

One of the most significant factors which must be recognized as influencing the interactions of mentally retarded individuals is their stigmatized identity. Retarded and nonretarded persons alike seek to present themselves as competent relative to the requirements or expectations operating in the social situation in which they are participating, as competent members of their society. For those who have been ascribed a special status by society specifically on the basis of their perceived incompetence, however, the problem of presenting a demeanor of competence becomes particularly salient. Virtually every social interaction in which they participate is affected by their awareness of the stigma attached to incompetence and their attempts to disguise or disavow it. In their interactions, such individuals often have a hidden agenda. They are not only trying to convey information, ask a question, or participate in a conversation, they are trying to protect their self-esteem by demonstrating competence or disguising incompetence (Kernan & Sabsay, 1993, p. 145).

Introduction

Forness and Kavale (1984) contend that the education of those with mental retardation has historically served as a catalyst for resolution of major issues in special education. Through efforts of parents and professionals working with individuals with mental retardation, issues such as zero reject education, early intervention, the misuse of intelligence testing, the pejorative effects of labeling, the efficacy of special classes, inclusion, and parental participation in special education placement have emerged.

The number of learners with mental retardation receiving services in public schools has decreased since the 1976–1977 school year, with a total decrease of over 37.69 percent, or approximately 308,611 students, between 1976–1977 and 1993–1994 (U.S. Department of Education, 1995). In 1993–1994, mental retardation, representing 11.6 percent of all learners with disabilities, was the third-largest classification of student disabilities, following learning disabilities and speech and language impairment. In 1976–1977, by contrast, learners with mental retardation accounted for 24.9 percent of all learners with disabilities and was the second-largest group of learners with disabilities, following only those with speech and language impairment.

In 1989, approximately one-half million students with mental retardation were served in special education programs (U.S. Department of Education, 1990). About 96 percent of these students with mental retardation were classified as mildly or moderately mentally retarded (Baroff, 1986); they are discussed in this chapter. The remaining 4 percent of students with mental retardation are classified as severely or profoundly mentally retarded; they are discussed in chapter 16, "Learners with Severe and Multiple Disabilities." According to Grossman (1983), the generally accepted prevalence of mental retardation in the United States is 3 percent, though estimates range from 1 percent to 3 percent.

The decrease in the number of learners identified as mentally retarded may be due to the reclassification of some of the children previously served as mentally retarded as learning disabled or developmentally disabled. In addition, the criteria for identification of mental retardation have become more exclusive, with the cutoff score for tested intelligence quotient being lowered to 70 in 1973 and the corequisite of deficits in adaptive behavior added in 1983. In addition, the emphasis on more valid evaluation of learners from diverse cultures who previously may have been identified as mentally retarded may contribute to decreased numbers of learners in this category. Yet African Americans continue to be overrepresented among learners identified as having mental retardation. Though only 16 percent of the total population of students are African American, 34 percent of those served in programs for learners with mental retardation are African American (Office of Civil Rights, 1992).

Learners with mental retardation are served in various instructional settings. These include general education classes (7.1 percent), resource rooms (26.8 percent), separate classes (56.8 percent), separate schools (7.9 percent), and residential centers, home, and hospital settings (1.4 percent) (U.S. Department of Education, 1995).

a closer look

Characteristics of Individuals with Down Syndrome

Down syndrome, a group of chromosomal abnormalities, occurs in approximately two in every one thousand live births. The condition was originally referred to as mongolism by J. Langdon Down in 1866. More than fifty characteristics of Down syndrome have been identified, including:

small skull with flat back of the head
slanting, almond-shaped eyes
flat-bridged nose and ears slightly smaller than average
small mouth with protruding, fissured tongue
shortness of stature
stubby hands
too little muscle tone
varied levels of mental retardation

All types of chromosomal abnormalities that cause Down syndrome result in an extra chromosome on the twenty-first pair of chromosomes, or trisomy 21. In some individuals who have "mosaicism," some cells may have forty-six chromosome cells and others forty-seven. These individuals may have normal intelligence and few of these characteristics (Koch & Koch, 1974; LeJeune, Gauter, & Turpin, 1963) ∎

Personal Characteristics

Objective One

To describe the personal characteristics of learners with mild or moderate mental retardation.

Etiology

The etiology, or cause, of mental retardation includes several factors, few of which are considered to be the single and sufficient cause of the disability. Among the possible causes of mental retardation are the following (Smith & Luckasson, 1992):

- biological factors
- infections and poisons (toxins)
- injury
- socioeconomic and environmental factors

Mental retardation caused by biological factors includes Down syndrome, Tay-Sachs disease, phenylketonuria (PKU), and tuberous sclerosis, among others. Down syndrome is the result of an extra chromosome that attaches to the twenty-first pair of chromosomes, causing mental retardation and other specific characteristics. It is described in the "A Closer Look" box above. Tay-Sachs disease is a metabolic disorder that affects the processing of fats and results in mental retardation. The child's life expectancy is approximately four years. PKU is a metabolic disorder that affects the processing of protein and results in mental retardation. PKU can be controlled with a special diet, although early diagnosis and intervention are essential (see the "A Closer Look" box on page 328). Tuberous sclerosis is a progressive neurological disorder that results in mental retardation accompanied by multiple disabilities.

There are many infections and toxins that can cause mental retardation. Three viruses that may result in mental retardation are rubella, meningitis, and measles. Alcohol, tobacco, and other drugs (cocaine, crack, and heroin) used by the mother during pregnancy may cause various degrees of mental retardation in the child. Children who live in older housing or housing being rehabilitated may ingest leaded paint; lead poisoning occurs most frequently in one- to five-year-old children who eat leaded paint. Far lower levels of lead ingestion than earlier

Even low levels of lead ingestion may cause mental retardation.

assumed may cause neurological problems and subsequent mental retardation. Lead levels below that which causes severe brain damage may cause more subtle behaviors and learning disabilities (Blouin, Blouin, & Kelly, 1983).

Mental retardation can be the result of traumatic brain and head injury. Injuries during the birth process may also result in mental retardation. The level of retardation is related to the location and extent of the injury.

Socioeconomic and environmental factors may also contribute to mental retardation. Menolascino and Stark (1988) found the major factor in 75 percent to 80 percent of persons with mild mental retardation without an organic basis was poverty. Many factors that accompany poverty may contribute to mental retardation, including poor sanitation, unsafe housing, lead-based paints, poor nutrition, and inadequate and insufficient child care.

Characteristics

Among the ways in which learners with mental retardation vary from their peers are cognition, language, and behavior and social skills. These factors impact social judgment, the development of learned helplessness, persistence in using ineffective strategies, outerdirectedness, self-concept, and transition.

Cognitive Skills Perhaps the most readily recognized characteristics of learners with mild or moderate mental retardation are those related to cognitive skills. Processing information may be less automatic for learners with mild or moderate mental retardation, and problems may emerge in integrating or generalizing

a closer look

Phenylketonuria (PKU)—An Example of Successful Early Intervention

Phenylketonuria (PKU) is an autosomal recessive inborn error of metabolism. Children with PKU are usually normal at birth, since prenatally the nutrients they ingest are already metabolized through the umbilical cord. Through universal blood-screening twenty-four to forty-eight hours after birth, the disorder may be diagnosed and treatment begun. If PKU is found, the infant is placed on a low phenylalanine diet, based on synthetic formula (phenylalanine is present in almost all proteins). The formula is the sole nutrient these infants receive.

Because phenylalanine is toxic only to developing brain tissue, treatment can cease or be relaxed when brain development is complete. Common practice is to return the child to normal food at about age eight, though some research suggests that longer dietary treatment may be helpful. Though the diet may prevent mental retardation, children with PKU may have learning disabilities with particular problems in perception (Brown, 1986; Brunner, Jordon, & Berry, 1983). For children who have been treated through the diet, the average adult tested intelligence quotient is about 90; for those who receive no treatment, severe mental retardation occurs by three years of age ∎

processes or information (Ashman, 1983). When deeper levels of cognitive processing are required, learners with mild or moderate mental retardation become progressively slower in processing and manipulating information (Schultz, 1983). As learners demonstrate more severe mental retardation, they expend more energy for coding and processing information.

Ellis and Wooldridge (1985) report that learners with mental retardation retain pictures better than words when processing more complex and abstract information. Problems emerge in changing from one mode of processing to another—for example, from pictures to written word or spoken word to written word.

Learners with mental retardation frequently demonstrate difficulties in paying attention. Brooks and McCauley (1984) state that such difficulties as attending sufficiently to the task at hand for an adequate period of time may contribute to these learners' challenges in developing cognitive skills.

Language Beitchman and Peterson (1986) suggest that many of the adaptive behavior problems in learners with mental retardation may be due to problems in language and communication strategies. Learners with mental retardation have been found to focus more on the formal, sequential processes of language than do their nonidentified peers (Abbeduto & Nuccio, 1991).

Though learners with mental retardation are proficient in simpler contexts, they become more challenged in terms of topic maintenance and other pragmatic skills when the number of speakers, number of utterances, and degree of appropriateness of the speakers' responses change (Koetting & Rice, 1991). In addition, learners with mental retardation have difficulty identifying the emotional state of other persons in complex situations and settings (Sternina, 1990). For example, individuals with mental retardation may continue to sit next to children on the bus who are continually making fun of them.

In research with adults with mild and moderate mental retardation, Kernan and Sabsay (1993) found that in context, learners with mental retardation understood and produced stories that were essentially the same in structure as those produced by persons who were not identified as disabled. In generating stories, they found that learners with mental retardation were well able to recognize the main points, judge the importance and relevance of information, and make inferences based on prior knowledge. Kernan and Sabsay contend that when understood in the context of the social situation in which it occurs, the communication of learners with mental retardation often demonstrates sensitivity and creativity not otherwise recognized.

Social and Emotional Characteristics   Learners with mild or moderate mental retardation demonstrate more behavioral and emotional problems than do their peers (Polloway, Epstein, & Cullinan, 1985). Weiss (1981) believes that learners with mild or moderate mental retardation may also demonstrate "learned helplessness," that is, a perception that behavior and its outcomes are independent of each other. Feedback from professionals and peers may suggest to these learners that some tasks are simply too difficult to try. As a response, learners may exhibit deterioration in applying strategies when compared to their peers. In the future, with early intervention and appropriate instruction, learned helplessness may become less evident among learners with mental retardation (Polloway & Smith, 1983). Perhaps related to learned helplessness is a greater incidence of the symptoms of depression among adolescents with mild mental retardation (Reynolds & Miller, 1985).

Learners with mental retardation may demonstrate a less-positive real and ideal self-image than do their peers (Leahy, Balla, & Zigler, 1982). Negative self-statements, withdrawal, and an apparent lack of motivation may be related to their diminished self-image.

Social Interaction   Though often perceived to demonstrate "deficiencies of social intelligence" (Greenspan, 1979), individuals with mental retardation, among themselves, share four "focal concerns." These concerns, which demonstrate social sensitivity, include the following (Turner, 1983):

1. A need for affiliative relationships, a need to belong, to have friends, to become engaged in romantic involvements.
2. The desire to find refuge from prevailing negative attitudes, pejorative labels, and unfavorable social comparisons of "being retarded" through deviance disavowal.
3. The need for social harmony and to repair conflicts.
4. The need to avoid boredom and to seek some novelty and stimulation.

Kernan and Sabsay (1993) write that, in addition to these four focal concerns, learners with mental retardation, as a result of their disability and the reaction of others to that disability, lack knowledge and experience in certain areas. To deal with this lack of knowledge and experience, learners with mental retardation use a variety of strategies. In terms of **deviance disavowal,** or denying the existence of any disability, Kernan and Sabsay report **normalcy fabrication,** which is telling stories concerning some aspect of personal life in which the teller claims to have had some experience that he or she has not actually had. The stories present the teller as leading a life more normal and less restricted than the life he or she actually lives. For example, an individual who lives in a group home and receives few visitors may have pictures of his "wife" and "children" in his wallet, and he may share stories about what the family did over the weekend. These stories are often presented following some event that has threatened or damaged the teller's self-esteem. For example, stories about Christmas shopping, caroling, and receiving large and multiple presents may follow the teller's remaining in the group home over the holidays while others visited their families.

High-interest activities typical of their age peers support the learning of individuals with mental retardation.

Another challenge in social interactions among learners with mental retardation is described by Graffam (1985). He indicates that adults with mental retardation place little belief in the concept of chance or accident, so that if a problem occurs regarding social relations, a responsible party is sought. When a speaker presents a problem, someone is usually "blamed." This blaming, though often accepted by peers who are also mentally retarded, causes stress in social interactions among others.

According to Coffman and Harris (1980), learners with mental retardation exhibit "transition shock" when entering new and unfamiliar settings. Transition shock is characterized by a generalized disorientation, regression, and emotional stress. The learner may exhibit cuing problems, value discrepancies, physical and emotional feelings of dissatisfaction, adjustment problems, and inappropriate emotional responses.

Identification and Evaluation

Objective Two

To describe the identification and evaluation of learners with mild or moderate mental retardation.

McLean and Snyder-McLean (1988) describe four critical features that are relatively consistent among the various definitions of **mental retardation.** First, the problem is developmental, that is, not the result of immediate trauma, and it is manifested throughout the developmental period. Second, the problem is "mental" in that it reflects impairments in general intellectual functioning. Third,

My Story

John Angelo
Indiana, Pa.

I am 21 years old. I graduated from Indiana High School in June, 1993. My high school program was special education, but I was "mainstreamed" in many classes like art, gym, health, music, "Chef's Corner," "Tots for Teen," "On Your Own" and "Pilot English." I also took part in four high school musicals, glee club, mixed chorus and the Key Club. I also served as an aide for the Guidance Office. I was the first special education student at Indiana High School to have so much mainstreaming.

Special education was good for me because I could learn more. Some of my regular education classes were too hard for me. Once I was placed in a regular history class, but the book was too hard for me to understand. Maybe with a book that was easier to read, I could have stayed in that class.

I was in special education because I have Down Syndrome. That makes it harder for me to learn some things, but I am able to read quite well, and that's a good thing. I also really got along well with everyone like my teachers and the other students. When I want to do something that's difficult, I can usually succeed because I try very hard.

I have a job now. I work at Gatti's Pharmacy Services. My job is pretty complicated. I fill orders for medicines for nursing homes, I package them and seal them with a sealing press. I also clean up empty cartons and cardboard. I pop pills from cards into bins, some to be destroyed and others to be recycled. I enjoy my job and can do it because I really want to do it and try hard to do a good job.

Besides my job, I volunteer at a nursing home, I am a manager for the IUP basketball team, I am a volunteer assistant for IUP football, I volunteer as an acolyte and usher at church, and I sing in a church choir.

I also enjoy playing golf and other sports, and I spend a lot of time with my brothers and sisters and nephews and nieces. I really enjoy my life •

From "A Celebration of the Impact of the Individuals with Disabilities Educational Act" in *The ARC, 20 Years of IDEA in America.* Reprinted by permission of the publisher and the author.

mental retardation is pervasive, in that the learner's ability to function in all activity spheres is affected. Finally, mental retardation if fully defined only when adaptive functioning, including independent self-care behaviors, language development, self-direction, and socialization, are considered.

The definition of mental retardation used in Public Law 94-142 is the definition originally adopted by the American Association on Mental Retardation (AAMR) in 1973. In 1983, this definition was modified to include a greater emphasis on adaptive behavior. The AAMR again revised the definition in 1993. The purpose of this revision was to clarify and develop a common understanding of mental retardation. According to this definition, mental retardation

> ". . .refers to substantial limitations in present functioning. It is characterized by significantly subaverage intellectual functioning, existing concurrently with related limitations in two or more of the following application adaptive skill areas: communication, self-care, home living, social skills, community use, self-direction, health and safety, functional academics, leisure, and work. Mental retardation manifests itself before age 18." (MR Express, 1993, p. 3)

This definition is grounded in four assumptions. First, identification must be based on valid assessment, which takes into consideration cultural and linguistic diversity as well as individual variations in communication and behavior. Second, limitations in adaptive skills must occur in the context of the community environments typical of the individual's age peers and related to the individual's need for support. Third, adaptive limitations are assumed to often co-exist with strengths in other adaptive skills or abilities. Finally, with appropriate supports over an extended period of time, it is assumed that an individual's quality of life will improve.

Despite the changes in the definition, two basic components remain unchanged. First, measured intelligence is significantly below that of the individual's peers, and second, social behavior is nonconventional when compared to age and cultural peers.

Wodrich and Barry (1991) surveyed a random sampling of school psychologists regarding the ways in which learners with mental retardation were identified. The Weschler Intelligence Scales were the most frequently used tool for describing intelligence quotient scores, which, with adaptive behavior scale scores, were rated as the most influential in identification and placement decisions. Of social behavior scales, the Vineland Adaptive Behavior Scales were the most commonly used.

Gold (1980) states that there are several assumptions implicit in the AAMR definition that put a limit on the potential of the individuals labeled mentally retarded. He points out that the AAMR definition assumes that intelligence, as defined by tests, is permanent and that defined intelligence is sufficiently general to describe a learner's potential or functioning. The AAMR definition assumes that a definable "developmental period" exists for all people, and that it is somehow meaningful to catalogue individuals according to their tested intelligence and tested adaptive behavior. Finally, Gold notes that the definition assumes that retardation is most meaningfully conceptualized as a phenomenon existing within the individual rather than the contexts in which the individual functions.

Gold proposes the following alternative definition:

> Mental retardation refers to a level of functioning which requires from society significantly above average training procedures and superior assets in adaptive behavior, manifested throughout life.
>
> The mentally retarded person is characterized by the level of power needed in the training process required for him to learn, and not by limitations in what he can learn.
>
> The height of a retarded person's level of functioning is determined by the availability of training technology and the amount of resources society is willing to allocate and not significant limitations in biological potential.

Gold's definition places the limitations imposed by retardation within the cultural and social contexts in which the individual functions.

From a systems perspective, mental retardation may be defined as the social role to which the individual is assigned and assumes within the ecological contexts in which he or she functions. According to Mercer (1973), an individual with mental retardation, from the social systems perspective, is one who "occupies the status of mental retardate and plays the role of mental retardate in one or more of the social systems in which he participates" (p. 27). This may be why many children classified as mildly mentally retarded may be classified as such during the school year and during the school day. However, these children may function within the normal limits of their cultural groups prior to entering and after leaving the school system and before and after the school day. These children were referred to as the "six-hour retarded child" in the report of the President's Committee on Mental Retardation (1970).

Reschley (1988) describes the overrepresentation of learners who are members of minority cultural, ethnic, or linguistic groups in classes for learners with mild mental retardation. During the early 1970s and 1980s, there was extensive placement-bias court litigation, which included efforts to address problems in the role of intelligence tests in the classification and placement decision-making process, the correctness of assertions concerning the nature of mild mental retardation, and conclusions regarding the effectiveness of special education programs for learners with mild mental retardation. The National Academy of Sciences, through a panel comprising leading scholars in academic disciplines, minority social scientists, and legal, mental health, and test-development experts, developed several recommendations for reform related to the overrepresentation of learners from minority cultures in programs for learners with mild mental retardation. These reforms included such actions as emphasizing prereferral interventions, increasing the emphasis on adaptive behavior in the identification process, and placing an emphasis on instruction rather than on the placement setting.

While recognizing the great diversity within the various levels of mental retardation, the AAMR has, nevertheless, grouped persons with mental retardation into four levels: mild, moderate, severe, and profound. Persons with **mild mental retardation** have a tested intelligence quotient of between 50–55 and 70. These persons typically master basic academic skills, independent functioning, and living independently as adults. Learners with **moderate mental retardation** demonstrate intelligence quotients between 35–40 and 50–55 on standardized measures, and usually acquire self-help, communication, social, and some occupational skills. Learners with **severe mental retardation** and **profound mental retardation** require close lifelong supervision. These learners may learn self-help skills, and those with severe mental retardation may learn simple vocational skills.

The Impact on Interactions in the Home and Classroom

Interactions in the Home

Ysseldyke, Thurlow, Christenson, and Muyskens (1991) report that the home environments of students classified as having mild mental retardation were less conducive to academic achievement than those of their nonidentified peers, particularly in the area of stress and valuing of education. According to Turnbull and Turnbull (1986), a child with mental retardation may cause family stress, which may result in negative reactions of guilt, grief, denial, overprotection, and avoidance.

The well-being of families with young children with mental retardation is significantly related to the child's behavior and well-being. In addition, the child's behavioral characteristics are significantly related to the child's progress as perceived by the parents (Dunst, Trivette, Hamby, & Pollock, 1990). Orr, Cameron, and Day (1991) found that a family's perceptions of the birth or diagnosis of a child with mental retardation are the most significant factors in their ability to cope with the child and the resulting circumstances.

Blacher and Bromley (1990) reviewed the literature on the placement of learners with mental retardation out of their biological homes. They found that out-of-home placements appeared to relate to social support available to the family, parent-child attachment, overall family adjustment, specific child characteristics, and the family's needs and resources.

Even when available, Salisbury (1990) found a low level of use of respite care across all levels of children's retardation. Though the child's level of functioning was found to have an impact on parent depression, social support, and personal well-being, Salisbury found a significant discrepancy between families' need for respite care and its use. Requests for community living services for young

Objective Three

To describe the impact of mild or moderate mental retardation on interactions in the home and classroom.

Positive outcomes have been reported for students with mental retardation in inclusive settings.

adults with mental retardation were found by Black, Molaison, and Smull (1990) to be more related to characteristics of the young adult or to a desire for the young adult to be out of the home for day activities than a desire to promote the young adult's independence.

An emerging out-of-home placement option for learners with mental retardation is adoption. Glidden (1990) investigated the long-term adjustment of families who have adopted children with mental retardation. Positive outcomes were reported for almost all of the 567 children placed adoptively.

Interactions in the Classroom

Ysseldyke, Thurlow, Christenson, and Muyskens (1991) found that students served in classes for the mildly mentally retarded, when compared to their non-identified peers, had less time allocated to academic activities and more to free time. McWhirter, Wilton, Boyd, and Townsend (1990) report that more individualized learning activities were implemented when the learners were in general rather than special education classes. The "Guidelines for Practice" box on page 335 suggests ways to modify instruction for learners with mild or moderate mental retardation.

Van Bourgondien (1987) studied the effects of socially inappropriate behaviors and the label "in a special class for the retarded" on the attitudes and behavior of eight- to nine-year-old and twelve- to thirteen-year-old girls in general education. The results indicated that a child's social behaviors had a significant effect on the attitudes and behaviors of peers, while the label "in a special class for the retarded" did not. Neither behavior nor labels affected the peers' performance as teachers of the target child. Older children and children who were acquainted with a child in special education were more positive in their attitudes.

Even after an instructional program related to friendship awareness, learners with mental retardation had little interaction with students who were not identified as mentally retarded. When interactions did occur among the children during lunch and recess, they were brief and inconsistent (Fritz, 1990).

guidelines for practice

Learners with mild or moderate mental retardation may profit from individualization in response to their learning style and rate. Some ways to modify instruction include the following:

- Provide several short sessions, rather than a single longer session.
- Slow the pace, allowing longer response times.
- Break an objective into subobjectives, and make sure each subobjective is achieved before moving on.
- Teach a single concept in a session.
- Provide ample opportunities for practice.
- Review before initiating another step or activity ▮

Mediating the Environment

Polloway, Patton, Smith, and Roderique (1991) argue that with changes in the population of learners with mental retardation and the discouraging findings in follow-up studies on adult outcomes of education interventions, curriculum must be modified to reflect students' long-term needs. They propose that the profession adopt an attitude of recognizing "subsequent environments." Using this approach, primary attention is given to variables that may influence vertical and horizontal transitions for these students.

Less-intrusive strategies—that is, strategies that are less remarkable in the general education classroom—are emerging for learners with mental retardation. Engaging peers in the education of these learners and using cognitive behavior modification strategies call little negative attention to the learner. The possibilities of technological aids are just beginning to be explored.

Peer Tutoring

Peers have been found to be helpful as mediators for learners with mental retardation. Vacc and Cannon (1991), for example, studied the use of cross-age tutoring in mathematics education with elementary school students with mental retardation. The results of the tutoring program indicated that these learners' mathematics skills increased. The teachers involved in the tutoring program evaluated it as a positive learning activity and evaluated all participants' academic and/or social achievement as increasing as a result of the tutoring session. In classwide peer tutoring, the rates and accuracy of learners' responses to academic tasks and performance on weekly spelling tests both increased. Students also increased their retention of spelling words. The peer tutors reported positive evaluations of the process and perceived positive social and self-esteem changes (Mallette, Harper, Maheady, & Dempsey, 1991).

Several variables must be taken into consideration for the effective implementation of peer-tutoring programs with learners with mild or moderate mental retardation. The instructional objective must be measurable. In addition, time must be available for the program. Tutors must be selected and trained, and both the tutor and tutee must be engaged in the evaluation process (Krouse, Gerber, and Kaufmann, 1981). An example program of classwide peer tutoring is described in the "Guidelines for Practice" box on page 336.

Objective Four

To describe ways to mediate the environment for learners with mild or moderate mental retardation.

Annual **Edition**

Article 12

Annual **Edition**

Article 5

guidelines for practice

Classwide Peer Tutoring

Peer support, cooperative learning, and group contingencies may be used in combination to support the learning of students with mild disabilities. The following process was explored by Maheady, Sacca, and Harper (1988) in the implementation and evaluation of classwide peer tutoring.

1. Weekly study guides were developed collaboratively by general and special educators through (a) examining the weekly content during forty-minute consultation sessions and generating lists of instructional objectives, (b) developing a series of comprehension questions and appropriate responses, and (c) having the study guides reviewed by another individual for accuracy and clarity.
2. New classroom materials were introduced each week via one to two days of teacher lecture/discussion followed by assigned readings and homework. During the remainder of the week, twenty to thirty minutes of peer tutoring were involved. The classroom was divided into two teams by drawing colored squares. Team membership was the same for two weeks. Teams competed for the highest point totals in social studies. The teacher randomly paired students within each team.
3. Teachers and students were trained through role-play sessions. In-class supervision was also conducted. Bonus points were awarded to tutors for displaying "good tutoring" behaviors of (a) clear and accurate dictation of questions, (b) appropriate use of error corrections procedures, (c) contingent and accurate delivery of points for correct responses, and (d) use of praise and supports.
4. Quiz responses also earned points. Each correct response on each student's quiz earned the team five points. Weekly results were posted, and bonus points rewarded extra efforts.

The procedures resulted in immediate and systematic increases in the weekly social studies test performance of both the learners with disabilities and those without disabilities ▮

Gottlieb and Leyser (1981) used team cooperative learning experiences to facilitate the social mainstreaming of learners with mental retardation. This was an effort to change the classroom climate from one emphasizing rewards based on competition to rewards based on achievement. The cooperative learning teams were heterogeneous and included learners with mental retardation. The teams' primary function was to prepare its members through peer tutoring. This approach resulted in reduced failure and increased success for the learners with mental retardation.

Cognitive Behavior Modification

Cognitive behavior modification techniques, including self-instruction and self-recording, have been used with success with learners with mental retardation. A six-step self-instruction package for use with learners with mental retardation was developed by Burgio, Whitman, and Johnson (1980). The steps in the program are as follows:

1. The learner asks, "What does the teacher want me to do?"
2. The learner decides the nature of the task in response to the above question.
3. The learner determines the sequential order of the steps required to complete the assigned task.
4. The learner reinforces his or her personal success.
5. Using self-cues, the learner stays on task and ignores distractions.
6. The learner decides how she or he will cope with possible failure.

Table 14.1 Generalization Strategies

1. Fade reinforcers in the original setting while increasing the power of reinforcement in new settings.
2. Vary directions, cues, and supports.
3. Modify materials.
4. Vary responses and response time.
5. Move from single to many stimuli, adding distractors and increasing the abstract level of the stimuli.
6. Vary the setting.
7. Vary instructors.

(Vaughn, Bos, & Lund, 1986)

Using these procedures, Burgio and associates produced direct and generalized changes in the behavior of learners with mental retardation on printing and mathematics tasks. In addition, learners' off-task behaviors decreased. In oral reading tasks, Rose (1984) found simple self-instructional techniques to be effective with learners with mild mental retardation.

Self-recording has been used successfully with learners identified as mildly and moderately mentally retarded in increasing both on-task behavior and productivity (McCarl, Svobodny, & Beare, 1991). In self-recording, learners are trained to observe and document their personal behaviors. Sugai and Rowe (1984) used self-recording procedures to increase the in-seat behavior of a learner with mild mental retardation.

An ongoing challenge with learners with mild or moderate mental retardation is the generalization of skills taught in one setting to another setting. Drew, Logan, and Hardman (1992) reported additional issues related to generalization of skills among learners identified as mentally retarded. Among learners identified as mentally retarded and their nonidentified peers, younger children appeared to transfer learning more readily than older children. Also, the learners with mental retardation usually transferred learning best when both the initial task and the transfer task were very similar. In addition, meaningful tasks were both easier to learn and transfer to a second setting among learners with mental retardation. Vaughn, Bos, and Lund (1986) suggest several strategies that increase the likelihood that skills will generalize. These strategies are summarized in table 14.1.

Technological Aids

Technology has also emerged as a means of mediating the environment for learners with mental retardation. Parette (1991) contends that technology can (a) support educational activities, (b) provide, restore, or extend a learner's physical abilities, and (c) provide opportunities for greater participation in the mainstream of society. Gardner and Bates (1991) report that learners with mental retardation positively evaluated the use of computers. The learners reported that they found computers attractive and that using computers increased their confidence, self-esteem, and ability to learn some tasks.

In an innovative use of technology, Flexer, Millin, and Brown (1990) found that when using sound field FM amplification of the teacher's speech (see chapter 12, "Learners with Hearing Impairments," for an explanation of this technology), learners with mental retardation were more relaxed and responded more quickly to the teacher's directions. With only a 10-decibel amplification, primary-level children increased their accuracy and performance on tasks related to verbal communication.

Annual **Edition**

Article *39*

Sweetest Matchup: 1 Vs. 2

Beating Hurricanes For Championship Would Be Special For Stallings And Son

Bernie Miklasz

Gene Stallings had a remote-control clicker in his right hand, running the play on the large video screen behind his desk, over and over again.

The coach, in a foul mood, was operating some kind of Telestrator from Hell. I'd written about a controversial call that hurt the Cardinals late in their loss at Buffalo the day before.

Stallings was exhaling flames. The phone rang in his office. Stallings listened a while, and for the next five minutes lowered his voice to a compassionate whisper.

A stranger had called, long distance: A man who had just fathered a child born with Down syndrome. The new parents were having a difficult time coping with their heart-break and were given Stallings' number by a mutual friend.

Stallings spoke about his own experience of raising an afflicted child, his son John Mark. Down syndrome occurs when a child is born with an extra chromosome in each cell. Children with the condition are mentally impaired and many develop heart defects.

The Stallings family has cherished every moment spent with John Mark.

"Just remember," Stallings told the man, "that your child has a one-way, express ticket to heaven. The rest of us aren't that lucky. You'll get nothing but unconditional love for as long as he's with you. You'll feel blessed that you have him."

Stallings had transformed himself from maniac coach to kindly hospital minister.

Who is Gene Stallings? The finest answer was written by the late, great sportswriter, Shelby Strother, who likened Stallings to a cowboy boot: rough and tough on the outside; soft, warm and protective on the inside.

Much of who Gene Stallings is can be explained by the presence of John Mark in his life for the last 30 years.

"From my relationship with John Mark, I have learned to listen to my players more," Stallings said. "I want to win every game, but this is a game, not life and death. I've got children of my own. It's not like I haven't been through a crisis from time to time.

"I've learned to be more tolerant of the less gifted. If I see a player who isn't as talented give me everything he's got, I'm going to be on his side. But by the same token, I'm also less tolerant of the gifted who are lazy. If you have God-given talent, there's no excuse not to give your best."

Alabama quarterback Jay Barker has heard Stallings sound off on that theme in practice. "If someone messes up," Barker told reporters in New Orleans this week, "Coach might point over to John Mark on the bench and tell the player, 'He doesn't have the gifts you have, but he's always trying.' To see Coach and his son, it gives you a real warm feeling. You can see the bond they have."

Parents usually shape the character of their children. In the Stallings home, John Mark has shaped the character of his parents and four sisters. John Mark Stallings is their touchstone.

"I've had the best of both worlds," Stallings said. "I've had four daughters and John Mark. I've been able to see my girls grow up, meet nice boys and go through all of their various stages. John Mark has had his accomplishments, too."

When John Mark was born on June 11, 1962, Stallings passed out in the hospital. The doctors told Stallings that the boy

Annual **Edition**

Article *13*

Social Skills Training

Thomas (1980) reviewed the application of Goldstein's Social Skills Curriculum with learners with mental retardation. The curriculum is based on the assumption that learners with mental retardation can solve social problems through reasoning. It uses direct instructional methods and stresses "survival" tasks and competencies. In a review of the instructional techniques applied in several social skills training programs, Davis and Rogers (1985) found that active rehearsal in combination with other instructional techniques was more effective than instruction, reinforcement, and demonstration alone. They found the most frequently applied and most successful training procedures were a combination of visual instruction, practice, and contingent reinforcement.

Instructional Strategies

Instructional strategies that have been used with learners with mental retardation include sequential prompting and individualized instruction. When using sequential prompting, teachers should provide learners with "just enough" support to ensure success, but not so much that the learner's personal resources are not challenged. The steps to sequential prompting are as follows (Schloss, 1986):

wouldn't live five years and recommended that they institutionalize him.

"No, we were going to raise him and be proud of him," Stallings said. "If we were going to a restaurant, John Mark was going. When the girls brought home their dates, we weren't going to hide him. If he wanted to go to practice with me, I put him right next to me on the sideline like any coach would his son. We wanted to make his life as normal as possible."

John Mark made it to 5, and the doctors said he wouldn't make it to 10.

John Mark made it to 10, and the doctors said age 20 was out of the question.

John Mark made it to 20, and the doctors stopped making predictions.

The love of a doting family can be a miracle elixir, stronger and more sustaining than a doctor's curative touch. John Mark is 30 now, and there is a sadness in Stallings' voice when he discusses him.

"John Mark has problems," Stallings said. "He's slowing down. But I try not to think about how much time he has remaining. I just appreciate every day we have together. He does more for us than what we do for him, because he raises our spirits every day.

"It's Christmas time, and every one we spend with John Mark makes it a little bit more special. You know, John still believes in Santa Claus, and he's always the first one down the stairs on Christmas morning."

John Mark believes he's the Alabama team trainer, and one of his new Christmas presents was a kit of medical supplies. "He thinks he has the most important job at Alabama," Stallings said. "I don't rate."

We all know, of course, that the No. 1 job *anywhere* in Alabama is head football coach for the Crimson Tide. And Stallings is fitting the role so well . . . with the voice that you could pour on pancakes . . . the slow walk . . . the down-home countenance . . . the old-fashioned belief in a strong running game and defense. The only thing missing is Bear Bryant's houndstooth-check hat.

The comparison to Bryant is inevitable. The two coaches who preceded Stallings, Ray Perkins and Bill Curry, couldn't deal with the aura of a state and cultural icon. But Stallings, who played and coached under Bryant, understands the Bear legacy and embraces it.

Stallings has taken Alabama back to its fundamental roots. His offense is conservative, but nervy just the same. In this period of gimmicky offenses, and self-promoting

college coaches throwing the ball 40 times a game—usually losing—Stallings has taken football back to its essence. Block and tackle.

While the pretty-boy coaches dare to be different, Stallings *is* different because he dares to be so elementary. It takes a secure man to call running plays on two-thirds of his offensive downs. Eventually, the young geniuses in college football might put away their toy offenses and learn something from this Bryant disciple.

"We play football Coach Stallings' way," Lassic said. "Stop them on defense, run the ball at them, control the clock, control field position, win the turnover battle. That's also the way Coach Bryant believed football should be played. This is an opportunity to bring back a little of the tradition that Alabama has lost."

It's also an opportunity for Gene Stallings to create his own history. Bear's coaching son deserves his own identity. Besides, there's that special Alabama trainer, John Mark Stallings. And he deserves one of those championship rings.

Excerpts from *Sweetest Matchup: 1 vs 2,* by Bernie Miklasz. Reprinted with permission of the St. Louis Post-Dispatch. Copyright © 1993.

1. Identify the target behavior.
2. Determine the sequence of tasks to be completed to attain the objective.
3. Determine the prompts that may be applied to assist the learner.
4. Determine the possible sequence of prompts that may be used.
5. Implement the instructional program beginning with the least obtrusive prompt.

Among the prompts that may be selected for implementation of sequential prompting are physical guidance, modeling, vocal prompting, and graphic prompts. The teachers, prior to implementation, must determine how the prompts will be faded.

Teachers should individualize instruction in response to the learner's style and rate. Among the modifications that may be made in an effort to individualize instruction for learners with mental retardation are (a) slowing the pace of the lesson, (b) shortening the length of instructional practice sessions, (c) breaking down instructional objectives into subobjectives, and (d) simplifying instruction, that is, teaching each concept separately (Darch & Thorpe, 1978).

Some citizens with disabilities live independently with others.

Langone (1981) argues for an ongoing, diligent effort to provide relevant instruction to learners with moderate mental retardation. He suggests that teachers ask themselves questions such as

- Where do my students go at the end of the day?
- Where will my students be in several years?
- What skills will my students need to live in the community?
- How can I include daily activities to address these skill?

The Impact on Participation in the Community and Society

Objective Five

To describe the impact of mild or moderate mental retardation on participation in larger social systems of the community and society.

Though many learners with mild mental retardation live independently in the community, a continuum of supported living environments is an increasingly available option for those who need assistance. Among these options are mentor or "special friend" programs, in which the individual lives independently with occasional visits, phone calls, or other contacts with a support person; supervised apartments, in which the individual lives in one of several units in a building, with either live-in or hourly supervisors; and group homes, which usually accommodate between five and ten persons and may be managed by houseparents or hourly employees. Though there has been difficulty locating these housing alternatives in some communities, the general population appears to be understanding and accepting of them.

Changes have occurred in order to help learners with mental retardation have a more typical "home" experience. Howard (1990) analyzed how changing the structure of group homes and reducing the unnecessary regimentation (for example, ordering bedspreads and blankets bulk so that they are all identical) could create a more "normal" home environment. She claims that the needs of parents and staff to "get things done" or to "stay on schedule" often obstructed the learners' ability to become more independent and more adult in their behavior patterns. Parents and staff members became uncomfortable in many situations when the residents themselves took the responsibility for some personal decisions.

Employment

Finding and keeping gainful employment is also a challenge for learners with mental retardation. The employment rates of persons with mental retardation are low. In a statewide survey of the employment rates of learners with mental retardation who graduated from high school between 1980 and 1984, Hasazi and associates (1985) found that only 41 percent of the graduates were employed full- or part-time in the competitive job market.

Hill, Seyfarth, Banks, Wehman, and Orelove (1987) used a mail survey to study parents' attitudes about the working conditions of their adult sons and daughters with mental retardation. In their sample, there was low interest in specific improvements in the working conditions of their children, particularly in increased wages. Most of the parents indicated a positive attitude toward work for their children, but only 12 percent reported a preference for competitive employment. Young adults with mental retardation, however, were not happy with their work experiences. In an interview study, Szivos (1990) found that the learners themselves described work in the sheltered work environment as boring and frustrating. When asked why they did not seek another job, four reasons emerged: unusual position, perceived incompetence, nonavailability of jobs, and fear of discreditation.

In her study of the transition from school to adult life for individuals with mental retardation, Gallivan-Fenlon (1994) reported several issues that challenged families, young adults with mental retardation, and service providers. Families, young adults, and service providers each had different expectations. In addition, inconsistency in the special education and amount of inclusive education the young adults received made transitions difficult for service providers. All three groups of stakeholders had restrictive views on employment and community-living opportunities. Though there were significant benefits of supported employments and community inclusion, most of the young adults experienced unemployment and social isolation.

With support, adults with mental retardation may assume more-complex jobs. Mann and Svorai (1994) describe a job-skills training program in which participants were trained in the use of technology, including computers and fax machines. Through individualized evaluation, job modification, and the "Job Club," a support group, approximately 60 percent of the participants were successful in gaining and keeping employment involving technology.

Family and Community Issues

Mothers with mental retardation have been found to be more likely to lose custody of their children to human service agencies than mothers not identified as mentally retarded. Tymchuk and Andron (1990) found that child removal frequently occurred if the mother had a problem in addition to her retardation or if she was unwilling to attend and actively participate in a training program or if she did not have someone who could provide support. Many mothers with mental retardation who provide good care to their children live with a relative who shares child-care responsibilities.

Riordan and Vasa (1991) studied the accommodations made for and participation of learners with mental retardation in religious organizations. They found that clergy were aware of few persons with disabilities in their congregations and were not very active in providing accommodations or services to parents and families of these individuals or the individuals themselves. Though some church-oriented programs were available for children, the number of proactive accommodations and programs for individuals with mental retardation decreased as the learners grew older.

Summary

The majority of learners with mental retardation—those with mild or moderate mental retardation—were discussed in this chapter. The field of mental retardation has served as a catalyst for development in other areas of special education. However, there are decreasing numbers of learners identified as mentally retarded.

The etiology of mental retardation is a complex issue. Possible causes include biological factors, infections and poisons (toxins), and injury. These learners may present problems in processing information, attention, and language development. A particular difficulty arises in the area of generalization, that is, applying skills learned in one setting to another setting.

The definition of mental retardation has three components, including generalized below-average cognitive functioning, concomitant problems in social adaptability, and occurrence during the developmental period. There is, however, an overrepresentation of learners who are members of minority cultural, ethnic, or linguistic groups in classes for learners with mild mental retardation. This overidentification is related to the ways in which learners are identified and assessed.

The home environments of students classified as mildly mentally retarded were less conducive to academic achievement than those of their nonidentified peers. In addition, the nature of the educational placement of learners with mental retardation may have an impact on their educational outcomes.

Several effective strategies have emerged for learners with mental retardation. The use of peer tutoring can support learners in less-restrictive environments. In addition, cognitive behavior modification and technological aids may assist them in the general education classroom. Social skills training has emerged as an ongoing instructional need for these students.

Greater opportunities are developing for learners with mental retardation to live in their community. Supported living assists individuals in being as independent as possible. Challenges remain, however, in that learners with mental retardation usually face limited employment opportunities. In addition, learners with mental retardation, as parents, are more likely to lose the right to parent their children than parents who are not identified as having this disability.

Building Your Professional Vocabulary

Match each word or phrase to its meaning.

_____ deviance disavowal

_____ mild mental retardation

_____ moderate mental retardation

_____ normalcy fabrication

_____ severe mental retardation

a. rejection of self-description as mentally retarded
b. telling stories to relate personal experiences the teller may not have actually had

c. the individuals typically master basic academic skills and live independently as adults
d. the individuals require lifelong support
e. the individuals typically acquire self-help, communication, and occupational skills

Comprehension Check

Select the most appropriate response.

1. The number of learners identified as mentally retarded has
   a. remained stable over the last twenty years.
   b. increased over the last twenty years.
   c. decreased over the last twenty years.

2. The major factor contributing to mental retardation in learners identified as mildly mentally retarded is
   a. traumatic brain and head injury.
   b. poverty.
   c. alcohol and drug use.

3. Many of the adaptive behavior problems in learners with mental retardation may be related to
   a. problems in language and communication strategies.
   b. problems related to traumatic brain and head injuries.
   c. social and emotional characteristics of mental retardation.

4. One critical feature among various definitions of mental retardation is
   a. school failure.
   b. the consideration of adaptive behavior before identification.
   c. ethnic validity of assessment for learners from diverse ethnic, cultural, and linguistic groups.

5. The most significant factors in a family's ability to cope with a child with mental retardation are
   a. the cause and severity of the retardation.
   b. the socioeconomic class and culture of the family.
   c. the family's perceptions of the birth or diagnosis.

6. The use of respite care
   a. is available for all learners with mental retardation.
   b. is not often used by families with members with mental retardation.
   c. is related to family well-being.

7. In using peer tutoring
   a. tutees should be allowed to choose their tutors.
   b. careful selection and training are required.
   c. the most capable students make the most effective tutors.

8. Generalization is facilitated by
   a. teaching the task again in the new setting.
   b. varying the settings for instruction.
   c. keeping the task and instructor consistent during training.

9. As well as evaluating their students, teachers should evaluate
   a. their instruction in view of potential life goals of their students.
   b. community supports available to their students.
   c. family supports and visions for the student.

10. As adults, learners with mental retardation may live
    a. in any of a continuum of supported living environments.
    b. independently.
    c. in group homes.

References

Abbeduto, L., & Nuccio, J. B. (1991). Relation between receptive language and cognitive maturity in persons with mental retardation. *American Journal on Mental Retardation, 96,* 143–149.

Ashman, A. F. (1983). Exploring the cognition of retarded persons: A brief report. *International Journal of Rehabilitation Research, 6,* 355–356.

Baroff, G. S. (1986). *Mental retardation: Nature, cause, management* (2nd ed.). New York: Hemisphere.

Beitchman, J. H., & Peterson, M. (1986). Disorders of language, communication, and behavior in mentally retarded children: Some ideas on their co-occurrence. *Psychiatric Clinics of North America, 9,* 689–698.

Blacher, J., & Bromley, B. E. (1990). Correlates of out-of-home placement of handicapped children: Who places and why? *Journal of Children in Contemporary Society, 21,* 3–40.

Black, M. M., Molaison, V. A., & Smull, M. W. (1990). Families caring for a young adult with mental retardation: Service needs and urgency of community living requests. *American Journal on Mental Retardation, 95,* 32–39.

Blouin, A. G., Blouin, J. H., & Kelly, T. C (1983). Lead, trace mineral intake, and behavior of children. *Topics in Early Childhood Special Education, 54,* 249–262.

Brooks, P. H., & McCauley, C. (1984). Cognitive research in mental retardation. *American Journal of Mental Deficiency, 88,* 479–486.

Brown, R. T. (1986). Etiology and development of exceptionality. In R. T. Brown & C. R. Reynolds (Eds.), *Psychological perspectives on childhood exceptionality* (pp. 181–229). New York: Wiley.

Brunner, R. L., Jordon, M. K., & Berry, H. K. (1983). Early treated PKU: Neuropsychologic consequences. *Journal of Pediatrics, 102,* 381–385.

Burgio, L. D., Whitman, T. C., & Johnson, M. R. A. (1980). A self-instructional package for increasing attention behavior in educable mentally retarded children. *Journal of Applied Behavior Analysis, 13,* 3–7.

Coffman, T. L., & Harris, M. C. (1980). Transition shock and adjustments of mentally retarded persons. *Mental Retardation, 18,* 3–7.

Darch, C. B., & Thorpe, H. W. (1978). An intervention strategy for teachers of the mildly handicapped. *Education and Training of the Mentally Retarded, 13* (1), 29–36.

Davis, R. R., & Rogers, E. S. (1985). Social skills training with persons who are mentally retarded. *Mental Retardation, 23* (4), 186–196.

Drew, C. J., Logan, D. R., & Hardman, M. L. (1992). *Mental retardation: A life cycle approach* (5th ed.). Columbus, OH: Merrill.

Dunst, C. J., Trivette, C. M., Hamby, D., & Pollock, B. (1990). Family systems correlates of the behavior of young children with handicaps. *Journal of Early Intervention, 15,* 204–218.

Ellis, N. R., & Wooldridge, P. W. (1985). Short-term memory for pictures and words by mentally retarded and nonretarded persons. *American Journal of Mental Deficiency, 89,* 622–626.

Flexer, C., Millin, J. P., & Brown, L. (1990). Children with developmental disabilities: The effect of sound field amplification on word identification. *Language, Speech, and Hearing Services in Schools, 21,* 177–182.

Forness, S. R., & Kavale, K. A. (1984). Education of the mentally retarded: A note on policy. *Education and Training of the Mentally Retarded, 19,* 239–245.

Fritz, M. F. (1990). A comparison of social interactions using a friendship awareness activity. *Education and Training in Mental Retardation, 25,* 352–359.

Gallivan-Fenlon, A. (1994). "Their senior year": Family and service perspectives on the transition from school to adult life for young adults with disabilities. *Journal of the Association for Persons with Severe Handicaps, 19,* 11–23.

Gardner, J. E., & Bates, P. (1991). Attitudes and attributions on use of microcomputers in school by students who are mentally handicapped. *Education and Training in Mental Retardation, 26,* 98–105.

Glidden, L. M. (1990). The wanted ones: Families adopting children with mental retardation. *Journal of Children in Contemporary Society, 21,* 177–205.

Gold, M. W. (1980). An alternative definition of mental retardation. In M. W. Gold (Ed.), *"Did I say that?" Articles and commentary on the Try Another Way system.* Champaign, IL: Research Press.

Gottlieb, J., & Leyser, Y. (1981). Facilitating the social mainstreaming of retarded children. *Exceptional Education Quarterly, 1* (4), 57–70.

Graffam, J. (1985). About ostriches coming out of Communist China: Meanings, functions, and frequencies of typical interactions in group meetings for retarded adults. In S. Sabsay, M. Platt, et al., *Social setting, stigma, and communicative competence: Practice and beyond, 6,* 9–40.

Greenspan, S. (1979). Social intelligence in the retarded. In N. R. Ellis (Ed.), *Handbook on mental deficiency research: Psychological theory and research* (2nd ed.). Hillsdale, NJ: Lawrence Erlbaum Associates.

Grossman, H. (1983). *Classification in mental retardation.* Washington, DC: American Association of Mental Deficiency.

Hasazi, S. B., Gordon, L. R., Roe, C. A., Hull, M., Finck, K., & Salembier, G. (1985). A statewide follow-up on post-high school employment and residential status of students labeled "mentally retarded." *Education and Training of the Mentally Retarded, 20* (6), 222–224.

Hill, J. W., Seyfarth, J., Banks, P. D., Wehman, P., & Orelove, F. (1987). Parent attitudes about working conditions of their adult mentally retarded sons and daughters. *Exceptional Children, 54,* 9–23.

Howard, M. (1990). "We don't have no say in our lives anymore": An anthropologist's study of group home life for adults with mental retardation. *Adult Residential Care Journal, 4* (3), 163–182.

Kernan, K. T., & Sabsay, S. (1993). Discourse and conversational skills of mentally retarded adults. In A. M. Bauer (Ed.), *Children who challenge the system* (pp. 145–184). Boston: Ablex.

Koch, R., & Koch, K. (1974). *Understanding the mentally retarded child: A new approach.* New York: Random House.

Koetting, J. B., & Rice, M. L. (1991). Influence of the social context on pragmatic skills of adults with mental retardation. *American Journal on Mental Retardation, 95,* 435–443.

Krouse, J., Gerber, M. M., & Kauffman, J. M. (1981). Peer tutoring: Procedures, promises, and unresolved issues. *Exceptional Education Quarterly, 1* (4), 107–115.

Langone, J. (1981). Curriculum for the trainable mentally retarded . . . or "What do I do when the ditto machine dies?" *Education and Training of the Mentally Retarded, 16,* 150–154.

Leahy, R. L., Balla, D., & Zigler, E. (1982). Role-taking, self-image, and imitativeness of mentally retarded and nonretarded individuals. *American Journal of Mental Deficiency, 86,* 372–379.

LeJeune, J., Gautur, M., & Turpin, R. (1963). Study of the somatic chromosomes of nine mongoloid idiot children. In S. H. Bayer (Ed.), *Papers on human genetics* (pp. 238–240). Englewood Cliffs, NJ: Prentice Hall.

Maheady, L., Sacca, M. K., & Harper, G. F. (1988). Classwide peer tutoring with mildly handicapped high school students. *Exceptional Children, 54,* 52–59.

Mallette, B., Harper, G. F., Maheady, L., & Dempsey, M. (1991). Retention of spelling words acquired using a peer-mediated instructional procedure. *Education and Training in Mental Retardation, 26,* 156–164.

Mann, W. C., & Svorai, S. B. (1994). COMPETE: A model for vocational evaluation, training, employment, and community for integration for persons with cognitive impairments. *American Journal of Occupational Therapy, 48,* 446–451.

McCarl, J. J., Svobodny, L., & Beare, P. L. (1991). Self-recording in a classroom for students with mild to moderate mental handicaps: Effects on productivity and on-task behavior. *Education and Training in Mental Retardation, 26,* 79–88.

McLean, J. E., & Snyder-McLean, L. (1988). Application of pragmatics to severely mentally retarded children and youth. In R. L. Schiefelbusch & L. L. Lloyd (Eds.), *Language perspectives* (pp. 255–289). Austin, TX: Pro-Ed.

McLoughlin, J. A., & Lewis, R. B. (1990). *Assessing special students* (3rd ed.). Columbus, OH: Merrill.

McWhirter, J., Wilton, K., Boyd, A., & Townsend, M. A. (1990). Classroom interactions of mildly intellectually disabled children in special and regular classrooms. *Australia and New Zealand Journal of Developmental Disabilities, 16,* 39–48.

Menolascino, F. J., & Stark, J. A. (Eds.). (1988). *Preventive and curative intervention in mental retardation.* Baltimore, MD: Paul H. Brookes.

Mercer, J. (1973). *Labelling the mentally retarded.* Berkeley: University of California Press.

MR Express. (1993, January). The AAMR Manual revisions: CEC-MR responds: Assessment of the changes and their implications for special educators (p. 3). Reston, VA: Council for Exceptional Children.

Office of Civil Rights. (1992). *OCR, the national and state summaries of data from the 1990 elementary and secondary school civil rights survey.* Washington, DC: Author.

Orr, R. R., Cameron, S. J., & Day, D. M. (1991). Coping with stress in families with children who have mental retardation: An evaluation of the double ABCX model. *American Journal on Mental Retardation, 95,* 444–450.

Parette, H. P. (1991). The importance of technology in the education and training of persons with mental retardation. *Education and Training in Mental Retardation, 26,* 165–178.

Polloway, E. A., Epstein, M. H., & Cullinan, D. (1985). Prevalence of behavior problems among educable mentally retarded students. *Education and Training of the Mentally Retarded, 20,* 3–13.

Polloway, E., Patton, J. R., Smith, J. D., & Roderique, T. W. (1991). Issues in program design for elementary students with mild retardation: Emphasis on curriculum development. *Education and Training in Mental Retardation, 26,* 142–150.

Polloway, E. A., & Smith, J. D. (1983). Changes in mild mental retardation: Population, programs, and perspectives. *Exceptional Children, 50,* 149–159.

President's Committee on Mental Retardation. (1970). *The six-hour retarded child.* Washington, DC: U.S. Government Printing Office.

Reschley, D. J. (1988). Minority MMR overrepresentation and special education reform. *Exceptional Children, 54* (4), 316–323.

Reynolds, W. M., & Miller, K. L. (1985). Depression and learned helplessness in mentally retarded and nonretarded adolescents: An initial investigation. *Applied Research in Mental Retardation, 6,* 295–306.

Riordan, J., & Vasa, S. F. (1991). Accommodations for and participation of persons with disabilities in religious practice. *Education and Training in Mental Retardation, 26,* 151–155.

Rose, T. L. (1984). The effects of previewing on retarded learners' oral reading. *Education and Training of the Mentally Retarded, 19* (1), 49–53.

Salisbury, C. L. (1990). Characteristics of users and nonusers of respite care. *Mental Retardation, 28,* 291–297.

Schloss, P. J. (1986). Sequential prompt instruction for mildly handicapped learners. *Teaching Exceptional Children, 18* (3), 181–184.

Schultz, E. E. (1983). Depth of processing by mentally retarded and MA matched nonretarded individuals. *American Journal of Mental Deficiency, 88,* 307–313.

Smith, D. D., & Luckasson, R. (1992). *Introduction to special education: Teaching in an age of challenge.* Boston: Allyn & Bacon.

Sternina, T. Z. (1990). Mentally retarded children's comprehension of another person's emotional state. *Soviet Psychology, 28,* 89–104.

Sugai, G., & Rowe, P. (1984). The effects of self-recording on out-of seat behavior of an EMR student. *Education and Training of the Mentally Retarded, 19* (1), 23–28.

Szivos, S. E. (1990). Attitudes to work and their relationship to self-esteem and aspirations among young adults with a mild mental handicap. *British Journal of Mental Subnormality, 36,* 108–117.

Thomas, M. A. (1980). Strategies for problem solving: A conversation with Herbert Goldstein. *Education and Training of the Mentally Retarded, 15* (3), 216–223.

Turnbull, A. P., & Turnbull, H. R., III. (1986). *Families, professionals and exceptionality: A special partnership.* Columbus, OH: Merrill.

Tymchuk, A. J., & Andron, L. (1990). Mothers with mental retardation who do or do not abuse or neglect their children. *Child Abuse and Neglect, 14,* 313–323.

U. S. Department of Education. (1990). *Twelfth annual report to Congress on the implementation of the Education of the Handicapped Act.* Washington, DC: Author.

U.S. Department of Education. (1995). *Seventeenth annual report to Congress on the implementation of the Individuals with Disabilities Education Act.* Washington, DC: Author.

Vacc, N. N., & Cannon, S. J. (1991). Cross-age tutoring in mathematics: Sixth graders helping students who are moderately handicapped. *Education and Training in Mental Retardation, 26,* 89–97.

Van Bourgondien, M. E. (1987). Children's responses to retarded peers as a function of social behaviors, labeling, and age. *Exceptional Children, 53,* 432–439.

Vaughn, S., Bos, C. S., & Lund, K. A. (1986) . . . But they can do it in my room: Strategies for promoting generalization. *Teaching Exceptional Children, 18* (3), 176–180.

Weiss, J. R. (1981). Learned helplessness in black and white children identified by their schools as retarded and nonretarded. *Developmental Psychology, 17,* 499–508.

Wodrich, D. L., & Barry, C. T. (1991). A survey of school psychologists' practices for identifying mentally retarded students. *Psychology in the Schools, 28,* 165–171.

Ysseldyke, J. E., Thurlow, M. L., Christenson, S. L., & Muyskens, P. (1991). Classroom and homelearning differences between students labeled as educable mentally retarded and their peers. *Education and Training in Mental Retardation, 26,* 3–17.

15

Chapter

Learners with Mild Disabilities

Objectives

After completing this chapter, you will be able to:

1. describe the personal characteristics of learners with mild disabilities.
2. describe the identification and evaluation of learners with mild disabilities.
3. describe the impact of mild disabilities on interactions in the classroom.
4. describe ways to mediate the environment for learners with mild disabilities.
5. describe the impact of mild disabilities on participation in the larger social systems of the school, community, and society.

Key Words and Phrases

collaborative consultation
high-prevalence disabilities

school survival skills
teacher-assistance teams

"I think you have to see them as another one of the children in class who has some strengths, some weaknesses, and you need to find out where they are at and how you can help them." (Comment made by a teacher discussing a child with a disability in her general education classroom, in Giangreco, Dennis, Cloninger, Edelman, & Schattman, 1993, p. 366)

Introduction

Algozzine and Korinek (1985) discuss the consistent increases during the five-year period from 1978 to 1982 in the number of learners with **high-prevalence disabilities,** that is, learners with mild behavior disorders, mild learning disabilities, and mild mental retardation. They write that these data could mean that there is an increasingly effective system to provide specialized educational experiences to students failing to profit from general education. However, they also suggest that these increases could be evidence of an increasingly ineffective system, in which it has become more profitable and socially desirable to find more students either learning disabled or mentally retarded.

In an effort to classify patterns of individual differences prior to school failure, Cooper and Speece (1990) studied children in the first grade before any disabilities were formally identified. They examined the role classroom environments play in modifying the course of school failure. They posit that young children who enter school without a diagnostic label do not "catch" a disability as one would catch a biophysiological disorder; rather, they bring with them as yet unspecified cognitive, behavioral, linguistic, and affective characteristics developed over time, which interact with the academic and social ecology. Cooper and Speece found that two classroom environments tend to be associated with school failure: (a) pencil and paper tasks, when the structure is diffuse and the teacher is engaged with the whole class, as in spelling tests, and (b) pencil and paper tasks, with focused structure and a disengaged teacher, as in working independently on seatwork.

Historically, learners with mild handicaps have been served in a wide variety of structures; however, research does not clearly support any one service delivery system over another (Kauffman & Pullen, 1989). In a study of forty special education classes for students with different categorical classifications of mild disabilities, Algozzine, Morsink, and Algozzine (1988) found few differences in the extent to which teacher communication patterns, learner involvement, and instructional methods were different in classes containing students classified as learning disabled, behaviorally disordered, or mildly mentally retarded. Regardless of the categorical identification of the program, there was a low occurrence of behaviors related to working with individuals and groups, little use of convergent/divergent inquiry, little development of problem-solving skills, and few efforts to facilitate generalization or the transfer of learning. Algozzine and associates found that instruction for learners identified as educable mentally retarded, learning disabled, or behaviorally disordered was more similar than different, though teachers of learners identified as mildly mentally retarded modified the instruction to meet individual learner needs about half as frequently as teachers of learners with other disabilities.

Personal Characteristics

Learners with mild disabilities are assumed to demonstrate academic achievement lower than that of their peers. However, remediating academic areas has not been demonstrated to meet the needs of all of these students. Sabornie and Beard (1990) state that special education practitioners have come to realize that learners with mild disabilities encounter social challenges in their everyday lives.

Social-Emotional Characteristics

Sabornie and Beard (1990), summarizing the findings of current research regarding the social competence of learners with mild disabilities, characterize these learners as (a) having low social status among their peers, (b) participating in few extracurricular activities, (c) being dissatisfied with their social lives, (d) having fewer friends, and (e) being lonelier and more isolated than their peers.

Objective One

To describe the personal characteristics of learners with mild disabilities.

In a comparison of three subgroups of learners with mild disabilities (that is, learning disabilities, mild mental retardation, behavioral disorders) using a teacher rating scale, Gresham, Elliott, and Black (1987) found a significant difference between all of the mildly disabled subgroups and a matched sample of typical students. No differences, however, were found between the subgroups of learners with mild disabilities. Analysis revealed that three-fourths of the learners with mild disabilities could be correctly classified on the basis of teacher-rated social skills.

Nonacademic activities may provide an alternative path to achievement and self-esteem for many learners with mild disabilities. Murtaugh (1988), in an investigation of nonacademic activities, found that learners with mild disabilities were much less likely than their general education peers to be seriously involved in activities outside of school. Individual case studies showed that the involvement in activities provided students means to demonstrate their abilities and talents in ways not usually afforded by their school achievement.

As learners with mild disabilities grow older, they may continue to vary from their peers. In an ethnographic study of typical adolescents and adolescents with mild disabilities, an account was obtained about the life of each student, both in the home and among friends outside the home. Murtaugh and Zetlin (1988) found that autonomy was achieved through a gradual process of negotiation during high school. Learners with mild disabilities generally lagged behind their general education peers in breaking away from the family. While about three-fourths of the typical learners made significant gains toward increased freedom, less than half of the learners with mild disabilities had negotiated less parental supervision. However, most of the learners with mild disabilities were satisfied with the amount of independence they had gained.

Language

Natsopoulos and Zeromeritou (1990) investigated the use and knowledge of language structures of learners with mild disabilities. They found no real problem in the use of syntactic information to process semantic information, in that typical learners of equivalent verbal mental age used the same processes as learners with mild disabilities. However, learners with mild disabilities were more challenged than were their typical peers when asked to describe the processes they applied to manipulate information.

It appears that learners with mild disabilities in the general education classroom vary from typical peers quantitatively rather than qualitatively. The instructional characteristics of both groups are similar with regard to frequency, intensity, and duration (Bauer & Shea, 1989). Learners with mild disabilities tend to be more impulsive and exhibit attentional problems in the areas of focusing, vigilance, and selectivity. Their temperamental patterns tend to differ from those of general education students with regard to activity level, distractibility, adaptability, responsiveness, and mood. They tend to be more cautious when approaching new activities. Motivational problems are related to their failure expectations, outer-directedness or reliance on others, learning set (that is, their basic approach to learning a new skill), and difficulty transferring what they have learned from one situation to another. Needless to say, these unique characteristics are not exhibited by all learners with mild disabilities who are served in general education classrooms.

Objective Two

To describe the identification and evaluation of learners with mild disabilities.

Identification and Evaluation

The categories used in special education for students with mild disabilities are not reliable or valid as indicators of the services or forms of services individuals receive (Reynolds, Wang, & Walberg, 1987). In an examination of the relationship between state-level financial and demographic characteristics and variability in the identification and degree of inclusion of learners with mild disabilities, Noel and Fuller (1985) found that much of the variance among states in terms of numbers of identified learners with mild disabilities and the use of special rather than mainstreamed placement was accounted for by the amount of financial resources that states and local districts commit to education, the state's minority enrollment, and the number of children living in or at the poverty level.

Though the long-standing belief is that, in most cases, we are unable to determine the cause of mild disabilities, Smith (1989) found that many of these problems are due to medically identifiable syndromes. Rather than "cultural familial" or unknown in origin, Smith suggests that fetal alcohol effects, chromosomal abnormalities, multiple anomaly syndromes, phenylketonuria, Tourette syndrome, and several other genetic syndromes may be the cause of mild disabilities.

Difficulties in differentiating learners with mild disabilities from those who demonstrate low achievement is a consistent problem in special education. The primary difference that has emerged in differentiating these two groups of learners is that learners who are mildly disabled score significantly lower in achievement than their low-achieving peers (Shinn & Marston, 1985). Aksamit (1990) believes that there is an apparent overidentification of learners as disabled and that changes in teaching, school organization, and staffing approaches might enhance the education of at-risk children and reduce the numbers labeled as disabled. Learners from minority cultures and ethnic groups are particularly at risk for misidentification.

The use of standardized assessment instruments with learners with mild disabilities has been continually problematic. Intelligence quotient scores, for example, are no longer perceived to be as stable as once assumed. Bauman (1991) found that children initially tested before eight years of age had a significant loss in intelligence quotient scores at a later age. This loss was particularly strong among those learners whose initial test scores approached the mean (100) on the verbal subtest of the Wechsler Intelligence Score for Children (revised).

Maheady, Algozzine, and Ysseldyke (1984) argue that many of the academic difficulties for which learners are referred may be directly attributable to problems in the learning environment. They recommend the use of a functional assessment perspective that involves assessing a child's performance in the context of the existing learning environment.

The Impact on Interactions in the Classroom

Objective Three

To describe the impact of mild disabilities on interactions in the classroom.

In a study of teachers' classroom interactions with learners with mild disabilities, these students were found to receive fewer teacher questions and were provided with less teacher feedback than their typical peers (Alves & Gottlieb, 1986). However, these findings may have resulted from teacher behavior rather than the student's challenges.

Armstrong (1994) suggests that by using Gardner's (1983, 1993) theory of multiple intelligences, teachers may view the interactions of learners with mild disabilities in a more-positive way. Gardner (1983) contends that our culture defines intelligence too narrowly and that there are at least seven different kinds of intelligences. Intelligence, in Gardner's framework, has more to do with problem solving and generating products than performance on a test.

Using the theory of multiple intelligences, a new perspective of learners with mild disabilities in the classroom emerges. Armstrong (1994) contends that when applying the theory of multiple intelligences, learners with mild disabilities are not viewed in terms of deficit, disorder, or disease. Rather, difficulties or disabilities are acknowledged within the context of regarding the learners as healthy individuals. The theory of multiple intelligences provides a way to envision positive

Intelligence, in Gardner's view, has more to do with problem solving and generating products than performance on a test.

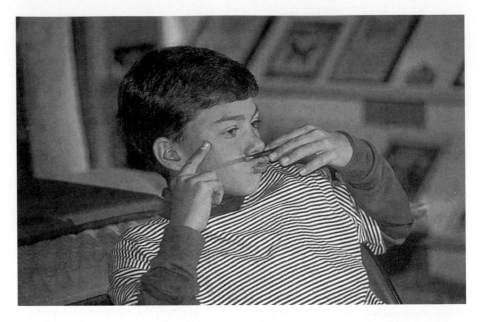

channels through which learners with mild disabilities can deal with their disabilities. For example, to understand fractions, a learner with a strength in spatial intelligence could be provided with diagrams of "pies" and draw pictures. A learner with a strength in intrapersonal intelligence could choose a favorite fraction and collect specific examples of it. A learner with a strength in interpersonal intelligences could divide the class into different fraction parts.

Mediating the Environment

Objective Four

To describe ways to mediate the environment for learners with mild disabilities.

Coleman, Pullis, and Minnett (1987) argue that the current research base on the education of learners with mild disabilities with regard to mainstreaming is problematic. They suggest that further research is needed that (a) provides a longitudinal analysis and assessment across environments, (b) uses multitrait-multimethod strategies, and (c) weaves a complex pattern from the personal, peer, family, and school factors involved.

Data suggesting that teacher certification made little difference in instruction or achievement caused Marston (1987) to question whether a categorical service delivery model for learners with mild disabilities was appropriate. O'Sullivan, Marston, and Magnusson (1987) found no differences in the instructional behavior of teachers with various categorical certifications. Jenkins, Pious, and Peterson (1988) also found that similarities in instructional level and learning rates were greater than differences in the categorical programs for learners with mild disabilities.

Several services have been used with learners with mild disabilities. These include remaining in general education, consultation, resource-room services, and self-contained programs.

Preschool

Jenkins, Speltz, and Odom (1985) contrasted the effects of integrated and segregated preschool programs for young learners with mild disabilities and found that the learners in both programs made significant gains across the year. The learners in integrated special education programs, however, scored significantly higher in terms of changes in their social play. The amount of time the learners spent with typical peers had no pervasive effect on the learners' development.

guidelines for practice

Adapting Textbooks for Use with Learners with Mild Disabilities

Meese (1992) presented three general areas in which textbooks can be adapted for use by learners with mild disabilities in general education classrooms. These areas, and related techniques, include the following:

Modify the textbook by
highlighting information
tape recording text segments
using an alternative, high-interest, low-vocabulary text

Alter instructional procedures by
teaching students how to use the textbook's structure
helping students preview the chapter or section
providing advance organizers for the student
teaching key words, phrases, or other critical vocabulary

Teach textbook reading strategies such as
self-questioning about the main idea, summaries, and themes
reading actively
making study cards

Inclusive Classrooms

In the last ten years, a significant change has occurred in educational programming for learners with mild disabilities. Rather than the formerly common special education classes or resource rooms, in which students were removed from their classrooms for specific periods each day to provide special instruction, learners with mild disabilities are now being served in inclusive classrooms. These inclusive classrooms have significantly altered the role of the general education teacher in regards to learners with mild disabilities.

In an inclusive classroom, several new responsibilities emerge for the general education teacher (Jenkins, Pious, & Jewell, 1990). General education teachers become responsible for the education of all of their students, they must make and monitor instructional decisions for all. Besides providing "typical" instruction, teachers must adapt instruction when the learner's progress is discrepant from what is normally expected. As the teacher manages instruction for diverse populations, he or she must seek, use, and coordinate the supports for learners who require more-intense services than those provided to their peers.

Ysseldyke, Thurlow, Wotruba, and Nania (1990) suggest that teachers make both structural and instructional arrangements in inclusive classrooms. Teachers in inclusive classrooms often have another adult in the room, even though that individual is typically used the same way as in general education classrooms that are not inclusive. The teachers do not change their instructional grouping and continue to use direct instruction, cooperative groups, and independent work. In terms of instructional adaptations, teachers usually hold students accountable for performance and quality of work and alter instruction so that the student can experience success.

In a study of general education teachers' perceptions of educational program modifications for learners with mild disabilities, simple modifications were found to be common (Munson, 1986). However, there were significant negative relations between general education teachers' age and years of teaching experience

guidelines for practice

Self-Monitoring in Arithmetic

The complex sequences involved in computation may be a challenge for learners with mild disabilities. Frank and Brown (1992) suggest using self-monitoring strategies to help students remember the steps that must be followed during computation. They recommend using the following steps to develop a personal self-monitoring strategy for a student:

1. Analyze the steps needed to successfully complete the task. For example, for addition, in which column should the student begin? Under which column should the student write the sum?
2. Write down the steps in a clear, concise sequence.
3. Create a mnemonic to help the student remember the steps (for example, for addition, **SASH**—**S**tart in the one's column, **A**dd, **S**hould I carry? **H**ave I carried correctly?).
4. Model using the strategy; use it verbally at the board, write the steps near problems, etc.
5. Fade the supports as the student begins to use the strategy independently.

and the number of modifications reported for learners with mild disabilities. Examples of modifications for using textbooks and for solving arithmetic problems are presented in the "Guidelines for Practice" boxes on page 355 and above.

Salend and Lutz (1984) surveyed general and special educators to determine the skills and competencies needed by learners with mild disabilities for success in general education classrooms. They found that three general areas of competency were necessary: (1) positive peer interaction, (2) ability to follow rules, and (3) appropriate work habits. In the area of positive peer interaction, learners needed to be able to work effectively with others, respect the feelings of others, avoid fighting and stealing, engage in cooperative play, and share materials and equipment. Specific class rules to be adhered to included remaining quiet while others were speaking, using appropriate language, and telling the truth. Appropriate work habits needed to function successfully in the general education classroom were following directions, seeking assistance when appropriate, initiating assignments independently, attending to and persisting at tasks, and attending class regularly. Several strategies for helping learners with mild disabilities become organized are presented in the "Guidelines for Practice" box on page 357.

During reading groups, Englert (1994) found that the nature of the discussion and dialogue between the teacher and the learners with mild disabilities was related to effective instruction. When dialogue, social interactions, and scaffolded instruction were involved, students made greater gains. Coaching also helped students learn to make explanations and promote their relational thinking (Scruggs, 1994). Using guided notes or outlines that the learners completed in class was also effective in supporting learning (Lazarus, 1993).

Peer Tutoring

Classwide peer tutoring has been suggested as an effective strategy for learners with mild disabilities. Implementation of peer tutoring has been associated with increases of approximately eighteen points on social studies examinations of learners with mild disabilities (Maheady, Sacca, & Harper, 1988). In addition, the implementation of classwide peer tutoring has been found to reduce failing grades. In one study, learners with mild disabilities received no grades below a C.

guidelines for practice

Helping Students with Mild Disabilities Become Organized

Students with mild disabilities may need additional supports to help them develop organizational skills. Shields and Heron (1989) suggest several strategies to help students become more organized (and maintain organization).

Provide students with a visual representation of what must be learned, what tasks need to be accomplished, and the time frame.

Teach students to use an assignment log. This log can be coordinated with a two-pocket work folder, in which one pocket is labeled "completed" and the other "to be completed."

Set up a work station for the student that signals academic engaged time.

Color code assignments: red flags can mean due immediately, yellow for due tomorrow, and green for due in the near future.

Provide "guided notes" that include a list of key terms, definitions of the terms, and comprehension questions **|**

Collaborative Consultation

West and Idol (1990) write that **collaborative consultation** can support learners with mild disabilities. Consultation is effective in (a) preventing learning and behavioral problems, (b) remediating these problems, and (c) coordinating instructional programs.

The purpose of collaborative consultation is to have the special educator and the general educator work as a team to develop specific management and instructional interventions for learners with mild disabilities and other difficult-to-teach learners who are served in the general classroom (Pugach & Johnson, 1988). Through consultation, the general educator is provided assistance in the identification, intervention, and evaluation of learner behavior.

In an effort to overcome the barriers to true collaborative consultation caused by differences in the professional roles and functions of the general and special educators, Pugach and Johnson have reconceptualized collaborative consultation on four dimensions:

1. Consultation should be a reciprocal process and involve mutual interaction among all professionals in the school.
2. Consultation should result in the development of independent problem-solving skills by the general educator.
3. Consultation should be a routine part of the function of all professionals in the school.
4. A common language that does not emphasize the specialized language used in special education or other professions should be used in consultation communications.

Teacher-Assistance Teams

The **teacher-assistance team,** whose members include teachers, school administrators, and professionals in psychology, social work, and special education, has been suggested as a strategy for serving learners with mild disabilities in the general education program (Hayek, 1987). As a prereferral support system, the teacher-assistance team can be of aid to students who are not eligible for special education services due to the mildness of their disability and to students who though eligible for special education services can be maintained in the general education classroom with services from the general education teacher.

The teacher-assistance team is "a teacher-centered instructional alternative support system" (Hayek, 1987). By engaging in problem-solving activities, the members of the team generate ideas, methods, techniques, and activities and develop a plan to assist the teacher in efforts to maintain the learner in the general education classroom.

In addition to reducing the number of unnecessary referrals to special education, the teacher-assistance team is an excellent in-service training or staff-development device for teachers and administrators unfamiliar with specialized instructional and management interventions. Team activities facilitate open communication among general and special educators and other support personnel.

Of course, the teacher-assistance team cannot function without the general education teacher who willingly agrees to participate and implement the interventions developed by the team. Membership in the team is fluid and varies from case to case and from setting to setting. It should be clearly understood by the members that the team is not a special education strategy but rather a way to prevent referral to and placement in special education services.

Prior to referral to the teacher-assistance team, the teacher should implement and document the interventions that have been used to assist the learner in the general education classroom. If these interventions have not been effective, then the teacher confers with the principal and together they determine the need for referral to the teacher-assistance team. The teacher then completes the proper forms and follows the accepted procedures to convene the team. When the team meets, the teacher presents his or her major concerns about the child and the team engages in collaborative problem-solving activities, leading to recommended interventions. The teacher implements the interventions for a predetermined period of time and documents implementation and results. If the interventions are not effective, then the team is reconvened to develop additional interventions or to refer the learner to special education for a diagnostic evaluation.

Social Skills Programming

An overriding concern for learners with mild disabilities is that of providing programming in social skills or, in some cases, what are referred to as **school survival skills.** Schaeffer, Zigmond, Kerr, and Farra (1990) state that instruction in school survival skills must be a part of the special education agenda if learners with mild disabilities are to succeed in school and, eventually, work. These critical skills, according to Zigmond, Kerr, Brown, and Harris (1984) include the following:

1. Going to class daily.
2. Being on time.
3. Bringing necessary materials to class.
4. Turning in work on time.
5. Interacting with teachers without "back talk."
6. Reading and following written directions and following oral directions.

The effectiveness of instruction in these skills is significantly enhanced if parents reinforce the lessons learned in school at home.

Cooperative strategies can enhance both social skills and academic skills. O'Melia and Rosenberg (1994) found that using cooperative homework teams increased the rate of homework completion and percentage correct on homework. These teams both practiced the content provided in the homework and learned to work together.

Learners with mild disabilities are full participants in their community.

The Impact on Participation in the School, Community, and Society

Objective Five

To describe the impact of mild disabilities on participation in larger social systems of the school, community, and society.

Putnam (1987) suggests that the most powerful interventions for learners with mild disabilities take place in the community at large as well as in the schools. These interventions require a cooperative and trusting working relationship between the school, the student's home, and the community. Secondary school counselors may serve to support the transition from school to work, through involvement in vocational planning and training in social skills, the coordination of services, and consultation with other professionals on progress and outstanding needs (Rose, Friend, & Farnum, 1988).

Learners with mild disabilities may need to learn to become their own advocates in the community. Sievert, Cuvo, and Davis (1988) demonstrated the effectiveness of a program that taught young adults with mild disabilities (1) to discriminate whether or not possible violations of legal rights occurred, and, if so, (2) to role play how to deal with these violations. Learners who completed the program showed marked increases in their knowledge of their personal rights, community responsibilities, human services, and consumer rights.

In a study utilizing participant observation, Zetlin and Hosseini (1989) spent one year studying six young adults with mild disabilities the year following their graduation from high school. All students reported that they were glad to have graduated. Five of the students were less than satisfied with the special education program and their experiences during high school. These adult learners experienced problems with typical peers, whose friendship they preferred. All six of the learners received only minimal vocational skills. After graduation they went to junior college, but they did not take challenging courses. In addition, they were all unwilling to acknowledge their disabilities and the complications their particular problems presented towards normative achievements. Though challenged in their participation in the community, all of the learners shied away from support services designated for the developmentally disabled as soon as they shed their special education label. These adult learners floundered from job to job, expressed discontent and frustration, but were at a loss to plan for the future and maintained an unrealistic appraisal of their skills.

Fardig (1985) also found that little specific vocational training was available to rural learners with mild disabilities. Okolo and Sitlington (1988) suggest that this low participation of learners with mild disabilities in vocational programs is related to several factors, including (a) the level of independence required in vocational programs, (b) reading and writing skills required, (c) primary modifications needed for effective participation, such as extra assistance or additional time, (d) lack of staff training for work with learners with disabilities, (e) minimal staff involvement regarding decisions in placements of learners with disabilities, and (f) low staff comfort level with individuals with mild disabilities.

In an interview study conducted six years after graduation, Scuccimarra and Speece (1990) reported that most of their respondents relied on self, family, and friend networks to secure employment. Most of the adults were single, resided at home, and were in primarily unskilled, semiskilled, or service positions. Scuccimarra and Speece state that these findings are consistent with thirty years of data documenting low-level employment for learners with mild disabilities.

Edgar (1988), paraphrasing Finn (1986), writes that special education for learners with mild disabilities has three primary purposes in the area of skills preparation. Special education should teach skills needed to function by preparing learners with skills to (a) function in the social system in which they live, (b) lead personally fulfilling lives, and (c) prepare for the next phase of their life, whether it be higher education or employment. In an extensive analysis of the research, Edgar concludes that learners with mild disabilities have more difficulty finding employment than do their peers. Learners labeled mildly mentally retarded do less well in the area of employment than any other subgroup. Females do less well than males. The positions obtained by learners with mild disabilities are low-paying and lack fringe benefits. There is little evidence to support the conclusion that differential education has an impact on future employment. However, special education graduates have greater success finding employment than dropouts.

Miller (1994) suggests a program to increase the life skills of adolescents with mild disabilities. This program emphasizes hands-on activities, small-group discussion, and self-discovery projects. Four phases of the program are involved. First, students are supported in choosing a career. Students review benefit packages and salaries of jobs available to students in the community. During the second phase, students learn to budget for an apartment at a specific income level. In the third phase, students furnish an apartment. During the fourth phase, students learn to take out a car loan, develop a plan for buying a house, open a savings account, purchase items on credit, and budget for a new baby. Miller reports that students benefit from the program and that attendance and positive behavior increase as does the students' knowledge of life skills.

Summary

In this chapter, learners with mild disabilities were discussed. There is concern over the consistent increase in the number of learners being identified as mildly learning disabled, mildly behaviorally disordered, and mildly mentally retarded.

Learners with mild disabilities may present academic and social-emotional challenges to teachers. Though research data is limited, it appears that a broad range of instructional and management interventions may be applied to facilitate the education and socialization of learners with mild disabilities. These interventions include preschool services, modified instruction in the general education classroom, peer tutoring, collaborative consultation, and teacher-assistance teams. Social or survival skills instruction appears to be essential to the effective functioning of learners with mild disabilities. This need for support continues when learners leave school and enter the workplace and community. Assistance through vocational training, higher education, and socialization to adulthood are needed.

Building Your Professional Vocabulary

Match each word or phrase to its meaning.

_____ collaborative consultation

_____ high-prevalence disabilities

    a. teachers and staff members who work together to support learners with mild disabilities in general education

_____ school survival skills

_____ teacher-assistance team

    b. a reciprocal process
    c. disabilities that occur most frequently
    d. required for success in schools

Comprehension Check

Select the most appropriate response.

1. Instruction in categorical special education classrooms for learners with mild disabilities has been found
   a. to be more similar than different.
   b. to be significantly different for learners identified as having learning disabilities.
   c. to be related to specific techniques developed for each disability category.
2. Learners with mild disabilities
   a. have the same social skills as their peers.
   b. have the same social status as their peers.
   c. have low status among their peers.
3. As they grow towards adulthood, learners with mild disabilities tend to
   a. appear more similar to their peers.
   b. lag behind their peers in breaking away from the family.
   c. resent the supervision of their parents.
4. In terms of language, learners with mild disabilities tend to
   a. verbally communicate more than their peers.
   b. vary in terms of quantity of language as compared to their peers.
   c. vary from their peers in terms of the quality of language they generate.

5. Differentiating learners with mild disabilities from those who demonstrate low achievement
   a. is based on social skills.
   b. is based on psychoeducational assessment.
   c. is based on learners with disabilities having significantly poorer achievement.
6. Categorical service delivery for learners with mild disabilities
   a. does not vary in instruction.
   b. does not vary in certification required.
   c. does not vary in the eligibility of learners served.
7. In the last ten years, more and more learners with mild disabilities are being served
   a. in special education programs.
   b. in resource rooms.
   c. in general education programs.
8. After graduation, learners with mild disabilities
   a. often access services for persons who are developmentally disabled.
   b. shy away from support services designed for persons who are developmentally disabled.
   c. are readily and successfully employed.

References

Aksamit, D. (1990). Mildly handicapped and at-risk students: The graying of the line. *Academic Therapy, 25* (3), 277–289.

Algozzine, B., & Korinek, L. (1985). Where is special education for students with high prevalence handicaps going? *Exceptional Children, 51,* 388–394.

Algozzine, B., Morsink, C. V., & Algozzine, K. M. (1988). What's happening in self-contained special education classrooms? *Exceptional Children, 55,* 259–265.

Alves, A. J., & Gottlieb, J. (1986). Teacher interactions with mainstreamed handicapped students and their nonhandicapped peers. *Learning Disability Quarterly, 9* (1), 77–83.

Armstrong, T. (1994). *Multiple intelligences in the classroom.* Alexandria, VA: Association for Supervision and Curriculum Development.

Bauer, A. M., & Shea, T. M. (1989). *Teaching exceptional students in your classroom.* Boston: Allyn & Bacon.

Bauman, E. (1991). Stability of WISC-R scores in children with learning difficulties. *Psychology in the Schools, 28,* 95–100.

Coleman, J. M., Pullis, M., & Minnett, A. M. (1987). Studying mildly handicapped children's adjustment to mainstreaming: A systematic approach. *Remedial and Special Education, 8* (6), 19–30.

Cooper, D. H., & Speece, D. L. (1990). Maintaining at-risk children in regular education settings: Initial effects of individual differences and classroom environments. *Exceptional Children, 57* (2), 117–127.

Edgar, E. (1988). Employment as an outcome for mildly handicapped students: Current status and future directions. *Focus on Exceptional Children, 21* (10), 1–8.

Englert, C. S. (1994). Lesson talk as the work of reading groups: The effectiveness of two interventions. *Journal of Learning Disabilities, 27,* 165–185.

Fardig, D. B. (1985). Postsecondary vocational adjustment of rural, mildly handicapped students. *Exceptional Children, 52,* 115–121.

Finn, C. E. (1986). A fresh option for the noncollege-bound. *Phi Delta Kappan, 68* (4), 234–348.

Frank, A. R., & Brown, D. (1992). Self-monitoring strategies in arithmetic. *Teaching Exceptional Children, 24* (2), 52–54.

Gardner, H. (1983). *Frames of mild: The theory of multiple intelligences.* New York: Basic Books.

Gardner, H. (1993). *Multiple Intelligences: The theory into practice.* New York: Basic Books.

Giangreco, M. F., Dennis, R., Cloninger, C., Edelman, S., and Schattman, R. (1993). "I've counted Jon": Transformational experiences of teachers educating students with disabilities. *Exceptional Children, 59,* 359–372.

Gresham, F. M., Elliott, N., & Black, F. L. (1987). Teacher-rated social skills of mainstreamed mildly handicapped and nonhandicapped children. *School Psychology Review, 16* (1), 78–88.

Hayek, R. A. (1987). The teacher assistance team: A prereferral support system. *Focus on Exceptional Children, 20* (1), 1–7.

Jenkins, J. R., Pious, C. G., Jewell, M. (1990). Special education and the regular education initiative: Basic assumptions. *Exceptional Children, 56,* 479–491.

Jenkins, J. R., Pious, C. G., & Peterson, D. L. (1988). Categorical programs for remedial and handicapped students: Issues of validity. *Exceptional Children, 55* (2), 147–158.

Jenkins, J. R., Speltz, M. L., & Odom, S. L. (1985). Integrating normal and handicapped preschoolers: Effects on child development and social interaction. *Exceptional Children, 52,* 7–17.

Kauffman, J. M., & Pullen, P. (1989). An historical perspective: A personal perspective of our history of service to mildly handicapped and at risk students. *Remedial and Special Education, 10,* 12–14.

Lazarus, B. D. (1993). Guided notes: Effects with secondary and post-secondary students with mild disabilities. *Education and Treatment of Children, 16,* 272–289.

Maheady, L., Algozzine, B., & Ysseldyke, J. E. (1984). Minority overrepresentation in special education: A functional assessment perspective. *Special Services in the Schools, 1* (2), 5–19.

Maheady, L., Sacca, M., & Harper, G. F. (1988). Classwide peer tutoring with mildly handicapped high school students. *Exceptional Children, 55,* 62–69.

Marston, D. (1987). Does categorical teacher certification benefit the mildly handicapped child? *Exceptional Children, 53,* 423–431.

Meese, R. L. (1992). Adapting textbooks for children with learning disabilities in mainstreamed classrooms. *Teaching Exceptional Children, 24* (3), 49–54.

Miller, D. (1994). "On your own": A functional skills activity for adolescents with mild disabilities. *Teaching Exceptional Children, 26* (3), 29–33.

Munson, S. M. (1986). Regular education teacher modifications for mainstreamed mildly handicapped students. *Journal of Special Education, 20,* 489–502.

Murtaugh, M. (1988). Achievement outside the classroom: The role of nonacademic activities in the lives of high school students. *Anthropology and Education Quarterly, 19,* 382–395.

Murtaugh, M., & Zetlin, A. G. (1988). Achievement of autonomy by nonhandicapped and mildly learning handicapped adolescents. *Journal of Youth and Adolescents, 17* (5), 445–460.

Natsopoulos, D., & Zeromeritou, A. (1990). Language behavior by mildly handicapped and nonretarded children on complement clauses. *Research in Developmental Disabilities, 11* (2), 199–216.

Noel, M., & Fuller, F. (1985). The social policy construction of special education: The impact of state characteristics on identification and integration of handicapped children. *Remedial and Special Education, 8* (3), 27–35.

Okolo, C., & Sitlington, P. L. (1988). Mildly handicapped learners in vocational education: A statewide study. *Journal of Special Education, 22,* 220–230.

O'Melia, M. C., & Rosenberg, M. S. (1994). Effects of cooperative homework teams on the acquisition of mathematics skills by secondary students with mild disabilities. *Exceptional Children, 60,* 538–548.

O'Sullivan, P. J., Marston, D., & Magnusson, D. (1987). Categorical special education teacher certification: Does it affect instruction of mildly handicapped pupils? *Remedial and Special Education, 8,* 13–18.

Pugach, M. C., & Johnson, L. J. (1988). Rethinking the relationship between consultation and collaborative problem-solving. *Focus on Exceptional Children, 21* (4), 1–8.

Putnam, M. L. (1987). Effective interventions for mildly handicapped adolescents in the home and the community. *Pointer, 31* (3), 19–24.

Reynolds, M. C., Wang, M. C., & Walberg, H. J. (1987). The necessary restructuring of special and regular education. *Exceptional Children, 53* (5), 391–398.

Rose, E., Friend, M., & Farnum, M. (1988). Transition planning for mildly handicapped students: The secondary school counselor's role. *School Counselor, 25,* 275–283.

Sabornie, E. J., & Beard, G. H. (1990). Teaching social skills to students with mild handicaps. *Teaching Exceptional Children,* 35–38.

Salend, S. J., & Lutz, G. L. (1984). Mainstreaming and mainlining: A competency based approach to mainstreaming. *Journal of Learning Disabilities, 17* (1), 27–29.

Schaeffer, A. L., Zigmond, N., Kerr, M. M., & Farra, H. E. (1990). Helping teenagers develop school survival skills. *Teaching Exceptional Children, 23* (1), 6–9.

Scruggs, T. E. (1994). Promoting relational thinking: Elaborative interrogation for students with mild disabilities. *Exceptional Children, 60,* 450–457.

Scuccimarra, D. J., & Speece, D. L. (1990). Employment outcomes and social integration of students with mild handicaps: The quality of life two years after high school. *Journal of Learning Disabilities, 23,* 213–219.

Shields, J. M., & Heron, T. E. (1989). Teaching organizational skills to students with learning disabilities. *Teaching Exceptional Children, 21* (2), 8–13.

Shinn, M., & Marston, D. (1985). Differentiating mildly handicapped, low-achieving, and regular education students: A curriculum-based approach. *Remedial and Special Education, 6* (2), 31–38.

Sievert, A. L., Cuvo, A. J., & Davis, K. (1988). Training self-advocacy skills to adults with mild handicaps. *Journal of Applied Behavior Analysis, 21,* 299–309.

Smith, S. M. (1989). Congenital syndromes and mildly handicapped students: Implications for special educators. *Remedial and Special Education, 10* (3), 20–30.

West, J. F., & Idol, L. (1990). Collaborative consultation in the education of mildly handicapped and at-risk students. *Remedial and Special Education, 11* (1), 22–31.

Ysseldyke, J. E., Thurlow, M. L., Wotruba, J. W., & Nania, P. (1990). Instructional arrangements: Perceptions from general education. *Teaching Exceptional Children, 22* (4), 4–8.

Zetlin, A. G., & Hosseini, A. (1989). Six postschool case studies of mildly learning handicapped young adults. *Exceptional Children, 55,* 405–411.

Zigmond, N., Kerr, M. M., Brown, G. M., & Harris, A. L. (1984). *School survival skills in secondary school age special education students.* Paper presented at the meeting of the American Educational Research Association, New Orleans.

Learners with Severe and Multiple Disabilities

Objectives

After completing this chapter, you will be able to:

1. describe the personal characteristics of learners with severe or multiple disabilities.
2. describe the identification and evaluation of learners with severe or multiple disabilities.
3. describe the impact of severe or multiple disabilities on interactions in the home and classroom.
4. describe ways to mediate the environment for learners with severe or multiple disabilities.
5. describe the impact of severe or multiple disabilities on participation in the larger social systems of the community and society.

Key Words and Phrases

augmentative communication
   systems
autism
dual sensory impairments

facilitated communication
multiple disabilities
pervasive developmental disorder
severe disabilities

The living quarters for older men and women were, for the most part, gloomy and sterile. There were rows and rows of benches on which sat countless human beings, in silent rooms, waiting for dinner call or bed time. We saw resident after resident in "institutional garb." Sometimes the women wore shrouds—inside out.

We heard a good deal of laughter but saw little cheer. There were few things to be cheerful about. A great deal of the men and women looked depressed and acted depressed. Even the television sets, in several of the day rooms, appeared to be co-conspirators in a crusade for gloom. These sets were not in working order. Ironically, the residents continued to sit on their benches, in neat rows, looking at the blank tubes.

We observed adult residents during recreation, playing "ring-around-the-rosy." Others, in the vocational training center, were playing "jacks." These were not always severely retarded patients. However, one got the feeling very quickly that this is the way they were being forced to behave. (Description of an institution for individuals with mental retardation in the early 1960s, from Blatt & Kaplan, 1966)

At The Seaside there is time, time for teaching a young child to use a spoon or fork, time for helping a child to learn to use a zipper, time to heal a wound—either of the body or the soul. But, at The Seaside, there is no time for tomorrow. There is a fight against inertia. Children must be helped today, for in too few tomorrows children become adults and residents become inmates.

At The Seaside, there is schooling. Some children attend school at the institution. The older and more capable youngsters attend school in the community—public school—with other children who are living at home. At The Seaside, it is not difficult to tell that this is an environment designed for children. The lawns are filled with swings and jungle gyms and bicycle paths. During Christmas time, each room is decorated, welcoming Santa Claus and the spirit of Christmas. Rooms are clean and orderly. Furniture that adults use is designed for adults.

There are adult residents at The Seaside. However, they are not in the same dormitories, or programs, with the children. Adults have other needs and the following may illustrate how some of these are met.

One of our difficulties in photographing activities at The Seaside was our inability to take very many pictures of adult residents. There is a very good explanation for this. Most of the adults at The Seaside worked during the day—they are on institutional jobs or out in the community. Some, who could not be returned to their own homes, live in a work training unit. Here, they are together with friends and co-workers, under the supervision of a cottage mother and father. During the day they are on placement—working in the community—and in the evening they return to their "home" where they can receive special help and guidance in their successful attempts to integrate into normal communities and become contributing members of society. (Description of an experimental institution for the severely retarded in the early 1960s, from Blatt & Kaplan, 1966)

Introduction

There are, without doubt, no individuals with disabilities who have been more positively affected by the litigation and legislation of the past two decades than those identified as severely or multiply disabled. Institutions similar to that described in the first vignette at the beginning of the chapter are, for the most part, a thing of the past. Today, the few adults and children living in residential centers and group homes reside in environments similar to The Seaside, described in the second vignette presented to open the chapter. Though the transition is not complete, these individuals have progressed in great numbers from institutions into the mainstream of the educational community and the community at large.

The number of learners identified with multiple disabilities increased and those with dual sensory impairments decreased between the 1992–1993 and 1993–1994 school years (U.S. Department of Education, 1995). During the 1993–1994 school year, 109,746 learners between six and twenty-one years of age were classified as multiply disabled and 1,372 were classified as demonstrating dual sensory impairments. Though inclusion is becoming more common, learners with multiple disabilities or dual sensory impairments are served in separate special education classes, separate schools, and residential facilities.

Another low-incidence disability discussed in this chapter is autism. The prevalence of autism has been estimated to range from 4 to 5 per 10,000 births (Ritvo & Freeman, 1978) to 10 to 15 per 10,000 births (American Psychiatric Association, 1987). Most learners with autism are served in public school special education programs, separate schools, and, in some cases, in general education classes with support services. The number of learners with autism served in the 1993–1994 school year was 18,903, an increase of 21.3 percent over 1992–1993. (U.S. Department of Education, 1995).

Personal Characteristics

Learners with Multiple Disabilities

There is great variation among individuals with severe or multiple disabilities. These learners frequently have severe to profound mental retardation as well as one or more significant motor or sensory impairments. Orelove and Sobsey (1987) indicate that learners with severe or multiple disabilities often present two or more of these concerns:

Objective One

To describe the personal characteristics of learners with severe or multiple disabilities.

> physical and medical problems
> restricted movement
> skeletal deformities
> sensory disorders
> seizure disorders
> respiratory difficulties
> the need for appropriate positioning and handling
> the need for augmentative communication strategies
> the need for a means to choose, that is, make personal decisions

For many individuals with severe or multiple disabilities, communication is a challenge. Finding a way for individuals with severe or multiple disabilities to communicate their personal needs is essential to their participation in the community (Ferguson, 1994).

Learners with Autism

In 1981, learners with autism were moved from the category "serious emotional disturbance" to "other health impaired" as a result of parental and professional efforts to emphasize the biological nature of the disorder. In Public Law 101-476 (The Individuals with Disabilities Education Act of 1990), autism was again reclassified as a separate category of disability. There is ongoing professional dialogue with regard to the personal characteristics of learners with autism. However, it is generally agreed that, in varying degrees, learners with **autism** demonstrate many of these characteristics (Simpson, 1992):

- difficulty relating to others and developing interpersonal relationships
- communication problems in both language and speech
- developmental delays in cognitive, social, and motor areas
- difficulties reacting appropriately to environmental events

Learners with autism, when compared to those with mental retardation and no identified disabilities, may demonstrate less diverse play, particularly in spontaneous and cued symbolic play (Sigman & Ungerer, 1984).

The incidence of autism is three times greater in boys than in girls. Its occurrence is fifty times as great in siblings than in the general population (American Psychiatric Association, 1987). Autism was first described as a clinical syndrome by Leo Kanner in 1943. Kanner's use of the word "autism," which had prior to his work been used to describe a symptom of schizophrenia, contributed to confusion surrounding the biological nature of the disorder (Rutter, 1978). The American Psychiatric Association (APA) has attempted to clarify this issue by referring to these children as having a "pervasive developmental disorder." In recent research, many organic factors have been associated with autism, including maternal rubella during pregnancy, celiac disease, tuberous sclerosis, metabolic disorders, and genetic conditions such as fragile-X syndrome (Rutter & Schopler, 1985). However, none of these factors accounts for more than a very small number of cases; in most situations, the cause of the disability cannot be determined.

Based on advances in research, Prizant (1984) conceptualizes autism from a communication perspective. In order to describe the functioning of these individuals, he delineates three levels of communicative functioning and the behaviors related to each level (see table 16.1). When autism is viewed from Prizant's communication perspective, many of the "bizarre" behaviors of learners with autism take on or can be ascribed meaning.

Learners with Dual Sensory Impairments

Originally referred to as "deaf-blind," learners with **dual sensory impairments** have both visual and auditory disabilities. As a result of these complex disabilities, learners with dual sensory impairments present severe communication deficits as well as developmental and educational problems.

Ninety-four percent of learners classified as dual sensory impaired have some residual hearing and/or vision (Fredericks & Baldwin, 1987). Andrews (1989) states that the essential issue with these learners is to facilitate their use of residual vision and hearing. However, he cautions against overestimating the value and use that a learner with dual sensory impairments can make of these senses.

There are special problems related to these learners. For example, because of lack of feedback from the infant, there may be challenges in attachment and parental overprotection.

Table 16.1 **Communicative Functioning of Learners with Autism**

Level of Communication	Description	Behaviors
Preintentional/early intentional	Active exploration of the environment; no direct signals or gestures; in early intentional begins direct signals, and develops ways to communicate which only significant other can understand; shows some persistence in signalling	Stereotypic manipulation of objects; orients to stimuli in the environment; inconsistent response to others' speech; in early intention will manipulate adults' hands to perform specific tasks; moves adult physically to initiate action; may use echolalia with intent
Prelinguistic, intentional/ emerging linguistic	Clear concept of communication; uses conventional gestures; more persistent if communicative goals not met; in emerging linguistic uses some words or signs; increased word comprehension	Signals, vocalizes, uses echolalia for a variety of functions; later uses words; greater flexibility in use of echolalia
Intentional/linguistic	Language primary means of communicating; problems in nonliteral forms of language	Initiates and responds to verbal interactions; demonstrates primary problems in pragmatics

Identification and Evaluation

Public Law 94-142 and its amendments did not include a definition of the term **severe disabilities.** One of the more widely used definitions is that of the Bureau of Education for the Handicapped (U.S. Office of Education, 1975):

> Severely handicapped children are those who because of the intensity of their physical, mental, or emotional problems, need educational, social, psychological, and medical services beyond those which are traditionally offered by regular and special education programs, in order to maximize participation in society and self-fulfillment. Such severely handicapped children may possess severe language or perceptual-cognitive deprivations and evidence a number of abnormal behaviors including failure to attend to even the most pronounced stimuli, self-mutilation, manifestations of durable and intense temper tantrums, and the absence of even the most rudimentary forms of verbal control. They may also have extremely fragile physiological conditions. (Sec. 121.2)

According to an analysis by Dollar and Brooks (1980), three criteria for identification as severely handicapped emerge from this definition. First, severe disabilities must be present. Second, an intense educational program with a wide range of resources is necessary. Finally, the focus of educational programs must be on independent functioning.

In 1990, The Association for Persons with Severe Handicaps (TASH) proposed an alternative definition for severe disabilities that refers to level, duration, and supports needed by the individual. In addition, the definition considers the goals and outcomes of service. TASH defines persons with severe disabilities as

> . . . individuals of all ages who require extensive, ongoing support in more than one major life activity in order to participate in integrated community settings and to enjoy a quality of life that is available to citizens with fewer or no disabilities. Support can be required for life activities such as mobility, communication, self-care, and learning, as necessary for independent living, employment, and self-sufficiency. (Lindley, 1990, p. 1)

Objective Two

To describe the identification and evaluation of learners with severe or multiple disabilities.

Age-appropriate activities support improved quality of life for learners with severe disabilities.

Another working definition of individuals with severe disabilities includes those who "have a significant functional discrepancy in (1) general developmental abilities, (2) caring and looking after themselves, (3) expressing thoughts, ideas, and feelings, (4) responding to environmental stimuli, and (5) interacting socially with chronological-age peers" (Brimer, 1990, p. 15).

Learners with **multiple disabilities,** as defined by Public Law 94-142 and its amendments, are those with

> . . . concomitant impairments (such as mentally retarded-blind, mentally retarded-orthopedically impaired, etc.) the combination of which causes such severe educational problems that they cannot be accommodated in special education programs soley for one of the impairments.

Learners with dual sensory impairments are not included in this group. Rather, they are identified as deaf-blind, with the term defined as "concurrent hearing and visual impairments, the combination of which causes such severe communication and educational problems that they cannot be accommodated in special education programs for either the deaf or blind student" (Federal Register, 1977).

The Federal Register does not provide a definition of autism, but refers to it as ". . . an autistic condition, which is manifested by severe communication and other developmental and educational problems." The APA, in the fourth edition of its *Diagnostic and Statistical Manual of Mental Disorders* (1994), refers to autism as a **pervasive developmental disorder (PDD),** which is usually evident in the first years of life and is often associated with some degree of mental retardation. The diagnostic criteria for autistic disorder are presented in table 16.2

In a description of the process used by the APA committees in determining the criteria for the diagnosis of autism, Denckla (1986) reports that social impairment was felt by some to be the core characteristic of the disorder. In addition, communication skills, both verbal and nonverbal, must be impaired for the diagnosis of autism. The presence of repetitive, ritualistic behaviors, in and of themselves, were not felt to establish a diagnosis of autism, but when present with social and communicative impairments, provide diagnostic confirmation.

Table 16.2 **Diagnostic Criteria for Autistic Disorder**

A. Total of six (or more) items from (1), (2), and (3), with at least two from (1), and one each from (2), and (3):

1. qualitative impairment in social interaction, manifested by at least two of the following:
   (a) marked impairment in the use of multiple nonverbal behaviors, such as eye-to-eye gaze, facial expression, body postures, and gestures to regulate social interaction
   (b) failure to develop peer relationships appropriate to developmental level
   (c) a lack of spontaneous seeking to share enjoyment, interests, or achievements with other people (e.g., by lack of showing, bringing, or pointing out objects of interest)
   (d) lack of social or emotional reciprocity
2. qualitative impairments in communication as manifested by at least one of the following:
   (a) delay in, or total lack of, the development of spoken language (not accompanied by an attempt to compensate through alternative modes of communication such as gesture or mime)
   (b) in individuals with adequate speech, marked impairment in the ability to initiate or sustain a conversation with others
   (c) stereotyped and repetitive use of language or idiosyncratic language
   (d) lack of varied, spontaneous, make believe play or social imitative play appropriate to developmental level
3. restricted repetitive and stereotyped patterns of behaviors, interests, and activities, as manifested by at least one of the following:
   (a) encompassing preoccupation with one or more stereotyped and restricted patterns of interest that is abnormal either in intensity or focus
   (b) apparently inflexible adherence to specific, nonfunctional routines or rituals
   (c) stereotyped and repetitive motor mannerisms (e.g., hand or finger flapping or twisting, or complex whole-body movements)
   (d) persistent preoccupations with parts of objects

B. Delays or abnormal functioning in at least one of the following areas, with onset prior to age three years:
1. social interaction
2. language as used in social communication
3. symbolic or imaginative play

C. The disturbance is not better accounted for by Rett's disorder or childhood disintegrative disorder.

American Psychiatric Association: *Diagnostic and Statistical Manual of Mental Disorders, Fourth Edition.* Washington, DC, American Psychiatric Association, 1994.

Students with severe and multiple disabilities are particularly susceptible to discriminatory assessment practices (Sigafoos, Cole, & McQuarter, 1987). In a study of the types of tests used with these students, there was found to be a lack of technically adequate norm-referenced tests that are appropriate. Generally, school systems do not select tests on the basis of technical adequacy. In addition, they found that criterion-referenced assessment and adaptive behavior measures are used rather infrequently.

Standardized tests are not appropriate for learners with severe disabilities in that they are not designed for them, they do not include these learners in the standardization sample, scoring does not allow for adaptive motor or language responses, and changes in behavior may be too small to be measured on such instruments (Linehan, Brady, & Hwang, 1991). In the alternative ecological approach, the teacher, family, and related service personnel determine the practical and functional skills needed in the home, school, community, and vocational setting. Linehan and associates found that ecological assessment reports generated higher expectations among professionals.

Based on his and others' previous work, Brown (1987) suggests that in order to appropriately assess learners with severe and multiple disabilities, the learner's daily activities should be broken down into a series of routines composed of different core skills. An emphasis on routines for these learners reflects the complex competencies needed to function as independently as possible in the community. These routines can be grouped within four domains: personal management, vocational/school, leisure, and mobility. The most appropriate strategy for this type of assessment is observation of the learner in the natural environment. In addition, parent or caregiver interviews are helpful in acquiring specific information regarding skills.

Snell and Grigg (1987) suggest a strategy for assessment grounded in an ecological inventory of the activities in which the learner engages and the skills required within those activities. The strategy includes the following:

1. Specify the curriculum domains. Rather than traditional academic categories, these domains represent the major life areas, lead to practical skills, and emphasize movement towards independence.
2. Analyze the environments and subenvironments in which the activities occur.
3. Assess the subenvironments for the relevant activities performed there, rather than identifying every possible activity. Emphasize those activities necessary for basic acceptable performance.
4. Examine the activities to isolate the skills required, then break down each skill into meaningful units.

An emerging area is the assessment of biobehavioral states of students with profound disabilities. Guess and associates (1988) define biobehavioral states as the general state of alertness and responsiveness described in the literature about infants. In discussing learners with profound disabilities, Guess and associates express a concern that program schedules followed regardless of student receptivity or responsiveness and even though the students may have very severe neurological, physical, and/or sensory impairments, may be susceptible to a variety of acute illnesses, or may be heavily medicated. They suggest that in working with these learners, understanding the patterns or clusters of periods during which the learner "shuts down" to external sensory or social stimulation is essential.

By using a variation of the Neonatal Behavioral Assessment scale (Brazelton, 1973), Struth and Guess (1986) describe six biobehavioral states: asleep/inactive; asleep/active; drowsy; awake/inactive/alert; awake/active/alert; and crying/agitated. It is important, however, to collect biobehavioral data over longer durations of the day so as to describe possible intrastudent fluctuations in state conditions. The data can then be compared on an across-day basis.

A comprehensive assessment approach is needed for learners with autism (Simpson, 1992). The approach is multidisciplinary and uses both formal and informal assessment techniques. The areas recommended for assessment are (a) cognitive skills, (b) family and environmental behaviors, (c) neurological, sensory-motor, and medical difficulties, (d) social and behavioral abilities, and (e) the curriculum (preacademic, academic, vocational, self-help, communication, and independent living).

The Impact on Interactions in the Home and Classroom

Objective Three

To describe the impact of severe or multiple disabilities on interactions in the home and classroom.

In the Home

Though management of daily household tasks and child-care routines in families with adopted children with severe disabilities was not identified as stressful, interactions with school, medical personnel, and other professionals were extremely stressful for all families interviewed (Todis & Singer, 1991). Medical crises and behavior problems were seen by the families as time-limited sources of stress; dealing with service providers and "figuring out the system," however, were perceived to be chronic problems. Household management routines, medical and hygiene routines, time away from the family, and social support from other families with special-needs children were viewed as ways of coping with difficulties.

In interviews with twenty-eight families whose children had dual sensory impairments, Giangreco, Cloninger, Mueller, Yuan, and Ashworth (1991) found that parent concerns clustered around a "good life" for their children, as well as their experiences with fear, frustration, and change. Parents expressed the frustrations that "dealing with schools can be tough" and that the sheer number of professionals working with their children was hectic and an invasion of their privacy. Parents viewed themselves as their child's case manager, though professional case managers could be helpful.

Attention has also been given to the siblings of learners with severe disabilities. Rodrique (1993) compared children with autism, siblings of children with Down syndrome, and children with siblings with no identified disability. He found that these three groups of children did not differ on measures of perceived self-competence or parents' reports of social competence. However, the siblings of children with autism did demonstrate more behavior problems than siblings of children with no identified disability.

In a review of twenty-seven studies of parental attitudes on the deinstitutionalization of a family member, Larson and Lakin (1991) found that in the studies in which the family member was still institutionalized, families indicated general opposition to deinstitutionalization. In those studies in which the family member had already moved to the community, parents who had retrospectively reported lower levels of satisfaction with earlier institutional placement reported lower levels of opposition to deinstitutionalization and high levels of satisfaction with community settings.

There was considerable research, prior to Public Law 94-142, on the reasons that individuals with severe and multiple disabilities were placed in out-of-home residential services. In 1991, Bromley and Blacher, as part of a parent interview study of out-of-home placement, reviewed the literature and concluded that parents had three major areas of concerns when placing a child out of home. Their concerns focused around the child's characteristics, family characteristics, and lack of supportive services. Child characteristics related to out-of-home placement included behavior problems and severe levels of mental retardation. Family characteristics were related to daily stress, parental health, marital status, and family size. The availability of supportive services, such as help in the home, babysitters, and respite care, also influenced the decision to place an individual out of home. In their study of sixty-three parents (primary caregivers) of individuals with severe disabilities between the ages of two and sixteen, Bromley and Blacher found that the decision to place out of home was not based on one factor but influenced by a number of factors working together. Of the twenty factors that emerged, the five most influential were (1) day-to-day stress, (2) the child's level of functioning and potential for future learning, (3) the child's behavior, (4) the feelings of nondisabled siblings, and (5) the spouse's attitude toward placement. The availability of supportive services was not found to be essential in the decision to place children out of home.

Parent involvement has been correlated significantly with many factors reflecting the home and quality of parenting (Meyers & Blacher, 1987). Overall family adjustment and the level of the mother's education have been correlated to parent involvement. Schools reportedly provided some respite for parents, and many parents felt they did gain techniques and skills for working better with their child through their involvement. When compared to mothers of children with milder disabilities, some mothers of learners with severe or

A Camp That Cares

When Jeffrey Erlanger was 10, his parents, Pam and Howard Erlanger of Congregation Beth El in Madison, Wisconsin, enrolled him as a camper at the UAHC's Olin-Sang-Ruby Union Institute in Oconomowoc. Today, Jeffrey, 21, is a counselor at the camp and a merit scholarship student at Madison's Edgewood College, majoring in journalism.

Jeffrey, a quadriplegic, lost the use of both arms and legs in infancy.

The Erlangers' decision to send Jeffrey to the Olin-Sang-Ruby camp led to the creation of an unusual program—an annual Kallah that enables Jewish families with disabled children to spend three days together at the camp to discuss mutual problems, enjoy recreational activities such as waterfront sports and horseback riding, and just hang out and have fun.

The Kallah was organized in 1984 by camp director Gerard W. Kaye with the help of Pam Erlanger, a professional occupational therapist. Held every August at the Union Institute camp, it is attended by between 10 and 15 families from various parts of the Midwest. Some 20 teenage members of temple youth groups from NoFTY and CFTY sign on as volunteer Kallah counselors—Jeffrey Erlanger himself was one—and receive an intensive orientation on working with the disabled. The teens are supplemented by college students and adult occupational and physical therapy professionals.

The Kallah is jointly sponsored by the Olin-Sang-Ruby camp and Keshet, a 200-member support group for Jewish families with disabled children. Disabilities run the gamut from visual impairment to serious learning disabilities to diseases such as muscular dystrophy. In fact, most of the children in the Keshet program suffer from multiple handicaps.

"As important as the Kallah is for the disabled youngsters," says Kaye, "it's no less so for their parents and brothers and sisters who rarely have a chance to enjoy a simple family vacation."

Another key aim is to make available to the disabled youngsters activities that normally would be denied them, such as horseback riding or taking their wheelchairs onto a pontoon boat. "No activity at the Kallah is off limits for a child because of a disability," he says.

For the temple youth teens who serve as volunteer Kallah counselors, the experience can be profound. "Many self-involved kids soon discover in themselves previously untapped wells of sensitivity," the camp director explains.

But the greatest impact is on the disabled youngsters themselves and their families. The opportunity to give and receive emotional support and practical advice can be an extraordinary experience, says Pam Erlanger. Equally important, she adds, is the chance for parents to have a mini-vacation "within a family context," secure in the knowledge that their children are being well cared for.

Jeffrey Erlanger observes that serving as a Kallah counselor gave him an opportunity to help disabled children, just as he himself had been helped, by giving them a sense of reassurance and determination. "Because of my own disability," he says, "I could honestly tell the younger disabled kids that they are capable of achieving a lot more than they may have hoped or even dreamed of."

As a camper, Jeffrey was able for the first time to establish ongoing relationships with children who were not disabled. "In school I could never do that," he says. "The other kids did not exactly make fun of me, but they found it hard to be my friend because they thought I was different. But at camp, I had something in common with the non-disabled kids—Judaism and the fact that we were all campers together."

Jeffrey contends that the annual Kallot gives other disabled children the same chance, even if only for three days. "Camping helped change my life," he says. "Perhaps it can help change their lives, too" ●

Reprinted with permission from *Reform Judaism,* published by the Union of American Hebrew Congregations, New York.

---

multiple disabilities were able to identify as many communication cues as the mothers of infants with milder disabilities, perhaps because they adapted to their infants' disabilities and were better able to interpret their behavior (Yoder & Feagans, 1988).

Though parent involvement in their children's education is clearly described in the law, efforts to engage parents of learners with severe disabilities beyond the mandated levels may be minimal. In their study, Hilton and Henderson (1993) suggest that parent involvement is both best practice and a forgotten practice. They found few efforts to engage parents beyond the level required by the law, and attitudes toward the ability of parents to contribute to the education of their children were poor.

Parents of learners with dual sensory impairments need practical help, advice, and resources, including contact with other parents who have had similar experiences. They frequently need information on hearing aids (Andrews, 1989).

Students use technology to communicate.

In the Classroom

Chadsey-Rusch (1990), using narrative recording procedures, studied the social interactions of secondary-aged students with severe disabilities by observing ten students attending a junior high school campus. She found that these students were involved in more task-related than non-task related interactions and that they were engaged more with teachers than with their peers. In addition, these adolescents were dependent on contrived or additional cues and feedback rather than those that naturally occurred in the school or vocational settings.

Schnorr (1990) studied how part-time integration of a learner identified as moderately mentally retarded was understood by his first-grade classmates. The part-time student was assigned to a special class for learners with moderate and severe disabilities for the remainder of the school day. While in the first-grade room he followed the cues of the other first graders quite well in routine situations, such as waiting in line, playing a game, and following directions. In discussions with the first graders, Schnorr found that they identified themselves as first graders and in Ms. _____'s class. The part-time student was not really regarded by the first graders as a member of the class, but as a visitor who "comes and goes." He was perceived as someone who had no grade, no teacher to speak of, whose desk was empty most of the day, who got his own stickers instead of the typical reward system; he was not considered to be a first grader like themselves. Schnorr concluded that for this student, being a part-time first grader was a different, not just briefer, experience.

General education adolescents who were integrated with peers with severe disabilities reported several benefits related to their relationships with classmates with disabilities (Peck, Donaldson, & Pezzoli, 1990). The general education students indicated that their experiences improved their self-concept, increased their growth in social cognition, increased their tolerance of others, reduced their fear about others' differences, and increased their interpersonal acceptance and friendships. These students, however, reported that they had difficulty and felt uncomfortable in dealing with the challenging behaviors demonstrated by the learners with severe disabilities.

York, Vandercook, Macdonald, Heise-Heff, and Caughey (1992), in an analysis of questionnaires regarding integration, reported that almost all of the classmates of learners with severe or multiple disabilities reported that integration was a good idea and made comments such as "they need to be around normal people" and "it teaches her more stuff." Special educators, general educators, and classmates all reported perceived positive changes, particularly in social and communication skills.

In a study contrasting peer-tutoring and "special-friends" interactions, Cole, Vandercook, and Rynders (1988) found that peer-tutoring interactions tended to be lopsided, with nonidentified students watching, teaching, and helping. Interactions with "special friends" were more reciprocal, though some distinct imbalance was apparent. Special-friend relationships were closer to best friends, whereas peer tutors were more like teacher-students. Students who were engaged in the "special-friends" program attended a training session where they learned rules and roles, how to play, how to communicate, what a friend is, why integration is implemented, what a prosthesis is, how a disabled person lives, and similar issues.

More naturalistic efforts to increase friendships between learners without identified disabilities and their peers with severe disabilities have emerged. There has been an increased awareness among general education teachers that friendships between students with and without disabilities are not only possible, but are also beneficial to all students and should be facilitated by adults (Hamre-Nietupski, 1994). Regular participation in general education classes may be an important source for meeting peers without disabilities who then become part of disabled students' social networks (Kennedy & Itkonen, 1994).

Mediating the Environment

The overall goal of education for learners with severe and multiple disabilities is the development of "functional" skills, that is, skills that can be used in the immediate and future domestic, vocational, community, and recreation/leisure environments. "Educational programs are future-oriented in their efforts to teach skills and behaviors that will enable students with severe handicaps to be as independent and productive as possible after they leave school" (Heward & Orlansky, 1992, p. 433). The "Guidelines for Practice" box on page 377 discusses appropriate curriculum for learners with severe disabilities.

Variables that must be considered when designing a curriculum for learners with severe or multiple disabilities are (a) functionality, (b) chronological age appropriateness, (c) varying levels of participation, (d) encouragement of decision making, (e) facilitation of communication, (f) vocational training, and (g) development of recreation and leisure skills. A functional curriculum includes skills that are useful and productive to the learner in the real environment in which the learner functions or will function in the future. It is essential that curricular activities are age appropriate for the learner rather than either contrived or appropriate for persons of a younger age. Activities should encourage the learner to participate to as great an extent as possible. Caregivers are cautioned not to assume the decision-making responsibilities of learners with severe and multiple disabilities. These learners should be provided with the means and be encouraged to make personal decisions and express personal preferences. Communication skills, either verbal, gestural, or

Objective Four

To describe ways to mediate the environment for learners with severe or multiple disabilities.

Annual **Edition**

Article *42*

Article *13*

guidelines for practice

Appropriate Curriculum for Learners with Severe or Multiple Disabilities

One of the key questions in working with learners with severe or multiple disabilities is "What should I teach?" With these learners, whose rate for learning and generalization may be significantly slower than other learners with disabilities, every instructional opportunity counts. "Preacademics" and "prevocational" skills have often been emphasized to the extent that one parent of a learner with severe disabilities stated, "Don't tell me he's still doing 'pre' skills. 'Pre' means never doing the real thing."

When designing programs for learners with disabilities, the curriculum content should be

- functional. Will someone eventually have to complete this task for the learner if he or she cannot do it himself or herself?
- age appropriate. Do other individuals the student's age do similar tasks?
- accepting of varying levels of participation. Even with partial participation and support, the task, if functional and appropriate, should be considered.
- encouraging decision making. It should help the learner understand choices and decrease passivity.
- demanding of communication. Communication attempts increase with opportunities.
- supportive of future vocational environments. Will the learner eventually need this skill in the world of work?
- supportive of leisure and recreational skills. Again, will the learner ever apply this skill in the community? ▮

through augmentative communication aids, are essential to learners with severe disabilities. Finally, employment-related and recreation and leisure skills are important to the present and future dignity and self-concept of learners with severe and multiple disabilities.

Inclusion in the general school community has emerged as a major trend in the education of learners with severe or multiple disabilities. York and Vandercook (1990) suggest several change strategies to generate a more unified and inclusive system of education for learners with severe and multiple disabilities. First, they argue for natural proportions, that is, distribution of learners with severe or multiple disabilities in school that reflects their diversity in the larger community. The second principle is one of natural supports, that is, using persons typically available in a given environment who can provide assistance to an individual with disabilities. For example, the teacher and classmates are natural supports to a learner with or without disabilities. In addition to these guiding principles, York and Vandercook suggest several change strategies, summarized in table 16.3, to facilitate the development of inclusive school environments.

An ongoing concern regarding the educational programs for learners with severe and multiple disabilities is that of educational validity. Voeltz and Evans (1983) write that educational validity is a concept that addresses these measurement questions:

1. Has behavior change occurred as a function of the educational intervention?
2. Did the educational intervention occur as specified in the treatment plan?

Annual **Edition**

Table 16.3   Change Strategies to Facilitate the Development of
Inclusive School Environments

A. Identify and recruit collaborators in the process
   1. develop a planning team to provide direction and leadership
   2. organize task forces or work groups
B. Communicate with all members in the school community
   1. communicate with all faculty—provide a vision
   2. communicate with students—involve and educate students
   3. communicate with parents—invite them in
C. Conduct an inventory of life within the school community
   1. study student life
   2. study faculty life
   3. study the general community's involvement
D. Share space
   1. integrate general education homerooms
   2. integrate general education classes

3. Is the resultant behavior change meaningful, that is, beneficial for the learner now and in the future, and considered to be valuable by those in the learner's natural environment?

These questions address the internal, educational, empirical, and social validity of an intervention.

The outcome of education for learners with severe disabilities should be participation in daily routines. The student should also experience increased, meaningful control over personal routines and events as a result of education (Brown & Lehr, 1993).

Learners with severe and multiple disabilities have several unique concerns that require mediation. These concerns include physical management and handling, including proper lifting, carrying, positioning, feeding, toileting, and dressing (Campbell, 1987). The goal of any physical management procedure is to allow the student to perform independently as many parts of a task as possible. In this way, the learner not only gets to practice selected movements, but the amount of physical stress on the person teaching or caring for the learner is reduced.

Leisure activities are also an essential part of programming for learners with severe or multiple handicaps. Moon and Bunker (1987) summarize the need of leisure programming to (a) increase community integration, (b) reduce inappropriate behaviors, and (c) increase skills in other areas.

Communication is an essential part of the program for learners with severe and multiple disabilities. Communication instruction should occur in the individual's natural environment throughout the day as an ongoing process. Kaiser, Alpert, and Warren (1987) describe "child-directed modeling" as one strategy to develop communication skills. In this process, the teacher first focuses his or her attention on what the student is interested in or gets the student to attend to something the teacher wishes to discuss. When the teacher has control over the object and can manipulate the object being discussed, he or she presents a model for the learner to imitate. If the student imitates the model, the learner is immediately praised and the requested material is offered. If the learner does not attempt to imitate the model or performs an unrelated response, the teacher reestablishes joint attention and presents the model again.

During communication programming, the environment must be arranged to increase the rate of requests and communication interactions. Objects and events of interest must be available. Snack and lunch as well as free play situations may be used for facilitating the development of communication.

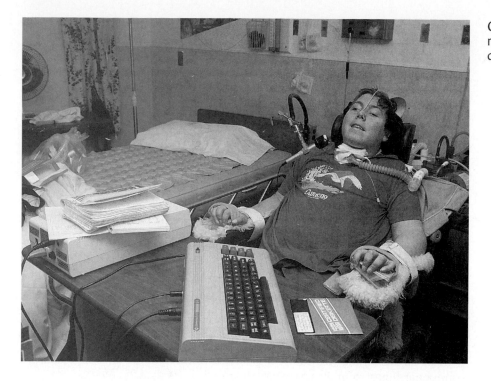

Communication systems may be necessary for learners who are challenged in verbal communication.

Augmentative Communication

When learners do not demonstrate the ability to use speech effectively, **augmentative communication systems** may be necessary. As Miller and Allaire (1987) suggest, these systems may be based on gestures or sign language or they may require an aid of some sort. Aided systems vary with regard to the type of motor response needed (whether it be to point, to blink an eye, or to press a button). Systems may include language boards or other electronic aids. Objects, photographs, pictures, rebus systems, or written words may be incorporated into these systems.

Whenever augmentative and alternative communication applications are involved, professionals should consider (a) the need for lifelong management, family and peer involvement, and current information about available options, and (b) the need for a well-coordinated interdisciplinary team that is able to treat other problems that may coexist (Mirenda & Mathy-Laikko, 1989). Bryen and McGinley (1991) suggest that even in using a system as common as sign language, professionals should ask the following questions:

1. Do significant others have the needed sign-language competence to be effective models?
2. Does the learner use sign language to communicate with peers?

In addition, when working with learners with physical handicaps such as cerebral palsy, positioning becomes a significant part of the communication intervention (McEwen & Lloyd, 1990).

A new application of technology in augmentative communication is facilitated communication. **Facilitated communication** is a teaching strategy for individuals with severe communication problems who are not able to independently use an augmentative communication device but for whom direct use of such a device is a goal (Crossley, 1992). In facilitated communication, the individual types with one index finger, first with hand or hand-at-the-wrist support and then later independently or with just a touch to the elbow or shoulder

Annual **Edition**

Article *21*

(Biklen, Morton, Gold, Berrigan, & Swaminathan, 1992). Over time, the individual moves from structured work, such as fill-in-the-blanks, to open-ended conversational text. In one study of facilitated communication, Biklen (1990) described cases of individuals with autism who, after years without an effective communication system, used facilitated communication to demonstrate unanticipated abilities.

Facilitated communication has provoked significant controversy. Silliman (1992) states that as proponents of the method suggest that the unexpected literacy of these individuals with autism is based in a relatively intact language-processing capacity and a neurological motor problem, opponents argue that these are only case studies rather than empirical evidence of the effectiveness of the method. Simpson and Myles (1995) state, "We are convinced that facilitated communication is not a miraculous phenomenon or a cure for disabilities. Nonetheless, it may be a potentially useful communication tool for some individuals with disabilities" (p. 14).

Learners with Autism

In recognition of the communication issues of learners with autism, Biklen and Schubert (1991) studied the effects of facilitated communication. With physical supports, successful training, and maintaining the students' focus, they used computer-supported communication. Biklen and Schubert hypothesize that it is perhaps far easier and less complex for these learners to use this augmentative communication system than to speak.

According to Simpson (1992), effective programs for learners with autism should use age-appropriate and functional curriculum strategies. Professionals should be sensitive to the multiple needs of these learners, and they should utilize the expertise of a multidisciplinary team.

As with all learners discussed in this chapter, community-based instruction is essential for learners with autism. To the maximum extent possible, instruction should take place in the environments in which the learner with autism functions or will function in the future, such as the home, places of employment, stores and shopping centers, restaurants, theaters, and recreation facilities.

Learners with Dual Sensory Impairments

Until federal legislation founded regional model centers for learners with dual sensory impairments in 1968, these learners were usually educated in private residential schools or remained at home or in residential facilities. Beginning in 1983, states were provided federal funds to develop programs for learners with dual sensory impairments.

Nearly all learners with dual sensory impairments (about 94 percent) have either residual hearing or residual sight (Michael & Paul, 1991). Working with these learners is complicated by the fact that relatively few data are available concerning the enhancement of residual vision and hearing of young learners with dual sensory impairments. Specialized services in modes of communication, functional sensory training, and orientation and mobility are essential to support these learners.

Downing and Eichinger (1990) suggest several instructional and curricular strategies for learners who are dual sensory impaired in integrated settings. They suggest the enhancement of visual and auditory stimuli because most students identified as deaf-blind have some residual vision or hearing, or both. The clearest information, however, is provided by tactile input, which is not meant to replace either visual or auditory information, but increases the amount of information available to the learner. Efforts to increase visual and auditory skills should occur within a meaningful context.

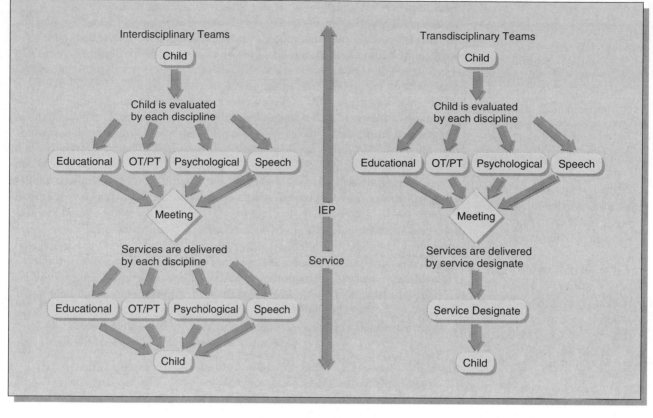

Figure 16.1

Comparison of interdisciplinary and transdisciplinary teams.

Annual **Edition**

Article 28

Learners with dual sensory impairments require small instructional groups. In these groups, cooperative learning strategies can be used to develop essential social skills, such as turn taking and accommodating to social interactions. Throughout all activities, the principle of partial participation should be applied; that is, students with severe disabilities who may not be totally independent in a given activity should be given the opportunity to learn those steps of which they are capable. However, Curtis (1982) found that over a four-year period, communication among his sample of learners with dual sensory impairments was found to be unchanged and adjustment and learning had deteriorated. Other researchers argue that the outcome is likely to be better than earlier predictions presumed (Freeman, Goetz, Richards, & Groenveld, 1989).

Transdisciplinary Teams

Due to the complexity of the educational challenges facing learners with severe or multiple disabilities, Lyon and Lyon (1980) argue for a transdisciplinary team approach. This approach involves a joint, team effort to meet the learner's needs. Through role release, two or three members of the team share general information regarding their individual expertise, duties, and responsibilities. Each team member teaches the other team members to make specific teaching decisions within his or her area of expertise. Each professional trains other team members to perform specific skills within his or her area of expertise. The teacher emerges as the actual implementer of much service, with other team members providing training, skill development, education, and support. The schematic in figure 16.1 depicts the differences between the traditional interdisciplinary team and the transdisciplinary team.

The National Parks

In search of access for all . . . disabled face fewer barriers to enjoying America's scenic wonders

By Wendy Roth and Michael Tompane
Universal Press Syndicate

In the wilderness, we all are physically challenged.

Whether hiking a backcountry trail, shooting the rapids or setting up camp under the stars, we must consider our physical abilities as well as preparations for a rewarding experience.

In the United States, our most precious wilderness settings are in national parks—treasures kept in trust for all. They afford each of us, including those with disabilities, the opportunity to remain in touch with our natural heritage.

With the passage of the Americans With Disabilities Act in 1990, the United States has recognized the rights of those with mobility problems, visual and hearing impairments, and developmental problems.

The National Park Service was the first federal agency to make accessibility a matter of policy. While much remains to be done, people with disabilities can explore many of the national parks.

We set out to visit a selection of wilderness treasures and evaluate their accessibility—for people with mobility problems, families with young children and senior citizens. We also noted opportunities for deaf and blind visitors.

Because we think wilderness is best enjoyed in undeveloped surroundings, we did not limit our journeys to automobile drives.

Michael, who does not have a disability, has been a backpacker on primitive wilderness trails. He began hiking in the national parks at age 8 with his father.

Wendy walked many of this country's natural trails until 10 years ago. During the past 18 years, since her early 20s, she has lost voluntary movement in her legs, hands and upper body because of multiple sclerosis. She uses an electric wheelchair and requires assistance when traveling.

On our journey, we drove more than 32,000 miles, stayed at more than 100 campsites and visited 45 parks. The resulting book, *Easy Access to National Parks* (Sierra Club Books), encourages people with disabilities to visit them.

Initially, we were concerned that many parks would not have adequate access. For example, we planned not to visit Chaco Culture National Historical Park. Having visited Chaco Canyon several years earlier, Michael thought the prehistoric pueblo dwellings would not give Wendy access to the Anasazi ruins. At the urging of a ranger in a nearby park, however, we decided to visit Chaco.

Although Wendy did get to Pueblo Bonito, the largest ruin in the park, it is not fully or legally accessible. Only the beginning portion of the trail is what we term fully accessible, one that meets the Uniform Federal Accessibility Standards.

From the parking lot, a paved path leads to the ruin's outer wall. It soon became steep and narrow, however, forcing us to retrace our steps. We entered Pueblo Bonito's central plaza through the other end of the trail, Michael assisting Wendy over the soft dirt to keep her chair from getting stuck.

Big Bend National Park in Texas has only a few short trails with wheelchair access. We began to wonder whether Big Bend, with its abundant desert wildlife, would be only a "windshield experience," a park viewed exclusively from inside an automobile. We could not even find a trail to the Rio Grande.

Then we learned that Big Bend River Tours guides visitors of differing abilities on eight-hour raft trips from Lajitas, Texas, through the park's Santa Elena Canyon. We started along banks lush with desert life, then entered the narrow canyon, with 1,500-foot walls. With the wheels popped off and the wheelchair frame securely strapped to the rubber raft's seat, Wendy felt like Cleopatra on her Nile barge.

The Impact on Participation in the Community and Society

Objective Five

To describe the impact of severe or multiple disabilities on participation in the larger social systems of the community and society.

As Bellamy (1985) reminds us, learners with severe and multiple disabilities require ongoing support throughout their lives. Employment of learners identified as severely and multiply disabled is a particular challenge. In their study of the employment status of 117 transition-age young adults with moderate, severe, or profound mental retardation, Wehman, Kregel, and Seyfarth (1985) found that 88 percent were unemployed, with only 14 of the 117 holding competitive jobs. Wage accumulation was seriously limited. Nearly 80 percent of the young adults had received no rehabilitation services.

Kennedy, Horner, and Newton (1989), in a study of the social contacts of adults with severe and multiple disabilities, found that the twenty-three

The tour climaxed with our shooting the white-water rapids at the "Rockslide." Twisting through the rolling river and diving perilously close to midstream boulders, the raft seemed close to capsizing. In hindsight, though, it was a thrilling and safe experience.

In addition to rafting, park experiences can include canoeing, boating, scuba diving and horseback riding.

One unique opportunity is the sit-ski program at Badger Pass in Yosemite National Park, Calif. Sit skis are designed for skiers with paralysis of the lower body. They sit in a kayaklike device and control the ski with upper-body movement and short poles.

Yosemite's famous valley features 8 miles of paved trails, and most of the developed facilities and trails are at least moderately accessible. At the west end of Lake Tenaya, we stood where Ansel Adams and Edward Weston took famous photographs.

Farther north, in Olympic National Park, Wash., another rewarding trail is Madison Falls Trail, designed for accessibility by everyone, including wheelchair users. The 200-foot asphalt trail ends at an observation platform overlooking Madison Falls, which tumbles 100 feet down a basalt cliff.

Less than 200 miles northeast of Olympic in North Cascades National Park, Happy Creek Trail is an elevated boardwalk that gives visitors a squirrel's-eye view of the forest.

If the trails in the Pacific Coast parks are not challenging enough, visit Haleakala National Park on the Hawaiian island of Maui. It is a huge shield volcano rising 10,020 feet above sea level. At lower elevations, the rocks-and-roots trail through the tropical woods is a real test of chair control.

The major attraction, however, is the rim of the crater, with a moderately accessible path at Puu Ulaula Summit. While wheelchair users may need assistance in certain areas, asphalt makes it pretty free-wheeling. On a clear day, it's easy to see why the early Hawaiians called Haleakala the "House of the Sun." On a cloudy day, it's still overwhelming.

Park visits need not be confined to developed facilities; people with disabilities can enjoy primitive areas, too. Ranger Steve Eide, who has a spinal cord injury, led us along Cascade Lake at Yellowstone National Park in Wyoming. Eide, who uses a manual wheelchair, negotiated logs and gentle hills into a meadow where bison graze. The trail has significant barriers but, for athletic or skillful wheelchair users, this can be an exhilarating experience.

Families with young children, senior citizens and visitors with mobility problems can use many of the boardwalks through Yellowstone's geothermal areas to view geysers, bubbling mud and hot springs.

On our travels, the sights were only a part of our fascination with the parks. We met many interesting people—people with and without apparent disabilities.

Parents often pushed young children in strollers behind us, assuming that strollers could go where Wendy could. Other wheelchair users shared with us their satisfaction in being able to travel park trails. We went canoeing with an expert canoeist, a triple amputee, and we shared paths with people who have vision and hearing impairments.

Several parks have sign-language interpretation for deaf visitors. On our visit to Theodore Roosevelt National Park in North Dakota, a ranger interpreted her tour of the Maltese Cross Cabin built by Roosevelt. The future U.S. president used it while hunting and raising cattle in the Dakotas.

While a great task remains to improve accessibility everywhere, opportunities in the parks clearly abound. Recreation and contact with nature can be great healers and should be available to all ●

participants in their study engaged in regular social contact with people other than those with whom they interacted due to proximity. Some participants engaged in social contacts only once a week, while others participated in activities with companions daily. One problem that emerged in their data, however, was the limited number of companions who remained a part of the participant's social sphere for more than a few months. Family members were the most stable companions, but it was rare for a participant to have contact with anyone other than his or her family for more than eighteen months.

In a national survey of the community involvement of persons with severe disabilities, Aveno (1989) found that individuals with severe disabilities spend more time in employment or day activities, using health-care services, walking or wheelchair strolling for pleasure, and using parks or zoos than do their nondisabled peers.

Summary

In this chapter, low-incidence disabilities, that is, severe and multiple disabilities, dual sensory impairments, and autism, were discussed. These learners, who just a few decades ago were either not served or served in restrictive settings, have made dramatic strides in inclusion in the community and general education classroom.

Learners with severe and multiple disabilities are an extremely heterogenous group. Standardized assessment instruments have scant validity and reliability in efforts to assess the strengths and needs of these learners. A comprehensive ecological approach for assessment is recommended as the most practical and useful basis for programming.

The impact of severe and multiple disabilities on the home and classroom is substantial. Parents experience stress when conducting everyday household and child-care tasks and extreme stress when interacting on behalf of their children with school, medical, and other professionals.

Integration of these learners into general education benefits both the learners with disabilities and their nonidentified peers. General education students, for the most part, accept learners with severe and multiple disabilities and state that they profit from the experience of associating with them.

To effectively mediate the environment on behalf of learners with severe and multiple disabilities, it is recommended that they be integrated into natural environments in proportion to their numbers in the general population and provided the natural supports available in those environments. Valid educational programs that are responsive to their physical management and handling, leisure, communication, and vocational needs must be provided for these learners.

Learners with severe and multiple disabilities require lifelong support systems. There is a continuing need for vocational training, rehabilitation, and employment services. Learners have limited social contacts with friends, other than family members, and their circle of friends is quite restricted.

Building Your Professional Vocabulary

Match each word or phrase to its meaning.

_____ augmentative communication systems

_____ autism

_____ dual sensory impairments

a. a pervasive developmental disorder
b. requiring intense services in order to maximize participation
c. having both auditory and visual disabilities

_____ multiple disabilities

_____ severe disabilities

d. concomitant impairments, the combination of which causes severe challenges
e. systems for communication that do not require speech

Comprehension Check

Select the most appropriate response.

1. Learners with severe disabilities
   a. require wheelchairs and augmentative communication systems.
   b. usually have mental retardation and one or more sensory impairments.
   c. have profound mental retardation.

2. Autism is now, according to federal law,
   a. another health impairment.
   b. a disability category unto itself.
   c. a serious emotional disturbance.

3. Most learners with dual sensory impairments
   a. have severe mental retardation.
   b. require institutionalization.
   c. have some residual hearing and/or vision.

4. In order to be identified as having severe disabilities, an individual must
   a. require an intense educational program with a wide range of resources.
   b. have severe or profound mental retardation.
   c. have severe or profound physical disabilities.

5. Identification as having multiple disabilities requires
   a. having severe challenges in two areas of functional skills.
   b. having two disabilities that make services strictly for one disability inappropriate.
   c. education in separate special education programs.

6. Standardized assessments
   a. are useful in identifying severe disabilities.
   b. may be used prescriptively for persons with severe disabilities.
   c. are not appropriate for learners with severe disabilities.

7. Inclusion of learners with severe disabilities
   a. becomes inappropriate as vocational needs emerge.
   b. benefits learners both with and without disabilities.
   c. can only be partial.

8. The concept of natural proportions suggests that
   a. learners should be accommodated in general education in proportion to the level of disability.
   b. the distribution of learners with disabilities in the school should reflect the distribution in the community.
   c. a four-to-one ratio of learners without identified disabilities to learners with severe disabilities is appropriate.

9. Augmentative communication systems
   a. should be based on the learner's skills.
   b. require the involvement of family and peers.
   c. require technology.

10. The concept of transdisciplinary teams suggests
    a. several team members should contribute their specific expertise.
    b. expertise should be shared through role release.
    c. professionals should provide direct service to individuals with severe disabilities.

References

American Psychiatric Association. (1987). *Diagnostic and statistical manual of mental disorders* (3rd ed. revised). Washington, DC: Author.

American Psychiatric Association. (1994) *Diagnostic and statistical manual of mental disorders* (4th ed.). Washington, DC: Author.

Andrews, A. K. (1989). Meeting the needs of young deaf-blind children and their parents. *Child Care, Health, and Development, 15,* 195–206.

Aveno, A. (1989). Community involvement of persons with severe retardation living in community residences. *Exceptional Children, 55,* 309–314.

Bellamy, T. (1985). Severe disability in adulthood. *Newsletter of the Association for Persons with Severe Handicaps, 11* (1), 6.

Biklen, D. (1990). Communication unbound: Autism and praxis. *Harvard Educational Review, 60,* 291–314.

Biklen, D., Morton, M., Gold, D., Berrigan, C., & Swaminathan, S. (1992). Facilitated communication: Implications for individuals with autism. *Topics in Language Disorders, 12* (4), 1–28.

Biklen, D., & Schubert, A. (1991). New words: The communication of students with autism. *Remedial and Special Education, 12,* 46–57.

Blatt, B., & Kaplan, F. (1966). *Christmas in purgatory: A photographic essay on mental retardation.* Boston: Published and distributed under the auspices of a group of parents and friends of the mentally retarded.

Brazelton, T. B. (1973). *Neonatal behavior assessment scale.* Philadelphia, PA: Lippincott.

Brimer, R. W. (1990). *Students with severe disabilities: Current perspectives and practices.* Mountain View, CA: Mayfield Publishing.

Bromley, B. E., & Blacher, J. (1991). Parental reasons for out-of-home placement of children with severe handicaps. *Mental Retardation, 29* (5), 275–280.

Brown, F. (1987). Meaningful assessment of people with severe and profound handicaps. In M. Snell (Ed.), *Systematic instruction of persons with severe handicaps* (3rd ed.), 30–63.

Brown, F., & Lehr, D. H. (1993). Making activities meaningful for students with severe multiple disabilities. *Teaching Exceptional Children, 25,* 12–16.

Bryen, D. N., & McGinley, V. (1991). Sign language input to community residents with mental retardation. *Education and Training of the Mentally Retarded, 26,* 207–213.

Campbell, P. (1987). Physical management and handling procedures with students with movement dysfunction. In M. Snell (Ed.), *Systematic instruction of persons with severe handicaps* (3rd ed.), 174–188.

Chadsey-Rusch, J. (1990). Social interactions of secondary-aged students with severe handicaps: Implications for facilitating the transition from school to work. *Journal of the Association for Persons with Severe Handicaps, 15,* 69–78.

Cole, D. A., Vandercook, T., & Rynders, J. (1988). Comparison of two peer interaction programs: Children with and without severe disabilities. *American Educational Research Journal, 25,* 415–439.

Crossley, R. (1992). Getting the words out: Case studies in facilitated communication training. *Topics in Language Disorders, 11* (4), 60–68.

Curtis, M. S. (1982). Study of behavioral change in 40 severely multi-sensorily handicapped children. *International Journal of Rehabilitation Research, 5,* 550–551.

Denckla, M. B. (1986). New diagnostic criteria for autism and related behavioral disorders: Guidelines for research protocols. *Journal of the American Academy of Child Psychiatry, 25,* 221–224.

Dollar, S., & Brooks, C. (1980). Assessment of severely and profoundly handicapped. *Exceptional Education Quarterly, 1,* 87–91.

Downing, J., & Eichinger, J. (1990). Instructional strategies for learners with dual sensory impairments in integrated settings. *Journal of the Association for Persons with Severe Handicaps, 15,* 98–105.

Federal Register. (1977), *42,* 42659–42688.

Ferguson, D. L. (1994). Is communication really the point? Some thoughts on interventions and membership. *Mental Retardation, 32,* 7–18.

Fredericks, H. D., & Baldwin, V. (1987). Individuals with dual sensory impairments: Who are they? How are they educated? In L. Goetz, D. Guess, & K. Stremel-Campell (Eds.), *Innovative program design for individuals with dual sensory impairments* (pp. 3–14). Baltimore, MD: Paul H. Brookes.

Freeman, R. D., Goetz, E., Richards, D., & Groenveld, H. (1989). Blind children's early emotional development: Do we know enough to help? *Child Care, Health, and Development, 15,* 3–28.

Giangreco, M. F., Cloninger, C. J., Mueller, P. H., Yuan, S., & Ashworth, S. (1991). Perspectives of parents whose children have dual sensory impairments. *Journal of the Association for Persons with Severe Handicaps, 16,* 14–24.

Guess, D., Mulligan-Ault, M., Roberts, S., Struth, J., Siegel-Causey, E., Thompson, B., Bronicki, G. J. B., & Guy, B. (1988). Implications of biobehavioral states of the education and treatment of students with the most profoundly handicapping conditions. *Journal of the Association for Persons with Severe Handicaps, 13,* 163–174.

Hamre-Nietupski, S. (1994). Regular educators' perceptions of facilitating friendships of students with moderate, severe, or profound disabilities with nondisabled peers. *Education and Training in Mental Retardation and Developmental Disabilities, 29,* 102–117.

Heward, W. L., & Orlansky, M. D. (1992). *Exceptional children: An introductory survey of special education* (4th ed.). New York: Merrill.

Hilton, A., & Henderson, C. J. (1993). Parent involvement: A best practice or forgotten practice? *Education and Training in Mental Retardation, 28,* 199–211.

Kaiser, A. P., Alpert, C. L., & Warren, S. F. (1987). Teaching functional language: Strategies for language intervention. In M. Snell (Ed.), *Systematic instruction of persons with severe handicaps* (3rd ed.), 247–272.

Kennedy, C. H., Horner, R. H., & Newton, J. S. (1989). Social contacts of adults with severe disabilities living in the community: A descriptive analysis of relationship patterns. *Journal of the Association for Persons with Severe Handicaps, 14,* 190–196.

Kennedy, C. H., & Itkonen, T. (1994). Some effects of regular class participation on the social contacts and social networks of high school students with severe disabilities. *Journal of the Association for Persons with Severe Handicaps, 19,* 1–10.

Larson, S. A., & Lakin, K. C. (1991). Parent attitudes about residential placement before and after deinstitutionalization: A research synthesis. *Journal of the Association for Persons with Severe Handicaps, 16,* 5–38.

Lindley, L. (1990). Defining TASH: A mission statement. *TASH Newsletter, 16* (8) (August), 1.

Linehan, S. A., Brady, M. P., & Hwang, C. (1991). Ecological versus developmental assessment: Influences on instructional expectations. *Journal of the Association for Persons with Severe Handicaps, 16,* 146–153.

Lyon, S., & Lyon, G. (1980). Team functioning and staff development: A role release approach to providing integrated educational services to severely handicapped students. *Journal of the Association for the Severely Handicapped, 5,* 250–263.

McEwen, I. R., & Lloyd, L. L. (1990). Positioning students with cerebral palsy to use augmentative and alternative communication. *Language, Speech, and Hearing Services in the Schools, 21,* 14–21.

Meyers, C. E., & Blacher, J. (1987). Parents' perceptions of schooling for severely handicapped children: Home and family variables. *Exceptional Children, 43,* 441–449.

Michael, M. G., & Paul, P. V. (1991). Early intervention for infants with deaf-blindness. *Exceptional Children, 57,* 200–211.

Miller, J., & Allaire, J. (1987). Augmentative communication. In M. Snell (Ed.), *Systematic instruction of persons with severe handicaps* (3rd ed.), 273–298.

Mirenda, P., & Mathy-Laikko, P. (1989). Augmentative and alternative communication applications for persons with severe congenital communication disorders: An introduction. *AAC: Augmentative and Alternative Communication, 5,* 3–13.

Moon, M. S., & Bunker, L. (1987). Recreation and motor skills programming. In M. Snell (Ed.), *Systematic instruction of persons with severe handicaps* (3rd ed.), 214–244.

Orelove, F. P., & Sobsey, D. (1987). *Educating children with multiple disabilities: A transdisciplinary approach.* Baltimore, MD: Paul H. Brookes.

Peck, C. A., Donaldson, J., & Pezzoli, M. (1990). Some benefits nonhandicapped adolescents perceive for themselves from their social relationships with peers who have severe handicaps. *Journal of the Association for Persons with Severe Handicaps, 15,* 241–249.

Prizant, B. M. (1984). Assessment and intervention of communicative problems in children with autism. *Communicative Disorders, 9,* 127–142.

Ritvo, E. R., & Freeman, B. J. (1978). National Society for Autistic Children: Definition of the syndrome of autism. *Journal of Autism and Childhood Schizophrenia,* 162–169.

Rodrique, J. R. (1993). Perceived competence and behavioral adjustment of siblings of children with autism. *Journal of Autism and Developmental Disorders, 23,* 655–674.

Rutter, M. (1978). Diagnosis and definition of childhood autism. *Journal of Autism and Developmental Disorders, 8,* 139–161.

Rutter, M., & Schopler, E. (1985). Autism and pervasive developmental disorders: Concepts and diagnostic issues. Paper prepared for the NIMH Research Workshop.

Schnorr, R. F. (1990). "Peter? He comes and goes . . .": First graders' perspective on a part-time mainstream student. *Journal of the Association for Persons with Severe Handicap, 15,* 231–240.

Sigafoos, J., Cole, D. A., & McQuarter, R. J. (1987). Current practices in the assessment of students with severe handicaps. *Journal of the Association for Persons with Severe Handicaps, 12,* 264–273.

Sigman, M., & Ungerer, J. A. (1984). Cognitive and language skills in autistic, mentally retarded, and normal children. *Developmental Psychology, 20,* 293–302.

Silliman, E. R. (1992). Three perspectives of facilitated communication: Unexpected literacy, Clever Hans, or enigma? *Topics in Language Disorders, 12* (4), 60–68.

Simpson, R. L. (1992). Children and youth with autism. In L. M. Bullock (Ed.), *Exceptionalities in children and youth* (pp. 168–195). Boston: Allyn & Bacon.

Simpson, R. L., & Myles, B. S. (1995). Facilitated communication and children with disabilities: An enigma in search of a perspective. *Focus on Exceptional Children, 27* (9), 1–16.

Snell, M. E., & Grigg, N. C. (1987). Instructional assessment and curriculum development. In M. Snell (Ed.), *Systematic instruction of persons with severe handicaps* (3rd ed.), 64–109.

Struth, J., & Guess, D. (1986). *Implications of biobehavioral states for the education and treatment of persons with severe and profound handicaps.* Unpublished manuscript. University of Kansas, Lawrence.

Todis, B., & Singer, G. (1991). Stress and stress management in families with adopted children who have severe disabilities. *Journal of the Association for Persons with Severe Handicaps, 16,* 3–13.

U.S. Department of Education. (1995). *Seventeenth annual report to Congress on the implementation of the Individuals with Disabilities Education Act.* Washington, DC: Author.

U.S. Office of Education. (1975). Estimated number of handicapped children in the United States, 1974–75. Washington, DC: Bureau of Education for the Handicapped.

Voeltz, L. M., & Evans, I. M. (1983). Educational validity: Procedures to evaluate outcomes in programs for severely handicapped learners. *Journal of the Association for Persons with Severe Handicaps, 8,* 3–15.

Wehman, P., Kregel, J., & Seyfarth, J. (1985). Transition from school to work for individuals with severe handicaps: A follow-up study. *Journal of the Association for Persons with Severe Handicaps, 10,* 132–136.

Yoder, P. J., & Feagans, L. (1988). Mothers' attributions of communication to prelinguistic behavior of developmentally delayed and mentally retarded infants. *American Journal on Mental Retardation, 93,* 36–43.

York, J., & Vandercook, T. (1990). Strategies for achieving an integrated education for middle school students with severe disabilities. *Remedial and Special Education, 11* (5), 6–16.

York, J., Vandercook, T., Macdonald, C., Heise-Heff, C., & Caughey, E. (1992). Feedback about integrating middle-school students with severe disabilities in general education classes. *Exceptional Children, 58,* 244–259.

Objectives

After completing this chapter, you will be able to:

1. describe the personal characteristics of learners identified as gifted, creative, or talented.
2. describe the identification and evaluation of gifted, creative, or talented learners.
3. describe the impact of giftedness, creativity, or talent on interactions in the home and classroom.
4. describe ways to mediate the environment for learners identified as gifted, creative, or talented.
5. describe the impact of giftedness, creativity, or talent on participation in the larger social systems of the school, community, and society.

Key Words and Phrases

acceleration	gifted imposter phenomenon
Cinderella complex	mentor
creative	talented
enrichment	underachievement
gifted	

17

Chapter

Learners
Who Are
Gifted,
Creative, or
Talented

Programs for able students simply did not exist in my school. I always knew I learned fast because I got my work done before everyone else most of the time, and I always felt the teachers were mad at me for doing this. I learned to not work so fast. I remember getting into trouble lots of times, mostly for talking or for disturbing other students around me. My sixth-grade teacher even rapped me on the knuckles once with a long wooden stick, which made me very angry and embarrassed. If only science class hadn't been so boring with so much sitting and lecturing, I might not have been doodling on my assignment sheet and bothering my neighbors.

You see, I didn't understand why I got into trouble so much, or why I began to dislike school, or why I felt I never fit in. I only felt alienated, different from my teachers and my classmates, and basically incompetent nine months of the year. (Carol Woodin Boyce, a resource teacher for the gifted, in a letter to a student, 1991, p. 10)

Introduction

Sapon-Shevin (1987) suggests that two assumptions underlie educational programming and the identification of learners who are gifted, talented, or creative. First, learners who are gifted, talented, or creative are assumed to represent an empirically identifiable population. Second, the needs of this population are assumed to be significantly different from those of children in general. Current definitions of learners who are gifted, creative, or talented limit the identified population to 3 percent to 5 percent of the general population. These limitations lead to severe restrictions on the selection of learners to be served and to charges of elitism (VanTassel-Baska, Patton, & Prillaman, 1989). Marjoram (1986) supports a broadening of the definition of giftedness and urges its application to the top 10 percent of the population, with a reconceptualization of education on youth services, open learning, and flexible study opportunities throughout the learner's life.

Salkind (1988) argues that learners who are gifted and talented are exceptional in the same sense of the word as those defined within Public Law 94-142 and that mandated services are appropriate for this population. In addition, in a survey of parents of school-age children identified as gifted, creative, or talented, there was strong support for programs addressing the special needs of these students, especially if those programs did not reduce service to average or slow learners (Larsen, 1994).

Personal Characteristics

Learners who are gifted and talented, though an extremely heterogeneous group, may be confronted with unique developmental challenges (Hilyer, 1988). These predictable developmental crises may include (a) society's contradictory treatment of learners who are gifted and talented, (b) labeling, (c) more rapid development, (d) heightened sensitivity or oversensitivity, (e) a discrepancy between intellectual and social skills, (f) unrealistic goals or expectations, (g) perfectionism, (h) stress, anxiety, and depression, and (i) difficulty dealing with failure and success. These crises are perhaps even more significant for gifted females, the highly gifted, gifted learners from various cultures, and gifted learners who underachieve.

Social-Emotional Development

In a study of self-concept, self-esteem, and peer relations, Janos, Fung, and Robinson (1985) found that 40 percent of the children who were gifted and talented thought of themselves as different and demonstrated self-esteem scores significantly lower than those who did not see themselves as different. Coleman and Fults (1983), however, suggest that studies related to the self-concept of children who are gifted and talented must take into account the learner's educational placements. Because children judge their capabilities in relation to others in their immediate environment and because that judgment is governed by the similarities between individuals, learners in separate programs for the gifted and talented may report a lower self-concept than similar children in integrated programs.

Other studies of self-concept support the heterogeneity of this group. Girls presented stronger self-concepts than boys on three self-concept measures in another study (Loeb & Jay, 1987). Forsyth (1987) found no significant difference between children who were gifted and talented and peers in self-concept, but children who were gifted and talented were found to be more anxious. In yet another study, children who were gifted and talented and in integrated programs demonstrated higher scores for academic self-concept and similar scores in social and physical self-concept when compared to their peers (Schneider, Clegg, Byrne, & Ledingham, 1989).

Objective One

To describe the personal characteristics of learners identified as gifted, creative, or talented.

Students who are gifted, creative, or talented are often more anxious in class situations.

Coleman and Fults (1985) examined the influence of instructional segregation on the self-concepts of children who were gifted and talented. All of the learners had robust self-concepts yet demonstrated higher self-concept scores prior to being placed in the segregated program. Coleman and Fults argue that the reduction in heterogeneity of ability in gifted classrooms forced some learners to see their abilities in a less favorable light. Students who were at the lower end of the distribution of children who were gifted and talented were most affected. This study supported earlier findings (Coleman & Fults, 1982) in which the measure of self-concept decreased on placement in a segregated program and increased when the students reentered general education. These findings support the issue of the developmental context: children's development is influenced by the program that they attend and the peers with whom they interact.

When the content of the self-esteem measure is academically oriented, children who are gifted and talented report higher self-esteem (Eccles, Bauman, & Rotenberg, 1989). Though learners who were gifted and talented were found more likely to be chosen as study partners, they were about as likely to be chosen as a friend or teammate. Depending on the criteria and context, peer acceptance of learners who are gifted and talented may vary.

Roeper (1982) describes several roles learners who are gifted and talented may assume to cope with their emotions. She describes

1. the perfectionist, who combines early omnipotence with later conscience development.
2. the child-adult, who combines the feeling of omnipotence with an unrealistic goal of total independence.
3. the winner of the competition, who combines feelings of omnipotence with a desire to achieve over others.
4. the exception, in whom the feeling of omnipotence remains an overpowering force that deters normal growth.
5. the self-critic, who is fixated on conscience development.
6. the well-integrated, who proceeds through the typical developmental social and emotional phases.

Though no one particular child may be completely described as being in one category, these roles may describe some of the approaches children who are gifted and talented use to cope with their emotions.

When presented with psychosocial dilemmas and open-ended questions, learners who were gifted and talented were found to be more likely to express internal attributions, heightened sensitivity to the protagonist's dilemmas, and a precocious moral and ethical reasoning (LeVine & Tucker, 1986). These findings suggest that learners who are gifted and talented may analyze and react uniquely to stressful situations and may demonstrate a unique sensitivity and distress. These findings concur with Su's (1982) research, which reported no differences between learners who were gifted and talented and their peers in emotional stability, but found stronger reactions to anger and sadness among learners who were gifted and talented.

The incidence of psychological problems among children who are intellectually gifted has been found to be comparable to the regularly achieving population (Gallucci, 1988). However, it must be recognized that learners who are gifted and talented do have personal concerns. Galbraith (1985) interviewed four hundred learners and summarized their concerns as evolving around being gifted, feeling different and unaccepted, peer relationships, parent and teacher expectations, and world problems.

Language Development

Children who are gifted and talented have been found to demonstrate higher scores on measures of receptive language than their peers (Chermak & Burgerud, 1983). Guilford, Scheurle, and Shonburn (1981) also found that learners who were gifted and talented demonstrated advanced receptive language operations in auditory memory and memory for linguistic information. Though the measure they used did not demonstrate significantly greater expressive language when comparing learners who were gifted and talented and their peers. Guilford and associates felt that the gifted learners were able to bring more-complex and deep language structures and rules to completion in comprehension and verbal syntax.

Cognitive Development

By definition, learners who are gifted exhibit advanced cognitive skills. These learners are intellectually capable and learn to speak fluently at an early age. Research by Carter (1984) using Piaget's stages of development suggests that learners who are gifted and talented demonstrate all operations earlier than children with normal ability. Davis and Rimm (1985) found among the cognitive characteristics of the gifted and talented good comprehension, good problem-solving skills, and ease in recognizing cause-and-effect relationships. These learners participate at an early age in reading, writing, mathematics, music, and artistic endeavors. They are capable of retaining and manipulating extraordinary quantities of information. They are analytic thinkers, capable of manipulating abstract concepts and acting intuitively.

Identification and Evaluation

The terms *gifted*, *creative*, and *talented* are used throughout this chapter to describe that heterogeneous group of individuals who demonstrate unique ability, skills, talents, leadership, or creativity. In general usage, **gifted** refers to the academically gifted, those learners whose tested intelligence quotients are within the superior range and who perform exceptionally well in academic areas. In reference to school, gifted learners are generally two or more grade levels ahead of

Objective Two

To describe the identification and evaluation of gifted, creative, or talented learners.

Talented learners often excel in art, music, or leadership.

their typical peers in achievement. Those judged to be **creative** are capable of expressing unique and novel ideas, solutions, and products; they excel in divergent thought processes. Learners who are **talented** exhibit special abilities, aptitudes, and accomplishments in various areas, such as art, music, leadership, or theater.

Public Laws 94-142, 99-457, and 101-476 mandated appropriate public education for all children with disabilities; those who are gifted, creative, or talented are *not* protected by these laws. However, the federal government recognized this group of learners in the Gifted and Talented Children's Education Act of 1978 (Purcell, 1978). This legislation defined this group of learners as

> children, and whenever applicable, youth, who are identified at the preschool, elementary, or secondary level as possessing demonstrated or potential abilities that give evidence of high performance responsibility in areas such as intellectual, creative, specific academic, or leadership ability, or in the performing and visual arts and who by reason thereof require services or activities not ordinarily provided by the school. (Sec. 902)

Renzulli (1978) offers a broader definition, which has been accepted by some factions within the field of gifted education. He defines giftedness as a condition that results when creativity, task commitment, and above-average ability are brought to bear on a field of learning. This definition brings together the several dimensions of giftedness (fig. 17.1). It requires that all learners be given expanded opportunities to demonstrate creativity or talent, with a subgroup then continuing for advanced work on the basis of their performance and interest.

Both the federal and Renzulli definitions of giftedness differ significantly from the original definitions offered by Terman (1954) and his contemporaries. Their definitions employed intelligence quotients as the indicators of giftedness. They were applied at a time when society was greatly concerned with academic performance and enamored with intelligence tests. Terman originally suggested that gifted learners were those who received an intelligence quotient of 140 or above on the Stanford-Binet Intelligence Test. Later, the academically talented were defined as those receiving an intelligence quotient (IQ) of 115 or more on the Stanford-Binet or a similar score on another instrument. At this time, students who were gifted were placed into these subcategories: academically talented (IQ above 116), gifted (IQ above 132), and highly gifted (IQ above 148) (Gallagher, 1985). Both the federal and Renzulli definitions are broader and make a concerted effort to include learners who are talented and creative as well as academically gifted. In addition, the definitions are an effort to respond to the identification of learners who are gifted in ways not generally recognized by the majority culture and learners who are not easily identified as gifted and talented. They are, as definitions, more democratic and more appropriate for application in American schools.

Karnes and Koch (1985), in an exploration of the status of the definition of giftedness, found that ten states used a form of the federal definition and two used variations of Renzulli's definition. In seventeen states, *gifted* with no inclusion of *talented* was used, and in five others, *intellectually gifted* was applied. Twenty-eight states used the term *gifted and talented,* though only three defined *talented.* Only twenty states indicated that those identified as gifted and talented were to be provided services beyond general education.

Because Public Law 94-142 and its amendments provided no protection for students who are gifted and talented, state legislation regarding this population is permissive rather than mandated. In *Roe vs. the Commonwealth of Pennsylvania* (1986), the courts determined that due process and "stay put" did not apply to programs for learners who were gifted and talented. The issue of contention for potential participants in these programs, then, was whether the

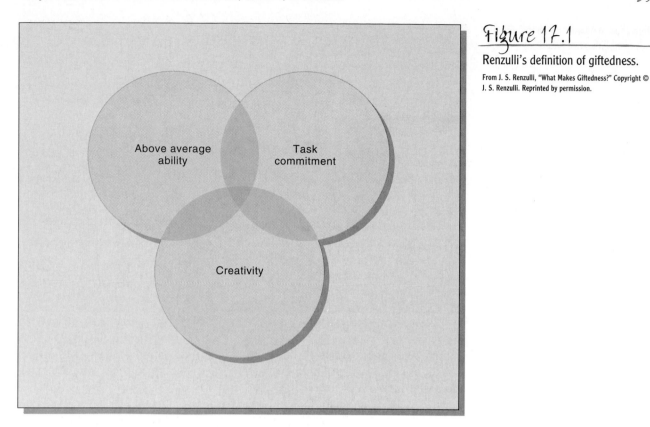

Figure 17.1

Renzulli's definition of giftedness.

From J. S. Renzulli, "What Makes Giftedness?" Copyright ©
J. S. Renzulli. Reprinted by permission.

criteria for eligibility were appropriate. Courts have, to this point, deferred to educational agencies in their implementation of programs for children who are gifted and talented (Rothstein, 1990).

Birch (1984) argues that identifying children who are gifted, creative, or talented should focus on assessment and education, with the application of curriculum-embedded processes. When general education classroom teachers and teachers of gifted and talented learners were asked to describe preferred criteria for referral for gifted programs, Schack and Starko (1990) reported an emphasis on criteria, learning quickly and easily, and initiating one's own learning. As teachers' experience with gifted and talented learners increased, a higher percentage of teachers chose intelligence quotient test scores as a basis for referral. Schack and Starko recommend the role of general education teacher as "talent scout" in seeking out learners not identified by other means.

The use of intelligence tests with learners who are gifted and talented has been controversial. Robinson and Chamrad (1986), however, believe that much of this controversy derives from professionals using tests in ways they were not designed to be used. They suggest that many of the criticisms of intelligence tests are based not on the tests themselves but on unrealistic expectations that they will accomplish what they were never intended to accomplish. Conventional intelligence tests have been shown to present problems in terms of cultural bias. Alternatives, such as assessing learning ability, have been suggested (Tyerman, 1986).

Feldhusen, Asher, and Hoover (1984) present an alternative procedure for the identification of giftedness, talent, or creativity. They contend that the identification process should begin as a program process. First, the program goals and types of youth to be served should be outlined, followed by the development of nomination and assessment procedures. Next, individual differentiation

More than 2 percent of all individuals with disabilities are gifted.

should take place, followed by an evaluation and validation of the identification; that is, are the learners for whom the program is designed those who are being identified and served?

Betts and Neihart (1988) provide further insights into the question of how to identify the gifted, talented, and creative by studying learner profiles. After conducting observations, interviews, and reviewing the literature, they developed six profiles of learners who are gifted and talented. The profiles include the following:

1. Successful students.
2. Underground learners, who have not and do not wish to be identified.
3. Divergently gifted students, who demonstrate their abilities in ways that are not necessarily recognized by the school.
4. Dropouts.
5. Double-labeled students; that is, those who demonstrate a disability as well as giftedness, talent, or creativity.
6. Autonomous learners, who are usually identified as intellectually gifted and successful in school.

Identification of Gifted and Talented Learners

Gifted Learners with Disabilities   Professionals are beginning to focus on the challenges presented by learners who are both disabled and gifted. The disability, which often masks the learner's giftedness, may be a learning disability, hearing or visual impairment, communication problem, physical disability, or other disability. Whitmore and Maker (1985) estimate that more than 2 percent of the disabled population are gifted and talented.

Children with learning disabilities who are also gifted and talented may not be identified for services for either exceptionality, in that they may appear to be functioning within the average range and neither their giftedness nor their learning disabilities are recognized (Suter & Wolf, 1987). Such children may demonstrate a combination of success and failure, which challenges teacher's stereotypes that gifted children are good at everything and that children with learning disabilities are only of average intelligence (Yewchuk, 1983). A particular challenge for teachers is to recognize the learning disability when the learner excels in some other area of learning or performance.

Minner (1990) found that teachers were significantly less likely to refer learners who had learning disabilities to programs for gifted and talented children. In a study using identical behavioral vignettes and descriptions, students labeled physically disabled were more likely to be described as gifted than those labeled learning disabled (Minner, Prater, Bloodworth, & Walker, 1987). According to Chermak and Burgerud (1983), children with learning disabilities who were gifted and talented did not perform as well as their peers who were gifted and talented on three measures of receptive language. Learners with learning disabilities who are gifted and talented may be defensive regarding their strengths and weaknesses, independent in their ways of thinking and problem solving, and perplexed regarding their own weaknesses (Yewchuk, 1985). Yewchuk and Bibby (1989) suggest that educational programs work towards helping these learners develop a strong self-concept and an accurate assessment of personal strengths and weaknesses.

Children with learning disabilities who are gifted and talented tend to have lower self-concepts than their peers who are gifted and talented. In addition, a relationship has been found between lower self-concepts and the level of hyperactivity or social interaction these learners demonstrate. Because these learners are not failing, few are reported by their parents or general education teachers as having learning problems (Waldron, Saphire, & Rosenblum, 1987).

Brown-Muzino (1990) lists the issues regarding learners with learning disabilities who are gifted and talented as follows:

a. Assessment—In addition to the assessment administered to all children, for these children additional concerns of perfectionism, feelings of inadequacy, unrealistic goals, hypersensitivity, demand for adult attention, and intolerance should be evaluated.
b. Early intervention—Specifically aimed at preventing underachievement.
c. Flexible placements—Designed to respond to individual needs, because traditional "gifted programs" may not meet the needs of these students.
d. The use of strategies—Positive reward systems and ways to increase a personal awareness of strengths and weaknesses should be used.

Students who are gifted and talented and have visual impairments have problems similar to those learners who are gifted and talented and learning disabled. Corn (1986) contends that the obstacles to the identification of these children include (a) stereotypic expectations related to persons with visual handicaps, (b) developmental delays, (c) incomplete information, and (d) a lack of opportunity to display superior abilities. In a similar manner, learners with hearing impairments may present information deficits due to their hearing impairment, learners with communication disorders may present problems in expressive language, and so on. Learners who are gifted and talented and have physical disabilities have been helped greatly through advances in technology, such as the personal computer and augmentative communication devices.

Gifted Learners Who Are Culturally or Socioeconomically Disadvantaged   Two neglected subgroups of learners who are gifted and talented are (a) individuals who may not actualize their potential because they are from cultural backgrounds that differ from the mainstream culture, and (b) individuals who are socially and economically disadvantaged (VanTassel-Baska, Patton, & Prillaman, 1989). Deschamp and Robson (1984) conceptualize "gifted disadvantaged" students as

1. high-achieving students in disadvantaged areas; with little contact with other more-capable students, they may not be challenged or presented opportunities.

Learners who are gifted and talented need contact with more challenges.

2.   underachievers, whose teachers may not recognize their potential or who may be in systems that do not intervene.
3.   high-achieving students from ethnic groups who have difficulty reconciling language and value differences between home and school.
4.   high-achieving students from socioeconomically or culturally diverse groups who have difficulties in the school-home cultural mismatch.

In addition, the group of learners who are gifted and socioeconomically disadvantaged may demonstrate giftedness or talent in ways that are not generally understood and accepted by the majority culture. Programming for these students includes focusing on maintaining their ethnic identity, cultural enrichment, counseling, parent-support services, and career education (Rimm, 1985a).

A study commissioned by the secretary of education cited four conditions that must be considered if the needs of learners who are gifted and disadvantaged are to be met:

1.   Learners from minorities represent 30 percent of the public school population but less than 20 percent of the learners selected for gifted programs.
2.   Learners from low-income backgrounds represent 20 percent of the school population but only 4 percent of the learners performing at the ninety-fifth percentile or above on standardized tests.

3. Seniors in high school who are from disadvantaged families (in which the mother did not complete high school) are over 50 percent less likely to have participated in programs for the gifted and talented than their more-advantaged peers.
4. Disadvantaged students are far less likely to be enrolled in academic programs to prepare them for college and are about half as likely to take courses in advanced math and science than are more advantaged students (U.S. Department of Education, 1989).

Interventions for learners who are gifted and disadvantaged should demonstrate the following generic characteristics (VanTassel-Baska, Patton, & Prillaman, 1989):

- Early and systematic assessment
- Parent involvement
- Effective school strategies—for example, time on task, school leadership
- Experiential and hands-on learning approaches
- Activities that allow for self-expression
- Mentors and role models
- Community involvement
- Counseling efforts that address the issue of cultural values as well as facilitating talent development

Underachieving Learners Who Are Gifted and Talented   Those learners who are gifted and talented yet do not achieve to their potential, usually referred to as "underachievers," are not a homogeneous group. As a group, however, these learners demonstrate a significant discrepancy between ability and achievement. The factors that influence their achievement are often situation specific and highly variable (Gonzalez & Hayes, 1988). Whitmore (1986) contends, however, that the school experience may be hazardous to the mental health and achievement motivation of young learners who are gifted and talented. Her work with children identified as underachievers, based on these learners' perceptions of the school experience, suggests that patterns of special socialization needs, personality attributes and emotional conflict, and low motivation are facets of classrooms that have a damaging effect on the achievement and performance of learners who are gifted and talented.

According to Rimm (1985b), accurate measures to determine **underachievement** are not available. He suggests assessing trends in behavior patterns to identify underachieving learners. The patterns of behaviors to be analyzed include (a) competition, (b) responsibility, (c) self-control, (d) interpersonal communications, and (e) respect. A parent report is suggested to obtain information on these five patterns. The characteristics of underachievement in the area of competition are bossiness, blaming others, avoiding competition, and depression. In the area of responsibility, the characteristics are seeking assistance with home assignments, postponing long-term projects, and trying to please perfectionist parents. The negative correlations to achievement are parent generosity, a close and somewhat dependent maternal relationship, conforming to peers, and being able to convince parents to change their minds. The underachievers have a tendency to "talk back" or to be disrespectful.

In a study comparing learners who were achievers and those who were perceived to be underachievers, Dowdall and Colangelo (1982) found underachievers to be less socially mature, have more emotional problems, demonstrate more antisocial behavior, and have a lower self-concept. Underachievement was found to be primarily a male phenomenon. The major characteristics of gifted and talented underachievers are summarized in table 17.1.

Table 17.1   **Characteristics of Underachievers Who Are Gifted or Talented**

Patterns related to achievement

poor performance on tests
at or below level in basic skills
daily work incomplete or poorly done
discrepancy between oral and written communication
little academic initiative

Patterns related to cognition

superior retention and comprehension when interested
large repertoire of facts
many interests, areas of expertise
interests are frequently rigid

Patterns related to personality

creative and imaginative
persistently dissatisfied with work
avoids new tasks to prevent imperfect performance
self-critical, with poor self-esteem
self-selects home projects
rationalizes and denies failure
impulsive emotional responses
immature
external locus of control
perceives environment as threatening
uncooperative, autonomous

Patterns related to social interaction

distrustful of overtures of affection
productive in groups
sensitive towards self and others
few friends
belligerent, intolerant, critical
low sense of personal and social work
perceives self as alienated and unlikable

Patterns related to school behaviors

withdrawn or aggressive in class
dislikes drill, practice, rote learning, memorization
distractible, difficulty focusing and attending
negative attitude towards school
difficult to motivate, reinforce, discipline
procrastinates
frequently absent, malingers
disorganized, poor study habits, little persistence

Sources: Whitmore, 1980; Gallagher, 1975; Shoff, 1984; Mamchur, 1982; Seeley, 1985; Rimm, 1984; Blackburn & Erickson, 1986; with the assistance of Faye Wagner.

Major emphasis of programs for gifted underachievers is on changing their counterproductive behaviors to productive behaviors. Whitmore (1980) urges the application of six principles when working with these learners. First, pressure should be reduced by deemphasizing grades and competition. Nonconforming behavior that does not interfere with programming should be tolerated. Second, the student's motivation should be analyzed to pair strengths and weaknesses with likes and dislikes. Third, independent activities that emphasize choice and self-evaluation should be used. Fourth, instruction in social skills and effective leadership should be provided. Fifth, activities should reward both long- and short-term goals. Finally, students should be assisted in developing a rational understanding of their personal limitations and demonstrating self-control over personal behavior and its consequences.

Girls and Young Women Who Are Gifted or Talented

Though they may perceive themselves as more scholastically competent than either boys who are gifted or talented or regularly achieving girls (Li, 1988), girls who are gifted and talented are confronted with a series of challenges in efforts to meet their potential. During elementary school, the interests of girls are more similar to the interests of boys who are gifted or talented than to the interests of their normal-ability peers. However, by the time they reach adolescence, young women who are gifted or talented develop lower career aspirations than those of young men who are gifted and talented (Kerr, 1985). This change in aspirations occurs at approximately fourteen years of age. At this time, young women are confronted with socialization patterns toward passivity and dependence.

Young women who are gifted, creative, or talented are pressured to conform to stereotypical roles, and recognize the inconsistent vertical development of the careers of men and women around them (Leroux, 1994). Girls identified as gifted, creative, or talented are viewed by their teachers and themselves as having lower intellectual capacity for math and science than boys (Marjoram, 1994). Even boys identified as gifted and talented report that they believe their wives should not pursue a career once children are born (Reis & Callahan, 1994). Because they frequently must balance professional interests and higher education with traditional sex roles, women who are gifted or talented are said to be "cultural underachievers," (Davis & Rimm, 1985); that is, they are forced to achieve at less than their potential due to their culturally relegated role as primary parent and home manager.

Personal causes of underachievement in girls and young women include two unique socialization patterns: (a) the **gifted imposter phenomenon** (a personal belief that one is not truly as successful as others believe and that this lack of success will be discovered), and (b) the **Cinderella complex** (waiting to be rescued from personal responsibilities by a male partner). According to Silverman (1986), women who achieve with a high degree of excellence combine the beliefs, values, behaviors, and expectations of both males and females. Facilitating the potential of females who are gifted and talented requires early identification, avoiding overprotection, fostering independence, ability grouping, which permits the expression of abilities and talents without fear, retaining high expectations, academic and career counseling, appropriate role models and mentors, and social-emotional support.

Gifted Learners from Various Cultures

If consideration is to be given to learners from various cultures, a multicultural perspective must be included in the identification process (Schlesinger, 1987). Diversity within cultures, as well as the search for data from multiple sources and an awareness of the different types of behavior manifested by gifted and talented learners from differing cultural backgrounds, must be considered (Frasier, 1987). Language may also emerge as an issue among Hispanic children, in that poor test performance limits referral to programming for learners who are gifted and talented (deBernard, 1985).

In their comparison of behavioral ratings of Anglo and Hispanic children who were gifted and talented, Argulewicz, Elliott, and Hall (1982) found significant ethnic differences in the areas of learning and motivation, with Anglo students being rated higher. No significant differences were found between the two groups in the areas of creativity and leadership. The use of this type of measure may, depending on the criteria used, result in the exclusion of Hispanic learners, by nature of their culture.

Annual Edition

Article *35*

Annual Edition

Article *34*

In their exploration of behavior rating scales, Elliott and Argulewicz (1983) found that differences between Anglo and Hispanic learners did not appear to be educationally significant. In addition, when they analyzed the data by socioeconomic status, there again were no significant differences. They contend that behaviors indicative of intellectual giftedness are similar across socioeconomic status and ethnic background, but support the position that ethnic, sex, grade, and socioeconomic status differences should be considered in the development of local and national norms.

In working with learners who are gifted and talented from various cultures, support in developing a bond between parents and school may be necessary, especially to assure parents that the development of the learner's abilities and the preservation of family and community values are addressed in the gifted program (Colangelo, 1985). In one urban area, a program was designed to provide an opportunity for socioeconomically disadvantaged children to receive intensive school-based activities that would prepare them for gifted education programs (Baldwin, 1994). In this program, the concept of multiple intelligences was used to generate thematic units that challenged the students.

Technology has contributed to meeting the needs of migrant children who are gifted and talented. Hamilton (1984) describes the Migrant Student Record Transfer System, which allows students who have been identified as gifted and talented in one district to be immediately eligible for services when moving to another district. With over 672,000 active files, the program often prevents migrant students from being lost in the system and helps them to consistently receive the programming needed to meet their potential. In addition, programming specific for "high-potential minority youth," such as the Skills Reinforcement Project (Lynch & Mills, 1990), which involves Saturday classes and a residential summer program, have been found to make significant differences in these learners' ability to match the achievements of their Anglo peers.

Very Young Children Who Are Gifted, Creative, or Talented

Children who are gifted, creative, or talented are frequently identified at very early ages. In a study of children identified between three and five years of age, parents reported early verbal expression skills, an unusual curiosity level, and long attention spans (Creel & Karnes, 1988). Perhaps of most interest was the finding that in retrospect, 96.3 percent of the fifty-three sets of parents interviewed supported a specialized gifted preschool program on at least a half-day basis.

As is true among older children who are gifted and talented, there are multiple factors beyond tested intelligence quotient that have an impact on the young child's skill performance and adaptation to social and nonsocial situations (McGuffog, Feiring, & Lewis, 1987). Among young children, however, it is at times difficult to differentiate children who have had a multitude of experiences and opportunities and have a broad base of general knowledge from young children who are truly gifted and talented.

The Impact on Interactions in the Home and Classroom

Objective Three

To describe the impact of giftedness, creativity, or talent on interactions in the home and classroom.

The majority of families with children who are gifted and talented experience moderate levels of adaptation and cohesion, suggesting that having a child who is gifted and talented in the home is not necessarily associated with extreme patterns of family functioning (West, Hosie, & Mathews, 1989). Family relationships may be affected, however, in the areas of the tempo of family interactions, family system makeup, sibling self-perceptions, and collective attitudes toward

It is difficult to identify young children who are gifted, creative, or talented.

the giftedness (McMann & Oliver, 1988). Children who were creatively gifted have been shown to come from family environments that stressed independence, were less child centered, and exhibited tense family relationships and more negative affect, resulting in motivation to attain power. Academic achievers came from cohesive, child-centered families with strong parent-child identification (Olszewski, Kulieke, & Buescher, 1987). Families with a child who was gifted and talented were shown to demonstrate higher levels of adjustment in problem solving, communication, roles, and affective responsiveness (Mathews, West, & Hosie, 1986).

Parents

Parents may experience stress associated with the increased demands of parenting children who are gifted and talented, and they may have a particular challenge in working with daughters who are gifted and who are confronted with stereotyping by their peers (Shaughnessy & Neely, 1987). Though all of the parents Cornell and Grossberg (1989) interviewed acknowledged thinking of their children as gifted, over one-fourth of them reported not using the term *gifted* in reference to their children. The families with parents who used the term were more achievement oriented and provided less freedom for expression of individual feelings.

In comparison with the general population, fathers of children who were gifted and talented were found to be more intelligent, independent, aloof, assertive, and tense (Fell, Dahlstrom, & Winter, 1984). In the same study, mothers tended to be more intelligent and independent, as well as conscientious, persistent, and more calculated and controlled in their approach to life as members of the general female population.

Braggett, Ashman, and Noble (1983) analyzed the type of support and assistance sought by parents of children who were gifted and talented. The parents (a) wanted to understand their childrens' development in terms of giftedness, intellectual ability, social-emotional development, and motivation; (b) were anxious that their children proceed at their own pace and avoid boredom; and (c) searched for enrichment activities. The parents consistently expressed the desire that their children, though gifted, be "normal." Parents of children who are gifted and talented tend to spend more time with their child on school-related activities, report unconditional love for their child, and encourage independence (Karnes, Swedel, & Steinberg, 1984).

The parents' recognition of their child's uniqueness and special needs may help the child avoid social and emotional issues. Sebring (1983) advises parents to value the individuality of their child and, while approving accomplishments, show acceptance of failure. He urges that these children be helped to enjoy being a child while being provided opportunities for choices and decision making that teach them responsibility. Parents' awareness of resources such as school staff, other parents, organizations, and literature is helpful in meeting the continuing needs of children who are gifted and talented (Conroy, 1987).

When engaged in problem-solving tasks, the mothers of young children who were gifted were significantly more likely to encourage metacognitive strategies such as predicting consequences than mothers of average children who provided more direct solutions to problems (Moss & Strayer, 1990). High self-esteem has been associated with the degree to which children who were gifted and talented viewed their mothers as likely to explain reasons for disciplining them (Enright & Rusicka, 1989).

Nontraditional Families and Families Representing Various Cultures

Gelbrich and Hare (1989) found that living in a single-parent home negatively affected the school achievement of children who were gifted and talented, with boys more affected than girls.

Families in rural areas are presented with a unique set of challenges related to their children who are gifted and talented. These families may need specific help including additional parent education, in overcoming obstacles that inhibit creativity in children (Strom & Johnson, 1989b).

Strom and Johnson (1989a), in their work with Hispanic parents, found that Hispanic parents were more likely to join their children in play, expressed a higher level of comfort during these periods, and assigned more importance to play than did their Anglo counterparts. Anglo parents reported more favorable perceptions towards their child's creativity, control, and teacher-learning activities.

Siblings

Labeling one child in a family as gifted, creative, or talented may have significant impact on the whole family system. Cornell (1983) found that in the majority of families with children in gifted programs, at least one parent did not perceive the child as gifted. Those parents who did perceive their child as gifted expressed pride in the child and described a closer parent-child relationship to their gifted child in comparison to his or her siblings. The siblings of children who were gifted and talented were significantly less well-adjusted than other children and were significantly less careful of social rules, less outgoing, more easily upset, shier, and more frustrated. Adjustment problems were found to occur primarily in general education students who were perceived as less gifted than their siblings by their parents (Cornell & Grossberg, 1986).

Siblings of children who were gifted and talented perceived themselves as happier about their gifted sibling's participation in accelerated programs than the gifted child perceived their siblings to be (Colangelo & Brower, 1987a). Siblings of children who were gifted and talented reported friction and pressure when the gifted child was older (Grenier, 1985). Large age gaps appeared to be beneficial to the sibling relationship, with highest scores for general positive relationship demonstrated between siblings who were more than three years apart in age. Siblings are typically fairly close in their tested intelligence quotients to their gifted sister or brother, although giftedness in a second child may be difficult to identify due to behavioral differences relative to first- and second-born children (Silverman, 1986). Ballering and Koch (1984) report that children who are gifted and talented are more likely to assign a negative affect to their relationships with their regular education siblings. As the child's intelligence quotient score increases, his or her perceptions of positive affect in relations with a gifted sibling decreases.

Colangelo and Brower (1987b), in a study of the long-term effects of the gifted label on siblings, found that though nonlabeled siblings scored significantly lower on academic self-concept, they did not differ from their siblings identified as gifted and talented on general self-esteem and, in fact, scored higher in the areas of personality adjustment and endurance.

Mediating the Environment

The range of educational alternatives needed to respond to the varied needs of learners who are gifted and talented is rarely available within a school system (Cox & Daniel, 1984). The possible exception to this assertion is a few major urban school systems.

Preschool

The early identification and programming for children who are gifted and talented has generated a broad range of concerns. Johnson (1983) contends that preschool learners who are gifted and talented are in a double-jeopardy situation because they are a minority and, historically, there have been few gifted programs for young children. Kitano (1985) describes issues related to parents' expectations and children's confidence and self-concepts in programs specifically for those who are gifted and talented.

It is difficult to identify young children who are gifted and talented by administering standard instruments such as intelligence and achievement tests. Such instruments are generally inappropriate for use with young children. In addition, the fact that young children develop rapidly and unevenly during preschool renders formal testing difficult. Perhaps the most-effective methods of identification are direct observations of the child's functioning and parent nominations.

Johnson (1983) suggests that an enriched, child-responsive preschool environment that affords opportunities for all children to demonstrate and develop the gifts specific to them would meet the educational and affective needs of children who normally would be identified as gifted or who would be overlooked. Karnes and Johnson (1987) also found that when programming to enhance divergent, convergent, and evaluative thinking skills was in place, both preschool children identified as gifted and talented and their nonidentified peers made gains in cognitive and creative functioning.

Early school entry has been suggested for young learners who are gifted and talented. Gallagher (1986) argues that administrative convenience should give way to developmental appropriateness in providing early admittance to school and other educational options for young children. Maddux (1983) maintains, however, that unless schools change so that children receive instruction from which they are ready to profit, early school entry will not address the needs of young children who are gifted and talented or, in fact, other children.

Acceleration and Enrichment

Two ways of mediating the environment for learners who are gifted and talented are acceleration and enrichment. The "Guidelines for Practice" box on p. 406 discusses these two mediation approaches. **Acceleration** refers to moving through the curriculum rapidly. **Enrichment** refers to the addition of activities to enhance the curriculum. Horowitz and O'Brien (1986) state that the evaluation of

Objective Four

To describe ways to mediate the environment for learners who are gifted, creative, or talented.

Annual **Edition**

Articles *33 & 36*

guidelines for practice

Acceleration and Enrichment

Two common strategies for working with learners who are gifted, talented, or creative are acceleration and enrichment. In acceleration, students move through the curriculum more rapidly. In enrichment, students complete additional activities to enhance the curriculum. A concern sometimes arises among children who are gifted, talented, or creative that they are punished for the speed at which they learn by having to do more work or extra assignments. One student, after being in enrichment programs through the middle grades, indicated that he "didn't want to be gifted anymore" because he was always expected to do more. Teachers must be sensitive to the balance of challenging students as opposed to simply adding assignments |

these two approaches and information on how best to mediate the instructional environment remain insufficient for professionals who plan, implement, and evaluate such programs. In addition, they argue that knowledge about the developmental course of giftedness remains sparse and that there is little information on the impact of acceleration, enrichment, or other strategies on intellectual, social, and personality processes in learners who are gifted and talented over the life span.

Acceleration   Acceleration options for children who are gifted and talented include early school entrance, fast-paced or accelerated classes, extra course load ungraded classes, or summer programs (Sisk, 1988). Sisk argues that acceleration is appropriate for most learners who are gifted and talented because they are usually advanced in overall development and successful when accelerated. Advanced achievement, high motivation, and a healthy self-concept are essential for this strategy.

In a survey of the attitudes of coordinators of gifted programs, school psychologists, principals, and teachers toward early admission and acceleration, Southern, Jones, and Fiscus (1989) found consistently conservative attitudes towards the value of acceleration as an appropriate intervention for young children. Though there were few negative reactions, even the group most favorably disposed toward acceleration, the coordinators of gifted programs, viewed the strategy as potentially hazardous to the child's development.

The primary purpose of acceleration is to speed up the educational development of budding professionals so that they will be in a position to make an impact on society when they reach a creative peak in their midtwenties. Among the most common strategies for acceleration are early admission to kindergarten, first grade, junior and senior high school, and college; grade skipping; and telescoping three years of academic work into two years (Davis & Rimm, 1985). Credit by examination and correspondence courses are also acceleration options. According to Pantus (1984), popular thought with regard to the social and emotional harm to students who have been accelerated has not been demonstrated in the professional literature.

Enrichment   Enrichment programs are designed to provide learners who are gifted and talented with additional experiences without placing them in a higher grade. This model has been criticized as simply adding more to the traditional learning context rather than modifying it and making it more responsive to the needs of the students (Kirschenbaum, 1984). Enrichment may take the form of classroom enrichment activities, consulting-teacher services, pull-out and

guidelines for practice

"Let's Build a Sailboat"

*L*earners who are gifted and talented are usually assumed to be intellectually gifted and to have exceptional achievement. However, learners may also be talented in other areas, such as leadership, planning, and construction. Forster (1990) describes the use of projects to facilitate the development of secondary school students' problem-solving skills and creativity. Projects can support students' learning by sharpening their planning skills and helping them effectively use their resources. He provides five questions to focus attention on whether or not a project is appropriate for learners who are gifted and talented:

1. Does the project challenge learners cognitively and affectively?
2. Does the project have a "student monopoly" on decision making?
3. Does the project measure experience gained through participating?
4. Does the project allow students to follow decisions with actions?
5. Does the project use self-regulation and self-evaluation?

For example, students were presented the task "Let's build a sailboat." Class was arranged into crews, and students wrote journals of what they expected to accomplish and how they planned to accomplish it. Basic plans were provided, but students were "turned loose" in planning, building, and testing their craft. Students used brainstorming, computers, models, spreadsheets, and other strategies to build their boats. Through the task, students in groups recognized the individual strengths of "crew" members, the need for a division of labor, how each of them varied in their abilities, and that leadership and cooperation themselves are talents ∎

resource-room programs, honors classes, special courses and seminars, independent study, research projects, special classes and schools, and community contributions such as mentoring programs (Eulie, 1983).

In-classroom enrichment activities are generally provided by the general education teacher who may or may not have specific training in the education of learners who are gifted and talented. Such activities may include special projects and assignments, studying more advanced materials than the other members of the class, assisting the teacher, or serving as a laboratory assistant (see "Guidelines for Practice" boxes above and on p. 408 for sample projects). In a few school systems, a consulting teacher is available to assist the general class teacher in programming for learners who are gifted and talented. Pull-out or resource-room programs allow the learner who is gifted and talented to leave the general classroom and attend programs with peers under the supervision of a specially trained teacher.

Honors classes and special courses and seminars allow the learners who are gifted and talented to interact in a learning environment with gifted peers and to engage in the study of various topics of interest in some depth. Such activities are generally under the supervision of specially trained teachers or experts in the study topic.

Special Classes and Schools

Special schools, sometimes called magnet schools (schools of performing arts, schools of science and technology, classical academies), expose gifted, creative, or talented students to in-depth exploration of their specific areas of giftedness or talent under the supervision of specially trained teachers and in the company of peers. Such schools also provide the student with the general knowledge and skills common to an education in the general classroom and school.

guidelines for practice

Storytelling

Young children who are creative or talented can build a greater awareness of themselves as creative individuals with valuable messages through storytelling. Sasser and Zorena (1991), in their "tell me a story" project, focused their students' efforts on real issues and problems. Students, by being urged to tell a story, could explore a wide range of subjects according to their interests.

Students were given basic guidance, but researched, organized, and wrote their stories independently. Though the students were familiar with research and writing a presentation, "tell me a story" required them to include a performance component. Emphasizing the performance aspect increased students' reevaluation, editing, and polishing of their work. Research skills were required; the story could not be told without a solid foundation and adequate supporting details. Stories involved the following topics:

the beginning of the earth (one student interviewed a local geology professor as part of her research)
town history
the remembrance of a grandparent, grounded in a historical event

Evans and Marken (1982) assessed the cumulative impact of special class in the public school on sixth through eighth grade students identified as gifted and talented. A battery of psychological and behavioral measures were used to assess five areas of functioning. Data were analyzed to determine any main effects of the program, sex, and grade on the five measures. No main effects of class placement were observed. As a group, females reported stronger intellectual achievement responsibility and self-perceived congeniality than did males. Males in special classes held somewhat less-positive attitudes toward school and teachers, as well as weaker commitment to classroom. Overall, females showed a more-positive school orientation. A meta-analysis of thirteen studies also supported sustained periods of instruction in like-ability groups for learners identified as gifted, creative, or talented (Rogers, 1993).

Mentoring Programs   A **mentor** provides individualized assistance to learners who are gifted and talented through his or her own expertise and time. Gray (1984) describes two model mentoring programs, a helping-relationship model and a four-phase mentoring model.

In the helping-relationship model, the community mentor plans, initiates, and directs activities based on background information from the learner and the teacher. The mentor then solicits the learner's reaction to the plan, and together they discuss and modify it to respond to the learner's specific needs. Next, the student and mentor, contributing equally, conduct the activity. As the learner's contribution increases, the mentor's influence decreases. During the final phase of the program the learner functions independently.

The four-phase mentoring model is more directive than the helping-relationship model. First, the mentor writes a proposal. Second, the proposal is presented to potential students who participate in writing a mutually agreed upon plan of action. Next, the mentor shares his or her personal expertise with the students. Finally, the activity is completed by the students and presented to the students' peers.

A mentor can help a child succeed.

Management and Curriculum Jones (1983) contends that the manner in which teachers approach classroom management has a significant effect on learners who are gifted and talented. He maintains that learners who are gifted and talented are sensitive to disruptive environments and that their unique needs require a particular style of classroom leadership to enhance their personal and academic potential. The classroom environment is critical because it must offer the student variety, stimulation, and challenge (Wyatt, 1982).

Inadequate feedback and the lack of reward for originality, which frequently occur in classroom assessment and testing procedures, may challenge learners who are gifted and talented (Smith, 1986). The typical testing and examination procedures used in classrooms may have a harmful effect on the student's attitudes and intrinsic motivation. A differentiated curriculum that (a) promotes higher thinking processes, (b) employs teaching strategies that accommodate both curriculum content and individual learning styles, and (c) provides special grouping arrangements appropriate for particular children may enhance the development of learners who are gifted and talented (George, 1990).

Society perceives women as less able to make major decisions and less serious about their careers.

The Impact on Participation in the School, Community, and Society

Objective Five

To describe the impact of giftedness, creativity, or talent on participation in the larger social systems of school, community, and society.

Popular theories about the social and emotional harm to learners who are gifted and talented caused by rejection by peers and the social isolation of accelerated programs are not supported in the literature (Pantus, 1984). Gifted and talented students rated positively their gifted programs as well as the gifted label. A significant impact on positive ratings included the use of computers, independent study, and increased contact with teachers in small-group discussions and lab activities (Midgett & Olson, 1983).

Reviewing the history of programming for learners who are gifted and talented may provide some insight into society's perceptions of these learners. Johnson (1986), in her review, indicates that in the early twentieth century, learners who were gifted and talented were identified primarily by their ability to excel on tasks measured by intelligence tests. These early programs focused on accelerating students through existing academic content. During the 1920s, enrichment became the preferred practice. By the 1950s, however, researchers began to recognize the limitations of intelligence testing and, as reflected in current definitions, the concept of ability and its various aspects became the focus.

Myths about giftedness continue to plague learners who are gifted and talented. Roedell (1986) suggests that these myths, unrealistic expectations, pressure to perform, constant criticism or praise, pressure to conform, and challenges in making friends and dealing with peers remain for these learners.

Society's perception of women who are gifted and talented is a significant challenge for these learners. As late as 1979, attorneys in a Sears Roebuck and Company sex discrimination suit argued that women did not want better paying jobs and could not handle stress, competition, or risk. The historical and accepted perception remains that women are not really suitable candidates for leadership (Tell, 1987). Historically, women are perceived as a powerless group, as is reflected in discrepancies in salaries and the numbers of females in executive positions or with doctorates (Curcio, Morsink, & Bridges, 1989).

Summary

Learners who are gifted, creative, or talented make up approximately 3 percent to 5 percent of the population. Many professionals suggest that present definitions and assumptions with regard to the gifted artificially limit the number of learners identified as gifted, creative, or talented. Some believe that this population of learners is closer to 10 percent of the school-age population.

Though an extremely heterogeneous group, learners who are gifted, creative, and talented are distinguishable from other learners in the areas of social-emotional development, language development, and cognitive development. Initially, services for learners within this heterogeneous group focused exclusively on the academically talented. With the development of broader definitions of giftedness, talent, and creativity, the number of students within this population expanded dramatically. Emphasis in identification is placed on the demonstration of unique abilities, skills, talents, leadership abilities, and creativity. Today, educators give greater attention to identifying and serving gifted, talented, and creative individuals who are disabled, socioeconomically disadvantaged, members of diverse cultures, females, very young children, and underachievers.

Society's response to individuals who are gifted, talented, and creative is mixed. On the one hand, society appears to appreciate the gifted and to desire their skills and abilities; on the other, society tends to resist providing programs and services. Society appears confused in its reaction to women who are gifted, talented, and creative. It provides them with fewer opportunities than their male counterparts, including fewer fellowships, lower salaries, and fewer employment opportunities.

Building Your Professional Vocabulary

Match each word or phrase to its meaning.

_____ acceleration

_____ Cinderella complex

_____ creative

_____ enrichment

_____ gifted

_____ gifted imposter phenomenon

_____ mentor

_____ talented

_____ underachievement

a. academically or intellectually superior
b. capable of expressing unique and novel ideas
c. special abilities, aptitudes, and accomplishments in various areas
d. failure to reach anticipated accomplishments
e. one is truly not as successful as others believe

f. awaiting rescue from responsibilities
g. moving through the curriculum rapidly
h. addition of activities to enhance curriculum
i. a person who individually supports a learner who is gifted, creative, or talented

Comprehension Check

Select the most appropriate response.

1. Placement in segregated programs for learners who are gifted, creative, or talented may result in
   a. increased perceptions of self-worth.
   b. greater anxiety.
   c. higher self-esteem.

2. The incidence of psychological problems among learners who are intellectually gifted is
   a. greater than the general population.
   b. lower than the general population.
   c. about the same as the general population.

3. Public Law 94-142
   a. provides legal protections for learners who are gifted, creative, or talented.
   b. requires due process for learners who are gifted, creative, or talented.
   c. does not refer to learners who are gifted, creative, or talented.

4. Originally, definitions of giftedness
   a. were based on IQ.
   b. were based on intellectual achievement.
   c. were based on academic achievement.

5. Learners who are gifted and talented and have learning disabilities may
   a. not be identified in that they appear to be functioning within average range.
   b. be identified at an earlier age due to the mismatch between intelligence and apparent achievement.
   c. not be identified according to Public Law 94-142.

6. School
   a. is typically a positive experience for learners who are gifted, creative, or talented.
   b. may be hazardous to the mental health of learners who are gifted, creative, or talented.
   c. generates increased ennui, or boredom, among learners identified as gifted, creative, or talented.

7. Young women who are identified as gifted, creative, or talented
   a. have interests similar to those of boys who are gifted, creative, or talented.
   b. have similar aspirations as boys who are gifted, creative, or talented.
   c. lower their aspirations during early adolescence.

8. Parents of learners identified as gifted, creative, or talented
   a. may revel in the success of their children.
   b. may feel incompetent to parent their children.
   c. may experience stress related to increased demands.

9. In families of learners identified as gifted, creative, or talented,
   a. at least one parent typically does not perceive the child as gifted.
   b. parents recognize their child's giftedness early on.
   c. little impact on siblings occurs.

10. Acceleration
    a. provides alternatives for learners who are gifted, creative, or talented.
    b. increases critical thinking of learners who are gifted, creative, or talented.
    c. speeds up typical programming.

References

Argulewicz, E. N., Elliott, S. N., & Hall, R. (1982). Comparison of behavioral ratings of Anglo-American and Mexican-American gifted children. *Psychology in the Schools, 19* (4), 469–472.

Baldwin, A. Y. (1994). The seven plus story: Developing hidden talent among students in socioeconomically disadvantaged environments. *Gifted Child Quarterly, 17* (2), 80–84.

Ballering, L. D., & Koch, A. (1984). Family relations when a child is gifted. *Gifted Child Quarterly, 28* (3), 140–143.

Betts, G. T., & Neihart, M. (1988). Profiles of the gifted and talented. *Gifted Child Quarterly, 32,* 248–253.

Birch, J. W. (1984). Is any identification procedure necessary? *Gifted Child Quarterly, 28* (4), 157–161.

Boyce, C. W. (1991). Dear Sam. *Gifted Child Today, 14* (4), 10.

Braggett, E. J., Ashman, A., & Noble, J. (1983). The expressed needs of parents of gifted children. *Gifted Education International, 1* (2), 80–83.

Brown-Muzino, C. (1990). Success strategies for learners who are learning disabled as well as gifted. *Teaching Exceptional Children, 23* (1), 10–12.

Carter, K. R. (1984). Cognitive development in intellectually gifted: A Piagetian perspective. *Roeper Review, 1* (3), 180–184.

Chermak, G. D., & Burgerud, D. M. (1983). Receptive language of gifted and learning disabled-gifted children. *Exceptional Children, 30* (3), 226–229.

Colangelo, N. (1985). Counseling needs of culturally diverse gifted students. *Roeper Review, 8* (1), 33–35.

Colangelo, N., & Brower, P. (1987a). Gifted youngsters and their siblings: Long-term impact of labeling on their academic and personal self-concepts. *Roeper Review, 10* (2), 101–103.

Colangelo, N., & Brower, P. (1987b). Labeling gifted youngsters: Long-term impact on families. *Gifted Child Quarterly, 31* (2), 75–78.

Coleman, J. M., & Fults, B. A. (1982). Self-concept and the gifted classroom: The role of social comparisons. *Gifted Child Quarterly, 26* (3), 116–120.

Coleman, J. M., & Fults, B. A. (1983). Self-concept and the gifted child. *Roeper Review, 5* (4), 44–47.

Coleman, J. M., & Fults, B. A. (1985). Special-class placement, level of intelligence, and the self-concepts of gifted children: A social comparison perspective. *Remedial and Special Education, 6* (1), 7–12.

Conroy, E. H. (1987). Primary prevention for gifted students: A parent education group. *Elementary School Guidance and Counseling, 22* (2), 110–116.

Corn, A. L. (1986). Gifted students who have a visual handicap: Can we meet their educational needs? *Education of the Visually Handicapped, 18* (3), 71–84.

Cornell, D. G. (1983). Gifted children: The impact of positive labeling on the family system. *American Journal of Orthopsychiatry, 53* (2), 322–335.

Cornell, D. G., & Grossberg, I. N. (1986). Siblings of children in gifted programs. *Journal for the Education of the Gifted, 9* (45), 253–264.

Cornell, D. G., & Grossberg, I. N. (1989). Parent use of the term "gifted": Correlates with family environment and child adjustment. *Journal for the Education of the Gifted, 12* (3), 218–230.

Cox, J., & Daniel, N. (1984). Comprehensive programs for able learners. *Gifted, Creative, and Talented, 32,* 47–53.

Creel, C. S., & Karnes, F. A. (1988). Parental expectancies and young gifted children. *Roeper Review, 11* (1), 48–50.

Curcio, J., Morsink, C., & Bridges, S. (1989). Women as leaders. *Educational Horizons, 67* (4), 124–130.

Davis, G. A., & Rimm, S. B. (1985). *Education of the gifted and talented.* Englewood Cliffs, NJ: Prentice Hall.

deBernard, A. E. (1985). Why Jose can't get in the gifted class: The bilingual child and standardized reading tests. *The Roeper Review, 8* (2), 80–82.

Deschamp, P., & Robson, G. (1984). Identifying gifted-disadvantaged students: Issues pertinent to system-level screening procedures for the identification of gifted children. *Gifted Education International, 2* (2), 92–99.

Dowdall, C. B., & Colangelo, N. (1982). Understanding gifted students: Review and implications. *Gifted Child Quarterly, 26* (4), 179–183.

Eccles, A. L., Bauman, E., & Rotenberg, K. J. (1989). Peer acceptance and self-esteem in gifted children. *Journal of Social Behavior and Personality, 4* (4), 401–409.

Elliott, S. N., & Argulewicz, E. N. (1983). Use of behavior rating scale to aid in the identification of developmentally and culturally different gifted children. *Journal of Psychoeducational Assessment, 1* (2), 179–186.

Enright, K. M., & Rusicka, M. F. (1989). Relationship between perceived parental behaviors and the self-esteem of gifted children. *Psychological Reports, 65* (1), 931–937.

Eulie, J. (1983). Wanted: A program for gifted and talented that meets individual district needs. *Thrust, 12* (May–June), 36–38.

Evans, E. O., & Marken, D. (1982). Multiple outcome assessment of special class placement for gifted students: A comparative study. *Gifted Child Quarterly, 26* (3), 126–132.

Feldhusen, J. F., Asher, J. W., & Hoover, S. M. (1984). Problems in the identification of giftedness, talent, or ability. *Gifted Child Quarterly, 28* (4), 149–151.

Fell, L., Dahlstrom, M., & Winter, D. C. (1984). Personality traits of parents of gifted children. *Psychological Reports, 54,* 383–387.

Forster, B. R. (1990). Let's build a sailboat: A differentiated gifted education project. *Teaching Exceptional Children, 22* (4), 40–43.

Forsyth, P. (1987). A study of self-concept, anxiety, and security of children in gifted, French Immersion, and regular classes. *Canadian Journal of Counselling, 21,* 153–156.

Frasier, M. M. (1987). The identification of gifted Black students: Developing new perspectives. *Journal for the Education of the Gifted, 10,* 155–180.

Galbraith, J. (1985). The eight great gripes of gifted kids: Responding to special needs. *The Roeper Review, 8* (1), 15–18.

Gallagher, J. J. (1985). *Teaching gifted children* (3rd ed.). Boston: Allyn & Bacon.

Gallagher, J. J. (1986). The need for programs for young gifted children. *Topics in Early Childhood Special Education, 6* (1), 1–8.

Gallucci, N. T. (1988). Emotional adjustment of gifted children. *Gifted Child Quarterly, 32,* 273–276.

Gelbrich, J. A., & Hare, E. K. (1989). The effects of single parenthood on school achievement in a gifted population. *Gifted Child Quarterly, 33* (3), 115–117.

George, D. (1990). The challenge of the able child. *Cambridge Journal of Education, 20* (2), 175–182.

Gonzalez, J., & Hayes, A. (1988). Psychosocial aspects of the development of gifted underachievers: Review and implications. *Exceptional Children, 35* (1), 39–51.

Gray, W. A. (1984). Mentoring gifted, talented, creative students on an initial student teaching practicum: Guidelines and benefits. *Gifted Education International, 2,* 121–128.

Grenier, M. E. (1985). Gifted children and other siblings. *Gifted Child Quarterly, 29* (4), 164–167.

Guilford, A., Scheurle, J., & Shonburn, S. (1981). Aspects of language development in the gifted. *Gifted Child Quarterly, 25,* 159–163.

Hamilton, J. (1984). The gifted migrant child: An introduction. *Roeper Review, 6* (3), 146–147.

Hilyer, K. (1988). Problems of gifted children. *Journal of the Association for the Study of Perception, 21,* 10–26.

Horowitz, F. D., & O'Brien, M. (1986). Gifted and talented children: State of knowledge and directions for research. *American Psychologist, 41,* 1147–1152.

Janos, P., Fung, H. C., & Robinson, N. M. (1985). Self-concept, self-esteem, and peer relations among gifted children who feel "different." *Gifted Child Quarterly, 29* (2), 78–82.

Johnson, L. G. (1983). Giftedness in preschool: A better time for development than identification. *Roeper Review, 5* (4), 13–15.

Johnson, S. (1986). Who are the gifted? A dilemma in search of a solution. *Education of the Visually Handicapped, 18* (2), 54–70.

Jones, V. (1983). Current trends in classroom management: Implications for gifted students. *Roeper Review, 6* (1), 26–30.

Karnes, F. A., & Koch, S. F. (1985). State definitions of the gifted and talented: An update and analysis. *Journal for the Education of the Gifted, 8* (4), 285–306.

Karnes, M. B., & Johnson, L. J. (1987). Training for staff, parents, and volunteers working with young gifted children, especially those with disabilities and from low-income homes. *Young Children, 44,* 49–56.

Karnes, M. B., Swedel, A., & Steinberg, D. (1984). Styles of parenting among parents of young gifted children. *Roeper Review, 6* (4), 232–235.

Kerr, B. A. (1985). Smart girls, gifted women: Special guidance concerns. *Roeper Review, 8* (1), 30–33.

Kirschenbaum, R. J. (1984). Examining the rationale for gifted education. *Roeper Review, 7,* 95–97.

Kitano, M. K. (1985). Issues and problems in establishing preschool programs for the gifted. *Roeper Review, 7* (4), 212–213.

Larsen, M. D. (1994). Public opinion regarding support for special programs for gifted children. *Journal for the Education of the Gifted, 17* (2), 131–142.

Leroux, J. A. (1994). A tapestry of values: Gifted women speak out. *Gifted Education International, 9* (33), 167–171.

LeVine, E. S., & Tucker, S. (1986). Emotional needs of gifted children: A preliminary, phenomonological view. *Creative Child and Adult Quarterly, 11* (3), 156–165.

Li, A. (1988). Self-perception and motivational orientation in gifted children. *Roeper Review, 10,* 175–180.

Loeb, R. C., & Jay, G. (1987). Self-concept in gifted children: Differential impact in boys and girls. *Gifted Child Quarterly, 31* (1), 9–14.

Lynch, S., & Mills, C. J. (1990). The Skills Reinforcement Project (SRP): An academic program for high potential minority youth. *Journal for the Education of the Gifted, 13* (4), 364–379.

Maddux, C. D. (1983). Early school entry for the gifted: New evidence and concerns. *Roeper Review, 5,* 15–17.

Mamchur, C. (1982). The reluctant learner. A paper presented at the annual meeting of NCTE. Washington, DC: ERIC. (ERIC document No. 219761)

Marjoram, T. (1986). Better late than never: Able youths and adults. *Gifted Education International, 4* (2), 89–96.

Marjoram, T. (1994). Are/should boys and girls gifted in mathematics be taught together? *Gifted Education International 9* (3), 152–153.

Mathews, F. N., West, J. D., & Hosie, T. W. (1986). Understanding families of academically gifted children. *Roeper Review, 9* (1), 40–42.

McGuffog, C., Feiring, C., & Lewis, M. (1987). The diverse profile of the extremely gifted child. *Roeper Review, 10* (2), 82–89.

McMann, N., & Oliver, R. (1988). Problems in families with gifted children: Implications for counselors. *Journal of Counseling and Development, 66* (6), 275–278.

Midgett, J., & Olson, J. (1983). Perceptions of gifted programming. *Roeper Review, 5,* 42–44.

Minner, S. (1990). Teacher evaluations of case descriptions of LD gifted children. *Gifted Child Quarterly, 34* (1), 37–39.

Minner, S., Prater, G., Bloodworth, H., & Walker, S. (1987). Referral and placement recommendations of teachers toward gifted handicapped children. *Roeper Review, 9,* 247–249.

Moss, E., & Strayer, F. F. (1990). Interactive problem-solving of gifted and non-gifted preschoolers with their mothers. *International Journal of Behavioral Development, 13* (2), 177–197.

Olszewski, P., Kulieke, M. J., & Buescher, T. (1987). The influence of the family environment on the development of talent: A literature review. *Journal for the Education of the Gifted, 11* (1), 6–28.

Pantus, P. (1984). Acceleration: More than skipping grades. *Roeper Review, 7* (2), 98–100.

Purcell, C. (1978). *Gifted and Talented Children's Education Act of 1978, Congressional Record.* Washington, DC: Government Printing Office.

Reis, S. M., & Callahan, C. M. (1994). Attitudes of adolescent gifted girls and boys toward education, achievement, and the future. *Gifted Education International, 9* (3), 144–151.

Renzulli, J. S. (1978). What makes giftedness? Reexamining a definition. *Phi Delta Kappan, 65,* 180–184.

Rimm, S. (1985a). How to reach the underachievement. *Instructor, 95* (1), 73–76.

Rimm, S. (1985b). Identifying underachievers: The characteristics approach. *Gifted, Creative, and Talented, 41,* 2–5.

Robinson, N. M., & Chamrad, D. L. (1986). Appropriate use of intelligence tests with gifted children. *Roeper Review, 8* (3), 160–163.

Roedell, W. C. (1986). Socioemotional vulnerabilities of young gifted children. *Journal of Children in Contemporary Society, 18,* 17–29.

Roeper, A. (1982). How the gifted cope with their emotions. *Roeper Review, 5* (2), 21–24.

Rogers, K. B. (1993). Grouping the gifted and talented: Questions and answers. *Roeper Review, 16* (1), 8–12.

Salkind, N. J. (1988). Equity and excellence: The case for mandating services for the gifted child. *Journal for the Education of the Gifted, 12* (1), 4–13.

Sapon-Shevin, M. (1987). Giftedness as a social construct. *Teachers College Record, 89* (1), 39–53.

Sasser, E., & Zorena, N. (1991). Storytelling as an adjunct to writing: Experiences with gifted students. *Teaching Exceptional Children, 23* (2), 42–44.

Schack, G., & Starko, A. J. (1990). Identification of gifted students: An analysis of criteria preferred by preservice teachers, classroom teachers, and teachers of the gifted. *Journal for the Education of the Gifted, 13,* 346–363.

Schlesinger, B. (1987). Considerations in the identification of the talented child from non-English speaking backgrounds. *Gifted Education International, 4* (3), 160–162.

Schneider, B. H., Clegg, M. R., Byrne, B. M., & Ledingham, J. E. (1989). Social relations of gifted children as a function of age and school program. *Journal of Educational Psychology, 81* (1), 48–56.

Sebring, A. D. (1983). Parental factors in the social and emotional adjustment of the gifted. *Roeper Review, 6* (2), 97–99.

Seeley, K. (1985). Facilitators for gifted learners. In J. Feldhusen (Ed.), *Towards excellence in gifted education.* Denver: Love.

Shaughnessy, M. F., & Neely, R. (1987). Parenting the prodigies: What if your child is highly verbal or mathematically precocious? *Creative Child and Adult Quarterly, 11,* 7–20.

Shoff, H. G. (1984). The gifted underachiever: Definitions and identification strategies. Washington, DC: ERIC. (ERIC Document No. 252092)

Silverman, L. K. (1986). Parenting young gifted children. *Journal of Children in Contemporary Society, 187,* 73–87.

Sisk, D. A. (1988). The bored and disinterested gifted child: Going through school lockstep. *Journal for the Education of the Gifted, 11,* 5–18.

Smith, D. J. (1986). Do tests and examinations alienate the gifted student? *Gifted Education International, 4* (2), 101–105.

Southern, W. T., Jones, E. D., & Fiscus, E. D. (1989). Practitioner objections in the academic acceleration of gifted children. *Gifted Child Quarterly, 33,* 29–35.

Strom, R., & Johnson, A. (1989a). Hispanic and Anglo families of gifted children. *Journal of Instructional Psychology, 16* (4), 164–172.

Strom, R., & Johnson, A. (1989b). Rural families of gifted preschool and primary grade children. *Journal of Instructional Psychology, 16* (1), 32–38.

Su, C. W. (1982). A study on the development of basic emotions of gifted children and adolescents. *Bulletin of Educational Psychology, 15,* 67–84.

Suter, D. P., & Wolf, J. S. (1987). Issues in the identification and programming of the gifted/learning disabled child. *Journal for the Education of the Gifted 10* (3), 227–237.

Tell, D. (1987). Disparity or discrimination? *Society,* (Sept./Oct.), 4–16.

Terman, L. (1954). The discovery and encouragement of exceptional talent. *American Psychologist, 9,* 221–230.

Tyerman, M. J. (1986). Gifted children and their identification: Learning ability not intelligence. *Gifted Education International, 4* (2), 81–84.

U.S. Department of Education. (1989). No gifted wasted: Effective strategies for educating highly able, disadvantaged students in mathematics and science. Washington, DC: Government Printing Office.

VanTassel-Baska, J., Patton, J., & Prillaman, D. (1989). Disadvantaged gifted learners at risk for educational attention. *Focus on Exceptional Children, 22* (3), 1–15.

Waldron, K. A., Saphire, D. G., & Rosenblum, S. A. (1987). Learning disabilities and giftedness: Identification based on self-concept, behavior, and academic patterns. *Journal of Learning Disabilities, 20,* 422–427.

West, J. D., Hosie, T. W., & Mathews, F. N. (1989). Families of academically gifted children: Adaptability and cohesion. *School Counselor, 37* (2), 121–127.

Whitmore, J. R. (1980). *Giftedness, conflict and underachievement.* Boston: Allyn & Bacon.

Whitmore, J. R. (1986). Preventing severe underachievement and developing achievement motivation. *Journal of Children in Contemporary Society, 18* (3–4), 119–133.

Whitmore, J. R., & Maker, C. J. (1985). *Intellectual giftedness in disabled persons.* Rockville, MD: Aspen.

Wyatt, F. (1982). Responsibility for gifted learners: A plea for the encouragement of classroom teacher support. *Gifted Child Quarterly, 26* (3), 140–143.

Yewchuk, C. R. (1983). Learning disabled/gifted children: Characteristic features. *Mental Retardation and Learning Disabilities, 11* (3), 218–233.

Yewchuk, C. R. (1985). Gifted/learning disabled children: An overview. *Gifted Education International, 3* (2), 122–126.

Yewchuk, C. R., & Bibby, M. A. (1989). The handicapped gifted child: Problems of identification and programming. *Canadian Journal of Education, 14* (1), 102–108.

A Look Toward
the Future

 Trends, Issues, and Directions

Trends, Issues, and Directions

**Shobha Chachie Joseph and
Sally Ann Zwicker
Contributing Authors**

Objectives

After completing this chapter, you will be conversant with:

1. issues, trends, and directions regarding the emerging paradigm shift in the education of learners with disabilities.
2. issues, trends, and directions emerging from the current dialogue regarding performance assessment.
3. issues, trends, and directions emerging from the current dialogue regarding challenges to self-concept and identity related to inclusion.

Key Words and Phrases

authentic assessment
normalization
paradigm shift
personal futures planning

performance assessment
self-concept
social identity

ven at best, efforts to turn rhetoric into reality too often focus on students who are able to learn the most with the least investment. . . . As with any effective school reform, we must seek to alter not just the curriculum but the climate and structure of the educational experience offered these children. (Edelman, 1990, p. ix)

Introduction

There are many issues confronting general education and special education as the twenty-first century is entered. These have arisen as a result of a reconceptualization of schooling and education. The issues include planning for learners with disabilities while the field is experiencing a paradigm shift, assessment, and inclusion. In this chapter, these three areas are addressed in detail, with discussions of controversial issues related to each topic. The resolution of these issues will have a significant impact on the future of both special education and general education and the role and functions of those working with learners with disabilities. Of greater significance, their resolution will affect the lives, present and future, of learners with disabilities. The issues selected for review and discussion are (a) the paradigm shift to person-centered planning, (b) performance assessment, and (c) challenges to self-concept and identity related to inclusion.

Emerging Paradigm Shift

Kuhn (1962), in a frequently cited scholarly work, describes a **paradigm shift,** as a new way of thinking, or a change from the standard of practice. A new paradigm is emerging regarding the education of learners with disabilities. This paradigm shift, Lipsky and Gartner (1991) suggest, attempts to assure quality outcomes for all students, including those now labeled disabled. This shift recognizes that what the student produces is the heart of the desired educational outcome: learning. It is a shift from *means* to *results* (Lipsky & Gartner, 1991). This shift is reflected in the move to empowerment and person-centered planning, described in this section, and in new considerations regarding assessment and self-concept, described later in the chapter.

Traditionally, the medical or deficit model has driven the education of learners with disabilities. This model contends that the disability should be diagnosed, prescriptive programs should be designed, and efforts should be made to remediate the disability. The new paradigm emphasizes individual empowerment and self-determination.

In *No Pity,* Shapiro (1993) describes the evolution of this new paradigm in a discussion of the poster child: "No other symbol of disability is more beloved by Americans than the cute and courageous poster child—or more loathed by people with disabilities themselves" (p. 12). He reports the evolution of the poster child, who in the 1940s was projected as someone who, if you sent your money, would be cured. Because cures were few, children with disabilities were perceived as damaged goods who had to try harder to prove themselves worthy of charity and respect.

As a result of this attitude of pity towards persons with disabilities, the "inspirational disabled person" emerged, someone who was presumed deserving of pity until proved capable by overcoming a disability through an extraordinary feat. As a consequence of this attitude and central to the civil rights movement for persons with disabilities is the concept that disability, itself, is not tragic or pitiable.

In the emerging paradigm, schooling is reconceptualized (Lipsky & Gartner, 1991). The new paradigm for schooling requires respect for students and their active engagement in the learning process. The role of education is to prepare learners for a lifetime of learning. In addition, schools must "do it right from the start"; that is, failure is recognized as the failure of the school to meet the students' needs.

Objective One

To be conversant with issues, trends, and directions regarding the emerging paradigm shift in the education of learners with disabilities.

Children with disabilities can get involved in activities.

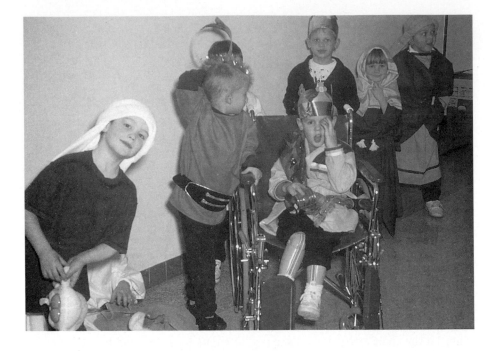

Personal Futures Planning

In recognition of the need for respect and dignity for individuals with disabilities and their families, **personal futures planning** has emerged. Personal futures planning recognizes that the individual with a disability and his or her family are capable of making choices about what services and supports they want and need (Mount, 1992). McKnight (1987) suggests that person-centered planning, the heart of personal futures plans, relies on personal relationships and promotes and nurtures connections between individuals with disabilities and their communities.

The McGill Action Planning System (MAPS) (Vandercook, York, & Forest, 1989) is a personal futures planning process in which the primary emphasis is the involvement of learners with disabilities in the school community. MAPS is structured around seven key questions, which structure planning. These questions, described in table 18.1, help learners and their families and teachers dream, brainstorm, and plan to further the inclusion of the learner with disabilities in the school community.

Rather than based on curriculum or the special education program, MAPS bases educational planning on a vision for the learner with disabilities. MAPS supports the development of the Individualized Education Plan (IEP) by providing a clearer sense of mission and a greater sense of a unified vision for the learner.

When working with adults with disabilities, personal futures planning may follow a lifestyle planning process (O'Brien & Lyle, 1987). Like MAPS, lifestyle planning engages family members and friends through the three-part sequence of (a) describing the learner's desirable future, (b) identifying activities and supports necessary to move towards that future, and (c) accepting responsibility for using available resources and engaging in problem solving when resources are not available.

The goals of lifestyle planning can be used to summarize the current paradigm shift in the education of learners with disabilities towards empowerment and self-determination. O'Brien and Lyle (1987) suggest that the quality of life for a learner with disabilities can be measured through (a) community presence,

Table 18.1 Description of Questions Related to MAPS

1. Family members and the learner, to the maximum extent possible, respond to the question, "What is the learner's history?"
2. Members of the team respond to the question, "What is the dream or vision for the learner?"
3. Members of the team respond to the question, "What is the nightmare—the least desirable outcome—for the learner?"
4. Members of the team respond to the question, "Who is the learner?" by describing the individual, then selecting the three best descriptors from the list generated.
5. The list generated through question 4 is then reviewed in response to the question, "What are the learner's strengths, gifts, and abilities?"
6. Team members respond to the question, "What are the learner's needs?" and set priorities among the needs.
7. Team members respond to the questions, "What would be the learner's ideal day at school, and what must be done to make that happen?"

Adapted from Vandercook, York, & Forest, 1989.

(b) choice, (c) competence, (d) respect, and (e) community participation. This model suggests that learners with disabilities are not pitied nor cared for; rather, they are respected and cared about.

Performance Assessment

Debates over the use of traditional and alternate forms of assessment have been the focus of recent reform movements. Performance assessment has emerged as an alternative to traditional testing.

Performance assessment is a form of direct assessment that allows students to demonstrate their knowledge in thoughtful ways and in a number of different contexts. It is an attempt to move beyond the traditional, norm-referenced, standardized testing. Cognitive psychology and behavioral assessment have made significant contributions to performance assessment (Elliot, 1994). Special educators have, for many years, used direct assessments with learners with severe disabilities and sensory impairments to make instructional decisions.

Three forms of assessment historically used in special education are behavioral assessment, mastery learning, and curriculum-based measurement. Both behavioral assessment and mastery learning have been criticized for their tendency to break behaviors into subskills for the purpose of instruction and then treat these subskills as isolated units. Some students with learning disabilities have difficulty integrating isolated activities and transferring them to other settings (Anderson-Inman, Walker & Purcell, 1984). The reliability and validity of mastery learning were perceived to have technical limitations. Curriculum-based assessment, also known as general-outcome measurement, enables teachers to evaluate and plan their instruction based on student performance. The curriculum of a particular school determines the content of the assessment, and an inadequate school curriculum could, in turn, define poor assessment practice. Since curriculum-based assessment occurs over longer periods of time, it takes longer to determine growth. The connection between assessment and instruction is less visible when compared with behavioral assessment or mastery learning. The teacher experiences fewer insights into actual student progress and less direction for the planning of subsequent lessons (Fuchs, 1994).

Performance assessment has come to be known by various terms, including authentic assessment, portfolio assessment, and direct assessment (Coutinho & Malouf, 1992; Worthen, 1993). Each of these terms refers to alternative

Objective Two

To be conversant with issues, trends, and directions emerging from the current dialogue regarding performance assessment.

assessments and allows students to be directly examined through tasks that are based in real life. Of these terms, *authentic* and *performance* are the two most frequently used. What differentiates performance assessment from traditional testing is the degree of involvement and the type of response that is required of the students. As the term suggests, performance assessment invites students to be active participants in the assessment process. They are required to demonstrate the behavior, knowledge, or skills being measured by creating a permanent product or engaging in some observable performance that can allow others to understand the processes of thinking and learning involved in the task (U.S. Congress, Office of Technology Assessment, 1992).

While student response is important in performance assessment, the key elements of **authentic assessment** are the nature of the task itself and the context within which it takes place (Coutinho & Malouf, 1992). The focus of authentic testing is to pose problems that are closely related to real life and to issues that are generalizable. Students are encouraged to demonstrate that they can apply their knowledge to tasks that are challenging, related to real-life experiences, and require analytical, thoughtful solutions. In addition, authentic tasks are intrinsically meaningful to the individual student. Authentic assessments encourage students to participate in self-assessment. Students are expected to assess and evaluate their performance and revise and improve on previous performance. A feeling of competence and the motivation to do better each time is made possible by this process. Students are encouraged to share their work with the school community and parents, and preparation for such occasions allows students to achieve greater mastery over their work. This sharing serves to build self-confidence and offers a sense of accomplishment (Darling-Hammond, Ancess, & Falk, 1995).

Authentic assessment originated in the arts. A musician, for instance, could be asked to perform a piece in order that others may watch the performance, listen to the music, and be able to offer an overall evaluation (Poteet, Choate, Stewart, 1993). Authentic tests provide for the interested and meaningful engagement of students in problem-solving tasks that allow measurement not only of factual knowledge, but of a wide range of skills and complex thinking (O'Neil, 1992).

It is possible that a performance task may not be authentic, but it is not possible that a task that is truly authentic is not performance based (Meyer, 1992). Assessment tasks vary in the extent to which they are purely performance, authentic, or both (Elliot, 1994). A low-performance task is one in which a student marks checklist items that support an argument for increased student participation in the planning of assessments. A similar high-performance task is one in which a student writes a paper supporting the same position and then presents it at a debate forum. When a teacher wants students to become fluent in the use of conversational sign language but encourages the practice of studying isolated vocabulary from a sign language textbook, the task has low authenticity. A highly authentic task requires the students to interact and converse with individuals who are deaf in natural communication situations.

Performance assessment is not new. Though first used in vocational education, it is used today to evaluate performances in academic areas such as mathematics and the language arts. Formal scoring criteria have now been developed for these disciplines.

In performance assessments, students show what they know in a variety of ways. Constructed-response items allow students to answer questions by writing a short answer, sketching a rough diagram, or solving a problem. Writing is an age-old means of testing, and essays are useful in assessing students' understanding of a concept or issue. Oral discourse is useful in evaluating oral skills or the command of a foreign language. Exhibitions allow students to show off their

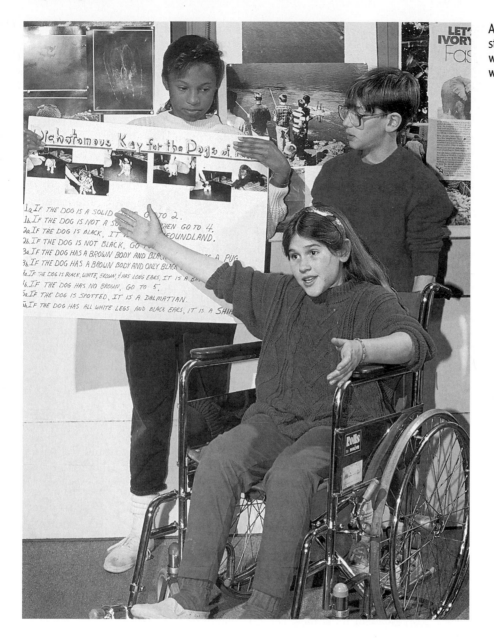

Authentic assessments encourage students to share their work with others and assess the work themselves.

creative talents as well as their understanding of various areas of knowledge. Hands-on performances of science experiments and similar projects are beneficial in evaluating a student's understanding of the concepts involved in the domain being evaluated. Portfolio assessment, collections of work done by the students that represent their best performances over a period of time, is also commonly used in classrooms (Fuchs, 1994). Other ways of demonstrating knowledge are audiotapes, interviews, collections, book and field trip reports, models, puppet shows, student self-assessments, and teacher observations (Fischer & King, 1995).

The Relationship Between Teaching and Testing

A hallmark of performance assessment is the relationship between instruction and assessment. Advocates of performance assessment contend that if assessments require the application of knowledge to problems in the real world, then curriculum will react to assessments and include outcomes that are valued for real life. This reactivity of performance assessment to instruction will, in turn, positively influence the students' learning (Archbald & Newmann, 1988; Wiggins, 1991a, 1991b).

In other words, in performance assessment, teaching is not separated from assessment. Teachers continually redesign their instruction based on student performance.

Performance assessment supports the belief that what should be tested is what should be taught (Elliot, 1994). While this may be dangerously limiting when dealing with traditional tests, this connection between instruction and assessment is the very cornerstone of performance assessment. Historically, emphasis has been on the technical aspects of curriculum and other procedures whenever standards for instruction have been considered. Little attention has been paid to the quality of instruction itself.

Newmann and Wehlage (1993) propose new standards for instruction that can lead to student involvement in work that is mentally challenging and has value beyond grades. Five standards are proposed to measure quality instruction: (a) higher order thinking, (b) depth of knowledge, (c) connectedness to the world beyond the classroom, (d) the degree to which students are involved in conversation during learning, and (e) the extent of social support to encourage student achievement. When instruction is authentic, students are actively involved in the creative performance of authentic tasks, teachers closely monitor these performances, and instruction and assessment can be viewed as one.

A key objective of performance assessment is to enable teachers to plan high-quality lessons. Teachers must carefully consider what and how they expect their students to perform if they intend to assess students based on performance. Anticipated learning outcomes must therefore always be kept at the forefront when planning. If tests influence what teachers teach, then tests that do not synthesize different areas of knowledge or measure only factual information lower the quality of education.

There are several advantages in integrating instructional decisions and assessment. Students receive ongoing and immediate feedback on performance and are motivated to become more involved in learning. Teachers continually modify their instruction to better meet the needs of individual students by noting where their students have problems and thereby getting feedback on the effectiveness of instruction (Fuchs, 1994). Performance assessments give teachers a greater voice in planning instruction and make it possible for them to become more involved in the assessment process (O'Neil, 1992).

Assessment must meet certain conditions if it is to be used to make instructional decisions. It should allow teachers to know at which level to place students so they will be challenged and yet not frustrated or bored. A teacher should be able to monitor students' learning and support them in their personal goal setting. Assessment must focus on important learning outcomes that require students to draw knowledge and experience from a number of different areas. A diagnostic function of assessment is the identification of the difficulties students face and the clear description and documentation of these so further instructional decisions can be made. Of course, assessment must be practical and feasible and allow teachers to use many instructional models or approaches (Fuchs, 1994).

Why Alternative Assessment?

Increased accountability and high-stakes testing have led to the current reform movement in educational testing (Wolf, LeMahieu, & Eresh, 1992). Communities have begun to recognize the need for educational outcomes that equip individuals with skills for the modern world. In addition, there has been a movement away from learning models that view learning as the process of accumulating discrete skills. The belief has emerged that learners should actively construct their own knowledge, resulting in learnings being approached in a more holistic and integrated manner (Shepard, 1989).

Across the country, test scores have become a way to monitor the performance of schools. Schools have fallen into patterns of maintaining minimal standards. In high-stakes testing, where test results affected decisions of placement, resource allocations, and other critical affairs, teachers tailored teaching to the test. Standardized tests were tempting tools for teachers due to ease of administration and scoring (Wiggins, 1989a). "Teaching to the test" resulted in instruction that failed to challenge higher order thinking and reasoning (Worthen, 1993). Traditional tests, such as multiple-choice, were thought to be biased against minority and non-English speaking groups (Fischer & King, 1995). Poor performances were viewed as the result of deficits in learners rather than teaching, and no efforts were made for devising greater varieties of teaching-learning strategies to accommodate individual differences (Darling-Hammond, Ancess, & Falk, 1995).

The demand for alternative forms of assessment increased with dissatisfaction over traditional testing. Standardized tests were regarded as limited measures of learning. Multiple-choice tests were seen as "one-shot tests," which provided no evidence of the consistency of a student's performance nor evidence of how the same student might perform at a different time (Wiggins, 1989a, 1991a, 1991b, 1992). Single measures of student performance were seen as incapable of predicting future performance (Fischer & King, 1995). Tests were judged to be unable to measure the real abilities of students since they did not test the whole person (Brandt, 1992). Instead, isolated outcomes that did not give insight into what the individual was truly capable of doing on various intellectual tasks were measured (Darling-Hammond, Ancess, & Falk, 1995; Wiggins, 1991a, 1991b; Worthen, 1993).

Traditional tests are indirect measures of what students really know and are largely based on decontextualized, factual information. Traditional tests do not draw on application or higher order thinking (Fischer & King, 1995). Moreover, standardized tests are not based in reality (Brandt, 1992; Fuchs, 1994; Wiggins, 1992). The statement that American students are the most tested but the least examined, made by Daniel Resnick and Lauren Resnick (1985), reflects the growing concern that traditional tests accept answers as correct or incorrect without requiring students to support their answers or demonstrate higher order thinking skills (Wiggins, 1989a, 1989b).

The manner in which tests are interpreted and used cause additional concern. Tests tend to be interpreted in ways that allow comparisons against a standard, with students who have taken the same test in the past. Comparing groups of students over time assumes that no changes have been made to curricula in the intervening period. These tests emphasize the differences in children, in turn, having a debilitating effect on their self-concept development (Wiggins, 1991).

Performance Assessment in General Education and Special Education

Several states currently use some form of performance assessment strategies. Traditional tests are now incorporating elements of performance testing to evaluate student skills, such as oral proficiency or fluency in the use of a foreign language (Pierce & O'Malley, 1992).

States vary in the inclusion of students with disabilities in standard testing programs. Students with disabilities are included in statewide performance testing in California, but some states, such as Florida and Ohio, excuse learners with disabilities. Other states, such as Virginia and Delaware, base application of standardized tests on the learner's IEP.

Performance assessment allows the student to demonstrate learning.

Performance assessment has had a positive impact on special education in several ways. Authentic tests expose students to experiences closely tied to reality, enabling learners with disabilities to rehearse a variety of real-life situations. Performance assessment allows students to demonstrate their knowledge in multiple ways (Fuchs, 1994). It also facilitates a sense of fairness and allows learners to demonstrate their knowledge in the best ways they can. Individual styles, interests, and aptitudes are accommodated in performance assessment (Darling-Hammond, Ancess, & Falk, 1995). Strengths can be identified through the variety of tasks available. For learners whose primary mode of communication may be sign language or facilitated communication, the freedom to use these modes may encourage them to become more involved in the assessment process. This increased participation builds self-confidence.

Learners with disabilities are frequently in directive environments, where they are taught fixed ways of approaching tasks and problem solving. Performance assessment broadens these limited perspectives and allows learners to see options and to be flexible.

The direct connection between assessment and instruction has many advantages for special educators. Since authentic assessments are tied to instruction and each sets the pace for the other, there is additional time for learning (Choate & Evans, 1992). The connection between assessment and instruction allows the teacher to tailor instruction according to the individual student's performance. In addition, with assessment and instruction closely related, accountability for learning outcomes becomes as much the responsibility of the teacher as it is of the students. Alternative assessments are sensitive to the needs of individual children, and as curricula increasingly adopt alternative methods of instruction and assessment, the possibility of general education and special education students working with similar curricula becomes an even-greater possibility (Elliot, 1994).

Performance assessment opens to learners with disabilities the community at large. For example, a learner with a disability tells of his experiences when asked to conduct a community-based research project. He describes his initial distress when he thought that nobody was going to help him, but then explains the overwhelming support for his project he received from various companies in the community. The variety of tasks, the breaking away from school conventions and routines, and the experience of negotiating his own learning were rewarding to the student. A sense of accomplishment and independence were other valuable outcomes of the experience (Darling-Hammond, Ancess, & Falk, 1995).

Limitations of Performance Assessment

Despite its potential positive impact and outcomes, several concerns have been expressed about performance assessment. These have led some to claim that performance assessment exists as a vision rather than a clearly defined assessment tool (Fuchs, 1994).

One controversy surrounding alternative assessments is the lack of specific, well-defined terminology. The use of different terms to describe the same tool makes it difficult for educators and the public to clearly visualize the concept of performance assessment (Worthen, 1993).

There is additional criticism over issues of measurement; performance assessment appears to be at odds with traditional psychometric measures. Merely saying that performance assessment measures students' performance over time and that the tasks are meaningful, are of interest to the individual, and challenge higher order thinking skills does not make it all directly measurable (Camp, 1993).

Evaluating the outcomes of performance assessment also poses some problems. Writing, for instance, is a form of performance assessment. Some students may have problems in writing as well as in the academic areas being assessed. It is difficult to attribute their poor performance to poor writing skills, ineffective problem solving, low creativity, or other variables. Well-defined quantitative or qualitative methods to describe and record these assessments have not yet been developed (Shavelson, Kobett, Heiss, & Fennell, 1992).

Another problem closely associated to evaluation is objectivity on the part of the examiner. Given the subjectivity of performance assessment, avoiding bias is a challenge (Siegel, 1986; Elliot, 1994).

The time involved in administering and scoring tests could make performance assessment more time consuming and expensive than traditional testing. The necessity of multiple tests to ensure validity is also time consuming. Training teachers to use performance assessment techniques effectively is expensive and the cost of materials for performance assessment can be high (Archbald, 1991; Fuchs, 1994).

Selecting and defining the domain to be tested is difficult. Since the real world is changing rapidly and constantly, it is a challenge to specifically define the anticipated outcomes of testing to closely match reality. Once the test has been administered, the extent to which it can guide further instruction is dependent upon the ability of teachers to accurately identify key elements of their students' performance, for without this they cannot plan effective instruction. Research suggests that this is not easy for teachers (Fuchs, Fuchs, Hamlett, & Stecker, 1991).

The lack of a theoretical base and absence of clear descriptions of performance assessment further add to the problem of justifying the feasibility of performance assessment (Coutinho & Malouf, 1992). It is an open-ended, all-encompassing approach with little empirical backing, and it therefore generates a degree of distrust among experts. Cizek (1991) states that the feasibility of performance assessment has still not been established on any substantial scale.

The question of generalizability of assessments has been debated. Making a task generalizable to equivalent tasks is difficult because of the number of complex issues and problems involved in any one given performance task. Finding equivalent tasks is difficult (Shavelson, Kobett, Heiss, & Fennell, 1992). Questions of reliability and validity, especially reliability, are yet to be resolved. The validity of these tests, however, cannot be counted on based on the assumption that they are drawn from criterion performances (Cizek, 1991). If students do well on a particular task, they may not necessarily do equally well on other tasks. Performance tests have low generalizability, thus lowering predictability (Madaus & Tan, 1993). Moving away from paper-pencil tests may not automatically eliminate biases based on differences among individuals from different cultural backgrounds (U.S. Congress, Office of Technology Assessment, 1992). There are therefore numerous questions that have been raised about the technical adequacies of performance assessment.

Within their classrooms, teachers may be unable to monitor even small groups of students when each of them is working at different levels on different tasks, all at the same time (Fuchs, 1994). Some doubts have been raised over whether performance tests really measure higher level cognitive abilities or whether they just measure students' motor skills (Siegel, 1986). Students could still be memorizing steps and formulae without really understanding the underlying concepts involved in the task. It cannot be assumed that a test is measuring higher order thinking just because it is a hands-on activity.

When considering performance assessment and learners with disabilities, other issues arise. The first of these has to do with the role of standards in educational reform and the concern that standards for learners with disabilities might be set lower than those for their nondisabled peers. As stated earlier, states vary in their decisions to include children with disabilities in statewide testing programs. The State of Maryland, for instance, includes learners with disabilities in statewide assessments, but does not expect them to achieve mastery over all of the tasks (Roeber, Bond, & van der Ploeg, 1993). Expectations for learners with disabilities should not be lowered and goals should not be compromised. Learners with and without disabilities may approach tasks differently or take more or less time to perform a task. Such flexibility must be allowed, even when it takes children with disabilities more than the average amount of time or effort to accomplish a task. This is particularly important when the task at hand is related to a critical learning outcome. Teachers must also be careful not to make generalizations about ability across all disabilities. A deaf or blind student may, for instance, be absolutely on par (or even better) than his or her nondisabled peers in ability to perform on some tasks. Until such time as critical skills for all learners are identified and developed, there is concern that standards may be compromised for learners with disabilities (Marzano, Pickering, & McTighe, 1993).

In regards to children with disabilities, another concern arises from the very flexibility that performance assessment affords. Since a task can be accomplished in a variety of ways, there is danger of repeatedly reinforcing only the strengths of learners with little attention to developing weaker but equally critical skills.

In the past, tests have been used to exclude students with disabilities. If performance assessment is to be fair to these learners, efforts must be made to prevent bias in testing and scoring. Objective documenting and reporting of performances is critical. Careful decisions about the educational outcomes included, the behaviors counted as progress, agreement on how to interpret test performances, and understanding the appropriate use of performance assessments with children with disabilities are critical (Elliot, 1994).

There is concern over the complexity of some of the more-involved and extended tasks in performance assessment (Choate & Evans, 1992). Some students simply may not have the ability to perform some tasks. Since performance tests require students to problem solve and are timed, the resulting pressure may be frustrating to some students (Elliot, 1994). In addition, with student self-assessment being an important aspect of authentic assessments, special efforts must be made to work with those learners with disabilities who need support to work through details of their performance.

The following example highlights how important it is that assessment for learners with disabilities is truly authentic and not just performance based. With the increased emphasis on inclusion, a child with a disability may be placed in a classroom with a teacher who has no prior experience or knowledge of the disability. A basic premise of authentic assessment is that the tasks involved are intrinsically meaningful to the individual child. This may not occur if the teacher is not familiar with the realities of the learner with the disability. For example, adequate language and writing skills are critical for a profoundly deaf child who may show little potential for developing intelligible speech skills. Spending hour after hour on speech therapy with such a child at the cost of time spent on reading and writing does not fit completely with the present and future realities of the child. Coutinho & Malouf (1993) suggest that research needs to look more carefully at the appropriate use of performance assessment with children with disabilities, including the issue of how teachers make decisions about tasks that fit the realities of their students.

Benefits of Performance Assessment

Wiggins (1991a) states that current educational reform is not an attempt to discard traditional forms of testing. One form of testing does not have to be used to the exclusion of others. The reform movement in testing draws attention to how the field of education is so completely dominated by standardized tests.

Advocates of performance assessment offer several suggestions in response to the criticism and concerns of its opponents. Validity can be ensured by having students perform several tasks within the same domain. To ensure reliability, teachers should identify target behaviors clearly. Information must then be collected over several occasions, while improving the scoring process each time. Reliability can be maintained by having multiple judges score the performance and by demanding high interrater reliability (Brandt, 1992). High interrater reliability can be achieved in written and oral performance assessments, even in large-scale assessments (Gipps, 1993). Cross-reading is an arrangement whereby teachers read samples of portfolios of students from one another's schools in order to ensure that quality evaluation standards are maintained. Audit committees comprising members of the community who represent different fields could evaluate portfolio presentations by the students (Wolf, LeMahieu, & Eresh, 1992). Before using a test, all or at least a part of it should be piloted so problems can be anticipated and revisions made. Reliability can also be maintained by having students perform several tasks that test the same domain (Brandt, 1992).

Sampling may reduce the overall costs and the time involved in performance assessment. Sampling allows for a comparison of instruments outside of the classroom. Following scientific procedures, it involves the selection of only a few tasks from the whole domain, along with a representative group of students who are to be tested. Limiting sample size and student sampling makes the testing process feasible and attractive (Elliot, 1994; Worthen, 1993).

While there is some concern about the blurring of instruction and assessment in performance assessment, Wiggins (1992) disagrees. Advocates say that despite the costs incurred by performance assessment, it is worthwhile largely because of the close relationship that performance assessment makes between teaching and testing (U.S. Congress, Office of Technology Assessment, 1992).

Since the success of performance assessment depends to a great extent on the teachers who administer it, concerns have been raised over the competencies of teachers in constructing these tests. Developing tool kits on a school-wide or district-wide level could be extremely useful, especially for teachers who are unfamiliar with performance assessment. Teams could brainstorm ideas for tasks that test different domains, and these ideas could be recorded and used as a resource for teachers.

Future of Performance Assessment

The future of performance assessment hinges on the degree of expertise that teachers can develop in its use and the extent to which they believe it can be successful. The more teachers are able to select tasks that are meaningful to the students and the more they can find ways to integrate past and present learning, the closer assessment is to authentic (Fischer & King, 1995). The skills teachers need to conduct alternative assessment are different from those needed to conduct traditional assessment. Teachers must change traditional instruction to match an authentic curriculum. Increasingly, the focus is on thinking and encouraging students to become involved in challenging, thoughtful kinds of work (Kirst, 1991). In order to support some students with disabilities in their efforts to employ higher order thinking, special educators must directly model skills and be prepared to provide feedback, prompts, and repetition as necessary (Moore, Rieth, & Ebling, 1993). Professional development for teachers to become better acquainted with performance assessment is critical (Fuchs, 1994), and teacher preparation programs will have to gear themselves to prepare teachers with the necessary competencies to be confident and informed when conducting assessments.

Teachers who are unfamiliar with learners with disabilities should seek information from agencies or contact adults with disabilities similar to those of a child in their program. This can give the teacher a better insight into the realities of the individual child. Inviting adults who have like disabilities to IEP meetings enables teachers to set more authentic goals for students. Parents of children with disabilities must be encouraged to record real-life instances in which their child could have coped more effectively if they had had a particular skill. Sharing such observations with the teacher can be beneficial in planning assessment and instruction. Learners with disabilities must be encouraged to participate in personal goal setting. Decisions should not always be made for them; they should be encouraged to negotiate personal goals.

Special educators should directly address and influence standards and ensure that they are appropriate for learners with disabilities. They must be informed and contribute to the direction of assessment as it affects children with disabilities (Fuchs, 1994).

The extent of technology's role in performance assessment is yet to be determined. It, however, suggests some promise in eliminating some of the labor-intensive, time-consuming tasks that are currently required of performance assessment. Certain network systems have already been found to be useful for individualizing instruction. Videos and other equipment could become central to alternative assessment practices in the future (Worthen, 1993).

The promise of performance assessment is great. However, performance assessment should not be viewed as the cure-all to the concerns of traditional testing. While there are educational outcomes that are not readily assessed with traditional tests, these tests should not be completely and hastily abandoned (Marzano, Pickering, & McTighe, 1993).

Self-Concept and Identity

Increasingly, the educational community is attempting to include all students in general education. With today's movement towards greater inclusion of students with disabilities in mainstream America, efforts are being made to provide all students with equal access to education.

Defining the term *inclusion* is difficult because it is a dynamic concept. Simply put, inclusion is society's way of ensuring equal rights for all individuals. In the context of this chapter, inclusion means giving people with disabilities the opportunities and choices to be who they want to be and do what they want to do. In terms of education, inclusion refers to the increasing involvement of learners with disabilities in general education programs (Fullwood, 1990).

Zigler and Muenchow (1979) point out that fundamental to the integration of learners with disabilities is normalization. **Normalization** relates to society's attempts to make the circumstances of everyday life for people with disabilities as ordinary as possible, by providing them with the skills and social image needed to fit into the mainstream (Fullwood, 1990). Zigler and Muenchow (1979) argue, however, that this does not allow the child with disabilities to express needs that might differ from those of the majority. The rights of some individuals to the most effective services may be taken away because of the attempt to provide normalization by treating everyone the same way.

The concept of normalcy and the persistent negative connotation, or stigma, related to disability contribute to the assumption that learners with disabilities can and should look like their "normal" peers based on the fact that these peers do not have a visible disability themselves. It is inferred that rather than acting like themselves, learners with disabilities should emulate "normal" behavior. This issue of what is "normal" for learners with disabilities is perceived by some as irrelevant or troublesome.

Separate programs for learners with disabilities have been criticized in the belief that interacting only with learners with like disabilities decreases the learning of appropriate behaviors. Not every educator, peer, or member of the school community, however, is willing to accept inclusion. Individuals in general education may feel threatened due to their unfamiliarity with learners' disabilities. The staff may be afraid and uncomfortable having children in their classrooms over whom they have no decision-making power. Teachers may feel frustrated, forced to comply with the laws providing for inclusion (Fullwood, 1990). Even when teachers see the value of inclusion, the time it takes to become knowledgeable and the efforts required to meet the needs of all students in the classroom could result in a delay in providing support and have a negative impact on the development of a learner with disabilities.

Schools have great influence on the growth and achievement of children. Much of what happens in schools is evaluative, and once the child has performed, his or her work is open to the judgment of teacher or peers. The ways in which learners with disabilities come to understand and see themselves is based largely on the feedback they receive from the environment (Gurney, 1988). Experiences of a learner with disabilities in an inclusive setting contribute to building or tearing down his or her self-esteem. The development of the self-concept of a learner with disabilities is greatly influenced by the dynamics of an inclusive setting.

Objective Three

To be conversant with issues, trends, and directions emerging from the current dialogue regarding challenges to self-concept and identity related to inclusion.

The term *identity* is reflective of a person's sense of self.

What Is Self-Concept?

Self-concept, according to Gurney (1988), is the image that each person has of self. Burns (1982) describes self-concept in terms of its descriptive element as well as its evaluative element. Terms such as *self-image* or *self-picture* are frequently used to refer to the descriptive element of self-concept. The evaluative aspect tends to imply certain emotional evaluations that individuals make of themselves. These evaluations may be called self-esteem, self-worth, or self-acceptance.

The term *identity* is reflective of the individual's sense of self and is the psychological term for what one thinks or feels about oneself (Bosma, Graafsma, Grotevant, & de Levita, 1994). Social behavior is determined by identity. For this discussion, it is useful to note the two kinds of identity that individuals may develop: personal identity and social identity. **Social identity** may force an individual to modify his or her personal identity in an effort to fit the expectations of society (Goffman, 1963). Therefore, an individual's identity is not a stagnant entity, but a dynamic process (Bonner, 1961).

Schowe (1979) defines identity as the process whereby individuals seek answers to these questions: Who am I? and Where do I belong? This is an attempt to create an internal picture of self in order to understand who one is, make decisions on how one wishes to present oneself to society, and how society in turn, sees one. By the age of four, children are able to recognize their personal differences and understand that these differences are viewed in certain ways by society (Branthwaite & Rogers, 1985).

The Importance of Self-Concept

Burns (1982) explains that self-concept determines the ways in which individuals interpret situations and the meaning that they give to experiences. Developing and maintaining a positive self-concept is important in light of the roles that self-concept plays in the lives of individuals. These roles include the following:

1. *Inner consistency.* Self-concept allows for individuals to maintain a sense of inner consistency. Every person operates in a particular way. Experiences that are in opposition to the way the person thinks or feels cause dissonance. Self-concept is, therefore, something that influences one to act in ways that are consistent with the way one sees oneself, allowing one to maintain consistently within oneself. For example, relatively calm children identified as emotionally/behaviorally disordered may become more agitated in a setting where people anticipate that they will be disruptive. The learners try to match their behavior with what they come to believe of themselves.

2. *Interpreting experiences.* Self-concepts are powerful influences in determining an individual's behavior because they allow for the interpretation of experiences. How a learner with a disability responds to the offer of an extra five points on every written test from a teacher in an inclusive setting depends on the way in which the learner interprets the offer.

3. *Setting expectations.* A poorly developed self-concept can result in low, average, or high self-expectations. This in turn can determine decisions that learners make and their future. Self-concept is important both in determining present behaviors and setting the direction for future development (Gurney, 1988).

The Development of Self-Concept

Self-concept is learned (Gurney, 1988). The raw materials for building self-concept are the messages received from parents, peers, teachers, and others in the environment. The ways in which these messages are interpreted determine how one interprets and defines oneself, including the degree of competence and worthiness that one attributes to oneself. Humans are social animals and look to society for approval. If an individual is to get approval, then he or she must abide by society's norms and standards (Burns, 1982).

Society is a powerful influence in the development of an individual's identity. In early studies of racial identity, Clark (1955) explained how an individual does not know his or her racial group until he or she acquires knowledge of how society perceives his or her race. A story is told by Bloom (1971) of a man who could not determine his identity until his society made a decision on the social category to which he belonged. He was a South African black man who grew up in a white neighborhood, always had white friends, and did not consider himself black. When it came time for him to make professional and life choices, a reevaluation of his classification as white or "colored" arose. He could not make any decision about job or residence until society decided his identity in a court of law. This incident demonstrates the power that society exercises in influencing the ways in which persons perceive themselves.

Phinney and Rotheram (1987) write about the impact minority/majority group membership has on the development of children. While minority-culture children may be more aware of their differences, majority-culture children may not have the same degree of awareness of their differences from other groups. They may tend to base their understandings of differences on stereotypes that they learn from the media and adults. The setting of the norms in society falls into the hands of the majority. In other words, the differences of minority members of a society may not be totally understood, respected, and accepted by majority members, and minority members often attempt to lessen the visibility of their differences in order to resemble "normal" people.

Society imposes its perceptions of disabilities on the individual. It then tries to help the individual find ways to overcome his or her undesirable characteristics (disabilities). Such continuing negative feedback becomes a part of the internalized picture the learner with disabilities has of himself or herself and contributes to his or her personal identity (Hallahan & Kauffman, 1994).

Individuals with disabilities have shared personal accounts of how society sees them. Athas (1956) writes of how she has no regrets about being blind. She lists the many things that she can do and doesn't dwell on her limitations. She tells how little society understands blind people and how it interprets a life of blindness as a life of despair. This lack of understanding by the larger group causes people who are blind to seek each other out. Leisman (1936) tells of the pity that he always receives from society because of his deafness, although he is proud to be deaf. Rousso (1984) describes how her mother, who had not accepted her disability, made her practice trying to walk normally for many years. Rousso later saw those early years as being an assault on her identity since she had accepted her walk as being a part of her personal identity. Grandin (1985) writes that her autistic behaviors, judged "perseverative" and "maladaptive," enhanced her ability to complete a doctorate and pursue a career. These stories emphasize how society and significant others in the environment can influence the development of personal identity.

Annual **Edition**

Article 2

Research on Self-Esteem and Inclusion

There is little empirical evidence of the effects of inclusion on learners with disabilities, and there are few researchers conducting studies in the area today (Stainback, Stainback, East, & Sapon-Shevin, 1994). Most of the literature available concerns previous efforts at mainstreaming and integration.

A series of studies suggest that the learner's self-esteem may be enhanced by segregation with like-peers (Gurney, 1988). Higgins (1962) found significant differences in the self-esteem of adolescent learners with mental retardation when placed in special schools. Lawrence and Winschel (1973) and Schurr, Towne, and Joiner (1972) reported increased self-esteem with respect to academic performances when learners with special needs were placed in segregated classes. These same studies showed lower self-esteem scores when the learners were reintegrated after a year in special classes.

A positive association has been consistently reported between academic achievement and self-esteem of learners with mild disabilities (Macmillan, Keogh, & Jones, 1986). Battle (1979) reports that learners with learning disabilities experience less frustration and anxiety and greater positive self-esteem when they are in special education classes.

Learners with physical disabilities did not show significant differences in self-esteem when compared to their nonidentified peers (Richardson, Hastorf, & Dornbusch, 1964). Ten- to twelve-year-old learners with emotional and behavioral disorders showed significantly lower levels of self-esteem in integrated settings (Gurney, 1988). Learners with mental retardation who spent half their time in inclusive settings reported lower self-esteem than those in separate settings. Similar findings were reported in studies conducted by Smith, Dorecki, and Davis (1977). Although early efforts at mainstreaming may be quite different from current efforts at inclusion, it remains essential to look at the potential effects of inclusion on the self-concept of learners with disabilities.

Society and significant others can influence the development of personal identity.

   Two theories, social comparison and reference group, offer a rationale for these findings. Individuals tend to compare themselves with others and measure their own worth in relation to the way in which they perceive others. Social comparison theory, in the case of learners with disabilities, refers to the way in which they compare themselves with other learners like themselves, when such a group is available. Reference theory, on the other hand, refers to learners with disabilities comparing themselves with a group different from their own. In the part-time inclusion setting, social comparison is facilitated because of contact with learners with disabilities; the reference group remains learners without identified disabilities. In completely inclusive settings, learners with disabilities use learners without identified disabilities as a reference group, contributing to lower self-esteem.

Self-Concept and Views on Inclusion

Learners with disabilities may enter school with negative self-concepts. Parents may be faced with feelings of personal inadequacy and disappointment, and depending on the parent and the quality of the relationship between the parents, the child may pick up various signals and messages that contribute to his or her developing self-concept (Gurney, 1988). Learners with disabilities do not grow up with other children like themselves in the home or community, and they have little opportunity to see and understand other children like themselves (Ferguson & Asch, 1989). When they arrive at school, they may become increasingly aware of their differences and struggle with social acceptance and academic performance. Many of these experiences negatively influence the self-esteem of these students and cause them to frequently feel that it is beyond them to succeed. Adults with disabilities recall few positive experiences of inclusion (Ferguson & Asch, 1989). Instead, they relate incidents of teasing, exclusion, and rejection. The effects of such experiences on the development of the self-concept of these individuals may be profound.

Views of the Disabled Community on Integration

Many deaf people do not have a positive outlook on inclusion and prefer segregated settings (Lane, 1987). The deaf and blind have resisted the movement towards inclusion for a number of reasons. First, both groups of individuals argue that separate education is necessary for the preservation of cultural values. The deaf and blind, who see their disability as a cultural aspect of their identity, believe that separate schools are conducive environments for passing on cultural information and other invaluable insights.

According to Phinney and Rotheram (1987), there are three criteria that define one's ethnic self-identification. The first criterion requires that a person be described by one of the following attributes: ancestry, national or religious background, language, skin color, or group label. Persons with disabilities tend to be labeled according to their specific disability. Some individuals may have their own language or mode of communication, such as American Sign Language, braille, or facilitated communication. Therefore, in this sense, persons with disabilities meet the first criterion of ethnic identification. The second criterion requires that a person distinguish himself or herself from another ethnic group. Persons with disabilities may group together on the basis of their disability. For instance, there are associations for the blind, community service centers for the deaf and hard-of-hearing, support groups for the mentally ill, and recreational leagues for individuals who use wheelchairs. The third criterion requires that one's culture remain a constant factor in all contexts. Obviously, persons with disabilities are disabled in all contexts other than their own. Therefore, one's disability may be seen as a part of cultural self-identification, such as membership in the deaf or blind communities.

Phinney and Rotheram (1987) state that children whose ethnicity is in the minority know more about the cultural aspects of the majority than they know about their own culture. The school curriculum is primarily responsible for this knowledge. This may suggest that the current school curricula do not include, for instance, the history and accomplishments of persons who are deaf or hard-of-hearing, information that may be invaluable to learners who are deaf and hard-of-hearing. Ramirez and Castaneda (1974) demonstrated that the self-esteem of Mexican American children was higher if they were taught about their culture in schools. Spekman, Goldberg, and Herman, 1992 suggest that individuals with learning disabilities may consider themselves part of a learning-disabled culture and view learning disabilities as part of their identity.

The time spent with each other is invaluable to individuals with disabilities. A student who is blind related the positive experiences of spending time with other blind individuals at camp. She told that campers were able to share stories of how parents, teachers, and peers treated them because of their blindness. They talked about common problems and struggles, developed friendships with individuals who were nonjudgmental about their blindness, and built relationships to collaborate in combating discrimination (Ferguson & Asch, 1989). The parents of a deaf girl shared their experiences of how their daughter, Lynn, developed her personal identity as a deaf person. They explained how Lynn began to see the world differently, from a perspective they could not share. Deaf friends could understand Lynn and were able to guide her towards a meaningful life as a deaf person (Spradley & Spradley, 1978).

Enhancing the Self-Concept of Students with Disabilities

Multicultural education models have clarified that it is not appropriate to ignore the differences that exist among individuals. In fact, individual differences play a significant role in the development of an individual's identity and role as a member of a group (Stainback, Stainback, East, & Sapon-Shevin, 1994). Similarly, in the attempt to create homogeneous environments for all children, unique, individual needs must not be compromised. Disability rights activists, therefore, share the same concerns as the civil rights activists of the 1960s. The most important things, they believe, are getting a good education, having positive feelings about oneself, and having options available. Just as simply attending a school with white students would do nothing in and of itself for the self-concept of African American students, attending a school with learners without disabilities but with no meaningful interactions would not contribute to making a wholesome person with disabilities (Ferguson & Asch, 1989).

Ferguson and Asch (1989) point out that there is evidence that, as children, adults with disabilities had exposure to and involvement with individuals with similar disabilities. Some educational reformers are becoming increasingly concerned over the lack of opportunities for learners with disabilities in inclusive settings to form friendships with other students and adults with disabilities (Ferguson & Asch, 1989). It appears that it is critical to involve individuals with disabilities in the school community if all learners are to develop and maintain positive self-concepts. This may increase the self-esteem of learners with disabilities, stemming from their association with others who share similar characteristics and interests (Stainback, Stainback, East, & Sapon-Shevin, 1994). Inclusive school settings should allow learners with disabilities to maintain their membership with the community of individuals with disabilities. Schools should be sensitive to processes that are involved in the development of the self-concept. The value of learners with disabilities engaging with others who share the same culture, abilities, struggles, and experiences must be recognized (Edgar & Siegel, in press).

The benefit of having adult individuals with disabilities as role models for children with disabilities is further elucidated by two theories: reflection, or mirror, theory, and imitation, or model, theory. Mirror theory maintains that the self is the product of how one believes one is seen by significant others (Burns, 1982). In that learners with disabilities may not have positive experiences in inclusive settings (Ferguson & Asch, 1989; Foster, 1989), the behaviors of those around them towards them may be reflected in feelings of low self-worth. Adults with disabilities who have a strong identity are in a position to understand and value these learners, especially since they share the same realities. These adults can be positive role models and promote the personal identities of the children. Positive feedback that communicates to the learners that he or she is valued and doing well can enhance self-esteem. The evaluations of these significant others is closely tied to a learner's sense of self-worth.

Making News

Jan Grieser
Coon Rapids, Minn.

"I am Matt Grieser's mom. Matt is a delightful 10-year-old, who loves to play Nintendo, baseball, kickball and basketball. He enjoys working on computers, teasing his older sisters, and pushing his mother's buttons. He also has Down syndrome, and uses special education services from the Anoka-Hennepin School District #11, where he is fully included in his neighborhood 4th grade classroom at Hoover Elementary School in Coon Rapids, Minn.

"I have dreams for Matt—that he will be happy, that he is an active participant in his community, that he some day will have a home of his own, and a job that he enjoys. These dreams are not really very different than the dreams I have for Matt's sisters, except that he will need help and support to fulfill them. Special education is helping me reach my dreams for Matt.

"Matt walks to school with his neighborhood buds, (no special education transportation costs here) and he enjoys his relationships with his classmates. He has a wonderful circle of friends who celebrate an all-star day with him, or they will let him know when they don't like his behavior. He knows his school community, and his community members know him. He is happy!

"Matt spends approximately 85 percent of his school day in the regular classroom. All of the modifications of the curriculum are based from Matt's learning level. He receives time every day in the resource room with a special ed. teacher working on reading and math skills. He is sounding out words and taking regular ed. math tests using a calculator. He is supported by children and a para-professional who does not hover over him, but is there when he needs her. Articulation (speech) services are provided in and out of the classroom, and OT and adaptive phys. ed. services are provided in the regular classroom.

"Matt is learning and playing along side his community members. He is also a wonderful teacher for the other kids. They are learning how to interact with someone with differences. They are learning how to modify and adapt in order to welcome someone who desperately wants to be a part of real life experiences. Matt's classmates are the neighbors, co-workers, bosses, parents and legislators of the future.

"His generation will not grow up, as mine did, being afraid of people with differences. Good, educated decisions will be made by people who understand that Matt, and others with special needs are an important part of the whole community." •

From "I am Matt Grieser's mom" by Jan Grieser, in *The ARC, 20 Years of IDEA in America.* Reprinted by permission of the publisher and the author.

Model theory, a social learning theory proposed originally by Bandura, Ross, and Ross (1963), asserts that children develop a concept of self from imitating and then internalizing the behaviors of those individuals who are important to them (Gurney, 1988). Adults with disabilities who are leaders, advocates, successes, or symbols of courage and hope can affirm a sense of self-worth for the students and a pride in the positive accomplishment of individuals with disabilities.

Suggestions for Fostering Positive Self-Concept

Self-concept is learned. Schools must make every effort to promote the positive development of the self of learners with disabilities. Self-concept has a pervasive influence in every aspect of learning and living in the individual's life (Gurney, 1988). A sense of autonomy is vital if learners with disabilities are to be successful. This autonomy cannot be developed without a strong sense of identity and self-acceptance (Meadow-Orlans, 1987).

It is a responsibility of schools to provide opportunities to learners with disabilities to spend time with other individuals with disabilities. Following are several suggestions to facilitate the development of positive self-identification in learners with disabilities.

1. Establish support groups that enable learners with disabilities to share information and support. This shared information could include strategies to confront and overcome prejudice, discrimination, frustrations, and other barriers. Support groups can also be useful in enhancing a positive self-concept. The purpose, focus, and duration of the groups must be determined by the students, and school personnel must be supportive, sensitive, and respectful of choices made by these learners (Stainback, Stainback, East, & Sapon-Shevin, 1994).

2. By facilitating mentoring relationships, the school can encourage positive self-concepts among learners with disabilities. Mentoring is a relationship between two unrelated individuals of different ages. The purposes of mentoring vary: it may facilitate an individual's awareness of his or her culture, may improve academic achievement, may teach about the world or work, or may increase the individual's resourcefulness. Mentoring activities must be meaningful and related to everyday life.

   Generally, the individuals in a mentoring relationship do not have similar characteristics. However, for the purpose of facilitating positive self-concept development among learners with disabilities, the school should consider, as mentors, adults with disabilities who have strong self-concepts and high self-esteem.

3. An educator with a disability can serve as a role model who not only enhances the self-concept of learners with disabilities, but communicates to individuals with and without disabilities that learners with disabilities are capable and not restricted by society's low expectations.

4. In order to provide opportunities for learners with disabilities in inclusive settings to meet with other learners with disabilities, school personnel can arrange field trips to various schools, such as those for the blind or deaf, where learners with disabilities are educated with persons with like disabilities. Arrangements can be made for students from these facilities to visit inclusive settings so that the general school community can see that they are competent students who have made a choice to be in school settings where all students share a similar culture.

   Kauffman (1994) argues that people who favor inclusive education tend to place their values on where the education takes place in the belief that society's acceptance and perception of learners with disabilities is dependent on this setting. There is, however, no one, perfect educational setting. Learners with disabilities must be judged on the basis of their competence rather than the setting in which they are educated. Differences in students and differences in the ways in which they learn must both be respected. This implies that educators in inclusive settings should provide both learners with disabilities and learners without disabilities the opportunity to interact with peers with and without disabilities in order to promote respect, understanding, and acceptance. This is also true for educators of learners with disabilities who are not in inclusive settings.

   In addition to visiting schools, students should have opportunities to visit places where adults with disabilities work and recreate. These may be Deaf clubs, associations for persons with disabilities, or supported employment settings.

5. Parents have a responsibility to enhance their child's self-esteem. Without a strong personal awareness of their child's disability and involvement in their child's education, opportunities for the enhancement of positive self-concept may be limited.

6. A final suggestion for fostering positive self-concept of learners with disabilities and to promote understanding and positive attitudes among nondisabled learners towards learners with disabilities is to adapt school curricula and lesson plans to create greater awareness of persons with disabilities. The curricula of inclusive schools have not actively made attempts to include information on disabilities. The significant contributions of persons with disabilities to society and the place of persons with disabilities from historical, societal, political, and cultural perspectives have not been considered. Books, movies and other resource materials that tell stories of various disabilities and the lives of individuals with disabilities are frequently unavailable. Making such information and materials available is critical for learners with disabilities so they can understand that people with similar characteristics lived before them, that these people made significant contributions to society, and that they played important roles in history. This also enables these learners to see, through the lives and experiences of these historical individuals, how important the attitudes and values of society towards disabilities are in their daily lives. Learning about the lives of other individuals with disabilities can be a source of inspiration to these learners in inclusive settings, who may not have the opportunity to interact with others like themselves. It is also encouraging to see that they do have the ability to overcome barriers and to accomplish anything they want. These resources are invaluable in the ways in which they can educate nondisabled learners to recognize the strengths of learners with disabilities.

The following are some examples of how issues relating to disabilities can be included in the curricula.

1. In a world history class, teachers can talk about the monarchy as part of a unit on government or talk about the contributions of Queen Victoria. Teachers can mention at this point that Queen Victoria had a close friend who was deaf and with whom she used British sign language to communicate. Teachers can also mention that Queen Victoria's daughter-in-law was deaf.

2. Teachers can compare and contrast the ways in which individuals with disabilities were perceived and treated in the past with the present by highlighting various events from history. The story of how people reacted to the first-born, deaf son of a count in France, a person with disabilities who had to fight for his every right, and the account of how his family and others in France got rid of him by putting him in the front line of battle could educate these students. Teachers can contrast this with the present-day issues of pride and rights of individuals with disabilities. For example, the power of deaf and hard-of-hearing individuals at Gallaudet University was apparent in their successful demand for a deaf president.

3. A well-stocked library of materials on individuals with disabilities is essential to give learners with disabilities a sense of who they are. Such materials are useful for nondisabled peers as well.

The placement of learners with disabilities in educational settings with peers without identified disabilities does not necessarily enhance their self-concept. For learners with disabilities to succeed in a world where the norms of the majority prevail, they must first have a strong sense of self and their identity, as an individual with a disability. They should be given access to role models, individuals with disabilities who can challenge them and instill confidence that barriers can be overcome. This contributes to the positive development of the individual's self-concept and affects their outlook on life.

Summary

In this final chapter, three issues that have a significant impact on the education of learners with disability and the education of all learners were discussed. The issues presented were (a) the emerging paradigm in special education, (b) performance assessment, and (c) the relationship of self-concept development and inclusion.

The emerging paradigm of person-centered programming is having a significant impact on society's perceptions of disability and education. With movement away from the medical model, self-determination and empowerment become essential for learners with disabilities. Through personal futures planning, the learner and his or her family are given a voice to express their dreams, fears, and needs.

Through performance assessment, students are allowed to demonstrate their knowledge in thoughtful ways and in different contexts. While student response is important in these authentic alternatives to traditional testing, the key element of performance assessment is the nature of the text and the context in which it takes place. In performance assessment, instruction and assessment are clearly integrated.

As we move towards an inclusive society that celebrates diversity, the self-concept and self-identity of learners with disabilities have emerged as issues. The need for individuals with disabilities to have role models with similar disabilities and the need to recognize one's strengths as an individual with a disability have emerged. Several suggestions for enhancing the self-concept of learners with disabilities were provided.

Building Your Professional Vocabulary

Match each word or phrase to its meaning.

_____ performance assessment

_____ authentic assessment

_____ social identity

_____ normalization

_____ self-concept

_____ paradigm

a. evaluation of a student by posing problems related to real life
b. attempts to make the circumstances of everyday life for people with disabilities as ordinary as possible

c. direct assessment of the products or accomplishments
d. standard or perspective on practice
e. image of self
f. modification of personal identity to meet the expectations of the larger society

Comprehension Check

1. In working with learners with severe disabilities and sensory impairments, special educators have for many years
   a. used norm-referenced measures for educational decisions.
   b. used standardized measures for educational decisions.
   c. used student performance for educational decisions.
2. Behavioral assessment has been criticized for its
   a. adherence to norm-referenced measures.
   b. tendency to break behaviors into subskills.
   c. holistic appraisal of skills.
3. The key element of authentic assessment is
   a. the task itself.
   b. the student's performance.
   c. the student's competence.
4. Through performance assessment, students are able to show
   a. how they compare to their peers.
   b. what they know in a variety of ways.
   c. critical thinking skills.
5. Self-concept is
   a. related to inborn personality traits.
   b. learned.
   c. dependent on the disability.
6. For the learner with disabilities, self-concept determines
   a. school achievement.
   b. the meaning attributed to an event.
   c. competence.
7. Ethnic self-identification
   a. is related to racial characteristics.
   b. is relevant for learners with disabilities.
   c. is relevant for learners with disabilities if their parents also have disabilities.
8. The traditional, medical model of special education
   a. assumes that learners with disabilities can plan their own future.
   b. assumes a deficit that must be remediated.
   c. assumes a systems perspective.
9. MAPS demonstrates
   a. personal futures planning as applied to educational environments.
   b. a model for remediating special needs.
   c. a model for vocational planning.
10. An emergent paradigm for serving learners with disabilities is
    a. "no pity."
    b. compensation, not remediation.
    c. individualized educational planning.

References

Anderson-Inman, L., Walker, H. M., & Purcell, J. (1984). Promoting the transfer of skills across settings: Transenvironmental programming for handicapped students in the mainstream. In W. L. Heward, T. E. Heron, D. S. Hill, & J. Trap-Porter (Eds.), *Focus on behavior analysis in education.* Columbus, OH: Merrill.

Archbald, D. A. (1991). Authentic assessment: Principles, practices, and issues. *School Psychology Quarterly, 6*(4), 279–293.

Archbald, D. A., & Newmann, F. M. (1988). *Beyond standardized testing: Assessing authentic academic achievement in the secondary school.* Reston, VA: National Association of Secondary School Principals.

Athas, D. (1956). *The fourth world.* New York: G. P. Putnam's Sons.

Bandura, A., Ross, D., & Ross, A. (1963). Imitation of film-mediated aggressive models. *Journal of Abnormal and Social Psychology, 66,* 3–11.

Battle, J. (1979). Self-esteem of students in regular and special classes. *Psychological Reports, 44*(1), 212–214.

Bloom, L. (1971). *The social psychology of race relations.* London: Allen and Unwin.

Bonner, H. (1961). *Psychology of personality.* New York, NY: Ronald Press.

Bosma, H. A., Graafsma, T. L., Grotevant, H. D., & de Levita, D. J. (1994). *Identity and development: An interdisciplinary approach.* Thousand Oaks, CA: Sage Publications.

Brandt, R. (1992). Overview. *Educational Leadership, 49*(8), 7.

Branthwaite, A., & Rogers, D. (1985). Development of social identity and self-concept. In A. Branthwaite & D. Rogers (Eds.), *Children growing up* (pp. 34–42). Milton Keynes, PA: Open University Press.

Burns, R. (1982). *Self-concept development and education.* Great Britain: Henry Ling.

Camp, R. (1993). The place of portfolios in our changing views of writing assessment. In R. E. Bennett & W. C. Ward (Eds.), *Construction versus choice in cognitive measurement* (pp. 183–212). Hillsdale, NJ: Lawrence Erlbaum.

Choate, J. S., & Evans, S. S. (1992). Authentic assessment of special learners: Problem or promise? *Preventing School Failure, 37*(1), 6–9.

Cizek, G. J. (1991). Innovation or enervation: Performance assessment in perspective. *Phi Delta Kappan, 72,* 695–699.

Clark, K. B. (1955). *Prejudice and your child.* Boston, MA: Beacon Press.

Coutinho, M., & Malouf, D. (1992). *Performance assessment and children with disabilities: Issues and possibilities.* Washington, DC: Division of Innovation and Development, U.S. Department of Education.

Darling-Hammond, L., Ancess, J., & Falk, B. (1995). *Authentic assessment in action: Studies of schools and students at work.* New York: Teachers College Press.

Edelman, M. W. (1990). Preface. In J. Knitzer, Z. Steinberg, & B. Fleisch (Eds.), *At the schoolhouse door* (p. ix). New York: Bank Street College of Education.

Edgar, E. & Siegel, S. (in press). Post-secondary scenarios for troubled and troubling youth. In J. M. Kaufmann, J. W. Lloyd, T. A. Astuto, & D. P. Hallahan (Eds.), *Issues in the educational placement of pupils with emotional or behavioral problems.* Hillsdale, NJ: Erlbaum.

Elliot, S. N. (1994). Creating meaningful performance assessments: Fundamental concepts. *ERIC Document Reproduction Service No.* ED375566.

Ferguson, P. & Asch, A. (1989). Lessons from life: Personal and parental perspectives on school, childhood, and disability. In D. Bilken, D. Ferguson, & A. Ford (Eds.), *Schooling and Disability* (pp. 108–140). Chicago, IL: The University of Chicago Press.

Fischer, C. F., & King, R. M. (1995). *Authentic assessment: A guide to implementation.* Thousand Oaks, CA: Corwin Press.

Foster, S. (1989). Social alienation and peer identification: A study of the social construction of deafness. *Human Organization, 48*(3), 226–235.

Fuchs, L. S. (1994). *Connecting performance assessment to instruction.* ERIC Document Reproduction Service No. ED 375565.

Fuchs, L. S., Fuchs, D., Hamlett, C. L., & Stecker, P. M. (1991). Effects of curriculum-based measurement and consultation on teacher planning and student achievement in mathematics operations. *American Educational Research Journal, 28*(3), 617–641.

Fullwood, D. (1990). *Chances and choices: Making integration work.* Baltimore, MD: Paul H. Brookes Publishing Co.

Goffman, E. (1963). *Stigma: Notes on the management of spoiled identity.* Englewood Cliffs, NJ: Prentice Hall.

Grandin, T. (1985). *Emergence.* New York: Basic.

Gurney, P. W. (1988). *Self-esteem in children with special educational needs.* Great Britain: Billing & Sons.

Hallahan, D. P., & Kauffman, J. M. (1994). Toward a culture of disability in the aftermath of Deno and Dunn. *The Journal of Special Education, 27*(4), 496–508.

Higgins, L. C. (1962). *Self-concept of mentally retarded adolescents.* Unpublished B. Litt. dissertation, University of New England.

Kauffman, J. M. (1992). Special education into the 21st century: An educational perspective. Challenge for change: Reform in the 1990's. *Proceedings of the 16th National Conference of the Australian Association of Special Education.* Perth, Western Australia: Author.

Kirst, M. (1991). Interview on assessment issues with Lorrie Shepard. *Educational Researcher, 20*(2), 21–23.

Kuhn, T. K. (Ed.). (1962). *The structure of scientific revolutions.* NY: Basic Books.

Lane, H. (1987). Listen to the needs of deaf children. *New York Times,* p. 35.

Lawrence, E. A., & Winschel, J. F. (1973). Self-concept and the retarded: Research and issues. *Exceptional Children, 39*(4), 310–319.

Leigh, I. W., & Stinson, M. S. (1991). Social environments, self-perceptions, and identity of hearing-impaired adolescents. *The Volta Review, 93*(5), 7–20.

Leisman, A. (1936). I am glad I am deaf. *American Mercury.*

Lipsky, D. K., & Gartner, A. (1991). Achieving full inclusion: Placing the student at the center of educational reform. In W. Stainback & S. Stainback (Eds.), *Controversial issues confronting special education: Divergent perspectives* (pp. 3–12). Boston: Allyn & Bacon.

Macmillan, D. L., Keogh, B. K., & Jones, R. L. (1986). Special educational research on mildly handicapped learners. In M. C. Wittrock (Ed.), *Handbook of research on teaching* (3rd ed.), (pp. 686–724). New York: Macmillan.

Madaus, G., & Tan, A. G. (1993). The growth of assessment. In G. Cawelti (Ed.), *Challenges and achievements of American education, 1993 Yearbook* (pp. 53–79). Alexandria, VA: Association for Supervision and Curriculum Development.

Marzano, R. J., Pickering, D., & McTighe, J. (1993). *Assessing student outcomes: Performance assessment using the dimensions of learning model.* Alexandria, VA: Association for Supervision and Curriculum Development.

McKnight, J. L. (1987). Regenerating community. *Social Policy, 18,* 54–58.

Meadow-Orlans, K. P. (1987). Autonomy for the deaf adolescent: Facilitative environments. In G. B. Anderson & D. Watson (Eds.), *Innovations in the habilitation and rehabilitation of deaf adolescents.* Little Rock, AR: University of Arkansas Rehabilitation Research and Training Center on Deafness and Hearing Impairment.

Meyer, C. A. (1992). What's the difference between authentic and performance assessment? In M. E. Diez, & C. J. Moon (Eds.), *What do we want students to know? . . . and other important questions* (pp. 38–41). Washington, DC: Association for Curriculum, Supervision, and Development.

Moore, P. R., Rieth, H., & Ebling, M. (1993). Considerations in teaching higher order thinking skills to students with mild disabilities. *Focus on Exceptional Children, 23*(7), 1–12.

Mount, B. (1992). *Personal futures planning: Promises and precautions.* New York: Graphic Press.

National Center for Research. (1994, Winter). Evaluation, Standards, and Student Testing. *CRESST Reporter, 8.*

Newmann, F. M., & Wehlage, G. G. (1993). Five standards of authentic instruction. *Educational Leadership, 50*(7), 8–12.

Newsletter of National Center for Research on Evaluation, Standards, and Student Testing. (1993, Winter). *CRESST Reporter, 8.*

O'Brien, J., & Lyle, C. (1987). *Framework for accomplishments.* Decatur, GA: Responsive Systems Associates.

O'Neil, J. (1992). Putting performance assessment to the test. *Educational Leadership, 49*(8), 14–19.

Phinney, J. S., & Rotheram, M. J. (1987). *Children's ethnic socialization.* Newbury Park, CA: Sage Publications.

Pierce, L. V., & O'Malley, J. M. (1992). *Performance and portfolio assessment for language minority students.* Washington, DC: National Clearinghouse for Bilingual Education.

Ramirez, M., III, & Castaneda, A. (1974). *Cultural democracy, bicognitive development, and education.* New York: Academic Press.

Resnick, L. B., & Resnick, D. P. (1985). Standards, curriculum and performance: A historical and comparative perspective. *Educational Researcher, 15,* 5–21.

Roeber, E., Bond, L., & van der Ploeg, A. (1993). *State student assessment program data base.* Washington, DC: Council of Chief State School Officers/North Central Regional Education Laboratory.

Rousso, H. (1984). Fostering healthy self-esteem. *Exceptional Parent, 14,* 9–14.

Schowe, B. M. (1979). *Identity crisis in deafness.* Tempe, AZ: The Scholars' Press.

Schurr, K., Towne, R., & Joiner, L. M. (1972). Trends in self-concept of ability over two years of special class placement. *Journal of Special Education, 6*(2), 161–166.

Shapiro, J. (1993). *No pity.* New York: Random House.

Shavelson, R. L., Kobett, B., Heiss, L., & Fennell, F. S. (1992). Performance assessments: Political rhetoric and measurement reality. *Educational Researcher, 21*(4), 22–27.

Shepard, L. A. (1989). Why we need better assessments. *Educational Leadership, 46*(7), 4–9.

Siegel, A. I. (1986). Performance tests. In R. A. Beck (Ed.), *Performance assessment.* Baltimore, MD: Johns Hopkins University Press.

Smith, M. D., Dorecki, P. R., & Davis, E. E. (1977). School-related factors influencing the self-concepts of children with learning problems. *Peabody Journal of Education, 54*(2), 185–195.

Spradley, L., & Spradley, J. P. (1978). *Deaf Like Me.* New York: Random House.

Stainback, S., Stainback, W., East, K., & Sapon-Shevin, M. (1994). A commentary on inclusion and the development of a positive self-identity by people with disabilities. *Exceptional Children, 60*(6), 486–490.

U.S. Congress, Office of Technology Assessment. (1992, February) *Testing in American schools: Asking the right questions* (OTA-SET 519, No. ED 340 770). Washington, DC: U.S. Government Printing Office. ED 340 770.

Vandercook, T., York, J., & Forest, M. (1989). The McGill Action Planning System: A strategy for building the vision. *Journal of the Association for Persons with Severe Handicaps, 14,* 205–215.

Wiggins, G. (1989a). Teaching to the authentic test. *Educational Leadership, 46*(7), 41–47.

Wiggins, G. (1989b). A true test: Toward more authentic and equitable assessment. *Phi Delta Kappan, 70,* 703–713.

Wiggins, G. (1991). Standards not standardization: Evoking quality student work. *Educational Leadership, 48*(5), 18–25.

Wiggins, G. (1991). A response to Cizek. *Phi Delta Kappan, 72,* 700–703.

Wiggins, G. (1992). Creating tests worth taking. *Educational Leadership, 49*(8), 26–33.

Wolf, D. P., LeMahieu, G., & Eresh, J. (1992). Good measure: Assessment as a tool for educational reform. *Educational Leadership, 49*(8), 8–13.

Worthen, B. R. (1993). Critical issues that will determine the future of alternative assessment. *Phi Delta Kappan, 74*(6), 444–454.

Zigler, E., & Muenchow, S. (1979). Mainstreaming: The proof is in the implementation. *American Psychologist, 34*(10), 993–996.

Appendix

Answers to Building Your Professional Vocabulary and Comprehension Check

Chapter 1
Building Your Professional Vocabulary

- i. accommodation
- g. behavior
- d. behavioral
- f. biophysical
- h. congruence
- c. development
- e. ecological contexts
- k. milieu
- b. psychoeducational
- a. special education
- j. transaction

Comprehension Check

1. c
2. a
3. b
4. a
5. c
6. b

Chapter 2
Building Your Professional Vocabulary

- d. ADA
- b. compensatory education
- f. disability
- g. handicap
- c. inclusive education
- a. stigma
- e. the wild boy of Aveyron

Comprehension Check

1. b
2. c
3. b
4. a
5. b
6. b
7. a
8. b
9. b
10. a

Chapter 3
Building Your Professional Vocabulary
b. appropriate education
g. screening
i. diagnostic evaluation
a. inclusion
c. IEP
f. IFSP
k. least restrictive environment
j. placement
e. prereferral activities
h. referral
l. related services
d. transition services
Comprehension Check
1. b
2. b
3. b
4. b
5. b
6. c
7. a
8. b
9. a
10. c

Chapter 4
Building Your Professional Vocabulary
c. collaboration
f. collaborative support for school programs
b. criteria of the least dangerous assumption
d. information-giving activities
e. information-sharing activities
g. nonparticipation
a. stage theory
Comprehension Check
1. b
2. b
3. a
4. c
5. c
6. c
7. c
8. a
9. c

Chapter 5
Building Your Professional Vocabulary
c. Civil Rights Act of 1964
g. The Education of the Handicapped Act of 1983
b. generalization

f. The Individuals with Disabilities Education Act of 1990
e. Perkins Vocational Education Act of 1973
a. transition
d. Vocational Education Act of 1963
Comprehension Check
1. c
2. c
3. a
4. b
5. b
6. b
7. c
8. a

Chapter 6
Building Your Professional Vocabulary
a. child abuse
c. child maltreatment
b. child neglect
f. fetal alcohol syndrome
e. foster care
g. possible fetal alcohol effect
h. prenatal drug and alcohol exposure
d. substitute care
Comprehension Check
1. b
2. a
3. c
4. a
5. c
6. c
7. c
8. c
9. a
10. c
11. a

Chapter 7
Building Your Professional Vocabulary
e. aggression
f. emotional/behavioral disorders
d. depression
h. disturbed behaviors
g. disturbing behaviors
b. externalizing behaviors
c. internalizing behaviors
j. levels systems
l. life space interview
i. seriously emotionally disturbed
a. suicidal ideation
k. token economy

Comprehension Check
1. c
2. a
3. b
4. b
5. a
6. b
7. b
8. a
9. a
10. b

Chapter 8
Building Your Professional Vocabulary
c. Anglo
d. Hispanic
a. ethnicity
e. migrant
b. minority

Comprehension Check
1. c
2. c
3. c
4. a
5. c
6. b
7. b
8. a
9. b
10. c
11. c

Chapter 9
Building Your Professional Vocabulary
h. cognition
e. expressive language
g. pragmatics
d. language
i. augmentative systems
j. speech disorders
f. receptive
b. speech
c. transactional model
a. communication

Comprehension Check
1. a
2. c
3. c
4. a
5. c
6. b
7. b
8. b
9. b
10. c

Chapter 10
Building Your Professional Vocabulary
b. spina bifida
a. cerebral palsy
h. orthotic device
e. epilepsy
d. hydrocephaly
g. prostheses
i. scoliosis
f. talipes
j. health impairments
c. catheterization

Comprehension Check
1. b
2. b
3. a
4. c
5. c
6. c
7. c
8. c
9. b
10. b

Chapter 11
Building Your Professional Vocabulary
g. amblyopia
f. astigmatism
b. blindness
h. cataracts
e. hyperopia
d. myopia
i. nystagmus
c. presbyopia
a. stereotypies
j. strabismus

Comprehension Check
1. b
2. c
3. a
4. c
5. a
6. b
7. c
8. b
9. c
10. b

Chapter 12
Building Your Professional Vocabulary
e. American Sign Language
f. tympanogram
d. Deaf culture
i. cued speech

j.　speechreading
h.　TDD
g.　FM system
b.　hearing impairment
c.　hard of hearing
a.　postlingual hearing impairment

Comprehension Check
1.　b
2.　c
3.　c
4.　c
5.　b
6.　c
7.　a
8.　c
9.　c
10.　a

Chapter 13

Building Your Professional Vocabulary
d.　ADD
c.　cognitive behavior modification
f.　curriculum-based assessment
b.　social skills training
e.　strategies training
a.　tutoring

Comprehension Check
1.　a
2.　c
3.　b
4.　b
5.　a
6.　b
7.　a
8.　c
9.　a
10.　a

Chapter 14

Building Your Professional Vocabulary
a.　deviance disavowal
c.　mild mental retardation
e.　moderate mental retardation
b.　normalcy fabrication
d.　severe mental retardation

Comprehension Check
1.　c
2.　b
3.　a
4.　b
5.　c
6.　b

7.　b
8.　b
9.　a
10.　a

Chapter 15

Building Your Professional Vocabulary
b.　collaborative consultation
c.　high-prevalence disabilities
d.　school survival skills
a.　teacher-assistance team

Comprehension Check
1.　a
2.　c
3.　b
4.　c
5.　a
6.　a
7.　c
8.　b

Chapter 16

Building Your Professional Vocabulary
e.　augmentative communication systems
a.　autism
c.　dual sensory impairments
d.　multiple disabilities
b.　severe disabilities

Comprehension Check
1.　b
2.　b
3.　c
4.　a
5.　b
6.　c
7.　b
8.　b
9.　b
10.　b

Chapter 17

Building Your Professional Vocabulary
g.　acceleration
f.　Cinderella complex
b.　creative
h.　enrichment
a.　gifted
e.　gifted imposter phenomenon
i.　mentor
c.　talented
d.　underachievement

Comprehension Check
1. b
2. c
3. c
4. a
5. a
6. b
7. c
8. c
9. a
10. c

Chapter 18

Building Your Professional Vocabulary
c. performance assessment
a. authentic assessment

f. social identity
b. normalization
e. self-concept
d. paradigm

Comprehension Check
1. c
2. b
3. a
4. b
5. b
6. b
7. b
8. b
9. a
10. a

Glossary

A

acceleration   moving through the curriculum at a more rapid pace [17]

accommodation   adaptation or adjustment [1]

Acquired Immune Deficiency Syndrome (AIDS)   a fatal viral disease transmitted through intimate sexual contact, contaminated blood or blood products, contaminated needles and syringes, and from mother to child; no known cure is available [10]

adapted physical education   physical education designed for the successful participation of learners with disabilities [10]

Adoption Assistance and Child Welfare Act of 1980   provided subsidies for families adopting special needs children; mandated state procedures for promptly terminating parents' rights when appropriate to facilitate permanency for children [6]

African American   an American whose ancestry includes individuals native to Africa [8]

aggression   behavior intended to dominate others [7]

allergy   abnormal reaction to a specific substance [10]

amblyopia   reduction or loss of vision in the weaker eye [11]

American Sign Language (ASL)   the native language most frequently used among persons with hearing impairments; it is not the signed equivalent of English [12]

Americans with Disabilities Act (1990)   mandates equal accommodations for individuals with disabilities in all businesses, public facilities, and transportation systems and bans discrimination [2]

amplification   increasing volume [12]

amputation   total or partial removal of a part of the body [10]

Anglo   the Caucasian middle-class culture [8]

Appalachian   an individual whose ancestry includes individuals native to the Appalachian region [8]

appropriate education   education that allows an individual to achieve commensurate with peers [3]

articulation disorders   difficulties with producing the sound system of oral language, or speech; also known as phonologic disorders [9]

Asian American   an American whose ancestry includes individuals native to Asia [8]

asthma   respiratory or breathing disorder [10]

astigmatism   a condition marked by variations in the cornea that result in blurred vision [11]

attention-deficit/hyperactivity disorder   a clinical disorder marked by difficulties in focusing and often concomitant hyperactivity [13]

augmentative communication systems   systems that serve as an alternative to spoken language, including gestures, sign language systems, or mechanical or technological aids of some sort [16]

augmentative systems   systems used to supplement communication [9]

authentic assessment   evaluation conducted through posing problems related to real life [18]

autism   a developmental disorder apparent before thirty months of age and demonstrated by a pervasive lack of responsiveness to other people and by communicative disorders [16]

B

behavior   the expression of the dynamic relationship between the individual and the environment [1]

behavioral perspective   a point of view from which the individual's behavior is seen as being maintained by stimuli in the immediate environment in which the individual functions [1]

behind-the-ear (BTE) hearing aids   hearing aids that fit behind the learner's ear [12]

The chapter in which these key words first appear is indicated in brackets following the definition.

bicultural-bilingual (Bi-Bi) education a philosophy regarding the education of learners who are deaf that uses American Sign Language as the primary language and educates students in the Deaf culture [12]

biophysical perspective a point of view that emphasizes neurological and other organic factors as the cause of the individual's behavior [1]

blind a visual impairment requiring alternatives to print and visual materials [11]

C

cancer a group of diseases of unknown cause that produce abnormal cell growth [10]

cascade of services the range of placement options available to learners with disabilities [3]

cataracts a clouding of the lens of the eye [11]

catheterization insertion of a tube into the urethra to drain urine from the bladder [10]

cerebral palsy a dysfunction of the neurological motor system [10]

child abuse physical or mental injury or sexual abuse of a child under the age of eighteen by a person responsible for the child's welfare under circumstances that indicate that the child's health or welfare is harmed or threatened [6]

Child Abuse Prevention and Treatment Act of 1974 provided mechanisms for the reporting and prevention of child abuse and neglect; included legal definitions of child abuse and neglect [6]

child maltreatment child abuse and neglect [6]

child neglect failing to provide for the physical, medical, emotional, or educational needs of a child by an individual responsible for the child's welfare [6]

Cinderella complex tendency of a girl or woman to wait to be rescued by a male partner [17]

Civil Rights Act of 1964 banned discrimination in education [5]

cluttering running together sounds, words, and phrases, producing rapid, jumbled speech [9]

cognition the process of knowing and thinking [9]

cognitive behavior modification strategies in which the learner overtly and eventually covertly practices a set script for addressing problems [13]

collaboration the participation of equal partners in the solution of problems [4]

collaborative consultation consultation in which the special educator and the general educator work as a team to develop interventions for learners with disabilities [15]

collaborative support for school programs family activities that support the in-class program of the learner with disabilities [4]

communication the verbal and nonverbal means of transmitting and decoding messages from one individual with the intention of stimulating meaning in the mind of another [9]

compensatory education a model of education that provides for "making up," or compensating, for weaker skills or ability [2]

conductive loss hearing loss caused by damage to the outer or middle ear [12]

congruence "match" or "goodness of fit" [1]

context setting [1]

creative capable of expressing unique and novel ideas, solutions, and products [17]

criteria of the least dangerous assumption the belief that assumptions made regarding individuals should be those least intrusive and least limiting [4]

criterion-referenced evaluation evaluation that focuses on the learner's mastery of specific skills [3]

cued speech a set of hand cues that, together with speechreading, permit visual identification of spoken sound [12]

curriculum-based assessment assessment grounded in the curriculum and materials in which the learner receives instruction [13]

cystic fibrosis a disease of the pancreas marked by abnormally thickened mucus and other glandular secretions [10]

D

d-amphetamine (Dexedrine) a stimulant sometimes used in the treatment of attention-deficit/hyperactivity disorder; brand name Dexedrine [13]

deaf learners unable to process auditory linguistic information [12]

Deaf a member of Deaf culture [12]

depression a dysphoric mood or loss of pleasure that lasts at least two weeks [7]

development the continual adaptation or adjustment of the individual and the environment to each other [1]

deviance disavowal efforts made by a learner with a disability to reject differences attributed to their disability [14]

diabetic retinopathy aneurysms in the retinal capillary blood vessels due to diabetes [11]

Diagnostic and Statistical Manual of Mental Disorders the manual for the classification system of mental disorders developed by the American Psychiatric Association [7]

diagnostic evaluation the process of studying a learner and the learner's developmental contexts to determine the nature of the problem if, in fact, there is a problem [3]

diagnostic evaluation team a group of individuals from various disciplines responsible for the evaluation of learners [3]

disability a reduction in function or the absence of a particular body part or organ, such as the loss of a limb [2]

disfluency behavior that inhibits the smooth flow and rhythm of speech [9]

disturbed behaviors behaviors that occur across settings [7]

disturbing behaviors behaviors that are person, setting, or task specific [7]

dual sensory impairments concurrent hearing and visual disabilities, the combination of which causes such severe communication and educational problems that the child cannot be accommodated in special education programs for either deaf or blind students [16]

E

ecological context   the setting in which an individual develops [1]

Education of the Handicapped Act of 1983   authorized grants and contracts to strengthen and coordinate education, training, and related services to assist youth with disabilities in the transition from school to community [5]

emotional/behavioral disorders   learners who, in the school environment, vary from their peers in terms of interaction and whose challenging behaviors persist despite interventions typically used in general education [7]

enrichment   additional activities that enhance the typical curriculum [17]

epilepsy   a condition marked by recurrent unprovoked seizures [10]

ethnicity   membership in a group of people who share a unique social and cultural heritage that is transmitted from one generation to the next [8]

expressive language   language for developing and sending messages [9]

externalizing behaviors   behaviors directed outward, such as stealing, lying, disobedience, and fighting [7]

F

facilitated communication   augmentative communication technique that permits the individual with severe disabilities (e.g., autism) to communicate; a specific method or strategy [16]

fetal alcohol syndrome   a birth defect resulting from maternal alcohol use that causes prenatal and/or postnatal growth retardation, central nervous system damage, and a set of common facial characteristics [6]

fluctuating conductive hearing impairment   the changing hearing loss that may occur as a consequence of otitis media [12]

FM system   a wireless amplification system in which speech is transmitted from a microphone via frequency modulated radio signals to a receiver worn by the learner [12]

foster care   substitute-care placement that is typically licensed and regulated by state human services agencies [6]

G

generalization   the demonstration of a behavior in a context in which it was not directly taught [5]

gifted   usually refers to learners who are intellectually or academically within the superior range [17]

gifted imposter phenomenon   a personal belief that one is not truly as successful as others believe and that this lack of ability will be discovered [17]

glaucoma   increased pressure in the eye [11]

H

handicap   disadvantage that results from a disability that limits or prevents fulfillment of a role [2]

hard of hearing   learners who have hearing losses that still permit them to process auditory information [12]

health impairments   chronic and acute physical conditions that impair strength, vitality, or alertness [10]

hearing impairment   condition whereby hearing is not typical for age and culture [12]

heart condition   a number of conditions that may cause cardiac malfunction [10]

hemophilia   a genetically transmitted disease marked by problems with blood coagulation [10]

high-prevalence disabilities   mild handicapping conditions such as mild mental retardation, learning disabilities, and mild behavioral disorders [15]

Hispanics   persons of all races whose cultural heritage is related to the use of the Spanish language and the Latino culture [8]

holistic communication-based approaches   intervention strategies that involve instruction in reading and writing as communication in context [13]

human immunodeficiency virus (HIV)   a virus that affects the immune system and impairs the individual's ability to fight infections; develops into AIDS [10]

hydrocephaly   a condition in which fluid accumulates in the ventricles of the brain [10]

hyperopia   farsightedness [11]

I

immitance   audiologic testing that includes tympanometry and acoustic reflex testing [12]

inclusion   the philosophy that all students, regardless of disability, are a vital and integral part of the general education system; special needs services addressing the IEP goals and objectives of students with disabilities may be rendered in the general education classroom [3]

Individualized Education Program (IEP)   a year-long plan of the services and activities conducted with a learner with a disability [3]

Individualized Family Service Plan (IFSP)   a year-long plan of services and outcomes for the family of a child with a disability who is younger than three years of age [3]

individual-referenced evaluation   evaluation that focuses on the learner's progress over time [3]

Individuals with Disabilities Education Act   reauthorized and amended PL 94-142; changed language to "person first"; added categories ("autism" and "traumatic brain injury"); extended related services to include rehabilitation counseling and social work services; added transition services [5]

information-giving activities   activities in which the family is the passive recipient of information [4]

information-sharing activities   activities in which the family shares and receives information [4]

internalizing behaviors   behaviors directed inward, such as physical complaints, phobias, social withdrawal, and fearfulness [7]

interpreter   a hearing individual who communicates spoken language, usually through one of the manual or signed systems, to learners who are hearing impaired [12]

in-the-ear (ITE) hearing aids   hearing aids that fit in the learner's ear [12]

J

juvenile diabetes   a metabolic disorder caused by inadequate production of insulin [10]

juvenile rheumatoid arthritis   a chronic childhood disorder marked by joint inflammation [10]

L

language the ability to communicate complex ideas through an organized system of meaning [9]

language disorders deviant or delayed development of comprehension and/or the use of the signs and symbols of a spoken, written, or other symbol system [9]

lead poisoning neurological damage resulting from the ingestion of toxic levels of lead [10]

learning disabilities a general term that refers to a heterogeneous group of disorders manifested by significant difficulties in the acquisition and use of listening, speaking, reading, writing, reasoning, or mathematical abilities [13]

least restrictive environment the setting that provides the maximum amount of interaction with learners without disabilities while providing enough support for the learner with disabilities to be successful [3]

levels systems organizational frameworks within which various behavior management interventions are applied to shape behaviors [7]

life space interview a technique in which the teacher and student interact in a guided interview with the aim of developing appropriate student responses to incidents in the environment; developed by Redl [7]

M

macular degeneration a breakdown of the macula, the central part of the retina [11]

mainstreaming participation of learners with disabilities with their typical peers [3]

mental retardation generalized subaverage intellectual functioning, concurrent with problems in adaptive behavior, that occurs before eighteen years of age [14]

mentor an established individual in a profession or field who serves as a model [17]

methylphenidate (Ritalin) a stimulant frequently used in treatment of attention-deficit/hyperactivity disorder; brand name Ritalin [13]

migrant person who moves frequently, following employment opportunities [8]

mild mental retardation retardation indicated by intelligence quotients on standardized tests of about 50–70 [14]

milieu an individual's environment or developmental context [1]

minority any group with unequal access to power [8]

moderate mental retardation retardation indicated by intelligence quotients on standardized tests of about 20–50 [14]

morphology the smallest units of meaning [9]

multiple disabilities concomitant disabilities (such as mentally retarded-blind, mentally retarded-orthopedically impaired, etc.), the combination of which causes such severe educational problems that the student cannot be accommodated in special education programs designed solely for working with one of the impairments [16]

muscular dystrophy a group of diseases characterized by the wasting and progressive weakness of skeletal muscles [10]

myopia nearsightedness [11]

N

Native American a descendant of the indigenous population of the Americas [8]

neural tube defect spina bifida; a defect of the spinal column in which the spine fails to close properly around the column of nerves it is designed to protect [10]

nonparticipation the option to not be involved in an activity [4]

normalcy fabrication a story told by an individual with a disability in order to appear more competent or "normal" [14]

normalization attempts to make the circumstances of everyday life for people with disabilities as ordinary as possible [18]

norm-referenced evaluation evaluation that compares a learner's performance with the performance of others [3]

nystagmus rapid and uncontrolled eye movements [11]

O

occupational therapy therapy designed to support the development of work, recreation, and self-care skills [10]

orthopedic disability a physical disability that challenges mobility, management of body functions, and social interactions [10]

orthotic device a device to enhance the partial functioning of a part of the body [10]

otitis media middle-ear infection [12]

P

paradigm shift a change in the standard way of thinking and acting [18]

parent training activities that increase parents' knowledge and skills [4]

partially sighted unable to use print and visual materials without the help of large print, optical aids, technological aids; usually requires education in the use of residual vision [11]

performance assessment direct assessment of the products or accomplishments of the learner [18]

peripheral vision seeing by means of the outermost portions of the eye, that is, the corner of the eye [11]

Perkins Vocational Education Act of 1973 provided for vocational services for individuals with disabilities; required client involvement in the design and delivery of services [5]

personal futures planning individualized planning based on the dreams and goals of the learner and his or her family [18]

pervasive developmental disorder (PDD) a psychiatric diagnosis that includes individuals who have autism [16]

phonemes the written representation of speech sounds [9]

phonology the study of the individual speech sounds characteristic of a language and the rules governing them [9]

physical therapy therapy designed to increase strength, endurance, and range of motion [10]

placement the assignment of a learner to special education services [3]

possible fetal alcohol effect   a group of mild birth defects caused by maternal use of alcohol, usually involving prenatal and/or postnatal growth retardation and central nervous system damage [6]

postlingual hearing impairment   a hearing impairment occurring after the development of language [12]

pragmatics   the social communicative consideration of language [9, 12]

prelingual hearing impairment   a hearing impairment present prior to the development of language [12]

prenatal drug and alcohol exposure   fetal exposure to drug and alcohol of any kind or amount by the mother's use during pregnancy [6]

prereferral activities   those strategies implemented in the general education classroom by the general education teacher to address the individual needs of a learner prior to referral for evaluation for special education services [3]

presbyopia   impaired or lost ability to focus for close work; usually occurs at about forty-five years of age [11]

profound mental retardation   the most severe degree of mental retardation, with intelligence quotients on standardized tests below the 20–25 range; persons with profound mental retardation require life-span care and supervision [14]

prostheses   artificial replacements for missing body parts [10]

psychoeducational perspective   a point of view that emphasizes the primary cause of the individual's behavior as being dynamic intrapsychic phenomena [1]

Public Law 94-142   The Education for All Handicapped Children Act; required a free, appropriate public education for all learners [3]

Public Law 99-457   Amendments to PL 94-142, which include permissive legislation for services for learners zero to two and require preschool programming for learners three to five years of age [3]

Public Law 101-336   Americans with Disabilities Act (ADA); bars discrimination; mandates equal accommodations for individuals with disabilities in all businesses, public facilities, and transportation [3]

Public Law 101-457   Amendments to PL 94-142, called the Individuals with Disabilities Education Act; provided for a transition planning for all learners sixteen or more years of age and person-first language [3]

Puerto Rican   an American whose ancestry was or who himself or herself is native to Puerto Rico [8]

R

receptive language   language for receiving and interpreting messages [9]

referral   the process of soliciting and accepting nominations for evaluation from others [3]

related services   transportation and developmental, corrective, and other supportive services required to assist the child with disabilities in special education [3]

retinitis pigmentosa   an inherited condition that begins with a loss of night vision and leads to gradually decreasing peripheral vision [11]

retinopathy of prematurity   an abnormal proliferation of blood vessels in the eye, causing scar tissue and bleeding and detachment of the retina [11]

S

school survival skills   skills necessary for successful interactions with teachers; for example, being on time, bringing materials, doing assignments [15]

scoliosis   a lateral curve of the spine [10]

screening   activities to identify at-risk learners for further study [3]

seizure disorders   disorders represented by any of various types of seizures; epilepsy [10]

self-concept   an individual's image of himself or herself [18]

semantics   the meaning of individual words and their relationship with each other [9]

sensorineural loss   hearing loss caused by damage to the neurological hearing system [12]

seriously emotionally disturbed   the label used in federal law for learners identified as emotionally/behaviorally disordered [7]

severe disabilities   intense physical, mental, or emotional problems that require educational, social, psychological, and medical services beyond those that are traditionally offered by general and special education programs [16]

severe mental retardation   an extensive degree of mental retardation; persons with intelligence quotients on standardized instruments in the 20–25 to 35–40 range; require life-span care and supervision [14]

sickle cell disease   a genetically transmitted disease marked by chronic anemia and sickle-shaped red blood cells [10]

social identity   modification of personal identity to meet the expectations of larger society [18]

social skills training   specific interventions, usually involving problem solving, aimed at increasing the ability of learners to interact with others [13]

social systems perspective   a point of view from which the individual is seen as developing in a dynamic relationship with and as an inseparable part of the settings in which the individual functions over the life span [1]

special education   a subsystem of regular education responsible for the education of learners with disabilities [1]

speech   the vocal system of language [9]

speech audiometry   a measure of a person's aural detection of speech [12]

speech disorders   impairments in the production of oral or spoken language [12]

speechreading   the process of following environmental cues related to a message and recognizing speech movements produced by another individual [12]

spina bifida   a congenital condition marked by a defect of the spinal column in which the spine fails to close properly; neural tube defect [10]

spinal cord injuries   injuries to the neural column; the extent of injury varies from case to case [10]

stage theory the theory that family members progress through a set pattern of reactions to the birth or diagnosis of a member with a disability [4]

stereotypies repetitive, inappropriate social behaviors such as rocking, swaying, and head posturing [11]

stigma an attitude towards others that discredits them in some manner [2]

strabismus the inability to focus on the same object with both eyes [11]

strategies training the teaching of specific strategies to complete academic tasks [13]

stuttering a disruption in the timing of speaking [12]

substitute care the placement of children for rearing with other than the biological parents [6]

suicidal ideation thoughts about committing suicide [7]

symbols the media through which communication occurs [9]

syntax the rule system for constructing sentences [9]

T

talented exhibiting special abilities, aptitudes, and accomplishments in various areas [17]

talipes the turning of a foot towards the midline of the body; often referred to as clubfoot [10]

TDD telecommunication device for the deaf; a teletypewriter connected to a telephone system that allows persons with hearing impairments to communicate [12]

teacher-assistance teams teacher-centered instructional alternative support systems [15]

token economy an exchange system that provides individuals or groups whose behavior is being changed with immediate feedback cues of the appropriateness of their behavior [7]

transaction an interaction in which each participant is altered by the other [1]

transactional model the development of the child is seen as the product of the continuous interactions of the learner and the experiences provided by the caregivers in the social context [9]

transition the movement from one system or service to another [1, 5]

transition services services to facilitate the individual's movement between educational and other service programs, from home to school, between school programs, from school to work, advanced training, or postsecondary education [3]

traumatic brain injuries injuries to the brain that impair functioning [10]

TTY teletypewriter; a device connected to a telephone that allows communication between persons with hearing and persons with hearing impairments [12]

tutoring one-on-one or small-group teaching of materials used in the learner's other instructional settings [13]

tympanogram a test of the function of the eardrum [12]

U

underachievement wherein a learner demonstrates a significant discrepancy between ability and performance [17]

V

visual acuity a measure of how well a person can see at various distances; sharpness, distinctiveness [11]

visual impairment a generic term for any of several conditions that limit vision [11]

visually handicapped having sight limited in any way and to such an extent that special services are required [11]

Vocational Education Act of 1963 legislation that mandated 10 percent of the funds allocated to vocational education for programs for persons with disabilities [5]

voice disorders difficulties in the resonant quality of speech [9]

W

wild boy of Aveyron Itard's student and the subject of a historically significant study of the treatment of a learner with mental retardation and autism [2]

Z

zero reject philosophy the philosophy that no student may be excluded from receiving educational services, regardless of the disability [18]

Credits

Chapter One
Opener: © Paul Conklin/PhotoEdit; p. 8: © Jane Williams/Unicorn Stock Photos; p. 9: © S. Feld/H. Armstrong Roberts

Chapter Two
Opener: © Tracy Siehndel/Unicorn Stock Photos; p. 19: © Anheuser-Busch; p. 20: © Deborah Davis/PhotoEdit

Chapter Three
Opener: © Tony Freeman/PhotoEdit; p. 37: © Alon Reininger/Unicorn Stock Photos; p. 40: © Deneve Leigh Bunde/Unicorn Stock Photos; p. 49: © Jeff Greenberg/Unicorn Stock Photos

Chapter Four
Opener: © J. Kent Gildey/University of Alabama; p. 71: © Paul Conklin/PhotoEdit; p. 72: © James L. Shaffer; p. 76: © Laura Dwight/Corbis; p. 79: © Martin R. Jones/Unicorn Stock Photos; p. 80: © CLEO

Chapter Five
Opener: © James L. Shaffer; p. 92: © Bill Bachmann/Photo Researchers, Inc.; p. 93: © SuperStock; p. 95: © James L. Shaffer; p. 99: © Jean Higgins/Unicorn Stock Photos

Chapter Six
Opener: © Deneve Leigh Bunde/Unicorn Stock Photos; p. 105: © Richard Hutchings/PhotoEdit; p. 110: © Charles Gupton/Stock Boston; p. 112: © Andy Levin/Photo Researchers, Inc.; p. 116: © John Griffin/The Image Works

Chapter Seven
Opener: © Skjold Photographs; p. 135, 137: © James L. Shaffer; p. 142 : © Jeff Dunn/The Picture Cube; p. 146: © CLEO

Chapter Eight
Opener: © James L. Shaffer; p. 165: © Mark E. Gibson; p. 167: © Alan Oddie/PhotoEdit; p. 170: © Jeffrey Aaronson/Network Aspen; p. 178: © Frank Siteman/Light Sources Stock; p. 183: © Paul Conklin/PhotoEdit

Chapter Nine
Opener: © Devaney Stock Photos; p. 198: © Bob Coyle; p. 199: © Elena Rooraid/PhotoEdit; p. 203: © Bob Daemmrich/The Image Works; p. 209: © Bill Aron/PhotoEdit

Chapter Ten
Opener: © Tony Freeman/PhotoEdit; p. 221: © James L. Shaffer; p. 229: © Michael Siluk; p. 231: © MacDonald Photography/Unicorn Stock Photos; p. 232: © Tony Freeman/PhotoEdit; p. 234: © James L. Shaffer; p. 235 top left: © Paul Conklin/PhotoEdit; p. 235 top right: © Tony Freeman/PhotoEdit; p. 235 bottom left & right: © Robert Brenner/PhotoEdit

Credits

Chapter Eleven

Opener: © Todd Korol/First Light; p. 251: © Martha McBride/Unicorn Stock Photos; p. 254: © Alan Oddie/PhotoEdit; p. 258: © Martha Holmes/LIFE Magazine © TIME Inc.; p. 259: © Tony Freeman/PhotoEdit; 11.4: © Zefa-U.K./H. Armstrong Roberts; 11.5A: © James L. Shaffer; 11.5B: © Martin R. Jones/Unicorn Stock Photos; p. 263 left: © Rhoda Sidney/PhotoEdit; p. 263 right: © David Frazier Photolibrary

Chapter Twelve

Opener: AP/Wide World Photos; p. 279: © Michael Newman/PhotoEdit; p. 281: © David Young-Wolff/PhotoEdit; p. 284: © Stephen McBrady/PhotoEdit; p. 287, 292: © James L. Shaffer

Chapter Thirteen

Opener: © J. Myers/H. Armstrong Roberts; p. 304: © Tony Freeman/PhotoEdit; p. 311: © James L. Shaffer; p. 313: © Skjold Photographs; p. 315: © Melanie Carr/Zephyr Pictures

Chapter Fourteen

Opener: © James L. Shaffer; p. 327: © Tony Freeman/PhotoEdit; p. 330: © David Young Wolff/PhotoEdit; p. 334: © Richard Hutchings/PhotoEdit; p. 340: © Gaye Hilsenrath/The Picture Cube

Chapter Fifteen

Opener: © Gale Zucker/Stock Boston; p. 354: © Tony Freeman/PhotoEdit; p. 359: © James L. Shaffer

Chapter Sixteen

Opener: © Alon Reininger/Unicorn Stock Photos; p. 370: © Paul Conklin/PhotoEdit; p. 375: © James L. Shaffer; p. 379: © Peter Bates/The Picture Cube

Chapter Seventeen

Opener: © Jeffrey Aaronson/Network Aspen; p. 392: © Myrleen Ferguson Cate/PhotoEdit; p. 394: © Jeffrey Aaronson/Network Aspen; 17.3: © Seth Resnick/Light Sources Stock; p. 398: © Bill Bachmann/Stock Boston; p. 403: © James L. Shaffer; p. 409: © David Young Wolff/PhotoEdit; p. 410 top: © Karen Holsinger Mullen/Unicorn Stock Photos; p. 410 bottom: © Mark E. Gibson

Chapter Eighteen

Opener: © Richard Hutchings/PhotoEdit; p. 424: © James L. Shaffer; p. 427: © Tony Freeman/PhotoEdit; p. 430: © James L. Shaffer; p. 436, 439: © Skjold Photographs

Name Index

Beltempo, J., 302
Bemporad, J. R., 81
Bender, W. N., 47–48, 302, 308
Bennett-Levy, J., 230
Berg, F. S., 271, 280
Berger, S. R., 108
Berlowitz, M. J., 171
Berrigan, C., 380
Berry, H. K., 328
Berryman, J. D., 22
Betts, G. T., 396
Bibby, M. A., 397
Bickel, D. D., 44
Bickel, W. E., 44
Bigelow, A. C., 245–246
Biklen, D., 380
Bingol, N., 116
Birch, J. W., 395
Bird, B., 171
Birenbaum, A., 73
Birns, S. L., 247
Bishop, D. V., 201–202, 207
Blacher, J., 70, 333, 373
Black, F. L., 352
Black, M. M., 334
Blackard, M. K., 21, 73
Blackhurst, A. R., 17
Blackman, J. A., 225
Blackorby, J., 86
Blakeslee, S., 107–108
Blatt, B., 27, 366
Blocksberg, L. M., 113
Bloodworth, H., 397
Bloom, L., 437
Bloom, R. B., 80
Bloom, S. D., 44
Bloome, D., 192
Blouin, A. G., 327
Blouin, J. H., 327
Bobo, J. K., 167
Bockern, S. V., 168–169
Bohan, D., 235–236
Boles, S. M., 98
Bond, L., 432
Bond, M. R., 96
Bonner, H., 436
Boodoosingh, L., 198
Bookstein, F. L., 119
Boone, D. R., 210
Boos, M., 222
Boothroyd, A., 280
Borman, K., 170, 171
Borman, K. M., 171
Bos, C., 313
Bos, C. S., 337
Bosma, H. A., 436
Boyce, B., 222
Boyce, C. W., 390
Boyd, A., 334
Boyle, J. T., 228
Brackett, D., 273
Brackin, S. R., 201
Braden, J. P., 310
Bradshaw, J., 71
Brady, M. P., 371

Braggett, E. J., 403
Braiman, S., 131
Brandt, R., 429, 433
Branthwaite, A., 436
Brassard, M. R., 104
Brazelton, T. B., 372
Breme, J., 35
Brendtro, L. K., 168–169
Bridges, S., 411
Brill, R. G., 271, 289
Brimer, R. W., 370
Brinton, B., 201–202
Brobeil, R. A., 117
Brod, R. L., 167, 176
Brodzinsky, A. B., 113
Brodzinsky, D. M., 113
Broen, P. A., 204
Brokenleg, M., 168–169
Bromley, B. E., 333, 373
Bronfenbrenner, J., 87
Bronfenbrenner, U., 5–7, 9, 35, 44, 69–70, 73
Bronicki, G. J. B., 372
Brooks, A. P., 146
Brooks, C., 369
Brooks, P. H., 328
Brower, P., 404–405
Brown, A. L., 314
Brown, C. L., 151
Brown, D., 204, 356
Brown, F., 371, 378
Brown, G. M., 358
Brown, L., 90, 337
Brown, R. T., 231, 328
Brown, S. H., 280
Browning, L. D., 280
Brown-Muzino, C., 397
Bruder, M. B., 223, 233
Bruininks, R. H., 97
Bruner, J., 196
Brunner, R. L., 328
Bryde, J., 169
Bryen, D. N., 379
Buchanan, M., 315
Budd, K. S., 200
Buenning, M., 164
Buescher, T., 403
Buhrmester, D., 312
Bunker, L., 378
Burbach, H. J., 236
Burg, I., 225
Burgerud, D. M., 393, 397
Burgio, L. D., 336–337
Buriel, R., 229
Burlow, A., 229
Burns, K. A., 116
Burns, N. J., 116
Burns, R., 436–437, 442
Bursuck, B., 132
Bursuck, W., 304
Bursuck, W. D., 316
Burton, J., 116
Butler, J. A., 50, 60
Butler, R., 224
Byrd, K., 200
Byrne, B. M., 391

C
Cabral, H., 116
Cain, D., 196
Calhoun, M. L., 47
Callahan, C. M., 401
Calvert, D. R., 271
Calvert, M. B., 204
Camarata, S., 284
Camarata, S. M., 133
Cameron, S. J., 333
Camp, B. W., 151
Camp, R., 431
Campbell, E. Q., 183
Campbell, P., 378
Campbell, S., 116
Candler, A. C., 303
Cannon, S. J., 335
Cantwell, D. P., 202
Caparulo, B. K., 119
Cape, J., 204
Capona, R. H., 298
Cappelli, M., 228
Carlson, C., 104
Carlson, P. E., 141
Carnine, D., 298, 301
Carr, R. P., 312
Carson, R., 155
Carson, R. R., 155
Carter, D. D., 247
Carter, J., 46
Carter, K. R., 393
Cartledge, G., 311, 315
Casby, M. W., 197
Caseau, D. L., 132
Casey, A., 45
Castaneda, A., 440
Cates, J. A., 273
Caton, H., 253
Caty, S., 222
Caughey, E., 376
Cazden, C. B., 192
Centers for Disease Control, 222
Chabessol, D. J., 280
Chadsey-Rusch, J., 92, 375
Chamberlain, S. P., 309
Chambers, J., 93
Chamrad, D. L., 395
Chandler, M. J., 9, 195
Chapman, R. S., 201, 303
Charlesworth, W. R., 44
Chasnoff, I. J., 115–117
Chattopadhyay, P., 222
Chavez, J. M., 229
Chavkin, N. F., 183
Chee, C. M., 223
Chermak, G. D., 393, 397
Chinn, P. C., 172
Choate, J. S., 430, 432
Christenson, S., 47
Christenson, S. L., 45, 333–334
Cicchetti, D., 109
Civelli, L., 246
Cizek, G. J., 431–432
Clancy, R. R., 223
Clark, D. M., 202

Epstein, M. H., 132, 134–135, 151, 304, 309, 329
Eresh, J., 428, 433
Erin, J. N., 246
Ernst, G., 210
Escobar, C., 144
Eulie, J., 407
Evans, E. O., 408
Evans, I. M., 76, 377
Evans, J. L., 202
Evans, R. C., 229
Evans, S. S., 430, 432
Everson, J. M., 96
Ewer-Jones, B., 309
Executive Committee of the Council for Children with Behavioral Disorders, 137, 141, 174

F

Fairweather, J. S., 95–96
Falk, B., 426, 429–431
Fardig, D. B., 360
Farmer, T. W., 142
Farnum, M., 359
Farr, M., 179
Farra, H. E., 358
Farrar, H. C., 115–116
Farrell, K., 245
Feagans, L., 374
Federal Register, 39, 50, 52, 61, 127, 247, 273, 305–306, 370
Fein, E., 113
Feinstein, S. C., 152–153
Feiring, C., 402
Feldhusen, J. F., 395
Fell, L., 403
Fennell, F. S., 431
Feoktistove, V., 260
Ferguson, D., 88
Ferguson, D. L., 38, 367
Ferguson, P., 440–441
Ferguson, P. H., 88
Ferrante, O., 259
Ferrari, M., 224, 228
Fessler, M. A., 131
Fewell, R. R., 72
Fiese, B. H., 195
Figueroa, R. A., 164
Filter, M. D., 200
Finck, K., 341
Fine, M. J., 10
Fink, A. H., 131
Finkelstein, D., 245, 248–249, 251, 263
Finn, C. E., 360
Fischel, J. E., 207
Fischer, C. F., 427, 429, 434
Fiscus, E. D., 406
Fisher, A., 286
Fisher, K. F., 246
Fithian, J., 224
FitzGibbon, C. T., 210
Fitzmartin, R., 154
Fleisch, B., 143
Fleming, L. A., 58
Fletcher, J. M., 307

Flexer, C., 271, 337
Flood, M. R., 112
Forest, M., 424–425
Forman, E. A., 308
Forness, S. R., 26, 140, 325
Forster, B. R., 407
Forsyth, P., 391
Fortschneider, J., 22
Foster, J., 154
Foster, S., 441
Fox, A. A., 119
Fradd, S., 164
Fraiser, M. M., 401
Frank, A. R., 155, 356
Frank, B. B., 223
Frank, D. A., 116
Fredericks, H. D., 368
Freeby, N., 207
Freedman, E., 304, 312
Freeman, B. J., 367
Freeman, B. M., 131
Freeman, F. J., 205
Freeman, R. D., 381
Frey, K. S., 72
Fried, L., 116
Friedell, S., 115
Friedman, D. L., 18
Friend, M., 359
Fritz, M. F., 334
Fuchs, D., 49, 312, 431
Fuchs, L. S., 49, 311–312, 425, 427–432, 434
Fuchs, M., 116
Fuhrman, W., 262
Fujiki, M., 201–202
Fuller, F., 353
Fullwood, D., 435
Fults, B. A., 391–392
Fung, H. C., 391
Fung, T., 109
Fuqua, R. W., 226

G

Galbraith, J., 393
Gallagher, J. J., 73, 394, 400, 405
Gallivan-Fenlon, A., 93, 341
Galloway, C. M., 44
Gallucci, N. T., 393
Gamel, N. M., 138
Garcia-Preto, N., 165
Gardner, H., 353
Gardner, J. E., 337
Garlonsky, R. M., 222
Garris, E., 304
Garrison, W. M., 273
Gartland, D., 145
Gartner, A., 57, 423
Gaston, G., 224
Gatlin, D., 308
Gatlin, H., 9
Gaudet, L. M., 228
Gaustad, M. G., 313
Gautur, M., 326
Gefen, S., 108
Gelbrich, J. A., 404
Gelzheiser, L. M., 307

George, D., 409
George, E., 110
George, K. A., 280
George, M. P., 143, 153
George, N. L., 90, 143, 153
Gerber, M. M., 50, 310, 335
Gerber, P., 302
Gerber, P. J., 306
Gerken, K., 50
Gershaw, N. J., 311
Gersten, R., 55
Geva, N., 108
Giancoli, D. I., 230
Giangreco, M. F., 350, 373
Giangreco, M. L., 56
Gibbons, J. P., 182
Gibbs, D. P., 302
Gibbs, J. T., 163, 165, 173
Giddan, J. J., 133
Gill, F. M., 224
Gilligan, C., 27
Gilliland, H., 176
Gillis-Olion, M., 163, 173
Gilmore, P., 179
Ginsberg, R., 306
Gittelman, R., 304
Glazner, J., 273, 280
Gleckel, L. K., 227
Glenwick, D. S., 154
Glidden, L. M., 334
Goetz, E., 381
Goffman, E., 28, 436
Gold, D., 380
Gold, M. S., 115
Gold, M. W., 332
Golden, L. B., 302, 308
Goldman, L. G., 202
Goldstein, R. P., 311
Gomez-Rubio, M., 232
Gon, M., 222
Gonzalez, J., 399
Gordon, L. R., 341
Gordon, M., 312
Gorenflo, C. W., 209
Gottlieb, A., 236
Gottlieb, J., 336, 353
Graafsma, T. L., 436
Graden, J., 45, 309
Graden, J. L., 45, 307
Graffam, J., 330
Graham, S., 317
Grandin, T., 438
Grant, J. O., 303
Graves, D., 313
Gray, W. A., 408
Grayson, D., 250–251
Green, J. L., 44
Green, L., 273
Greenbaum, B., 317
Greenbaum, E., 21
Greenberg, M. T., 72
Greenspan, S., 329
Greer, B. G., 73
Greer, S., 114
Gregg, S., 303

Subject Index